THE LIFE OF A REGIMENT

THE LIFE OF A REGIMENT

THE
HISTORY OF THE GORDON HIGHLANDERS

VOLUME VIII
1787–1994

THE PEOPLE WHO MADE THE REGIMENT

BY

LIEUTENANT-COLONEL D.M. NAPIER

First published in Great Britain in 2016 by
Balmoral Group
Aberdeen

ISBN 978-0-9933657-1-3 (hardback)
ISBN 978-0-9933657-2-0 (paperback)

A catalogue record for this book is available
from the British Library

Printed in Great Britain by

J. Thomson Colour Printers
Glasgow

INTRODUCTION

by

Lieutenant-General Sir Peter Graham, K.C.B., C.B.E.
Colonel, The Gordon Highlanders 1986 to 1994

THE Gordon Highlanders are extremely fortunate to have a regimental historian of the calibre of Lieutenant-Colonel Derek Napier. Few regiments have such a dedicated, knowledgeable and enthusiastic retired officer with the ability to write well, research carefully and the determination to ensure the history and activities of his regiment are well recorded.

Volume VIII is a compilation 'of the bits and pieces I took from so many sources ... and covers the people who made the Regiment and the form that the Regiment took'. From the Regiment's romantic beginnings its history has been filled with wonderful characters, much action and many anecdotes. After the demanding and relentless campaigning of the Napoleonic Wars a more peaceful and less exciting period ensued until the 2nd Afghan War of 1879, which was soon followed by the amalgamation in 1881 of the 75th and 92nd; the former adding further laurels to the overall history with its gallant and distinguished service in India. The amalgamated Regiment then went through a period of considerable success: possibly its greatest period. During this golden period it saw active service in Egypt, on the North-West Frontier of India, the Boer War and World War I. The name and reputation of the Regiment grew, recruiting was excellent and, in spite of a reluctance to allow officers to attend the Staff College, this small Regiment produced an extraordinary number of senior officers. They included such famous names as Field-Marshal Sir George White, V.C., General Sir Ian Hamilton, General Sir Charles Douglas, Chief of the Imperial General Staff in 1914, General the Rt Hon Sir Neville Macready, last Commander in Chief Ireland and General Sir Aylmer Haldane, Commander-in-Chief Mesopotamia 1920–1922. But rank is not everything, and in the same period the Regiment produced many fascinating characters of all ranks; men such as William Robertson, V.C., who rose from Private through Regimental Sergeant Major to Colonel; or Pipe Major G.S. McLennan, who became world-famous as a piper and composer. World War II produced some amazing characters, such as Colonel Sir Hugh Boustead, Colonel Dougie Usher, Lieutenant-Colonel Ivan Lyon and many others. Throughout the Regiment's history its soldiers, the 'Jocks' of The Gordon Highlanders, were regarded by many as the best in the Highland Brigade. Their characteristics are clearly articulated in this book; their calm steadiness, reliability, courage, extraordinary determination, professionalism and sense of humour provide many stories. How lucky the British Army was to have such a wonderful Regiment.

Derek Napier has brought many of our Regimental characters to life as well as shedding light on the way the Regiment developed. He has produced stories and information that would have been lost, probably for ever, had it not been for his interest and careful research. He is owed a huge debt by all Gordon Highlanders for producing this unusual and fascinating volume of the Regiment's history—a true labour of love.

AUTHOR'S PREFACE

WHILE writing Volume VII of *The Life of a Regiment* I spent much time studying back numbers of the regimental magazine, *The Tiger and Sphinx*, to remind me of events that had happened when I was present, and to clarify what had been happening in the years I served outside the Regiment. My attention kept getting diverted to earlier periods when I read accounts by the 'old and bold' of incidents during their service. The earliest, from a *Tiger and Sphinx* of 1895, gave a first-hand account of the siege of Delhi during the Indian Mutiny! Many of those first-hand accounts went into more detail than was contained in *The Life of a Regiment*, and I became absorbed with the descriptions of events that I had known only through abbreviated versions. I realised that these accounts would be seen only by those who read back issues of *The Tiger and Sphinx*, a not very extensive readership that would only decline as the years went by. I therefore formed the intention of gathering some of the accounts, alongside material from other sources, to add flesh and bones to the official history and remind readers of just how remarkable a regiment The Gordon Highlanders had been.

My intention was not to provide a comprehensive chronological history of the Regiment, but to look at its life in peace and war, and highlight it by categories. This book looks at events, situations, people, impressions and values. It will infuriate those who believe that it should have had a different emphasis, and has missed out items that they would have included. I cannot disagree with them but can only say that the choice was mine and I made it. I apologise to those who feel I have omitted too much, or placed emphasis where they would not, but it is my earnest hope that all who dip into this book will find *something* that will please them.

The original aim was to publish a single volume of the bits and pieces I took from so many different sources, but I found that, like Topsy, the book 'just grew and grew'. I set about reducing it in size by cutting out anything that might be categorised as 'surplus to requirement', and I sought advice from a number of friends to whom I showed the manuscript. The advice was not to cut anything but keep it all! Not only that, but they pointed out some omissions that clearly had to be put right. While this was flattering, it left me with the prospect of publishing a book that would be so large that it would discourage people from picking it up, let alone reading it. The solution was to break it down into two separate volumes. Volume VIII covers the people who made the Regiment and the form that the Regiment took, while Volume IX covers what these people did to establish and sustain its reputation.

Much of the material in the section covering 'Special Forces' came from the excellent display at The Gordon Highlanders Museum in 2011, prepared and organised by the curator, Jesper Ericsson, to whom I am indebted. Jesper was of great assistance with many other aspects of this book, and, with his willing and talented team, unearthed much of the archived material that has been used. Without Jesper's generous help and willing assistance in so many matters, this book would have had great difficulty in seeing the light of day.

The extracts I have used come from more than 200 years of written records and display widely varying approaches to grammar, punctuation and spelling. Rather than try to adapt them to conform with modern views of the written word, I have retained them in their original form, with one or two acknowledged exceptions where the original was too abstruse or ambiguous. The reader will come across contrasting examples of English language usage, often on the same page where a modern narrative accompanies an older text. I hope that readers will show understanding when such instances occur and not see them as an indictment of a classical Scottish education!

The official title of the Regiment was 'The Gordon Highlanders', with a capitalised 'The'. I have used this when the formal title is indicated, but otherwise have used the colloquial form with a lower case 'the'.

I am grateful to the many Gordon Highlanders, of every vintage, who passed time with me, reminiscing about their time in the Regiment and laughing along with me at the memories of how much fun we had. In particular, I should like to thank Lieutenant-General Sir John MacMillan and Lieutenant-General Sir Peter Graham, under each of whom I had the privilege of serving when they commanded the 1st Battalion. They kindly agreed to plough through the voluminous manuscript and came up with welcome and sensible suggestions for correction, amendment and inclusion or exclusion of material.

Eileen Cox, who compiled the Index, a task I had dreaded, did a wonderful job, as did Ann McCluskey, who proofread the manuscript, pointing out many errors that I had missed, and making sensible suggestions to clarify the script. Eileen and Ann saved me much time, laborious work and heartache, and I am indebted to them both.

I am particularly indebted to Jim Milne, C.B.E., and his company, Balmoral Group. Jim's support of and generosity to The Gordon Highlanders in so many ways has been quite remarkable, and is much appreciated by all who have benefited (even though many are unaware of where and how his help has been given). Without Jim Milne this book could never have been published, and it is only fair that those who read it should realise that it is thanks to him that publication was possible. I should also like to acknowledge the unfailing assistance in preparing the book for publication of Steve Gibb and Ewen Milne of Balmoral Group and David Stewart of J. Thomson Colour Printers.

My wife, Helen, as ever, has been a constant support and never-failing source of encouragement. She has put up with me closeting myself with books, regimental magazines, internet searches and an ever-expanding electronic manuscript, when she would really far prefer that I was outside helping her with her beloved garden. My children, Jackie and Mark and their respective spouses, Jarrod and Rhona, looked at my efforts with tolerant amusement ('It keeps him out of the way, and he can't get up to any mischief!'), while my grandsons Cameron, James and Jack looked on me as a relic of a *very* bygone era (as Jack was often wont to say, 'How times have changed!') but tolerated my regimental obsession with good grace and humour. I am grateful to them all.

CONTENTS

CONTENTS

CONTENTS

CONTENTS

CONTENTS

LIST OF ILLUSTRATIONS

Key:

APC – Armoured Personnel Carrier
BM – British Museum
BW – Black Watch
GH – Gordon Highlanders
NTS – National Trust for Scotland
Prov unknown – Provenance unknown
SA Scottish – South African Scottish
SNPG – Scottish National Portrait Gallery
Seven in Seventy – pictorial record of 7th Battalion, Royal Australian Regiment's
        Vietnam tour, 1970–71
T&S – *The Tiger and Sphinx* (Regimental magazine of The Gordon Highlanders)

Prov unknown – some illustrations were found on the Internet, but they figured on numerous different websites, none of which claimed unique ownership. If the copyright holder of any of these illustrations informs the author, corrected attribution will be included in any future editions of this book.

LIST OF MAPS

SECTION 1

RAISING THE REGIMENTS

IN the sections dealing with the raising of the 75th and its activities over the ensuing forty years, much of the content has been taken from the *Manuscript Records of the 75th Regiment*. In these regimental records the spelling, grammar and punctuation conform to the norms of the late eighteenth and early nineteenth centuries. As far as possible I have reproduced the records as they appear, with minimal corrections, and these only where I deemed them necessary to make sense of the text. There will, therefore, be inconsistencies in spelling, much capitalisation of words, and other anomalies. I hope the reader will understand that these represent the actual way in which the record was written, and are not necessarily careless grammar or poor proofreading by the author!

CHAPTER 1

THE RAW MATERIAL

THE Gordon Highlanders achieved so much during their history thanks to the quality of the men in their ranks. Recruited initially throughout the extensive Highland estates of the 4th Duke of Gordon and in the north-east counties of Aberdeenshire and Banffshire, the early reputation that they gained for excellence was due in no small part to the non-commissioned officers and men who made up the Regiment. This section 'The Raw Material' looks at who these men were and what made them so special.

WHO WERE THE HIGHLANDERS?

Highlanders have long featured in Scotland's history. They fought in the Wars of Independence, providing a sizeable part of Robert the Bruce's army at Bannockburn. Bruce deserves the credit for bringing a large part of the Highlands to the king's side, a feat which his successors, the Stewarts, found less easy. To most Scottish sovereigns the Highlands seemed remote and inaccessible, and the Highlanders a threat rather than a support. Within the Highlands, however, there was support for the Stewarts that they perhaps did not deserve, and the Highlands provided the most significant military backing for James VII, his son James (the Old Pretender) and his grandson, Charles Edward Stuart (the Young Pretender).

The Jacobite risings had two significant effects on the Highlands. First came the demise of a social system that had existed for centuries. Proscription of the kilt and tartan, and disarming of the people, were the first steps. The value placed on sheep over men led to population decline through emigration, breaking the link between Highland chiefs and their people. The sale of land by Highland chiefs to pay off debts led to a new breed of landowner to whom profit and status mattered more than people. Clearing people from the land to make way for sheep was the inevitable result. The second effect, surprisingly, was the rehabilitation of the Highland fighting man in the eyes of the British public through his exploits in the ranks of the British Army.

The Highlander's traditional form of warfare was close combat. The Highlander preferred to look his enemy in the eye and use a blade to dispatch him. The following article gives the lie to the misplaced belief that the Highland charge was a disorganised affair carried out by untrained berserkers of great size and strength.

There is a general impression that Highlanders were men of great stature and strength. Contemporary evidence bids us modify this opinion.

While the evidence regarding their strength and agility is overwhelming, their average stature was on the small or medium side. In this connection it is interesting to note that when the 92nd was raised the height standard for the recruits from Uist and the Outer Hebrides had to be lowered to 5 ft. 2 in.

William Sacheverell, Governor of the Isle of Man, writing in 1688 from Tobermory, states: 'During my stay I generally observed the men to be large bodied, stout, subtile, patient of cold and hunger. No nation goes better armed, and I can assure you they can handle them with dexterity.' The author of *Certayn Manners* writes: 'They have large bodies and prodigious strong, and two qualities above all other nations, hardy to endure fatigue, cold and hardship, and wonderfully swift of foot.'

In 1759 two Highland regiments served in Germany against the French. Our German allies of those days described them as of small stature. Marshal de Broglio,[1] who fought against them and was himself of diminutive size, states when writing of the Highlanders in 1759 that he once wished he were a man of six-feet high, but that now he was reconciled to his size since he had seen the wonders performed by the little Highlanders.

There is a very old print of the time of Gustavus Adolphus showing four Highlanders (shown on previous page). They are depicted as large bodied and thick set, but of medium height, with sturdy muscular legs. Their agility and swiftness were remarkable, and we know that they were

---

1   Victor-François, 2nd Duc de Broglie, Marshal of France.

sometimes employed in the Scottish wars to act along with cavalry, and we are informed that they kept pace with the horses in their movements. The soldiers of McKay's regiment in the wars of Gustavus Adolphus acted as auxiliaries to the cavalry in the same manner. In the historic incident of the Gordons and Greys at Waterloo, it would therefore appear that the Highlanders were only reverting to an old type of warfare of their ancestors.

The chief reason for the impression that they were men of immense strength must be attributed to the terrible nature of the wounds inflicted by the Highland broadsword. We have several accounts of these wounds. After the skirmish of Achadalew, where 35 Camerons defeated 140 veteran English soldiers of the civil wars, we are told from an English source that 'the wounds inflicted appeared to be above the strength of ordinary men'. An officer present at Killiecrankie, after describing the charge of the Highlanders, proceeds: 'And I dare be bold to say there were scarce ever such strokes given in Europe, as were given that day by the Highlanders. Many of General McKay's officers and men were cut down through the skull and neck to the breast. Others had their skulls cut off above the ears like night-caps. Some of the soldiers had their bodies and crossbelts cut through at one blow. Pikes and small swords were cut like willows.'

In another English version we read: 'The English officers had formerly occasion to see the Highlanders of several clans and counties, but they appeared to be no extraordinary men neither in size nor strength, and they were at a loss to understand how such an odd variety of surprising wounds were inflicted by them.'

What English observers failed to understand was that timing was as much art as strength in producing these strokes. When the Highlander laid it on full, he drew the sword, which was sharpened to a razor edge, not straight down as was commonly supposed, but across with the whole blade in a sheering cut, at the same time throwing his whole strength and the full weight of his body into the stroke. It was the same with the back stroke (for it must be remembered the Highland claymore was double edged, not single edged like the present officer's claymore[2]). To use a golfing phrase, the old Highlander 'followed through' with his stroke. Many are under the impression that the Highlanders were an undisciplined mob, unskilled both in tactics and in the use of their

---

2 The Highlander's sword is often erroneously called a 'claymore'. The name 'claymore' comes from the Gaelic *claidheamh mòr* (great sword). The two-handed claymore was a large sword (almost 5 ft in length) used in the constant clan warfare and border fights with the English from circa 1400–1700. The basket-hilted sword carried by Highlanders in the seventh and eighteenth centuries, and in modern Highland regiments, is more correctly known as a 'broadsword'.

weapons. We have historical proof, however, that this idea is erroneous. They constantly practised sword play and sword exercises, and we have records of their astuteness in devising the tactics best suited for the occasion.

T&S, September 1934.

Highlanders first appeared in British uniform in the independent companies raised to police the Highlands. In the wake of the 1715 Jacobite rising, companies of trustworthy Highlanders were raised from loyal clans. Six companies were formed from 1725 and stationed in small detachments across the Highlands to prevent fighting between the clans, deter raiding and assist in enforcing the laws against the carrying of weapons.

In 1739 King George II authorised the raising of four additional companies and to form them all into a regiment of the regular army. The men were to be 'natives of that country and none other to be taken'. The new regiment was dressed in the Highland manner, in the kilt, which was of the tartan specially designed for it and known as the Government tartan. This was a simple tartan based on three colours—green, blue and black—that gave it a very dark appearance, and it was from the dark kilt that the regiment took its name *Am Freiceadan Dubh* (The Black Watch), the term 'Watch' meaning a 'guard' or 'police' force.

Soldiers of The Black Watch, 1739

After the 1745 rising tartan was proscribed, and the kilt banned by law. The only way the kilt could be worn was in a Highland regiment. Fortunately, some in government saw the wisdom of reconciling these former enemies of the state. The only way that the Highlanders could be won over was by adopting a liberal policy that employed the clan chiefs in the military service of the government, and actively supporting the raising of Highland regiments to fight in Britain's cause. It was William Pitt (Lord Chatham) who had the wisdom to understand the disaffection of the Highlanders and, by suggesting a remedy, made practical use of their military qualities. In 1757 Pitt recommended to King George II that Highlanders should be recruited in his service. The king agreed, and letters of service were issued for raising several Highland regiments, which served with distinction during the Seven Years War, in Europe, India and North America. Some in the British Army regarded Highland regiments as little more than expendable cannon fodder, but others recognised them as outstanding soldiers who were trustworthy and reliable.

The performance of Highland soldiers in the Seven Years War led to the raising of more regiments to serve in North America during the American Revolution, and in India. The onset of war with France after the French Revolution led to yet more regiments being raised. It was during this phase that the 75th was raised for service in India and the 92nd (originally 100th) for service in Europe and the Mediterranean.

Who were these Highlanders, and what made them so different from other British soldiers? From 1817 to 1825 Major-General David Stewart published three editions of his book *Sketches of The Character, Manners, and Present State of the Highlanders of Scotland; with details of The Military Service of The Highland Regiments*. He started writing mainly about The Black Watch, but he came to realise that the characteristics he recognised in The Black Watch applied to all Highland regiments:

> It struck me, that I could give similar details of the other Highland regiments. I met in all of them the same character and principles. The coincidence was striking, and proved that this similarity of conduct and character must have a common origin. Investigation confirmed that the strongly marked difference between the manners and conduct of the mountain clans and those of Lowlanders, and of every other known country, originated in the patriarchal form of government, which differed so widely from the feudal system of other countries.
>
> In forming his military character, the Highlander was not more favoured by nature than by the social system under which he lived. Nursed in poverty, he acquired a hardihood which enabled him to sustain severe privations. As the simplicity of life gave vigour to his body, so it fortified his mind. With a frame and constitution thus hardened, he was taught to consider courage as the most honourable virtue, cowardice the most disgraceful failing; to venerate and obey his chief, and devote himself to his native country and clan. Thus prepared to be a soldier, he was ready to follow wherever honour and duty called. With such principles, and regarding any disgrace which he might bring on his clan and district as the most cruel misfortune, the Highland soldier had a peculiar motive to exertion. When in a national corps, he is surrounded by the companions of his youth, and the rivals of his early achievements; he feels the impulse of emulation strengthened when every proof which he displays, of bravery or cowardice, will find its way to his home. He thus learns to appreciate

a good name; and in a Highland Regiment of men from the same country, whose kindred and connections are mutually known, every individual feels that his conduct is the subject of observation, and that, as one member of a systematic whole he has a reputation to sustain, which will be reflected on his family and district or glen.

Major-General David Stewart.

The years leading to the Napoleonic Wars saw a gradual change in the make-up of the Highland regiments. The following article explains how economic factors in the Highlands affected recruiting to Highland regiments. The Earl of Selkirk identifies similar characteristics in the Highland soldier as did General Stewart:

When the Gordon Highlanders were raised in 1794 a great change had come over the Highlands since 1745, not only as concerned disarming, but also through the introduction of sheep farming, which altered the economic face of the Highlands.

This was clearly stated by Thomas Douglas, 5th Earl of Selkirk (1771–1820), an upholder of emigration as a cure for the condition into which the Highlands had fallen. He wrote a remarkable book on the subject, *Observations on the Present State of the Highlands* in 1805. He found that one of the great objections offered by the Chiefs to his emigration scheme was that it would cut down the supply of soldiers, and he dealt with the matter in a chapter, which is essential to all students of Highland soldiering, though, strange to say, no regimental historian seems to be acquainted with his views:

Prior to 1745 the power of Highland chieftains over their followers was derived from the low rent of their lands. This was the essential circumstance on which the subsequent state of the country has chiefly depended. Those proprietors who continued to exact rents inadequate to the real value of the land, maintained all their former authority on tenantry, for this authority was tempered by the dependence of the gentry on the affection of their followers for personal safety. After 1745 the tenantry had no such return to make for the subsistence they derived from the indulgence of their landlord. They felt at the same time that he must be under frequent temptations to discontinue that indulgence and therefore were more anxious to merit his favour.

The only opportunity they had of rendering him any important obligation was when he undertook to raise men for the Army. The zeal with which the followers of a chieftain came forward to enlist was prompted not only by affection and enthusiasm of clanship, but likewise by private interest. The tenant who refused to comply with the wishes of his landlord could expect no further favour, and would be turned out of his farm. The more considerable the possession he held, the more was it his interest as well as his duty to exert himself. The most respectable of the tenantry would be among the first to bring forward their sons; and the landlord might select from among the youth upon his estate most suitable for recruits. The Highland gentry were too good politicians to make a wanton display of this power; and were well enough acquainted with the temper of their people to know that they would come forward with more alacrity if allowed to indulge the flattering idea that their exertions were the spontaneous effect of attachment to the chief; yet no man of penetration in the country ever doubted the real cause of the facility with which the Highland landlords could raise such numbers of men with such magical rapidity.

It is easy to see how superior [such] a body of men must be to a regiment recruited in the ordinary manner in other parts of the kingdom. As long as the old system remained, and rents continued at their old standard, the Highland regiments were composed of hardy mountaineers, whose life was a perfect school for the habits of a soldier. They were men for whose fidelity and good conduct there was a solid pledge in the families they left at home and in the motives that induced them to enter the Service; men with much stronger motives of obedience to their officers than the lash can enforce; who were accustomed, from infancy, to respect and obey the superiors who led them into the field; who looked on them as protectors no less than commanders; men in whose minds the attachment of clanship still retained its ancient enthusiasm.

Besides this, each corps being from the same neighbourhood, the men were connected by ties of friendship and blood; and everyone saw in his companions those with whom he would pass the rest of his life, whether in a military capacity or not. Everyone was therefore more solicitous to maintain an unblemished character than he would have been among strangers. The same circumstance gave that *esprit de corps* which is so powerful an engine in the hands of a judicious commander. The attachment of the Highland soldier to his regiment was not casual or transitory—it was not a matter of indifference to him, or the result of accident, whether he belonged to one regiment or another—his regiment was derived from his clan, inseparably connected with it; in the honour of his regiment he saw that of his name; and to it he transferred those sentiments of glory which early education had connected with the achievements of his ancestors.

Military men well know the effect which the established character of any regiment has in moulding the mind of the recruit: and how long a peculiarity may thereby be preserved, though perhaps originating from mere accident. The reputation acquired by the old Highland regiments has probably had no small effect on their successors, and perhaps also on the opinion of the public.[3]

T&S, July 1930.

The men of the original Highland regiments were different from the rest of the British Army. In 1805 Sir John Moore said that he considered the Highlanders, under an officer who understood and valued their character, among the best of Britain's military materials. Under such an officer they would conquer or die on the spot: 'But it is the principles of integrity and moral correctness that I admire most in Highland soldiers, and this was the trait that first caught my attention.'

The Highland regiments were renowned for their achievements on the battlefield—and humanity off it. That the men who formed their ranks could go in one generation from the foremost enemies of the state and objects of fear, to among the most valuable assets in the British military arsenal, is a tribute to the inherent fighting qualities and sense of loyalty that were second nature to them. As the years passed the number of Highlanders would gradually decrease, their place taken by Scotsmen (and others) from outwith the Highlands, but the spirit and ethos of the original Highland soldiers were passed on to, and adopted by, their successors. The groundwork laid by those original Highland soldiers, the last remnants of a fast-disappearing social order, formed the bedrock on which their successors built the high reputation that the Highland regiments enjoyed throughout their existence.

---

3   The Highland regiments' reputation for excellence and outstanding fighting qualities derived from their performance and Highland origin. Their standards were passed on, and generations of soldiers, many originating outwith the Highlands, were imbued with the spirit of their predecessors.

CHAPTER 2

RAISING THE 75TH

WHILE the origins of the 92nd are well documented, the events leading to the raising of the 75th are not so well recorded. We know that the 75th was one of the regiments raised specifically for service in India, and a brief account of this background is given below.

Tipu Sultan, the eldest son of Hyder Ali, ruler of the Indian state of Mysore, was trained in the art of warfare and from the age of 15 accompanied his father on campaign. Hyder Ali aggressively expanded his domains, using his French-trained army to defeat the Marathas, the rulers of the Carnatic and other Indian powers. Mysore faced opposition from the British, who were allied to several rulers in conflict with Hyder Ali. A clash for control of southern India was inevitable and two wars were fought: the First and Second Mysore Wars (1767–69 and 1780–84).

In 1780, during the second war—in which Mysore allied with Britain's rival in India, France—Tipu's 10,000-strong army surrounded and defeated a British-Indian force of 4,000 men at Pollilur. Tipu's French-trained regulars fought in column and broke through Colonel William Baillie's lines, forcing him to surrender. It was the worst British defeat in India up to that time. Many of the prisoners were carried off into an appalling captivity. One of them, Captain David Baird, was held prisoner for four years before returning to his regiment and eventually leading the force that defeated Tipu in 1799.

The Second Mysore War dragged on with neither side able to claim a decisive victory. In December of 1782 Tipu become ruler of Mysore after the death of his father. As well as building a modern army Tipu encouraged road construction, the growth of trade, a new coinage, the introduction of the French system of weights and measures and other reforms. He was implacably opposed to the British and saw the French as useful allies. It was clear to Britain that the uneasy peace after the Second Mysore War would not last, and the government recognised the need for more British troops in India. The decision was taken to raise new regiments specifically for service there. Four regiments were raised, which were paid for by the Honourable East India Company. These were the 74th (Highland) Regiment of Foot, the 75th (Highland) Regiment of Foot, the 76th (Hindoostan) Regiment of Foot and the 77th (Hindoostan) Regiment of Foot. These regiments would see a lot of each other over the coming decade.

The 75th Highland Regiment was raised on receipt of a Letter of Service addressed to Colonel Robert Abercromby,[1] the opening sentence of which states, 'Sir, I have the honor to acquaint you, The King has been pleased to order that a Regiment shall be forthwith raised under your Command, for His Majesty's Service abroad.'

In the autumn of 1787, Colonel Robert Abercromby (pictured), son of the laird of Tullibody, was appointed colonel of a regiment to be raised by

him in the north of Scotland. The army was unpopular in the south, but English ideas had little effect in Scotland, still less in the north, where Highlanders were neither jealous of the power of the Crown, nor cared much for the liberties of the people; they disliked manual labour, and though a man who claimed gentle blood despised mercantile pursuits, he did not consider it derogatory to be an innkeeper, a drover, or a soldier; thus men of a superior class often enlisted in the Highland regiments. The Highlands were in transition—the new order of relations between landlords and tenants had begun, but the clan system survived in the great power and influence over the people still possessed by the gentry, several of whom, among them MacKenzie of Seaforth, assisted Colonel Abercromby in his levy. Not many Highland officers appear to have been appointed, but some received commissions for raising men, while though Abercromby had no territorial influence in the Highlands, his character as a leader brought a considerable body of experienced soldiers who had served under him in a light brigade[2] which he commanded in the American War. These men had belonged to the 76th (MacDonald's Highlanders) and other Highland regiments, which had been disbanded after the peace in 1783–4.[3]

---

1   The Letter of Service for the raising of the 75th is at Appendix 1.

2   The experience gained in America led to the formation of a corps of Light Infantry, picked for their marksmanship from various regiments and trained in tactics that were regarded as a strange innovation—advancing in loose order and taking cover.

3   Although composed chiefly of young Highlanders, the tenantry of those gentlemen who forwarded the views of the Family of Tullibody, yet there were also to be found in the ranks of the 75th several old soldiers who had known Col Abercromby in America and who gladly availed themselves of this opportunity of again serving under his auspices. (*75th Regiment Record Book*) Officers of the 76th Regiment (MacDonald's Highlanders) were also appointed in the 92nd in 1794.

The regiment was embodied at Stirling,[4] that place being no doubt chosen as convenient to the colonel's home at Tullibody; there is, however, no evidence that it was recruited particularly in that district; had it been so, it would not in those days have been designated, as it was, the 75th Highland Regiment, sometimes called Abercromby's Highlanders. The regiment moved immediately to England and embarked for Bombay, where it landed, 700 strong, in August 1788.

The Life of a Regiment, Volume II, pp 183–4.

Apart from one captain, two lieutenants and two ensigns, whose appointment was in the gift of Robert Abercromby, all the officers were appointed by the War Office. Of these, the lieutenant-colonel, four captains, eleven lieutenants and four ensigns were appointed from the British Army. The remaining officers were named, but their appointment was conditional upon their recruiting a specified number of men.

The lieutenant-colonel appointed was James Hartley (pictured as a major in the army of the East India Company), a Scot born in 1745, who had served with the East India Company from 1764 to 1781, and then in the regular army in India. Although he is shown as commanding the 75th from 1788 to 1795, when the 75th arrived in India he was appointed Quartermaster-General in Bombay, and day-to-day command of the 75th fell upon the senior captain, Captain Robert Craufurd. Hartley became a major-general in 1796 and died in 1799 after thirty-five years' service in India.

The major appointed was George Vaughan Hart, born in Donegal in 1752. He served in the American War and in India from 1781 to 1795. He was promoted to lieutenant-colonel in 1795 and commanded the 75th from 1795 to 1801. He died in June 1832, having reached the rank of lieutenant-general.

The senior captain was Robert Craufurd, the third son of Sir Alexander Craufurd of Kilbirnie, later to gain fame as Major-General Robert Craufurd, commander of the Light Division during the Peninsular War and known among his contemporaries and his men as 'Black Bob' Craufurd.

The nominated officers were clearly successful in raising their quotas of men, for in March 1788, when the 75th sailed for India, all the officer posts had been filled. They were:

---

4   Volume I of *The Life of a Regiment* states that 'The Regimental Record gives no date.' However, the *75th Regiment Record Book* quite clearly states that the 75th was raised on 12th October 1787.

Colonel: Robert Abercromby.

Lieutenant-Colonel: James Hartley.

Major: George Hart.

Captains: Robert Craufurd, Charles Madan, John Wood, Daniel Seddon.

Captain-Lieutenant: Alexander Cumine.

Lieutenants: Zachariah Hall, Colville Learmonth, George Mackenzie, Benjamin Forbes, Charles Anderson, David Maxwell, John Charles Halkett, Gabriel Trotter, Adam Davie, John Cuningham, John Forbes, James Dunsmore, John Ross.

Ensigns: Alexander Steuart, George Laye, Donald Cameron, Alexander Wallace, Creighton McRae.

Chaplain: John Pritchett.

Adjutant: Benjamin Hill.

Quartermaster: Charles Stewart.

Surgeon: Charles Kerr.

CHAPTER 3

RAISING THE 92ND

W E know more about the raising of the 92nd. This is summarised in the following extract from John Malcolm Bulloch's book *The Gordon Highlanders, Their Origin*. In particular it details the remarkable record of the 4th Duke of Gordon, who raised no fewer than four regiments in the service of the Crown.

With the exception of the Black Watch and the Scots Greys, it may be questioned whether any British regiment has had more written about it, or holds a higher place in the affections of the people than the Gordon Highlanders. Something like a saga has risen round the Gordons. Now a saga is never very rational; it dislikes definitiveness; and though much has been written about the Gordon Highlanders, the origins of the regiment have been much overlooked. This is all the more curious because the early records of the regiment are unusually complete, and the archives of the Duke of Richmond and Gordon are available. They had not been touched by any historian till His Grace was good enough to permit the present writer to examine them.

The 100th Regiment was the fourth big contingent of troops raised for the Government, over nearly forty years (1759–94), by Alexander, 4th Duke of Gordon. The military activity of his Grace was conditioned by two facts: first, the desire of his wise mother (a Gordon by birth) to wipe out the stigma of Jacobitism which had made his family more than suspect; secondly, the straits to which the country was reduced by the necessity of holding her own all over the world. The regiments he raised marked crises in this struggle:—

1759–65:	89th Regiment.	Canada won from France 1763
1778–83:	Northern Fencibles	American War 1775–1781
1793–96:	Northern Fencibles	Coalition against France 1792
1794:	Gordon Highlanders	Coalition against France 1792

The raising of the Gordons was the most difficult task that the Duke undertook, because his first three regiments were all of the militia type, raised for a limited period for home service. The Gordons were raised as a regular regiment of the line, which men were shy of joining, all the more as the countryside had been drained dry by half a century of vigorous and often unscrupulous recruiting. At first, the whole adventure possessed all the charm of novelty. The levy of 1759 had been comparatively easy, for the Duke, a fatherless boy of thirteen, got the full benefits of orphanism and of the removal of the years of severe repression which followed Culloden. But in the ensuing half century much had occurred. Men came back to their native heath disillusioned. The glory of war had become a little dusty at the hem. The rivalry of contending recruiters had made them more demandful. The dislike of foreign service had increased.

The Duke's fourth and final effort, difficult as it was, received a great fillip from the fact that the regiment was raised not only in face of the menace of France, but also because it was to be commanded by his heir, the handsome and popular Marquis of Huntly, and because the equally popular Duchess and her daughters took the warmest interest in the corps, even if she did not actually kiss the recruits as tradition maintains and will not abandon in face of any evidence to the contrary.[1]

Young as he was (only four and twenty), the merry Marquis was not without experience. He began his career (1790) in the 35th Regiment, of which his brother-in-law, the future Duke of Richmond, was colonel. In the following month he raised an Independent Company for the Black Watch. In 1792, he joined the 3rd, now the Scots, Guards, and fought with them in Flanders. His father was 'a little vexed about his going to Holland,' and John Stuart, of Pittyoulish, in March, 1793, shared the same feeling—'not that I wou'd be affraid [for] his lordship if 20,000 well disciplined Highlanders was about him.' Short of being a King or a Croesus, it was not possible for the Duke to raise 20,000 men, but he did the next best thing: he raised a regiment of regulars for his boy.

The Gordon Highlanders, Their Origin.

The French Revolution had caused alarm in European monarchies. After the execution of Louis XVI, the great dynastic powers of Europe[2] tried to reverse the revolution and restore the French monarchy. This period, known as the War of the First Coalition (1793–97), saw the rise of Napoleon Bonaparte. In 1793 the British Government determined to increase the size of the Army to counter the growing French threat.

The Regiment that was to win undying fame as The Gordon Highlanders was originally numbered the 100th. It became the 92nd in 1798 after a renumbering process within the Army to make use of the regimental numbers of regiments which had previously been disbanded.[3]

In 1793 it was a not very well-kept secret that the Duke of Gordon might raise yet another regiment for the British Army. In January 1794 it became

---

1 Fact or myth? See Chapters 6, 21 and 30.
2 Austria, Prussia, Great Britain, Spain, Sardinia and the Netherlands.
3 To avoid confusion, the Regiment will be referred to as the '92nd' except when quoting from original documents that use the number shown in the relevant Army List.

official when the Duke received a letter from Lord Amherst, Commander-in-Chief of the Army.

St. James' Square,
24th January, 1794

My Lord,

The King, having been pleased to approve of the raising of some regiments in N. Britain agreeably to the plan of Lord Seaforth's in the last war, I beg the favour to know if it will be agreeable to Your Grace to raise a regiment of 1,000 men, the regiment having a Lieut.-Colonel Commandant and two Majors, the two Majors appointed by the King, and leaving to Your Grace the recommendation of the other officers. The plan of the particulars shall be transmitted immediately to Your Grace if it meets with your accepting the offer.

I have the honour to be, my Lord, Your Grace's most humble and most obedient Servant,

Amherst.

Alexander, 4th Duke of Gordon

In his reply the Duke wrote from Gordon Castle, 2 February 1794. (It seems that delays in delivering mail caused by inclement weather are not confined to our day and age!)

My Lord,

I had not the honour to receive Your lordship's letter of the 24th of last month till yesterday owing to the great fall of snow which retarded the course of the post for several days. Upon every former occasion it made me very happy to prove my zealous attachment to the King by promoting his wishes as far as lay in my power, and I think it my duty, more particularly on the present emergency, to comply with His Majesty's pleasure by accepting of the offer he has made me, and I shall do my utmost endeavours to assist Lord Huntly in raising the regiment, to whom I wish the command to be given. He will set out for London as soon as the roads are passable for a carriage, in order to settle the terms with Your Lordship, of which I am ignorant, but I trust they will be such as not to put me to great expense on account of my circumstances, which really will not admit of it.

Once the Duke of Gordon's reply had been received, the Letter of Service[4] for the raising of the regiment was sent from the War Office, on 10 February 1794, by Sir George Yonge, Secretary for War.

Unlike the 75th, the Letter of Service for the 92nd did not allocate any officers from the Army, apart from the two majors, but delegated 'the nomination of all officers' to the Duke of Gordon. The first task, therefore, was to allot commissions, as it fell to the officers appointed to find the men who would fill the ranks. The difficulty was not to get officers but to weed out unsuccessful candidates, for the applications were far in excess of the vacancies. Indeed, in November 1793 (three months before the raising of the regiment was officially authorised) thirty applications for commissions were sent in. The disappointed applicants for the first allotted commissions included four majors, eleven captains, two captain-lieutenants, two ensigns, two surgeons and five chaplains.

The man appointed as the first captain-lieutenant (effectively the senior lieutenant) was John Gordon of Coynachie, who had entered the Northern Fencibles in 1778. He gave two sons (including General John Gordon of Culdrain) and four grandsons (including General Cosmo Gordon of Culdrain) to the services. On 16 February 1794 he wrote to the Duke:

My Lord Duke,

When I had the honour of seeing your Grace at Gordon Castle the other week, I mentioned that I had made proposals to Lord Huntly for raising

---

4   The Letter of Service for the 92nd is at Appendix 1.

what number of men might be required for the Captain-Lieutenancy of his regiment, and, altho' his Lordship did not positively say that that was to be the appointment, yet he was pleased to say that I should be in his regiment in some line or other. As the raising of the regiment must be an expensive undertaking, if your Grace and Lord Huntly would trust me with the paymastership I would cheerfully do the business for one half of the emoluments that might arise from the office. I cannot pretend to be a good accountant, but shall be answerable for the accounts of the regiment being kept exact, and I am certain that I would have his lordship's interest in view as [well as] any other that can be appointed.

He was given the captain-lieutenancy and was duly appointed paymaster. On 24 June Captain Finlason the Duke's recruiter in Aberdeen, wrote:

Our friend Coynachy [sic] was put in orders as paymaster. I certainly did say everything in his favour is possible. I think well of him, and I was the more inclined to do him good offices that you joined and wished it. I shall be happy to give him all the instructions in my power. I went and ordered the proper books for him.

One of the successful applicants was Lieutenant Simon MacDonald of Morar from the half pay of the 76th Regiment.[5] On 15 February 1794 James Fraser of Gortuleg wrote to Charles Gordon of Braid soliciting a commission for MacDonald:

[He] is in point of friends and connections extremely well calculated to raise a company: and it would be particularly agreeable to him to be promoted in any corps to be raised by the Marquis of Huntly, as his brother is a captain in the first Royals, and owes much to Lord Adam Gordon, both from his original introduction and promotion in that regiment. Independent of his own tribe, which are numerous, and his remaining property by no means inconsiderable, he is by intermarriage particularly connected with the Glengarry branches.

The officers appointed to the new regiment were:

Lieutenant-Colonel Commandant: George, Marquis of Huntly.

---

5   At the moment Lord Cornwallis was giving the order to charge, a Highland soldier rushed forward and placed himself in front of his officer, Lt Simon MacDonald of Morar, afterwards Major of the 92nd Regiment. Lt MacDonald having asked what brought him there, the soldier answered; 'You know, that when I engaged to be a soldier, I promised to be faithful to the King and to you. The French are coming, and while I stand here neither bullets nor bayonet shall touch you except through my body.' Lt MacDonald had no particular claim to the generous devotion of this trusty follower, further than that which never failed to be binding on the true Highlander—he was born on his officer's estate, where he and his forefathers had been treated with kindness. He was descended of the same family, and when he enlisted he promised to be a faithful soldier. (from *The 76th MacDonald's Highlanders, 1777–1784*)

Majors: Charles Erskine of Cardross, Donald MacDonald of Boisdale.

Captains: Alexander Napier of Blackstone, John Cameron of Fassiefern, Honourable John Ramsay, Andrew Paton, William Macintosh of Aberarder, Alexander Gordon, Simon MacDonald of Morar.

Captain-Lieutenant: John Gordon.

Lieutenants: Peter Grant, Archibald MacDonell, Alexander Stewart of Achnacone,[6] John MacLean of Dochgarroch, Peter Gordon, Thomas Forbes, Ewan MacPherson, George Gordon (illegitimate son of 4th Duke of Gordon), James Henderson.

Ensigns: Charles Dowle, George Davidson, Archibald MacDonald, Alexander Fraser, William Tod, James Mitchell.

Chaplain: William Gordon.

Adjutant: James Henderson (adjutant was a separate rank).

Quartermaster: Peter Wilkie.

Surgeon: William Findlay.

Officers appointed to the new regiment purchased their commissions, and the money raised went towards the bounties paid to recruits. On 1 March 1794 Cox and Greenwood, the Army agents in London calculated (on the basis of other new regiments), that £22,850 could be raised from commissions and £5,586 due from the government. The sale of commissions was based on a rate of £2,000 each for the two majors, £1,500 each for the seven captains, £800 for the captain-lieutenant, £300 each for the two senior lieutenants, £250 for the next seventeen lieutenants in rank, £200 each for the two junior lieutenants, £350 each for the two senior ensigns, £300 each for the next two ensigns in rank and £250 each for the remaining four ensigns. This brought a total of £22,850 The levy money allowed by the government for 1,064 men was £5 5s., a total of £5,586, giving a grand total of £28,436. When divided by 1,064, the number of men to be raised, a bounty of £26 14s. per man was reached.

Recruiting officers was comparatively simple when compared with recruiting the men who would make up the regiment. The government allowance varied with different regiments according to the state of the labour and bounty markets. Unfortunately for the Marquis of Huntly, the amount paid to recruits was raised sometimes to four times the government bounty

---

6 Lieutenant Stewart served in Holland in 1799 and went on to have a distinguished career in the Rifle Corps. One of his descendants, Lt Alexander Stewart of Achnacone, fought with distinction with the Gordon Highlanders at Mons in 1914 and was taken prisoner with most of the 1st Battalion a few days later.

by the recruiting rivalry of the 109th Regiment being raised by Colonel Alexander Hay of Rannes, which had captured the patronage of the town council of Aberdeen.[7] The burden fell upon Captain Finlason, who was conducting not only the financial affairs of the Northern Fencibles in Aberdeen but the recruiting for the Gordons. Within a month of the issue of the War Office mandate, Finlason wrote:

> I struggle hard to make a good bargain, but I may as well attempt to change the system of the whole army as to ask recruiting officers here to alter their terms; but I flatter myself no other party has done the same execution here in the same time, and I give you my word there have not been ten minutes past this day without my knocker going to all fellows, drunk and sober.

The rivalry was felt in the country districts, for Gordon of Coynachie wrote on 14 March:

> If Colonel Hay's beating orders come to this country before the Marquis makes his appearance, it will knock recruiting on the head. Every man that has any inclinations expects such high bounty money from him.

It was essentially true of recruiting in those days that every man had his price. Recruiting officers paid varying bounties according to the expectations in different districts. For example, in Badenoch, bounties to recruits varied from £21 to £5 5s. The price tended to rise as time went on and the date for embodying the regiment approached. The total paid out for bounties in 1794 from the exchequer at Gordon Castle (the amount found by the Duke of Gordon in addition to the funds raised by the sale of commissions and the government bounty) was £2,478 12s. 5d. This figure does not include the men raised by other captains of companies and refers only to those whom the Marquis of Huntly was directly responsible for recruiting. It is probable that those recruiting individual companies would face similar additional expenditure.

In addition to bounties, the Marquis sometimes had to acquiesce in a *quid pro quo*, such as the following, which was propounded by James Gordon, who wrote from Croughly on 14 June 1794:

---

7   The keenness of the rivalry was strikingly shown by Hay's adopting the name 'The Aberdeenshire Regiment', which Finlason had suggested to the Duke on 1 March as the name which should be adopted by his Grace's corps. On 11 March Finlason reported that Hay 'is to assume the name of the Aberdeen Regiment. I once hinted that to your graceful Marquis.'. In all likelihood the Duke's new regiment would have been known as 'The Aberdeenshire Regiment' but for Hay's intervention. The first time the name 'Gordon Highlanders' appears is in an account of 17 June 1794. To this serendipitous result of recruiting rivalry is owed the far more romantic and marketable name by which the regiment would become famous around the world!

I find Peter Gordon cannot prevaill on either of his younger broyrs. to go with the Marquis. In my presence he used all his endeavours to perswade his younger broyr. to goe, but to no purpose; and as that is the case, to please the Marquis, he will goe himself. He wishes to get possession of Fourdmouth, as he has nothing to support his wife and two orphants, except to possession and small cover there, one which is reather greatly under burden, so that his wife, et cetera, cannot be supported without the possession in his absence: and in the event of his going he wishes if his friends can find anoyr. passable man to goe in his place some time hereafter to gett his discharge.

On 15 June the Marquis gave a bounty of £2 2s. to Gordon and £18 18s. to his wife. In some cases the relations had to be pacified. In this way the father of Neil McMillan got £12 12s., while Neil himself got £8 8s., bringing up his price to £21.

Sometimes the *quid pro quo* was put forward on behalf of the community. Thus, George Bell, writing from Coclarachie, speaks about the clothing of the regiment:

I think the profits of a Huntly regiment should be given to Huntly folks, and I hope you are of the same opinion, and will on proper occasions say so.

Huntly himself clearly recognised this method of bargaining, for he wrote from Edinburgh on 23 March, that 'Forsyth should exert himself, as he is to have the shirts to make.'

Even when he had captured his men, the Marquis had to humour them. In certain cases he even increased the bounty, as shown in the entry under date of 3 July: 'To Donald Macpherson, enlisted on March 12, ordered by your lordship over and above £8 8s. formerly paid by Menzies, and £7 7s. at Aberdeen, the further sum of £5 5s., Bringing up the price of Macpherson to £21.'

Everything seems to have been done to make the recruits as happy as possible, and payments are shown for 'playing the fiddle to the recruits at Gordon Castle', for 'four hogsheads of porter for the recruits' and for 'price of bull, baited and roasted and given to the recruits'.

In the end all difficulties were overcome, and the Marquis or, rather, his helpers and servers—who lacked his easy-going philosophy—had the satisfaction of seeing the rival 109th eliminated within two years, by being drafted into another regiment, the 53rd. The Gordons were embodied, 750 strong, at Aberdeen on 24 June, a red letter day in the military history of the North, for it was the date chosen for laying the foundation stone of the barracks on the Castle Hill, which were to become the depot of the regiment from 1881 until 1936.

The regiment was reviewed next day by General Sir Hector Munro, who had been an officer in the Duke's first Regiment 35 years previously, and set out at once for Fort George, where on July 8, 9 and 10 it embarked with the second battalion of the 78th Regiment and the Inverness-shire Highlanders for Southampton, which was reached on 16 August. The *Aberdeen Journal* recorded the embarkation:

> The men went on board in the highest spirits. The Marquis of Huntly, who may boast of one of the finest bodies of men in the service, embarked with them. He showed an alacrity of service by jumping into the first boat, and so great was the eagerness of his men to follow their noble commander, that the boat had nearly been overset; and the area resounded with cheers from those left on the beach until his lordship was on board the transport. Every man appeared to be perfectly sober, an Irish gentlemen excepted, who swore by J— that though he was half-seas over already, he would not quit the land without a quid of tobacco!

The transport set sail on 18 July, and passed Aberdeen, which must have been on the outlook for them, on the evening of 21 July. The regiment was not to set foot again in Scotland for eight years.

CHAPTER 4

THE MOTTO AND THE UNIFORM

THE Gordon Highlanders were inextricably linked with the motto *'Bydand'*. The link, through the Duke of Gordon, goes back to the founding of the Regiment, but its regimental use dates only from 1872, when the motto was officially used in the cap badge. Since then the word *Bydand* brings to mind The Gordon Highlanders far more readily than it does the Duke of Richmond and Gordon. Carved in granite, it is proudly displayed on war memorials throughout the north-east of Scotland, and will remain as a poignant reminder of the north-east's own regiment for generations to come.

There was always discussion as to the actual meaning of *'Bydand'*. There was acceptance that the motto hovered between 'watchful' and 'waiting'. *The Life of a Regiment* states:

> The form of the word is simple; it is an old form of present participle that occurs in hundreds of Scottish documents up to the seventeenth century. The exact shade of meaning of the present participle of 'To bide' or 'To byde'—sixteenth century spelling is extremely varied—may change with context, but as a broad rule can be little else than 'Standing', 'Staying', 'Biding'—hence 'Standing fast', which is as good a regimental motto as need be.'

The Life of a Regiment, Volume III, p 359.

The following article is a useful background to the meaning of the motto:

> The late Reverend John Grant Michie, M.A., historian and antiquarian writer, was responsible for inquiry into the meaning of the much-discussed motto *'Bydand.'* The translation, he wrote, of *'Bydand,'* as it appears above the crest of Lord Huntly in *Debrett's Peerage*, is 'Abiding.' The sense in which 'Abiding' is used in this instance is generally held to approximate to the well-known *'non obliviscar injuriam'* i.e., if you have been injured by anyone and are unable at the moment to avenge the insult you will abide your time until opportunity places your enemy in your hands, and then exact vengeance to the full. This meaning having regard to the formidable character of the Gordon family of old is likely to be the true import of *'Bydand.'*
>
> A much older interpretation of the word—in view of the services of the Gordon Highlanders—is by Capt. Douglas Wimberley in his book *Four Old Scottish Families*. The Captain's definition is:—

'*Bydand*' is an old Scotch form of the particle '*Byding*' i.e., 'standing firm'.

This meaning is, to some extent, supported by the variations of '*Byding*' used as the mottoes of several branches of the Gordon family. The motto of the Gordons of Avochie was '*Byde Together*,' that of the Gordons of Craig '*Byde*'.

Against those may be put the motto of the Gordons of Badenscoth, '*Still Bydand*,' which may mean either 'Still abiding firm' or, more singularly, 'Still waiting for vengeance.' The '*Victrix Patientia*' of the Gordons of Glenbuchat is likewise of dubious significance. The true meaning of '*Bydand*', however, has also been a matter of dispute. The word has been obsolete for a very long time. Philologists probably alone can tell when it ceased to be used as a part of speech.

In his introduction to the late Mr. John Mitchell's *Bydand, Poems of War and Peace* (1918), Dr. John Malcolm Bulloch, the historian of the Gordon family and its regiments, states:

'*Bydand*' has been the motto of the House of Gordon from time immemorial, but its origin and its meaning raise as much doubt as faced the famous Berlin lawyer, Justizrat Dr. Adolf von Gordon, who told the *Tageblatt* shortly before the war that his family motto, which he described as '*Byid Dand*', has puzzled the pundits of the Fatherland, who knew it only as an old Scotch motto.

The most generally accepted explanation of '*Bydand*' is that it is simply the word 'abiding,' indicating standfastness and 'siccarness.' Another explanation separates the words, much as the German family does, suggesting a warning: Bide—and see what you will get for your trouble.

Whatever the origin of the word, the Gordons have given it an indelible character. It stands for everything implied in the word grit.

T&S, March 1930.

UNIFORM

The kilt

The 75th and the 92nd were raised as kilted regiments. Less than 50 years before, the kilt, and tartan itself, had been proscribed by law, with the sole exception of Highland regiments recruited into the British Army. Had it not been for Pitt the Elder's foresight in calling into service those whom the British Government had so recently sought to destroy, then the kilt would probably have vanished from Scottish life. It was thanks to those regiments that the kilt and tartan were rehabilitated and, through the achievements of the soldiers who wore them, raised to a position of high esteem and acceptance as dress suitable for royalty itself.

Early prints of Highland soldiers show that the kilt worn was the traditional form of the garment, comprising a long tartan plaid wrapped around the waist, fastened with a belt and with the remaining length looped over the shoulder where it was held by a pin.[1] The drawing illustrates this process.

The kilt worn by the Highland regiments of the British Army soon took the form of an adaptation introduced in Scotland, ironically, by an Englishman. A letter from Ivan Baillie, Esquire of Abereachan,[2] dated 22 March 1768, published in the *Edinburgh Magazine* for March 1783, was the source of some misunderstanding about the origin of the kilt:

> This letter has often been quoted to support a belief that the kilt formed no part of Highland dress, but was introduced in later times by an Englishman, a misapprehension arising from not recognising the various senses in which the word *kilt* was used. The Englishman merely cut the kilted plaid in two and used the lower part separated from the upper, which was apt to fall down and inconvenience a working man. This form of the dress was called the *feile-beg* to distinguish it from full Highland garb, which continued to be worn for some time. The shirts were of home-

---

1 The belt was laid down, and the plaid laid over it; it was neatly pleated, leaving a part at each end uncompleted; the belt was fastened around the waist, so that the lower half of the plaid formed the *feile* or kilt. The uncompleted part became the apron; the upper half, falling over the belt, formed the *breacan* or plaid, fastened on the left shoulder, or thrown round the shoulders as a cloak. By loosening the belt, the whole became a blanket (*Plaide* is Gaelic for blanket.)

2 Abriachan on Loch Ness.

made woollen cloth. General Stewart refers to this kilt without pleats as the *fealdag*:

> 'to the best of my knowledge and the intelligence of persons of credit and very advanced years, the piece of Highland dress termed in the Gaelic *felie-beg*, and in our Scots *little kilt*, is rather of late than ancient usage. The upper garment of the Highlanders was the tartan plaid termed in Gaelic *breacan*. When buckled round by a belt, the lower part pleated and the upper loose about the shoulders, the dress was termed in Gaelic *felie*, and in Scots *kilt*. It was a cumbersome, unwieldy habit to men at work, and the lower class could not afford the expense of the belted trousers or breeches. They wore short coats, waistcoats, and shirts of as great length as they could afford, and such parts as were not covered by these remained naked to the tying of the garters on their hose.
>
> 'About fifty years ago, one Thomas Rawlinson, an Englishman, conducted an ironwork in the countries of Glengarrie and Lochaber; he had Highlanders employed in the service, and became fond of the Highland dress and wore it in the neatest form, which I can aver, as I became personally acquainted with him above forty years ago. He was a man of genius, and thought it no great stretch of invention to abridge the dress and make it handy and convenient for his workmen, and accordingly directed the wearing of the lower part, plaited, of what is called the *felie* or *kilt* as above, and the upper part was set aside; this piece of dress so modelled as a diminutive of the former was in the Gaelic termed the *felie-beg* (*beg* in that tongue signifies *little*) and in our Scots termed *little kilt*. And it was found so handy and convenient that in the shortest space the use of it became frequent in all the Highland countries and in many of our northern low countries also. The great *felie* or *kilt* was formed of the plaid double or twofold, the *felie-beg* of it single.'

The Life of a Regiment, Volume II, Appendix VII.

Some in the Army seem to have borne a marked antipathy to the kilt, and attempts were made to put Highland soldiers into trousers: irritations that commanding officers could have done without:

> In reading the history of the Highland regiments one comes across attempts to deprive them of their national garb. The medical authorities appear to have been the chief instigators. In view of our present-day knowledge of hygiene, it is difficult to understand why the kilt was considered unsuitable, and inimical to health, not only in cold countries, but in hot climates as well. Even so late as the South African War,

objections were raised because a large number of men in the Highland Brigade suffered from blisters, and horns of their knees and legs, through long exposure to the sun. The men affected, however, were reservists recalled to the Colours, whose knees and legs had not become hardened to exposure to the sun and air. In hot weather, the kilt has the advantage that a fresh current of air is constantly playing round the lower limbs, lessening the danger of heat-stroke. It is easier to understand why it was considered unsuitable for cold climates, for to the Englishman, who has never worn the kilt, it is natural to consider it a chilly garment. He fails to grasp the important fact that the kilt, instead of lowering the temperature of the body, actually maintains it, by efficiently protecting the abdomen with its vital organs against cold.

A distinguished Highland officer, who served in the trenches in France throughout that first terrible winter of the Great War, unhesitatingly asserted that, if he had to go through the same experiences again he would wear the kilt in preference to trews, which, when wet, clung to the limbs like a wet poultice, causing them to be constantly cold and chilled. When wearing the kilt, the knees soon dried from exposure to the air, and, in addition, the middle portion of the body was always warm and dry.

McIan's Costumes of the Clans states that it was the custom of the Highlanders when herding cattle, and watching them by night, to wet their plaids before wrapping them round them and lying down in the heather, the idea being that, by so doing, the plaid was rendered less pervious to the cutting winds.

An English officer writing from the Highlands in 1725 was surprised when places where Highlanders had spent the night were pointed out, cleared of snow which the heat of their bodies had melted. One can imagine the advantages such men had over more effeminate troops in times of war. In Col. Stewart's *Annals of the Highland Regiments* it is recorded that during the march through Holland and Westphalia in 1794 and 1795, when the cold was so intense that brandy froze in the bottle, the 78th, 79th[3] and the young recruits of the 42nd, with limbs exposed to the severity of the winter, scarcely lost a man, while better-clad troops were knocked up during the march.

Another advantage of the kilt from a purely military point of view is that, however old and worn, it never looks shabby. This has often been commented on at the end of long and arduous campaigns, when line regiments looked like tatterdemalions, while kilted corps looked smart and spruce even if the tartan was faded and worn. The following extract from Col. Stewart's *Annals* is interesting. He says:

---

3   78th: Ross-shire Buffs, later 2nd Battalion, The Seaforth Highlanders, 79th: The Cameron Highlanders.

> The effect of this garb on Highlanders even of the present day is curious. However clownish a young man appears in his pantaloons, walking with a heavy awkward gait and downcast look, if he dresses in the kilt and bonnet on a Sunday, he assumes a new character, holds his head erect, throws his shoulders back, and walks with a strut and mien that might become a Castilian Knight of old Spain.

Most of us who served at the Depot at Castlehill have observed the same metamorphosis when the latest-joined 'loon' first dons the kilt and obtains permission, after a final meticulous scrutiny by the Sergeant-Major, to swagger down the Castlegate and up Union Street!

In 1757 the Fraser Highlanders, raised and commanded by Lord Lovat, were serving in North America. When the regiment landed there, it was proposed to change the uniform as the kilt was thought unsuitable for the severe winter and hot summer in that country. Quoting from Col. Stewart's account, we find that:

> the officers and men vehemently protested against any change and Colonel Fraser explained to the commander-in-chief the strong attachment which the men cherished to this national dress, and the consequences that might be expected to follow, if they were deprived of it. Their representation was successful.

So far we find no hint as to who was responsible for the suggested change. But we are not left in doubt long, for, further on, as we read, we find the following:

> A veteran [of] the regiment was heard to say: 'Thanks to our generous chief we were allowed to wear the garb of our fathers and in the course of six winters showed the doctors did not understand our constitutions, for in the coldest winters our men were more healthy than those who wore breeches and warm clothing.'

So the doctors were the culprits! On referring to the list of the regimental officers, we find that the regimental surgeon was John McLean, a good old Highland name. No doubt he was a Gaelic-speaking Highlander. He had to be, for 90 per cent of the men neither spoke nor understood English. We are pretty safe in assuming that the suggestion did not emanate from him, but from a more senior medical 'brass hat' who knew not 'The Gaelic' nor the speakers thereof.

The next record of any importance we come across should be of interest to Gordon Highlanders, for it refers to the old 92nd. Again Col. Stewart is our authority, and again the doctor was [the cause]!

In 1800, on the voyage from England to Minorca, the 92nd suffered much from sickness. Before embarking in England a number of young recruits joined from the Highlands whose constitutions suffered a severe shock from the confinement and heat on board the transport in a Mediterranean summer and from the salt provisions so different from the milk and vegetable diet in their native country. A notion was prevalent that Highland dress was improper for soldiers, particularly in hot climates. Colonel Erskine, the commanding officer, gave in to this opinion and put his men in pantaloons of the strong thick cloth of which greatcoats were made. In this he was supported by his surgeon and others. The new dress did not have the result anticipated. To young men who had been recently so thinly clothed even in a cold climate, the increased warmth and confinement of the lower limbs had a disastrous effect, and gave rise to an inflammatory fever which broke out in all the transports. Of this malady a number of the finest young men died, and many were so debilitated as to be totally unfit for service in Egypt.

We then read the somewhat pathetic sentence: 'The commanding officer saw the mistake of following the advice given him, and declared he would never again alter the uniform.'[4]

In reading this account, it is easy to read between the lines. There are two statements in particular to be noted, viz., (1) 'the commanding officer gave in', from which we conclude that great pressure was brought to bear on him; and (2) 'In this (i.e., changing the kilt) he was strongly supported by his surgeon, etc.' The latter—his name was Findlay,[5] and therefore evidently a Scot if not a true Highlander—must not be treated too harshly by us. He was up against it, and in giving the advice he did, he no doubt was actuated by what he conscientiously believed was best for the regiment. But the man to whom our sympathy goes out most is the commanding officer, forced, as he evidently was, against his will to give in to what he believed, on expert advice, to be best for his men, and then later to find that he had been wrongly advised. The feelings of the officers and men can be better imagined than described, as also their deep resentment at what they must have considered the gross indignity to which they were subjected. These feelings must have been further accentuated while the regiment lay in Minorca, for we read that:

> the men made a most unmilitary appearance in their gray pantaloons, which, in addition to the thick texture of the cloth, were loose and badly fitting. The 42nd, which had been some time stationed in the Island, was quartered in the same Barrack, and had been recently

4   Erskine put the 92nd into pantaloons at Bastia in 1796, not during the voyage to Minorca in 1800. *The Life of a Regiment*, Volume I, p 31.
5   William Findlay was appointed surgeon of the 92nd when the regiment was raised in 1794.

supplied with new clothing. The martial appearance of the men, their erect air, walk and carriage were striking.'

Now, from this statement, we can imagine a lot. Two regiments in the same barrack, one in all the pride of new uniform and good health, the other bitterly resentful in an alien uniform, and with much sickness. Truly the 92nd's cup was indeed full to overflowing![6]

It speaks volumes for the spirit and discipline of the Regiment that, despite these trials, it covered itself with glory in Egypt a few months afterwards. There is a sad sequel, for we find that the two chief actors in it both died a few months later. Col. Erskine was killed while gallantly leading his regiment into action on March 13th, 1801, 'leaving,' as Col. Stewart relates, 'few officers of higher spirit and greater promise.' William Findlay, the regimental surgeon, died in Egypt in the same year[7].

F. McL.

T&s, January 1931.

The Tartans of the 75th and 92nd

There is no doubt as to the tartan the 92nd Gordon Highlanders wore. There is less certainty about the tartan the 75th Highland Regiment wore, but the article below raises an intriguing possibility:

In *The Life of a Regiment*, Col. Greenhill Gardyne says that it is not known what tartan was worn by the 75th when they were raised. He goes on to say that Capt. John MacRae-Gilstrap of Baltimore has a portrait of his grandfather, Major Colin MacRae of Conchra, in the uniform of the 75th. In it the colour is faded, but the tartan looks like the Gordon.

When the Black Watch was embodied in the Regular Army about 1740, a tartan called the '42nd Tartan' was invented and issued. This tartan was worn by all ranks except the grenadier company and the drums (who always wore the uniform of the grenadiers). These latter added a red stripe making a sett similar to the present Athol Murray. This habit of altering tartans for special purposes went on. As other Highland corps were raised they were issued with this Government tartan, and some added a stripe or stripes (often of the colour of their facings) to differentiate it from other corps. The Black Watch and the Argyll and Sutherland Highlanders still wear the original tartan (the Sutherland tartan is merely a lighter shade of

---

6 This account is fantasy. In 1796, when the 100th was put into trousers in Bastia (not Minorca), the 42nd remained in Gibraltar, when five companies were sent to the West Indies. The two regiments met in Minorca in 1800, but both wore the kilt. The 42nd 'received [the 92nd] with the hospitality so characteristic of the Scot abroad. Wine flowed, the quaint old streets of Mahon re-echoed Highland toast and song, and no doubt many a Highland head ached next morning!'

7 Sgt Robertson records Findlay's death in his account of the Battle of Alexandria. See Volume IX, Chapter 16.

the 42nd tartan). The 73rd (MacLeod's) Highlanders in 1777 added red and buff lines to the 42nd sett. The 78th (Ross-shire Buffs) added red and white lines and later called it 'Mackenzie Tartan.' The 79th invented a tartan of their own. It was issued to all the Lowland regiments and is still worn by the Royal Scots Fusiliers. The other Lowland regiments have since assumed tartans of their own for various reasons.

A.N. Edmonston Browne, in his *Notes on the Dress of the 71st Regiment*, bears out this suggestion. He also states that the Duke of Gordon chose the pattern now called the 'Gordon Tartan' from three samples. The others had two and three yellow lines respectively.

In view of all this evidence, it seems reasonable to suppose that the 75th took the 42nd tartan and added a line of their facing colour, i.e., yellow, anticipating their present tartan by some hundred years!

P. D. Clendenin.

T&S, June 1936.

The *Tiger and Sphinx* goes on to say:

The invention of Gordon tartan is fixed for us by a letter, preserved at Gordon Castle, which William Forsyth, Huntly, who had recruited for the Marquis' Black Watch Company, wrote on April 15th, 1793:

When I had the honour of communing with his Grace the Duke of Gordon, he was desirous to have patterns of the 42nd Regiment plaid with a small yellow stripe properly placed. Enclosed [are] three patterns of the 42nd plaid, all having yellow stripes. From these I hope his Grace will fix on some of the three stripes. When the plaids are worn, the yellow stripes will be square and regular. I imagine the yellow stripes will appear very lively.

On April 20th the Duke fixed on pattern No. 2—'the same with the 42nd Regiment with the alteration of the yellow stripe properly placed, the quality of the plaid same in every other respect.' Forsyth sent three patterns to the Duke—one yellow stripe, two yellow stripes and three yellow stripes. The single yellow stripe is the most familiar. I do not know if a two-yellow stripe was ever woven: but the three-yellow stripe is worn by the Wolrige-Gordons of Hallhead and Esslemont. It was also used by the late Duke of Richmond and Gordon, and is to be seen as a carpet in the entrance hall at Gordon Castle. The present Duke adopted the single stripe, as you see in the picture of him by Sir A.S. Cope, painted in 1919. By doing so he reverted to the sett worn by the 5th Duke of Gordon, as seen in portraits painted by Raeburn and Sanders.

J. M. Bulloch.

T&S, July 1929.

Gordon Highlander kilt showing yellow line on each pleat.

The uniform of the 75th

Raised as a Highland regiment, the 75th wore the Highland uniform:

The uniform was red with yellow facings, with the Highland dress, much the same as that of other Highland regiments, but whether in the ancient form of the *breacan an fheilidh* or of the *feile-beg*[8] does not appear. The officers were armed with sword and dirk, the latter holding a knife, fork, and spoon, the sergeants with sword and halbert—a light kind of battle-axe with a long shaft (replaced in 1792 by the pike). Officers and sergeants of flank companies carried fusils.[9] Officers wore silver epaulettes, but they had no lace on their jackets; belts at that period were generally black, with the buckle; the hair was curled at the side and tied back with a ribbon at the neck, till queues were introduced. Sergeant's rank was shown by the sash and laced shoulder-knot, or aiguilette, till chevrons were introduced in 1797–8.

The Life of a Regiment, Volume II, p 184.

---

8   The *breacan an fheilidh* was the traditional kilt, where the long plaid was wound and pleated round the waist and then looped over the shoulder. The *feile-beg* was the cut-down version of the kilt, now universally worn, where the length of pleated tartan was wound round the waist and buckled, with the shoulder loop removed.

9   A fusil was a short flintlock musket closely resembling a carbine.

Private soldier of 75th Highland Regiment, 1788

In *The Life of a Regiment*, Col. Gardyne expresses doubt as to the tartan worn by the 75th and states that black belts were worn. I have evidence that the tartan was Gordon. The Regiment was raised when white belts were regulation for all the Line; it is probable that they were issued with these, as all Highland corps wore white belts. Apart from this, the uniform was almost identical with that of the 92nd, with the exception of lace on the men's coats, which was plain. Officers wore a thin line of yellow silk twist to the buttons, and white waistcoats.

In 1787 the 75th were ordered to wear white hats in India. Apparently they changed to the uniform worn by English regiments at this period. There is a picture of Lieut. Branton[10] in the print of the Storming of Seringapatam. He is wearing English uniform with a waist-sash while the 'Scotch Brigade' wear Highland dress.

On their return from India in April, 1807, the 75th resumed Highland dress, as Hastings Irwin records: '1808 P.R.O. 75th, shoes with straps for buckle with Highland dress.'

In 1809 they ceased to wear the kilt, but retained certain Highland characteristics.[11] The late S.M. Milne had a portrait of Lieut. H. Malone showing him wearing a silver thistle with four leaves instead of the usual shako-plate, and a Highland sash and claymore. Whether the Regiment still retained their pipers I have been unable to find out.

P.D. Clendenin.

T&S, June 1936.

---

10 Charles Branton is shown in the Army List of 1788, but not later. Lt Nicholas Brutton is shown in the Army List covering 1799, when the second siege of Seringapatam took place.

11 See Chapter 5, p 42.

Uniform of the 75th in 1840

[In 1862 Horse Guards] acquainted the officer commanding that, at the recommendation of H.R.H. the Commander-in-Chief, Her Majesty had been graciously pleased to approve the 75th Regiment 'being in future distinguished as the "Stirlingshire," it having been raised in that county.'

Colonel Radcliff having applied to change the regimental forage caps, he received a letter informing him that Her Majesty had been pleased to authorise the 75th Stirlingshire Regiment to wear the round Kilmarnock forage cap with diced border, similar to that worn by non-kilted Highland regiments, [to] mark its national origin.

The Life of a Regiment, Volume II, p 232.

The uniform of the 92nd

The 92nd wore full Highland dress (*breacan an fheilidh*)—plaid and kilt in one, called in Regimental Orders 'the belted plaid.' Officers had twelve yards of Gordon tartan, but a smaller sett than was afterwards used. Rank and file had a smaller quantity. The officer's purse was badger-skin, with a silver rim on top, and six silver-mounted white tassels. Rank and file purses were grey goat-skin, with six white tassels. Hose were of strong red and white tartan cloth known in the Highlands as *cathadh* or 'battle colour,' worn by all Highland corps, and by civilians in Highland dress. Rosettes and garters were scarlet; the crimson sash was worn over the left shoulder by officers and sergeants. Officers wore a gilt gorget. All ranks had long hair, tied with a black ribbon, powdered on Sundays, special occasions, and on guard. Moustaches or whiskers were not worn.

The head-dress consisted of the round bonnet then commonly worn in Scotland, cocked and ornamented with ostrich feathers, with a diced border of red, white, and green, representing the *fess chequé* in the arms of the Stuart kings. It had a hackle fastened over the left ear by a black cockade, with regimental button on it.

The jacket was scarlet for officers and sergeants, red for the rank-and-file, with lapels turned back with yellow, showing the waistcoat, laced two and two; lace silver with blue thread; silver or plated buttons, with the number of the regiment in the centre.

Officers carried the Highland claymore, worn at the back, in the buff belt, fastened by a silver oval breast-plate, having a crown and thistle, surrounded by the words 'Gordon Highlanders'; they had a silver-mounted dirk. Sergeants with claymore and pike. Rank-and-file carried flint-lock muskets, the barrels brightly polished, and bayonets. Musicians were armed with the claymore. Knapsacks were goat-skin.

The Life of a Regiment, Volume I, pp 19–20.

The uniform of the 92nd (1794–1808) is illustrated below:

Private, Light Company; Sergeant, Grenadier Company; Private, Battalion Company.

Officer, Light; Mounted Officer, Battalion; Officer, Grenadier Companies.

Piper; Bandsman; Drummer.

The uniform of The Gordon Highlanders (75th/92nd)

The new regiment adopted the 92nd uniform, with amendments to acknowledge the 75th. The two theatre honours recognising the 75th's achievement in India and the 92nd's in Egypt were used to display the linking of the two regiments. The tiger and the sphinx were displayed together on uniform buttons, on cross belt plates and on sporran badges. The tiger was shown on the high-buttoned collar of the dress uniform. When khaki Service Dress jackets came to be worn, officers wore the sphinx on the collar. The two honours gave their name to the regimental magazine: *The Tiger and Sphinx*.

Some took issue with the portrayal of the symbols of their Regiment:

DESIGN ON 75TH BREASTPLATE, 1842.

We reproduce a sketch of the design on a 75th breastplate. In a letter from Major-General G.F. de Berry, who joined the 75th in 1842, he says, 'Please notice the tiger in the sketch. I call your attention to it because I believe in the badge now worn the tiger's tail is curled over his back, which is wrong and I think ought to be rectified. I know we used to be most particular about this. We wore on our forage caps the same badge as on the breastplate, without the battle honours.'

Can any reader explain why and when this alteration was made? There does not appear to be any information about it in any of the documents preserved at the Depot.

T&S, January 1925.

SECTION 2

RECRUITING

RECRUITING practices changed over the two centuries that The Gordon Highlanders existed. Both the 75th and the 92nd were recruited through the efforts of the men charged with raising the respective regiments. One was a successful military man while the other was an aristocrat with extensive estates and a tenantry that depended on him. They delegated responsibility to family members, members of their personal staffs and the officers appointed to the new regiments. Success depended upon the reputation and standing of the man given the task and the esteem in which he was held.

Once a regiment was raised, responsibility for recruiting lay with it, although drafts could be posted in from other regiments. There was no formal recruiting organisation, and regiments had small recruiting parties, headed by an officer, that traversed the countryside to persuade young men to enlist. As the years went on, a recruiting organisation grew. This section covers recruiting for the 75th and the 92nd throughout the years.

CHAPTER 5

RECRUITING FOR THE 75TH

THE man who raised the 75th, Sir Robert Abercromby, had an established military reputation, having served with distinction in America.

The Life of a Regiment implies that the 75th was not recruited from the area around Stirling ('there is, however, no evidence that it was recruited particularly in that district'). The *75th Regiment Record Book* states that the 75th 'was raised in the Town of Stirling in the year 1787, [and] Recruited chiefly in that neighbourhood, and from the Highlands'. The 'neighbourhood' of Stirling includes the southern edge of the Highlands, and it seems likely that this area and the southern Highlands into which it merged is where most of the local recruiting would have taken place. The comment that 'several of [the gentry], among them MacKenzie of Seaforth, assisted Colonel Abercromby in his levy' implies that bodies of men came from the MacKenzie lands north of the Great Glen. The title of the regiment, 'The 75th *Highland* Regiment', appears to have been an accurate description of its early composition.

Recruiting for the 75th while it was in India was a problem. The Regiment suffered considerable losses in the battles and sieges in which it was engaged in the nineteen years it spent in India, and while there was an occasional draft from Britain, these were made up of men recruited across the country and not necessarily from the Highlands of Scotland. Drafts from Highland regiments returning to Britain helped keep up the numbers and preserved the Highland character of the 75th, but, after the losses suffered at Bhurtpore in 1805, 300 men were drafted in from the 76th,[1] an English regiment (not the former 76th also known as 'Macdonald's Highlanders'), and this 'caused the first great change in the nationality of the 75th'.

When it returned to Britain in 1807 the 75th lost most of its soldiers, who were drafted into regiments remaining in India. The 75th was stationed at Dunblane, 'where several recruits and volunteers from the Militia joined, and by November the effective strength exceeded 300, but among them "were but few Highlanders" '.

In 1809 Horse Guards decreed that, along with three other Highland regiments, the 75th should cease to be Highland and would become an infantry regiment of the line. The Horse Guards memorandum that brought this into effect was unthinking and unfeeling, causing grave offence in the Highlands:

---

1   Later 2nd Battalion, The Duke of Wellington's Regiment.

41

As the population of the Highlands of Scotland is found to be insufficient to supply recruits for the whole of the Highland corps on the establishment of His Majesty's army, and some of these corps laying aside their distinguishing dress, which is objectionable to the natives of South Britain, would in a great measure tend to facilitate the completing of their establishments, as it would be an inducement to the men of the English Militia to extend their service in greater numbers to those regiments, etc.

Following this undiplomatic memorandum, the 75th, then quartered at Haddington, adopted the uniform of regiments of the line and was no longer designated as a Highland regiment.

In 1831, when the 75th went to South Africa, 'the reserve companies were moved from Sheerness to Plymouth, and subsequently to Bristol, enlisting recruits at all these places'. With the reserve, or depot, companies in England, the 75th was no longer predominantly Scottish, although it still had many Scotsmen in its ranks. There is evidence that, although the depot companies were in England when the 75th was on service overseas, the regiment maintained a recruiting station in Scotland. The 75th was in Ireland from 1845 to 1849, a period when 'a large number of recruits' were enlisted. In 1849, prior to leaving for India, the 75th received two sergeants and 105 rank and file volunteers from the 73rd and 79th regiments,[2] which boosted the Scottish character of the regiment. The 75th went to Ireland again in 1866–67. In the latter part of 1866 many recruits were attested, and at this time some sixty percent of the rank and file were Irish. In 1877, during the period when regiments were 'linked', the 75th sent a draft to the 39th Regiment,[3] which was in India. In the following year, with fears about a possible war with Russia, the 75th, its establishment having been raised to 1,000 rank and file, received 350 men from the Army Reserve and 177 from the Dorset and Somerset Militia and Reserve. Later in 1878, the threat of war having subsided and the reserves being no longer required, they were released, leaving the 75th nearly 200 rank and file below the establishment of 600 After amalgamation with the 92nd in 1881, recruiting was largely confined to the new regimental area in the north-east of Scotland.

2   73rd (Highland) Regiment of Foot, later 2nd Battalion, The Black Watch; 79th Cameron Highlanders.
3   39th (Dorsetshire) Regiment of Foot.

CHAPTER 6

RECRUITING FOR THE 92ND

THE 92nd (100th) was part of a remarkable feat by the 4th Duke of Gordon in raising troops for the Crown:

> Nothing illustrates more tellingly the intense activity of the ducal line and the family in raising troops than the fact that between 1759—the year when Quebec fell and Robert Burns was born—and 1794, a period of only thirty-five years, the fourth Duke of Gordon raised two regiments of the line and two of Fencibles, besides contributing a company for his brother-in-law in the Fraser Highlanders, and one in the Black Watch for his own son and successor.
>
> J.M. Bulloch
>
> *T&S, December 1935.*

Responsibility for finding the men who would form the new regiment lay with the Marquis of Huntly, who was to command it. Normally, he would have led the drive to secure recruits, appearing in person throughout the widespread Gordon estates, but having been injured, and being laid up in Edinburgh, he could not appear personally in the north:

> The Duke, aided by his family, put in a great deal of work, for the difficulty of getting men from a countryside bled white with a quarter of a century of recruiting was greater than ever. He was handicapped by the absence of his son, the Marquess of Huntly, who was lying ill in Edinburgh with an injured leg. His absence was a source of great anxiety to Capt. William Finlason, the chief recruiting officer, whose mother was a Gordon of Aberdour, and who had held a commission in the Duke's first regiment. For, at his wits' end, he wrote of the Marquess: 'Good God, why will he not come and be the Lion in his own cause?'[1] Even more serious was the fierce opposition by a rival recruiter, Alexander Leith-Hay of Rannes, who was raising the 109th, or Aberdeenshire Regiment.
>
> J.M. Bulloch
>
> *T&S, December 1935.*

---

1   On March 24 Finlason wrote: 'I got on very slowly in numbers here. Had it not been for the enterprises of a new corps, I had been about 40 strong, instead of 32 as I stand. Had the Marquis come among us long ago, it would have been above 100 men in his way taking the country all over. Every gauger in Scotland is employed for [Graham of Balgowan]. So between that and the Hay Corps we are sadly off: and no Marquis to support [us].'

The impetus to the Duke's drive to raise another regiment came from his remarkable Duchess, Jane Maxwell (known within the Regiment as 'Duchess Jean'). She had supported all previous efforts, taking:

> an active part in helping to raise his two regiments of Fencibles, in 1778 and 1793, and was even more absorbed in the single companies for the Fraser Highlanders and Black Watch. Every time the demand for more reinforcements came she took a very prominent part in helping her husband, who was an easy-going man, to raise and equip them.
>
> J.M. Bulloch

T&S, December 1935.

Her efforts to help raise a regiment for her beloved son, the Marquis of Huntly, transcended energy and devotion, turning the raising of The Gordon Highlanders into legend and endowing a prosaic and down-to-earth process with a romanticism and charm of Hollywood proportions:

Jane Maxwell, Duchess of Gordon, helping to raise The Gordon Highlanders

The celebrated Duchess Jean, still a beautiful woman, lent to it all the prestige of her high position, and all the grace and charm of manner in which she was famed alike in Court and cottage.

She rode in the country fairs in Highland bonnet and regimental jacket (it was not unusual, in those days of military enthusiasm, for ladies to wear the uniform of their husbands' or brothers' regiments). It is told how she gave a kiss to the men she enlisted—a fee more valued than the coin by which it was accompanied, as in the case of a smart young farmer at Huntly market, who took the shilling and kiss, and then paid 'smart,'[2] saying, 'A kiss from your Grace is well worth a pound note.'

Sometimes she is said to have placed a guinea between her lips. There was in a Highland village a young blacksmith, remarkable for his strength and good looks. Recruiters for the Guards and Line had in vain tried to enlist him, but he could not resist her Grace! He took the kiss and the guinea; but to show it was not the gold that tempted him, he tossed the guinea among the crowd.[3]

The Life of a Regiment, Vol I, p 11.

The 92nd had to be kept up to strength. Though it did not see any major action in its early years, there were losses through discharge, illness and misfortune, and the Duke of Gordon had to recruit to keep the Regiment up to strength. It was commonplace for drafts from regiments not on active service to make up the strength of regiments in the field. To a Highland Regiment, raised on the premise of serving alongside friends and fellow countrymen, this drafting practice was mistrusted and abhorred:

When the Gordon Highlanders were stationed in Gibraltar in 1796 a rumour got abroad that they were to be drafted into another corps, and only the great influence of the Marquis of Huntly, commanding them, stopped the suggestion. In January, 1797, the Marquis had an advertisement posted on the kirk doors of Kingussie and Advie—

His Lordship, being anxious to have a few young handsome fellows to complete his Regiment, entreats and expects the assistance and support of his friends in Badenoch. He can assure such young men as are willing to go along with him that the Regiment is not to be drafted during the war[4] and that they may depend upon every attention from him while they continue in service; and that on their return to the country they and their relations will have preference upon equal terms from the Duke of Gordon for such farms on his estate as they are inclined to settle upon. His Lordship will be at Aviemore the whole day on Monday.

T&S, May 1931.

---

2   If a recruit repented his bargain before being sworn in, he paid £1, 'smart money'.
3   For more about this remarkable woman, see 'Jane Maxwell, Duchess of Gordon' in Chapter 30.
4   Lord Huntly was successful in this guarantee as no Gordons were drafted, although several regiments with them at Gibraltar shortly after, including the 42nd Highlanders (Black Watch) and the 90th Regiment (Perthshire Volunteers), did have drafts taken from them.

A letter bearing on recruiting for the Gordons was written by Col. Duncan Macpherson of Cluny (1750–1813).[5] Writing on February 22nd, 1797, to William Tod, the factor for the Duke of Gordon in Badenoch and Lochaber,[6] he said:

> My namesake, Thomas Macpherson, the refractory fellow in Balgowan, has at last come to his senses and brought his son Malcolm here this morning, a volunteer for the Marquis' Regiment. His terms[7] are as moderate as could be expected (I have promised him they should be granted), as he only asks what Lord Huntly offers to every other person, viz., half aughten part of land (free of services) where he at present resides or in the place of Gorstial with as much land contiguous to it as will make up an half aughten part. The latter of the two he would prefer, and I think by far the most eligible situation for him, as our friend Mr. Grant has already two pensioners saddled upon him, and in my opinion it would be a hardship to burden him with any more.
>
> I shall accommodate his eldest son with an half aughten part at Glaskinloan, near the farm which his father wishes to get. I need not mention that the place of Gorstial and Blergiebeg is part of the farm of Delchallie, at present occupied by sub-tenants of which Mr. Mitchell is manager, as factor for Parson Robert's son; and I make no doubt he will readily provide for Thomas Macpherson on your applying to him, for he is a very good tenant, although he happened to forget himself upon the present occasion.
>
> With respect to Bounty money, the father leaves that matter totally to his lordship. I mentioned to Lord Huntly at Gordon Hall that, as the boy was young and weak, I wished his lordship to take him into his own service, but, as he had no way for him at the time, he promised to write to your son to employ him, or to get one of his brother officers to take him as a servant. I must, therefore, beg your attention to this matter, and procure a letter for the boy. His father requested me to say he hoped you would have the goodness to antidate his attestation, and, as the boy attends school, he hopes Lord Huntly will indulge him with remaining in the country as long as any of his other recruits.
>
> If the Marquis is at the castle, pray make my best respects to him, and tell him that I have not forgot my toast when we were all so tipsy at Pitmain, and I can with truth assure you that few of his lordship's friends has a higher esteem for Gillidow Glenamore than your humble servant.

---

5   Macpherson of Cluny was married to Huntly's sister, Catherine.
6   Tod's son, Ensign William Tod, was one of the original officers of the 92nd in 1794.
7   In those days recruits bargained for bounties.

The interesting point about these letters is the light they throw on soldiering at this time as a family affair.

J.M. Bulloch

T&S, May 1931.

The commanding officer was responsible for recruiting, and parties were kept in Scotland for this purpose. Some were employed because of ability, while others were there to recover from wounds or illness. In 1800 six officers, seven sergeants, one drummer and fifteen privates were recruiting in Scotland. These made up the 11th, or 'Recruiting Company'.

After the Treaty of Amiens in 1802, it was expected that the Army would be reduced, and the 92nd would be disbanded. Sir John Moore, writing to Major John Cameron, said 'I am sorry to find it is determined to reduce the 92nd. Their gallant services entitled them to a better fate.' It soon became clear, however, that Bonaparte's intentions would lead to resumption of the war, and talk of reductions and disbandments ceased:

> Recruiting was actively carried on. The standard height was lowered to 5' 5"; levy money was £6 6s., of which the recruit received £5 5s. Recruits were enlisted at headquarters, and parties sent to various places, such towns being chosen as were frequented by young men from the north in search of employment, from which they visited fairs and feeing markets throughout the neighbouring districts. They received volunteers from the Highland Fencibles, among them 28 from the 'Regiment of the Isles.'

The Life of a Regiment, Volume I, p 111.

When the French broke the Treaty of Amiens in 1803, the government agreed to raise 50,000 additional men by conscription, under the Army Reserve Act; a quota from each county was chosen by ballot (6,000 for Scotland) to serve only in Great Britain and Ireland, but could volunteer for general service with bounty. Men raised in Nairn, Inverness, Moray, Banff and Aberdeen formed a second battalion of The Gordon Highlanders. This battalion became a nursery of good recruits to make up the casualties suffered by the 1st Battalion until the peace of 1814. The 2nd Battalion 92nd Regiment was placed on the establishment on 9 July 1803.[8]

Recruiting was now better organised and the 92nd had recruiters throughout the regimental area. Scotland was divided into four military districts, each with its own headquarters: Northern (Aberdeen),[9] Central (Dundee), Western (Glasgow) and Southern (Musselburgh and West Barns). Recruits were enlisted at headquarters, and parties were sent to places

---

8   The 2nd Battalion, which was permanently based in Great Britain and Ireland, was disbanded in 1814, an unfortunate step that made keeping the 1st Battalion up to full strength more difficult.
9   Commanded in the early years of the nineteenth century by Maj-Gen the Marquis of Huntly.

frequented by young men from the north in search of employment. They visited fairs and feeing markets throughout neighbouring districts.

In 1803, 92nd recruiting stations were in Fochabers, Dundee, Aberdeen, Huntly, Paisley, Stirling, Inverness, Perth and Fort William, commanded respectively by Major John Gordon, Captains John Ramsay, Peter Grant[10] and Peter Gordon; Lieutenants James Mitchell,[11] Donald MacDonald,[12] William McKay and William Phipps; and Ensign Donald McBarnet. Recruiting good men was a very important task, especially when the Regiment had sustained heavy casualties, and the officers heading recruiting teams were usually men of ability. Sometimes they were sent to recover from wounds, sometimes to give hard-working officers a break in home surroundings, but always with the interests of the Regiment at heart. Captains Ramsay and Grant and Lieutenant MacDonald had been wounded in Holland in 1799. James Mitchell and Donald MacDonald went on to command the 92nd. Major John Gordon and Captain Peter Gordon were two of the original officers of the 92nd, and were no doubt due a break after nine years' service.

Recruiting parties had a non-commissioned officer, usually a sergeant, in charge. These were old soldiers, with the confidence, swagger and abundance of tales that goes with years of service. The ability to entrance potential recruits with their presence and their 'patter' gave rise to many tales. The example below is apocryphal, but is not atypical:

> When a party of [a] Highland Regiment was recruiting during the French War, the Sergeant in charge was a thoroughgoing specimen of the true born Highlander. His usual harangue to his gaping audience was:—
>
> 'Noo then, my praw lads, come awa' and list in this auld bauld corpps—often tried, but never found failing—and ca'ed the Twa-and-Forty Royal Hielandman's Feet and Black Watches. It is commanded by His Royal Grace, Prince Frederick, King o' the Highlands and Emperor of all the Europes in Scotland. And she'll give you the praw claes and the muckle bounty.' He would then flourish a bundle of bank notes, which rarely failed to glamour a recruit, on which he would count out his bounty, saying—
>
> 'There, my praw lad—sax and twa's ten and—awa' wi' ye noo, ye tamned scoonrel.'

T&S, June, 1893.

---

10 Promoted major in 1806; served in Peninsula 1810 to 1812; lost left arm and left leg at Fuentes d'Onor, May 1811; retired 1812; died in 1817 due to wound complications.

11 Commanded 92nd when Cameron of Fassiefern was killed at Quatre Bras, but was himself wounded the same day.

12 Commanded 92nd when Mitchell was wounded. Led 92nd during Battle of Waterloo.

Recruiting Poster from 1811–12

THE GALLANT
NINETY-SECOND
OR Gordon Highlanders

who have so often distinguished themselves

at COPENHAGEN, SPAIN, on the plains of HOLLAND and sands of EGYPT, and who are now with LORD WELLINGTON in PORTUGAL, want to get a few Spirited Young Men, Lads, and Boys, to whom the greatest Encouragement and HIGHEST BOUNTY will be given.

From the character of the officers of the Regiment who are from this part of the HIGHLANDS, they can depend that the Interest and Advantage of High-Spirited and Well-Conducted soldiers from this part of the country will be particularly considered.

Recruiting was carried on principally in the north of Scotland, with care as to the class of men taken. Throughout the Napoleonic Wars the 92nd recruiting organisation kept The Gordon Highlanders up to strength with Highland recruits. The 2nd Battalion, formed in 1803, provided a source of trained replacements for the 1st Battalion, which helped to maintain its Highland character:

> Since the formation of the 2nd Battalion, it had never been necessary to receive volunteers from other regiments of the line as had been the case on several previous occasions, and notwithstanding the great drain of constant campaigning, the 1st Battalion had been kept complete with men in whose keeping its character was safe, both in quarters and in the field.

The Life of a Regiment, Volume I, p 345.

One of the best ways of keeping regimental strengths up and reducing pressure on the recruiting organisation is encouraging men at the end of their engagement to sign on for a further period, thus retaining experienced trained men who would otherwise have been lost. The 92nd, in the Peninsular War, knew this only too well:

> While at Banos the men who had enlisted in 1806 for seven years were given the opportunity of renewing their engagements. Men not above

thirty-five years of age were allowed to enlist for life, and received sixteen guineas of bounty; those above thirty-five, for seven years only, and received eleven guineas. These were large sums in those days, sufficient to send a welcome help to the old folks at home, and leave enough to drink their health in many a cup of Spanish wine. There seems to have been a charm about the constant variety and adventure characteristic of the Peninsular campaign, which appealed powerfully to manly natures and outweighed the occasional hardships and dangers; and most of those who could do so re-engaged for unlimited service, which also entitled them to a pension.

The Life of a Regiment, Volume I, p 269.

The depot did not have a permanent home, but was located in the district where the 92nd was based, and remained in that district when the Regiment went overseas. There were four companies, commanded by a field officer, with an adjutant and a paymaster who acted as quartermaster. There was a corps of drums and fifes—and pipers. Two of the colour-sergeants acted as sergeant-major and quartermaster-sergeant, paid and clothed as such. The depot served as a battalion for general military service, but the principal responsibility lay in the selection and training of recruits and young officers.

During the Crimean War, the 92nd was left undermanned when 234 men volunteered for active service and were sent to the 30th, 44th and 55th Regiments.[13] This was exacerbated when shortages in the 42nd (Black Watch) and 79th (Cameron Highlanders) were made up by volunteers from the 92nd depot: 'a particularly fine body of young men, and almost everyone that was fit volunteered for service, all choosing the 79th, except ten, who went to the 42nd.'[14] Volunteers were attracted by the prospect of active service. With some, enthusiasm went beyond the bounds of practicability:

> As usually happens in war-time, young men of mettle wanted to see the fighting. One young fellow was found, on being measured, not to touch the standard.[15] 'Go home, my lad,' said the colonel, 'take more milk to your brose, and come back when you've grown.' 'Oh, sirs,' entreated the lad, 'an' ye'd juist tak' me! I'm *wee*, but I'm *wicked*!'

The Life of a Regiment, Volume II, p 83.

---

13 30th (Cambridgeshire) Regiment, 44th (East Essex) Regiment, 55th (Westmorland) Regiment.

14 This was because the 92nd and 79th were raised in the same district, and because in the 42nd the men appeared in the kilt at morning, and in *good* trousers at evening parade, which caused extra expense, while the 79th customs were less costly, like those of the 92nd.

15 A recruit was deemed tall enough if, standing next to the Regimental Colour with the staff on the ground, his head reached the lower corner of the flag on the staff. This height equated roughly to 5½ feet.

Training and recruiting group at the 92nd Depot, Stirling Castle, 1861

Until the Childers reforms of 1881, regimental depots were based in the area where the regiment was posted, and when the regiment went abroad they remained at a permanent garrison location. When the 92nd left Ireland for Corfu in 1852 the depot remained in Ireland. Even here, however, the policy laid down by General MacDonald was that only natives of Scotland should be recruited, and this was achieved by having recruiting parties throughout Scotland.[16]

No matter how successful recruiting parties might have been, until a recruit had been attested into his regiment, there was always the possibility that he might be 'diverted' elsewhere:

> Great exertions were made to recruit. Besides the regular parties, all n.c. officers and men were allowed to enlist (the recruiter's fee for each recruit was a guinea). It became known that the regiment was particular as to the class of men taken, which had the best effect. Officers were sent to the Scottish militia regiments, getting many volunteers. The Inverness Militia had few townsmen, but was filled with country-bred Highlanders, and the officer commanding the depot wished to get some of these men from the districts where the regiment had been raised, and with which it had kept up its connection. An officer who spoke Gaelic offered to undertake the journey (by coach from Perth), but the recruiting sergeant at Inverness wrote that it was not necessary, as over seventy men had given him their names for the 92nd; on the volunteering parade, however, the son of their adjutant, who had the promise of a commission in another

---

16 In 1855 there were recruiting parties in Stornoway, Tain, Inverness, Campbeltown, Huntly, Perth, Edinburgh, Glasgow and Hawick.

regiment on condition of bringing men, induced them to go with him, and the Gordons only got about seventeen.

The Life of a Regiment, Volume II, pp 82–83.

In Scotland, soldiering was seen as an honourable calling, and fathers, particularly those who had themselves served, often encouraged their sons to enlist:

> So many joined that the tailors could not clothe them fast enough, and on the 30th January 1855, a draft of 4 officers and 135 n.c. officers and men, under Lieut.-Colonel Lockhart, left for Gibraltar, where their equipment and drill were completed. Many parents came to see these young lads off. Among others I spoke to was an old man with white hair and a blue bonnet, giving his son his blessing and telling him in Gaelic 'never to turn his back on friend or foe.' He was a farmer from Rannoch, who had served at Waterloo as sergeant in the 92nd.

The Life of a Regiment, Volume II, p 83.

In 1855 the 92nd depot returned to Scotland, where 'great exertions were made to recruit'. From then on the depot remained in Scotland when the Regiment was overseas. In 1868, when the 92nd set off from Ireland for India, its depot companies joined the 15th Depot Battalion at Aberdeen, and the regiment established a presence in the city where it had been embodied that would last for the remainder of its days.

Directives from London sometimes led to unsuitable recruits being sent to Highland regiments. The system whereby regiments returning from India could see drafts of men wishing to remain in India sent to regiments arriving there still existed, but wherever possible drafts from Highland regiments were sent to sister Highland regiments:

> *August 20th*, 1867.— A Horse Guards letter informed the commanding officer that 156 volunteers from the 42nd [were to] join the 92nd on its arrival in India. A Horse Guards letter informed inspecting officers of recruiting districts that recruits for general service were to be posted to the 77th and 92nd Regiments. The consequence was an influx of general service men, of whom very few were Scots. Major Forbes Macbean, in Lieut.-Colonel Hamilton's absence, wrote to remonstrate, and a memo was received, stating that the Commander-in-Chief had directed that recruiting for the 92nd should be stopped, except in Scotland. The want of a second battalion was felt; whenever the recruiting was taken out of the hands of the officer commanding the regiment, its nationality suffered.
>
> I remember, in 1852, a sergeant-major telling me that Grant's *Romance of War*, lately published, had brought several recruits to the regiment, and

Mr Ross Martin,[17] formerly sergeant, who joined at the Curragh, 1867, tells how, when he was a boy, the minister at Inverness gave him Grant's book, and how he and his young friends got a man to read it aloud to them in the evenings. He determined to be a soldier when old enough, and that there might be no mistake about the regiment, had '92' tattooed on his arm! When the time came, he and twelve other lads agreed to go together. Not wishing to enlist at Inverness, where most of them were apprenticed, they walked to Fort William, took steamer to Glasgow, where they knew the recruiting sergeant, who had been stationed at Inverness, and enlisted with him.

The Life of a Regiment, Volume II, pp 88–89.

In 1868 the 92nd moved to India. After a long journey on HMT *Crocodile* to Alexandria, by train to Suez, on HMS *Malabar* to Bombay, then by train, boat and route march, they arrived at their destination, Jullundur:

From [Amritsar] they marched, getting a view of the Himalayas by the way, to Jullundur, where they arrived 30th of March. A number of men who had volunteered from the 42nd came out to meet their new regiment, and three of them who were pipers played them in. 'These volunteers were splendid men.'

The Life of a Regiment, Volume II, p 90.

Castlehill Barracks

For almost a century and a half the main barracks in Aberdeen was at Castlehill, but for eighty years it had only a passing acquaintance with The Gordon Highlanders (as when the 92nd depot companies joined the 15th Depot Battalion at Aberdeen in 1868). It was not until 1881, with the amalgamation of the 75th and 92nd, that The Gordon Highlanders' permanent depot became Castlehill Barracks. From that point on Castlehill was closely linked with the Regiment, training its recruits and hosting its recruiting parties. It remained so until 1935 when Castlehill was finally closed and the depot moved to the newly built barracks at Bridge of Don.

Castlehill Barracks was built in the latter half of the 18th century. As early as 1770, Aberdeen Town Council agitated for a barracks, offering to supply 'the site, stone and a supply of the town's water in a leaden pipe'. In 1792 the Lord Provost met the Commander-in-Chief, Lord Adam Gordon, uncle of the 4th Duke, but two years elapsed before anything was done. Recruiting carried on feverishly, so that 1794, when the foundation stone was laid, also saw the raising of The Gordon Highlanders.

---

17 See Sgt Martin's account of treatment of the Colours in Chapter 9.

The foundation stone was laid on Tuesday, 24 June 1794, by the good-looking young Marquis of Huntly. The date was of double interest, for on the same day the Gordon Highlanders were embodied in Aberdeen. The Marquis himself was a soldier. He began his career in 1790 as an ensign in the 35th Foot, closely identified with the Duke of Richmond, who had married the Marquis' eldest sister, Lady Charlotte Gordon; in 1815 she gave the famous ball on the eve of Waterloo. Within a few weeks of being gazetted to the 35th, the Marquis raised an Independent Company for the Black Watch, becoming a captain of them in January 1791. On 10 February 1794, he became Lieutenant-Colonel of the 100th, afterwards the 92nd, or 'Gordon Highlanders'.

The building was 192 feet long and 46 feet wide, with two wings (66 feet x 46 feet), with accommodation for 606 men. A Town Council minute of 8 December 1794 describes the mason work, which cost £16,000, as 'now built and erected'. On 24 May 1796, the Argyle Fencibles marched into it from Fort George.

Castlehill Barracks in the 1840s

Until 1881 The Gordon Highlanders had little contact with Castlehill Barracks—and then only as temporary visitors. When the 75th and 92nd were amalgamated in 1881, however, Castlehill became the home of the Gordon Highlanders' depot and, as such, became an indelible part of the life of the Regiment and every Gordon Highlander.

In 1935 the Gordons marched out of Castlehill and, led by Sir Ian Hamilton, into the new depot at Bridge of Don. The new depot was very different in every respect from Castlehill, which was as old as the Regiment itself. It differed in point of situation, of area and of equipment. Castlehill Barracks, built in 1794, covered two-and-a-half acres on a hill-top, so that expansion was impossible. The new depot, instead of looking down on the sea, was almost level with it, and occupied nearly fifty-four acres.

T&S, September 1934; June 1935.

The depot at Bridge of Don trained recruits for The Gordon Highlanders for a quarter of a century, before becoming the depot for the whole Highland Brigade and then, the training depot for junior soldiers of the whole Scottish Division.

CHAPTER 7

RECRUITING FOR THE GORDON HIGHLANDERS (75TH/92ND)

AMALGAMATION

THE lack of a second battalion posed problems in keeping regiments overseas up to strength. A system was introduced whereby two separate regiments were 'linked': one based in Britain while the other served overseas. The home-based regiment conducted all recruiting and training, posting drafts of trained men to the overseas regiment. The system was not perfect:

> In 1873, a system of linking two one-battalion regiments was introduced. They would retain individuality in number, name, and uniform, but officers and men were liable to serve in either, and the latter would no longer have regimental, but brigade numbers. The 92nd was fortunate in being linked with so good a Highland corps as the 93rd, and the recruits were enlisted for the 56th Depot Brigade. It had long been evident that a regiment of one battalion is unworkable in wartime, but it was not generally considered that linking was a satisfactory solution. Colonel Kenneth MacKenzie, Assistant Adjutant-General at Horse Guards, who had been adjutant of the 92nd, and who had great experience of the discipline and recruiting of a Highland corps, expressed his opinion in the strongest terms. 'It will never do,' he said; 'far better unite all the kilted battalions into one regiment, with one title and uniform; in time they will agree as well as the battalions of the Rifle Brigade, but two separate regiments linked will never answer.'

The Life of a Regiment, Volume II, pp 94–5.

'Linking' was not ideal and amalgamation became the favoured solution:

> The 'linked Battalion' system was unsatisfactory, and experienced soldiers agreed that a regiment of one battalion cannot be made ready for active service without completing one regiment by depleting another—of which the 92nd had such unhappy experience in Crimean days. Mr Childers, Secretary of State for War, concluded that the best way out of the difficulty was to adopt the recommendation that instead of *linking* two still separate regiments, they should be *welded*, as it were, into one, each of the newly organised regiments having a district appointed for its recruiting.

The Life of a Regiment, Volume II, p 177.

On 30th June 1881, an extract from General Orders of 1st May was published in Regimental Orders:—

> The following changes in the organisation, title, and uniform of the regiments of the line having been approved, are promulgated for general information.
>
> The 75th and 92nd will be localised together at Aberdeen. Soldiers serving in any of the battalions, previous to the 1st of July 1881, will not be liable to serve in the other line battalion of the new territorial regiment without their own consent.
>
> The composition and title of the Regiment will be—

The Gordon Highlanders

1st Battalion	75th Foot
2nd Battalion	92nd Foot
3rd Battalion	Royal Aberdeenshire Militia

The Life of a Regiment, Volume II, p 177.

Amalgamation must have been viewed with some unease in the two regiments, but both approached it with good grace and a desire to make it work. For the 75th, which had kept a significant Scottish representation and identity throughout the years of its existence as a line regiment, there was the satisfaction of seeing it restored to its Highland status, and for the 92nd the knowledge that merging with such a distinguished Scottish regiment would solve the problems of maintaining a full establishment when serving overseas. Determined to make the merging of the regiments a success, each regiment marked the amalgamation with humour. When amalgamation came, the 75th was in Malta, at Floriana Barracks:

> The order for the redistribution was issued on 11 April 1881, effective on 1st July. On that day the following epitaph was found in Sa Maison Gardens near Floriana Barracks:—

EPITAPH ON THE 75TH, 30TH JUNE 1881.

> Here lies the poor old Seventy-Fifth,
>   But, under God's protection,
> They'll rise again in kilt and hose,
>   A glorious resurrection!
> For by the transformation power
>   Of Parliamentary laws
> We go to bed the Seventy-Fifth
>   And rise the Ninety-Twa's!

The Life of a Regiment, Volume II, p 238.

Though the 92nd was to retain its own designation of 'The Gordon Highlanders,' all ranks determined that the obsequies of the dying number should be celebrated with due pomp and respect; accordingly, representatives of other corps were invited by the officers to the funeral feast, and at midnight of June 30th, when the number ceased to exist, the funeral oration was pronounced by Lieut-Colonel Luck, 15th Hussars; a torchlight procession was formed, the coffin containing a flag inscribed '92' was borne shoulder high, with the officers in full Highland dress as chief mourners, and proceeded, the band playing the *Dead March*, to the grave. Three volleys were fired over it, and the pipers played a Lament.

Next morning the 'body' had been exhumed, and on the flag, in addition to '92' were the words 'No' deid yet,' while many tents had flags flying with similar mottoes. Some of the English newspapers were foolish enough to find fault with this innocent and harmless ebullition of *esprit de corps*.

The Life of a Regiment, Volume II, p 177.

'Burial' of the 92nd

The amalgamation proved to be particularly successful. There were critics. While in Malta the 75th was mockingly called the '*Strada Reale Highlanders*' (after the main thoroughfare in Valletta) to distinguish it from the 'Real' Gordon Highlanders, the so-called '*Reale Highlanders*'.

After the amalgamation, the 92nd was particularly helpful in aiding the 75th make the transition from a trousered regiment to a kilted Highland one. Interchangeability of officers and men was commonplace. The home battalion endured shortage of men and a constant inflow of young recruits whom it had to train, only to see them posted to the overseas Battalion, but as all wore the same uniform this was accepted. The home battalion played a significant part in attracting new recruits to the Regiment:

When the [Boer] war broke out the 1st battalion had been less than a year in Edinburgh Castle when it had arrived from abroad on 9th December 1898. Most of its men were due for discharge but it found waiting for it 345 immature soldiers left by its sister battalion.

The officers, accustomed to the impressive numbers and physique of a foreign service corps, had to readjust their ideas to accord with half the number, most of them raw recruits. Even the feather bonnets which many donned for the first time could not make up for the lack of men; but if the winter winds of the Castle were trying, the warm welcome throughout the country more than compensated for such drawbacks.

Lack of ground has always made Scottish stations bad for training; musketry was mostly done at Barry, but company training at Stobs Camp, then in the first years of its existence—while for battalion training the Commanding Officer proposed a three weeks' route march through the regimental district. The scheme, I believe the first of its kind, was approved; it met with such success that almost every Scottish regiment has since familiarised its tartan in its home country by similar marches.

The Life of a Regiment, Volume III, p 85.

The Gordon Highlanders held such a place in the affections of the public that recruits from all over Scotland joined them. Some wanted to join but were prevented in the oddest manner!

Colour-Sergeant W.J.D. Pryce, a 'Fifer' by birth, was awarded the D.C.M. [for his actions at Caesar's Camp outside Ladysmith in the Boer attack of 6th January 1900]. His watch was struck by a bullet and his dangerous hurt was complicated by parts being carried into the wound, but he eventually recovered to hold the post of Garrison Sergeant-Major at Aldershot. Later he became the first Quartermaster of the Royal Flying Corps and finally went to New Zealand. He was one of three apprentices of St Andrews who enlisted together. One, Pirie, died as Quartermaster, 2nd Battalion; the third, Jock Menzies, became a Glasgow park-keeper. Sandy Herd (Golf Open Champion, 1902) had arranged to enlist with them but 'his mither hid his claes'!

The Life of a Regiment, Volume III, p 60.

Recruiting poster for The Gordon
Highlanders, 1906

Original photo for 1906 recruiting poster.
Pte H. Hefferon, Pipe Major C. Dunbar,
Pte ? McGeechan

Enlistment in The Gordon Highlanders was the ambition of many, and the recruiting staff often had to console those who were unsuccessful. Some refused to take 'no' for an answer!

One Anderson was rejected for 'hammer toes'. On dejectedly quitting barracks he left £7 in charge of the Quartermaster, but ten days later reappeared.

'Ah, my lad, come for your money, eh?'

'Na, na, I'm back tae 'list; the taes is aff!'

Following the best biblical analogy, he felt it profited him more to be a *sodger wantin' twa taes* than to remain a *civvy* with the full complement!

The Life of a Regiment, Volume III, p 356.

This was not the only example of self-removal of offending digits. In Calcutta in 1909, the 2nd Battalion saw a similar solution to foot problems during a long route march as part of 'Test Manoeuvres'!

No man fell out during the Test, but once he was sure that a sick man no longer lost marks to his corps, Sergeant Brittain, who had returned from two days' leave on 10th January, fell out with a sore foot. It transpired that he had been suffering much from a bad toe. He had gone into a private hospital, had the toe amputated, and marched next day!

The Life of a Regiment, Volume III, p 381.

The First World War saw men patriotically flocking to the ranks of The Gordon Highlanders. Eager to play their part in their own Regiment, they put up with shortages of uniform and equipment, inadequate accommodation and unfamiliarity with military customs and procedures. These citizen soldiers proved to be excellent fighting men, upholding the best traditions of the Regiment, to which they added further glory:

The 15th Division was the senior division of 'K.2', or the 'Second Hundred Thousand'. Its troops had undergone greater discomfort and faced more handicaps in their preparation for war than those of the 9th Division. Recruiting swelled to a flood, so that accommodation became hopelessly inadequate. One battalion had, on September 15th, 1914 one officer—commissioned from the rank of Quartermaster-Sergeant—and 900 men. A little later the first uniforms arrived, the jackets being of red serge. The first handful of obsolete rifles for drill were issued in early October.

'K.2' was given its start by recruits surplus to the needs of 'K.1'. 9th Gordon Highlanders was formed from surplus personnel of the 8th Battalion and a draft of 400 recruits from the depot. It formed part of the 44th (Highland) Brigade, the only one in the division bearing that title. Squad drill without arms was the only form of training at the start because there were no arms. The behaviour of the men was good, not so much from natural virtue as because they took their enterprise so seriously. They made no complaints, though all they had was the suit of clothes they had joined in and one blanket apiece.

The 9th and 10th Battalions lay side by side in camp at Rushmoor, so that their experiences must be practically identical. On September 23rd two horses were issued to the 9th, one for the commanding officer, Colonel W.A. Scott,[1] the other for the adjutant. However, the battalion might have been worse off. Nearly all tents had floorboards, and it did not take long to provide a paliasse for every man. October 7th, greatcoats (civilian) issued; October 8th, 800 D.P. (drill purposes) rifles issued; November 5th, though the men looked well on parade their knowledge was very slight and the simplest military term had to be carefully explained; December 2nd, six bicycles issued; December 7th, a notification that the battalion would wear drab kilts. Apparently it preferred to wait until its own tartan could be obtained.

The Life of a Regiment, Volume IV, pp 52–3.

---

1   Col Scott joined the 92nd in 1874, aged 18. He served in the Boer Wars of 1881 and 1899–1902, taking command of 2nd Gordons at Ladysmith in 1900 after Lt-Col Dick-Cunyngham, V.C. was killed. Having retired in 1907, he returned to the colours on the outbreak of the Great War and commanded the 9th Service Battalion of The Gordon Highlanders.

Drafting of men to other regiments still raised hackles in the 20th century. Gordon Highlanders awaiting discharge after the First War were warned for draft to the Cameron Highlanders. With no disrespect to the Camerons, the Gordons objected to this forcible transfer, particularly as the Camerons were bound for India. Once again, the intercession of a senior Gordons officer, Colonel W.E. Gordon, V.C., calmed tempers, brought the authorities to see reason, and placated the aggrieved soldiers:

> Two hundred men of the Gordon Highlanders, stationed near Aberdeen, who had been ordered to proceed to Invergordon on Saturday morning, refused to parade and leave for their destination, though the band was in attendance and all arrangements had been made for their departure. The men, of whom many have been on active service and some have been prisoners of war, objected to being transferred to the Cameron Highlanders, under orders for India. Most of them belong to the 51st Division and, being all 1916 and 1917 Derby men, argue that they should be kept in this country until they are discharged.
>
> They marched into the town and a deputation, appointed to interview the magistrates, pointed out that there were sufficient re-enlisted and short-service men who had been called up within the last two years, to form the necessary garrisons for foreign service.
>
> Colonel Gordon, V.C., made an official inquiry. The men report that their grievances are to be removed and express entire satisfaction with the result of the investigation. Colonel Gordon was loudly cheered on leaving camp.

The Times, June 1919.

Life in Scotland in 1930 was not easy. The Stock Market crash of 1929 led to the Great Depression that stretched through the 1930s. Service salaries were not excessive, but the army offered a secure job and a life of adventure. The following was 'overheard in the Castlegate':

Geordie: 'Hullo, Tam! Yer lookin' braw. Far did ye get the new shuit?'

Tam: 'Oh, I'm in the Gordon Heilenders noo ; an' I get fourteen bob a week, an' as I've got naething tae dae wi' it, I bocht this shuit.'

Geordie: 'Gosh, man! I hae twa pown ten a week an' it taks me aboot twa year tae buy a shuit like that.'

Tam: 'Oh, aye. I dare say, but ye hae lodgins, claes and beets an' a' yer extras tae buy oot o' that, an' I get the hale lot for naething.'

Geordie: 'Fin yer a sodger I aye thocht ye hid tae weer yer sodger claes.'

Tam:	'Sae I hiv; but gin ye behave yersel' they lat ye weer civvies fan yer oot, and fin I ging hame they gae ye a cheeper ticket on the train.'
Geordie:	'Fat dae ye dee wi' a' yer siller fin ye hinna got onything tae buy?'
Tam:	'Och, I files send puckles hame tae ma mither an' I'm keepin' the rest o't for ma month's holiday fin I get it.'
Geordie:	'Man, yer a richt lucky divil! I've hid an affa time wi' weet weather an' I'm fair scunnert. Fu auld hive ye tae be tae jine?'
Tam:	'Oh, echteen tae five and twenty if yer teeth's gweed. Come awa' up tae the berrecks if noo an' get yer denner wi' me and we'll see the recruitin' mannie. Mebbie I'll get ye inta ma room if ye pass.'
Geordie:	'Come awa', Tam.'

T&S, November 1930.

It might be expected, during the Depression, that recruiting would not be a problem, and the figures for The Gordon Highlanders in 1933 bear this out. It is interesting to note how the physical and educational standards of the recruits obtained met or surpassed the average for the army as a whole, while wastage during training was significantly lower than the average. A letter to General Sir Ian Hamilton from the Depot in July 1933 showed the following results:

Strength on July 1st, 1932: —

1st Battalion (India)	890
2nd Battalion (plus recruits at Depot)	669
Depot Staff (less recruits)	70
Total	1,629

Strength on July 1st, 1933: —

1st Battalion (India)	897
2nd Battalion (plus recruits at Depot)	731
Depot Staff (less recruits)	70
Total	1,698

The average strength of all infantry battalions at home, including recruits under training at Depots on July 1st, 1933, was 702.

During the first quarter ending June 30th, 1933, 85 recruits were obtained, of which 82 were county men.

The average height and weight of the recruits obtained during this quarter was 5ft. 6¾ in. and 133lb., as compared with the general infantry standard of 5ft. 4in. and 115lb. for the same period. During the quarter ending June 30th, 1933, the net recruit wastage at your Depot was 3 (3.0%), of the average number of recruits under training. During the same period the average net wastage at all infantry depots was 9.9 (6.8%), of the average number of recruits under training.

During the quarter we obtained our full quota of infantry recruits. The quality of recruits accepted, both physically and educationally, is well up to the average. We propose to maintain the existing standards throughout the next quarter.

T&S, September 1933.

The reputation of the Regiment, and the esteem in which it was held by the public, were of great assistance in attracting recruits:

An officer of another regiment, seeing some fine-looking Scotsmen standing talking near a recruiting station outside our Regimental Area, asked them why they did not join the Army. They replied, 'We have tried, but are told the Gordon Highlanders are closed for recruits.' The officer suggested they should join some other regiment, mentioning some that were short of recruits, amongst them his own. But the men replied, 'No, we will only join the Gordon Highlanders. We have heard how well they treat you while you are serving and, when you have finished, they try to get you a job.'

T&S, March 1934.

In 1935 The Gordon Highlanders left Castlehill and marched to their new depot at Bridge of Don. The citizens of Aberdeen lined the streets, and throngs of proud men and women clapped and cheered as men of their Regiment left their spiritual home for the last time. Led by the pipe band playing regimental tunes, a long column of Gordon Highlanders, young and old, serving and retired, marched out of Castlehill, through the Castlegate into King Street on to the long road leading out of Aberdeen to Bridge of Don. This historic event was a major milestone in the history of the Regiment:

In 1935 the Gordons marched out of Castlehill and, led by Sir Ian Hamilton, into the new depot at Bridge of Don. The new depot was very different from Castlehill, which was as old as the Regiment itself. It differed in point of situation, of area and of equipment. Castlehill Barracks, built in 1794, covered two-and-a-half acres on a hill-top, so that expansion was impossible. The new depot, instead of looking down on the sea, was almost level with it, and occupied nearly fifty-four acres.

The north side of the parade ground was flanked by three double-storey barrack blocks, and a fourth, single-storey block. The total accommodation held 238 men and 7 N.C.O.s. There were Sergeants and Officers Messes, and married quarters for married members of staff.

T&S, June 1935.

Aerial view of Bridge of Don Barracks, 1935

Regimental soldiers have always known that the best way to attract recruits was to have serving soldiers seen in their home towns in the regimental area. Even better was when soldiers were seen in the groupings in which they served and with the 'tools of the trade' in their hands. The recruiting march through the regimental area—a concept pioneered by the Gordons in 1899—was repeated in 1937, but this one was mechanised: the composite company involved was carried in Battalion transport. It was a great success, and it showed, as ever, how much The Gordon Highlanders were appreciated in their home area:

On 9th August a mechanized company at war strength under Major G.E. Malcolm, M.C., left Redford for a march round the Regimental District.

The first day we reached Buddon in time for a late lunch, and as we did not leave until next morning everyone could sample the attractions of Dundee and Monifieth. Next day we arrived at Stonehaven, having met Col. Hamilton and done a tactical exercise *en route*. After lunch the Provost inspected us and gave us the much appreciated freedom of Stonehaven swimming-pool.

We moved to the Depot in Aberdeen, where we spent the night, and thanks are due to Major Norman and all concerned for their hospitality. As practically everyone present had friends in Aberdeen, our stay there was a very enjoyable one.

On Wednesday we moved to Keith, our first stop being Banchory, where the Company was inspected and entertained by the Provost and Council. We could not stay very long and moved on to Alford, where the Company marched through the town.

Our next stop was Huntly, where we were given tea after we had been inspected by the Provost. Finally we reached Keith, where we spent the night. Everyone enjoyed the entertainments which had been arranged for us. Any Gordon was allowed into the cinema at half-price, and a large dance was held, which, judging from some of the haggard expressions seen next day, must have been a great success.

On Thursday we moved to Ellon, stopping at Banff, where we were inspected by the Provost, who invited the officers to lunch with the Council. Next stop was Turriff, where the Provost inspected the Company. We were unable to stay long at Turriff or at Peterhead, our next stop, as we had to get to Ellon. There we were inspected by the Provost, accompanied by Lord Aberdeen.

The next day we returned to Buddon, via Old Meldrum and Inverurie, where the Provosts inspected us. We could only stay a short time at these hospitable places, as we had to get back to Stonehaven, where Col. Hamilton met us and we did another scheme between there and Laurencekirk, where we were inspected by the Provost before returning to Buddon, where we spent another night before returning to Edinburgh on Saturday.

And so ended a very pleasant week, for which we must express our sincere gratitude to the Provosts, Councillors and people of all the places we stopped at and passed through for their kind hospitality and the wonderful welcomes they gave us. Everywhere we went we met old friends, many of whom were asking how they could get back to the Regiment to complete their twenty-one years' service. Our thanks are also due to Col. Buchanan-Smith, Col. Ledingham, Capts. Hutchins and Christie, and all the P.S.I.s[2] who gave us such valuable assistance.

This was the first time that the Battalion had moved with mechanical transport, and it is interesting to reflect that we covered 600-odd miles in five days, which would have taken nearly as many weeks in the old foot-slogging days. Until the last day the weather was ideal and even the vehicles behaved themselves. Our one misfortune, when an unfortunate

---

2 P.S.I.–Permanent Staff Instructor.

D.R. [despatch rider] had a slight difference of opinion with a truck, occurred within fifteen miles of barracks on the return journey.

In conclusion, we are hoping that this march will bring smiles to the faces of Sergt. Wisley and other recruiters in our district, but whatever the result it has with recruiting, it was certainly a very valuable experience for our transport drivers.

T&S, September 1937.

In 1939, with war looming, recruiting for Territorial units was stepped up. The encouraging response was typical of the pride and belief the people of the north-east had in their Regiment:

The districts from which the 5th/7th Gordons drew their recruits were Buchan, Mar and Mearns, with the addition, authorised in 1937, of Fraserburgh. The Shetlands had always been in the 7th Battalion area, but no attempt had been made to draw upon the islands since the end of the First World War. Now, in spring 1939, the assistant adjutant of the 5th/7th paid the Shetlands a visit, and in a very short time recruited 100 men. The 5th/7th beat up for recruits in Skene, Dunecht, Newmachar, Kingswells, Fintray, Fetterangus, and New Pitsligo, and many old 5th Battalion men rejoined. The 5th/7th Gordons were the first battalion in Scotland to reach a double establishment, and the commanding officer received from the War office a mild reproof for having exceeded the requisite number.

The Life of a Regiment, Volume V, p 29.

After the Second World War, National Service provided the recruits who kept private soldier strengths at the required levels. Recruiting objectives were therefore to provide a steady input of regular soldiers to keep a core of trained and experienced soldiers around which the National Servicemen could reach their potential quickly in the relatively short period that they served. The core of regular soldiers was also needed to provide the junior N.C.O.s who would fill vacancies in senior N.C.O. and Warrant Officer ranks. In 1954 another tour through the regimental area was organised. The Commanding Officer, Lieutenant-Colonel J.E.G. Hay, D.S.O., wrote of it:

This was unique in that it was not only the first post-war tour, but the first ever completely self-contained and mobile tour to have been undertaken—certainly by any Highland Regiment.

The tour, under Major George Morrison, D.S.O., included a complete display of the weapons and equipment in use at that time by the Battalion. Anti-tank guns, mortars, carriers, signal jeeps—the lot! The route was carefully planned to cover highways, byways, towns and villages throughout the Regimental Area. Frequent stops were made when, to the accompaniment of Pipe and Military Bands, the exhibits were laid out and explained. There was even a display of captured Malayan Bandit uniforms, equipment and weapons.

The tour, sponsored by Scottish Command and The Regiment, covered some hundreds of miles and throughout its progress was frequently visited by the Colonel of the Regiment whom I, of course, accompanied. Civil dignitaries were always asked to put in an appearance, which they gladly did.

The enthusiasm displayed wherever the tour went was tremendous. It was a great success and well worthwhile both from the short-and long-term point of view, as the recruiting figures show.

The Life of a Regiment, Volume VI, p 60.

Recruiting poster for The Gordon Highlanders, 1959

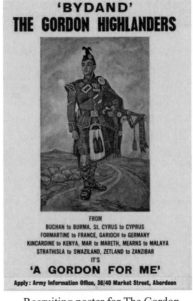

Recruiting poster for The Gordon Highlanders, 1966

When National Service ended in 1960, unit strengths were no longer maintained by a never-ending throughput of conscripts. The Regular Army now depended on volunteers to fill the ranks. Recruiting once again became an important part of regimental life. Recruiting offices were sited throughout the regimental area, with the head office in Aberdeen. These were Army recruiting offices, recruiting to all branches of the Army, but each office had at least one Gordon Highlander whose task was to get infantry recruits to join the Regiment. It was not easy, as representatives of Corps and Services, of the Scots Guards, Parachute Regiment, Royal Engineers, Royal Artillery and Royal Armoured Corps all vied for the finite source of recruits. Major Norrie

Donald, a distinguished Gordon who won the British Empire Medal in Belfast in 1978, and who had served with the Regiment in a long career all round the world, recalled how he became a Gordon Highlander when he decided to join the Army:

I always fancied driving around in a tank, and when I went to the recruiting office in Market Street I spoke to the Cavalry rep, who was in the Scots Greys. He painted such a rosy picture of life in the Greys that I signed up there and then. I went home and announced that I was going to be a cavalryman and would drive tanks. My father popped next door to see our neighbour, Bill Craig an old long-Service Gordon Highlander.[1] He came in, put his arm around my shoulder, and said 'Come on wi' me, son.' He took me back to Market Street where he went in to see the Recruiting Officer, Major George Slater (a distinguished and respected Gordon Highlander). After a few minutes Major Slater called for my enlistment papers and took me into his office. 'I see you made a small mistake there, Norman.' he said. 'I know you want to be a Gordon, so we'll do it again.' He tore up my original enlistment form, had me fill out another one, this time specifying The Gordon Highlanders, got me to sign it, and witnessed it himself. And that's how I became a Gordon—but on looking back it was the best thing that happened to me and I wouldn't change it for all the world!

Major Norman Donald.

Like Colonel Hay in 1954, commanding officers had to find recruits. The recruiting tour, preceding or following an operational tour or overseas posting, was a major event. When a recruiting tour could be combined with training, the best of both worlds was obtained. In 1973:

Buchan Wander consisted of a number of company exercises and ended with a test exercise. Planned by the Second in Command, Major Graham, it relied on the co-operation of local Councils, the Police and business concerns. Major Graham travelled around the area, explaining what would be involved, and enlisting the help of the authorities and the local people.

The Chief Constable of Aberdeen, Alex Morrison, was instrumental in getting the exercise accepted by local authorities. He instructed all his Divisional Commanders to assist the Regiment as much as possible. He contacted the Provosts and Town Clerks of Huntly, Keith, Fraserburgh

---

1 Bill Craig had been a sergeant in the 1st Battalion when it was captured in August 1914. He spent the rest of the First War as a prisoner. In 1940, as a major, he was Quartermaster of the 5th\7th Battalion when it was captured at St Valery. He spent the rest of the Second War as a prisoner.

and Turriff to get permission to use their towns. The townspeople co-operated willingly and many volunteered to take part.

When the exercise began the whole of the North-East had heard about it and watched with interest. 'A' Company moved into Keith, 'B' Company to Peterhead, 'D' Company to Huntly and Support Company to Fraserburgh. In each of these towns soldiers practised patrolling, checking vehicles, searching buildings and questioning and 'chatting up' the public. The latter art was the hardest to come by. Many Jocks found it difficult to start conversations with total strangers and keep them going, but as the exercise progressed it became easier. This was to prove invaluable in the months to come. *Buchan Wander* finished with each company moving to Fraserburgh for a one-day test exercise controlled by Major Graham.

The Jocks enjoyed *Buchan Wander* immensely. It was a novel way to train, and the audience of their own folk spurred them to perform at their peak. The success of an exercise is often measured by the tales told afterwards, and by this yardstick *Buchan Wander* was a triumph. Many were the stories of the goings on in the towns. One in particular illustrates the manner in which the local community threw itself into the exercise in Fraserburgh, the scene of the most intense activity.

Corporal 'Tucker' Duncan played the part of an IRA sniper, and arranged with the local fish factory to be kitted out in the full working outfit of a fish gutter. Complete with hat, apron and wellington boots he took up position in the factory. Outside the factory a small group of agitators started fighting, drawing Lieutenant Christopher Price's Reconnaissance Platoon into the area to try to break up the disturbance. When the platoon was fully committed Corporal Duncan and his accomplice, Private Taylor, opened fire from the factory. Quickly hiding the weapons, the two 'snipers' returned to the fish processing line where they started to gut fish.

Lieutenant Price realised where the shots had come from and led a follow-up party into the factory to search for the snipers. The party was met by hostility and lack of co-operation as the factory workers threw themselves into the part. As the Jocks scanned the faces a string of verbal abuse rang around their ears. This went on until Corporal Duncan was identified, which was the signal for a hail of prawns, kippers, half filleted haddock and fish entrails to descend on the Jocks trying to arrest him. Lieutenant Price was showered in prawns hurled by Mrs McQueen, the mother of Colonel MacMillan's driver.

There were occasional red faces. Major Graham had promised the Police that there would be no bomb incidents. On the third day the Police received a telephone message that there was a bomb in Woolworth's store in Fraserburgh. The Gordons confirmed that they had not planted an exercise bomb, and the Police initiated the full bomb alert procedure. The area was cordoned off, shops and buildings evacuated and the Bomb Disposal Team in Edinburgh called out.

Major Graham was talking to a policeman in front of the watching crowd, which had formed at a safe distance. As he stood there a voice said in his ear, 'It's good fun, isn't it? I laid the bomb!' Turning round he saw a lady, the mother of a Gordon Highlander taking part in the exercise. She was a leading organiser of the public effort to help the Gordons in the exercise, but got carried away with enthusiasm and decided to liven things up even more. With some embarrassment Major Graham went to the senior Police officer and told him that the whole thing was a mistake. The Police were not amused.

Training to recognise wanted suspects was done with the help of the Royal British Legion. Each company was tasked to find a particular wanted 'IRA' man and given some information about him. The 'IRA' men were members of the Fraserburgh British Legion branch who were briefed to go into the town centre at least once a day. It was amazing how, when the local population discovered who was wanted that day, they went out of their way to protect him, giving the soldiers false information and shielding the wanted man from observation. It was exactly the sort of behaviour that the Gordons would come across in Belfast, and was good training for the task.

Enormous benefit accrued from *Buchan Wander*. Apart from exercising the Gordons in skills they would need in Ulster—patrolling in towns, VCPs, riots, pub raids, searches, sniper incidents and chatting up techniques—the benefit in community relations justified the whole exercise. The community also took part in the exercise, with the Fraserburgh Royal British Legion, the Army Cadets and the Women's Institute playing significant parts. The North-East saw its own Regiment at close hand, and the goodwill and affection felt for the Gordons was evident. There were the 32 applications to join the Regiment as a result of seeing it doing its job. This gave some people cause to ponder whether official and more traditional recruiting methods might be less than cost effective when compared to a short, sharp, high profile military presence. The people of Fraserburgh in particular were magnificent, and the Battalion owed them a great debt. With their help, and that of the populations of the other towns, the Gordons had achieved realism in their training unequalled by any other unit in Britain. The subsequent Northern Ireland training at Lydd and Hythe, in the south of England, put the final touches to the preparation, and the Gordons were ready to move to Belfast in the best possible form for another demanding tour.

The Life of a Regiment, Volume VII, pp 96–8.

Recruiting was not only for soldiers. A steady supply of young officers was needed, and while many applied to join—some of them sons, grandsons and even great-grandsons of Gordon Highlanders—their wide age-spread meant that there would always be vacancies for new young officers. Suitable young men were identified through regimental contacts, schools in the regimental area and universities. Those who showed interest were invited to visit the Regiment, where they were sometimes the subject of innocent fun, as this account from 1974 tells:

One day in August a party of potential officers arrived at Inverness station to begin a two-day visit to the Battalion. Met by a rather untidily dressed driver who told them to throw their luggage into the back of a mini-van, they were driven at breakneck speed to Fort George, all the while listening to a running and somewhat indiscreet commentary on life in the Regiment. The van arrived at the Fort in the early evening, before dinner, and as the young hopefuls unloaded their bags they saw officers taking the evening air on the lawns.

A small fiery looking man with a bristling moustache, was practising golf strokes, sending balls soaring into the distance to bounce off the rampart walls. Every so often he stopped and called out in a peppery tone, 'Colour Sar'nt!', at which the Officers Mess Colour Sergeant, resplendent in scarlet Mess Jacket and trews, marched out carrying a silver salver on which rested a large glass of gin. After polishing off the gin the officer resumed smiting golf balls, to the accompaniment of ribald comments from other officers watching.

'Watch me get the Padre!' muttered the fiery officer, sending a ball screeching towards a figure on the distant ramparts pacing up and down and gesticulating to the heavens. 'Practising another of his bloody sermons. That'll make him cut about a bit!' The ball bounced some way from the figure, which carried on, oblivious to the attempt to maim him.

The visitors were shown to their rooms, and afterwards gathered in the Ante Room, which filled up as the living-in officers. They introduced themselves and called for drinks for their guests. When the small, peppery officer came in, now decidedly redder of complexion, he was introduced as the Battalion Second in Command. He presented a somewhat eccentric appearance, wearing an old suit in Regimental tweed, a checked Vyella shirt and a Highland Brigade Club tie that bore evidence of numerous breakfasts and spilled drinks. He was jovial and hospitable, if short of patience with the younger officers.

In one corner, sprawled on a leather chair with a copy of *The Field* draped over his face, a long, lanky figure emitted soft snores as he slept, oblivious to the gathering crowd. The Second in Command whipped the magazine away and shook the sleeping figure. 'Come on Archie, it's damned rude to sleep when we've got guests. On your feet!' Then, to the guests, 'This is Sir Archie, chaps. Doesn't really do much, but he adds a bit of tone to the place—when he's awake! That right, you old bugger?' The languid, lanky figure shook his long blonde hair and casually waved a hand to the visitors.

'Ah! the Padre!' went on the small bucolic major as the figure from the ramparts came in. 'Been practising another of your love-your-neighbour sermons, have you? Give 'em a bit of blood and guts, eternal damnation and all that stuff. Here, what'll you have to drink. One of those pathetic cream sherries, I'll wager!' The Padre smiled nervously and squirmed in embarrassment, then moved to a corner of the room to escape the gaze of the amused officers.

The door swung open and the Mess Colour Sergeant marched in, crashing to a halt in the middle of the room. 'Dinner is served, gentlemen!' he announced. 'You'd better take your seats before it gets cold.' He started to usher in the younger officers, whipping unfinished drinks from their protesting hands. With muttered imprecations the officers and their guests took their places at the table, where steaming bowls of soup sat before them. 'Grace, Padre!' called the Second in Command. 'Keep it short and to the point this time.'

The Padre got to his feet, stretched out his arms and launched into a grace that seemed to go on forever. From a call for blessings on the gifts of the table it went on to troubles at home and abroad, industrial relations, international tension, political dissent, racial discrimination, female emancipation and the sins of the world in general and the occupants of that Dining Room in particular. At last, with a ringing condemnation of rank and privilege that left everyone at the table with a guilt complex, he sat down and tucked into his bowl of, by now cold, soup. The visitors sat, stunned.

The Mess Colour Sergeant went round filling wine glasses, but could be seen polishing off unfinished bottles in the servery. As the meal went on he became more and more unsteady until he slipped as he swept into the Dining Room and ended up spreadeagled on the floor. Then the duty piper came in. Into the room came a small man with thick-lensed spectacles, dressed in grubby overalls and playing on practice pipes that consisted of no more than a bag, a mouthpiece and a chanter. Round the table he went, playing excruciatingly badly, stopping every so often to mutter to himself in Gaelic and then go back to try a difficult phrase again. At the table the Padre tried to look as if he were enjoying the music, the Second in Command kept shouting 'The man's a fool!' and Sir Archie slumped forward, his face on his plate as he snored contentedly.

It could not go on, of course, and after dinner the grotesques revealed themselves. The Mess Colour Sergeant turned out to be the Paymaster, Captain Ian Clarke, the piper was the Medical Officer, Captain Roddie MacLeod, Sir Archie was Private Shand, one of the Mess waiters, the fiery Second in Command was Lieutenant Dick Lamb, and the Padre was Captain Derek Napier. The relief on the faces of some of the more gullible visitors was plain to see. Of the potential officers, two were eventually to join the Regiment, and one went on to command the 1st Battalion.

The Life of a Regiment, Volume VII, pp 128–30.

Aberdeen was always a good source of recruits. Employment in the oil industry had slowed the flow, but had not stopped it altogether. Nothing was better to stir the hearts of prospective recruits than a sight of the Regiment on its own home ground, and events in the city were always at the heart of recruiting drives, such as the one in 1976:

The Regiment exercised its right, as Freemen of Aberdeen, to march through the City with Colours flying, bayonets fixed and drums beating. The streets were packed as the Gordons swung down Union Street led by the Drums and Pipes and Military Band. The companies followed, immaculate in their kilts, sporrans swinging jauntily and Glengarry tails whipping behind them. The Reconnaissance and Signals Platoon Landrovers came next, their crews wearing combat dress to remind watchers that it was a fighting regiment passing by. The crowds, as ever in Aberdeen, were generous in their applause, clearly appreciating the opportunity to welcome their own Regiment. Many proudly singled out sons and husbands among the marchers, for the North-East representation in the Battalion was strong.

The Battalion was treated to a Civic Lunch. The Jocks enjoyed this gesture but there was some unrest among Councillors, who felt that the main course of 'mince an' tatties' was demeaning to the Regiment. They felt embarrassed, they said, that the Gordons should be offered such simple fare on such a grand occasion. Colonel Graham defused the situation by replying that 'mince an' tatties was good wholesome North-East food for a good wholesome North-East Regiment!'

After lunch the Lord Provost produced a photograph of Colonel Graham's grandfather, in the robes of a senior Baillie of the City, and pointed out that as a Baillie he sat on the Bench administering justice. He told the Jocks that if they appeared before their Commanding Officer they would be getting good Aberdeen discipline!

The interest shown surpassed expectations and over 500 enquiries were received. Much of the ground work for the campaign, the advice and guidance given to companies during it, and all the responsibility for following up enquiries fell on the Regimental Recruiting Team led by Captain Arthur Heffren, a dedicated, tireless worker whose contribution to the ability of the Regiment to continue to attract recruits from the North-East, despite the lure of North Sea oil, was immense.

The Life of a Regiment, Volume VII, pp 178–79.

During the last twenty years of The Gordon Highlanders' existence, recruiting for the Army become more and more centralised. Army Recruiting Offices took volunteers for every branch of the Army, but unless a recruit specified another infantry regiment volunteers would automatically go to the home regiment of that particular area.

In the 1980s and nineties all that changed. Infantry recruiting in Scotland became a Scottish Division responsibility, and recruits were sent to the regiments that most needed them. Some postings required battalions to be of higher strength than others, and the Scottish Division tried to keep regiments at the appropriate level. If a recruit had family connections with a regiment then he would be allowed to go to it, but otherwise he could find himself in a regiment from another part of Scotland. Recruiting for other Arms and Services was based on Army priorities, and recruits with the specific skills were to be encouraged to join these.

In an area of high employment, with the oil industry in Aberdeen looking for suitable men to whom it could offer high wages, the flow of men to The Gordon Highlanders fell from the sufficiency it had enjoyed for many years to a level that made manning the Battalion a never-ending struggle. It was only when the Scottish Division decided that The Gordon Highlanders were the first priority for infantry recruiting that sufficient numbers were found. Because Army policy kept diverting high quality north-east recruits to technical Arms and Services, infantry recruits to The Gordon Highlanders came from all across Scotland, diluting the distinctive north-east character of the Regiment, although the majority of soldiers in the Regiment still came from its home recruiting area.[2]

---

2   From 1990 to 1993 the author was in charge of recruiting for the Army in Scotland, and can recall the efforts made by Recruiting Officers and Gordon Highlander Recruiting Sergeants to persuade prospective recruits to join the Regiment. They enjoyed no small measure of success.

.

SECTION 3

THE COLOURS

THE colours play a central role in every British regiment. In most regiments there are two colours: the King's (or Queen's) Colour and the Regimental Colour. Except in the Brigade of Guards, the Sovereign's Colour is based on the Union Flag, and the Regimental Colour has a background colour associated with the regiment. In The Gordon Highlanders the background of the Regimental Colour was always yellow.

The colours traditionally went into action with the regiment, the Regimental Colour (originally known as the Colonel's Colour, which carried the motif or emblem of the Colonel, whose name was also given to the regiment) providing an easily identifiable rallying spot for the regiment. If the Colonel was killed, or gave up the colonelcy, both the name of the regiment and the Regimental Colour were changed. By the time the 75th and the 92nd were raised the concept of the Colonel's Colour had been replaced by that of the Regimental Colour, and the two regiments when raised carried a King's Colour and a Regimental Colour.

When colours were carried on campaign and in battle, there was considerable wear and tear, not to mention battle damage. On occasions, severely damaged colours were replaced, but from the 19th century on, it became the practice for colours to be carried for a period, usually between twenty and thirty years, after which they were replaced.

CHAPTER 8

PRESENTATION OF COLOURS

THE dates of provision and replacement of colours for the 92nd are easily determined from the regimental history, but these events are not found for the early days of the 75th. The *75th Regiment Record Book*, covering 1787 to 1831, mentions the colours only when authority is received to display the Royal Tiger with the word 'India' superscribed, and the Battle Honour 'Seringapatam', in 1807 and 1818 respectively. The known dates on which new colours were presented to each regiment are:

75th	1787	
	1863	
92nd	1794	(King's Colour, replaced in 1801 by the new Union Flag)
	1807	(Regimental Colour damaged at Waterloo replaced in 1815 by that of 2nd Battalion)
	1830	
	1864	
2nd Battalion	1804	
	1813	(Disbanded 1815)

Gordon Highlanders (75th/92nd):

1st Battalion	1898	
	1937	
	1961	
	1988	
2nd Battalion	1894	
	1911	

It is not intended to cover every presentation of new colours, but extracts from contemporary accounts are given where available.

1794 – presentation of first Colours to the 92nd

In December, 1794, the Regiment received its first stand of Colours on Windmill Hill [Gibraltar]. After consecration by the Garrison Chaplain, the Marquis of Huntly gave an impressive address, calling the attention of officers and men to the duties which King and country expected from them, and to the honours which he trusted they would acquire under these Colours.

These Colours, altered at the Union in 1801, and retired in 1807, now rest in the chapel at Gordon Castle.[1]

Each Colour had in the centre the Star of the Order of the Thistle in proper colours: the scrolls and medallion were of crimson silk, edged with gold, the letters being black: the whole within a wreath of roses and thistles. The tassels and cords were of crimson and gold; the regimental colour was yellow. The medallion bore the figures '100' on it, the original number of the Regiment, changed a few years later to '92'.

T&S, September 1926.

First stand of Colours of 92nd Highland Regiment, 1794

Honours on Colours of 75th

Although it is not recorded when the Colours presented in 1787 were replaced, the awarding of campaign honours is recorded in 1807:

Horse Guards, 10th July 1807

Sir,

I have the honor to acquaint you that His Royal Highness the Commander in Chief has been pleased to obtain His Majesty's most gracious permission, that the 75th Regiment may assume (in addition to any other Devices or badges to which it may be entitled) and wear on its

---

1   The Regimental Colour presented in 1794 is in a good state of preservation. This set went through Holland in 1799, where the King's Colour was severely damaged in the fighting. When the Union of Great Britain and Ireland took place in 1801, it was replaced by a new Colour. The Regimental Colour was altered to bring it into line with the new pattern. The original number of the Regiment—100— had been changed to 92 in 1798, and the alterations consisted chiefly of shamrock leaves added to the existing wreath of roses and thistles.

    The only active service which these Colours saw was in Egypt. By their valour at Alexandria and Mandora the Gordons won the right to bear the sphinx on their Colours, and the badge was placed on all four corners of the Regimental one—a very rare thing. *Tiger and Sphinx, September 1926.*

Colours and appointments the "Royal Tyger" with the word "India" superscribed as an honourable and lasting Testimony of the distinguished service of that Corps in India.

I have the honor to be with great Respect

Sir

Your very Obedt Humble Servant

(Signed) Harry Calvert, A.G.

75th Regiment Record Book

1830—presentation of new colours to the 92nd

December 13, 1830—The Regiment was formed in Palatine Square to receive His Excellency Lieut-General Sir John Byng, commanding the forces in Ireland; a new stand of colours (the gift of the officers), on which were emblazoned the seven additional badges of distinction conferred on the regiment, was escorted by the grenadier company from the lieut-colonel's quarters. His Excellency then made a most appropriate and flattering speech, in which he alluded to the battle of the Nive (St Pierre), of which that day was the anniversary, and to the brilliant and distinguished conduct of the 92nd on that occasion, as well as on many others of which he himself was an eye-witness. After receiving the colours from the officers of the grenadiers, and remarking how delighted he was to see the names of so many well-earned battles emblazoned on them, he placed them in the hands of the ensigns, and the regiment saluted. Addressing the Regiment, he observed 'that he made no allusion to the necessity of defending those colours—any such remark would be out of place when addressing the 92nd; however, he could not give the young officers and soldiers a better advice than to follow the steps of those who preceded them.' To which the lieut-colonel[2] replied, that if anything could enhance the value attached to those colours by the regiment, it was their being placed in the hands of the ensigns by one who had, that day seventeen years, shown himself so very conspicuous in placing the colour of a regiment on the enemy's redoubt,[3] and that he pledged himself in the name of his brother officers and soldiers for their honour and safety.

The Life of a Regiment, Volume II, p 21.

By common assent the old colours were presented to Lieutenant-Colonel MacDonald for 'your great exertions in revising the records of the regiment,

---

2   Lt-Col John MacDonald (later Gen Sir John MacDonald).
3   Sir John Byng, afterwards Field-Marshal the Earl of Stafford, led his brigade at the battle of St Pierre to the assault of a strong height occupied in great force by the enemy and having himself first ascended the hill with the colour of the 31st Regiment in his hands, planted it on the summit, and the enemy was driven down the ridge.

and in obtaining the grant of these badges, you should be requested to accept the old colours as a mark of respect for your indefatigable zeal in their cause.'

Colours of the 92nd presented in 1830 and retired in 1864

1863 – new colours for the 75th

On May 15th, 1863, new colours were presented to the regiment by Mrs Hutchinson, the wife of the Major-General commanding the district, and in September the Royal authority was received for the words 'Delhi' and 'Lucknow' to be borne on the colours and appointments, in commemoration of the distinguished conduct of the regiment at Delhi and the relief of Lucknow.

The Life of a Regiment, Volume II, p 232.

1864 – new colours for the 92nd

April 16th, 1864.— [At Edinburgh Castle] the regiment was formed in Review order to be presented with new colours. Major-General Walker, C.B., and Staff, General Sir John MacDonald, the veteran and revered colonel of the regiment, accompanied by Lady MacDonald and other members of his family, were present. After the marching past and trooping the old colours, the religious ceremony was performed by the Rev. James Miller, chaplain. The colours were then placed by the Major-General in the hands of Lady MacDonald, who addressed the Regiment, alluding to their past career, and concluding by referring in a few touching words to 'the many happy years I spent among you, and the pleasure it gives me to see you again.' Lieut-Colonel Lockhart, after thanking Lady MacDonald, shortly addressed the regiment, and the Major-General having expressed his satisfaction of the way the ceremony had been performed, the regiment returned to quarters. In the evening a ball was given by the officers in honour of the occasion.

The Life of a Regiment, Volume II, p 75.

In August 1894, a hundred years after the first colours were presented to the 100th Gordon Highlanders, new colours were presented to the 2nd Battalion (the old 92nd). The following excerpts are from a Glasgow newspaper report of the day:

1894 – new colours for the 2nd Battalion

A most interesting and imposing ceremony took place at Maryhill Barracks yesterday, 9th August 1894, when the Gordon Highlanders celebrated the centenary of the formation of the regiment with a trooping of colours and presentation of new colours. The event was made doubly interesting through the presence of the Duke of Richmond and Gordon, whose great-grand-father had the honour a hundred years ago of forming the regiment. The officers on parade included Lieut.-Col. Oxley, Major Napier,[4] Captain Wright,[5] Captain Fraser, Captain Sinclair-Wemyss, Captain Staunton,[6] Captain Hunter-Blair, Captain Neish,[7] Captain Macneal, Lieutenant Forbes, Lieutenant Buchanan, Lieutenant Meyrick,[8] Lieutenant McConnel, Lieutenant Gordon,[9] and Second-Lieutenants Munroe [Monro], Maitland, Simpson,[10] Rowland, Lieutenant-Adjutant Bethune, and Lieut.-Quartermaster Anderson.

The regiment was drawn up in line on the parade ground. The two lieutenants had handed to them the old colours, which were marched down in front of the line. The old colours were afterwards escorted to the rear. The regiment formed three sides of a square, the drums piled in the centre. The new colours, in their cases, were brought forward and laid on the drumhead. They were then uncovered and held aloft. Prayers followed, and the new colours were formally presented by the Duke of

---

4   Maj Hon John Scott Napier, 14th Laird of Merchiston, commanded 2nd Gordons (1895–97).
5   Capt Harry Wright fought in Afghanistan and Majuba. In the 2nd Boer War he was awarded the D.S.O. He commanded 2nd Gordons (1903–07), and 8th Gordons (1914–15) until severely wounded at Loos.
6   Capt G. Staunton commanded 2nd Gordons (1907–11).
7   Capt F.H. Neish commanded the 1st Battalion at Mons and was captured along with the Battalion during the retreat from Mons.
8   Capt St. J. Meyrick was killed at the Battle of Doornkop in 1900.
9   Lt A.F. Gordon, not Lt W.E. Gordon, who would win the V.C. in the Boer War in 1900 and be captured with the 1st Battalion after Mons.
10 2Lt C.J. Simpson was wounded as a major at Mons in 1914. He commanded the 1st Battalion after the war, in Constantinople.

Richmond and Gordon, two officers, Lieutenants St. John Meyrick and F.B. McConnell, receiving them kneeling.

The Duke of Richmond and Gordon said:

> 'Colonel Oxley, officers, non-commissioned officers, and men of the Gordon Highlanders, I esteem it a great honour to have been entrusted with the duty of presenting new colours to the regiment which has so nobly illustrated the name of Gordon in every quarter of the globe. It is just one hundred years since my great-grandfather raised this regiment, and the names of the various battles blazoned on your colours bear testimony to the distinguished services of the regiment during the century that has elapsed. "Egypt," "India," "The Peninsula," "Waterloo," and "South Africa" make up the history of Great Britain during that period, and justify me in addressing to you the eloquent words of the Speaker of the House of Commons to the great Duke of Wellington:—"You have written your names with your conquering swords in the annals of the world, and we shall hand them down with exultation to our children's children."
>
> 'I have presented new colours in place of those you received thirty years ago at the hands of Lady MacDonald, the wife of a distinguished colonel of the regiment, with full assurance that if this country should unfortunately be engaged in war the 92d Gordon Highlanders will be found, as of old, in the forefront of the battle, and will maintain the honour and glory of Scotland, as their predecessors have done on many a well-fought field.'

Colonel Oxley, replying, said:

> 'I thank you, in the name of the Gordon Highlanders, for presenting these colours. The regiment will be proud to enter into the records of its history the honours which your Grace has presented to them. The grand history has been built up at a cost of 109 officers and upwards of 1,600 men[11] who have fallen, killed or wounded, from its ranks. I trust those now serving will bear in mind the glorious record of the regiment, maintain its reputation, and be true to their colours, Queen, and country.'[12]

T&S, September 1894.

The old colours were lodged in the care of the county of Aberdeenshire. This was very appropriate, and Colonel Oxley emphasised how closely the

---

11 These figures were to be horrifically eclipsed in the two World Wars.

12 These colours were replaced in 1911. In 1930 they were deposited on loan in the Scottish National War Memorial in Edinburgh Castle. They hung there until replaced by those of the 1st Battalion, when its new colours were presented in 1937.

Regiment was tied to the north-east of Scotland when he recalled the kindness and support the people gave to families of Gordon Highlanders:

> The colours and escort were loudly cheered as they passed through the streets to the Municipal and County Buildings, where they were met by Lord Provost Stewart and the Town Council in their robes. Lieut-Colonel Oxley addressed the Lord Provost, alluding to the Regiment having been embodied at Aberdeen, and that in 1881, when the 92nd went from India to South Africa, while the women and children returned to Great Britain in a very severe winter, lightly clad from a hot climate, a fund was raised in Aberdeenshire to help them.
>
> 'We now wish to mark our appreciation of the kindness shown to the regiment on that occasion by presenting to Aberdeenshire the old colours with which we now part. I would remind you, my Lord Provost, that these colours are very dear to us. They have been an emblem of our duty to our Queen and to our country, and we have endeavoured to do our duty consistently and well. We now place them in your keeping, sure that you and those who succeed you in the high office of Lord Provost of Aberdeen will watch over and protect and guard them.'
>
> He alluded to the neighbouring statue of George, Fifth Duke of Gordon, first Colonel of the Gordon Highlanders; he 'did not know if all who passed the statue knew how much had been done for Scotland and for Europe by raising the Gordon Highlanders. If not, they should read the History of the Regiment.'

The Life of a Regiment, Volume II, pp 318–9.

1899 – new colours for the 1st Battalion

Field-Marshal H.R.H. the Prince of Wales, Colonel-in-Chief,[13] graciously consented to present to the battalion new Colours in place of those carried since 1863 which Indian and African sun and rains had reduced to a few tattered scraps of silk.

Two hundred rank and file under Lieut.-Colonel G.T F. Downman, with Brevet Lieut-Colonel Forbes Macbean and eight other officers, plus chaplain and doctor, started on 11th September and spent two pleasant days at Stonehaven under the aegis of the Lord Lieutenant of the County, whose son, Lieut. A.W.F. Baird[14] was with the 2nd battalion. Thence they

---

13 H.R.H. The Prince of Wales (the future King Edward VII) was appointed Colonel-in-Chief in 1898, when he told Lt-Col Dick-Cunyngham that he felt it proper to be connected with the Gordons, Aberdeenshire being his own county.

14 Later Brig-Gen A.W.F. Baird, C.B., C.M.G, D.S.O., and father-in-law of Col C.M. Usher (see Chapter 39).

marched via Banchory and Aboyne, where they were welcomed to Gordon territory by the Marquis of Huntly, to Ballater, which they reached on the 16th.

Two days later, at Brackley House, the Prince presented new Colours in the presence of T.R.H. the Dukes of York and Connaught and many distinguished personages, and of spectators estimated at seven thousand—and this before the days of motors!

One hundred and ten old Gordons, who had come from as far as Devonport, whose oldest member had enlisted fifty-nine years before and among whose medals were those of Crimea and Indian Mutiny, stood on parade beside the serving generation. They were under the command of Captain Harry Brooke of Fairley, to whom old soldiers of the north-east owe so much; three of whose sons were to serve—and to fall—in the Gordon ranks fifteen years afterwards.

The old Colours being first trooped to the music of *The Garb of Old Gaul* and *The British Grenadiers*, the chaplain, the Rev. J. Robertson, blessed the new ones: 'Forasmuch as men at all times have made for themselves signs and emblems of their allegiance to their rulers and of their duty to uphold those laws and institutions which God's Providence has called them to obey,' the soldiers were, he said, met before God to ask His blessing on the new Colours; and with a short prayer he dedicated and set them apart that they might be a sign of the regiment's duty towards Queen and Country in the sight of God.

His Royal Highness handed the Colours to Lieutenants K. Dingwall[15] and H. Scrymgeour–Wedderburn.[16] He said that he trusted that when the corps was called to active service, it would be their part to carry these Colours to victory; and that they would feel it was the honour of Sovereign and Country that was committed to their charge.

> 'It has been given to your Regiment to perform distinguished service in the past, and this is amply illustrated by the record inscribed on your Colours; the ever-memorable Peninsular War and those most important campaigns in India, in South Africa, in Egypt; and lastly the Indian Frontier campaign in which occurred the splendid achievement of the storming of the Dargai heights. I am glad to inform you that an additional name will now be inscribed on these Colours—that of "Tirah".'

In thanking the Prince, Colonel Downman ended: 'Be it our duty to preserve their honour in the future as those who have gone before us, and as we ourselves, have endeavoured to do in the past.'

---

15 Wounded at Dargai in 1897.
16 The future Hereditary Standard Bearer for Scotland.

After the troops had marched past the Princes, followed by the two companies of veterans—who were received with the greatest warmth—and before breaking up the parade, Colonel Downman[17] brought his men to the 'Present' in honour of the old soldiers, with the words, 'Captain Brooke, and Veterans of the Gordon Highlanders, the Young Soldiers salute the Old,' which act of appreciation is still remembered warmly. The Prince afterwards inspected the party at Brackley House and reminded Captain Brooke that the latter had commanded a 92nd Guard of Honour at Lahore on the Prince's Indian tour of 1875.

The Life of a Regiment, Volume III, pp 85–7.

The colours presented at Brackley House would be carried by the 1st Battalion for nearly forty years. In that time, they would see many battle honours added, hard won during the First World War.

Colours presented to 1st Battalion at Brackley House, 1899

---

17   Lt-Col Downman was killed exactly three months later, on 11 December 1899, at Magersfontein.

1911 – new colours for 2nd Battalion

Although only seventeen years had passed since the 2nd Battalion received new colours, the State Visit to India in 1911 of George V, the King-Emperor, offered a chance to present new colours to regiments serving in India, including the 2nd Battalion:

On 11th December 1911 the 1st Northumberland Fusiliers, 1st Durham Light Infantry, 2nd Black Watch, 1st Highland Light Infantry, 2nd Gordons, and 1st Connaught Rangers received new Colours from the Royal and Imperial hands. The impressive ceremony commenced at ten o'clock; the Trooping massed into a single march, then each Colour Party advanced in turn from its own part of the hollow square with appropriate music from the massed bands; spectators came away with an impression of military pomp and circumstance very rarely to be witnessed in the twentieth century.

On return to camp Lieut.-Colonel Staunton read to the Battalion his Majesty's address:

'Lieutenant-Colonel Staunton, Officers, Non-Commissioned Officers, and the men of the 2nd Battalion, The Gordon Highlanders:

'I am very glad to have this opportunity of giving new Colours to your Battalion.

'The presentation of Colours is a solemn occasion. For you then bid farewell to the old flag which bears the records of past achievements, receiving in return a new flag, upon which it lies with you to inscribe the names of future victories. Recalling with pride the deeds of those who have gone before you, you look forward with hope into the coming days. Remember that this is no common flag which I am committing to your keeping. A Colour is a sacred Ensign, ever by its inspiration, though no longer by its presence, a rallying point in battle. It is the emblem of duty, the outward sign of your allegiance to God, your Sovereign, and your Country, to be looked up to, to be venerated, and to be passed down untarnished by succeeding generations.

'The whole Empire knows your reputation and record, I better than most, for my beloved Father was your Colonel. No regiment in the Army has a harder task before it than you, for you have to maintain the high standards and ideals which you have created for yourselves. But I know that you will maintain them because you are The Gordon Highlanders.'

George, R.I.

The Life of a Regiment, Volume III, p 401.

PRESENTATION OF COLOURS

1937 – new colours for the 1st Battalion

On 28th April, at Redford Barracks, Colinton, H.R.H. The Duke of Gloucester presented the 1st Battalion with new Colours to replace those which had symbolized the soul and honour of the Regiment for thirty-eight years. The spectacle was the brightest that has been seen at Redford for many years, witnessed by 3,000 spectators.

His Royal Highness' arrival in the uniform of the Gordon Highlanders was the occasion for a burst of cheering from the spectators. He and the Duchess were received by Lieut.-Col. J.M. Hamilton, D.S.O., the Commanding Officer, and shook hands with General Sir Ian Hamilton, Colonel of the Regiment, Lieutenant-General Sir Charles Grant, G.O.C Scottish Command, and Brigadier J.L. Weston, D.S.O., Scottish Command.

Majors W.J. Graham[18] and G.E. Malcolm were the field officers who handed the Colours to the Duke. While Lieuts. D. Stuart and E.C. Colville[19] knelt, His Royal Highness placed the Colours in their hands. The Duke then made his address:

'In presenting you with these colours I am proud to be with you for the first time as your Colonel-in-Chief. The world changes as the years pass by, but the colours remain the outward and visible signs of the traditions of the Regiment, a record of its service and triumph, the link uniting all ranks.

'Since the Regiment was raised nearly a century and a half ago, the two Battalions can proudly claim in peace and war a splendid record of devotion to duty. I am glad that the old colours presented by my grandfather, King Edward VII, are to find a resting-place in your National Memorial. I am confident that these new colours which I entrust to your care and keeping will inspire you to uphold the great and honourable traditions you have so worthily attained.'

In reply, Colonel Hamilton said:

'We are proud to have your Royal Highness with us to-day for such an important event in the Battalion's history. I am confident that these young soldiers will maintain the great traditions of the Regiment, and the high standard bequeathed to us by our predecessors of devotion to duty.'

General Sir Ian Hamilton spoke to the old Gordon Highlanders on parade. They came from all parts of Scotland. Sir Ian reminded them that

---

18 Colonel of the Regiment 1948–58.
19 Later Maj-Gen E.C. Colville.

he had been born into the Regiment which had at one time been commanded by his father.

'I have seen a good many regimental celebrations, but to-day has been one of the most momentous. It will be an outstanding date in our history. We have received our new colours from the hands of our new Colonel-in-Chief.

'The clan spirit of the North of Scotland, and the old feudal system, the shadow of which still persists in the country districts of the South of Scotland, gave them a big pull over English or Irish in the new world shortly to dawn.

'We are far more united in blood. To an Englishman tracing his pedigree it means a lot whether his ancestor was a squire, a gardener or a groom. To a true Scot it means very little whether his ancestor was a chief or a clansman. The blood is the same, and when we are adopted into a clan we feel the same. We are all brothers together for all time.'

T&S, June 1937.

Duke of Gloucester addresses the 1st Battalion after presenting new Colours, 1937

1961 – new colours for The Gordon Highlanders

In 1961 the 1st Battalion, The Gordon Highlanders, was in the last year of its three-year tour with the British Army of the Rhine. In addition to training for war the Gordons were preparing for a major ceremonial parade in April when new colours were to be presented by their Colonel-in-Chief, HRH The Duke of Gloucester. Ken Peters, Managing Director of the *Aberdeen Press and Journal*, reported:

Under a cloudless German sky, with a kindly sun shining on the kilts and bonnets of the Gordons, a big crowd packed the stands around the parade ground to see the intricate marching and formations associated with the colourful ceremony. This is the last major parade they will hold at Celle in Germany. At the year's end the 1st Battalion will exchange the plains and forests of North Germany for the Highlands of Kenya. So it was natural that there was sadness in the air as the pipes wailed their wild music in the keen morning. Kilts swung bravely, sporrans gleamed, white spats glistened as men marched, to make the most stirring sight a Highland Regiment can present.

The Colonel-in-Chief arrived, heralded by a Royal Salute. While the Drums and Pipes played slow marches, the Inspection was carried out. The old colours were trooped and marched off the Parade for the last time. The Parade formed hollow square, the drums were piled and the new colours laid on top. After they had been consecrated . . . they were presented by the Duke of Gloucester, who then addressed the Battalion. The Commanding Officer replied and the Battalion re-formed line to receive the new colours with the Royal Salute . . . the Battalion marched past in slow and quick time; re-formed line once more; advanced in review order . . . and gave a third Royal Salute. Three cheers for the Colonel-in-Chief, and the Battalion marched off.

The Life of a Regiment, Volume VI, p 401.

Duke of Gloucester presents new Colours to the 1st Battalion, Celle, 1961

1988 – new colours for The Gordon Highlanders

In July 1988 the 1st Battalion had been at Fort George, on the Moray Firth, for just over three months after four-and-a-half years in the British Army of the Rhine. With little time to prepare, they faced a major parade to receive new colours from their Colonel-in-Chief, HRH The Duke of Rothesay. Hard work saw them ready:

The rhythmic drum beat wove its way into the consciousness of the crowd, the sound of pipes, brass and woodwind, grew louder. Then the music burst forth as the Drums and Pipes and the Regimental Band led The Gordon Highlanders into view. Behind the swinging kilts and swirling plaids of the bands came the Gordons, dark kilts matched by dark green doublets set off by white belts and spats, colour added by the red and white hose and the officers' red sashes and white crossbelts. Sporrans swung in unison, bayonets glinted and swords glittered as the Gordons marched on, proud and erect, and crashed to a halt as one.

Entering with GOC Scotland, Lieutenant-General Sir John MacMillan, KCB, CBE, MA, and Lady MacMillan, was Lady Gordon Lennox, widow of Lieutenant-General Sir George Gordon Lennox. When they reached the saluting dais General MacMillan was received with a General Salute. As he stood there acknowledging the warm greeting from the Gordons, his thoughts must have strayed to those days in Cyprus, Northern Ireland and in Fort George itself when he had commanded the Battalion in front of him. For Lady Gordon Lennox, so recently widowed, it was a poignant moment, her thoughts inevitably of her late husband, that gallant and loyal Gordon Highlander to whom the Regiment owed so much.

The arrival of the Colonel-in-Chief, His Royal Highness, The Prince of Wales, Duke of Rothesay, KG, KT, GCB, accompanied by the Colonel of the Regiment, Major-General P W Graham, CBE, was greeted with a hum of expectation. The Prince cut a splendid figure in his Gordon Highlander uniform as he stood on the saluting dais to acknowledge the Royal Salute. As the national Anthem rang out the Standard of the Duke of Rothesay, eldest son of the Scottish Sovereign, broke out over the Fort. It was a proud moment for a regiment which had given unstinting loyal service to the Crown.

After the inspection Number 1 Guard moved forward to receive the old colours, which were handed over to the Ensigns, Second-Lieutenants R McArthur and J D Tink by the RSM, WO1 Jaffray. The old colours were trooped for the last time as the battalion stood at a long present arms. They were then marched off in slow time to the strains of *Auld Lang Syne* played by the Drums and Pipes. As the colours disappeared slowly through the sally port of the fort and into history there were few dry eyes in the crowd, and it was an unusual Gordon Highlander who did not have a lump in his throat as such an integral and symbolic part of regimental life left the battalion for ever.

The presentation of the new colours spoke of the continuity of service and unbroken traditions of the regiment. The drummers piled their drums and the battalion formed a hollow square. With the new colours draped over the drums, the Chaplain General to the Armed Forces, the Reverend Jim Harkness, O.B.E., QHC, led the service of consecration. After the Colonel-in-Chief handed over the new colours to the kneeling Ensigns, Lieutenant N J Buchanan and Second-Lieutenant C J Hay, he addressed the Battalion:

'Colonel Stenhouse, Officers, Warrant Officers, Non-Commissioned Officers and Men of the 1st Battalion, The Gordon Highlanders. It is a source of great pride to me, as your Colonel-in-Chief, that I am able to be here today to see the Battalion on parade in such a magnificent setting, and to present you with new colours on behalf of The Queen.

'A ceremony such as this is a very important occasion in the life of a regiment, and helps to remind its members of these proud traditions of service to the nation which have been handed down to us through successive generations of Gordon Highlanders during the last 200 years. You have certainly lived up to those traditions today by your bearing and smartness, and I congratulate you on the obvious effort you have all put into this parade.

'This occasion is also, above all, a family occasion, when you are surrounded by wives, children, girl-friends and former members of the regiment, many of whom have come from far away to witness such an historic event. Ever since I was fortunate enough to become your Colonel-in-Chief eleven years ago, at the time of The Queen's Silver Jubilee, you have made me feel very much a part of your regimental family, and I was most touched last year when it was decided that my tenth anniversary as Colonel-in-Chief needed commemorating![20] Having spent a considerable proportion of my life in the Gordons' main recruiting area around Balmoral, and having known so many Gordon Highlanders as a child, I felt I knew the regiment quite well.

'In the past few years I have followed your activities and service abroad with great interest and admiration, and have been in no doubt

---

20 The tenth anniversary was celebrated by having a party for all ranks and parts of the Regiment at the Craigendarroch Hotel in Ballater to which Prince Charles came. This was repeated in 1992, his fifteenth anniversary, and again in 2007, his thirtieth.

about those standards and qualities for which the Regiment is renowned—particularly the irrepressible sense of humour of the Scotsman, which can sometimes be the most effective weapon in your armoury! The reputation you have has been developed by the selfless service of successive generations of Gordon Highlanders in times of war and peace.

'Such qualities as steadfastness, courage, loyalty and forbearance have earned the regiment distinction in campaigns all over the world, and the battle honours which adorn these colours bear witness to our proud heritage. But today, for those of you on parade, and for those Gordon Highlanders yet to join our ranks, the same qualities are as relevant and as vital as ever before.

'Today, thankfully, we live in peace, but to preserve and safeguard that peace our Armed Forces must remain vigilant and be able to respond at short notice to whatever emergency may arise. During the last 25 years the 1st Battalion has been called upon to fulfil a wide variety of commitments, and by showing the same professionalism and dedication to duty of your forebears it has reinforced that reputation for dependability, resolve and good humour for which the regiment is so widely respected.

'No one can tell what the future has in store, but one thing is certain: the 1st Battalion will face new tasks and fresh challenges. Let these colours serve as an inspiration to you as they have to your forebears in earlier times. I charge you to safeguard these colours, and I am confident that in serving the Crown you will uphold the finest traditions of our regiment, and in so doing you will add new laurels to the illustrious history of The Gordon Highlanders.'

In reply, Colonel Stenhouse said:

'The presentation of new colours is a rare occurrence. This is only the fourth occasion this century that the 1st Battalion has received new colours. It is an historic and nostalgic event.

'The colours once played a vital role in the life of a battalion in that they identified the position of the commander in battle, which was invariably in the centre of the formation. Today they remain at the heart of battalion life, but their role is a more symbolic one. They embody the very spirit of the regiment, which endures from generation to generation.

'A few moments ago we watched the old colours being marched off parade for the last time. These colours were presented in 1961 and have accompanied the battalion on active service and around the globe for the last 27 years. I imagine that there were many on parade, and probably many more sitting in the stands who will have contemplated for a moment on the way the battalion has served the Crown during these intervening years.

'We now have new colours, and in whatever commitments the battalion faces in the years ahead—in times of peace or in times of conflict, I assure Your Royal Highness that the 1st Battalion will not be found wanting. These colours bear witness to our proud heritage. We will endeavour to live up to the high expectations of those who have gone before.

'It is with great pride that we receive these new colours. We are proud to serve our Queen and our Country in the cause of peace, and we are proud, each and every one of us, to be Gordon Highlanders.'

After the National Anthem the Battalion received its new colours with a General Salute as the two Ensigns marched in slow time to take their place. The Parade marched past in slow and quick time, and Advanced in Review Order, concluding with three cheers for the Colonel-in-Chief. The cheers rang out, staccato sharp. The precision with which the parade was carried out was epitomised by those cheers, so precise that it seemed as though just one vast voice had sounded them. The ceremony completed, The Gordon Highlanders marched off, giving a proud eyes right to their Colonel-in-Chief.

The Life of a Regiment, Volume VII, pp 398–403.

The new Colours are trooped past the 1st Battalion, Fort George, 1988

CHAPTER 9

EVENTS INVOLVING THE COLOURS

THE colours were carried by junior officers, known as ensigns. Ensign was the lowest commissioned rank, equating to second-lieutenant. Until the last quarter of the 19th century the colours were carried on the battlefield, and inevitably attracted much enemy fire. The casualty rate among ensigns was high.

1813—Pass of Maya

At Maya, [in] the Pyrenees, the Colours fell to the ground time after time, every officer but two being either killed or wounded, and carried from the field.

T&S, November 1927.

1815—Quatre Bras

The Grenadiers and First Company took the high road, the other companies to the right advanced upon the house and hedge, and some upon the garden, the enemy pouring a deadly fire on them from the windows and from the hedge. The officer with the regimental colour was shot through the heart, the staff of the colour was shattered into six pieces by three balls, and the staff of the Kings, by one.

The Life of a Regiment, Volume I, p 355.

A wounded Ensign

Two ensigns were killed and four wounded at Quatre Bras. When an ensign carrying a colour was shot another would step forward to take his place. Ensign John Bramwell (whose father, Gaelic speaking Captain John Bramwell, fought in the American War of Independence) was born at Inverkeithing in 1796, commissioned into the 92nd, and joined it in Ireland in 1814. On 16 June 1815, Bramwell, with one of the colours, was in the thick of the battle:

Early in the battle he had some narrow escapes and at great risk succeeded in saving the life of a brother officer who was badly wounded; but he was at last shot down. Fearful lest his standard should fall into the hands of the enemy, he tore the colours from the staff and wrapped them round his body for safety. He was carried to Brussels where he was laid up for some time. His wound disabled him from further service and he retired from the Army with the rank and pay of a Lieutenant. He died on the 18th June 1881, aged 85 years.

Memorials of Sanquhar Churchyard.

Lieutenant John Bramwell in 1816

Carried from the battlefield, Bramwell asked a brother officer to inform his father of his wound, and that he would recover:

Camp near Valenciennes
22nd of June 1815

To Captain Bramwell

Dear Sir,

It is with sincere regret that I communicate to you, at the particular request of your son, that he received a wound above the right knee when carrying the colours of the Regiment on the 16th June when we were engaged with the enemy in front of the village Genape when I carried him out of the field and got a waggon to bring him to Brussels, he begged I might communicate his situation to you and I regret it was not sooner in my power, the Regt being continually on the move.

It is a satisfaction to reflect that no one could behave with more cool and determined courage than Mr Bramwell did on the 16th, the whole day till he received his wound he was most conspicuously placed, in the front, with the Standard in his hand, an example to all round him.

He is gone I believe to Antwerp, and though the wound is severe, I trust he will soon get the better of it and be restored to the society of his friends, who here regret his absence much. We had five officers wounded on the 16th with 260 men, so that with what we lost on the great day of the 18th few remain.

I feel confident that before this reaches you, you will have received a letter from himself, but should it be otherwise I shall be most happy to give you any further information in my power.

I remain, dear sir
Your faithful servt
Thos Gordon
Lieut 92nd Regt

The Waterloo colours of the 92nd

The early colours put in a further appearance in 1966 when the Marquis of Linlithgow, whose family had guarded them since 1816, returned them to the Regiment:

On Tuesday, 19th July [1966], at Hopetoun House, South Queensferry, an event of historic importance took place. The Marquess of Linlithgow, M.C., returned to The Gordon Highlanders, after close on a century and a half, two Regimental Colours, carried during the Napoleonic Wars. One certainly was carried at Waterloo in 1815.

Since 1816 when Lieutenant-General, The Hon Sir John Hope, KB, Colonel of the 92nd Gordon Highlanders, accepted the Colours for safekeeping, successive generations of his family have safeguarded these relics at Hopetoun.[1]

Colours of the British Army carried at Waterloo are now rare, and these colours are unique in another way. It was under one of these Colours that the Regiment linked with the Scots Greys to charge and rout the French to the cry of 'Scotland for Ever'; a story which stirred the pride of every Scot at home, at a time when the then new Scottish Regiments were laying the foundations of professional skill, martial ardour and *élan* for which in the years following they have become famous.

One Colour, believed to have been carried at Waterloo, is almost entirely shot away, but the Regimental cypher is clearly seen, and the fragments are preserved in a glass case. The other Colour, the Regimental

---

1 Sir John Hope, to whom the colours had originally been entrusted, was the 4th Earl of Hopetoun. The 7th Earl was created the 1st Marquess of Linlithgow, and it was his grandson, the 3rd Marquess, who returned the colours to The Gordon Highlanders.

Colour, formerly carried by the 2nd Battalion of the 92nd until 1815 when it was carried by the 1st Battalion until 1830, is mounted on a pike.

The Commanding Officer headed a representative party from the 1st Battalion. Captain R.G.D. Bruce commanded a Guard of Honour of 2Lt F.D.H. Irvine, 2Lt M.P. Taitt and 48 Other Ranks, headed by the Drums and Pipes, from Redford Barracks.

At 3 p.m., the official party being in a position on the top of the staircase leading from the forecourt to the main entrance, Lord Linlithgow, accompanied by the Colonel of the Regiment, appeared outside the main entrance and was received with a General Salute. Lord Linlithgow inspected the Guard and returned to the main entrance where he handed the fragment of the Regimental Colour in its glass case to the Colonel of the Regiment, who in turn handed it to Captain I. Fleming. Next, the Regimental Colour, mounted on a pike, was handed over to 2/Lt M.P. Taitt, ensign to the Colour.

Lord Linlithgow addressed the parade in these words:

'General Gordon-Lennox, Officers, non-commissioned Officers and men of the Gordon Highlanders:

'We meet today to do honour to a great Regiment. These historic Colours which, on behalf of my family, I now return to you, are a symbol of the gallantry and devotion of your regiment during the Napoleonic War. During that war these Colours were carried on many fronts—the Low Countries, Spain, Portugal and Egypt and, of course, finally at Waterloo, and in these campaigns no Regiment earned greater honour than The Gordon Highlanders.

'It must have been a great joy to my ancestor, the 4th Earl of Hopetoun, when the 92nd Regiment handed these battle-scarred Colours to him for safekeeping at Hopetoun.

'As Lieut-General Sir John Hope, he had fought alongside the Gordons in all these areas except at Waterloo. He had been severely wounded at the siege of Bayonne in the last days of the Peninsular campaign, and from then on was unfit for active service. It will have been a compensation to him that the Regiment expressed their trust and admiration with such a significant gesture.

'Succeeding generations of my family have preserved these Colours ever since, and it is a duty they have been proud to discharge. Nevertheless, I have reluctantly come to the conclusion that, in these uncertain times, it is now our duty to return them to the Regiment, part of whose history they represent, and in whose hands they will now find a more lasting home.

'Please receive them with our best wishes for the future of the Gordon Highlanders.'

Second Lieutenant M.P. Taitt receives 'Waterloo' Colour from Marquis of Linlithgow, 1966

Lieutenant-General Sir George Gordon-Lennox replied:

'Lord Linlithgow,

'On behalf of the Gordon Highlanders I accept with great pleasure these historic Regimental Colours of the 92nd Regiment, consecrated and carried in the service of King George III; one of them being present with the 1st Battalion at Waterloo. [They] represent a fighting tradition which even in those early days of the Regiment's history was a proud one and of which, after many more wars in many lands in the services of the Sovereign, we today are prouder still.

'Little did your ancestor, who took over the Colonelcy of the Regiment from mine in 1806, think that you would be handing them back to the Regiment through me for safekeeping 160 years later.

'They will be preserved in honour in the Regimental Museum in Aberdeen in the heart of the Gordon country.

'For this very gracious act on the part of you and your family all Gordon Highlanders everywhere are most deeply grateful. We thank you, Sir, for making possible this memorable occasion.'

T&S, November 1966.

Regimental Colour of 2nd Battalion, 92nd Regiment, which replaced the badly damaged Colour carried at Waterloo. Displayed by Captain Robin Fogg-Elliot, curator of the Regimental Museum.

1879 – unusual treatment of the colours

In the author's day the colours were treated with respect bordering on reverence. When not on parade they were kept in the Officers Mess, and displayed throughout the day. At the end of the day the Orderly Officer ensured that the colours were cased and deposited in the Silver Room, which was always kept locked. The treatment of the colours attributed to officers and N.C.O.s in the following account would cause great consternation in the Officers and Sergeants Messes of a later generation!

Mr C.R. Martin,[2] late Sergeant of the 92nd, writing from Toronto to the *Scottish American*, says of the old colours deposited in the safe

---

2   This is Sgt Charles Ross Martin, whose enlistment in 1867 is covered in Chapter 6.

keeping of the city of Aberdeen, that they were only under fire on one occasion during the Afghan War.

It was on 8th October 1879, just two days after the battle of Charasia. At this engagement which resulted in the capture of Cabul, I was the centre-sergeant of the colour party. When trying to outflank the enemy we were marching in column of fours until we got into a ploughed field, when as we turned the corner we, to our great surprise, encountered the enemy strongly posted on the top of some hills behind the city. They had fifteen guns, and when they noticed us they opened fire with a vengeance. Seeing how matters were the Colonel at once gave orders for the colours to be uncased and the column to 'Front Form Companies'. In going through this formation a round shot just grazed the Queen's colour, carried by Lieut Donald Stewart, a son of Sir Donald Stewart, KCB. etc. 'By Jove!' cried the young lieutenant, 'won't my father be glad when he hears of that?' After two hours' fighting darkness came on, and we lay all night on the cold ground we had taken. Sergt M. Thompson, Corporals Donald Macphail, Macdonald and myself lay below the colours that night. During the night many of the officers and non-commissioned officers came and snapped small pieces of the colours (the writer among the number) to send to their friends at home; but this practice is carried on in times of peace, as well as in war, in all British regiments on occasions of any great event at which the colours are present.

T&S, February, 1895.

The days of carrying colours into battle drew to a close in the 1880s, although there still remained occasions when the colours were flown on the battlefield. By and large, however, British soldiers would no longer go into battle with colours flying.

Tel-el-Kebir was the first battle in which colours were not carried. A Horse Guards circular of March 1882 conveyed Her Majesty's command that, in consequence of the altered formation of attack and the extended range of firing, in the event of a battalion being ordered on active service, the colours 'will be left at the base of operations, unless the General Officer Commanding should be of opinion that the nature of the services are such as to render the possession of colours with the battalion undoubtedly expedient.' Both colours, however, were retained 'as affording a record of the services of the regiment, and furnishing to young soldiers a history of its gallant deeds.'

The Life of a Regiment, Volume II, p 75.

£ 67926

61 53409

Multico

Lloyd Loyd Mail

07940 491384 PTO

Joe John — 1826 — 1897

George John — 1857 — 1899

EVENTS INVOLVING THE COLOURS

The soul of a regiment is embodied in its colours, which display the most important battle honours and emblems won throughout its history. Loss of the colours is a matter of great shame for any regiment. On 10 February 1942, just before Singapore surrendered to the Japanese, the Regimental silver and Colours of the 2nd Battalion were lodged in the vaults of the Hong Kong and Shanghai Bank. Under normal circumstances they would have been sent home to Britain for safekeeping, but the rapid Japanese advance made this impossible, and the colours were left in the bank when the 2nd Battalion went into captivity. When the Japanese surrendered in 1945, the Commanding Officer of 2nd Gordons, Lieutenant-Colonel J.H. Stitt, was a prisoner in Thailand. On his release, he flew to Singapore to recover the Battalion's property and, miraculously, found the silver and colours still in the bank vaults. The Japanese had ransacked the bank but failed to recognise the significance of their find, as they would certainly have taken them back to Japan as a war trophy or displayed them in the museum they opened in Singapore to glorify their victory. The colours came back safely to Britain aboard HMS *Nelson* and were returned to the 2nd Battalion.

SECTION 4

VOLUNTEERS

FROM their earliest days The Gordon Highlanders worked with or alongside volunteers. We are used to thinking of volunteers as part-time soldiers such as the Territorial Army, but in the late eighteenth and early nineteenth centuries the word 'volunteer' had a very specific meaning. Volunteers were 'men of superior education, who enlisted and served in the ranks as private soldiers, but without pay and at their own expense, in the hope of getting commissions. They were included in the rank and file.'

The Napoleonic Wars saw volunteer units, in addition to existing Militia units, being raised in Britain for the defence of the United Kingdom. Like the Militia, they had no obligation to serve outside Britain, but they could do so by transferring to a line regiment. In the second half of the 19th century, volunteer units became formally established, and links were formed with local regiments. This system evolved into volunteer battalions of regular regiments—and eventually led to the formation of the Territorial Army.

CHAPTER 10

VOLUNTEERS THROUGH THE AGES

JAMES Hope,[1] whose letters and memoirs are quoted in this book, was a volunteer during the Napoleonic Wars. He joined the 92nd Highlanders as a twenty–year–old volunteer and served from 26 July to 1 November 1809, when he went with them on the Walcheren Expedition. On their return to Great Britain, he was commissioned into the 92nd as an ensign and posted to the 2nd Battalion in Ireland. He transferred to the 1st Battalion and served with it in Spain, France and at Waterloo. He was one of a number of officers who gained commissions in this way.

When The Gordon Highlanders were raised, the Militia had long existed in England, but there was none in Scotland before 1797. Fencible Regiments were raised, some for service in Scotland only, others for the defence of the United Kingdom while the regular army was abroad. They were disciplined and armed as troops of the line. Fencible officers ranked junior to those of the line but took precedence over the Militia.

The Duke of Gordon raised two regiments of Fencibles, one in 1778 and the second, the Northern Fencibles, in 1793. The Quartermaster of the Northern Fencibles records his first impressions, of the commanding officer—and of an officer recruited from the local gentry:

> I found Lieutenant-Colonel Woodford, an active clever officer and a great disciplinarian, in command. In a month we were ready, 600 strong, a fine body of young men. We went to Edinburgh, where the forming of flank companies excited no little jealousy among several Highland officers, especially one who had no conception, when he brought fourscore of his clan as volunteers, that they were to be disunited, and said, 'If the commanding officer dared to draft any of his men to other companies, he would order his piper to sound the gathering, and march them back to Lochaber'; that his men were gentlemen, and he would not have them associate with '*Bodach nam briogais*.'[2] It was explained that his men were now soldiers and must go to the company they suited, and that a court-martial might prove a disagreeable start to his military career.

The Life of a Regiment, Volume I, p 8.

---

1   James Hope was a nephew of Sir John Hope (later Earl of Hopetoun), eminent soldier and Colonel of the 92nd.

2   'Churls with breeches'.

TRAINING THE VOLUNTEERS

Modern-day Territorial Army soldiers attend a set number of training evenings and weekends throughout the year. The early Militia had similar obligations, although not all observed them. The author, at one period in his career Training Major of 3rd Battalion, 51st Highland Volunteers, remembers the counting of heads at training evenings to see just who had turned up. The Royal Aberdeenshire Volunteers in 1801 clearly faced similar problems and the following despairing letter addressed to his Commanding Officer expresses the frustration felt by an enthusiastic volunteer who saw efficiency degraded by lack of numbers and suitable training. Although couched in respectful tones, the letter implies a rebuke to the officer who has allowed this situation to develop. It is akin to the modern-day phrase 'With respect, sir . . .' which means exactly the opposite!

Wednesday afternoon
July 22 1801

Dear Colonel,

Perhaps you may be surprised, though I hope not offended, at my taking this method of addressing you on the following subject. I am a member of that honourable and respectable corps which you command— and as several Gentlemen who serve in same company with myself have expressed a wish that you, as colonel, should be made acquainted with the internal state of the corps, I have presumed to give the following hints: sincerely hoping that you will not be offended as they are the dictates of some real well-wishers to the cause, and who have the greatest veneration and esteem for you.

With sorrow I beheld our few number on the Day of Inspection—and still fewer on the preceding Drill—hardly one half of our number! I am surprised that men who ought to have understanding, and who should know their Duty, are so shamefully negligent. I lament that a spirit of discontent has prevailed in the corps, since his Majesty's Birthday—the cause of which probably you know. Without inquiring into the circumstances and reasons which an Officer of the corps, now high in office, might have had for not giving the usual invitation on the occasion—many imagined that as the corps was not invited as formerly, they had fallen in the esteem of those in office; and have absented themselves on that account. But what, in the name of wonder, have drinking and discipline to do together—surely no man of sense, who has any notion of honour, could give as a reason for his non-attendance 'That as he was not invited to drink, he would not attend Drill'. Yet many, to their shame, could give no other reason. Such men should be in a corps called The Bacchanalian Battalion.

It remains for me to thank you in the most sincere manner for your attention on the Inspection—for if it had not been for the uncommon attention of the officers, and especially you, we would have cut but a sorry figure. Indeed, I thought that it was to be the day on which the Aberdeen Volunteers was to lose all their former character, and which was to stigmatise them with sloth and inattention—yet everything went smoothly, and very well. On the drill prior to the Inspection you found fault with the marching of the Battalion—which way could it have been otherwise?—you know that marching is solely attained by practice— practice we had not. And several Gentlemen reflected on your conduct that night, in you not ordering one single drill in the month of June, notwithstanding the fineness of the weather—I hope you will never give them cause to complain so again.

It is the opinion of every wellwisher to the corps, that some method should be taken to ascertain the reason why so many members were absent on the Day of Inspection—either by a circular letter to those who did not attend, or in any other manner which you might be pleased to order. All those who could not show sufficient reason for non-attendance should be dismissed from the corps.

To a corps like the Royal Aberdeen Volunteers, who is among the oldest in Scotland, it is shameful not to be in a better state of discipline— instead of being better than some years ago, they are actually worse, altho' the danger be greater. The reason is obvious—'Seldom, if ever, ordered out to Drill; and when there, very careless in general.'—yet they boast serving without pay—but where is the service? Perhaps they imagine that to be out eight or ten times in the year is sufficient service. Indeed it may do to learn how to fire on a Birthday—but will never make them expert in the field. If a man has not three hours to spare in six days, he ought not to take up arms—he degrades himself, and shows a bad lesson to others. But I am happy to hear there is a plan for more effectual marching attendance of the corps; which I hope will be brought about by your good judgement; for without attendance we can never arrive at correctness.

At a time like the present, when a foreign enemy is threatening us with invasion—when we have reason to dread commotions in our own country—and when every corps and class of men are trying to see how much superior to one another they will rise in military affairs—it surely becomes the Royal Aberdeen Volunteers to be at least equal in point of discipline with a corps of a later date. It is therefore wished by many that you would order weekly drills in the usual manner, at such hour as you may think fit—as it is the only way that the corps can retrieve their former steadiness and alertness.

I shall only add, that as there is an order from the Commander in Chief, and when most Volunteers are practising themselves in leveling, that it would be highly proper, if there is ammunition in store, to order a morning or two for the purpose of firing at a target—as it would be very beneficial to the corps.

If any of those hints be just, I hope you will attend to them; and forgive any improprieties that may happen to be, as the whole are really designed for the use of the corps—and I remain (hoping to be at drill next week),

your most obedient

and very humble Servant,

A Volunteer—who was <u>never</u> absent.

Gordon Highlanders Museum.

W.S. GILBERT IN GORDON TARTAN

All sorts of people were to be found in the Militia, Volunteer and Territorial Army units connected with The Gordon Highlanders. A complete cross-section of trades and professions served in the ranks. One of the Gordons' oddest volunteer connections must surely be that of one half of Britain's most celebrated operetta duo, Gilbert & Sullivan!

As this happens to be the fiftieth anniversary of the creation of Savoy Opera by the production at the Royalty Theatre, London, on March 25, 1879, of *Trial by Jury* it is very interesting to remember that as an officer of the Royal Aberdeenshire Highlanders W. S. Gilbert wore the Gordon kilt for thirteen years. Having missed getting into the regular army owing to the curtailment of the forces after the Crimean War, Gilbert satisfied his instinct for soldiering, which figures so largely and pungently in his operas, by getting an ensigncy in the 5th West Yorks Militia, stationed at Knaresborough, on March 10th, 1859. Here he stayed till June 15th, 1865, when for some reason never explained was transferred as lieutenant to the Royal Aberdeenshire Highlanders, who became the 3rd Battalion of the Gordons in 1882. He got his company on July 7th, 1868, and did not retire until April 24th, 1878.

I have very little doubt that it was himself he pictured in the drawing signed Bab in the pages of *Fun* (March 30th, 1867), in the eighth of a series of articles he contributed on 'Men we Meet' by the 'Comic Physiognomist'. In this article the 'CP.' is described as going to a levee, and he does so with the remark: 'The CP. has invariably noticed that, with all their faults, Scotch gentlemen are more accessible to strangers than any other inhabitants of the British Isles.'

Gilbert knew a good deal about soldiering in this round-about way, and he always looked like a soldier. But the fun he made of soldiers incensed General Arthur Lambton so much that that proud guardsman barred his admission to the Garrick Club for years, as you will find duly noted in the amazingly frank book by the General's son.

The Aberdeenshire Militia raised in 1798, under the Scots Militia Act of 1797, were known from 1855 to 1882 as the Royal Aberdeenshire Highlanders, and in 1858, while stationed at Dublin, they adopted the Gordon tartan as a compliment to the Earl of Aberdeen, Lord-Lieutenant of Aberdeenshire at that time.

J.M. Bulloch

T&S, May 1925.

Gilbert himself wrote of his joining the Royal Aberdeenshire Highlanders:

> I was intended for the Royal Artillery, and read up during the Crimean War. Of course, it came to an end just as I was prepared to go up for examination. No more officers were required, and further examinations were indefinitely postponed until I was over age. I was offered a line commission, but declined; but eventually, in 1868, I was appointed Captain of the Royal Aberdeenshire Highlanders (Militia), a post I held for sixteen years.[3]

WATERLOO AND WHISKY

Many Gordon Highlanders went on to achieve great things in civilian life. They featured in politics, diplomacy, business, the arts and community life. One particular family has seen five generations serve in the Regiment. Of those, the representatives of the first and fifth generations served as regular soldiers, while the remainder served in the Volunteer battalions of the late 19th century and the Territorial Army of the twentieth. Those in the Territorial Army fought and suffered in the First and Second World Wars. In civilian life the family founded and ran one of the most successful whisky distilling firms in Scotland: William Grant and Sons. Their connection with The Gordon Highlanders dates back to the Napoleonic Wars.

---

3   If Gilbert is correct, and he served for sixteen years, then he must have spent time as a Gordon Highlander.

Old Waterloo

William Grant, the founder of the world-famous whisky distiller, William Grant & Sons, was born on 19 December 1839 in Conval Street, Dufftown. He came from a family with a strong military tradition; his grandfather had fought at Culloden and his father, William Grant (1784–1877), master tailor, was known as 'Old Waterloo' because he had served in the 92nd Gordon Highlanders during the Walcheren Expedition (1809), the Peninsular War (1810–13), and had stood in line with the 92nd at Quatre Bras and Waterloo, where he was wounded. As shown in the following extract from the list of Gordon Highlanders wounded (w) at Quatre Bras and Waterloo in June 1815, seven Grants were among the 408 non-commissioned officers and men wounded in the two battles. Of the seven, two were named William, and of these the one listed as a labourer from Inveravon is almost certainly 'Old Waterloo', as Inveravon is only a few miles from Dufftown, where the founder of Grant's Whisky was born.

Grant, Alexander (carpenter, Talbert)—Brussels (w.); d. August, 4.
Grant, James (labourer, Strath)—(w.).
Grant, James (tailor, Granton)—(w.).
Grant, John (labourer, Longside)—Brussels (w.).
Grant, Lewis—at Brussels (w.); d. July 24.
Grant, William (labourer, Inveravon)—(w.), on duty.
Grant, William (labourer, Kingussie)—(w.).

He is shown as wounded but remaining on duty, which, although his wound clearly did not fall in the 'grave' or 'serious' categories, speaks highly of his fortitude, his willingness to soldier on and his reluctance to leave his comrades.

William Grant was in the ranks of the 92nd Regiment, The Gordon Highlanders, when it marched out of Brussels in the small hours of 16 June 1815, some of its officers having come directly from the Ball given by the Duchess of Richmond, sister of their first commanding officer. They marched to Quatre Bras, where they met and checked the French, but lost six officers killed and twenty wounded, and thirty-five other ranks killed and 245 wounded. William Grant, standing in the firing line, was faced with the full fury of the French, exposed to musket fire, cannon fire and the charges of the French cavalry. The following glimpses of the 92nd at Quatre Bras and Waterloo are taken from *Sergeant Robertson's Journal*:

The 92d was now brought to the front of the farm-house, and formed on the road, with our backs to the walls of the building and garden, our right resting upon the crossroads, and our left extending down the front. We were ordered to prime and load, and sit down with our firelocks in our hands, at the same time keeping in line. The ground we occupied rose with a slight elevation, and was directly in front of the road along which the French were advancing.

The column of French cavalry reformed, and prepared to charge our regiment; but we took it more coolly than the Brunswickers did. When the Duke of Wellington saw them approach, he ordered our left wing to fire to the right, and the right wing to fire to the left, by which we crossed the fire; and a man and horse affording such a large object for an aim, very few of them escaped. The horses were brought down, and the riders, if not killed, were made prisoners.

A volley was fired at the Duke of Wellington from behind a garden hedge. I got a section and went into the garden, when, after a short contest, we succeeded in driving them out, after having killed a good many of them. By the time I got out of the garden and came to the road, the regiment was closely engaged with the bayonet.

We sustained considerable loss from the enemy's cannon, as we had none with which to oppose them. Our regiment was now very much cut up both in officers and men, as we had been first in the action, and, along with the other Highland regiments, had for a long time to resist the attack of the whole French army. We continued very warmly engaged until about eight o'clock in the evening, when we rallied, and made another effort to capture some of the enemy's guns.

We do not know if William Grant was among the wounded at Quatre Bras. We do know that, apart from those who had lost limbs or were severely wounded, many of the 92nd wounded returned to the ranks and stood with their comrades at Waterloo. Some of them died there or were wounded again. It is difficult to determine from the roll of the wounded in which battle the wounds were received. As William Grant was known as 'Old Waterloo' for the rest of his days, it is safe to assume that he survived Quatre Bras and faced the French again at Waterloo. Sergeant Robertson speaks for William Grant and all the soldiers of the 92nd when they rose, cold and hungry, to face the huge French army again.

We were aroused by daylight, on the morning of the 18th, and ordered to stand to our arms, till the line should be reconstructed. During the time I never felt colder in my life; every one was shaking like an aspen leaf. An allowance of gin was served out to each of us, which had the effect of infusing warmth into our almost inanimate frames, as before we got it, we seemed as if under a fit of ague. We had scarcely got breakfast discussed, when a shot from the French killed one of our pioneers. We were ordered to stand to arms, prime and load, fix bayonets, wheel into line, and be ready to act in any manner required. Beyond the hedge in front was a fallow field, having a gentle ascent towards it; and being placed rather in rear of the slope, the French cannoniers could not hit us, but they made some shells to bear upon us, which made great havoc in our ranks. As yet we had not fired a shot, but what had been discharged by our out-posts.

The French were forming columns to their right, directly in our front, and we were expecting to be attacked, as all on the right of our division were warmly engaged. We were well cautioned to be steady and keep together, as we would be first attacked by cavalry, who would try to break our line; and, above all, to mind what word of command was given— whether to form square, or whatever else the order might be. At this time, our men were falling fast from grape shot and shells, while as yet we had not discharged a musket. Our artillery commenced a brisk fire, which drew French fire upon our ranks, as we were immediately in rear of the artillery. A large column of French infantry was seen advancing in our direction. Every one was eager to be led on, and as the way which they were taking indicated that it was upon that part of the line where the 92d was that the attack would be made, General Pack ordered us to advance, and line the hedge, to oppose the advance of the column. But when we got to the hedge, we found the French were there as soon as we. We cheered loudly, and called to the Scotch Greys, who were formed up in our rear, 'Scotland for ever!' Upon which some person in the regiment called out to 'charge,' when, all at once, the whole regiment broke through the hedge, and rushed headlong on the French column. The onset threw them into confusion. At this critical moment, the Greys flew to our assistance, and having got round on the flanks of the column, they placed themselves between the enemy and our own line. While we pushed them hard in front, the other cavalry regiments came at full speed to our aid, when it was fearful to see the carnage. The dragoons were lopping off heads at every stroke, while the French were calling for quarter. We were also among them busy with the bayonet, and what the cavalry did not execute we completed; owing to the position taken up by the dragoons, very few of them escaped. It was here that some of the 92d and the Greys had a struggle for the eagle, which a sergeant of the Greys bore off.[4]

About four o'clock the enemy made another attack on our line, by a large body of lancers, who rode up to our squares with as much coolness as if subjecting us to a regimental inspection. We kept up a smart fire upon them, and put them to the right-about. But before we had succeeded in turning them, they did us considerable damage by throwing their lances into our columns, which, being longer than the firelock and bayonet, gave

---

4   This is an interesting observation, in view of the belief in some quarters that the Eagle captured by Ensign Ewart of the Scots Greys was in fact originally taken by a Gordon Highlander, when Ewart, 'on his big grey horse, relieved him of it.'

them a great advantage over us. At this time we could see large columns of infantry forming in our front, with numerous bodies of artillery, when we expected we were to be called upon to sustain a charge from all kinds of arms. We were ordered to line our old hedge in readiness to receive them. When we saw the dense masses collecting in our front ready to rush upon us, we looked for nothing but that our line would be broken, and utter discomfiture would be the consequence. The bodies of our brave artillerymen lay beside the guns which they had so bravely managed, and many a cannon had not a gunner left to discharge it.

While in this state, with life and death in the balance, the French column began to move forward. An awful pause ensued! Every man, however, was steady. They came within pistol-shot, when a volley of rockets was let off by a brigade formed in the hedge, which threw them into confusion. We gave a loud huzza, and poured a well-directed volley upon them. This unexpected and rough reception made them turn and run, leaving behind them a number of killed and wounded. When this brush was over, we sent out skirmishers, along the hedge, to keep up the fire, and give information of what was passing among the French, who were keeping up a distant cannonade. We opened our files along the hedge, as the wider they were, there was less danger to be apprehended from round shot, and in this way we remained for a long time. Notwithstanding this precaution, they were occasionally taking off some of us.

. . . the Duke was standing in the stirrups with his hat elevated above his head. Every eye was fixed upon him, and all were waiting with impatience to make a finish of such a hard day's work. At last he gave three waves with his hat, and the loud three cheers that followed the signal were the heartiest that had been given that day. On seeing this, we leapt over the hedge that had been such a protection to us during the engagement, and in a few minutes we were among the French lines. Nothing was used now but the bayonet, for, after the volley we gave them, we set off at full speed, and did not take time to load. All was now destruction and confusion. The French at length ran off, throwing away knapsacks, firelocks, and every thing that was cumbersome, or that could impede their flight. One division at the farm house of Le Belle Alliance made an attempt to stand, and came to the charge. When the three Highland regiments saw the resistance offered by this column, we rushed upon it like a legion of demons. Such was our excited and infuriated state of mind, and being flushed with the thought of victory, we speedily put an end to their resistance. The Prussians were now among us—the one nation cheering on the other, while the bands were playing their national anthems.

Sergeant Robertson's Journal.

William Grant, like so many of his comrades, wounded, but remaining with his regiment, stood throughout that long day, in the face of cannon fire, cavalry charges and assaults by overwhelming numbers of French infantry. Ignoring their wounds, they took everything the French could throw at them and gave as good as they got. Their dogged determination not to yield earned the admiration and respect of all, on the battlefield and at home and, for William Grant, the affectionate nickname that he was known by for the rest of his life, 'Old Waterloo'. (He was a small man at 4'11" and boasted that 'All the bullets went over my head.') An ordinary man from Inveravon, he had joined the ranks of immortals, and established the links with The Gordon Highlanders that his family maintained for generations.

William Grant

Born in Dufftown in 1839, Old Waterloo's son, William, at the age of seven, herded cattle at a farm on the upper reaches of the River Deveron. Apprenticed to a shoemaker, and after a spell as a clerk, William took a job in 1866 as a book-keeper at Mortlach distillery. He set about learning the art of distilling and in a short time was appointed clerk and manager. In 1886 William Grant bought a field beneath the towering shadow of Balvenie Castle and laid the foundation stone of his own distillery.

Undoubtedly inspired by his father's tales of soldiering with The Gordon Highlanders, William joined the Banffshire Rifle Volunteers (which became the Sixth Volunteer Battalion, The Gordon Highlanders), in which he rose to the rank of Major. A portrait of him in his Gordon Highlander uniform was used for many years on the label of Grant's Whisky. William Grant was a man of extraordinary capacities. One of the Dufftown Volunteers, William Ramsay, described the old Major: 'Mr Grant was always busy with something. Oh yes, he was a very bright man—a very live cove. He wasn't a particularly tall man but he was a broad man that could carry himself, and always with dignity—nothing proud about him.'

Although he spoke in the broad Scots of his native Banffshire, Grant had a withering command of English, particularly with pen in hand. Highly efficient, energetic and ambitious, he would not stand incompetence, and his bluntness was legendary. On the other hand, he was a model of consideration with his staff. He always whistled loudly when moving around the distillery, especially when approaching a warehouse where he might have stumbled on one of the workers extracting a dram from a convenient cask.

William Grant remained active until his death in 1923 at the grand age of 83. Following in his steps, many in subsequent generations of Grants served in The Gordon Highlanders and fought in both World Wars. Between them they endured wounds, captivity and appalling conditions, but, like 'Old Waterloo', survived.

William Grant, founder of Grant's Whisky, in the uniform of The Gordon Highlanders

Charles Grant

Captain Charles Grant (1872–1926) was William Grant's sixth son. He was quick to offer his services in 1914, and as an officer in 6th Gordons (his father's battalion), he went to France in November 1914. He went into action on 6 December, the day after the battalion manned the trenches. They went into the trenches 'wearing shoes, spats and hose . . . the shoes useless in such conditions because they were dragged off and lost in the dark, 15 pairs disappearing in a single night.' The 6th Gordons fought in the Battle of Neuve Chapelle in March 1915, where Charles Grant was severely wounded:

> 6th Gordons was brought up to the old German front line. It was ordered to attack on the left of the 2nd Battalion, and its objectives were pointed out to the officers on the ground. It seems an extraordinary action to send a battalion across the open in broad daylight when the general attack was clearly held up by heavy fire. It shared the fate of the 2nd in losing its commanding officer, Lieut.-Colonel C. McLean.
>
> Captain J.M. Cooke assumed command. He ordered the advance to be carried out by two companies, in lines of half companies, the other two following 200 yards behind. Artillery, machine-gun, and rifle fire was encountered, but the companies moved at speed without losing formation and, though suffering heavily, were not as hard hit as might have been expected. However, the fire grew hotter, till they came to a halt on a line a little in advance of the 2nd Battalion. Captain Cooke received a message from brigade to the effect that howitzer fire would be turned on to the houses at Moulin du Pietre in order to allow the advance to continue.

Despite this bombardment, the German fire did not slacken. Finally, at 5·45 p.m. orders were received to hold the position reached. The battalion brought in all wounded men under cover of darkness, and in the early hours of March 14th was relieved by the 2nd Borders. The losses of the 2nd Battalion numbered 255 killed, wounded and missing, and those of the 6th, 270 [Captain Charles Grant was one of the 9 officers and 217 other ranks wounded.]

The Life of a Regiment, Volume IV, p 39–40.

William Grant Gordon

William Grant Gordon (1899–1953), the son of William Grant's daughter, Isabella, was commissioned, aged eighteen, and sent to France as a 2nd Lieutenant in 6th Gordons after the German offensive of March 1918. The 6th Gordons had performed well in opposing the German assault on the Somme and the Lys but had suffered heavy casualties. In the 51st Highland Division, it fought under French command at the Second Battle of the Marne in July 1918. William Grant Gordon celebrated his nineteenth birthday as the great British counter-offensive started that was to drive the Germans back in a steady retreat and lead to the end of the War. He fought with the 6th Battalion until 5 October, when the 6th and 7th Battalions were amalgamated to form 6th/7th Gordons, and fought in the 6th/7th until the end, which was not reached without heavy fighting:

The attack was fixed for noon on October 12th. The 6th/7th Gordons reached their objective without difficulty. When, however, they tried to advance to the second, they were sharply checked by fire from Lieu-Saint-Amand. The Germans were making a fresh stand.

Though they were showing signs of demoralization their better divisions were not to be trifled with. The 51st Division was ordered to push parties over the Selle, three miles ahead, to cover the throwing of bridges. They advanced after a bombardment of Lieu-Saint-Amand but without a rolling barrage. The result was calamitous. Again the 6th/7th were badly shot up. Altogether they had upwards of 300 casualties, though a high proportion of these were suffering only from whiffs of mustard gas, from which recovery was normally quick. Among the wounded was Lieut.-Colonel Thom, a fine commanding officer.

. . . The 152nd Brigade now took over the right half of the front of the 153rd and the two attacked at seven a.m. on October 25th. 6th/7th Gordons was on the right of the 152nd. The first objective, a line of German rifle pits, was captured without difficulty. The next objective, the Le Quesnoy-Valenciennes railway, was reached despite hot machine-gun fire from Famars and a wooded knoll, Rouge Mont, south of it. The final objective, a road running into Famars from the South, was captured with about 100 prisoners. No exploitation was possible in face of strong resistance a few hundred yards ahead.

At 5 p.m. the enemy launched a counter-attacked behind a heavy barrage. The 6th/7th Gordons and 6th Seaforths were driven back to the railway, but made a stand behind it. The 4th Gordons relieved the Seaforths after dark and orders were issued for the renewal of the offensive at 10 a.m. on the 26th under a creeping barrage, fired on the whole divisional front by six field artillery brigades and one heavy.

The two battalions of the Gordons, 6th/7th on the right, 4th on the left, attacked side-by-side. The 6th/7th worked round the south side of Rouge Mont and killed or captured all its defenders. The 4th Gordons came in for stiff opposition . . . but by 11.30 a.m. the objective had been secured.

The two battalions of the Gordon Highlanders in the 51st Division could be well satisfied with what they had accomplished. The 6th/7th in particular had had a gruelling time and had been highly successful.

The Life of a Regiment, Volume IV, pp 251–52, 253–55.

Although he missed most of the First World War because he was too young, William Grant Gordon faced all the dangers of the war, both in attack and defence. Like the young soldiers sent out with him to make up the losses suffered in the German March offensive, he had proved himself able to stand against the best that the German Army could throw at him and, overcoming all obstacles, emerge victorious at the end.

George Gray Grant

Captain George Gray Grant (1914–1999) was the only son of Captain Charles Grant and served with 6th Gordons before the Second World War. He was posted to 2nd Gordons, where he was joined by his school friend from Huntly, Lieutenant Forbes Sandison. He was captured in Singapore and worked as a prisoner on the Burma railway.

Working on the railway was a nightmare. Only hand-held tools were provided, with no hydraulic or mechanical equipment. Men were driven to work long hours, carry heavy burdens and endure physical and mental abuse from their captors. There was no time off. The conditions they worked in, and the ordeal they endured are described in Chapter 20.

British and Australian prisoners of the Japanese went through a living Hell. Captain George Gray Grant suffered and endured along with his men, and, like them, emerged into a new world, bloodied but unbowed, with the horrors he had seen etched on his memory. With the fortitude that had sustained the Gordons he faced the future undaunted.

Eric Lloyd Roberts

Captain Eric Lloyd Roberts (1909–1980) served with 8th Gordons (100th Anti-Tank Regiment, RA) during the Burma Campaign. He married Janet Gordon, a grand-daughter of Major William Grant, who celebrated her 110th Birthday in August 2011, and died in 2012. The 8th Battalion, The Gordon Highlanders, was one of the two Gordon battalions re-roled during the Second World War. The 9th Battalion was re-roled as a tank regiment while the 8th Battalion became an artillery regiment, titled the 100th (Gordon Highlanders) Anti-Tank Regiment, Royal Artillery.

It fought at Kohima, at the Irrawaddy and in the capture of Mandalay. During the Irrawaddy operations the 100th Regiment was organised as infantry, their original role, and while in that role was designated '8th Gordons'. They sent out patrols, laid ambushes, and harassed the Japanese as they withdrew to the Irrawaddy. The Japanese put up a fierce resistance. On one occasion 'a troop moved in towards Myinze but were caught by machine-gun fire at short range. The Japanese then brought a mortar and a grenade discharger into action, and the volume of fire was such that the troop were unable to withdraw until darkness fell. The losses amounted to two killed, two wounded and seven missing . . . Gordon patrols continued to prowl about Yawayhitgyi, and on the night of the 31st [January 1945] the 4th Brigade put in an attack against the village but could not secure the whole of it. The mortars of the 169th [Gordons] Battery were in action and silenced a Japanese field gun.'

Captain Eric Lloyd Roberts, Gordon Highlander infantry officer, filled the role of an artillery officer competently and confidently. He helped the 8th Gordons maintain the high reputation the Battalion had built in the First World War and continued in the Second. He went on to become Chairman of William Grant & Sons.

Euan Gordon

Lieutenant-Colonel E.F.(Euan) Gordon (1933–2005) served in 1st Gordons. He married Elizabeth Alexandra Grant Howard, a great-grand-daughter of Major William Grant. Euan Gordon brought yet another link with The Gordon Highlanders in the Napoleonic Wars. His great-great-grandfather, Reverend William Gordon, was the first Chaplain of the 100th Regiment (Gordon Highlanders), later renumbered the 92nd. Euan Gordon was a regular soldier for twenty years, during which he saw active service in the Cyprus Emergency. When he retired he ran the very busy Army Careers Information Office in Edinburgh, where, although responsible for recruiting for the whole Army, and the local infantry regiments in particular, he gently convinced uncommitted recruits to join The Gordon Highlanders.

VOLUNTEERS

Grants in the Gordons through two centuries

Members of the Grant family in the uniform of The Gordon Highlanders served through five generations; four of which saw active service. Some bled for their country, suffered appalling treatment and degradation at the hands of a brutal and inhumane enemy, and endured the privations and hardships of prolonged campaigning. All of them, however, did their duty and maintained the honour and the glory of The Gordon Highlanders.[5]

VOLUNTEERS IN THE BOER WAR

During the Boer War many Volunteer units offered volunteers for the front. In December 1899 it was decided that each regular battalion could receive a company from its territorial corps. Service was to be for one year or the duration of the war (whichever was longer), and service was restricted to unmarried men between twenty-five and thirty-five. The Gordons, having both regular battalions engaged, needed 232 of all ranks for their first companies. Fortunately, besides having five territorial battalions, they had long been closely connected with the London Scottish, to which they had given a succession of adjutants and sergeant-majors. The London Scottish gave four officers and eighty-six other ranks to the Gordons, cementing bonds between the two regiments that would be further strengthened in two World Wars, and which would see the London Scottish become an integral part of The Gordon Highlanders. Three Volunteer companies were formed, although only two were on active service at any given time.

The Volunteer companies played a full part in the battalions to which they were posted. They shared the hardships, the dangers and the comradeship of their regular counterparts:

> [At Doornkop] all officers in the Volunteer Company were hit, 3 other ranks were killed and 11 wounded. Col. Macbean eulogised the gallantry of the Volunteers, and wrote a congratulatory letter to Col. Douglas Dawson, commanding 1st V.B. [The company had been raised mainly from the 1st Volunteer Battalion.]

The Life of a Regiment, Volume III, p 434.

At the action to take a Boer position at Paardeplaats Mountain, above Lydenburg in 1900, the Volunteer company of the 2nd Battalion faced the reality of modern warfare when they suffered casualties before they came within range of the Boer rifles:

---

5   The Grant family continued to help The Gordon Highlanders through the years. When the Regiment was raising funds to establish The Gordon Highlanders Museum, Grant's Whisky produced a specially distilled whisky that they named 'Gordon Highlanders Bicentenary Whisky', released in 1994, the bicentenary year, and provided stocks at cost price for sale in the Museum. The whisky produced significant sums for The Gordon Highlanders Museum.

Kitchener sent the Devons ahead with 2nd Gordons in support and as the latter cleared the town they came under fire; shells burst close. The battalion formed into column of companies at double distance, the men in single rank; there was some distance to go before cover was reached. But 'as the rear company (the Volunteers), followed by the pipers and drummers, emerged from a *donga*, a shell burst in the air some twenty feet above the right flank of the company, which it swept from end to end. The Volunteers reeled for a moment from the shock, but instantly recovering, marched on as if nothing had happened. There was a moment's unsteadiness, but the captain having ordered the company to dress by the right, it moved forward.' There were nineteen killed and wounded, of whom two were pipers and the rest Volunteers.

['The range of the shell was over 11,000 yards, the extreme distance for the weapon and the epoch. All writers commend the admirable steadiness of the Volunteers; both Buller and the divisional general complimented them; while Lord Roberts' dispatch of 9/9/00 repeats the encomium. An officer serving with the Volunteers stated to the writer soon afterwards that the wounded fell against others who themselves fell, while the shock knocked others over; so that the first impression was almost one of annihilation.' *General Sir Nevil Macready*.]

The Life of a Regiment, Volume III, p 208.

Having acquitted themselves with flying colours, the Volunteers, at the end of the war, returned home:

At Aberdeen the Gordons sections [of the 1st Battalion company] were received by the Lord-Lieutenants of the County and the City. The thronging populace admired bronze limbs and faded tartans; at each home centre of a group there was repetition of the reception.

A few days later the 2nd Battalion's company was due. Great was the reception when the train came, but the formalities of disbanding a hundred men are not long and all were civilians again that night. Several of both companies had been so happy in their campaigning that they re-engaged in succeeding companies; a third had been embodied on 1st February 1901, while a fourth was to follow. The first companies paraded once more, when at Castlehill Barracks, on 14th September 1902, war medals were presented by Lord Aberdeen to the men of the Counties and by Lord Provost Fleming to those of the City.

The Life of a Regiment, Volume III, pp 250, 251.

THE TERRITORIAL ARMY

The militia and Volunteer units of The Gordon Highlanders, comprising four battalions; 4th (City of Aberdeen), 5th (Buchan and Formartine), 6th (Donside and Deeside, with Kincardineshire) and 7th (Banffshire) were assimilated into the Territorial Army when it was formed in 1908.

In the north-east of Scotland, while there was pride in The Gordon Highlanders and in the volunteers who had served in South Africa, there was not yet the universal acceptance and adoption of the Regiment and its traditions that large-scale recruitment to and service in the Regiment in two World Wars would bring. There was even, in some quarters, a belief that 'going for a soldier' was not the best option for a young man!

Miss N.—'Tarrable thing aboot Mistress Tamson's loon, is't no?'
Miss M.—'Oh, fit was thon? I didnae hear o't!'
Miss N.—'He's jined the sodgers up tae Castlehill!'
Miss M.—'Jined the sodgers! *Eh, my*! His mither'll be sair pitten aboot!
　　　　Aye, an' this her washin' day an' a'!'

Territorial soldiering in North-East Scotland. (J.M. Bulloch, 1914)

The Territorial battalions, and three 'Kitchener' battalions, (8th, 9th and 10th Gordons), fought with distinction in the First World War alongside the Regular battalions. The accounts below of actions of the 8th and 8th/10th Gordons are a sample of what the Territorial battalions achieved and show how these citizen soldiers followed the example of their regular brethren.

First World War

The 8th Battalion, The Gordon Highlanders was raised in 1914, part of Kitchener's 'First Hundred Thousand'.

Jules Compte-Calix (photo below) was attached as interpreter to the 8th Gordons when it arrived in France on 10 May 1915. He was a young Frenchman of good birth and education and had travelled extensively; he possessed a charming personality and a keen sense of humour—and immediately became a favourite with everyone. On his part he reciprocated by taking the greatest interest in the Battalion; he was proud of its appearance and spirit and had a warm and enduring affection for its officers, non-commissioned officers and men, as his reminiscences show. A loyal Frenchman, he nevertheless saw himself as an integral part of 8th Gordons:

Bagpipes playing and drums beating, the 8th Bn. Gordon Highlanders, marched towards Boulogne. The 9th Scottish Division had arrived, and without delay was sent to the front; the 2nd Battle of Neuve Chapelle was raging and units melted like snow in the sun. The 8th Gordons, which I joined in Boulogne as French Interpreter, belonged to the 26th Brigade, along with the Black Watch, Camerons and Seaforths, men of splendid physique all wearing the kilt. I was often asked if

Highlanders wore any garments under their kilt. I must answer in the negative. Even in the coldest winter days only this kind of skirt covers their legs. Mounted officers had tartan breeches, but the Colonel had not adopted this custom; when he mounted his pony a silent smile lit the faces in the ranks.

We were commanded by Col. Wright,[6] 'Hurricane' Wright [photo], a fine old warrior, and very popular; Capt Maxwell was the Adjutant and the Second-in-Command was Major Cox, whose chief duties were centred on preparing the salad, which he did in state and with great care. Our other officers, of whom many were veterans of Ladysmith and Paardeberg, had various origins: some were ex-Regulars and Militia men, but mostly Kitchener's. The Scots are a very sympathetic race, friendly, hospitable; they have several points in

6   Col Harry Wright, see 'A Kitchener Battalion in France' in Volume IX, Chapter 20. His son, also Harry Wright, commanded the 1st Battalion in 1940 throughout the withdrawal of the 51st Highland Division to St Valery and was captured there along with most of his Battalion.

common with us. I cannot describe them as Puritans, because I found them to be much cuter in their ideas and doings than the English.

J. Compte-Calix

T&S, March 1935.

Compte-Calix felt at home with 8th Gordons, and the Gordons regarded him very much as one of their own. When it came to regimental authority catching out young officers enjoying themselves, Compte-Calix's loyalties lay with his fellow officers:

> One evening after dinner I was sitting in the Mess when Maxwell stated that he was going to have a night alarm and parade the Battalion at ten. A general routine order forbade all ranks to leave their billets after eight o'clock, so as to be at hand to answer any sudden emergency. The CO grunted his approval. It was 9.30 My decision was quickly taken. I wished the Colonel and Maxwell good-night, but once outside I galloped through the dark streets towards the merrymakers' haunts. I descended into the *caveau*; rejoicings were in full swing, and the Gordons greeted me with great roars of welcome, but taking Capt.— into a corner, I warned him of the impending peril. Sam Brownes were buckled and a steeplechase of Gordon officers careered through the *Grande-Rue.* When the alarm took place everybody was present!
>
> The next day Capt.— thanked me warmly on behalf of all his comrades. I told him I knew I had been indiscreet by communicating a conversation overheard, but had no remorse, as I thought I had acted to everybody's benefit. It would have annoyed our fatherly Colonel very much to have to lecture the defaulters the next day, and on the other hand the officers would have been displeased to be told off by Maxwell, who was their junior. After that day I was considered as belonging to the big 8th Gordons family.

J. Compte-Calix

T&S, March 1935.

In May 1916 the 8th and 10th Battalions were merged to form the 8th/10th Battalion, and they soldiered on under this title for the rest of the war. The 8th/10th fought at the Somme and in all the major battles that followed until, in the dark days of the Ludendorff Offensive in 1918, when so many units were under strength, it was assimilated into the 5th Gordons. The 8th/10th Gordons Territorials upheld the best fighting traditions of the Regiment, in major battles and in small-scale raids, a shining example of which was the raid on the Butte de Warlencourt.[7]

---

7   See Volume IX, Chapter 20.

Second World War

In 1940 another Territorial battalion, the 11th, was raised. In 1942, after the 2nd Battalion was captured in Singapore, the 11th was renumbered 2nd, and replaced the regular Battalion that had gone into captivity. As in the First War the Territorial battalions distinguished themselves.

The 5th/7th Gordons, along with the 1st Battalion, was in the 51st Highland Division in the British Eighth Army in North Africa. Their first taste of battle was at El Alamein in which both battalions of The Gordon Highlanders, regular and Territorial, distinguished themselves. The 5th/7th achieved further success in Tunisia in 1943 that surprised even themselves:

> Just before dark an enemy aircraft flew low over D Company, who promptly opened fire with Bren gun and rifle. Such fusillades generally achieved nothing, but to the surprise of the Jocks the aircraft was brought down. The machine, a Messerschmitt of a type not captured hitherto, was little damaged; and the Corps commander, Sir Oliver Leese, paid a special visit to congratulate the Gordons.

The Life of a Regiment, Volume V, p 159.

Everyone in an infantry battalion ran the risk of death or injury, and through the years the Gordons lost more than one commanding officer, killed or wounded. In January 1943 it was Lieutenant-Colonel H.W.B. Saunders, Commanding Officer of 5th/7th Gordons, who, even when wounded, demanded high standards from his soldiers!

> The commanding officer, Major Barlow, Major Cochrane, R.A., Lieutenant McAndrew, a machine-gun officer and three other ranks had already gone forward. One party followed the main road where a man trod on a mine, the explosion killing the machine-gun officer and wounding Barlow and McAndrew. Lieut.-Colonel Saunders and Major Cochrane were using a track some distance from the road when another mine explosion killed Cochrane and severely wounded the commanding officer.
>
> The two stretcher-bearers carrying him from the scene of the incident, thinking he had breathed his last, stopped for a smoke and no sooner were their cigarettes alight, than a voice from the stretcher crisply ordered, 'Put out those cigarettes, I am still your Commanding Officer!'

The Life of a Regiment, Volume V, p 157.

In the advance through Sicily in 1943, 5th/7th Gordons, battle-hardened in the North African desert, showed they were as professional, well-trained and experienced as any regular unit. They were more than capable of dealing with determined German resistance:

This thrust of the Gordons into hostile territory was attended by considerable risk, for they were beyond artillery support and had no knowledge of the enemy's strength and dispositions. Soon heavy fire opened away on the left, where eight *spandaus* were in action. The Gordons showed that they 'knew their stuff': mortars covered skilful manoeuvring by C Company which resulted in white flags at four machine-gun posts, while the opposition faded away. Thirty Germans of the Hermann Goering Division and two Italians were captured; six of the enemy lay dead. C Company had three men wounded, despite their opponents' prodigal expenditure of ammunition.

The Life of a Regiment, Volume V, p 205.

1943 – 1st and 5th/7th Gordons capture Sferro

It was half-an-hour short of midnight when our guns opened on the road and railway and Sferro itself: five minutes later the attack went in, 1st Gordons and 5th/7th Gordons side-by-side.

The enemy's defensive fire caught the tail of the leading companies, and the rest were heavily shelled while crossing the wadi. All agreed that this was the fiercest bombardment they had ever endured.

Despite the shelling and fire from rifles and automatics, B and C Companies of 1st Gordons pressed on over bare stubble fields. The railway was reached and the Highlanders forced their way across sidings packed with goods wagons. Some wagons had been loaded with tar, and this was flowing in a molten mass. Neither these obstacles nor the enemy resistance prevented B and C Companies from reaching the road. They established themselves 300 yards beyond it.

A and D Companies were following up. Captain W.M. MacFarlane, the new commander of A Company, was badly wounded and Lieutenant Morrison again proved himself a good leader of men. The railway station was cleared and Battalion headquarters established in the station yard; but when the commanding officer conferred by wireless with the Brigadier, it was agreed that the night was too far advanced for the attack to go through to Point 151 [beyond Sferro].

A and B Companies of 5th/7th Gordons, on the right of the road, forced their way into Sferro village, which proved larger than expected. Confused fighting went on among the houses, and as the wireless sets with the companies were either hit or rundown, no communication was possible either with the 1st Gordons or with Major Napier.[8] Runners sent by 1st Gordons had failed to reach the companies.

---

8   Maj B.C.A. Napier, 24-year-old second-in-command of 5th/7th Gordons, was commanding the Battalion after Lt-Col J.E.G Hay, had been wounded.

And then, as day was breaking, the Germans made a determined effort to turn the Gordons out of Sferro. An 88-mm. gun fired from one of the houses, seeking to demolish one building after another, while armoured cars began to shoot straight down the main street. Perhaps the 5th/7th Battalion have nothing finer to show than the performance of A and B Companies, who held on until the enemy tired of the struggle and withdrew. His going was hastened by the appearance of a troop of Sherman tanks, sent to the assistance of the Highlanders.

The bridge at Sferro

During this action Major Napier sent forward a truck of much-needed ammunition. As the bridge over the river was known to have been mined, and was registered by the German artillery, his orders were that the vehicle should leave the main road well short of the bridge and make for Battalion headquarters in the wadi. There the ammunition was to be loaded into carriers who would take it forward into Sferro. To save precious time Captain J.W. Ritchie intervened. He stopped the truck before it left the main road, and, all alone, drove across the bridge under heavy shell-fire and so into Sferro. Having delivered the ammunition safely he walked back to Battalion headquarters.[9]

The Life of a Regiment, Volume V, pp. 209–10.

---

9   Capt Ritchie had won a Military Cross at Alamein. He gained a Bar to his M.C. for this action.

Thirty years later Brigadier Charles Barker, who had been a major in 1st Gordons during the battle, returned to Sicily and recorded his recollection of the battle:

The Sferro bridgehead was never an inviting spot as many veterans of the Sicilian campaign can testify, but it looked most attractive viewed in May, 1973 from the 51st Highland Division Memorial nestled in the flat, green Catania Plain beneath Mount Turkisi and backed by a massive white-capped Mount Etna.

Thirty years after the campaign, General 'Nap' Murray and I found ourselves re-tracing the steps of the Division from the beaches on the Pachino Peninsula to Messina. We were guest speakers on a NATO battlefield tour of some 60 officers. Other guest speakers who had fought in the campaign included Major-General Faldella (Chief of Staff to the Italian Army Commander), Col Von Bonin (Chief of Staff HQ XIV Panzer Corps), Lt Col Rebholz (Commander Recce Bn, Herman Goring Division) and Lt Col Von Benda (Artillery Observer at Sferro).

The country looked superb—green and carpeted with wild flowers: by the time we left it was burnt up and reminiscent of July, '43.

We stood near the lighthouse on Portopalo overlooking the landing beaches and were most impressed with the near-perfect spot chosen for the initial beach-head. The Italians admitted of complete surprise at the decision to assault over the rocky parts of the coast in very rough weather, avoiding the main beach. The defenders, second and third line Italian units, had little stomach for the fray. Had a very strong Italian-held pillbox complex on the Portopalo/Pachino road resisted things would have gone much more slowly on the first day. It was interesting to hear from Lt Col Rebholz that our progress was reported back continuously and that his forward elements kept in close touch with our march inland.

One has pondered why we, in 51st Division, were unmolested by enemy ground forces until we reached Vizzini. The answer is that General Guzzoni only had sufficient forces to deal with one assault area at a time. He chose to counter-attack the Americans at Gela first and then to switch his thrust against landings at Syracuse. There were thus no forces left to deal with our bridgehead in the centre.

The Germans were surprised at the speed of our advance, the dynamic leadership of the Division doing much to unbalance them. The Herman Goering Recce Bn had to re-group hurriedly to put up even minor opposition. Lt Col Rebholz told us how a large Italian contingent poured into Vizzini and begged to be put in the safest part of the line. He ordered them into the railway tunnel which they could defend on a one-man front in depth! Later 1 Gordons took them all prisoner!

Lt Col Rebholz only had sufficient forces to hold the east end of Vizzini. He covered the south and west thinly with OPs but could not engage our advance against this mountain fortress as his guns were on the Sferro line and out of range—hence our easy move forward to the outskirts of the town. The Germans held on to Vizzini until dusk as their withdrawal north was uphill and they feared our artillery fire. They were clear of the town well before our assault at midnight. It was interesting to hear the view that had the Americans thrust north-east from Gela for Sferro, the Germans might never have had time to link up on the Etna line.

Vizzini was too far forward of the main German defensive position south of Etna to be held for long. The enemy plan was to hold the line of the Simeto River, with a forward line on the railway running through Sferro and Gerbini and outposts on the high ground south of the River Dittaino, where the 51st Division Memorial now stands.

Our night advance from Ramacca was remarkable—audacious and brilliantly executed—the enemy suffering severe casualties from our artillery before they retreated behind the Dittaino. The success of the advance encouraged the ambitious plan to force the Dittaino the next night and reach the Simeto by dawn, but the Germans had other plans and the battle for Sferro and Gerbini began.

The Germans had the equivalent of two Battalions plus in the area of Sferro and Gerbini, supported by howitzers whose OPs were in the railway stations and on the high ground north of the railway. They considered that the Gerbini area was their most dangerous flank as it was good armoured country and our tanks had been seen in this area. The German reserves were not committed to re-take Sferro as they were to counter any attack on Gerbini which, as we know, was a very tough engagement, for which Lt Col Rebholz won the Iron Cross.

The bridge at Sferro was not blown due to faulty orders. The Germans suggested that, with the bridge intact and Sferro in our hands, an attack against Gerbini from the Sferro bridgehead would have spelt disaster for the Germans. This is easier said than done when one considers time and space problems. As it was they held their ground and are still puzzled as to why we went on the defensive in this thinly-held sector for ten days, enabling them to re-group and organise withdrawal to Italy. There was little to stop us pressing on to the Simeto. Our left flank, admittedly very exposed, contained few enemy but we were not to know that in 1943!

Before we left Sicily we laid a large wreath, inter-twined with thistles, on the 51st Division Memorial in a simple ceremony. We also visited the war cemeteries—a moving experience—our friends lie in the British War Cemetery outside Catania.

T&S, February/March 1974.

6th Gordons at Anzio

6th Gordons landed in Algeria in March 1943 and took part in the Allied advance through Tunisia. They landed in Italy, at Taranto, in December 1943, and in January 1944, took part in the 1st Division assault landing at Anzio. On 3 February, 6th Gordons was on the eastern face of a salient about four-miles deep and a mile-and-a-half broad. They were spread out along the thinly held sector and, to cover as much area as possible, had deployed all the companies, leaving no reserve. Hitler issued a special order: to drive the Allied forces at Anzio back into the sea. The 6th Gordons, outnumbered and outgunned, would suffer dreadfully:

As a result of attacks along the axis of the Anzio-Albano road the [1st] Division now formed a salient which extended north as far as the main railway from Rome to Cisterna. It was approximately 4 miles deep and 1½ miles wide at its apex, in which was concentrated the whole of 3 Infantry Brigade. 2 Infantry Brigade, less 2nd North Staffs, but with elements of the Recce Regiment, was responsible for the east flank, and [6th Gordons] was east of the Anzio-Albano road, with 'A' and 'C' Companies forward just south-east of 3 Infantry Brigade and 'D' and 'B' Companies echeloned back, 'D' Company approximately 600 yards south of 'A' and 'C' Companies, and 'B' Company approximately 800 yards south of 'D' Company. Battalion Headquarters was about 400 yards in rear of 'B' Company, forward of some farm buildings, later remembered as Horror Farm.

The position was unsatisfactory. Owing to the nature of the ground companies could not give each other mutual support. The enemy was in strong defensive positions on the flank of the Battalion, and his forward defended posts extended well to the west of the Divisional boundary. The Battalion area, which sloped sharply towards the east, was under observation by the enemy who was assisted by the numerous deep ditches running north and south, which offered cover from ground observation and good assembly points for offensive operations.

The remainder of 2 Infantry Brigade was well to the right rear of Battalion Headquarters, thinly stretched out on the ground.

On the left the same situation prevailed. The Irish Guards held a position approximating to the Battalion's, extending along the ridge west of the Anzio-Albano road. This ridge dominated the positions held by 'A', 'C', and 'D' Companies.

1st February passed quietly, apart from some heavy shelling of 'A' Company's area, where the slightest movement drew fire. Immediately to the east of Battalion Headquarters, about 500 yards away, four houses drew attention, and a patrol from the Recce Regiment went out on the night of the 1st/2nd to investigate. They returned with information that the area appeared to be occupied by approximately two companies of enemy infantry. Application had been made for wire and mines, but these were not forthcoming, despite repeated requests.

At 23.30 hours on 3rd February the ominous calm was broken, and the enemy commenced his offensive. The battle opened with heavy shelling, the worst the Battalion ever experienced. The Battalion stood to and awaited the attack, which was not long in coming. Infiltration between 'B' and 'D' Companies started shortly after midnight, and the 3-in. mortar positions were overrun. The position was restored very quickly by a counter attack by Lt. J.W.S. Fordyce and his platoon. Infiltration continued, and battle raged for some time. The M.M.G.'s of the carrier platoon, under Capt. R.D. Bain, inflicted heavy casualties on the enemy crossing the wadi to their front. The forward companies were ordered to hold their fire, unless directly attacked, and to send out patrols to ascertain the extent of penetration. They reported that about two companies of enemy infantry were digging in between 'B' and 'D' Companies. At the same time, a battle was raging on the ridge on the left, where the Irish Guards were being subjected to a heavy attack.

Immediately before dawn on 4th February, a squadron of tanks appeared at Battalion Headquarters, and these were quickly briefed and sent forward to assist in a counter attack against the enemy positions. This was put in by 'B' Company and was immediately successful. A large number of casualties was inflicted on the enemy, and approximately 80 prisoners taken.

The enemy reacted violently, and a heavy barrage was put down on the Battalion, causing some tank casualties. All was far from well with the forward companies. Communication had been excellent by wireless throughout the night, except that messages for 'C' Company had to be relayed via 'A' Company, which now reported six Tiger tanks deploying on their front. Then all communication with 'A' and 'C' Companies ceased. Shortly afterwards 'D' Company went off the air.

Once 'A' Company's position had gone, 'C' and 'D' Companies, surrounded as they were by enemy closely overlooking their positions on both sides and to the rear as a result of the successful infiltration during the night, now found themselves completely enclosed. The enemy poured a hail of fire into the trenches at almost point blank range, and tanks and infantry overran the positions fairly easily.

6th Gordons 1935 – 1945.

One of the 'A' Company platoon commanders, Lieutenant H. Garioch, recalled his part in the action:

I was commanding 9 Platoon on the right flank. At 23.00 hours, 3rd February, a heavy artillery barrage was put down on 'A' Company. Shortly afterwards an enemy patrol approached my position and was fired on. The two leading men were killed, and the patrol withdrew.

Soon after midnight a strong enemy force came up behind the ridge to my right rear and started to dig in. We could hear the noise distinctly. They were in dead ground, and I reported to Company Headquarters. I received orders to attack this party at 04.00 hours, but at 03.30 hours this was cancelled, and I was told that 'B', 'C', and 'D' Companies were to attack the ridge at 06.15 hours, supported by 'A' Company.

We were all prepared to give the necessary support when I was I told that this attack, too, had been cancelled. This was a great disappointment, as we felt that the attack would have been successful, and it was this force that later proved our undoing.[10]

At 06.20 hours I went to Company Headquarters, and found we were out of touch with Battalion Headquarters. It was then that we observed seventeen[11] enemy tanks coming down the road from the east. They came to dead ground where their own infantry were, then opened out and came over the ridge from our rear. Our anti-tank guns opened fire, but were spotted quickly, and put out of action in next to no time. By this time, the tanks were about to overrun my position, and I was ordered to withdraw behind a ridge near 'C' Company.

We succeeded in getting back to a ditch beside 'C' Company, and I went forward to report to Major Hutcheon. He ordered me to go to Battalion Headquarters and report the situation, and I set off down the only covered approach leading to 'B' Company. I had not gone very far, however, when I ran into an enemy M.G. post dug in, and I was taken prisoner. As good luck would have it a barrage came down around the position shortly after I had been captured, and I managed to get away. I returned to Major Hutcheon and told him what had happened, and warned him there was no way back. He decided to attempt to get back to Battalion Headquarters himself to explain the situation, and ordered me to take over the Company in his absence.

As he got up to go he was killed by a burst of M.G. fire.

I immediately got hold of the C.S.M., and we tried to get through to Battalion Headquarters by wireless again. Our only hope now was smoke

---

10 This attack was cancelled after the unexpected arrival of tanks. It was felt that 'B' Company, supported by these, could clear up the situation. When the tanks attempted to get forward to 'D' Company they could not cross an intervening ridge owing to heavy anti-tank fire, and some tanks were lost. Contact had been lost with the forward companies, and it was impossible to revert to the original plan. No infantry could cross the ridge against fire from enemy infantry and tanks.

11 This should probably read 'seven' rather than 'seventeen'. Maj J.C. Williamson's account of the action states, " 'A' Company now reported that six Tiger tanks were deploying on their front".

and a barrage, but as we were attempting this we were overrun from behind by enemy infantry.

6th Gordons 1935 – 1945.

'C' and 'D' Companies had suffered a similar fate, being overrun by German infantry and tanks. 'B' Company and Battalion Headquarters were all that remained of 6th Gordons:

> The outlook was grim. Although heavy loss had been inflicted on the Germans, the salient had become untenable, for the Anzio-Albano road was being swept by enemy fire. Now the pressing need was to extricate the 3rd Brigade, still in their positions south of Campoleone.
>
> About 11.30 a.m. the Gordons—what was left of them—learned that the 1st London Scottish were coming through to counter-attack. The Gordons did all they could to help their friends in their preparations; and in the afternoon, when the London Scots attacked with two squadrons of tanks, enough ground was gained to enable 3 Brigade to withdraw. After they had done so, and the London Scottish, mission accomplished, had pulled back, the Gordons could be taken out of battle. Consisting of little more than 'B' Company and Battalion headquarters, they assembled three miles back. The day closed in showers of hail and sleet, heralding a night of bitter cold.
>
> The Gordons had seven killed and eighteen wounded, and ten officers and 319 other ranks missing. Four mortars and four anti-tank guns and the complete fighting equipment of three rifle companies had been destroyed or left on the field. Besides Major Hutcheon—a very gallant and capable soldier who had come from the 1st Battalion and had been adjutant before commanding A Company—Lieutenant J.M. Blandy was among the killed.
>
> Although the Campoleone salient had been lost, the 1st Division had taken terrible toll of the enemy and prevented a break-through.

The Life of a Regiment, Volume V, pp 227–29.

The 6th Gordons received reinforcements to bring them up to strength sufficient for them to maintain their place in the line of battle, although it was some time before they would be at full strength again. This did not stop them playing a full part in the slow advance northwards through Italy. Late 1943 saw them in the mountains north of the River Arno:

> From the time that the Gordons had left the Arno in September they had had their fill of mountain warfare in autumn and winter. It had been a great ordeal. The soldier, heavily laden with weapons, ammunition, tools and rations, was called upon to make his way along slippery tracks and

climb steep mountain sides in order to get to grips with his enemy. In the small actions which ensued, sometimes only patrol or platoon affairs, no spectacular success could be achieved. In every kind of advance progress was slow, and the utmost effort appeared to be unrewarding. Even when the Battalion reverted to the defensive round Monte Grande their lot was ceaseless vigilance in mud and rain and frost and snow with only the bare necessities of life to sustain them. Conditions were, indeed, hard, 'but', as their commanding officer could truly say, 'not hard enough to beat the Gordons'.

The Life of a Regiment, Volume V, p 245.

More than Infantrymen

As infantry soldiers the Gordon Highlanders were second to none. In the Second World War, however, two Territorial battalions found themselves in unfamiliar roles. The 8th Battalion was re-roled as the 100th (Gordon Highlanders) Anti-Tank Regiment, Royal Artillery, and the 9th Battalion was re-roled as the 116th Regiment (Gordon Highlanders), Royal Armoured Corps. Each battalion mastered the unfamiliar role given it, and played its part in the fight against the Japanese in India and Burma.

8th Gordons man the guns

The 8th Battalion fought as artillery at Kohima and on the Irrawaddy. At Kohima the Gordons fought in small detachments, sometimes of a single gun, sent up in close support of an infantry battalion:

On 2nd May [1944] Lieutenant Hall got a 6-pdr up to Garrison Hill, the centre of the 2nd Division front, to engage the bunkers at Kuki Piquet. After being towed forward by a tank the gun was run up a ramp built by the infantry, fired a few destructive rounds, and was then run back under cover to escape the fire of Japanese snipers only 100 yards away. One Gordon gunner was killed and two wounded. At night the gun detachment acted as stretcher-bearers and next day the gun knocked out three bunkers. . . . Hall's gun destroyed six bunkers on or near Kuki Piquet and with armour-piercing shot knocked down a number of trees which hindered observation.

On 9th May the Gordons had four guns in action under Lieutenant I.B. Nicolson to assist a 4th Brigade attack at G.P.T. Ridge. This was a night operation. One gun was dismantled, man-handled piece by piece for half a mile up a steep and muddy slope, and then reassembled in the dark so as to ensure surprise.

Hard fighting continued throughout the 10th when 33 Brigade, 7th Indian Division, obtained a hold of Pimple Hill and Jail Hill. One of

Nicolson's guns was run further forward to deal with a fresh target. A gunner was wounded, and snipers were so active that the gun was ordered out of action, its gun shield pitted with bullet marks. In this affair Gunner J.D. Satchell won the Military Medal for his efficient gun laying under constant and accurate enemy fire. On G.P.T. Ridge Lieutenant Hall had one gun man-handled under a smoke-screen to within fifty yards of a bunker. Two bunkers were engaged, but the gun detachment had to be withdrawn under a shower of Japanese grenades and the gun was protected by booby-traps and light machine-guns firing on fixed lines.

... The Regiment had been in action for over a month. With his battery scattered over the battle area Lieut.-Colonel D.B. Anderson could exercise little control, so that the leadership of subordinate commanders, the standard of training, and the fighting spirit of all ranks, were well tested. The anti-aircraft gunners proved themselves masters of their weapons: the anti-tank guns and the mortars brought comfort and support to the infantry. Officers and men were entitled to be proud of the part they had played in the Battle of Kohima

The Life of a Regiment, Volume V, pp 374, 375, 376.

On 17 January 1945 8th Gordons were on the outskirts of Shwebo, near the Irrawaddy River, when they received 'new and rather surprising orders'. Two batteries organised as infantry, were to operate south of the Irrawaddy and 'kill any Japanese retreating from the 20th Indian Division advancing from the west':

They lost no time in sending patrols along the Mu, laying ambushes at likely crossing places. ... the inhabitants of the numerous villages were friendly and gave information concerning the movements of the Japanese. The latter seemed to have little knowledge of our dispositions, but before long it became obvious that they were by no means ready to retreat from the Irrawaddy river line.

Typical of the Regiment's activities was the investigation of Yawathithyi, on the near bank of the Irrawaddy, by 169 Battery on 24th January. Two sections, each of nine other ranks with one Bren gun were led by Captain F.A.C. Noble, and Captain A. McKenzie-Smith commanded a mortar troop. As soon as the Gordons deployed they were sniped at, and as they worked forward towards the village, which was surrounded by a thick belt of trees, a machine-gun opened on them. Then a mortar came into action. The Gordon mortars fired twenty rounds into a cotton mill and then covered the withdrawal of the patrol.

... On 27th January one troop moved in towards Myinze but were caught by machine-gun fire at short range. The Japanese then brought a mortar and a grenade discharger into action, and the volume of fire was such that the troops were unable to withdraw until darkness fell. The losses amounted to two killed, two wounded and seven missing.

At dawn of the 28th Lance-Sergeant Sutherland, who had been twice wounded, advanced with one gunner and reached the outskirts of the village. On his return he was able to report that the enemy had retreated across the Irrawaddy during the night. For his gallantry and enterprise he was awarded the Military Medal; Captain McKenzie-Smith, who on this and other occasions proved himself a particularly capable and fearless leader, received the Military Cross.

The Life of a Regiment, Volume V, pp 382–383.

9th Gordons in tanks

In 1942 the 9th Battalion, The Gordon Highlanders, commanded by Lieutenant-Colonel Jim Blackater, arrived in India, where it was told that it was to be equipped with tanks and renamed 116 Regiment (Gordon Highlanders), Royal Armoured Corps. The news was received with 'very mixed feelings', but the Gordons got down to the task and, throughout the conversion process, proved willing, hard-working, and accomplished armoured soldiers. The enemy was the Japanese, who by that time had occupied most of Burma, with India lying under threat of invasion.

After conversion training 9th Gordons took part in the XIV Army drive through Burma that comprehensively defeated the Japanese. William Hannah, from Shotts in Lanarkshire, was called up in 1940 and posted to 9th Gordons. The extracts below are taken from *The Life of a Regiment*, Volume V, the *Recollections* of William Hannah and of Bryan Smith, a squadron commander in 9th Gordons.

The Gordons proved to be versatile and adaptable, and mastered the technical intricacies of their tanks, although technical ingenuity did not always bring them any rewards!

At the end of 3 weeks they moved on to Calcutta where they were introduced to their Sherman tanks,

These fine, hardy machines were armed with a 75mm main gun, an Oerliken 05″ ball mounted machine-gun and a turret mounted machine-gun as well. They had engines with five banks of six-cylinder General Motors petrol engines slaved to a common shaft to give sufficient horsepower. Tracing a spark plug fault on 30 cylinders could be a long job, but an inventive signaller called Baxter found an easier way, which comprised a handful of wires and neon lights. When connected to the ignition system, a 'Pink Mouse' would run all over the engine banks, as each cylinder fired in turn. In this way, the faulty plug could be traced and replaced easily.

An officer noticed it, took it to Brigade for evaluation, and the invention later turned up after the war as a standard piece of army kit. The inventor did not receive credit for his innovation, as it was invented in Army time.

Recollections of William Hannah.

Ask an Aberdonian which is the finest infantry regiment in the world and he will gaze upon you with incredulity and pity. That anyone should ask such a question is beyond comprehension, when, in his view, the whole world is aware that the finest infantry in the world are without doubt, The Gordon Highlanders.

Few Aberdonians are aware however, that Gordon Highlanders during World War II forsook kilts and foot slogging for tanks.

In July 1942, two months after the fall of Burma to the Japanese, the 9th Battalion, Gordon Highlanders landed in Bombay to undertake a role as strange as any the regiment had ever tackled. After nearly two hundred years as foot soldiers, the Gordons were converted to armour. After the initial shock they buckled down to learning the new skills of tank gunnery, wireless, driving and maintenance, and armoured tactics.

Japanese control of South East Asia taxed their lines of communication, and they were suffering increasing shipping losses. They needed a new victory and a new supply source. Japanese High Command launched an audacious plan to break out of Burma. They would attack Assam and push on to India. If India could be taken China would be isolated and might even sue for a separate peace.

In March 1944 the Japanese struck at the Imphal-Kohima sector, the very place that Slim had decided to make a stand. The battle raged back and forth in a savage bloody confusion, where hand to hand fighting was commonplace. By June it was over and the Japs, beaten and battered, were retreating back to the line of the River Chindwin.

T&S, 1984.

After the Japanese had been stopped at Kohima the 9th Gordons played a full part in Slim's offensive that drove the Japanese out of Burma:

Three summers ago I visited Eddie Peace, an old friend from Orkney, in Aberdeen Royal Infirmary. We had first met fifty years previously on the North West Frontier of India, the only two Orkneymen in the 9th Gordons (Strathbogie, Garioch and Strathdon Highlanders) a very 'hame-ower' Territorial battalion. The senior officers were local businessmen and farmers from Huntly, Keith, Turriff, Alford and surrounding areas; the junior officers came mainly from the Aberdeen University Graduate Class of 1939. The men were mostly Aberdeenshire farm servants. Uniquely, both officers and men communicated in the broad pre-war Doric of Buchan, the richest, most musical dialect of Scotland. The parochial nature of our battalion gave rise to one of the best stories of the Second World War—a story adopted and adapted by other regiments since: Rev Jock Tennant, padre of our 8th Battalion, a blacksmith in Gartly before taking the cloth, told it at a battalion reunion in Inverurie in 1950. Waddy (presumably so named after his association with the Irrawaddy), who had been third horseman at Drumdelgie pre-war, was shot in the leg by a Zero fighter whilst crossing the Irrawaddy. Shortly afterwards the great man, General Bill Slim, was visiting wounded at a Casualty Clearing Station when he spotted this odd-looking soldier in a green tank suit, Gordon Balmoral, pipe in mouth, engulfed in clouds of XX Bogie Roll. Moving rapidly over, accompanied by the Chaplain General, a Presbyterian Scot, he bent down and enquired solicitously, 'Tell me, my good man, where exactly were you wounded?' Waddy sat up, pondered for a moment and then replied, 'Weel, Sir, I jalouse hid wid hiv been about twa tae three miles the Huntly side o' the Irrawaddy'.

They say the most traumatic experience a woman can have is to give birth to a child. That of a man is to go forward at a range of less than a hundred yards and kill a man who is trying to kill you. After the war Colonel Jim Blackater was chosen to sit at the right hand of General Geoffrey Evans at reunions of the 7th Indian Division. He was told that our battalion, all civilians, had killed in the space of nine months more men at close range than any other unit in the British Army. We had the latest Sherman tanks in the daytime and rifle and bayonet at night and the Japanese all died rather than surrender.

Out at Oyne the other day, visiting an old comrade, George Stuart, retired master builder, I mentioned that statistic. 'Damn the bit', said George gazing up at the hill, 'That wis nae bad goin' for a puckle orra loons fae the Back o' Bennachie'.

On 12 April 1945 our battalion, spear-heading the advance to Rangoon, put in an attack on Pyinmana, a town the size of Huntly. We encircled it, killed three hundred Japanese and destroyed many vehicles. Two unusual events occurred. Firstly, we met Japanese tanks which we blew up; secondly a Japanese soldier stood up waving a white flag. He was a clerk in the Army Headquarters we had overrun. General Honda and his staff officers crawled away down a ditch. They had heard our tanks approaching, stripped naked and prepared to commit Hara-Kiri. Suddenly our tanks stopped and moved into laager across the Rangoon Road. Tropical darkness descended with its usual rapidity. During the night we heard a convoy coming down the road. We switched on searchlights, set fire to every vehicle and shot up the crews.

Sherman tank of 116 Regt RAC (9th Gordons) comes out of action near Taungtha, March 1945, Cpl J. Picken of Cults in turret.

Wullie, one of my machine-gunners, had gone back to 'keepering' after the war. He was helping at a Shooting Lodge on Speyside when he found himself alone on the hill with a Japanese businessman waiting for the stags to move upwind. Always polite the Japanese enquired, 'Is this what you have been doing all your life—shooting stags?' 'Aye', replied Wullie in his dry fashion. 'That's fit Ah've been dee'in a' my life, sheetin' stags—except for five years'. 'And what were you doing during those five years?' 'Sheetin' Japanese'.

Bryan Smith

T&S, 1993.

Although an armoured regiment, 9th Gordons kept their pipe band. In Burma the band was employed in a combat role, but was always ready to re-form and play. Pipers, in particular, kept their instruments close to them:

Andrew Hare was the Pipe Major, having replaced the original Territorial Pipe Major who was considered too old for overseas service. Andra' was a tank commander, and played the pipes hanging from his Sherman turret as we were rolling down the main street of Rangoon, having liberated it. Andra' was famous for playing the pipes from his turret as they advanced and was once rebuked for it as the Japanese would hear them coming. Andra's reply was that he was sat on top of 1,000 horse power of roaring engine, and that anyway, they wanted them to know that they were coming, as if the Japs had any sense, they would have legged it before they got there!

Recollections of William Hannah.

Techniques for living and fighting in the jungle became second nature. On one occasion defensive procedures were employed to make a point to an over-zealous N.C.O.!

At night, the tanks laagered with the soft skinned vehicles inside. Slit trenches were dug to protect against attack, and the men reminded not to sleep under the tank, as it could settle in the night. The duty officer set up machine-guns demounted from the tanks on fixed lines of fire, and at the sound of gunfire, the machine-guns would open up in interlocking fields. One martinet of a sergeant decided to check the troops were standing to, and although he was recognised, every time he showed his head over the slit trench wall, the guns would open up. He was still there in the morning.

Recollections of William Hannah.

The Gordons were enthusiastic tank soldiers, eager to engage the enemy, and forward thinking in anticipating orders:

A sortie was planned for the tanks of 255 and the infantry of 7th Division to advance and take Pakoku. A high chimney was spotted on the opposite bank of the river with a sniper engaging the troops from a position on top.

The officer commanding got as far as 'Chimney stack, right . . .' when the first 75 mm cannon fired. Some enterprising soul had it already dialled in, awaiting the command.

'Who fired that shot . . . charge that man!' was the retort. Then . . . 'No! damn fine shooting'. Willie Blackwood was the man, his small frame marking him for duty on the main gun in the cramped confines of the Sherman's turret.

Recollections of William Hannah.

The Japanese were deadly foes, whose fanatical readiness to die rather than fail meant that British and Empire troops had to be fully alert at all times. On this occasion alertness and the Doric saved the day:

A sortie of tanks were returning when a perimeter guard noticed one tank too many. The Japanese had repaired it and tagged onto the end, hoping to cause carnage inside the laager. The tank had the wrong squadron emblem on its side. 255 wore a white bull on a black background. This one wore a Deccan horse emblem which was suspicious and incorrect. After checking on the tank radios, which regularly switched frequencies, the intruder was identified.

As it entered the harbour, an armour piercing rocket through the lightly armoured engine doors put paid to their scheme. When talking on the radio net, broad Scots at full speed is difficult enough to understand, coupled with frequent radio frequency changes. If the information was critical, one could use morse code. If really secret, they reckoned they could use Gaelic speakers. I've never seen a Japanese/Gaelic Dictionary. In practical terms, broad Scots at normal speed defeated the English officers, never mind the Japs.

Recollections of William Hannah.

After the Second War some Gordon Territorial battalions were disbanded while others were merged. They had a significant role in Britain's reserve forces. All National Serviceman had a commitment to serve in the reserve forces after their engagement, and they made up a large component of Territorial battalions. Successive Defence Reviews cut the number of battalions, and the ending of National Service in 1961 led to an inevitable fall in numbers of Territorial soldiers. In 1967 the last of the Gordon Highlander Territorial battalions ceased to exist, and all Highland Territorial soldiers served in a single unit: 51st Highland Volunteers.

The Territorial Army had not been mobilised for war since 1945 when, in 1991, some Territorial units were mobilised to take part in the First Gulf War. Gordon Highlanders, with droll humour, reacted in typical fashion to the mobilisation hysteria that seemed to grip some parts of the media:

The British Army was preparing for operations in the Arabian Gulf after Iraq's invasion of Kuwait. There was a large TA medical element in the force sent to the Gulf but no TA infantry units. That did not stop many Jocks clamouring to go and wanting to know if they should bring their kit in for mobilisation. In Shetland interest reached the stage where the local newspaper, observing Colour Sergeant A Buchan organising the Lerwick platoon to go to the mainland for weekend training, asked if that was part of the Gulf build-up! One wag remarked, 'If they think wan 4-tonner and five men fae Lerwick are gaun tae put the fear o' Gaud into Saddam Hussein, just think whit wid happen if they sent the Keith platoon!'

The Life of a Regiment, Volume VII, p 589.

No Territorial Army Gordon Highlanders would ever be deployed on active service again.

For two hundred years Volunteers had played a part in the life of The Gordon Highlanders. They had shown, whenever called to battle, that they were every bit as committed and effective as their regular compatriots.

Through their service and the regimental ethos that they took back into civilian life, they helped to engender and maintain the remarkable family feeling that was so evident throughout The Gordon Highlanders' regimental area.

SECTION 5

DUELLING

THE Gordon Highlanders do not appear to have been too prone to duelling as a means of settling disputes, and there are only four recorded instances of duels taking place in the 92nd, and one in the 75th.

All duels were serious affairs, although the cause could often be minor and petty. Of the five duels recorded in the history of The Gordon Highlanders, two resulted in the death of one of the participants. The sanction taken against the surviving duellists differed significantly. Although forty years separated the incidents, and there was a great difference in the rank of the survivors, the differing treatment might be attributable to the fact that the first was dealt with by a military court-martial while the second was dealt with by a local coroner's enquiry.

CHAPTER 11

DUELS

IT appears that a duel was fought between two officers of the 75th in late 1791 or early 1792. Lieutenant George Douglas[1] was appointed to the 75th with regimental seniority from 9 March 1788. Lieutenant James Brugh was appointed on 25 January 1791. There was probably a clash of personalities between the new subaltern and his more experienced brother officer, and within a year of Brugh joining the 75th the two apparently met in a duel. The unfortunate Brugh lost his life, but Douglas lost his livelihood.

There are no details of what sparked the duel, or indeed any statement in the *75th Regiment Record Book* that the duel even took place, but the concluding paragraph of the report of the court-martial, in referring to 'the influence of false ideas of honour' implies that this was indeed a duel. The following report is from the *Madras Courier*, 23 February 1792. The Commander-in-Chief's finding follows the report.

Court Martial
G.O. Headquarters, Camp at Siddapore
28th January, 1792

The Court Martial, of which Major Sterling is President, having tried Lieut. George Douglas of his Majesty's 75th regiment, confined for the wilful murder of Lieut. James Brugh of the same regiment, has passed the following sentence:

The Court not finding sufficient proof from the respective evidences that have appeared, to substantiate the charge of wilful murder against the prisoner, Lieut. George Douglas, acquits him of that charge; but is of opinion that he is guilty of taking away the life of Lieut. James Brugh by his, the prisoner's, outrageous and unjustifiable conduct, being a breach of his Majesty's peace and of the Articles of War in that case made and provided, does by the virtue of the powers and authorities in it vested by the 4th. art. of the 23d sect, of the Articles of War, sentence him, the said prisoner, Lieut. George Douglas, to be cashiered his Majesty's service in the most public and ignominious manner; and, further, that he be imprisoned in any of his Majesty's gaols either in India or in Europe, at the discretion of the Commander in Chief, for the space of two years; at the expiration of which, he shall find security for his good behaviour in

---

1   The Army List of 1790 shows George Douglas as a lieutenant, while the 1791 List shows him as a captain, and Brugh as the junior lieutenant. Neither appears in the Army List of 1792!

all parts of his Majesty's dominions for the space of three years, himself in 200 £ sterl and two sureties of 100 £ each,

(Signed) Wm. Williamson, Judge Advocate.

M. P. Sterling, Major and President,

The Commander in Chief approves the sentence and dissolves the Court. Lieut. Colonel Hartley will be pleased to order the European part of the reserve under arms this evening at five o'clock. The Judge Advocate will in his presence, and in front of the colours of the 75th. regiment, read the sentence to the prisoner, after which Lieut. Colonel Hartley will order the Provost Martial to break his sword and cut his sash to pieces. The prisoner will then return to his confinement, and tomorrow morning he will be sent under a guard from post to post to Tellicherry, where he will be imprisoned until an opportunity offers of sending him to Europe.

Provided the bonds ordered by the Court are entered into, the remainder of the prisoner's confinement, after leaving India, the Commander in Chief will remit.

This awful example the Commander in Chief is convinced will make a deep impression upon the army and will prove to the young and inexperienced the danger in indulging impetuous and intemperate passions, which, under the influence of false ideas of honour, may terminate in an ignominious death, or a miserable and disgraceful existence.

T&S, November 1951.

The punishment awarded, and the public humiliation in being cashiered from the regiment, would have been sufficient to deter most young officers from becoming involved in duels, but feelings of honour slighted could still lead to 'meeting at dawn' as John MacDonald of Dalchosnie found in 1831!

FIRST DUEL IN 92ND

The first recorded duel in the 92nd involved none other than Cameron of Fassiefern, at that time a captain. Both parties appear to have escaped injury:

About the end of the year 1794, the 92nd (or 100th as it was still numbered) were ordered to Gibraltar. While stationed here, some dispute, the nature of which we know not, arose between Cameron, and then Lieutenant, afterwards Sir John Maclean, likewise of the 92nd, which, according to the barbarous fashion of the times led to a duel. Fortunately the combatants parted without serious injury, and this was the only instance in which Cameron had a hostile encounter with a brother officer.

Memoir of Colonel John Cameron of Fassiefern.

DUELS

DUELLING SUBALTERNS

A duel took place in 1815 between two officers of the 2nd Battalion in Cork. Colonel Cameron's comments seem somewhat ironic in view of the duel that he had fought in 1794!

> It appears that a quarrel in a ball-room, resulting in a duel, took place between two officers. 'It is with a feeling of deeper regret than he can express that Colonel Cameron has heard of an occurrence which, as it is the first of its kind in the 92nd regiment he has heard of since he has been in command, he sincerely hopes it may be the last . . . He has been accustomed to feel proudly conscious of the high sense of propriety of conduct, together with the unanimity and harmony which prevailed among the officers of the 92nd. . . . It is some palliation that this interruption proceeded from very young men, of but short service in the regiment, though by no means a sufficient excuse'; the Order continues 'that while he has the honour to command the 92nd, he will use his power to rid it of parties concerned in such transactions either as principals or accessories, the latter being frequently more to blame than the former.'

The Life of a Regiment, Volume I, p 346.

A DUEL IN KELSO

There is no record of any further duels within the 92nd until December 1829, when the *Kelso Mail* reports a duel between two officers of The Gordon Highlanders. The splendid historian, John Malcolm Bulloch, has added some notes that throw light on what happened to the participants:

> On Thursday last, an affair of honour took place in a field near Kelso Race Course, between Captain Stewart and Ensign Pringle, both of the 92nd Regiment; the former attended by Captain Noel, of the same regiment, and the latter by George Baillie. Jun. Esq. Both parties fired at the same time, and Mr Pringle received his adversary's ball in the upper part of the right thigh. He was conveyed to the Stand House, where he still lies; and as the ball has not yet been extracted, his medical attendants cannot pronounce him free from danger. The affair having come to the knowledge of the local authorities, Captain Stewart and his Second were taken into custody, and after a judicial investigation, committed to the Castle of Jedburgh, where they will be detained until Mr. Pringle is pronounced to be out of danger. Mr. Baillie, against whom a warrant was also issued, has hitherto evaded the search made for him. Various reports, are of course, in circulation as to the cause of the affair; but in the present situation of the parties, it would be highly improper to notice these rumours, or to indulge in any vague conjectures on the subject.

And later in the same Journal, date unknown:

> We are happy to state that Ensign James Pringle, who was wounded in the late duel here, is doing well, and is now considered out of danger; but he has not yet been able to be conveyed to Stitchel House. Mr. Baillie and Captain Noel the seconds, have been admitted to bail, and it is expected that Captain Stewart will forthwith be liberated, under the usual forms of the law in similar cases.

J. M. Bulloch.

Scottish Notes & Queries, May 1930.

> When the *Mail* appeared again, on December 14th, it stated that Pringle was doing well and was out of danger, though he had not been removed to the house at Stitchel where his father, Sir John Pringle, 5th Bart., lived. It was expected that Stewart would forthwith be liberated 'under the usual forms of the law in similar cases.'
>
> I have not found out what happened under the civil law to Stewart, who had got his company in the Gordons in November, 1826, but he left the Regiment, placed on half pay on June 12th, 1830 His second, Captain Noel, continued in the Gordons till put on half pay on October 5th, 1841. Young Pringle exchanged on March 16th, 1830, into the 83rd Foot, now the 1st Royal Irish Rifles.

J. M. Bulloch.

THE FINAL RECORDED DUEL

The most notorious duel fought in the 92nd involved its commanding officer, Lieutenant-Colonel John MacDonald of Dalchosnie:

> A Distinguished colonel of the Gordon Highlanders, Sir John MacDonald, shot Capt. Robert Markham, of the 58th Foot, dead at Fermoy at five o'clock on the morning of Thursday, May 31st, 1832. Even in the days of duelling that was a notable episode; in retrospect it seems far more dramatic. Yet to this day the facts of the case are meagre and obscure, not least in the history of the Gordons, as told by the late Col. Greenhill Gardyne, in his highly individualistic book, *The Life of a Regiment.*
>
> He names neither the victim nor his regiment, simply noting that
>
> > . . . a regiment on the march was billetted in the town and the officers dined at the barracks. One of them made a remark which seemed to Colonel MacDonald to be disparaging to his men, and with which he declined to agree. The retort was such that the Colonel rose from table and left the room, accompanied by one of his officers. An apology was asked for and refused. They met at dawn on the banks of

the Blackwater. MacDonald fired in the air,[2] when his adversary exclaimed, 'I did not come here for child's play' and demanded another exchange of shots. This time the Colonel fired with fatal effect,[3] which was regretted by none more sincerely than by the surviving principal and his second.

Colonel Greenhill Gardyne was given this account of the affair with the expression used by the officer at Mess and on the ground, 'by an officer who was present with the Regiment at the time, though not present at the duel.' The [second] edition of *The Life of a Regiment* adds that, in 1903, the late Major-General Forbes Macbean 'brought to the notice of the author a detailed account of the duel written by the second of the officer who was killed,' and that it 'entirely bears out' the Colonel's statement.

The *Aberdeen Journal*, of June 13th, 1832, stated that Captain Markham was attended by Lieutenant Pack of the 58th, while Colonel MacDonald's second was Lieutenant Archibald Inglis Lockhart,[4] of the Gordons. Markham was Commander of the Depot of the 58th at Fermoy, which had arrived the day before the duel from Limerick. He accepted an invitation to the 92nd Mess. 'After dinner a conversation took place. It is not exactly known what were the words used which called forth the challenge, but they must be more strong than anything we can yet conjecture, to justify the host and his guest being arrayed in mortal combat against each other.'

The *Dublin Evening Mail* went on to state that 'upon the first fire Colonel MacDonald's pistol having misfired, he exclaimed that he trusted 'the matter would rest there,' or words to the same effect. Captain Markham, however, would not admit of such a termination to the affair, and insisted upon another fire, saying that 'he did not come there for child's play.' Consequently, the pistols were again put into the hands of the parties, and upon the discharge the result proved fatal instantly to Captain Markham.'

The report of the inquest in the *Times* of June 6th, throws no light whatever on the actual duel, for nobody who witnessed it gave evidence.

---

2 Firing in the air was a not uncommon way of concluding a duel, honour being deemed to have been satisfied. It depended, of course, on the opponent following the same course. There is at least one recorded instance of a duellist firing in the air only for his opponent to take careful aim and fire a shot from which the gallant, but misguided, gentlemen died.

3 This says much for MacDonald's marksmanship, for he either used his right hand, on an arm that was so severely disabled by war wounds that he received a pension for it, or he used his left hand, which he would have learned to use for everyday matters, but could hardly be expected to become an expert shot with.

4 Lockhart's participation in the duel did not harm his subsequent career, as he went on to command the 92nd from 1857 to 1865.

The only mention of MacDonald as the duellist occurs in the opening sentence, which was merely the introduction of the report, and stated that 'as soon as the report of the duel between Colonel McDonald and Capt. Markham was received, Richard Foott, the coroner, proceeded to Fermoy where he summoned a respectable jury, who, having viewed the body of Captain Markham, immediately commenced hearing the evidence which closed that night, May 31st, with the examination of two witnesses. On Friday, June 1st, the inquest was resumed, and did not terminate till an advanced hour that day.' . . . the evidence of eight witnesses called was all second-hand.

Despite two days of evidence, we know nothing officially about the actual duel itself. It is small wonder that the jury, after a short deliberation, returned the following verdict: —

> 'That the deceased Captain Robert Markham was killed by a bullet discharged from a gun or pistol, but by whom is uncertain; and we find that the deceased was found dead yesterday morning shortly after five o'clock, at a place called the race course in barony of Condons and Congibbons in the County of Cork aforesaid.'

This disposes of Colonel Greenhill Gardyne's statement that Colonel MacDonald and his second 'obtained leave and retired for a time to the wilds of Rannoch.' Why, if he was not indicted by the coroner's jury? Colonel Greenhill Gardyne adds: 'As Colonel MacDonald soon returned to his command, it is evident that the result of the inquiry proved him to have acted according to what was then considered the code of honour.' [5]

What was the real cause of the quarrel between MacDonald and Markham? I have an idea that it was a remnant of an old grudge between the 92nd and 58th. In 1821, when the 58th and 61st Foot were to return home from Jamaica, their men were permitted to volunteer for a corps serving in the island, 'which, notwithstanding yellow fever, seems not to have been an unpopular quarter with thirsty souls.' The Gordons were ordered to receive 33 men from the 58th and 47 from the 61st, and a note in the Gordons' Description Roll describes them as '80 men of the worst character and description.' Colonel Greenhill Gardyne states that none of them appears to have been Scotsmen. It is just possible that this memory lingered with the Gordons, and may have been the cause of the quarrel at

---

5   By the mid-nineteenth century, duelling was in decline as a means of settling disputes, partially because victory could lead to a jail term for assault or manslaughter. The interesting point here is that although the inquest acknowledged that the duel was between Col MacDonald and Capt Markham, the finding was that the death was caused by a bullet discharged from a gun, 'but by whom is uncertain'. It appears that the jury preferred not to jeopardise the freedom of a person involved in what was still seen as 'a matter of honour'.

Fermoy, for as every soldier knows, traditional antipathies die hard in the Army.

John Malcolm Bulloch

T&S, November 1929.

An account of the duel was unearthed by former Gordon Highlander Arnold Henderson, expert on medals and the early years of the 92nd. This account, perhaps closer to the truth, is by the son of the barrack master at Fermoy, where the duel took place. His account of MacDonald's fiery reaction to a perceived slight on his honour, driven by his 'hot Celtic blood', is totally in keeping with the man who, clutching his Portuguese regiment's colour, rode within musket range of the French and brandished the colour, while musket balls tore at his clothes, to wipe out the shame of his troops falling back in the face of the enemy.[6]

About the year 1834 a very sad event took place in the exercising ground behind our house in the barracks of Fermoy. A company of infantry under the command of Captain Markham marched in, and as is usual when an officer of a regiment is passing, where a regimental mess is in place, the officers were invited to dine in the mess. Captain Markham had been previously stationed in Fermoy, and when my father invited him to dine he thanked him, but said he was engaged to dine at the mess of the 92nd Highlanders, but promised to call on my mother and sisters next day. Alas, his death prevented the fulfilment of his promise.

After dinner, the conversation turned on the Peninsular Campaigns, and the Captain said, 'the victories were all gained by the Household troops and the Cavalry.'

'Oh no,' replied Colonel McDonald, who had shared many of the battles in the Peninsula and left an arm at Busaco,[7] 'you are quite mistaken, the victories were won by the line.'

'Colonel McDonald,' replied Captain Markham 'there is no use in arguing with you, you know nothing at all about it.'

This was too much for the Peninsular veteran's hot Celtic blood. He rose instantly from his chair, and tapping one of his officers, Major Lockhart, passed into the ante-room. When joined by Major Lockhart[8] he said, 'Lockhart, you heard how I was insulted. You must demand either an apology or a meeting.' The Major tried to induce the Colonel to attribute the words to too much wine, and to pardon the offender as his guest, but in vain. The Colonel was peremptory, so the Major had to try

---

6   See 'The MacDonalds of Dalchosnie' in Chapter 34, 'Remarkable People'.
7   MacDonald did not 'leave an arm at Busaco', although he was in receipt of a pension for a wound that restricted the use of his right arm.
8   Lockhart was a lieutenant at the time.

to get Captain Markham to apologise. This was also in vain, and the alternative was accepted. A duel was arranged to take place at six o'clock next morning in the exercising ground at the back of the new barracks. The principals, with their seconds, and many who were aware of the fracas, were on the ground. The twelve paces were measured and the signal given. One pistol alone, that of Captain Markham, was discharged, without effect. Colonel McDonald's having burned priming therefore did not explode. Immediately Markham asked for a fresh pistol.

'What' exclaimed Colonel McDonald, 'is Captain Markham going to fire again?' 'Yes' replied the Captain hastily; 'I did not come here for child's play.'

A.J. Henderson.

An Octogenarian Literary Life by J.R. O'Flanagan,[9] 1896.

The latter account is the more likely version of the cause of the duel. Such a slur on the honour of the 92nd would inevitably warrant the ire of the Commanding Officer, who had fought through the Peninsular War and knew how wrong and misguided the allegation was. His family and regimental pride aroused, and with Markham's dogged refusal to retract, he was left with no other course of action.

The Gordon Highlanders appear to have got the message after MacDonald's duel, and observed the law from then on, for there are no more recorded instances of duels being fought.

---

9   J.R. O'Flanagan was the son of Capt O'Flanagan, the Barrack Master at Fermoy at that time.

SECTION 6

THE MUSIC OF THE REGIMENT

FROM the beginning both the 75th and 92nd were provided with music. The Letters of Service that raised them authorised drummers and fifers on the establishment, and the officers who were recruited to the regiments on condition of bringing men with them, brought their own pipers. The transition from individual pipers to pipe bands, and from drummers and fifers to military bands took some time, but by the middle of the 19th century the respective bands had begun to take on a form recognisable to this day.

When the 75th and 92nd were raised they were authorised to recruit respectively twenty-four drummers and two fifers, and twenty drummers and two fifers. The Letters of Service did not authorise pipers, and it was not until 1854 that pipers were officially recognised by the War Office. Pipers, however, formed an important part of the Regiment from its first days. Officers, who as part of the purchase of their commissions undertook to recruit a given number of men, often brought with them their own piper, who became that officer's company piper. Pipers were taken on strength as private soldiers or, interestingly enough, as drummers. Regimental Orders of 11 May 1805 state, 'Alexander Cameron the piper is to be taken on the strength of the Grenadiers as drummer from the 25th of last month' (probably to get him drummer's pay, to which, as a piper, he was not entitled).

In purely historical terms the drums took precedence over the pipes, having been on the official establishment of units for much longer, and it was for this reason that the Pipe Band in the post-Second War 1st Battalion of The Gordon Highlanders was known, alone among all the Scottish military pipe bands, as the Drums and Pipes rather than Pipes and Drums.

Irrespective of the name, the pipe bands of The Gordon Highlanders played a vital role in the life of the Regiment, and pipers and drummers distinguished themselves, not only in the field of music, but more importantly on the field of battle.

CHAPTER 12

THE PIPES

BAGPIPES played an important role in The Gordon Highlanders from their earliest days. Each company had its own piper, who played in camp, on the march, and at the head of the troops in battle. They played the music of their homeland, with familiar tunes that marked out times of the day, routine activities and, in times of war, could rouse them to a battle pitch that made them the most effective soldiers in the British line of battle, instilling in their enemies awe, apprehension and often terror.

Where did it come from, this instrument that played so prominent a part in the life of Scotland and her fighting men?

Much controversy has centred around the origin of the bagpipe in Scotland. As a result of two Irish colonisations in A.D.120 and A.D.506, the bagpipes were introduced into Scotland. Caledonia was peopled by Irish colonists who brought the bagpipe along.

From the eleventh to the fourteenth century, the bagpipe in Scotland was equally popular as in Ireland. We have record that bagpipes were played at Bannockburn (1314). Robert Bruce (from his *Exchequer Rolls*) employed his own pipers. What was considered to be the oldest set of pipes is in the National Museum of Antiquities in Edinburgh. It is dated '1409' and bears the initials 'R.McD.' It has two small drones and a chanter. It is probable that the pipes were played at the Battle of Harlaw on St. James's Eve 1411.

Inasmuch as the Romans employed bagpipes, which they named *tibia utricularis*, it is not surprising that many of their writers refer to it, including Virgil. Judging by the sculptured bronze found at Richborough Castle, in Kent, the Romans introduced the bagpipes into Britain. In this bronze the piper is represented as a Roman soldier in full marching order, implying that Roman soldiers marched to the sound of pipes. Roman soldiers wore kilts, but these were not pleated.

The bagpipe evolved by a long process through the ages. There have been many forms, from the simple chanter to the small three-droned pipe that was played over the arm. As late as 1548, droneless pipes were common; but pipes of two drones were making their appearance. The Irish maintain that their soldiers were marched into battle by pipers in the sixteenth century, and there is mention of such in the seventeenth and eighteenth centuries. During this period the bag-inflated pipe was gaining ground, while the bellows pipe was also very much in vogue. To the

Highland piper of the eighteenth century, however, belongs the credit of placing the [drones] on his shoulder.

The era of the 'Great Highland Pipe' began in the early seventeenth century, with the development of clan pipers in the retinue of the important Highland chiefs. The most celebrated of the hereditary pipers were the MacCrimmons, who were attached to the family of Macleod of Dunvegan. Many of our well-known *piobaireachdan* date from this period, when undoubtedly the best pipe music was written. The MacCrimmons founded a College for the study of pipe music at Boreraig, Isle of Skye, where the piping was taught in a dark cave entirely by ear. To this *Oilthigh,* or College, resorted students from all parts of the Highlands. As long as six to twelve years were devoted to the acquirement of the *piobreachd* alone; today less than a third of this time is considered adequate!

The Gaelic name for the bagpipes was *Piob Mhala*, as distinguished from *Piob Shionnaich* for the bellows pipe. Contrary to general belief, the harp [*clarsach*], and *not* the bagpipe, was the musical instrument of Gaelic legend and history.

Piobaireachd is the classical music of the pipes. Quicksteps, reels and strathspeys are of very modern origin. To the uninitiated, a *Piobaireachd* may seem rather dull and monotonous, but to the Highlander it tells its story of a gory battle, or perhaps of sweet repose amidst purple heather hills beside a Highland burn.

To-day we find the bagpipes providing the most inspiriting martial music and thrilling the heart of every Scot within hearing, at home and, more especially, overseas.

T&S, July 1927 and November 1950.

There is little record of the part played by pipers in the early years of the 75th's service in India, but this extract from the records of the Hawick Archaeological Society suggests that pipers played a full part in the life of the 75th, with a pipe major at their head:

In April, 1802 the Town Council engaged one John Kennedy, late Pipe Major of the 75th Highlanders, as town piper at a salary of forty shillings *per annum*. His duty was to march through the town at seven o'clock at night, playing the bagpipes.

T&S, August/September 1971.

The first mention of pipers in the Gordons occurs in a regimental order of 27 October 1796, at Gibraltar, which stated that pipers were to attend all fatigue parties. An interesting sidelight on the use of the pipes occurs in a regimental order of 12 November 1812, at Alba de Tormes:

The pibroch will never sound except when it is for the whole regiment to get under arms; when any portion of the regiment is ordered for duty and a pipe to sound, the first pipe will be the warning, and the second pipe for them to fall in. The pibroch only will, and is to be considered, as invariably when sounded, for every persons off duty to turn out without a moment's delay.

Pipers were in the foremost ranks of the regiment in battle, exhorting the men to deeds of heroism by the exhilarating hypnotic tones of the war pipes, or, if their pipes were out of action, by engaging the enemy themselves:

As Cameron the pipe-major was giving forth his most warlike notes, a bullet pierced the bag of his pipe, causing it to emit a piteous and unwarlike skirl. Filled with wrath at the insult to his music, and with the desire to avenge the wound of his beloved instrument, he first tied it round his neck, and then, exclaiming '*Bheir sinn ceol dannsaidh eile dhaibh!*' (We will give them a different kind of dance music), seized the musket of a wounded man, and discharging it at the offending foe, drew his sword and rushed into the thick of the fight amidst the laughter and cheers of his comrades.

The Life of a Regiment, Volume I, p 210.

Piper and drummer of the 92nd at Edinburgh Castle, 1846

As many pipers found, their presence on the battlefield attracted enemy fire. In 1879, like Pipe Major Cameron in the Napoleonic Wars, one piper had a miraculous escape while his pipes suffered in his place:

> The enemy were on a ridge towards the village of Pir Paimal, and their musketry became so hot, that the regiment was held for a few minutes. General Macpherson remarked on the severity of the fire, and marksmen were told off, who by their steady shooting to some extent checked it; the General then asked the commanding officer to bring up the pipers. Piper Middleton struck up, being quickly joined by others, and the regiment, inspirited by the strains of *The Haughs of Cromdale*, rose from cover, dashed on with a cheer and pushed the enemy back. 'Fat's wrang wi' the auld wife the day?' wondered Middleton as, after a few paces, his pipes refused to speak—a bullet had pierced the bag!

The Life of a Regiment, Volume II, p 151.

Pipers were keen to engage the enemy. At of the Pass of Maya, as General Stewart was trying to block the advance of the French:

> Pipe-major Cameron, thinking a little music would be grateful to his comrades, made the hills re-echo the *Pibroch of Dhonuil Dhu*. The effect was electrical. The weary Highlanders were on their legs in an instant anxiously looking to their wounded General, who was a few paces in rear, for the order to advance. He at once ordered the piper to stop, and warned them of the fatal consequences that might follow a forward movement at that particular moment. Meanwhile the French below were increasing in numbers, and in ten minutes the piper, probably impatient of the general's tactics, tuned up again, and again his comrades jumped up eager for action. The angry General peremptorily ordered him not to play without orders, on peril of his life. He obeyed, but was heard muttering, with a sublime confidence in the power of his own music, '*Mur leig e leom a phiob a chluich cha'n eil Frangeach 's an duthaich nach bi nuas oirn*' (If he'll not let me play, every man in the land of France will be here).

The Life of a Regiment, Volume I, p 296.

> Fresh troops were advancing from Urdax. Our troops were from 2,000 to 2,500 men, their opponents 8,000 to 9,000; and about 7 p.m. General Stewart, in order to stop further bloodshed, proposed to retire, and sent an order to the troops on the rock to abandon it; but, before the bearer of the message could deliver it, the cheers of the troops at the base of the hill reached the summit. These were occasioned by the arrival of General Barnes with the 6th Regiment and some Brunswick infantry. A more seasonable reinforcement was never received. The tired soldiers were

resting when it arrived, but rose to cheer—'Our lads were perfectly frantic with joy.' General Stewart, having regard to the extraordinary loss and fatigue sustained by them, desired that the 92nd should not join in the charge of Barnes' troops. But this time the pipe-major was not to be denied. He struck up the charging tune of *The Haughs of Cromdale*, his comrades, seized with what in the Highlands is called *mire cath*—the frenzy of battle—without either asking or obtaining permission, not only charged, but led the charge, and rushed down on the enemy with irresistible force, driving back their opponents in the most splendid style. The power of the national music over the minds of Scottish soldiers was never more conspicuous

The Life of a Regiment, Volume I, p 297.

The battle of St Pierre in December 1813 was a desperate affair where the French fought ferociously in a final attempt to stem the inexorable advance of Wellington's army. The 92nd played a full and gallant part in the battle and suffered heavy casualties. An incident in this battle saw the 'Three Pipers of St Pierre' gain immortal fame when, as they went into battle at the head of the regiment, one piper died, his place to be taken by another. When that second piper was hit, a third took up the air, and continued to play the Highlanders into battle:

The British were in imminent danger, when General Barnes brought forward the 92nd. As the battalion cleared the houses of St Pierre, one of the pipers was killed at its head. The right wing extended on the moor to the left; the French skirmishers fell back before them, while the left wing, led by Colonel Cameron, charged down the road on the two regiments composing the column. 'The charge,' says Napier, 'was rough and pushed home; the French mass wavered and gave way.' The Highlanders pursued and took many prisoners. Abbé immediately replaced the beaten column with fresh troops, and Soult, redoubling the play of his heavy guns, sent forward a battery of horse artillery, which opened fire at close range with destructive activity. Cannonade and the musketry rolled like one long peal of thunder, and the second French column advanced with admirable steadiness, regardless of their loss by Ross's guns. The Highlanders, unable to resist this accumulation of foes, were born back, fighting desperately hand-to-hand, and even charging again and again with most determined fortitude and audacity, till General Barnes ordered them to retire, while all the time the pibroch *Cogadh na sith*[1] rang in their ears.

The Life of a Regiment, Volume I, pp 319–20.

---

1   War or Peace.

The three pipers of St Pierre

The conduct of the pipers, whose prominent position at the head of the troops brought concentrated enemy fire upon them, was acknowledged with acclaim in Scotland. A letter from Archibald Campbell suggests that Sir John Sinclair (President of the Highland Society) 'ought to communicate to the Highland Society the fact that two out of the three pipers of the 92nd Regiment were killed while playing *Cogag na shee* [sic] to encourage their comrades'; as one fell another took it up; this 'should be made known all over the Highlands'.

Apart from playing the Regiment into battle, the pipes were used to pass instructions; particularly to muster the remaining soldiers after battle. Gathering the survivors of Quatre Bras together after the battle was a sobering experience, particularly as they all knew that they would have to face the French again (at Waterloo, little more than a day later):

At ten o'clock the piper of the 92nd took post at the garden in front of the village, where, after tuning his chanter, and setting his drone in order, he attempted to collect the scattered members of his regiment. Long and loud blew Cameron; but although the hills and the valleys echoed the hoarse murmurs of his favourite instrument, his utmost efforts could not produce above a half of those whom his music had cheered in the morning on their march to the field of battle.

The Military Memoirs of an Infantry Officer.

'Cameron' was Pipe Major Cameron, who led the Gordons into battle throughout the Peninsular War, in France and at Quatre Bras and Waterloo. He died only two years after Waterloo. His actions during the war had made him well known, and his death was reported on 5 November 1817:

Death of Sergeant Cameron—At Belfast, on the 18th ult., died Sergeant Alexander Cameron, pipe-major of the 92nd Highlanders. He served in the Peninsula during the whole of the late war, and by his zeal attracted the notice of several officers of high rank.

Lieutenant-General Sir William Erskine, in a letter to a friend after the affair of Rio del Molinas [Arroyo del Molinos], says, 'The first intimation the enemy had of our approach was the piper of the 92nd playing *Hey, Johnny Cope, are ye waukin' yet?*' To this favourite air from Cameron's pipe, the streets of Brussels re-echoed on the night of the 15th of June, when the regiment assembled to march out to the field of Waterloo. Once and once only, was this brave soldier missed in his accustomed place in the front of the battle, and the occasion strongly marks the powerful influence which the love of fame had upon his mind. In a London newspaper, a very flattering eulogium had appeared on the conduct of a piper of another regiment. Our gallant musician, conscious that no one could surpass him in zeal or intrepidity, felt hurt that he should not have gained this flattering distinction; and declared, that if his name did not appear in the newspapers, he would no more play in the battle field! Accordingly, in the next affair with the enemy, Cameron's pipe was mute! Some insinuations against the piper reached his ear. The bare idea of his motives being misunderstood was torture to poor Cameron, and overcame at once the sullen resolution he had formed of remaining silent in the rear. He rushed forward, and not content with gaining his place at the head of the regiment, advanced with a party of skirmishers, and placing himself on a height in full view of the enemy, continued to animate the party by playing favourite national airs. For the next two years his health seriously declined. He was afflicted with an asthma, which the blowing of the bagpipe tended to aggravate. Notwithstanding, he could not be induced to resign his favourite enjoyment, but continued till very lately to play *The Gathering* for the daily assembling of the regiment. His remains were attended to the grave by several Officers, all the non-commissioned officers, and the grenadier company to which the deceased belonged.

The Times, 5th November, 1817.

Pipers saw themselves as something special. They were well aware of the position they held in the Regiment and of the part they were expected to play in battle. They were respectful to officers and N.C.O.s but never overawed by them. They had a well-developed sense of humour, which could bring a smile to the face of the weariest troops or pierce the self-important bubble of the pompous. They were looked on by their comrades with proprietorial affection. The pipe major was a highly regarded member of the Regiment, not only as a piper of great skill, but also as a highly individual and often eccentric character:

The battalion of which the 92nd depot company formed part was under the command of a Lieut.-colonel on the Staff. The piper of the company was a quaint specimen of the old-fashioned Gordon Highlander, named Duncan Smith. The first time the battalion marched out for exercise, the drummers and fifers of all the depots played together at the head of the

column, but the Gordons, who were the rear company, were marching to the strains of Duncan's pipe. The colonel thought the piper should also be at the head of the column, and ordered accordingly, desiring him to play up, but Duncan could not bear the idea of playing to soldiers in 'chacos.' 'She's nae mair wind,' he replied, with a respectful salute, but a twinkle in his cunning old eye. Presently the notes of *Gillean an' fheile* were heard from the rear; again he was ordered to the front. With an innocent look he again excused himself by, 'She has nae mair wind.' The colonel gave it up, and never asked the piper again to play away from the bonnets. A portrait of Duncan by the late General Archibald Inglis Lockhart (illustration) hangs in the room where I write. Many stories have I heard of him. When asked how he felt at Waterloo—'the which is Och! Shust plaw awa', no gie a d— whether she'll be shot or no.' On another occasion he had to give evidence on some trial. The lawyer who was badgering him asked, among other questions, if he had fought at Waterloo—'Hoo cud I be fechtin' when I was plawing the pipes a' the time? It was mair wind than wark wi' me, like a lawyer!' On no account would he wear the fatigue trousers which formed part of his kit. He was never known to wear anything but the kilt except once, when, having been ill, a lady presented him with a warm pair of trousers. Out of compliment to her he put them on, but got so bothered by the unaccustomed buttons and braces, that he threw them away in a rage. He wore the shoe that was on his left foot one day on the right the next, his hose alternately in the same fashion, and was altogether an eccentric character, but a first-rate musician of the old Highland school. He became lance-sergeant and pipe-major, and served till quite an elderly man; he retired, in 1831, to his native place in the Black Isle, with Waterloo medal, pension, gratuity, and good conduct medal. The officers presented him with a set of bagpipes.

The Life of a Regiment, Volume II, pp 10–1.

Most senior officers had no doubt about the part played by pipers, and the effect their music had on the Highland troops. The Duke of Wellington's response to an Inspecting Officer's report on the 92nd in 1847 showed that he, for one, appreciated the pipers:

Major-General J.E. Napier, commanding at Limerick, while highly approving, in his report to the Commander-in-Chief, of the regiment in general, called attention to the pipers shown in the state, as not being allowed by regulation. The Duke of Wellington answered that he was surprised that an officer who must have seen the gallant deeds performed by Highland regiments, in which their pipers played so important a part, should make such a report.

The Life of a Regiment, Volume II, p 49.

Until 1854 pipers were not officially on the strength of a regiment (as General Napier, above, pointed out) and were paid for by the officers. The pipe major held a junior non-commissioned rank, although his honorary rank earned him great respect. In 1854 the Army finally recognised the value of pipers and brought them on the establishment of Highland regiments. This brought about a radical change in regimental piping:

[In 1850] Sergeant Duncan MacPhail was appointed pipe-major. Up to this time the pipers were in charge of the drum-major, though for musical purposes they were under a lance-sergeant or corporal, who had only the honorary title of pipe-major. He carried on grand occasions the regimental banner on his pipe, each company piper carrying that of his captain; still, they were not officially acknowledged by the War Office till 1854, when six of their number were ranked as 'pipers,' and received pay accordingly. On guest nights one piper only, generally the pipe-major, played a pibroch in the officers' mess-room; no quick-step or reel was allowed unless by permission of the senior officer. No drum was played with the pipe at any time. Band, drums and fifes, and pipes played separately, except in marching past in slow time, when each piper played a 'salute' as his company passed the General.

The Life of a Regiment, Volume II, p 50.

When pipers were finally taken on establishment the practice of drummers accompanying pipers began to take hold, and the pipe band came into being. The pipe band evolved into a form where side drummers provided a rhythmic accompaniment, given depth by tenor drums, and a bass drum gave the beat that gave timing to the performance. Military pipe bands needed more pipers, who were required to play in unison and provide music for soldiers to march to:

MacKay-Scobie says that about 1854 there was a radical change in regimental piping. Up to that time regiments had marched to fife and drum bands, and the pipers had been company pipers, who played principally in camp, in barracks, and in action, rarely on the line of march, and usually solo, their music being almost exclusively *piobaireachd*. The change came about by the abolition of the fifes, and the joining of the drums to the pipes.

At this stage it became necessary to increase the number of pipers, and thereby to lower the general standard of playing, for it would obviously be impossible to teach hastily manufactured pipers the old *piobaireachd* calls as well as the music required for the band. Thus it may have come about that adaptations of Lowland songs were substituted for the former *piobaireachdan*. The question suggests itself why should so many Lowland tunes have been selected? And why should an air like *Highland Laddie* have been chosen for the march past with the pipes? The answer may be that these airs were survivals from the fifes and drums, as many of the old tunes were retained as could be made suitable for the pipes. Another answer, which I suspect to be equally near the mark, is that old Highland marching tunes were not chosen because there were none to choose.

Well into the nineteenth century there were at least two different forms of bagpipes in Scotland, the Highland bagpipe and the Lowland, or 'ordinary,' bagpipe. Joseph MacDonald, the earliest known writing piper, records in 1760 that there were then only three forms of music for the Highland pipe, *piobaireachd*, reels and jigs, but that performers on the Lowland pipe (of which he speaks disparagingly) played Scottish song airs and 'various other things'. As late as 1832 we have the Highland

Society of Scotland complaining to the Highland Society of London that Highland pipers persisted in viewing strathspey and reel playing with contempt, accompanied by a strong belief that it was detrimental to pibroch-playing. Since then the ousting of the Lowland pipe by the Highland pipe has been complete, but the process was probably accompanied by the transfer to the Highland pipe of a good deal of Lowland pipe music. On the whole, it seems open to question whether what we now call pipe marches have been played on the Highland bagpipe for more than about 100 years. There are plenty of allusions by old writers to pipes and piping, but the difficulty is that we do not know of what particular kind of bagpipe they are speaking. Unless regimental records can help us, we seem to have nothing more solid than the two facts (a) that Joseph MacDonald specifies in 1760, *piobaireachd*, reels and jigs, as the only kinds of Highland bagpipe music, and (b) that in the series of competitions from 1782 to 1844, by which the Highland Society sought to revive Highland piping after the proscription, there was never any competition for marches, nor even any suggestion for such a competition.

A. Campbell.

T&S, March 1932.

Pipers of the 92nd under Pipe Major Gregor Fraser at Jullundur, 1870 Note that Fraser and two pipers play left-handed!

In 1880, at Kandahar on the North-West Frontier of India, a young piper's musical future was brought to an untimely end:

Among the wounded was a young man from Strathspey named Grant, an enthusiastic musician, whose ambition it was to become a regimental piper. Two of his fingers had been shot off; the surgeon, while addressing the wound, observed a tear in the lad's eye, and remarked that the pain would soon be over. 'I don't mind the pain, sir,' replied Grant, 'but that I will never more play the pipes.'

The Life of a Regiment, Volume II, pp 155–56.

At Dargai, in 1897, pipers played a significant part in the inspiring charge of the 1st Battalion up the precipitous hillside to clear the Afridi tribesmen who held the summit. Pipers taking part were Lance Corporal Milne and Privates Findlater, Fraser, Kidd, Walker and Wills, who were at the front of their respective companies. Findlater later wrote:

I remember the Colonel addressing the regiment, telling them what they were expected to do. I remember the order for the regiment to attack, and the order 'Pipers to the front'. I am told that the *Cock o' the North* was ordered to be played, but I didn't hear the order, and using my own judgement I thought that the charge would be better led by a Strathspey, so I struck up the *Haughs o' Cromdale*.[2] The *Cock o' the North* is more of a march tune and the effort we had to make was a rush and charge.

The battle fever had taken hold of us and we thought not of what the other was feeling. Our whole interest being centred in self. Social positions were not thought of, and officers and men went forward with eagerness shoulder to shoulder.

www.findlater.org.uk

During the assault three pipers were hit: Lance Corporal Milne was shot through the lung, Piper Findlater through the left ankle and Piper Kidd through the leg (later amputated). Findlater said of his wounding:

Milne was shot down and rendered helpless, shot through the lung. I got about half across when I was struck on the left foot, but as the bullet only grazed my toes that did not matter. Then a stray shot broke my chanter [but] the break did not make it impossible to play. I had not gone much further when a third bullet went through my right ankle—the feeling was as if I had been struck heavily with a stick. My leg went under me, and my pipes slid off my shoulder. But I managed to keep on playing to cheer on the other fellows. I got my back against the stone, and that helped me wonderfully, but I was bleeding profusely and in a few minutes sickened. I am told that the time I continued playing after falling was about five minutes. After the hill was taken I was taken to the field hospital with the other wounded. My first thoughts on recovery were how lucky I had been in getting off so easily.

---

2   There has long been debate about the tune that Findlater played at Dargai, many maintaining that it was *The Cock o' the North*. Findlater's own account here, that it was *The Haughs o' Cromdale*, settles this debate.

Sometime before the New Year Colonel Mathias came to me and said he was going to put me in for the Victoria Cross. It never occurred to me that I had done anything to merit reward. What I did I could not help doing.

The pipers wounded at Dargai.
From left: Lance-Corporal Milne D.C.M., Piper Kidd, Piper Findlater V.C.

Victoria Crosses were awarded to Private Findlater and Private Lawson (Lawson had carried wounded officers and men to safety, sheltering them with his body). Lance Corporal Milne was awarded the medal for 'distinguished service in the field' (the Distinguished Conduct Medal). Findlater's Victoria Cross was presented to him personally by Queen Victoria when she visited the Military Hospital at Netley.

During the Boer War the Pipe Major of the 2nd Battalion, Charles Dunbar, wounded at Elandslaagte,[3] was awarded the Distinguished Conduct Medal for conspicuous bravery at the battle. On three other occasions he was mentioned in despatches. Pipe Major Dunbar was not the only piper to be decorated for gallantry at Elandslaagte. Corporal-Piper Kenneth Macleod (later to be Pipe Major) took the lead after Pipe Major Dunbar was wounded, exposing himself to heavy enemy fire as he piped the Gordons into the charge. The *Natal Advertiser* said, 'This gallant Scot was twice struck, once in the arm and once in the side. He however, continued to pipe and advance

---

3   When he recovered from his wounds Pipe-Maj Dunbar was posted to the 3rd Battalion, The Gordon Highlanders. Discharged in 1911, he emigrated to Canada and returned to the colours for the First World War, in which he was wounded at Courcelette in 1916. He was given an honorary commission in 1917.

with the Gordons to their final rush. Presently came more bullets, smashing his drones, chanter and windbag, whereupon the splendid fellow had to give in.' The Adjutant wrote, 'Corporal Macleod, shot through the arm, stood up in the hottest of fire and blew like mad and the men advanced.'

At times there were misunderstandings about Highland courtesy! In 1909 the 2nd Battalion was stationed in Calcutta. At a dinner at which Lord Minto was present, the Pipe Major played:

> The Pipe-Major [Kenneth Macleod] was a magnificent specimen of Hebridean manhood. Just at the end of a big *tamash* at which Lord Minto was present, he was playing a *piobaireachd* and continued a *very* long time. His Excellency's time was up but as a good Scot he didn't like to leave before the pipes stopped playing. At last he was driven to approach the musician, who ceased to sound and stood at attention. 'Pipe-Major, you're playing is splendid, but I have to leave, and I don't like doing so till you stop!' 'Your Excellency, I canna be stoppin' till your Excellency is leaving.'[4]

The Life of a Regiment, Volume III, p 354.

Visitors, particularly foreign visitors, to the Officers Mess often found pipe music strange to the ears, and their reactions were usually interesting:

> Lieutenant von Koppelow of the Mecklenburg Grenadiers dined in the 1st Battalion Officers Mess in 1911. He made a good impression, showed the keenest interest in trophies, plate, etc., and handed the Pipe-Major his glass of whisky with a speech, the translation of which is: 'Herr Pipe-Major, I thank you for your most delightful music, but may God grant I never hear it in battle!' Against this may be placed a yarn of a Russian naval officer dining . . . at Colombo in 1890, who, at first stunned and dazed by the crash and volume of the pipes, gradually became alert, fingers drumming in time more and more certainly, till he turned on his host excitedly: 'They're playing a tune!'

The Life of a Regiment, Volume III, p 354.

Tinkers were 'gentlemen of the road', once widely seen across Scotland. They did odd jobs, sang with varying degrees of musicality, or played musical instruments, again with varying skill, all for a few coins to provide sustenance. The piper in the following article was typical of the breed—and a good Gordon Highlander:

---

4   Lord Minto was Viceroy of India. Kenneth Macleod succeeded Charles Dunbar as Pipe-Maj, and held this post from 1901 to 1912. The Crown Prince of Germany, in India, impressed by Macleod's playing, presented him with the Order of the Red Eagle. Macleod returned this decoration in August 1914.

Rab Stewart was a clansman before he became a Huntly Highlander.[5] He was one of the Tinker Stewarts, who travelled Aberdeenshire, playing bagpipes and doing odd jobs.

Freedom was the motto of the clan and the open air its worshipping place. The clan spirit, or a sense of patriotism, was probably responsible for each male Stewart of military age being enrolled in the Militia or the Huntly Highlanders as a piper.

Rab never believed in half-measures, so, previous to the South African War, he enlisted into the ranks of the Huntly Highlanders, a piper in the Militia not being the *pukka* place for him. As he was tall, well-proportioned, and of erect carriage, after a brief spell of training he was considered one of the smartest soldiers in the regiment.

He was wounded in the South African War, and invalided home. Soldiering at home when the war on was alien to Rab, so he deserted and joined the newly formed Irish Guards, under an assumed name, hoping to be sent to South Africa. His scheme failed, as his appearance and ability marked him for promotion, [and] he [soon] became a Corporal. A Sergeant transferred from the Huntly Highlanders was responsible for Rab being court-martialled, reduced to the ranks, and sentenced to a term of imprisonment. On release he was returned to his former regiment and drafted to South Africa as an infantryman. His period of service in the infantry was a happy time for Rab, a very efficient scout. On the return of peace, Rab joined a battalion of Huntly Highlanders in India, and being known as one of the Tinker Stewarts, he was appointed piper. For twelve years in India and Egypt[6] he was a distinguished member of the pipe band, competing and gaining prizes for piping and dancing at Regimental and Highland Gatherings.

Rab was not only a piper and dancer, he was a regimental 'worthy.' He possessed the Scottish pawky humour, could sing Scottish songs, so he was one of the star artists at regimental concerts and canteen 'sing-songs.' His care-free manner, appearance, pronounced Scottish accent and wit made him an outstanding character wherever he went, and he was as well-known and popular with English or Irish regiments in the garrison as he was in the Huntly Highlanders. He had no inferiority complex.

In India he had two glorious months as instructor to the pipers of a native regiment in a hill station, a three days' journey from his own battalion, being made a Lance Corporal for the occasion. When the two months expired, the Colonel of the native regiment sent a report to the Colonel of the Huntly Highlanders, stating that 'Corporal Stewart was a

---

5   Huntly Highlanders—a pseudonym for The Gordon Highlanders.
6   This places him in the 2nd Battalion.

first-class piper and instructor, but he was also exceedingly thirsty.' He had been a missionary of other things than piping!

In Egypt, at the outbreak of the Great War, Rab had mellowed considerably: his thick black hair and moustache were streaked with grey, and he seemed inclined to rest on his laurels earned during the many years he had been an 'unpaid regimental comedian.'

Rab was one of the few men who at times really enjoyed the war, full rope being given to the primitive element in him. In a letter he wrote to the writer of this article, he said that the war was O.K., though he greatly missed the old comrades who were killed or too badly wounded to return—men who had been bound closer to him with years of regimental association than blood ties. He had a roving commission in France, being the Colonel's runner, and he was often to be met going with an important message, sometimes carrying a rifle and sometimes a revolver. He fought through Ypres, 1914, and Neuve Chapelle; great yarns are told of his deeds in these battles. The Battle of Loos gave a fitting end to Rab of the Lion Heart. He was killed going 'over the top' with the Colonel, the latter being mortally wounded,[7] Rab dying like a clansman of old alongside his chief. The old Tinker Piper died as a Sergeant, and the possessor of the Distinguished Conduct Medal.

T&S, May 1931.

John Malcolm Bulloch describes an interesting family of pipers. It is just possible that Rab Stewart, in the article above, was connected with this family:

The Gordons have enjoyed the services of one particular family of hereditary pipers, the Stewarts. They came from Perthshire, where one of them was a piper to the Duke of Atholl, while his brother, known as 'Piper Jamie,' crossed time hills into the Parish of Kirkmichael, Banffshire—the cradle of a remarkable military family, the Gordons of Croughly, where seven sons were born to him. All of these strapping fellows entered the Aberdeenshire Militia, now the 3rd Battalion of the Gordon Highlanders, six of them becoming pipers. The best known of these was the eldest, Donald (1849–1913), who migrated to New Deer, Aberdeenshire, and was known all over Scotland as a champion piper. The family has been supplying pipers to the Gordons for more than half a century.

from *The Pipes of War*, Seton and Grant (1920), p227.

---

7   Lt-Col J.R.E. Stansfeld, commanding 2nd Gordons. Before he died he sent from the casualty clearing station the message, 'Well done, dear old 92nd!'

The custom of a piper playing after the meal was an old one, rooted in the traditions of the old Highland society, where the Chief's piper would play not the sprightly marches strathspeys and reels familiar to modern audiences, but the pibroch (Gaelic *piobaireachd*); the evocative classical form of piping:

The word *piobaireachd* is Gaelic. If we dissect it we find *piob* the pipe, *piobaree* the piper, the termination *-eachd* being simply the case ending, signifying the act of piping. Hence we may also take the word to mean pipe music, which is, in short, the classical music of the bagpipe. Pipe music is divided into two main classes, *ceòl mòr* meaning the great music, and *ceòl beag* the lesser music. The former means *piobaireachd*, while the latter comprises marches (quick and slow), strathspeys and reels.

Piobaireachd is undoubtedly the oldest form of pipe music; included in it we find salutes, laments, welcomes, warnings and also marches.

All are written in the same form. They commence with the *urlar* or ground. This is the melody which runs through the whole tune. Then come the variations, generally three or four in number, which increase in difficulty and speed until the composition concludes with the *creanludh* (pronounced *crunloo*), which is the most difficult of all the movements.

Piobaireachd is a story or poem. If one uses one's imagination it is possible to follow the story or poem as the tune is being played. One must, however, know the story before hearing it played.

On all subjects handed down through the ages there is controversy. *Piobaireachd* has not escaped. There are two schools of thought. The *Piobaireachd* Society upholds the theory that a *piobaireachd* cannot be marched to. Yet in *Ceòl Mòr*,[8] which is recognised by the Society, we find several *piobaireachdan* called marches. For example, *Glengarry's March* and others with time signatures suitable to marching.

The other School could be called the McLennan School. The late Lieut. John McLennan held an entirely opposite view from the Society. He said there was rhythm and time in *piobaireachd* and therefore the piper could march to his playing, his foot coming down with the beat. This, he maintained, simplified the playing of the tune and made it more intelligible to an audience.

His son George, late Pipe-Major of the 1st Battalion and the Depot, has followed his father. He is admitted everywhere to be one of the finest, if not the finest, march, strathspey and reel player that Scotland has ever produced, but he has never got justice in *piobaireachd* competitions for the reason stated.

T&S, March 1926.

---

8   *Ceòl Mòr*, by Gen C.S. Thomason, R.E., the standard work on *piobaireachd*, published in 1900.

The Gordon Highlanders produced many fine pipers across the years, renowned in piping circles and respected by their peers. Part of the skill of the piper is the ability to create new pipe music that can stand on its own merits. One of the greatest composers is commonly held to be George Stewart McLennan.

The history of pipe music is rich with the names of men who sustained the art and added new dimensions. In the early twentieth century none

shone so bright as George Stewart McLennan (known in the Regiment and in piping circles as 'GS'), perhaps the most complete player and composer of modern times.

From a long line of pipers, GS (photo) was born to Lt John McLennan (Edinburgh Police) and Elizabeth Stewart on 9 February 1884. He was not robust, walking for the first time only at four and a half years, about the same time that his father had him playing *Kenmure's On and Awa'*! Five years later, he had won the Amateur National Championship for marches, strathspeys and reels (1893) and the Scottish Amateur Championship for piping (1894). Word reached Queen Victoria, who summoned GS to give a performance at the age of ten. What GS thought of meeting the queen is not recorded, though he appeared to be far more interested in the cakes she served!

On 3 October 1899, his father sent GS to Edinburgh Castle with a note to Sgt Mitchell of the Gordon Highlanders that read 'Please enlist my son the bearer George Stewart McLennan in the 1st Gordon Highlanders and send him up to the Castle as soon as possible.' George duly reported for duty. As a small man, only five-two and a half, he was subjected to bullying, but he taught himself jujitsu and it soon became well-known to leave young McLennan alone. He was disappointed to be left behind [aged 15!] when the Battalion shipped out to war in South Africa but he quickly rose through the ranks, becoming the British Army's youngest Pipe Major in 1905. While serving in Colchester he met his wife, whom he married in 1910 before being posted to the Regimental Depot in Aberdeen in 1913. He had two sons, George (born 1914), who as a medic elected to stay with his comrades at St Valery-en-Caux in 1940 and was taken prisoner, and John (born 1916), killed in action at St Valery-en-

Caux. GS returned to the 51st Division in France in 1918, serving not only as a piper but also as a Lewis gunner. He was well-known in the Battalion for sitting in his trench, making pipe reeds to be sent home and sold. It was during this time that GS fell very ill, but refused to leave the Battalion in the trenches; when the Gordons rotated out of the front, he reported sick and fluid was removed from his left lung. After the Armistice, GS retired with 22 years' service. He returned to Aberdeen, opened a piping shop and carried on with his competitive career. At 40 scarring in his left lung led to failing health. At age 45, he lost consciousness, chanter in hand, while teaching his boys to play *Dancing Feet*. He never recovered, and died on 1 June 1929.

His funeral was the likes of which Aberdeen and Edinburgh have rarely seen. More than 20,000 people lined the streets, with the Depot and British Legion pipe bands leading his coffin, borne on a gun carriage. His body was returned to Edinburgh and interred at Echobank Cemetery to the strains of his favourite *piobaireachd*, *Lament for the Children*.

In all, Pipe Major McLennan won over 2,000 piping awards. It is unfortunate that recording equipment was not widely available during his lifetime. It was written of him, '. . . a little finger which seemed as if it had been part of a mechanical contrivance placed in the chanter to make it trill in marches, strathspeys, and reels. George's playing gave me the impressions of the supernatural and kept one spellbound.' His competitive career carried on much as it had in his early years with him winning virtually every contest in the United Kingdom. Part of what sets him apart was his skill at composing fresh, bright, and very musical tunes, and he set the bar to which everyone else aspired.

www.bydand.com

Pipers were killed and injured in such numbers in the First World War that the War Office banned the practice of playing in the trenches. This ban was not always observed, as with the 1st Gordons at Longueval, of whom it was told: 'They were out of sight right over the parapet, but we could hear at intervals the shouts of "Scotland for Ever" and the faint strain of the pipes.' But, although pipe bands accompanied battalions into the trenches, pipers were no longer exposed to murderous fire as they led assaults. In the Second World War pipe bands again accompanied their battalions on deployment, and despite War Office strictures, on occasion led them into battle. General Montgomery, recalling the opening night of the Battle of Alamein, said, 'I well remember that night on 23rd of October when the Highland Division went into battle with its bagpipes'; and J.B. Salmond in his *51st Highland Division* says: 'So the reincarnated 51st Highland Division moved forward to its first battle, and in front of each Battalion marched its pipers playing.'

Brigadier Howard Kippenberger, commanding the 5th New Zealand Brigade, later wrote of Alamein: 'Far away on our right I could hear clearly the skirling of the Highland pipes, warlike stirring music.' Three months after Alamein, British forces entered Tripoli; 1st Gordons were the first troops to enter the city. On 4 February 1943 a Victory Parade was held in the presence of Winston Churchill, when the 51st Highland Division, to the music of the massed pipes and drums (including the bands of the 1st and 5/7th Gordons), marched past. Brigadier Kippenberger wrote|: 'The previous afternoon the Highlanders had marched past General Alexander in Tripoli. They had brought their kilts with them—where they found the room in their transport I cannot imagine. As the battalions turned into the square they caught the skirl of the pipes, every man braced himself up, put on a swagger, and they went past superbly.'

After the war the drums and pipes continued to play a major part in the life of the Regiment. They were an integral, important and cherished part of day-to-day life, and they represented the Regiment in many engagements in both army and civilian circles.

Internal security operations in Northern Ireland in the 1970s and 1980s saw the Drums and Pipes employed in new, differing ways. The commanding officer in 1972 and 1973, Lieutenant-Colonel John MacMillan, explains how he approached the problem:

> The Drums and Pipes held the longest serving and most versatile members of the battalion. Because they were originally company pipers, there was a pull to split them up so that the companies had their own, to the dismay of the Pipe Major, was left without a command, and knowing his pipers would lose their musical skills unless he had them in his hand. I don't know how this was played in Borneo, but in the first Armagh tour I went for the split to companies and the search team while Pipey Kerr and the remainder were my escort; great company and very efficient, but he was unhappy with his empire scattered.
>
> In Andersonstown the Drums and Pipes were just another platoon, but an extremely good one, and Joe Kerr personally made the most important arrest of our tour, Micky McMullen, who was convicted of killing Pte Marr. The Drums and Pipes always prided themselves on being both musicians and fighters, and looked down (in a comradely way) on the Military Band as musicians only.

Lieutenant-General Sir John MacMillan (writing to author).

Pipers were used to playing before, and conversing with, distinguished personages. There was little that threw them off their stride or overawed them, and they dealt with senior officers, politicians and even royalty with quiet confidence. Pipe Major Joe Kerr gave a perfect example when he played for Her Majesty The Queen at a function in Japan in 1975:

On April 29th the Military Band and a party from the Drums & Pipes set off for Japan, where they were to give a number of performances during a visit there by Her Majesty The Queen. A pipe band, 11 strong, accompanied the Military Band while the remainder of the Drums & Pipes was split into two groups that performed in Tokyo and Osaka.

The Military Band provided fanfare trumpeters and a woodwind quartet for the State Banquet, while Pipe Major Kerr and his pipers played the pipes. The Pipe Major had complained that 'the Japanese waiter was a bit tight with the Highland Dew'. When he reported to Her Majesty after a pipe set, she asked him if he were teetotal! 'I'm working on it, Ma'am,' he replied, 'but not at the moment!' When the waiter was asked to fill the *quaich* with whisky the poor man was so nervous that the whisky went everywhere but the vessel. The Duke of Edinburgh laughed openly at Pipe Major Kerr's attempts to get the *quaich* underneath the stream of whisky, but at last it was full enough for the Pipe Major to give the Regimental Gaelic toast. This so impressed the Queen that she asked for a translation, which the Pipe Major duly gave her. He subsequently got a letter from the Queen's Piper saying that Her Majesty had asked him to learn the toast, and could Pipe Major Kerr send it to him. The answer, only slightly tongue in cheek, was that it was The Gordon Highlanders' own toast, and if he wanted one, to get his own![9]

The Life of a Regiment, Volume VII, p 169.

Pipe-Major Kerr's successor, Gaelic-speaking Pipe-Major Brian MacRae, was appointed in 1980 as Queen's Piper, personal piper to Her Majesty The Queen, a post he held for 13 years. He played for The Queen wherever she was in residence—Buckingham Palace, Windsor, Sandringham, the Palace of Holyroodhouse or Balmoral. He established an easy, familiar yet respectful relationship with the Royal Family, and became a well-loved figure in the Royal Household. When he retired as Queen's Piper he worked as Judge's Clerk for Sir William Macpherson, the renowned High Court Judge, who regarded Brian MacRae as 'the best Judge's Clerk he ever had'.

In the fifty years that remained to The Gordon Highlanders after the Second World War the Drums and Pipes played a full part in representing the Regiment and building on their reputation as fine musicians, and as trained riflemen on active service. Their performance in action, on the parade ground, in the concert hall and recording studio, and in the daily life of the Regiment, earned them the respect and affection of all Gordon Highlanders.

---

9   The Regimental toast is shown at the end of this Chapter.

Drums and Pipes of 1st Battalion, Singapore 1974

Back row: Dmr R. Calder, Dmr M. Taylor, Cpl W. Gow, Dmr A. Thomson, LCpl S. Alexander, Cpl I. Whyte, Dmr J. Harper, Dmr J. McSeveney, Dmr J. McGregor.
Centre row: Ppr G. Blythe, Ppr W. Milne, Ppr B. Ewan, Ppr J. Anthony, Ppr W. Rugg, Ppr G. Mellay, Ppr J. Lovatt, Ppr I. Macey, Ppr R. Gregson, LCpl K. Knox
Front row: Cpl D. Davies, Cpl A. Cruickshank, LCpl R. Dailly, P/M J. Kerr, Maj D.M. Napier, D/M B. Huntington, Ppr M. Dailly, Cpl A. Stewart, LCpl A. Kelly

Regimental Toast of The Gordon Highlanders

Tir nam beann nan gleann's nan gaisgeach,
Far an cinnich an t-eun fionn
's far am faigh am fiadh fasgadh;
Cho fad 'sa dh'iadhas ceo mu bheinn
's a ruitheas uisge sios Ie gleann
Maridh cuimhn' air luchd nan treun;-
Biodh slaint' is buaidh gu brath
Aig gillean Moirear Hundaidh.

Land of bens and glens and heroes,
Where the ptarmigan flourishes
And the stag finds shelter;
While mist enfolds the mountain
And water flows down the glen
The memory of the brave shall endure;
'Health and Victory' for ever
To the lads of the Marquis of Huntly.

CHAPTER 13

THE DRUMS

PIPERS had a musical role in war, sounding the various calls to action. Drummers in Highland Regiments did not take their drums into action, but played an active part as medical orderlies or riflemen.

Drummers of the 92nd – 1815 and 1866

Drummers and pipers wore broadswords, and during the Afghan campaign of 1879–80 they were quite prepared to use them:

The enemy retired slowly, fighting, but a number of Ghazis stood to receive a bayonet charge of the Highlanders while many shut themselves up in the houses and fired on our men as they passed, and some splendid hand-to-hand fighting occurred. In the melee Lieutenant Menzies found himself in a courtyard, at the end of which was an open door, and beyond it another door which was locked, but voices being heard within, the lock was burst by a shot from the officer's pistol and the door swung open; instantly a shot from inside hit Menzies in the groin, and he fell. The only man near at the moment was Drummer Roddick, whom he asked not to leave him. 'You're all right, sir, as long as this blade lasts', replied Roddick, as with his drawn claymore he stood over his wounded officer. A number of Afghans rushed out, and the leader fired, the bullet knocking off Roddick's helmet: the man then made for him with the muzzle of his rifle, but the stalwart drummer parried the blow, and ran him through with his sword. At this moment Private Dennis came up; not liking to put the wounded man in the house, where a lot of bags of grain might conceal a foe, they laid him in the slight shade given by the wall of the court. Just as they had done so an Afghan rushed from behind the bags, making a slash at the officer as he passed and cutting his shoulder, but, fortunately, his blade hit the wall, which broke the force of the blow, and the man was shot dead by Dennis. More men joined them, Roddick and Dennis carried the lieutenant to a doolie, and immediately rejoined their company.

The Life of a Regiment, Volume II, pp 149–50.

By the second half of the 19th century the British Army had introduced awards for acts of gallantry that had not been available to soldiers in earlier wars. Drummer James Roddick was awarded the Distinguished Conduct Medal for his bravery in saving the life of Lieutenant Menzies.

Drummer Roddick saves Lieutenant Menzies

In the First World War great heroism was shown by all ranks of The Gordon Highlanders. One of them—Drummer (later Drum-Major) William Kenny—was awarded the Victoria Cross.[1]

The colours are not the only medium on which battle honours are displayed. The battle honours and emblems shown on the colours are reproduced on the drums of the Drums and Pipes, which are treasured and guarded like the colours.

Misplaced Drums

Early in both the First and Second World Wars, regimental drums stored in Belgium and France were left behind during the fighting withdrawals that marked the opening stages of each war. These drums were lost to the enemy, not in battle, but when the towns where they were stored were taken by the Germans. Some of the drums found their way back to their rightful owners years later. In the first instance the drums were returned in 1934, not long after the Nazi party, led by Adolf Hitler, came into power in Germany.

Return of the Drums of the 2nd Battalion, lost in 1914.

This article, telling how the drums of the 2nd Battalion were lost in 1914, and how they were returned to The Gordon Highlanders in January 1934, is interesting in its air of camaraderie, fellow feeling between soldiers and sense of honour. The knowledge that Adolf Hitler was already in power and that Hindenburg would be dead within months puts such sentiments, the relics of a Germany that would soon show itself willing to discard all such concepts of honour and decency, into chilling perspective:

The 2nd Battalion landed at Zeebrugge on 4th October, 1914. It marched to Bruges, to Ostend the next day, and the following day entrained for Ghent.

At Ostend Major W.J. Graham, M.C. (then 2/Lieut.), who was Transport, reported to Lieut.-Col. Uniacke that the Transport wagons were much overloaded. Major H. M. Sprot (then Lieut.) was ordered to deposit the drums in the Police Station at Ostend.

As soon as possible after the Armistice, Major Graham went to Ostend to recover the drums. He was told that they had remained in Ostend until shortly before its evacuation by the Germans, who found the drums during a house-to-house search, and took them away.

Until recently the drums lay in the Armoury Museum at Berlin, but upon representations by the Colonel of the Regiment, the German Government graciously decided to return the drums to the Regiment.

---

1 See Chapters 25 and 27. It is fitting that out of the 19 Victoria Crosses awarded to Gordon Highlanders, one went to a piper and one to a drummer.

General Sir Ian Hamilton and Lieut. Col. S.R. McClintock went to Berlin on the 29th January, 1934, to receive the drums. They were entertained during their stay in Berlin by the German Government, and were much impressed by the kindness and hospitality shown to them by everyone whom they met.

Sir Ian Hamilton described the ceremony.

> To put down, in cold blood, an account of our meeting with the War Minister of Germany, His Excellency General von Blomberg, and of my reply to his speech, is not easy. The circumstances of the occasion were entirely unexpected; nothing had been prepared; some partial reports which have already appeared in the German and British Press were, so I have been informed, obtained by private enterprise from a sentry after he had been relieved.

> Here is what happened. When the great folding-doors on the first floor of the *Reichswehr Ministerium* were thrown open, we—Lieut.-Col. McClintock and myself—were gently shepherded through and found ourselves in a large room, he following me about two paces on my left. As the doors closed behind us we saw, five paces in front of us the War Minister, General von Blomberg. His Excellency is tall and slim; he looks, as the Germans say, 'through and through' a soldier; his smile is sympathetic and his attitude conveys the impression that he is ready for anyone or anything. Immediately behind him were our drums, decorated with bay leaves and guarded on either hand by sentries in service kit, steel hats, fixed bayonets, motionless as statues; even their eyes had been switched on half-right and half-left respectively, and appeared to be fixed upon me. To the left were grouped about thirty senior officers, amongst whom were General von Fritsch (Chief of the Army), Admiral Raeder (Chief of the Navy), General Beck (Chief of the *Truppenampt*), General von Schaumberg (Commandant of Berlin), Col. von Striphagel (Director T.3), and General von Reichenau (Chief of the War Minister's Cabinet). I think the Director of Civil Aviation was also present. After salutes had been exchanged, the War Minister addressed me as follows:

> > It is a special joy and honour for me and, with me, the whole German Army that I am in the position at this moment to satisfy a wish which was transmitted from you through the German Ambassador in London.

> > Nearly twenty years ago, at the beginning of the tremendous struggle which we call the World War, there were left at Ostend, where they had been stored after the disembarkation, the drums of one of the most famous regiments of the British Army, the Gordon

Highlanders. It was only some time afterwards that they were found there by the German troops in occupation and were sent to the *Zeughaus* in Berlin.

Only too gladly do we recognize that these drums are not battle trophies; the *Reichspresident*, Field-Marshal von Hindenburg, has therefore approved of their being restored on this day and in this manner into your hands, my dear General, as Colonel of the Gordon Highlanders.

We honour the Gordon Highlanders one of the bravest and most famous British regiments, which has carried its colours from India to South Africa, from Flanders to Italy, and displayed them, as I am specially pleased to remember, side by side with the Prussian Army at Waterloo. The memory of that historic day and the recollection of the four years in which our armies lay opposed to one another as chivalrous enemies makes this occasion for me and the German Army a symbolic act.

The handing over of these historic drums of your regiment should be a token to you personally, and to the British Army, that above the political strife and political interests of the nations there lives in the soldiers of both armies a common sympathy, respect for the chivalrous opponent, recognition of his feats and bravery, and the feeling of an inner tie in the high calling of defending country and people.

You are present to-day in a Germany which has found itself again after long dark years of misfortune and division. May you now recognize that the German nation has no other wish than to take her place in the concert of nations in honourable peace as a free country with equal rights.

I pray you, General, to accept these drums at the hands of the German Army and with them to convey to the Regiment, which proudly bears the Royal Tiger as its badge, its respect for its bravery and for its fallen comrades. To have crossed swords with such troops is an honour for the German Army.

Although the *Reichsminister* had read slowly and clearly, I had hardly taken in what he was saying, my mind being preoccupied with what I should say myself, and of whether I should speak in German or in English.

The first word that came to my mind was '*Ereignis*,' or 'Excellency,' and with that word I commenced my address, in German, in reply to General von Blomberg. At its conclusion General von Blomberg signed his name upon the big drum.

General Sir Ian Hamilton and Lieutenant-Colonel S.R. McClintock with the drums and
General von Blomberg

After the ceremony Sir Ian Hamilton was received by the President,
Field-Marshal von Hindenburg, and had a private conversation with him.
The President came out, and Lieut.-Col. McClintock was presented. The
Field-Marshal gave him the following message:—

> 'I am very glad to meet an officer of the active list of your famous
> regiment. Please give my best regards to the officers and men, and tell
> those young soldiers that a very old soldier has very much pleasure in
> sending them back their drums.'

T&S, March 1934.

Efforts had been made at the end of the War to recover the drums, but to
no avail. After return of the drums a letter to *The Times* from the widow of
Lieutenant-Colonel J.R.E. Stansfeld threw some light on these efforts:

> Sir, — I have just read with the greatest pleasure in *The Times* of today
> that Sir Ian Hamilton has been successful in recovering the drums of the
> 2nd Battalion, The Gordon Highlanders, from Germany.
> Sir Ian says he never heard of their capture, but in 1918 I did my best
> to get them back. My late husband, Colonel J.R.E. Stansfeld, who was
> killed at Loos in 1915, was Adjutant when the drums were handed over to
> the officials at Ostend for safekeeping in October, 1914. After the
> Germans occupied Ostend his anxiety for the drums was very great. When
> on leave after being wounded, he constantly referred to them and hoped

they would not be taken, especially those with battle honours on them. He recounted the whole episode and told me to remember that the official receipt for them had been sent to the depot.

Nothing could be done during the War, but in October, 1918, when our Fleet was going to Ostend, I wrote to Admiral Sir Roger Keyes, asking him to make inquiries as soon as he arrived there. This he most kindly did, and in three letters dated October 23, 29 and November 9 I have all the details of his efforts. I sent out the receipt for the drums, and this enabled the Burgomaster, M. August Siebaert, to find out what had happened to them; but as they had been taken to Germany he could not restore them.

It is indeed a matter for congratulation that they have been restored, and I am grateful to everyone concerned, including the President, who has acted in such a friendly way. This conclusion would have given much joy to my husband.

Yours faithfully,
C.G. Stansfeld

T&S, March 1934.

Return of a drum of the 4th Battalion, lost in 1940

In 2012 a French family visited The Gordon Highlanders Museum in Aberdeen to return a drum, kept lovingly in the family since 1940 The drum belonged to the pipe band of the 4th (City of Aberdeen) Battalion, The Gordon Highlanders, which was a Divisional machine-gun battalion during the retreat to Dunkirk. On 27 May 1940 the Battalion covered the canal linking Comines and Ypres:

> The machine-gun support of the Gordons never faltered, and as the day wore on it seemed the whole front of the 5th Division was covered only by the fire of the Battalion. At night, however, very gallant counter-attacks drove the Germans back and made the line secure.

The Life of a Regiment, Volume VI, p 56.

On the following day, 28 May, Belgium surrendered and the order came to withdraw. At this point 'all documents and nearly all trucks and motorcycles were destroyed before the 4th Gordons moved'. It was at this point that the drum was hidden.

A French policeman, Seraphin Boulet, 'noticed a small mound of earth and unearthed the drum hours after it had been buried by the retreating Gordons'. He took it home to give it to his grandson, Jean Pierre, for his fourth birthday, but 'with the Nazi occupation in full swing, Jean's Pierre's mother, Raymonde, hid it in an attic'. When she died in 1995, Jean Pierre discovered the drum was to have been his birthday present 55 years earlier.

He displayed it prominently in his home before he died in 2007 and the drum passed to his sister, Mrs Pascale Osson. She and her husband Pierre, deciding that the drum should be returned, spoke to representatives of a nearby town, Hem, which is twinned with Mossley near Manchester. Their contacts in Mossley helped them research the drum's origins, and put them in touch with The Gordon Highlanders Museum.

Jesper Ericsson, curator of The Gordon Highlanders Museum, and representatives of the Regiment travelled to Hem in November 2011, when the drum was handed over in a moving ceremony. Prince Charles, Duke of Rothesay, former Colonel-in-Chief of The Gordon Highlanders, sent a message. The drum was brought back to its home city and, to complete the handover, the family travelled to Aberdeen in 2012 to see the drum in its new surroundings.

Return of a drum of the 5th Battalion, lost in 1940

In May 1940, the 5th Battalion, The Gordon Highlanders (along with the 1st Battalion) was in 153 Brigade of the 51st Highland Division. The 5th Battalion stored its drums in the town of Metz just before the German *blitzkrieg* began, which led ultimately to the 51st Highland Division's withdrawal through France, south around Paris and then north to the coast, to its last stand at St Valery-en-Caux, and capture. Inevitably, once the withdrawal began, the drums had been left behind. Little did the men of the 5th Battalion think that after the war ended one of those drums would be found again:

On 23rd March, 1945, Capt. Thomas O'Rorke, 10th U.S. Armoured Division, Seventh U.S. Army, found a drum in the officers' quarters in the Kasserine Artillery near Baumholden. The drum belonged to the 5th Battalion and had been presented by Capt. W. Stephens, of Peterhead.

Lieutenant-General A.M. Patch, Commander of the Seventh U.S. Army, decided to present this drum back to the Battalion and invited a representative party to take part in a historic ceremony in Munich on 7th June, 1945.

Brigadier J.R. Sinclair, D.S.O., commanding 153rd Infantry Brigade, represented the Regiment. The Battalion party was represented by the Commanding Officer, Lieut.-Colonel C.F. Irvine, M.C., Capt. D.A. Thorn, commanding the guard of honour, and 2/Lieut. D.A. Craig. The guard of honour consisted of C.S.M. Nicol, C.Q.M.S. Runciman, six N.C.Os. and twenty-four other ranks. The Pipes and Drums were under Drum-Major Ferguson and Pipe-Major Macgregor. There were fourteen pipers and nine drummers on parade.

The party arrived at Seventh U.S. Army Headquarters at Augsburg on Tuesday, 5th June, 1945. On Wednesday evening the Pipes and Drums beat Retreat on the main square of Army Headquarters. The Chief of Staff and many senior officers of Army Headquarters were present. General Patch had been recalled to Washington, but Brigadier Sinclair, Lieut.-Colonel Irvine and officers of the Battalion party were presented to him before his departure. General Patch expressed his regret at being unable to take part in the ceremony, and introduced his successor, Lieutenant-General Wade H. Haislip.

The ceremony at Munich took place on the Konigsplatz on 7th June in brilliant sunny weather. The following units of the United States Forces were on the parade: an infantry regiment of the 45th ('Thunderbird') Division; a company of the 42nd ('Rainbow') Division and a carrying party of the flags of the forty-eight American States; a guard of honour of the 10th Armoured Division carrying the drum on to the parade; a troop of tanks and tank destroyers.

The parade was formed up with the company of the 42nd Division and flags of the States forming an arc behind the saluting base. Drawn up in front were the troops on the parade, with the Pipes and Drums and guard of honour of the 5th/7th Bn The Gordon Highlanders on the right of the line. In the centre were the Colour parties of the United States Forces, with the infantry regiments on either side. The Band of the 45th U.S. Infantry Division was on parade.

At 1500 hrs. General Haislip reached the saluting base, with [the US Army Divisional Commanders], Brigadier J.R. Sinclair, D.S.O., The Gordon Highlanders, Lieut.-Colonel C.F. Irvine, M.C., The Gordon Highlanders, Lieut.-Colonel R.F. Daubigny, M.B.E., M.C., commanding British Increment, Seventh U.S. Army.

After the General Salute, Lieut.-Colonel Irvine gave a short history of the 5th Battalion and the drum. Capt. O'Rorke handed the drum to General Haislip, who after a short speech presented it to Brigadier Sinclair, who thanked General Haislip for the honour done to the Regiment by the United States Forces. He mentioned the pleasure it would give to the officers and men of the old 5th Battalion, who had so recently returned home, to know that this drum had been found and handed back to the Battalion.

The drum was handed to Cpl. W. Sim, and the parade came to the present. Cpl. Sim marched across the square to a position immediately behind the Drum-Major. The Pipes and Drums then 'Trooped the Line,' returning to their original position. After the 45th Division Band had played the two National Anthems, the whole parade marched past.

The Gordons' guard of honour, headed by the Pipes and Drums, led the march past, and took up a position on the other side of the square, where they remained whilst the United States Forces marched past, headed by the Band of the 45th Division.

The whole ceremony lasted thirty-five minutes, and was broadcast by the B.B.C. and all American radio networks.

When the GIs were getting into trucks to return to camp, one was heard to say, 'I sure as hell hope they don't lose that drum again!'

T&S, August 1948 and February/March 1974.

Corporal Sim sounds the returned 5th Battalion drum

CHAPTER 14

THE MILITARY BAND

Military Band, 1867

AT the end of the 18th century military bands were already in existence—a record from the period refers to the purchase of 'clarionetts, a bassoon, a bass drum head, a tamborrin and reeds'—and we know that bandsmen served in the Napoleonic Wars, for shortly after Waterloo a Court of Enquiry was established to investigate, amongst other things, why some of the bandsmen lost their instruments during the battle! We know that at least two musicians—a German, Augustus Sochling, and a Dubliner, Andrew Hollingsworth—were among the original men recruited for The Gordon Highlanders in 1794, and from this we can infer that a band was formed when the Regiment was raised.

Following the defeat of Napoleon, the 92nd returned home for a brief period, before being posted to Ireland and then Jamaica. In 1827 it came back to Scotland, with the band still engaged on regimental duties: 'On 12 July 1827, after the death of the 4th Duke of Gordon, his body was removed from Holyrood on its journey to Gordon Castle, being escorted by two companies of the 92nd with their band playing the Dead March from *Saul*.'

The early days of the band of the 75th are undocumented, though the regiment was censured in 1834 for having more N.C.O.s than was permitted in the band. The first Bandmaster of whom there are any records was William Collender, appointed in January 1869. Later that year Charles Farrell took up a similar position in the 92nd.

Military Band, 2nd Battalion, Aldershot 1897

Bandsmen of both battalions served as stretcher-bearers in the Boer War and in the two World Wars. In the years between the First and Second Wars both bands spent time overseas. The band of the 1st Battalion served in Malta, Turkey, Egypt, India and Palestine and, though it returned to Britain with the Battalion in January 1935, it was soon off again on a trip to Brussels.

In 1936, along with the drums and pipes, the band went to South Africa, playing for six weeks at the Empire Exhibition in Johannesburg and then going on tour. Thirty-nine concerts and ceremonies at twelve war memorials were played in four weeks. Whilst there, an unofficial mascot was adopted in the form of a dog, whom the bandsmen named 'Champ'. They claimed that Champ could recognise the drum roll for the National Anthem and would stand to attention. 'He has an ear for music and likes the bagpipes,' commented Bandmaster Campbell, in what some bandsmen regarded as a contradiction in terms! So attached did the men become to Champ that permission was given for him to accompany them home.

In 1937 a visit to France saw the band attend the opening of the British Pavilion at the Paris Exhibition.

The 2nd Battalion band was also active, playing at the 1932 British Exhibition in Copenhagen and moving to Gibraltar in 1934. To commemorate the visit, the Danish composer Hermann Pecking wrote the march *92nd in Copenhagen*, later shortened to *Copenhagen*.

The Second World War saw disaster overtake both Battalions and their bands: the 1st was captured with the 51st (Highland) Division at St Valery, whilst the 2nd was taken prisoner in Singapore by the Japanese in 1942. Bandmaster Reg Ashton was amongst those who died in the construction of the notorious Siam-Burma railway.

In anticipation of the disbandment of the 2nd Battalion in 1948, Bandmaster Bill Lemon was not replaced when he left to join the Royal Tank Regiment in September 1947.

The late 1940s saw the band active in Germany, France, Belgium and Denmark, as well as Scotland, where the Regiment received the Freedom of Aberdeen on 20 August 1949.

In 1951 it embarked on the *Empire Halladale* for Port Said, before moving on to Malaya. Massed band performances were given with the Seaforths and the Cameronians, but there were also military duties; Band Notes from the regimental journal of the period read: 'At the moment of writing, the whole Band excluding the scribe are out on a forty-eight-hour operation chasing the elusive Yong Hoi, the area bandit commander.'

On 6 October 1951, the British High Commissioner, Sir Henry Gurney, was killed on the Kuala Kubu Road near Fraser's Hill in an ambush by Communist Terrorists (CTs) while on his way to a meeting at Fraser's Hill. Gurney was riding in his Rolls Royce Silver Wraith with his wife, private secretary and Malayan chauffeur in a convoy. As the convoy rounded a curve in the road, it was ambushed by thirty-eight CT guerrillas, who opened a withering fire on the convoy with three Bren guns, Sten guns and rifles. Down that same road, earlier that day, had come a truck carrying members of the Military Band to an engagement in a local village. The bandsmen on the open back of the truck faced outwards, weapons at the ready, covering the jungle-clad hills on either side. After completing the engagement, they returned by the same route. The terrorists did not open fire on them. Official opinion afterwards was that the ambush on Sir Henry Gurney was a random, non-targeted attack and it was pure bad luck that the High Commissioner was killed. The fact that the CTs allowed a truck full of soldiers to pass when, with a sizeable ambush party, they could probably have killed all of them, seems to indicate that they were waiting for a specific target. Whatever the reason, the Gordon bandsmen, alert as they were, could consider that they had indeed had a narrow escape.

During the Battalion's operational tours in Northern Ireland in the 1970s, 1980s and 1990s, the Military Band played its part as medical assistants, and carried out guard duties in the fortified bases. It played a full part in community relations, giving concerts and performances, where the security situation allowed, to a wide range of civilian audiences. On non-operational tours in Scotland, England, Germany, Singapore and Belize the Military Band maintained the highest musical and regimental standards and brought joy and happiness to local communities and fellow Gordons alike.

Military Band leads a pageant through Chester, 1978

The Band, and Drums and Pipes, had a highly successful tour of Japan in 1986. There was a slight hitch when Japanese Customs officials were reluctant to allow two broadswords, sixteen dirks and seventeen *sgian dubhs* into the country, but diplomacy and the blandishments of the Pipe Major won the day, and the tour went ahead as planned. It culminated in a concert at the British Embassy in Tokyo, where the guests included the Prince and Princess of Wales and the Crown Prince and Princess of Japan.

In November 1990 the bandsmen saw active service in the First Gulf War (the only formed body of Gordon Highlanders to take part in that conflict), where they served as medical assistants with 32 Field Hospital, RAMC. The following account of the Band during the Gulf War was written by Lieutenant David Knox, who was Bandmaster during that period:

At about 3 am that morning we were awoken by the NBC alarm. The training we had undergone was suddenly a reality, even to the extent of loading our rifles—although, what effect the SA80 would have on a Scud missile remained to be seen! As we all looked at each other and checked that we were correctly dressed, Cpl Ronnie Taylor had the good sense to turn on the radio which gave us confirmation that the war had indeed started. During the coming days our confidence grew as the coalition air strikes took their toll. Gradually, we began to move north from Al Jubayl in convoys of ambulance buses.

After many exercises testing the whole medical chain from the point of wounding to the evacuation of a casualty our briefings indicated that we were now on a countdown to the ground offensive and we knew that we were as prepared as we were ever going to be! Later that afternoon two Scud missiles exploded in mid-air about 20 kms north of our location and we were assured that the now famous Patriot missile had yet again proved its worth. However, it was revealed later that evening that Patriot had not in fact taken out these two Scuds but they had broken up in mid-air for no good reason. More alarming, it was revealed that Patriot was not deployed in our area at all!

When the ground offensive began, we were relieved to hear, from briefings and from the American Forces Network Radio that the battles were going our way. This was reinforced by the lack of allied casualties in comparison to Iraqis who began to arrive by helicopter after a couple of days. At last the system we had trained with was being used, thankfully not by our own troops, but nevertheless allowing us to save lives and repair some serious wounds. The Hospital treated over 1,200 casualties, from a soldier with a bum boil, to major surgical cases.

Operation *Granby* was an experience which we will never forget and to those who say that Bands cannot justify their existence merely by training as medical assistants, we say 'The Gordons Band were a tiny part of the largest military operation in recent years and together with a large number of other Bands, fully justified the need to retain individual Bands within individual Regiments'.

Our sincere thanks go to our wives, girlfriends, families, the Regiment, the Regimental Association, and the people from the Regimental area and beyond, for their support during what was for us, a very uncertain period. We leave you with a short extract from a letter received from a school child from the North-East,

> 'Dear Gordons Bandsman, I hope that you get this letter in your desert home and that you also get lots of other letters from Scotland. Thank you for what you are doing for peace in the world. Love Kirsty, aged 8.'

The Regimental Band flew home on 26 March. A day or two later found them nearing Fort George. Outside Ardersier the coach was stopped and they were met by Major Chant-Sempill, who got them out of the comfortable coach and loaded them onto the back of an open-topped 4-ton truck. The truck was met at the Sally Port gate by the Drums and Pipes, who played it into the Fort where the whole Battalion and the Bandsmen's families were waiting to greet the returning Gordons. The reunions were emotional and the Bandsmen were clearly touched by the welcome given them by their Regiment.

The Life of a Regiment, Volume VII, Appendix 3.

The last major tour abroad came in October 1993 when a visit to Italy ended in Lucia, home of Puccini, where a concert was attended by 2,500 enthusiastic fans.

In June 1994 the Military Band gave a farewell concert in the Music Hall in Aberdeen, to say goodbye to the Gordons' home city; the city that had been inextricably linked to the Regiment from the day it was formed. The citizens of Aberdeen filled the Music Hall to overflowing to savour the quality of the band and were treated to a virtuoso concert in which every section of the band was given a chance to demonstrate the perfection of the parts that made such a memorable whole. There were few dry eyes in the theatre by the time the Military Band (assisted by pipers from the Drums and Pipes) played their last piece, and the music of The Gordon Highlanders faded into memory—but the echoes lingered in the mind for years to come.

In 1994, as the Regiment was amalgamated, the Band of The Gordon Highlanders was assimilated into the new Highland Band, a single band formed from the bands of all the Highland regiments.

SECTION 7

REGIMENTAL LIFE

THE life of a regiment when not on active service tended to follow formalised and even ritualised routines. Soldiering standards were kept as high as realistic training, commitment and professionalism could make them. The off-duty and social sides of regimental life were important in keeping interest and enthusiasm at the forefront of everyday life—and in avoiding boredom, complacency and a gradual erosion of standards. Rest and relaxation was achieved for officers, warrant officers and senior N.C.O.s in the respective officers and sergeants messes, while the soldiers could relax in their canteen. In overseas stations regimental canteens were run by civilian contractors who provided the facilities, food and drink and charged for them accordingly. The contractor paid a fee and often a percentage of his takings to the regiment, which used such funds to provide further amenities for the soldiers. In the 20th century many facilities were provided by the NAAFI (Navy, Army and Air Force Institute). Soldiers, and officers, enjoyed themselves as much as circumstances would allow. Sometimes their enjoyment got out of hand!

CHAPTER 15

REGIMENTAL LIFE

A Subaltern in Ireland, 1850

SUBALTERNS with time on their hands need no excuse to enjoy themselves, especially if they have money to spend. A posting in Ireland around 1850 seems to have afforded ample opportunity to enjoy local hospitality and endeavour to win money, at the card table or on the race track. Lieutenant John Cunningham, who joined the 92nd in 1846, appears to have enjoyed a good social life, as his diary (below) shows. It also shows that wine and spirits were enjoyed, not in small measures but on an almost industrial scale! Cunningham appears to have been a good judge of horseflesh and an accomplished jockey. The sums wagered are high at 1850 rates, which suggests that Cunningham was a man of means:

27th March—No parade. Get up at 10 o'ck and breakfast. Drive to Curraghmore by invitation from Lord Waterford. Stroll grounds for half an hour while he finishes a letter. He takes us round stables and shows us every animal in his possession, about one hundred horses in the most beautiful condition. Go to Race Course which is irrigated to make it soft or hard at pleasure. See about 30 horses gallop. Go round the Home Farm and see the stock which is first rate. Visit the Kennels, Deer Park and Fox Preserve and return to House for dinner at 4 o'ck. Six of us sit down to as nice a dinner as was ever cooked. Claret called for and bottle after bottle disappears. The Lord and some guests begin to show that the 12th bottle has taken effect. Make a match with him for £50 'Chronometer' and 'Regalia,' 14 st. each over the Whitefield Course in May, owners up. He tells us of all his feats and is wonderfully kind. Retire into the Library to see the Block he took by force from Eton when there at school. Consumed up to 11 o'ck. 21 bottles of Claret, 3 bot. Sherry, 1 bot. Port—25 bottles among six. Cup of Coffee and a glass of Liqueur and start for Carrick. Tattnall and myself only two sober, the rest mortal. One fellow gets four falls from his horse in a couple of minutes. Get home to Carrick at ½ p 12 o'ck after having passed a most delightful day. Perfectly sober.

2nd May—Up at 9 o'ck. Breakfast and start in Ross's phaeton to the race course. Get there by 12 o'ck. A tremendous crowd and a most lovely day. See the first race and then go into a tent and put on my things. Mount at 2 o'ck to run my match for £50 p.p. with Lord Waterford. Canter past the stand and get fairly started. Take the lead at starting but my horse refuses and is passed. Beautiful finish for last half mile and after a good deal of whipcord and persuaders win by a couple of lengths. Congratulations on victory from all ranks. Refuse £100 from Waterford for my horse. Start him an hour afterwards for the Welter Race, 13 st. 7 lbs. Fine start, I make a waiting race and win in a canter the others having all come to grief. The day's sport over, we all dine at Kilfane and have a glorious dance in the evening. Keep it up till 4 o'ck a.m. and after having spent a most agreeable day and night and won clear of all expenses £120, go home to Kilkenny and get to bed at 6 o'ck a.m.

It appears to have been no great problem to travel from Ireland back to London for short periods, as Cunningham's diary entry covering attendance at the Epsom Derby suggests:

29th May, Wednesday.—'The Derby Day.' Get up at 9 and go to the Club at 10 and breakfast. Go by steamer to the London Bridge Station and thence per rail to Epsom. The crowd something overpowering. A most glorious day and every promise of first rate sport. The race before the great event but no one pays it any attention. Davies makes himself known to all in the ring from his infernal voice. At 4 o'ck 24 horses come to the Post and after a beautiful start away they fly. Tremendous excitement as they near Tattenham Corner. 'Voltigeur' from the distance has the race in hand and wins very easily by several lengths. Pocket a good round sum on the race, always satisfactory. Smith, a brother officer of mine who came over with me drops a cool £1,200 Tremendous squash to meet the train. Drive from the Course to the railway with Lord Cantilupe (now departed this life). Get to town without any mishap at 8 o'ck. Have a Champagne dinner at the Club. Go to the Casino in the evening and then to a 'Hell.' Drop £50 in half the number of minutes. Have a good supper for my money at all events and go home to bed at ½ p 3 a.m.

Diary of John Cunningham, 92nd Regiment.

The Messes

Officers, warrant officers and senior N.C.O.s relaxed in their respective messes, which contained accommodation, eating and drinking facilities, and lounges. Management of staff was overseen by a senior N.C.O. Responsibility for running the mess lay with a committee led by the President of the Mess Committee (P.M.C.), with individuals holding responsibility as Mess Secretary, Food Member, Wines Member, Silver Member and House Member. If any member of the mess was dissatisfied with the running of the mess he could take it up personally with the respective Mess Member, or, particularly if he wished to make a point publicly, could enter his complaint in the Mess Complaints Book. The relevant Mess Member would take steps to rectify or explain the problem, writing his response in the book. These entries could often be very amusing, both in the complaint and the response:

What does the Orderly Officer do when he does not like his own food? Unlike the procedure in the Men's Dining Hall the Food Member is not invited to approach each officer in turn and ask if he is well satisfied with his meal. Food Members are hard to come by and cannot yet be regarded as expendable. Verbal warfare at the expense of any member of the Mess Committee is frowned upon. The Medical Authorities and Astrologers both agree that to eat whilst angry is bad for the digestion and, were the complaint not reduced to writing, the choicer *bon mots* would be lost for ever to posterity. That is why a book, suitably bound in leather with *Complaint Book* in bold gold lettering on its outer cover, is placed in the Officer's Mess. The book at present in use in the Mess was inaugurated by Lieutenant-Colonel A.M.B. Norman, then a Captain, on the 23rd of December, 1928. It may appear surprising that it has lasted so long, but it is a very large book. It contains the signatures of many very famous names in the Regiment. It is into this book that we are delve, to capture the thoughts of the officer, be he Saint or Subaltern, as he sits before the fire with his feet on the chimneypiece, dressed in Mess Kit, dreaming of ways to outwit the P.M.C.

The flies in the Mess at luncheon today were not only a direct menace to the health of officers, but proved quite definitely that adequate steps are not being taken to cope with them. No fewer than five died in my food. Cannot the Mess Committee deal with these pests. (Delhi. July 1929).

Which pests?

There was only one pen provided for the two writing tables in the Ante Room, and it was quite unfit to write with. May I suggest that the junior member of the Mess Committee occasionally attends to his duty. (Delhi. October 1929).

Ouch!

My ginger beer tonight was filled with five small pieces of broken glass which I nearly swallowed. I request that drastic action should be taken against those responsible for this gross negligence. (Landi Kotal. May 1931).

How can you be sure that it WAS negligence?

It took 20 minutes this evening before I was able to obtain a whisky soda. I found a new waiter on duty who was unaware where the barman lived. The latter had left no whisky in the bar and I found him asleep in bed at 6 p.m.! (January 1933).

No whisky left in the bar? No wonder he was in bed.

The oatcakes at supper absolutely ruined what would otherwise have been a most excellent meal. The Khansamah evidently submits them to some secret hardening process, the finished result of which compares most favourably with granite. A well cooked oatcake, if lifted by one extremity should just show signs of cracking, but not actually break. The present articles would bear considerable stress before showing any signs of weakening. (December, 1933).

Ah yes, but who wouldn't show signs of stress if lifted by an extremity?

The sauce provided with the fish at dinner has for some time past been like poor quality Target Paste. May the Khansamah be forbidden to co-operate with the Range Chowkidar in future, and also may a sauce less redolent of the stop butts and musketry season be provided please. (February, 1934).

I think the Weapon Training Officer may be the source of the trouble.

India Rubber cheese has yet again managed to displace the gorgonzola and insinuated itself into the dining room where it now holds complete sway. K.A. Gai stocks the following cheeses:—Stilton, Gorgonzola, Gruyere, Parmesan, Ordinary Dutch and Cheddar, Cream Cheese, Roquefort, Camembert. What about entering a team from these and ousting the India Rubber? (Peshawar. February, 1934).

A strong team, but would they answer to the whistle?

I should like to complain about the description of the chops this evening. They were called Lamb whereas Old Goat would be more accurate. (Haifa, September. 1934).

The Food Member has instructions to adapt his nomenclature to existing circumstances. An umbrella in sheep's clothing, perhaps?

There are only two billiard cues with tips on them and one of these is not straight. This interferes very considerably with the progress of the game. (June, 1937).

I should think so too. Who ever heard of trying to play billiards with a bent tip?

I wish to complain that the ration bread produced in the dining room to-day was quite disgusting. It was covered with blood (Human or animal I have not ascertained). I realise that in peace it is desirable to inure junior untried officers like myself to the rigours and horrors of breakfast, lunch or tea on the field of battle, but the training and manoeuvre areas are the place for that. The Officers Mess dining room is not. The Food Member should be forced to eat all such fouled bread and given nothing else in the Mess until the matter is improved. This is not the first time that we have been subjected to this martial diet. (June, 1938).

The Feast of the Passover?

At Argos yesterday the breadrolls issued as Officers haversack rations were so hard that they were rejected as fodder by a wide, though hungry, range of animal kingdom—by Officers, batmen, War Dogs, Cypriot donkeys and peasants. I do not know if the Padre ate his even. Would the P.M.C. please consider reverting to the attractive sandwiches issued for the sack of 'Polystipos'—or alternatively issuing one gas-check and one balistite cartridge per bread-roll, so that they can at least be used as a solid shot for the demolition of terrace walls being searched? For many lonely hours in the cordon I was sustained by the thought of the bar of chocolate so loudly promised by the P.M.C. for my breakfast. At first light I was heart-broken to find no chocolate in my nose-bag.

May my mess bill please be credited with the value of one bar? A return to the practice of using newspaper as wrappers for hard-boiled eggs would be appreciated, so that we have something to read with our breakfasts in the field.   (Platres, November 1956)

See the next but one above (June 1938). '. . . I quite realise that it is most desirable to inure officers to the rigours and horrors of breakfast, lunch or tea on the field of battle.' Obviously a case of maintenance of the aim.

T&S, October 1958.

School meals

Providing meals for children in school is commonplace nowadays. It was not always so, and it was not until the 1920s that provision of meals for schoolchildren was brought into law. The Gordon Highlanders provided school meals for their soldiers' children on their own regimental initiative:

Whenever I pass through Ardersier on my way to The Fort,[1] I pass the village school, and although my eyes and attention are concentrated on

---

1   Fort George, near Inverness.

the road I am conscious of considerable additions to the building as I first remember it: though I have never got out of my car to inspect, I am sure what I see out of the corner of my eye are kitchens and dining halls for the scholars. I wonder just how many remember the conditions obtaining in 1923–24 when The Gordon Highlanders were stationed at The Fort. In those days the children from the Married Quarters ran to school with their piece and that was all for the day, the distance not admitting of children returning home for dinner. My late wife realised how hard it was on the children and she organised a system to give the children a hot bowl of broth at mid-day, ably assisted by Mrs. Johnnie Pope. I just don't know who else was not roped into the scheme, Jim Sutherland, the QM, was the main supporter, and where the bones for the stock, the split peas and the barley came from, he alone knew. This had to be transported down from the barracks to the school in a vehicle known as the Maltese Cart, whose driver laid the fire and started it up in the bin stove provided for the purpose. So the scheme for giving our Regimental children a hot meal was initiated and invariably a child from the barracks would lead up a child from the local population who too had come a long distance.

I believe it would that this was the start of 'school meals', the first scheme of what is now at times a political issue.

I should mention that the married families whose children benefited from the scheme did give a small contribution to a fund to pay for the ingredients of the broth. On packing up to move to Bordon there was a small balance left in this fund and a most charming presentation was made by the families to my wife as a christening present to our daughter.

Lt Col R.A. Wolfe-Murray

T&S, February/March 1973.

Off Duty

Keeping soldiers out of trouble in off-duty hours has been a constant concern for officers from time immemorial. Some soldiers, commendably, tried to improve themselves through learning, and as the 19th century wore on it became common practice to provide a quiet room for study, or a place to sit and chat quietly and peaceably. For most soldiers, however, something more lively was desired, usually entailing the consumption of alcohol. When stationed near a town, taverns were frequented. As these were also used by the local population, there were occasional brawls between soldiers and locals, and this gave rise to the popular perception of the military as 'a brutal and licentious soldiery', an epithet that, with some basis in reality, was nevertheless a gross calumny on the majority of soldiers. In an attempt to minimise confrontations when alcohol was involved, canteens within barracks, where some control could be exercised, were established.

The canteen became a place where soldiers could relax and enjoy themselves within easy distance of their barrack-rooms. When brawls did erupt, the violence and damage was contained within the barracks, did not impinge upon the local population, and could be dealt with in a military environment. Canteens, particularly when regiments were overseas, were usually run by a local contractor, who sold food and drink, and in return paid a fee, part of which was based on a percentage of turnover, to the regiment employing him.

Discipline in the canteen was in the hands of a duty N.C.O. Apart from the Orderly Officer, whose task it was to ensure the canteen closed at the appointed hour, officers were never seen there. This was not class or rank distinction, but a very practical avoidance of contact between high-spirited soldiers in the grip of alcoholic fervour and officers. If a soldier, inflamed by drink, sought an argument or confrontation with an officer and struck him, he would be court-martialled; whereas a drunken misdemeanour that did not involve an officer could be settled by a good night's sleep or by a minor punishment. The Orderly Officer often had to tread a fine line in clearing the canteen. George MacDonald Fraser, who wrote a number of books based on his time as a subaltern in The Gordon Highlanders, recounts in *The General Danced at Dawn* how he was helped by an old soldier to clear the canteen. The old soldier, known as Wee Wullie, is described thus:

> Between his massively booted feet at one end, and the bonnet on his grizzled head at the other, there was about six and a half feet of muscular development that would have done credit to a mountain gorilla. On another occasion he did me a great service. I was orderly officer and was supervising the closing of the wet canteen. The joint was jumping and I hammered with my walking-stick on the bar and shouted, 'Last drinks. Time, gentlemen, please.' which was always good for a laugh. Most of them drank and went, but there was one bunch, East End Glaswegians with their bonnets pulled down over their eyes, who stayed at their table. Each man had about three pints in front of him; they had obviously been stocking up.
>
> 'Come on,' I said. 'Get it down you.'
>
> There were covert grins, and someone muttered about being entitled to finish their drinks—which strictly speaking they were. But they were trying it on: on the other hand, how does a subaltern move men who don't want to be moved? I know, personality. Try it sometime along the Springfield Road.
>
> 'You've got two minutes,' I said, and went to supervise the closing of the bar shutters. Two minutes later I looked across; they were still there, having a laugh and taking their time.

I hesitated; this was one of those moments when you can look very silly, or lose your reputation, or both. At that moment Wee Wullie, who had been finishing his pint in a corner, walked past and stopped to adjust his bonnet near me.

'Tak' wan o' them by the scruff o' the neck and heave 'im oot,' he said, staring at me, and then went out of the canteen.

It was astonishing advice. About the most awful crime an officer can commit is to lay hands on an other rank. Suppose one of them belted me? It could be one hell of a mess, and the scandal. Then one of them laughed again, loudly, and I strode across to the table, took the nearest man (the smallest one, incidentally) by the collar, and hauled him bodily to the door. He was too surprised to do anything; he was off-balance all the way until I dropped him just outside the doorway.

He was coming up, spitting oaths and murder, when Wee Wullie said out of the shadows at one side of the door:

'Jist you stay down, boy, or ye'll stay down for the night.'

I went into the canteen again. The rest were standing, staring. 'Out,' I said, like Burt Lancaster in the movies, and they went, leaving their pints. When I left the canteen Wee Wullie had disappeared.

The General Danced at Dawn. (1970) pp 69, 74–6.

Education

A letter was received from G.O.C., Northern Command, congratulating 1st Battalion, The Gordon Highlanders on being the only regiment in India with no uncertificated men in their unit. This record is unique and believed to be a record in the British Army. Educational Training is one of the most important subjects in the Battalion, and men are made to realize the benefits of a 2nd Class Certificate of Education. It means an increase in pay, a better chance of being employed or receiving a Vocational Training Course at the end of his service.

Educational statistics of the Battalion are as follows:

Total strength of Battalion.—917

1st Class Certificates	64	(6.98%)
2nd Class Certificates	559	(60.96 %)
3rd Class Certificates	294	(32.06%)

T&S, March 1934.

Fighting the Demon Drink

Soldiers and alcohol are synonymous in the minds of some civilians, and the picture of a 'brutal and licentious soldiery' inflamed by drink is one assiduously promoted in disapproving sections of the population. That this is an exaggeration is occasionally acknowledged publicly.

From the *Aldershot News* of May 7th, 1898.

Temperance has taken such a firm hold in the Gordon Highlanders that Mrs. Dick-Cunyngham, wife of the Officer Commanding, had the great satisfaction, the other evening, of presenting as many as sixty medals. In the battalion branch of the Army Temperance Association and the Bydand Lodge, which was formed during the Afghan War, there are together 170 members, and Lieutenant-Colonel Dick-Cunyngham, V.C., in an encouraging speech at the presentation, praised both Sergeant-Major Robertson and Sergeant Raffan for their excellent work in a good cause.

[Sergeant-Major Robertson was awarded the Victoria Cross in the first battle of the South African War.—Ed.]

T&S, June 1938.

Thespians

Appearing on stage is not normally associated with the profession of soldiering, but a moment's reflection will suggest that in barracks and outposts in Britain and throughout its erstwhile Empire soldiers had to look to themselves for entertainment. Amateur theatricals were the rule rather than the exception in most military stations. The Gordon Highlanders were no exception and from time to time accounts of officers and soldiers 'treading the boards' appear.

Stationed in Cairo after Tel-El-Kebir, and before they set out on the Nile Expedition in the abortive attempt to relieve Khartoum, the men of the 1st Battalion 'enjoyed' themselves in Cairo. Much of their entertainment was self-generated:

The barrack square was large enough for cricket and football, though the ground was stony and hard. One of the difficulties was to provide attractions to counter the temptations of the drink shops in the town, where the most poisonous liquor was sold—poisonous in the literal sense! Happily, Lieut. Downman,[2] who had been at the Depot during the war, joined the Battalion, and in him we had an expert in the organization of theatricals and sing-songs. The old Hall of Justice at the back of the Bijou Palace was handed over to the garrison, and developed into a most excellent theatre. It had been unused for ages, and when handed over no key could be found. Slade Thomson and the doctor were lowered from a skylight, and, after some difficulty, unfastened the rusty bolts. They were

2 G.T.F. Downman, who went on to command the 1st Battalion, and was killed at Magersfontein in 1899.

wearing flannels, and on emerging were black to the knees with a heaving mass of the largest Egyptian flea.

The floor was several inches deep in dust and fleas! Willing hands, aided by scrubbers, disinfectants, whitewash and paint, soon had the place clean, the old cells providing excellent dressing-rooms, and the pioneers ran up a stage large enough for a big cast. Fortunate, too, we were in having a real artist in Major Woodward to undertake the scenery.

Downman collected talent from the units in the Citadel. The Camerons produced several good actors and singers, one especially, who had studied elocution, was a first-rate amateur actor. He had one failing—the canteen. One night at the dress rehearsal for *The Ticket of Leave Man*, in which he played the lead, he arrived 'blind to the world.' Downman locked him up in one of the cell dressing-rooms, wrote to his company officer to get him a pass, and in the cell he stayed until next evening, when, after a cup of weak tea, he played his part to perfection.

The Gordons had some really good performers—Sergeant-Major and Mrs. Skelly, whose performances in *The Blossoms of Churnington Green* always brought down the house; Slade Thomson, who introduced *The Boys of the Old Brigade*, then a novelty, to Cairo; Boy Maundy, who stood about four feet nothing and always got an encore.

And lastly, Private Bishop, a first-class comic and a great draw, who had been on a music hall stage in Scotland. He brought a tragic note into our usually successful performances.

To Cairo came in the winter of 1883–84 Captain Speedy, Abyssinian traveller, who had been tutor to Prince Alamayu, son and heir of Theodore, King of Abyssinia. Cairo was at the height of its season, and people were anxious that Speedy should lecture on his experiences. It was to take place in the Citadel theatre, and was in three parts, the interval between the first and second being filled by a song by one of our officers, and that between the second and third by a comic song by Private Bishop. Now our CO of that day[3] had not only no spark of humour, but a holy fear of 'Brass Hats.' The hall was packed. The elite of Cairo society and the gilded staff in the stalls, and men of the Gordons, Camerons, etc. at the back, to whom Bishop and his songs were well known. All went well until Bishop appeared. He started with *When Noah hung out in the Ark*, quite harmless, even if not sung in London drawing-rooms. The men, who of course formed the bulk of the audience, encored him again and again, and after he had bowed several times the music struck up and he launched out on a song called *I'm a deserter from the Salvation Army*, which described the advances of a lady Captain to the singer. Many ladies in the audience

---

3   Lt-Col D. Hammill.

had to go outside for a breath of fresh air, and the Colonel's face was a study. But the men simply would not let Bishop go. The curtain was lowered time and again, still they stamped and shouted, and finally Bishop reappeared and sang, *Those old fatigue Trews*, of which I cannot venture to give an adequate description. Suffice it to say that the house was cleared of high society, who only trickled back when Captain Speedy was well into the third part of his lecture.

A champagne supper and dance in the officers' mess did not entirely dispel the effects of Bishop's efforts. Poor Downman, as manager of the theatre, was for orderly room next day, when it appeared that the most heinous part of the offence was that the singer had appeared dressed in the livery of the officers' mess!

General Sir Nevil Macready.

T&S, January 1933.

Not every use of the theatre in Cairo was attributable to artistic temperament or theatrical ability:

The 1st Gordons after Tel-el-Kebir marched with Sir Archibald Alison to Tantah and thence to Cairo, where they camped, with the rest of the brigade, on the present Cairo racecourse, and the Gordons and Camerons were soon afterwards sent to the Citadel, where they lived together for two years. The cholera broke out in 1883, and the Gordons were left on duty in Cairo. One hot summer day an officer in the regiment was on 'main guard' in Cairo. The guard-room was a little theatre in the Esbikieh quarter, and many a romp has taken place on its empty stage and over its deserted seats and stalls. The officer had gone to bed, and was vainly attempting to defeat the mosquitoes, when a knock at his door heralded the sergeant of the guard with the information that the black servant of the guard-room had suddenly succumbed to an attack of cholera.

'And what have you done with the body?' quoth the officer.

'Weel, sir,' replied the sergeant, 'I just pet him in the formaist row o' benches. He'll do fine there for the night.' Probably so gruesome an object had seldom been seen in the stalls of any theatre.

T&S, February/March 1970.

Soldiers can always be found who will jump at the opportunity to perform in front of an audience, and Gordon Highlanders were no exception. At times, however, over-enthusiasm got in the way, leading to performances that were unscheduled and unrehearsed:

A performance by two of 'our talented amateurs' was a howling success, though not quite in the way they intended. The scene was an incident in the recently-finished Zulu War. It had been produced at home on the music hall stage with great success. One of the performers acted as a sentry on the camp while his comrades were, presumably, out having a romp with 'Fuzzy-Wuzzy.' In his chorus, he declares, 'Here upon guard am I, willing to do or die,' and while rendering the last verse the other performer, acting the Zulu, appears from behind a rock to rush him. The black warrior was in the most approved fighting kit—for a Zulu—absolutely naked except for a breech clout, armed with shield and assegai. His face and body was as black as burnt cork could make it; his head adorned with the 'ring' and feathered headdress. He was, indeed, a fearsome sight, and 'put the wind up' the sentry; so much so, that instead of firing the blank cartridge in his rifle over his enemy's head, he blazed straight at him, and filled his body and face with powder grains, fortunately without touching his eyes. Annoyed—as he had every right to be, the Zulu warrior closed and forthwith began a terrific struggle in which real blows were heftily exchanged, and the fight continued until one of the combatants—the Zulu—was knocked clean off the stage into the laps of the front row of the audience. Dressed as he was, after his fight, he made 'quite a hit' among the officers and others who broke his fall. Tableau—Curtain and 'howls for the Provost Sergeant.'

W. H. Patterson.

T&S, September 1925.

Between the First and Second Wars Regular and Territorial battalions formed concert parties which performed for their battalions, and also in the local community. Although totally amateur, these performances frequently reached almost professional standards. The concert party of the 2nd Battalion called itself the Dandy Bees, a play on the regimental motto, *Bydand*.

In the 1950s Ronnie Hilton was a popular singer whose career coincided with the onset of rock'n'roll in the ballad-dominated hit parade. But for a time Hilton was a star, with nine top 20 hits between 1954 and 1957, the transitional era between 78 and 45 rpm records. Not many people knew that at one time he had been a Gordon Highlander. He gave a résumé of his military career in response to a letter from Major M.H. Burge in 1967:

Dear Major Burge,

Very many thanks for your letter of the 26th April. I am delighted that you enjoyed my recent television show so much, in '*The Good Old Days*'.

I have no objection to you using something about me, in your regimental magazine. I should be most honoured.

First however, I should tell you that of the five years which I served in the Army, only the last eighteen months were with the Gordon Highlanders, but I shall start from the beginning.

I joined the Army in 1942, at sixteen having stated a falsehood regarding my age, but this came to light later. I went into the Cameron Highlanders at Fort George, and was then transferred to the 10th H.L.I, in the 15th Scottish Div. I went with them to France eight days after D Day. During the action in Normandy it was discovered, through one of my brothers being wounded, that I was not of age to be in action and was sent back to the U.K. However, within two months I was back in action, now being of age, and was posted to the 6th H.L.I, in the 52nd Mountain Div., with whom I served until just after the end of the War. About Christmas time, 1946, I was transferred to 1st Gordons, at Essen in Germany, where I was for about the first six months provost corporal in the Regimental Police and then was put on the staff of the Officers Mess, mostly in charge of the bar. This is probably where I obtained my drinking education.

I was demobbed from the Gordons in June 1947 and incidentally, did a couple of songs on occasion, with the regimental band on their visits to our Battalion in Germany.

You will gather from all this therefore, that I did not serve with the Second Batt.

I am afraid that the only photograph available is one which I have enclosed from a magazine, but I doubt if this will reproduce, plus, a current give-away photograph, which may be of some use.

I would very much appreciate your sending me a copy of the magazine, when it is published.

Thank you for your interest and you may be pleased to know, since the T.V. show I received many requests during my cabaret performances to sing '*A Gordon for me*'.

Yours very sincerely,

Ronnie Hilton.

T&S, July 1967.

The Gordons could even boast a future Hollywood star in their ranks, albeit for a short time. Stewart Granger, the well-known film actor with a Scottish background, enlisted in The Gordon Highlanders at the start of the Second War, but transferred to The Black Watch when commissioned.

Film stars

Not everyone gets the opportunity to take part in a cinema production seen around the world, but Stewart Granger was not the only Gordon Highlander to appear on the large screen. The pipes of the 1st Battalion, The Gordon Highlanders achieved that distinction when they played their forebears at the *Battle of Waterloo* in the film named after the battle:

One day in 1968 Captain Nigel Oxley, on holiday in Elba, was sitting in a restaurant with his wife when a man came up to him and said, 'Don't I know you? You're a Gordon Highlander, aren't you?' He was the British Military Attaché in Rome, who had met Nigel Oxley before, and he had an unusual proposition. Dino de Laurentiis, the film producer, was making a film about Waterloo, and wanted it to be as authentic as possible. The Gordons were at Waterloo. Would they be interested in sending a party for two weeks in Rome, and two months in Russia, where the outdoor battle scenes would be filmed?

'Interested?' replied Captain Oxley. 'I should think so! We'll give you the whole Battalion! And the Scots Greys too—they were at Waterloo. Do you think they'd want the Greys as well?'

On his return to Minden Captain Oxley put the request to the Commanding Officer (Lieutenant-Colonel J Neish). Receiving an encouraging response he then sent off a signal to the Ministry of Defence, informing them that 1st Gordons would be spending a month in Italy and two months in Russia the following year. The reply came back almost before the ink was dry on the original signal. Under no circumstances was anybody to go to Russia, and it was out of the question for a whole battalion to be out of BAOR on a commercial venture. Eventually however, agreement was reached that a party of 50 Gordon Highlanders could take part in filming in Italy.

In March 1969 the Drums and Pipes, with 15 dancers, set off for Rome under Captain Oxley. On arrival at its hotel, an eager and solicitous manager welcomed them, hoped they would enjoy their stay and would not break up his hotel!

The embryo actors, fitted out in period uniforms, made a film to demonstrate how to march and counter-march to the pipes. This was sent to Russia, where hundreds of extras made up the respective armies, in order, as Pipe Major Joe Kerr commented, 'tae teach the MacIvans tae march'. The Drums and Pipes recorded the pipe tunes to be played in the film, including some that many in the Band had never played before. They were learned during the lunch break and recorded that afternoon. The Band drew the line, however, when asked to sing to pipes accompaniment, and refused, much to the Director's chagrin. He reluctantly removed from the score what he had thought was a traditional Highland activity.

The most demanding task was the Highland dancing scenes at the Duchess of Richmond's ball on the eve of Quatre Bras. Five teams danced the 'Argyll Broadswords' in the middle of the Ballroom, surrounded by hosts of pretty girls and Italian extras playing British officers. Hemming in the dancers were cameras, microphones, arc lights, and 3,000 candles, all of which produced an intense heat that made dancing exhausting. The dance was repeated no less than 43 times in one day so that different shots could be taken from a variety of angles. The film 'rushes' were viewed afterwards through the critical eyes of Drum Major Hall and Pipe Major Kerr, both of whom agreed that the dancing instruction and practice under the tutelage of Sergeants R Harman and R Harrop had been eminently successful.

There was an awkward moment when the Producer included one of the extras, a six foot four inch New Zealander, Roger Green, as the centre-piece of the dance scene. As Green's only previous experience of Highland dancing appeared to have been taking part in an impromptu sixteensome at a Newtonmore *ceilidh* the year before there was some concern among the real dancers, but Pipe Major Kerr agreed to try to teach him the steps. It soon became clear that Green's talents lay not on the dance floor, and his presence threatened to turn the scene into catastrophe The Pipe Major refused to have him in the set; the Producer insisted that he should appear. Eventually a compromise was reached, with the Gordons doing the dancing, interspersed with close-ups of the upper half of Green's body as he hopped from leg to leg. Honour was satisfied when a full length shot of Green was included as the dancers marched out of the Ballroom.

During the filming of the battle the pipers worked long hours to provide the footage for the few seconds they would be on the screen. One morning, after being kept waiting for hours while camera angles were tested and changed, they were rehearsed well into the lunch break until they were finally told that the next time would be a 'take'. Their protests of malnutrition and starvation were dismissed and they were told to get on with it. Off they marched to their cue positions, stomachs rumbling in time with the drumbeat.

The Jock has his own way of making a point. 'Action!' cried the Director. Cannon roared, smoke billowed, Colours fluttered in the breeze and the pipers of the 92nd, in the dress of 1815, swept over the brow of the hill playing *Arrivaderci Roma*, a popular Italian song of the 1950s. 'Cut!' screamed the Director, tearing at his hair. 'Okay wise guys, go get your lunch, and next time let's have a different tune!'

When the battle scenes were being filmed Captain Oxley pointed out to the Director that all the extra Gordons in the party had their kilts with them, and, fitted out with period costumes, could fill out the infantry awaiting the French charge. The suggestion was received enthusiastically, and it was agreed that the footage of the Regiment waiting in line would consist of real Gordons on the right wing and Italian extras on the left.

When filming started the battle effects were set off. Explosions filled the air, clods of earth shot upwards, and smoke billowed across the field.

At the first explosion the extras shrieked in terror, turned and fled the battlefield to their bus. The Director had a frantic dialogue with their spokesman and eventually they agreed to return.

This time the deployment was changed. The Gordons would form the front rank with the extras in the rear. As a bonus, they would be allowed to hold the Colours! The special effects men replaced their explosives and waited. 'Action!' cried the Director. Once again earth flew into the air and the smoke generators pumped out great drifting clouds of smoke, and once again the extras, screaming in terror, fled to the safety of their bus, this time streaming the Colours behind them! The Gordons standing fast on the 'battlefield' grudgingly admitted that the effects were realistic, not least Pipe Major Kerr, whose false moustache was blown off![4]

The Jocks enjoyed the luxury of their hotel, although there were moments when Captain Oxley had to act as a conciliatory go-between, such as when he was woken by the manager at three in the morning to be told that a group of Jocks returning from a night out had paid the taxi with Embassy cigarette coupons, and what was he going to do about it? 'Just you pay it, and I'll sort it out in the morning.' was the sleepy reply.

Although the hotel had a fine restaurant, Italian cooking did not always go down too well with the Jocks. There was a mutiny on the day when the hotel produced a very appetising chicken dish, but one smothered in garlic. To a man the Jocks downed utensils and refused to eat 'this foreign muck'. Captain Oxley mollified the stricken manager, telling him 'Steak, egg and chips. That's what to give them. I'll tell them that's on the menu tonight, and that'll keep them quiet.'

That evening the Gordons trooped into the Dining Room looking forward to a meal they could recognise, to be confronted by thin strips of leathery meat, potato crisps and a boiled egg. Once again Captain Oxley stepped into the breach. 'If you really don't want your hotel broken up, you should get the menu right. I can hold them for half an hour—after that you're on your own!' Within half an hour plates of succulent steak, with fried egg on top, and piles of chips were served to the starving Jocks.

The Life of a Regiment, Volume VII, pp 6–9.

Heard in Church

The Church of St Andrew in a certain fort stands in its own grounds, thickly wooded, in the centre of which are two large ponds. The church is infested with mosquitos.

---

[4] The film, while spectacular, was inaccurate in some historical portrayals. Scenes of the pipe band on the battlefield were anachronistic. Pipers were attached to companies, and played on their own, and certainly did not play accompanied by drums.

The Gordon Highlanders had just relieved an English regiment in the fort, and on the first Sunday after their arrival four hundred Gordon Highlanders were marched to a parade service in the church. The most optimistic mosquito had never in its dreams imagined such a succulent banquet as that afforded by the four hundred kilted Highlanders, and made the fullest use of this unique opportunity. Soon the church was resounding with the smacks of hands on bare thighs and knees as the men endeavoured to destroy a few of their tormentors. The Minister, hearing the loud clapping, but entirely misapprehended in its purport, paused in his sermon, and said, 'My brethren, it is verra gratifying to a minister of the Word of God to meet with approbation of his hearers; but, I bid you all to remember that applause is strictly oot o' place in the Hoose o' God.'

T&S, November 1925.

Heard in the Married Quarters

Mrs McClusky will gie they Drumkilloch loons something for pittin' dirt an' stanes on her verandah.

Nae doot it costs Mrs Green a tidy penny for sape aifter her twa loons hae been fishin' in the dust bin a' day.

If some fouk had as much siller as they hae swank, there wad be nae need for their men to be in the sodgers.

T&S, November 1925.

The Regimental Dinner

The Gordon Highlanders have played their part in shaping the destiny of continents. The following account shows how, in a very small way and at very short notice, The Gordon Highlanders helped to ensure the smooth running of a World Economic Conference!

The Regimental Dinner was held in the Grosvenor House Hotel on Monday, June 12th, 1933, and a large number of officers attended. It so happened that a dinner was being given the same night to the delegates attending the World Economic Conference, and, on hearing this, Sir Ian Hamilton immediately sent a message through to the Prime Minister, who was presiding at the dinner to the delegates, to ask if they would care to hear the Pipers who had been playing at the Regimental Dinner.

The Prime Minister replied that he would very much like to hear them, and the Pipers proceeded to play a set round the tables in the delegates' dining-room.

At the opening of the new Gordon Highlanders depot at Bridge of Don in 1935 Sir Ian Hamilton referred to this event:

At the World Economic Conference in London the 500 delegates, dining in the Dorchester Hotel, were regaled by the pipers of the Gordons, who, without warning, suddenly entered and marched round the banqueting hall playing *Cock o' the North*.

For a moment the delegates were terror-stricken, thinking that massacre was about to commence, and in the relief of discovering that this was an entertainment, became so amenable to the arguments of our Prime Minister that he wrote their Colonel a letter praising the Gordons' pipers for the excellent service they had rendered!

My dear Sir Ian,

I cannot tell you how pleased I am that you suggested those Pipers last night and how grateful everybody is to them for the contribution they made to our enjoyment. We did not get nearly enough of them, but the hour had got rather late and we had, as you will have seen in the newspapers this morning, a meeting of the Cabinet after we finished dinner.

Is there any way in which you can convey my personal thanks to them for coming in? They made a very brave show.

With kindest regards,

Believe me,

Yours very sincerely,

J. Ramsay MacDonald.

T&S, July 1933, December 1935.

Keeping Track of Equipment

In 1948 Lieutenant John Durbin was responsible for Bren gun carriers in the 1st Battalion. Before he took over the post, when a number of carriers had broken down and were off the road, the Gordons had borrowed a carrier from a neighbouring unit. One by one the errant carriers were repaired and returned to duty, and the number of working vehicles increased until the full establishment was achieved. The neighbouring unit did not seem to want its carrier back and it was retained as a useful backup if one of the Gordons' carriers again malfunctioned {a not unusual event!). In the course of time the extra carrier was taken for granted, its origin was forgotten and it went unnoticed in the crowded vehicle compound.

The time came when the annual Administrative Inspection came round. The Motor Transport (MT) Sergeant pointed out to Lieutenant Durbin that they appeared to have an extra Bren gun carrier, and that, to an Inspecting Officer, one item too many was just as bad as one too few, and would inevitably lead to some embarrassing questions. They would have to dispose of it. There was a lengthy discussion and investigation, but no one seemed to know where the carrier had come from. 'We'll just have to get rid of it.' said

Lieutenant Durbin, and, in a clandestine night operation, the carrier was taken to a cliff overlooking a deep lake. With furtive glances over their shoulders to ensure that no-one could see them, the carrier was pushed by John Durbin and the MT Sergeant to the edge of the cliff. With eerie mechanical groans, as if the machine knew what was coming, it was dispatched over the cliff, plunging down to the waiting waters, into whose murky depths it disappeared with an awe-inspiring splash that sent a column of water almost as high as the intrepid watchers. In due course the MT officer of the neighbouring unit turned up and said to Lieutenant Durbin, 'We lent you one of our Bren carriers some time ago. With our Admin Inspection coming up we need it to make up our numbers. Can we have it back please!'

Major J.T.D. Durbin (narrated to author).

Regimental Pride

> A Gordon for me, a Gordon for me,
> If ye're no a Gordon ye're nae use to me.
> The Black Watch are braw, the Seaforths and a'
> But the cocky wee Gordon's the pride o' them a'.

The song is familiar to all Scots. The Gordons adopted it, and it became a part of the Regimental Band repertoire. The last line summed them up. Every Scottish regiment believed itself better than the others; as for English, Welsh and Irish regiments, good though they might be, they were not Scottish! This common conceit did no harm, but played a part in enabling regiments to reach and maintain the highest standards. The 'cocky wee Gordons' certainly had a 'guid conceit o' themsel's' as the following illustrate:

> A certain Grenadier, whose overnight potations and morning dram, though they prevented his being allowed to take his place in the ranks, did not make him forget that *esprit de corps* which, drunk or sober, is ever present in a Gordon Highlander—'I ken fine,' he said, 'I'm naething but a drucken grenadier, but I wad rayther be a grenadier o' the 92nd than Gustavus Adolphus, King o' Sweden.'

The Life of a Regiment, Volume II, p 43.

> For the Coronation of King George VI troops from many regiments, British, Commonwealth and Empire, were called to London. Among them was a detachment of 1st Gordons, who bore themselves with proper pride. Asked what 'mob' he belonged to one private made the crushing retort: 'I dinna belong to any mob. I'm a Gordon Highlander.'

The Life of a Regiment, Volume V, p 24.

The ultimate expression of regimental pride, however, is seen in the contemptuous retort of the last survivor of the small group of Gordons who fought against overwhelming odds at the ambush of the train at Naboomspruit in 1901 when asked by the Boers why they had not surrendered. 'Why, man, we are the Gordon Highlanders.'[5]

Sport

The Gordon Highlanders have a proud sporting history, and for two centuries Regimental teams featured prominently in garrison and formation competitions around the world. Many were the trophies won, and ancient photographs show teams of Gordons in the languid posture adopted in the rigidly posed photographs of the day, with everyone but the team captain staring in every direction except at the camera. Silverware of every description can be seen, cups, shields, bowls, statuettes and an assortment of individually manufactured trophies.

When the Gordons won the Army Football Cup

The years 1897–98 saw the star of the Gordon Highlanders high in national esteem. The deeds of the 1st Battalion on the Indian Frontier chased by irate natives in 1897 had stirred the nation deeply to the realization of the fighting qualities of the Regiment, and it was left to the 2nd Battalion to prove that in the realms of sport the same fighting qualities predominated.

On the football field they proved that the 'Gordons hae the guidin' o't,' carrying all before them. In the Army Cup they reached the final, and won or reached the final of several others, notably the Hampshire Senior Cup, in which they were beaten by Southampton St. Mary's, a professional side now known as Southampton F.C. The Gordons' success was due to Lieut. Outhwaite (Jacky Outhwaite, beloved by the men of the Regiment). He was in charge of the team, and spent much time and money guiding its efforts to success. He died of enteric fever the following year in Umballa, to the sorrow of all ranks.

This regimental team was probably the best looked-after in the history of Army football in those days. They had a private trainer, who had been with Preston North End. They lived in a separate barrack room, and their messing was considerably augmented. Prior to the Army Cup final, the team were taken to London to the final of the English Cup. It was only natural that the team made every endeavour to bring the coveted Army Cup to the Regiment. Even in those days the English League clubs were on the look-out for talent, and it was not surprising that two of the team

---

5   See Volume IX, Chapter 17.

were bought out of the Army. To their lasting credit they refused to leave until the final had been played.

The writer joined the 2nd Battalion on Good Friday, 1898, with a draft from the Depot, in good time to participate in the excitement. Easter was the period of attachment of the Volunteer units, and our friends the London Scottish were with the Battalion. What pals the 'lads in hodden grey' were!

What a fine battalion the 92nd was—led by that handsome martinet (a just one), Col. Dick-Cunyngham, V.C., known to the men as 'Dick,' with Sergt.-Major W. Robertson, who was to receive the Cross later in South Africa. We were brigaded with the Loyal North Lancashire Regiment, Scottish Rifles, King's Royal Rifles, and the Dublin Fusiliers (the dear old 'Dubs'). The regiments got on well together, but the greatest friendship existed between the 'Dubs' and the Gordons.

Easter Monday dawned with a glorious morning, and excitement reached fever-point as the hour drew near. A hurried mid-day meal and then off to the Army Athletic Ground. The field was roped off and surrounded by Army Service Corps wagons, forming a grandstand all around the ground. All the troops in Aldershot were there in the vast crowd, and a fair proportion of civilians were mingled, as many old soldiers came down from London to witness the Army Cup final.

The team we had the honour of opposing was the Royal Artillery from Portsmouth, which had for some years been the strongest in the Army, and had won the cup in a previous year. They were hot favourites, and outside the Regiment not many favoured our chances. The teams lined up and the game commenced. It was a hard, fast game, with the Gordons scoring twice in the second half, victors by 2–0

At the finish pandemonium broke loose, the victory being popular in Aldershot; and while the presentation of cup and medals was being made, the pipe and brass bands of the Regiment were hurriedly summoned from across the Queen's Parade. Then with the whole Regiment, reinforced by the North Camp troops, surging around, the team were carried shoulder-high back to barracks. At their head, shoulder-high and carrying the cup, was Jackie Outhwaite, tears streaming down his cheeks. At Malplaquet Barracks, the procession, played all the way by the bands, went straight to the Officers Mess, where the cup was filled in traditional style, the troops cheering to the echo.[6]

Later, Lieut. Outhwaite walked down the lines, exhibiting the cup and telling one and all that it was the proudest day of his life. His delight was unbounded and rightly so, as it was to him in great measure that the

---

6 In 1901 3rd Gordons won the Aldershot Football Cup, beating the Highland Light Infantry, who had won the Army Cup that year.

victory was due. All Gordons were happy, as he was the type of officer to whom soldiers gave of their best.

The final scene of this memorable day took place in the evening, when the London Scottish took their departure. The Gordons lined the square as the Scottish paraded, and before marching off the latter were called to attention and gave three cheers for the Gordon Highlanders. These were replied to with tremendous enthusiasm by the 92nd, and there can be little doubt that the mutual friendship was greatly cemented.

T&S, January 1931.

Victory on the sporting field is sweet, especially when it is the result of arduous training and great effort, but there were occasions when the Gordons enjoyed the fruits of victory through less traditional methods. The following account of sporting activities in the 1960s displays a less competitive approach than some, but is an example of initiative and a desire to enjoy life to the full. The events are related by Captain R.M. Kinghorn and cover his time with the 1st Battalion in Kenya and as a training subaltern at the Highland Brigade Depot, Bridge of Don:

The East Africa Command Swimming Championships

One day I was called into the Commanding Officer's office where Charles Napier[7] told me that the Battalion had been instructed to enter a team in the East Africa Command Swimming Championships in Nairobi. As I could swim I was to put together a team to enter in the relay. We'd have to do the butterfly stroke, the breast stroke, the back stroke, and the last lap was freestyle, which invariably meant the crawl. Organising the team and taking part in the Championships seemed an ideal opportunity to get away from the routine in camp, and I accepted readily—not that there was any option!

I got the Pay Sergeant because he seemed pretty competent in the pool, and also asked Robin Fawcus. 'I'll do the breast stroke!' Fawcus announced, which was to be expected as it was the only stroke he knew and he could do it without getting his hair wet. I thought I'd get David Hendry in the team as he'd been confined to camp for weeks and I thought he could do with a break. He was always in trouble of some sort, and once you fell foul of the Adjutant[8] it was almost impossible to get off the Orderly Officer roster, because you were bound to miss something, or make some mistake that earned you another dozen duties. David was desperate to get to Nairobi where he could chat up the girls, and he jumped at the offer. 'Can you swim?' I asked him. 'Is that essential?' he replied.

---

7   Lt-Col B.C.A. Napier.
8   Capt P.W. Graham.

As the event was only a week away I'd have only one opportunity to practise, and accordingly I organised transport to take us to Lanet, where there was a swimming pool. We set off in great spirits, as was the norm whenever we had a chance to get out of camp. We arrived at Lanet to find that the pool had been emptied, so we retired to the bar of the Rift Valley Sports Club at Nakuru and spent the rest of the day enjoying ourselves— David Hendry chatting up any girls who came past. We got back to camp late at night and sneaked in to avoid the Adjutant's beady eye.

When we fronted up at the Championships I thought we'd better decide who' would swim each leg. Fawcus bagged the breast stroke. The Pay Sergeant agreed to do the butterfly as he'd seen it done and reckoned he could get the hang of it. I asked David Hendry to do the back stroke and he agreed. 'Front or back, it's all the same to me.'

When the race began the Pay Sergeant launched into the butterfly. It was most unorthodox, but it could, I suppose, be described as a 'butterfly' stroke. His arms were OK and he was pretty powerful, but his legs were all over the place using an ever-changing variety of movements to propel him along while his hips undulated in what he thought was the approved style. He got to the end and handed over to Fawcus, who set off at his slow, steady breast stroke, holding his own, but little more—but more importantly, keeping his hair dry. He eventually reached the handover point and David Hendry pushed off for the backstroke. It was pretty obvious that it was the first time he'd ever tried it, and he spent most of the length under water, his arms appearing above the surface in a frantic threshing and the white blob of his gasping face showing below. He came up for air a couple of times and ploughed on (he coughed up water for about three days after that!) and at last came to the end where I was waiting, all alone as all the other teams were in the water 10–15 yards ahead. I went in to the water and almost drowned because I was laughing so much at Hendry that I took in a lungful of water, but I managed to get going and struck out after the others. It was just as well that the other teams, although better organised than the Gordons, were no better at swimming, and there were no real competitors in that last lap. I managed to overhaul them and touched first, to give the Gordons a thoroughly underserved first place.

When I went up to receive the Cup, the GOC, General Dick Goodwin, remarked dryly, 'An interesting team you've got there, Roddy!' to which I replied, 'Ah yes General—it's all in the training!'

Orienteering

It was when I was at the Depot at Bridge of Don as a training subaltern that the Commanding Officer, John Davie, called me to his office. John Davie was a splendid man and a good commanding officer, but he could be pretty hard on you if you cocked up. He had this habit of shaking his left fist up and down when he was tearing a strip off you, so my first words to the Adjutant, Euan Gordon, were 'How's his hand?'

'It's all right, Roddy, he's quite calm.' came the reply. 'Just go on in.'

I went in and saluted. John Davie looked at me. 'Ah, Roddy. D'you know what Orienteering is?' I replied that I'd heard of it and didn't it involve running around with compasses and maps? Orienteering was a relatively new sport, imported from Scandinavia and taken up eagerly by many civilian clubs. Someone in the Army had decided that this was an Army-type activity—maps and compasses, and finding your way over the countryside—bread and butter to soldiers!

'Scottish Command has organised an Army orienteering competition,' said John Davie, 'and we're going to enter. I want you to put together a team, train it, and take part.' This was a not unusual command for a subaltern, and I went away to find out what I could about the sport. The top civilian clubs had taken to it, and used special lightweight compasses and 1:5,000 or even 1:2,500 maps. We had the standard issue 'compass prismatic', an excellent compass for soldiers, but bulky and heavy compared to the civilian versions; and we used the 1:63,360 (one inch to the mile) map which was the standard military map in those days.

I couldn't get any adult recruits for the team as they had a quick turnover and were at a critical stage in their recruit training. We did have junior soldiers, however, who spent up to two years at the Depot before coming of age to join the Battalion, and I got three of these. Training was a nightmare—they got lost every time they went out and I spent most of my time trying to find them. I decided on a simple plan. When we turned up for the Scottish Command competition in Perthshire I got the team together and briefed them. Runners were sent off individually, not as a team, and not in succession. The order was drawn out of a hat, and your team could set off say, 13th, 21st, 58th and 70th. I arranged that I would set off last, and I said to the team 'You see that silver birch in the distance? I want you to set off and run to it, then wait until I get there.'

Which they did. They all set off in their appointed order and got to the tree, where they waited. When I got there, in typical Jock fashion they were all asleep. I woke them up and led them around the course, from check point to check point, where they got their cards stamped. All the other teams had their members running individually, and inevitably some in each team had difficulty finding some check point or another. We, on the other hand, went round as a group, and eventually reached the finishing line together, where we found that ours was the first team to get home complete. Accordingly, we won the first Scottish Command Orienteering Competition!

John Davie was delighted! So delighted that he called me back into his office a few weeks later and told me that Scottish Command wanted some Army teams to enter in the Scottish National Orienteering Championships, and that as we were the Scottish Command Champions we were to represent the Army!

Never break a winning formula, and we repeated the tactics for the Scottish Championships. There wasn't a silver birch, but I found another landmark, and we went round the course in the same manner. We didn't win, but came third, which was highly creditable in the face of highly skilled and experienced civilian teams. The GOC was delighted, John Davie was delighted, and we all felt pretty good, although I hoped we wouldn't be rumbled for our unorthodox and probably illegal method.

The sting in the tail came some time later when an international orienteering competition was to be held in Belgium, and on the basis of my 'training' of the Scottish Command Champions I was invited to compete as an individual. I was pretty chuffed at this chance to get to Belgium and I went to John Davie to get his approval.

'What? You want time off to go running about Belgium with a compass and map? Your job is to train recruits. Of course you can't go!'

Captain R.M. Kinghorn (narrated to author).

Subalterns on the loose

In 1963 the Gordons carried out a successful operation in Swaziland that settled a situation that had threatened to escalate into a major political crisis sparking off widespread violence and destruction, with the likelihood of heavy loss of life. The operation was carried out by a well-trained, well-led and well-motivated Battalion, supremely confident in its own ability to confront and deal with unfamiliar situations in a strange country.

The impression gained by outsiders looking at a successful operation usually belied the turmoil and minor crises that attended both the routine and the emergency activities of the Battalion. The following account is a transcription of an after-dinner conversation conducted by, among others, Captain R.M. Kinghorn (Roddy Kinghorn), Lieutenant-Colonel R.S. Fawcus (Robin Fawcus) and the author. The occasion was relaxed and the account was greeted with much hilarity. It is, however, an affectionate and dubiously accurate account of life in The Gordon Highlanders' Officers Mess in Kenya, life in a rifle company preparing for operations in Swaziland and off-duty moments in Borneo. Subalterns in every British regiment across the years have at times found their high spirits leading them away from the straight and narrow path—and have so often reflected on how lucky they were to get away with it!

Kenya

Roddy Kinghorn: It was at Christmas 1962. We drove off to pay a visit to some of the married officers, but on the way we rolled over. We took a bend too quickly, on the *marram*, the dust roads. They are wicked old things, and Fawcus was probably saying 'Faster, faster,' and I said 'I really shouldn't', and we rolled, and it finished up on its side. We got out and we somehow pushed and pushed and we finally got it up, and surprisingly it started. We then got to this house looking like Korky the Kat, we didn't realise how dusty and dishevelled we were, and we said 'We've come to wish you a Merry Christmas'. 'That's good of you, but we're having a lunch party,' they said. They weren't impressed at all. So we went off to find somewhere else to visit. We rolled over again, and that was the end of the car, it wouldn't start.

Carol Kinghorn to Robin Fawcus: Why did you let Roddy drive all the time, Robin? You're a much better driver!

Robin Fawcus: I didn't let him drive *all* the time. He was so *awful* at driving.

Author: It wasn't that he had accidents when he was driving. It was, when he was driving he had accidents!

Roddy Kinghorn to Robin Fawcus: And you used to keep saying 'Mix the gears a little', but I didn't bother with that too much—I was concentrating too much on steering.

We were all a bit short of money and we went on this grand holiday. We left Gilgil to go back to Zanzibar and we had to go through Tanganyika to get to Dar es Salaam and we came to a *wadi* and it was all too much for the car. We went into the *wadi* but we couldn't come out. There were a lot of interested natives gathered, and we said 'Will you help us pull the car out?' Well, of course Tanganyikans aren't keen on white men at all because they had a very tough time under German colonialism, and they were very aggressive. They said 'How much?' and we said 'Oh well, how much do you think?' Now, we didn't have a ha'penny on us, and we haggled away, and got the money right down, and they pulled and pushed us out, and the time was nearing when we would have to pay them, and we didn't have any money. We got Fawcus into the driver's seat and I was out there purporting to look in my pockets for the appropriate amount of money, and he had the engine running and then as fast as I could I leapt into the seat and we were off. My gosh, they chased us for quite a long way. It wouldn't have been a good time to run out of petrol!

Carol Kinghorn: That was a terrible thing to do!

Roddy Kinghorn: Well it was all we could do! Anyway, we got down to Dar es Salaam, where we spent one night on the beach, because we couldn't afford a hotel, and then we booked our flight across to Zanzibar in the morning. We had three or four nights in the English Club there, that was frequented by a lot of people we knew. We left the car at the airport in Dar es Salaam.

The trip back was along the coast, and we were making good time—it wasn't too far to the Kenya border—we were just a little north of Tanga, a coastal town in Tanganyika. It was a *marram* road, with a gentle hump in the middle of good hard earth, and on either side of the road was sand and grit. I was driving, when I saw a bus coming towards us. Normally when you meet another vehicle on these roads you slow down and pull to the side so that one set of wheels is on the *marram* road while you pass. You're going slowly so there's no problem. Anyway, this bus, filled with passengers and driven by a mad Indian wasn't giving way to anyone. It stuck to the centre of the road, and I had no option but, at the last minute, to drive off the road out of the way of the bus. There was a great big ditch there and we somersaulted a couple of times and landed upside down with our few possessions scattered around. Fawcus was moaning about his back, and I was bleeding profusely because my ear was hanging off. It was my left ear, which had been cut by the roof light as we were thrown about inside the car. We disentangled ourselves, gathered what little we owned and went to the side of the road. We were basically all right, Fawcus still moaning about his back, and we waited about an hour and a half or even more, for a vehicle to take us either back to Tanga or on to Mombasa, which was a good long drive.

The first vehicle to come along, heading north towards Mombasa, was a pick-up with fish in it, probably from Tanga going, no doubt, to Mombasa to sell the fish in the market. It was driven by two Indians who were not remotely sympathetic to our state and condition. We asked them if they would take us to Mombasa (because they did at least stop), and they said 'Yes, how much?' Well, how much didn't really matter, as we had no money. The good honest Robin would have told them there and then that we had no money, but I preferred to start haggling about the price, which might suggest that we did have money. We got the price down, and jumped on the back of their truck, with all the fish—I'm still bleeding profusely, and may I say an ear bleeds and bleeds and bleeds, and Fawcus still moaning about his back—and off we went. It was a long drive, and we finally got to the hospital—they knew where that was, which was more than we did. They were keen to drop us at the entrance, but we said 'No, you've got to take us to the front door, we are injured.' The closer we got to the front door the happier we were. So they did that, reluctantly, and we clambered down and started the bit about payment. I started to haggle again, trying to get the price down further, and urging Fawcus to go to the front door with the bags, and go in, and I would make a bolt for it. But there was no need for any of that for within half a minute out came Matron, a truly Hattie Jacques[9] type, who said 'You two, inside, and you two (meaning the Indians) go!' They said 'But we haven't been paid.' 'It doesn't matter if you've been paid or not,' retorted the Matron, 'you're not allowed in the hospital, so go!' So they went, meekly, and we went into the hospital. Things had gone very well, thanks to the Matron.

We were taken to a room for some attention, and the Matron sent for the doctor to come and look at my ear. He had already gone off to lunch— it was Saturday and the end of his working day, and he had gone to the Mombasa Club. When he arrived it was apparent that he had been there quite a long time. He looked at my ear and said 'We'll just take that off. We'll snip that and just tidy it up for you.' I said 'No, we'll stitch it back on.' He wasn't very keen on that, because he wanted to get back to the Club, and it was going to take too long. He kept saying 'It probably won't take, so I'll just snip it off.' I said 'No! no!', at which point Fawcus locked the door and said, 'You've got to stitch it on, and if it doesn't take, it doesn't take!' So he did, and I needed no anaesthetic because the fumes from his whisky breath were overpowering enough, and he put in a lot of stitches. He attended to Fawcus in another room and just told him what he already knew, that his back was sore.

Then we went off to a ward, and we were there for four or five days. We were well accommodated, lovely views of the Indian Ocean, but they were a bit light on the rations. I don't know if that was their policy or not, but we were always hungry, perhaps because we were only twenty-two years old. But there was one fellow there who seemed to be in a perpetual coma, and he wasn't being fed because he was never awake, but then we told the orderly, who was a good Kenyan woman, that he had woken up and did want to be fed, but he'd fallen asleep again. I don't know if she believed it or not, but anyway she gave him breakfast the following morning, which we ate. We told her how much he had enjoyed it. I don't know if she believed that, but he got another meal later on in the day, and we had that too. This went on for a couple of days until he died, and that was the end of our extra rations. Poor fellow, he never did wake up.

We got the train and returned to the Battalion at Gil Gil, to be summoned before Charles Napier, who took our licences away because that was the third or fourth accident we had had. He said 'Hand them into the Adjutant,' who of course was delighted to grab them. Into the safe they went, and that was the end, we couldn't drive. In total we wrote off three cars, and I have to say, I was at the wheel every time it happened!

---

9   Hattie Jacques was a film actress, of large frame (what Africans would call 'traditionally built'), who often played the matron in British hospital comedies.

Swaziland

Roddy Kinghorn: When the news came out and we told the Jocks that we were going to fly down to Swaziland, some of them looked overjoyed, and excitedly started talking about ski-ing. That was when I realised that they'd never heard of Swaziland and thought we were going to Switzerland! Anyway, we all piled into the aircraft and flew off to Southern Africa.

Once in Swaziland we were told we were going on an operation to cordon off the Havelock mine and arrest the ring-leaders of the strike that was taking place. It was a big operation, and we'd been waiting for orders from Tony Brown,[10] who had been called to an orders group by Charles Napier. This was at muster parade, ten to eight in the morning. Nothing happened all day, and about quarter to three in the afternoon Chalky[11] and I, who were pretty bored just waiting around, wandered off to a nearby hotel for, believe it or not, afternoon tea, just to get away from the boredom. We were there for longer than we should have been, about an hour and a half. We came back and there were Jocks rushing around everywhere looking for us, and we were summoned to Tony Brown. The moment we had gone, back he had come. 'Get everyone ready for orders,' and of course Chalky and I weren't there! We got there into the room, and Tony had about fifteen huge Ordnance Survey maps rolled up, and they are very heavy when you roll them up tight in the form of a club, and as soon as Chalky walked in he hit him hard. It surprised Chalky, and he was hit again before he decided that he didn't want to keep on getting hit. There was a table there where we were going to have the orders group, and Chalky began to run round it and Tony chased him, ready to hit him again. Dick Murison[12] was quite surprised at this; Du Boulay[13] was smug because he'd never left the place, and I'm standing there wondering if I was going to be hit, but Tony was concentrating on Chalky and Chalky was running for his life—you wouldn't believe that this was the British Army!—and then it stopped because Tony was getting tired. I was spared because I was always point platoon, and I was about the only chap who could read a map, and he didn't want me damaged. Finally, the chase stopped, and Tony announced that we were both to be placed in close arrest. Then he realised that he would have to go on operations without two platoon commanders, so he gave us a huge bollocking instead and then got on with the orders.

---

10 Maj A.T.C. Brown.
11 Lt D.H. White.
12 Capt R.W.C. Murison.
13 Lt D.M.H. Du Boulay.

Borneo 1965

Roddy Kinghorn: The Borneo hotel was the place to go, all the ex-pats who had well-paid jobs went there. It was about the only place in Sabah that had air conditioning!

There was this restaurant in the town, and we were there on Robin Fawcus's birthday. (*Aside from Author*: 'If I remember right, Fawcus ended up that evening wandering around with a toilet seat draped round his neck!') He had a massive birthday card from his platoon, about three or four feet long. He had rolled it up and carried it around with him all day. It was a big instrument, and quite a powerful thing, and if you hit someone with it he got quite a wallop, and he was doing this all the time because he had been fu' all the day. Every member of his platoon had been anointed with it, not to mention the barman and the waiters.

When we had finished our meal we were leaving, and there was a function room there. He went in and went round the whole table of local dignitaries. He started to sing 'One potato, two potato, three potato, four etc', while going round the table, and with each 'potato' he would tap a dignitary on the top of the head with his rolled up birthday card. They seemed bemused, but not amused!

It turned out that they were the Sabah Cabinet having a working dinner. Well of course the police were summoned, and we all had to scarper in every direction, and two or three people who hadn't been in the room didn't know why we were suddenly fleeing the place, but they all took the hint and we got away.

Captain R.M. Kinghorn and Lieutenant-Colonel R.S. Fawcus.

Cyprus 1971

Major Duke took some sailing dinghies from Lara Point on a four-day trip round Akrotiri Point and on to Dhekelia. On the second day he saw a raft some distance off and signalled his flotilla to tack in succession and follow him to investigate. As they approached, a Vulcan bomber appeared on a course heading directly towards the raft. To Major Duke's horror a column of spray erupted from midway between his boats and the raft.

'Oh Lord,' thought the intrepid traveller, 'Duke's done it again.' With commendable disregard of Nelson's dictum he put as much distance between his flotilla and the sound of gunfire as he could and sped off to the security of the shore. As he approached Episkopi he was met by a rather agitated RAF officer. Somewhat apprehensively Major Duke greeted the obviously upset airman. He presumed that every sailor was supposed to know that the raft was the target in a designated bombing range, and expected to bear the brunt of the righteous wrath of an outraged

Service. To his relief, however, the RAF officer apologised profusely for failing to warn the aircraft that the range had not been clear. In the lively seas the four little sails of Major Duke's fleet looked just like waves from where he was standing.

The Life of a Regiment, Volume VII, p 63.

SECTION 8

WHAT WERE THEY DOING THERE?

THROUGHOUT their two centuries of existence The Gordon Highlanders saw men from every walk of life in the ranks. Many served a full military career as Gordon Highlanders, and when they eventually left the Army found employment in civilian life. Some went on to forge successful careers in business, law and industry, often rising to the very top.

Some serving Gordon Highlanders found themselves in action outside the Regiment in places where Gordon Highlanders might not expect to be found, and others came across fellow Scots where least expected.

This section covers some interesting people whose Gordon Highlander background was not generally known, and some Gordon Highlanders who were found in surprising places.

CHAPTER 16

A MISCELLANY

A Turkish Highlander

SCOTS have always found employment outwith their own country. They have achieved positions of prominence in foreign courts, professions, political circles and armies, and often popped up when least expected:

> A curious story was told of two officers of the 92nd, who, while at Marmorice [in 1801], met during a walk a very magnificently dressed Turk, followed by a number of retainers. One of the officers, with British contempt for this display of Oriental grandeur, and thinking it possible the grandee might understand English, but certainly would be ignorant of Gaelic, said to his companion, '*Co a ghalla is mathair d'on chu leisg so*?' ('Do you see the fellow with the tail?' It is easy telling who his mother was, the lazy dog!') What was his astonishment when the Turk answered, '*Seadh a' ille agus gu'de an seorsa mathair dh'araich thusa mar chuilean*?' ('Aye, my lad, and what sort of mother may own you for her whelp?')
>
> After mutual apologies and explanations, the Celtic Turk dined on board with the officers, and afterwards sent boatloads of fruit and vegetables for all the men. His name was Campbell, and, having in a quarrel killed a school-fellow at Fort William, he had fled the country, entered the Turkish service, and had risen to high position.

The Life of a Regiment, Volume I, p 81.

Wives on campaign

In the Napoleonic Wars wives often accompanied their husbands on campaign. Military wives were expected to earn their keep, and often performed cooking and laundry duties:

> During their marches the troops were accompanied by the wives and children of the n.c. officers and soldiers, who received rations; and though they sometimes caused anxiety, both to their husbands and the commanding officer, were of great use in nursing the sick, washing the linen of the officers and men, etc., while their presence gave something of a homelike appearance to the camp or cantonments. They generally had donkeys, which they rode, or which carried panniers with their children and possessions; they were capital foragers, were as full of *esprit de corps*

as the men, and bore the fatigues of the campaign with the patient fortitude of their sex. I knew an old lady who used to tell how, when a sudden order to march came while the linen of the men she washed for was in the tub, she took advantage of the fact that she was billeted on a wood merchant to make a roaring fire, and succeeded in giving every man his dry shirt as he stood on parade, emerging, like Wellington at Fuentes d'Onor, undefeated by the difficulties of the situation. She gave brandy to the wounded in the ensuing engagement, made her husband's breakfast before the fight of the next day, and ended her eventful life as the respected hostess of a hotel in Argyll.

The Life of a Regiment, Volume I, p 246.

92nd men in the Rifle Brigade

The use of rifled muskets was pioneered during the American War of Independence by Major Patrick Ferguson, the Scottish designer of the first breech-loading rifled weapon. Ferguson was killed during that war, and his invention was not taken up by the British Army. During the Napoleonic Wars regiments were raised to use the Baker rifle, a muzzle-loaded rifled weapon with longer range and greater accuracy than the standard smooth-bore Tower musket. The new regiment proved extremely effective and was taken on the establishment of the British infantry. Rifle and light infantry regiments were distinguished by their marching pace, which was faster than line regiments, and more particularly, Highland regiments. Gordon Highlanders formed part of the *ad hoc* regiment that tested the concept:

H.R.H. the Commander-in-Chief had been impressed by the rapid movements and accurate fire of the enemy's riflemen, and by the execution they had done in Holland; he determined to constitute a similar corps as part of the British establishment. The commanding officers of fourteen regiments of the line were directed to select 2 sergeants, 2 corporals, 30 privates, and 1 bugler to compose a rifle corps; and to send the names of 1 captain, 1 lieutenant, and 1 ensign willing to volunteer for this service. These detachments were assembled at Horsham, under Colonel Coote Manningham of the 41st Regiment and Colonel Stewart of the 67th,[1] as an 'Experimental Corps'. Three companies, made up of the

---

1   Col Coote Manningham, and Lt-Col the Hon. W. Stewart (formerly of the 42nd), fourth son of the Earl of Galloway, addressed a letter to the Secretary for War urging 'the importance of having in the British army a regiment armed with a rifled arm.' The 'Experimental Rifle Corps' was a success, and it was decided to raise a 'Corps of Riflemen'. This corps had many men from the Scottish Fencibles; out of it grew the 95th Rifle Regiment, which became the Rifle Brigade. The Baker Rifle, by London gunmaker, Ezekiel Baker, was 2 feet 6 inches long in the barrel, 7 grooved, and rifled one quarter turn. The balls were 20 to the lb (smooth bore bullets were 14 to the lb); weight of [rifle] 9½ lbs; sighted by a folding sight to 200 yards. Small wooden mallets were supplied to assist in ramming down the ball. A horn for powder and a pouch for bullets. In the rifle stock was a brass box for the

detachments of the Royals,[2] 23rd, 25th, 27th, 79th, and 92nd Regiments under Lieut-Colonel Stewart, embarked with the force under Sir J.M. Pulteney, and landed at Ferrol in Spain on the 25th August 1800; they covered the advance, and particularly distinguished themselves in the two skirmishes which took place near that fortress, the Spaniards being defeated in both. This was the first day a British rifleman ever fired a shot at an enemy.[3]

The 79th and 92nd detachments formed the Highland Company, wearing their own dress. When the Rifle Corps was afterwards formed, the officers and men of the 'Experimental Corps' were allowed to volunteer for it, but with two exceptions the men of the Gordon Highlanders elected to return to their own Regiment. Lieutenant Alexander Clarke, Ensigns Charles Cameron and Alexander Cameron volunteered, but Lieutenant Clarke was killed in Egypt, and only the two ensigns donned the 'green jacket' as lieutenants. The latter[4] eventually became General Sir Alexander Cameron, K.C.B., of Inverailort, Colonel of the 74th Highland Regiment, and his son, Arthur Wellington Cameron, served in the 92nd from 1844 till 1876, and commanded the regiment in India.

The Life of a Regiment, Volume I, pp 74–6.

The men of the 92nd in the Experimental Rifle Corps went as fully fledged Highland soldiers. A Routine Order of February 22nd, 1800 directs:

The men who have been fixed upon to be detached as Rifleman will take with them their new clothing, and they will immediately set about cocking and making up their new bonnets. The officers will take care that they be neatly cocked.

The Life of a Regiment, Volume I, p 74.

A Routine Order two days later, on February 24th, directs that:

---

greased rag in which the ball was wrapped. A picker to clean the touch-hole and a brush were suspended by brass chains to the belts. A triangular sword-bayonet was fixed by a spring.

2 The Royal Scots.

3 There had previously been only foreigners in British pay armed with the rifle. The 60th were Germans.

4 In the eighteenth century, when Ensign Cameron joined, candidates for commissions did not sit difficult examinations, and young Highland gentlemen, instead of being sent south, were educated at home, and brought up among the country people, joining in their sports and the work of the estate or farm. Young Cameron was clipping a sheep when the letter was brought to him, then a rare event in the distant Highlands. It announced his commission in the Gordon Highlanders. '*Cha rùisg mi caoraich tuilleadh*,' ('I'll clip no more sheep') said he, tossing aside the shears, and left the Highlands, to return a general with a 'Sir' to his name. Lt Alexander Stewart of Achnacone, an original officer of the 92nd, became captain in the Rifle Corps. *The Life Of A Regiment*, Volume I, p 76., One of Stewart's descendants was Capt A.D.L. Stewart of Achnacone. (see Volume IX, Chapter 12.)

The detachment of riflemen will march tomorrow at 10 o'clock under command of Ensign Cameron. The major expects that the detachment will conduct themselves in such a manner as to do credit to the regiment they belong to, and that Ensign Cameron will so exert himself on the march, and after he has arrived at Horsham, that his detachment will appear as respectable in the corps they are to join, as the regiment has always done among other regiments.

The Life of a Regiment, Volume I, p 74.

It did not take long for the Experimental Rifle Corps to establish itself as an invaluable addition to the British Army's line of battle, and in 1801 it was titled the Rifle Corps. In an acquittance roll of Captain Alexander Stewart's company in 1801 there are sixty-seven men, and their names show them to have been almost all Highlanders. A letter to him from his commanding officer in 1802 desired him to enlist as many as possible in his own country (Appin). In 1803 the Rifle Corps became the 95th Regiment of Foot (Rifles) with one of its companies known within the regiment as 'the Highland company'.

The Forgotten Scots

Gordon Highlanders, sometimes in small groups, found themselves on detached duty in many places around the world. On conclusion of their duty they returned to the Regiment and resumed their duties there. The tale below is a rather sad one, where Gordon Highlanders doing their duty appear to have been 'mislaid' by the authorities!

One of the first things to strike a visitor to the Channel Islands is the great number of little round towers found all over the archipelago. They stand, squat and forbidding, at all points on the coast line which are not protected naturally. Most are in Guernsey. They remain as a memorial to the fear in which Great Britain held Napoleon, to the forgetfulness of the British Army, and the discipline of the Gordon Highlanders.

At the beginning of the nineteenth century Britain faced isolation, for Napoleon had deprived her of active allies, and it seemed that his next move in the conquest of Europe would be to attack British territory. The Channel Islands were the most likely victims, for to the French they were still *Les Isles Normandes*. The population spoke a Norman dialect of French, which still survives, and owed allegiance to no one. Their sole connection with Britain was that the King was first the Duke of Normandy. They had their own Parliament, their own laws and customs, and their own militia for service on the island. A few miles separated them from the ports of France, and they looked easy victims for a Napoleonic invasion.

Had it been only a case of losing a few islands the British administration might have worried little, for the material advantage to the Crown was very slight. The great advantage of Guernsey lay in the harbour of St. Peter Port, for it had strategical value in blocking the Channel, and in attacking the coast of France. Alternately, it would have been of great value to Napoleon had he planned a landing in Dorset as it was thought he would.

The British Government were scared, and with the cooperation of the States built the squat grim little fortresses which still ring the coast. Only a few people remember the story of these fortresses now. You might search the archives of Whitehall long enough without finding a trace. I came on the story by accident.

It happened when I was staying in Guernsey, not far from St. Peter Port. It was my habit in the afternoons to walk down the water-lane which leads to the shore, and bask in the sunshine at the foot of the Martello tower. Beside the tower was a little teashop; I knew it well, taking tea there every day at four, but for the hundreds of times I had visited it, I had never troubled to find out the name of the owner. The sign above the door was dusty and faded, and it was only by chance that a shaft of sunlight caught it one day and I made out from the cracked paint, instead of the usual De La Mère, or Mauger, a surprising 'J. Ferguson, Proprietor.'

I had a sudden spasm of nostalgia, quickly followed by one of curiosity. I went to the woman in the shop and asked what her name was. It was Ferguson. Yes, her husband was J. Ferguson, Proprietor. Certainly, she would get him to tell me how a Scottish name came to the last remnant of the Duchy; And this is the story.

When the Martello towers were built the Government decided that the Militia might not be able to withstand the Emperor's attack, so they sent to man the towers some three dozen Gordon Highlanders. It was a magnificent tribute to the fighting powers of the Scots, even if it underestimated those of the French. The Gordons arrived and manned the towers. Private Ferguson went to the one at Fermaine. Then they waited for Napoleon, but he did not arrive. Years went by. Waterloo was fought, and Napoleon went into exile. But still the Gordons manned their towers. A desire to see the homeland again stirred in them, and they sent word to London. London wrote back to say that there were no instructions for the recall of the Gordon Highlanders, and they were to remain at their posts.

They did. Some of them, like Private Ferguson, married Guernsey girls, and reared families. All of them settled down, and in the course of the seasons died, Scotland lost to them. No word came from London and none has come since.

Here and there over Guernsey you come across families with Scottish names and almost all of them own a Martello tower. Like J. Ferguson, Proprietor, they are descendants of the Gordons who stuck to their posts.

J. Carroll, ex-Band Sergeant, 1st Battalion.

T&S, June 1938.

The Martello tower frequented by Sergeant Carroll

A world-famous ship

The SS *Great Britain* was a revolutionary ocean-going ship. Built by Isambard Kingdom Brunel, it was one of the first screw-driven ships in the world, one of the earliest iron-built ships and was the largest ship of its day. Still in existence, and restored, it lies in the Bristol dry dock where it was built. At its launch the 75th played a ceremonial role.

[In 1843 the 75th] furnished the guard of honour to H.R.H. Prince Albert at Bristol on the occasion of the launch of the *Great Britain*, the largest steamship then known.

The Life of a Regiment, Vol II, p 212.

CHAPTER 17

GORDON HIGHLANDERS IN THE CRIMEAN WAR

THE 92nd, stationed in Gibraltar, was not one of the regiments initially sent to Crimea, and it played no part in the main actions of the Crimean War, finally arriving there the day after Sebastopol fell. It did, however, provide a large contingent of soldiers who volunteered to make up the strength of other regiments:

> Orders came to Gibraltar that the battalions who had been longest on the Rock were to be made up towards strength by volunteers from those lately arrived; consequently, the n.c. officers and men of the 92nd were offered the opportunity of seeing active service by volunteering. The offer was accepted by three sergeants, five corporals and 226 private soldiers, leaving the service companies with under 300 privates.
>
> The 93rd was the first Highland regiment in readiness, and was made up by volunteers from the 42nd and 79th. Shortly after, these regiments were added to the expedition, and the 92nd depot was called upon. It consisted of a particularly fine body of young men, and almost everyone volunteered, all choosing the 79th, except ten, who went to the 42nd. Thus a corps avowedly unsurpassed in efficiency was for the time destroyed, while its soldiers went as strangers to other regiments. When their regiment was thus broken up, the feeling of grief, amounting almost to despair, may be imagined better than described. By some it was never forgotten. The disappointment was increased by the arrival of a letter by which the 92nd was excepted from the volunteer offer. It was too late, the men had departed!
>
> In availing themselves of what they supposed to be their only chance of active service, the men behaved like the good soldiers they were; so good that I have heard an officer of the Regiment to which a number went speak of them as men of a very superior class, and that most of the privates were fit to be n.c. officers. Many distinguished themselves, and after the war numbers of those who were able to do so rejoined the 92nd, saying they volunteered to see service, not for leaving the Regiment. One, who speaks of his time in the 92nd as 'the brightest and happiest of all my service,' says, 'Those volunteers could not take the colours of the regiment with them, but they went themselves.'

The Life of a Regiment, Volume II, pp 55–6.

A GORDON HIGHLANDER AT THE CHARGE OF THE LIGHT BRIGADE

Gordon Highlanders in Crimea served their adoptive units faithfully; one of them winning one of the first V.C.s. It would not, however, be expected that a Gordon Highlander should take part in one of the most famous cavalry actions of the Crimean war:

The Gordon Highlanders did not serve in Crimea, although over 300 NCOs and men volunteered for service with other regiments. Some officers also served; Captain A.M. MacDonald,[1] aide-de-camp to General Pennefather, was wounded at the Alma, Captain Walter Charteris was aide-de-camp to Lieutenant-General the Earl of Lucan, and Major K.D. MacKenzie was the hard working and popular Deputy Quartermaster General at Balaclava.[2] It may surprise some to learn that the Gordons lost an officer in 'The Charge of the Light Brigade.'

In the Tiger and Sphinx of Autumn 1982 there appeared an account of Captain Walter Charteris's death. Research had been carried out by Mr Barrie Stevens, with acknowledgement of the assistance given by The Right Honourable The Earl of Wemyss and March, KT, LLD, who provided documents proving the battle damage to Charteris's sword.

Captain The Honourable Walter Charteris, sometime Deputy Adjutant of the 92nd Gordon Highlanders, was the third son of the 9th Earl of Wemyss and March. His mother was a sister of the Earl of Lucan, and Walter secured the post of aide-de-camp to his uncle, Lord Lucan, during the Crimean War. He had to purchase a Captaincy, and also purchased the uniform and cocked hat of a cavalry staff officer as well as the regulation 1821 pattern sabre, obtained from Wilkinsons of Pall Mall.

He arrived in Turkey on 13 August 1854 and moved with the army to Crimea on 14 September. His description of the battle of the Alma, and of Lord Lucan's key part in it, was in a letter to his brother, Lord Elcho, a member of the War Cabinet. This letter was read out in Parliament when Lord Elcho spoke out in Lord Lucan's defence.

Apart from a brief mention in Volume II of *The Life of a Regiment* there does not appear to be any named mention of Charteris in any other history book, and yet he played as important a part as Captain Nolan, who brought the order to charge. Charteris brought the message that Lords Cathcart and Cambridge, commanding the infantry, had no orders to support the cavalry. Lord Lucan therefore had to order the charge without support. Walter Charteris also took part in the lesser known but more successful Charge of the Heavy Brigade earlier in the day.

---

1   Alastair MacIan MacDonald, son of Gen Sir John MacDonald. See Chapter 34.
2   Volume II, p 57.

Without mentioning his name, Cecil Woodham Smith does cover his death briefly:

'At this moment the Heavy Brigade came under the withering cross-fire that had just torn the Light Brigade to pieces. Lord Lucan, leading the Brigade, was wounded in the leg and his horse hit in two places; one of his aides was killed, and two of his staff wounded.'[3]

Walter Charteris was with Lord Lucan and three other staff officers at the head of the two regiments of heavy dragoons that made up the third line several minutes behind the Light Brigade. When within range, the Russian guns fired a barrage of grapeshot. Forty or fifty troopers went down as did Charteris, killed by a grapeshot that struck the blade of his sword. Out of Lord Lucan and four staff officers, only one was unscathed. Lord Lucan had the body of Captain Charteris, and his accoutrements recovered.[4]

The officers of The Gordon Highlanders erected a memorial in Aberlady Church, which reads:

THIS TABLET TO THE MEMORY OF
CAPTAIN THE HONBLE WALTER CHARTERIS
THIRD SON OF FRANCIS EARL OF WEMYSS AND MARCH
IS ERECTED BY HIS BROTHER OFFICERS
OF THE 92ND GORDON HIGHLANDERS
ON OCTOBER THE 25TH 1854 IN HIS 26TH YEAR
HE FELL GLORIOUSLY AT BALAKLAVA
WHEN AIDE DE CAMP TO HIS UNCLE
LIEUT GEN THE EARL OF LUCAN

The Life of a Regiment, Volume VII, pp 654–5.

---

3   *The Reason Why* by Cecil Woodham Smith, p 247.
4   The dent made by the Russian grape shot can be clearly seen on the sword, which is held in the h National War Museum in Edinburgh Castle.

CHAPTER 18

GORDON HIGHLANDERS IN THE ZULU AND 1ST BOER WARS

IN 1879 the 75th was stationed in the Channel Islands and the 92nd in Afghanistan. When war broke out in South Africa against the Zulus it was reasonable to assume that no Gordon Highlanders would be involved. In fact, there were Gordon Highlanders at Isandlwana and Rorke's Drift.

The career of Edward Essex is not covered in the regimental history. He gains just one entry in Volume II, covering his appointment to command the 2nd Battalion in 1887 and relinquishing command in 1891. His name crops up in the *Tiger and Sphinx*, in a letter regarding 75th regimental tunes and in the lists of subscribers, right up to 1939. This lack of information is regrettable, as he had an interesting career and was present at some significant events in the 1870s and 1880s. The following section, based on an article, *Lucky Essex*, by Graham Alexander, in *The Journal of the Anglo Zulu War Historical Society (AZWHS)* (December 2003), *Memories of Forty-Eight Years' Service* by General Sir Horace Smith-Dorrien and extracts from one of the most informative books on the Zulu War of 1879, *Zulu Rising* by Ian Knight, gives hitherto unrecorded details of his career, and his part in battles in which The Gordon Highlanders played no part.

In 1847 17-year-old Edward Essex entered the Royal Military College Sandhurst. He was a hard-working, intelligent cadet, and he passed out in third place. He wanted to join the 75th Stirlingshire Regiment, but as there was no vacancy in the regiment he was gazetted into the 9th (East Norfolk) Regiment. Within a month a vacancy occurred in the 75th and he transferred to his first choice of regiment. In November 1867 he purchased his lieutenancy and presented to the Officers Mess a silver goblet inscribed '*Presented by Lt. Edward Essex on promotion November 27th 1867*'.[1]

Essex saw service in Gibraltar and the Far East (to which the 75th sailed in the troopship *Himalaya*). In 1869, having impressed by his hard work and meticulous attention to detail, Essex was made adjutant. In 1871 a vacancy occurred for a captain and Essex, after negotiating and paying the requested price, purchased the captaincy on 31 May. (Within weeks the Regulation of the Forces Bill, which abolished the purchasing system, was passed. Essex

---

1   These goblets, showing the Bengal tiger and number 'LXXV', were presented by officers on promotion, on leaving the Regiment, or sometimes in memory of friends. When the 75th and 92nd amalgamated in 1881 the 92nd adopted the custom, its officers presenting similar goblets, but with a sphinx and the number 'XCII'. When the 1st and 2nd Battalions were amalgamated in 1947 the goblets showed both the tiger and the sphinx. These goblets were used on formal occasions until The Gordon Highlanders disappeared from the Army order of battle in 1994.

was therefore one of the last officers in the British Army to purchase his rank.) As a captain, Essex should have relinquished the role of adjutant, but he continued until 8 September 1871, when the 75th moved from Hong Kong and Singapore to South Africa. Mention of Essex is found in *The Tiger and Sphinx*, in an article in the Natal *Daily Dispatch* published by Dr. A.W. Burton of King William's Town, Natal:

> In 1871 the 75th came to Natal from China and Singapore, losing two men during the voyage. After calling at Mauritius, they proceeded to Natal, where head-quarters were established at Pietermaritzburg. Shortly after their arrival, a wing of the 75th was sent by the steamship *Tamar* to King William's Town. After landing at East London, the 75th camped in tents and on 23rd October set out on foot for King William's Town (a distance of 37 miles). Not long after reaching King William's Town, Lieut. Essex was promoted Captain,[2] and Lieut. A. Cross succeeded him as Adjutant. The regiment was often referred to as the 75th Stirlingshires.

T&S, March 1937.

Essex appears twice more in Dr Burton's article, as a judge of events at a Sports Meeting at King William's Town in February 1872, and in charge of the firing party at the funeral of a fellow officer in January 1873.

Essex returned to Britain on leave in April 1873. He rejoined the regiment in February 1874. The 75th had been on garrison duties until November 1873, when a mixed force under Major Anthony Durnford was involved in a skirmish with amaHlubi warriors at Bushman's Pass. It was a minor affair, with slight injuries on both sides, but the reaction in Natal was extreme. It was decided that a decisive blow had to be struck at the amaHlubi and an expedition, with 200 men of the 75th, set off. An amaHlubi settlement was attacked, and over 200 people were killed. Essex would later meet Durnford in circumstances that he would never forget.

In 1875 the 75th returned to Britain and was posted to Ireland. Essex applied to attend Staff College. Career advancement would be certain and employment in a staff role would be assured, but it was unusual for an officer to request to go to the Staff College. His brother officers would ask if the regiment was no longer good enough for him, and they would have to shoulder his responsibilities while he was 'enjoying himself'. The Staff College was not seen as the way forward for regimental officers.

Essex began the two-year course in 1876, and successfully passed out of Staff College. He was appointed Garrison Instructor at Manchester, but his

---

2   There is a slight discrepancy between this date and that in the biographical details above, but this could be accounted for by something as simple as the official War Office approval of the purchase not being published in orders until the latter date.

staff job was of short duration because, with war against the Zulus looming in South Africa, staff officers with a knowledge of the country were needed. Essex was seconded from his garrison duties and on 31 October 1878 boarded ship for Natal, for an experience that few would survive, and luck would play a large part for all those who did.

Affairs in South Africa were volatile. In 1877 the Transvaal became a British colony. Sir Theophilus Shepstone, the dominant voice in the management of Natal's African population for nearly half a century, was its administrator. British South Africa was a disorganised collection of colonies and protectorates, with very little unity, and unrest in the disparate African communities. The High Commissioner, Sir Bartle Frere, backed by Shepstone, felt that British interests called for the destruction of the independent Zulu Kingdom. Frere believed that a short, successful war would demonstrate British determination to remove all threats to confederation. He did not have British Government approval to start a war that it did not seek, but in 1878, after a Zulu incursion into Transvaal, Frere decided on a war that he believed would be won quickly, with British superiority of firepower ensuring a comparatively bloodless victory. Not for the first (or last) time, the fate of British soldiers was determined by political ambition and manipulation of events by men who would never smell the gun smoke.

The task of destroying the Zulu kingdom fell to Lieutenant-General Frederic Thesiger (within a few months he inherited the title of Lord Chelmsford). Thesiger felt that he had too few regular troops for the task, but his request to London for more men was rejected.

The invasion required a strong and versatile army to confront Chief Cetswayo's *impis*.[3] There were few regular British regiments in South Africa, and white colonial volunteers formed some irregular units. Local natives were recruited, but the quality of many of these units was not high. Officers for the campaign included not only British officers of regiments in South Africa, but also some who had obtained leave from their units in Britain. These 'special duty' officers volunteered after Lord Chelmsford issued a request for assistance. Ambitious young officers, eager for active service, would even accept a reduction in rank to do so. They accepted any position offered them. Among them were Major Redvers Buller, Captain Edward Essex[4] and Lieutenant Horace Smith-Dorrien.

Essex's role was not one an experienced infantry officer might have expected. He was made Director of Transport of one of the five columns that

---

3 *Impi*–Zulu regiment.
4 Essex was not the only 75th officer to volunteer. Lt D.L. Baynes also volunteered and travelled out to South Africa with Essex. He was on the lines of communication and at base but was not at Isandlwana. Promoted to captain, he became a Gordon Highlander when the 75th and 92nd amalgamated in 1881. He contracted dysentery and died when with the 1st Battalion in Egypt.

Chelmsford formed for his invasion of Zululand. This involved a transport method unfamiliar to the British Army, which used mule-drawn 'general service' wagons. These were unsuited to terrain where their narrow wheelbase led to frequent upsetting. Chelmsford relied on civilian transport wagons: long, heavy vehicles that were the mainstay of the colonial transport system. These needed sixteen oxen to pull them—more, when crossing rivers, hauling up rocky hillsides or through difficult *dongas*.[5] The oxen were worked for no more than four hours a day, with long periods of rest and grazing to maintain their strength. The Army hired civilian drivers and *voorloopers*— young African boys who walked beside the team controlling the oxen with long whips.

Chelmsford appreciated the importance of logistics and directed that each column should have one Transport Officer in overall charge of the baggage train, assisted by a civilian head conductor and a sub-conductor for every ten wagons. Each wagon had a driver and *voorlooper*, and wagons moved in sections of ten or columns of twenty. Each column carried ten days supplies and covered ten miles each day

Essex was in charge of the transport of Chelmsford's centre column. He had to ensure that the wagons were correctly loaded and sited where needed. Each company had its own wagons, with seventeen in each battalion. Supplies were taken to Helpmekaar, forward base and headquarters camp of No 3 column. Assisting Essex was Lieutenant Smith-Dorrien, fresh from England and inexperienced in transport matters.

Helpmekaar quickly grew from an insignificant collection of tin huts to a sprawling encampment overlooking the Buffalo River and the hills of Zululand beyond. Four companies of the 1/24th Regiment were based there and Essex was invited by the officers to join their Mess.

On Saturday 11 January 1879, Chelmsford's troops crossed the river at Rorke's Drift to enter Zululand. Because his wagons could not cross the river, Essex remained at Rorke's Drift. By 20 January the track could take the wagons to Isandlwana, where the site became a vast tented area, with some 350 tents carefully aligned. A wagon park was established, where wagons were unloaded and sent back for more supplies. Overseeing and supervising the wagon park were Essex's prime responsibility.

On 21 January Essex was organising wagons to return to Rorke's Drift on the following day to collect fresh supplies. In the early hours of 22 January Chelmsford cancelled the convoy. With Zulus in the area, the troops to guard the convoy would be better employed at Isandlwana.

Before dawn on the 22nd Chelmsford rode out with the 2nd Battalion of the 24th, four guns and mounted troops. His aim was to find and engage the

---

5   *Donga*—a deep gully.

Zulu army. The 1st Battalion of the 24th, with one company of the 2nd Battalion, was left to guard the camp at Isandlwana.

Isandlwana showing camp laid out

Essex, with no immediate duties, took the opportunity to write home. This was his first day off since his arrival in South Africa. He was wearing a dark-blue patrol jacket: the usual dress for officers when not in a tunic. At 7.30 the bugles sounded for breakfast. The men were still at breakfast when distant firing was heard, and a horseman was seen galloping towards the camp. This was an officer of the Natal Native Contingent who brought news that a large body of Zulus was advancing towards the camp.

The men of the 24th fell in and stood to. One company took up a defensive position on the spur connecting the camp to the plateau. Essex returned to his tent to continue with his interrupted letter and was there when the Zulus launched their attack. He recalled:

> About noon a sergeant came into my tent and told me that firing was heard behind the hill where the company of the 1st Battalion 24th had been sent. I had my glasses over my shoulder and thought I might as well take my revolver, but did not trouble to put on my sword, as I thought nothing of the matter and expected to be back in half an hour to complete my letters. I got on my horse and galloped up the hill, passing a company of the 24th on its way to the front.

Essex had just arrived at the company on the spur when the troops opened fire at the Zulu regiments which had run to the edge of the plateau and launched themselves down its steep sides.

On arriving at the top I saw the company in extended order firing on a long line of Zulus 800 yards distant. I had been living with the 1st Battalion 24th and knew their officers very well, and the men knew me. I therefore acted as a company officer, directing the men what to fire at and not to waste their ammunition.

The main body of the 24th was lined up in front of the camp. It was now attacked by the massed ranks of Zulus, which were received with volley fire. Essex admired the skirmishing skills of the Zulus.

Captain Mostyn moved his company into the space between the portions of that already on the hill, and his men extended and entered into action. This line was then prolonged on our right along the crest of the hill by a body of native infantry. I did not notice the latter much, save they blazed away at an absurd rate.

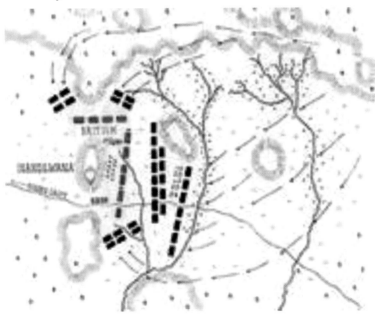

Isandlwana – British and Zulu positions

Melvill, the 1/24th's Adjutant, who had stayed behind after he had injured his leg on a reconnaissance, visited the line. He had been instructed by Pulleine to order the companies on the ridge, which were out of sight of the camp, to fall back, as a real threat was developing. Essex wrote:

I was informed by Lieutenant Melvill that a fresh body of the enemy was appearing in force in our rear, and he requested me to direct the left of the line formed, to fall slowly back, keeping up the fire. This I did; then proceeded to the centre of the line. I found, however, that it had already retired. I therefore followed in the same direction, but being mounted had great difficulty in descending the hill, the ground being very rocky and precipitous.

Some native cavalry units had been deployed in front of the firing line to engage the Zulus, but were themselves in danger of being overrun. They therefore pulled back. Wyatt Vause, of the amaNgwane Horse, wrote:

> The Zulus were shooting very badly and as yet few casualties had occurred on our side. As soon as the Zulus perceived we were in retreat, they came on with a shout and were gaining on us when we regained our horses. As soon as the men were mounted, we retired slowly, dismounting every few yards and firing a volley but without holding the enemy in check as they did not seem to mind our fire at all.

The battle on the spur had been conducted at rifle range. Essex noted that 'the enemy's fire [was] wild and ineffective' and 'up to this time no soldiers had fallen'. Men on the ridge now withdrew to join the main body. At the bottom of the spur Essex 'found the two companies of 1st Battalion 24th Regiment drawn up at about 400 yards in extended order, and Captain Younghusband's company in similar formation in echelon on the left'.

Essex noted that when the companies on the ridge retired they were 'getting short of ammunition'. They had been in action for half an hour, or more, but had not been profligate with their ammunition. Essex had helped to direct the fire and noted that most of the 24th were experienced men who had been in battle before—and were 'old steady shots'.

The 24th battle line was a long arc, curving from the northern edge of Isandlwana towards a *donga*, to which Durnford's men were falling back. The line stretched for nearly two miles, the soldiers spaced several yards apart. They were spread as thinly as possible, and relied on steadiness and firepower. Essex thought that things were becoming serious:

> The enemy's left had been concealed by a hill, but the attack now developed, and I could see their troops formed a dense black semi-circle, threatening both flanks. Their line was constantly fed from the rear, which seemed to be inexhaustible. Affairs now looked serious as our little body appeared insignificant compared with the enormous masses opposed to us. The 24th men, however, were as cheery as possible, making remarks to one another about their shooting, and the enemy opposed to them made little progress; but they were now within 500 yards of our line.

The soldiers fired volleys from their Martini-Henry rifles (over 4,000 rounds per minute). This held the Zulus, but the black powder cartridges created clouds of smoke that obscured targets in the still conditions. Such fire required a steady supply of ammunition to replenish the 70 rounds in each soldier's pouches. The companies firing from the beginning had used over half their ammunition and more was needed.

As the Zulu attack developed, Essex organised ammunition resupply: 'I got such men as were not engaged, bandsman, cooks etc, to assist me, and sent them to the line under an officer.' That officer was Lieutenant Horace Smith-Dorrien. In his memoirs Smith-Dorrien gives a vivid description of his attempts to organise a resupply, which has been much quoted—and even more misunderstood:

> I will mention a story which speaks for the coolness and discipline of the regiment. I, having no particular duty to perform in camp, when I saw the whole Zulu army advancing, had collected camp stragglers, such as artillery men in charge of spare horses, officers' servants, sick etc, and had taken them to the ammunition-boxes, where we broke them open as fast as we could, and sent the packets to the firing line. When I had been engaged at this for some time, and the 1/24th had fallen back to where we were, with the Zulus following closely, Bloomfield, the quartermaster of the 2/24th, said to me 'For heaven's sake, don't take that, man, for it belongs to our Battalion.' And I replied, 'hang it all, you don't want a requisition now, do you?'

Memories of Forty-Eight Years' Service,

This anecdote is the source of the myth of a zealous quartermaster refusing to issue rounds to companies from another battalion. But this was not what Smith-Dorrien meant. His aim was to stress the regiment's professionalism under fire. Smith-Dorrien had brought the men assembled by Essex to the closest ammunition wagon. With the 1/24th's camp further away, they had found the 2nd Battalion's supply, the ammunition wagon clearly marked, according to Chelmsford's standing orders, by a small red flag. Bloomfield's response, when he saw them breaking open the boxes, was perfectly correct; this was the reserve supply Chelmsford had directed to be kept ready for rapid dispatch to his battalion. To let it be used without authorisation would have made Bloomfield guilty of serious dereliction of duty—the more so because the true nature of the threat to Chelmsford was not at all clear. If Bloomfield had given up his supply to the first young lieutenant who asked for it, the consequences if Chelmsford had suddenly called for the ammunition might have been very severe indeed.

Essex persuaded Bloomfield to overrule Chelmsford's instructions. After sending Smith-Dorrien to the firing line with some ammunition, Essex 'followed with more ammunition in a mule cart. In loading the latter, I helped the Quartermaster of the 2nd Battalion to place the boxes in a cart, and while doing so the poor fellow was shot dead. The enemy's fire was increasing and I could hear the whiz of bullets all over the place.'

After delivering the ammunition Essex rode back to the line. The companies were closer to the camp. As the day wore on Zulus went round the flank of the firing line, heading for the rear of the camp. Durnford, who had been trying to stem this flanking movement was himself outflanked, and his troops fell back. This had serious consequences for the 24th as there was now nothing between the Zulus and the tents but open ground.

Aware that they were about to be outflanked, the 24th fell back. The bugles sounded 'Cease Fire' and then 'Retire'. 'Then, at the sound of a bugle, the firing ceased at a breath, and the whole British force rose from the ground and retired on the tents. Like a flame the whole Zulu force sprang to its feet and darted upon them.'

The auxiliary units, which had been steadied by the rock-like bearing of the 24th line, broke when they saw the line falling back:

[Essex} noticed some native infantry retreating towards the camp, their officers endeavouring to prevent them, without effect. On looking to our right and rear I saw the enemy was surrounding us. I rode up to Lieutenant-Colonel Durnford, near the right, and pointed this out. He requested me to take the men to that part of the field and endeavour to hold the enemy in check; but while he was speaking, those men of the Native Contingent who had remained in action rushed past us in the utmost disorder, thus laying open the right and rear of the companies of the 1st Battalion 24th Regiment on the left, and the enemy dashing forward in the most rapid manner poured in at this part of the line.

When the troops deployed on first sighting the Zulus, the tents had been left standing. If a full-scale engagement had been anticipated at that stage, Lieutenant-Colonel Pulleine, in command of the camp, would have ordered the tents to be struck. Left standing, they now presented an obstacle to troops falling back and trying to regroup. (The tents left standing also deceived Chelmsford, who could see them by telescope from his position. Seeing the tents standing, he assumed that there was no serious threat to the camp, and accordingly made no moves to support it.) In order to avoid being outflanked and taken in the rear, the order was given for the line to fall back. The tents were to prove a fatal obstruction.

As the 24th reached the tents their cohesion was broken as they tried to pass through. Many tents collapsed under the weight of struggling figures, and the fallen canvas, poles and ropes slowed the soldiers down and prevented them from forming a coherent line. Zulus got in between groups of soldiers and much hand-to-hand fighting took place. Where soldiers managed to congregate, they formed a ragged square and fired volleys into the rampant Zulus. Many Zulus ran close and threw their *assegais*. As the soldiers reloaded their single-shot Martini-Henrys, a process that was taking longer as breeches became fouled by the black powder cartridges, Zulus ran in and dragged down stragglers and wounded men. Essex saw the officers struggling to keep their men under control:

> The men became unsteady. A few fixed bayonets, and I heard the officers calling on their men to keep together and be steady.

That they did so under such impossible circumstances is a tribute to their courage and discipline. Lieutenant Stafford of the 1st Natal Native Contingent heard one officer calling on his men to 'Fix bayonets!' and went on, 'The only orders that I heard given out were by a young Imperial officer of the 2nd/24th Regiment, who was endeavouring to rally the remnants of his men, and actually got them into some sort of formation.'

Groups of soldiers stood shoulder to shoulder, facing the Zulus, steadily losing men to both gunfire and spear thrusts. The only option left was retreat, but as they neared the *nek* they saw Zulus on the skyline. The right horn of the Zulu attack was closing behind Isandlwana.

As the remnants of the 24th faced the final onslaught, Essex, outside the small groups facing the Zulus with little more than bayonets, took his life in his hands and made his escape down the route known to this day as Fugitives' Drift. This in itself was a perilous task.

Left behind in the camp in addition to the infantry soldiers were many non-combatants—wagon-drivers, *voorloopers* and civilian contractors. They had abandoned the camp and made off down the road to Rorke's Drift long before the Zulus reached the tents. But, on the winding track down to the river Manzimnyama, a greater horror awaited them. While the British had been occupied in dealing with the Zulu centre and left, the Zulu right had looped round behind Isandlwana and had cut off the road to the drift. The fleeing survivors had to run a gauntlet of battle-crazed warriors. The killing began. A Zulu warrior, interviewed after the war, stated:

> While the Kandampemvu were driving back the horsemen over the hill north of the camp, we worked round behind Isandlwana under cover of long grass and *dongas*, intending to join the Ngobamakosi on the 'neck', and sweep in upon the camp. Then we saw the white men beginning to run along the road to 'kwaJim';[6] many were cut off and killed, down in the stream which flows through the bottom of the valley. When they saw the valley was full of our warriors, they turned left and ran along the side of the hill; those who had not got horses were soon overtaken. The Nodwengu pursued the mounted men, numbers of whom were killed among the thorns and *dongas*, but I heard that some escaped.

---

6   Rorke's Drift.

Essex described the last moments in the camp as the Zulus surrounded small groups of red-coated infantrymen, who stood valiantly and fought their attackers, literally to the last man:

> We were driven up through the camp towards the road by which we had arrived, men falling right and left. The road immediately in rear of our camp led across a sort of *nek* between two hills. By the time we arrived here the retreat had become a stampede, horses, mules, oxen, waggons, all being carried in the same direction. The worst was yet to come. On gaining the *nek*, we found the circle our enemy had drawn round us was nearly complete, the only space not yet occupied by them being a rugged and deep dry water-course to the left of the road. A rush was made to gain this before the enemy, and I gave myself up for lost. I had, thank God, a very good sure-footed horse, but I saw many poor fellows roll over, their horses stumbling over the rocky ground.

The fugitives rushed towards the river, intent on survival. Individuals were ripped from their mounts and quickly butchered. Essex noticed that:

> The Zulus kept up with us on both sides, being able to run down the steep rocky ground quite as fast as a horse could travel. It was an awful ride of ten miles, and I cannot describe the terrible scenes I witnessed further than to say that the Zulus take no prisoners, but employ the *assegai* in every case.

As he raced along the boulder-strewn track on his sweating horse, a voice in Essex's head kept repeating, over and over again, the words he would recall in future years:

> Essex, you bloody fool, you had a chance of a good billet at home, and now, Essex, you are going to be killed!

Essex fired his revolver at any Zulu who came close, keeping the others at a distance, until he ran out of ammunition. Hurling away the useless revolver he now relied on the speed and endurance of his horse. Zulus remained alongside, cutting down more fleeing men until the Buffalo River came into sight. There was a steep decline where the river crashed over half submerged rocks, creating strong currents. After waiting for a moment as he assessed the situation, Essex drove his horse down the bank and into the water:

> There was no ford and many plunged in only to be carried away by the strong stream. I chose what seemed to be the best place for crossing, though there was not much time for deliberation, and luckily passed over in safety, my horse swimming with me in the saddle. Our pursuers kept

up with us until near the river, where they appeared to halt, but still kept firing on us.

On the Natal bank, some forty exhausted men, with just four regular officers,[7] still clutching their horses, gathered together to decide on the best course of action. They could head for Rorke's Drift, but Zulus had been seen crossing the river further up. Few had firearms, and they would not be able to protect themselves against any Zulu attacks. The alternative was to make for Helpmekaar, where a company of the 24th was based. Essex, as senior officer, took command of the small group of survivors. He wrote a note in pencil and sent it with a rider to Rorke's Drift, warning them of the approach of the Zulus who had been seen crossing the river.[8] Essex then ordered the men to ride the fifteen miles to Helpmekaar.

The group set off for Helpmekaar, but some of the volunteers, local men, rode off to their homes instead. When the remaining group reached Helpmekaar they found that the infantry company left to protect the stores was no longer there. The area was unusually quiet. Essex recorded:

> We saw Zulus on our right for five miles after crossing the river, and arrived at Helpmekaar between 5 and 6 o'clock. A large depot exists at that place, and we had determined to entrench and hold this, hoping to do so with the assistance of the company of the 24th we expected to find there. On our arrival we learnt that two companies of that regiment had left a few hours previously for Rorke's Drift, so we had to depend on our own resources. I found I was the senior officer present, so I took command and caused some waggons to be drawn up at a short distance all round the storehouse, a zinc building, quite indefensible. I had sacks of oats placed under the waggons and now had a barrier.

Essex deserves credit for organising a defence at Helpmekaar, inadequate though this might have been in the face of an all-out Zulu attack. Everyone there had seen what the Zulu army was capable of, and it was remarkable that any of the traumatised survivors could be induced to stay and defend Helpmekaar, which was a sprawling area of tents, huts and supplies. At Rorke's Drift, alerted by Essex's warning, the troops there had built the same sort of barricades that Essex was building at Helpmekaar. It was well that

---

7   These officers were special duty or volunteer regular officers, and unlike the officers and men of the 24th, they wore not red jackets, but dark-blue patrol jackets. It has been suggested that the Zulus, ordered to destroy the 'red-coated soldiers', took this instruction literally. It is certainly true that of the red-coated soldiers who fled down Fugitives' Drift, the majority were killed. While Essex in his dark coat would have been a tempting target, he might well have been ignored when a red-coated fugitive offered a more attractive one. Whatever the reason, the luck that was to earn Essex his nickname of 'Lucky Essex' was certainly with him this day.

8   The receipt of this timely warning gave the small garrison time to start preparing the defences they would so soon need.

they had, for by this time over 4,000 Zulus were throwing themselves at Rorke's Drift. Essex summarised his command:

We mustered about 25 Europeans, the others, about 10 volunteers and camp followers, continued their retreat. Two or three farmers with wives and children, arrived, and my little garrison numbered 48 men, of whom, only 28 had rifles. We expected the Zulus every moment, but we had plenty of ammunition, and I told every one to fire away as hard as he could in the event of attack, to deceive the enemy as to the number with whom he had to deal. We had an anxious time after dark, as we could not see ten yards in front of us. Several false alarms were given.

During the night some volunteers deserted, leaving Essex with even fewer men to defend Helpmekaar. But help was at hand. The two companies of the l/24th which had left for Rorke's Drift, having been unable to get there, returned and added much needed strength.

One more man was added to the defences when, after dark, a figure stumbled into the depot. Lieutenant Horace Smith-Dorrien had managed to get across the Buffalo River but lost his horse in the crossing. He was close to collapse, having ridden some thirty miles and run another twenty.

Throughout the night the weary defenders peered into the darkness, expecting to see Zulus at any moment, but as dawn broke, the likelihood of attack grew less and tired men tried to snatch some sleep.

The defence of Helpmekaar

Later in the morning a messenger brought news that Rorke's Drift had held out against sustained Zulu attacks, and that Chelmsford had arrived at the post with the remainder of his troops. Essex and Smith-Dorrien, with some mounted men, rode to Rorke's Drift to report to Chelmsford. When they arrived they saw what a desperate fight the defenders had put up. Lying in front of the defences were over 350 Zulu bodies.

Although employed to control Chelmsford's transport, Essex put his infantry experience to good use during the battle at Isandlwana, and behaved with courage, enterprise and initiative. He was certainly fortunate to escape from Isandlwana, but that his professionalism, enterprise and readiness to confront the enemy did not desert him is shown by his actions to defend Helpmekaar. As it happened, the Zulus did not attack, having, in obedience to Cetswayo's orders, halted at the Mzinyathi River which formed the border between Zululand and Natal. The survivors were not to know this, however, and Essex's efforts to form a defence at Helpmekaar, although probably doomed if the Zulus had launched an attack similar to that at Rorke's Drift, were highly creditable.

A GORDON AT RORKE'S DRIFT

Curiously enough, to complement Captain Edward Essex's presence at the battle of Isandlwana, another Gordon Highlander claimed to have been at Rorke's Drift. The following article, from a South African newspaper, appeared in the *Tiger and Sphinx* in 1957:

> Mr. Hugh Fraser Ross, the oldest Gordon Highlander in the world, died in Addington Hospital at the age of 104. Sailor, soldier, farmer, railwayman, he first saw Durban in 1874, and spent 83 of his 104 years in South Africa.
>
> Mr. Ross was born at Portmahomack, a little fishing village in Ross-shire, Scotland, on November 25, 1852, the year the *Birkenhead* sank off the Cape Coast. Aged 14 he went to sea in a windjammer, and in five years before the mast he sailed to South America, Africa and the Far East. He might have remained at sea, but aged 19, he celebrated too well with some shipmates during a night ashore at Glasgow. One of their companions that evening was a recruiting sergeant—and next morning Ross and his friend found themselves in the Army.
>
> Ross was posted to the Training Depot of The Gordon Highlanders at Aberdeen. He completed his training there, and in 1874 he sailed with his regiment for the Colony of Natal.
>
> The Gordon Highlanders [75th] moved north from Durban to the 'interior,' to the small centre of Pinetown, where the regiment was to do garrison duties. Later, Ross transferred from the Gordons to the Army

Service Corps.[9] It was with his new unit that he saw action at Rorke's Drift and in the historic Battle of Ulundi. Then followed more service in the Anglo-Boer War of 1880–1881.[10]

Ross was back in uniform again for the campaign in Mashonaland in 1896 and not long after that he was fighting against the Boer Commandos in the South African War.

Hugh Fraser Ross was 62 when the Kaiser's war started. 'Too old,' they told him when he went to join up again. But the 'Old Man' had an officer friend who knew that the experienced campaigner from the Highlands would be helpful in training recruits. Ross joined as a private. In two weeks he was a corporal, and in a month a sergeant.

In retirement Hugh Ross lived quietly and simply. It was through *The Sunday Tribune* that The Gordon Highlanders first knew that Hugh Fraser Ross was still alive. He was then 97 years old. The Gordon Highlanders Regimental Association sent him a goodwill gift, followed by others in later years. They acknowledged him as the oldest Gordon Highlander in the world.

T&S, November 1957.

Hugh Ross died in 1956, aged 104. His ashes were brought back to Scotland where they were consigned to the sea:

With a piper playing the lament, and soldiers and sailors standing to attention, the ashes of Mr. Hugh Ross the world's oldest Gordon Highlander, were scattered in the Moray Firth on 20th December.

The ceremony took place on board the *Britannia,* flagship of the Lossiemouth Seine net fishing fleet, with which 104-year-old Mr. Ross had gone to sea as a boy.

The *Britannia*, with flag at half-mast, tossed in a foam-flecked sea as Provost Lyon Dean consigned the ashes to the waters of the firth, thus fulfilling Mr. Ross's last wish before he died in Durban last September.

---

9   Presumably the transfer took place when the 75th returned to Britain in 1875.

10 There is an anomaly here. In 1874 the 92nd was in India, while the 75th, which seven years later was to become the 1st Battalion, The Gordon Highlanders, was in its last year of service in South Africa. Neither Regiment 'sailed . . . for the Colony of Natal' in that year, and it was unlikely that recruits from the Gordon Highlanders depot would be sent to the 75th, rather than to the 93rd, the 92nd's linked Regiment. It is possible that volunteers might have been called for a draft for the 75th, and that Ross took the chance for service in Africa; alternatively, Ross might have been part of a draft for the 92nd going out to India and was diverted to the 75th when the troopship staged through Cape Town. Ross clearly served in South Africa, and just as clearly considered himself a Gordon Highlander, but just how he got to the 75th is unclear. As to his claim to have been at Rorke's Drift, the incomplete roll of those present at the battle does not show his name under the Army Service Corps, although as only one name is shown for that Corps, that does not necessarily preclude his presence. Ulundi, the battle that broke the Zulu army, was fought some five months after Rorke's Drift and there would have been a substantial supply system requiring a significant Army Service Corps presence.

Before the ashes were taken on board, a short service was conducted at the local fisherman's institute. Then, headed by Piper T. Smith, playing the march, and watched by a large crowd, the company marched in procession to the *Britannia,* Lieutenant Charles Michie,[11] Keith, bearing the casket containing the ashes.

Mr. Ross, a native of Portmahomack, lived in Lossiemouth until the age of 20

T&S, March 1958.

ESSEX AT ULUNDI

Essex saw action against the Zulus again when Chelmsford defeated the Zulu army at Ulundi in July 1879. As at Isandlwana, Essex placed himself in the battle line. This time he was secure within the British square.

On the night of 3 July Essex wrapped himself in his blanket and tried to sleep. As Transport Officer he would have no duties, so he chose to accompany the soldiers across the river Mfolozi to be present when the battle opened. It was a cold and misty night, and many found difficulty in sleeping. At 4 a.m. Essex was awake, sipping a hot drink to ward off the chill. A thick white mist reduced visibility to a few yards. The infantry started to cross the shallow waters at 6 a.m. after the cavalry had crossed. The infantry regiments, once across the river, cleared the short scrub along the riverbank, then started to form an enormous hollow square (it was actually a large rectangle). Within an hour the column had crossed the river and was taking position in the square. There was no sign of any Zulus as Chelmsford's force formed upon the ground he had selected to fight from.

Shortly before 9 a.m. two strong columns of Zulus were seen coming down from the hills and then disappearing into the valley. A third strong column emerged from Ulundi, and further bodies of Zulus gathered to the sides and rear of the square. The vast Zulu host, some 20,000 strong, closed in and surrounded the soldiers standing to await them.

Essex, one of the few survivors who had seen the same tactics employed so successfully at Isandlwana, could be forgiven for a cold shiver of fear, but he was reassured by the imperturbable infantry, four rows deep on every side, who waited for the order to fire.

They did not have long to wait, as the Zulus launched their attack against all sides of the square. They were met with steady, controlled volleys from infantry rifles, repeating fire from Gatling guns and canister fire from artillery. As a contest it was hardly fair. Overwhelming numbers of Zulus

---

11 Charlie Michie served in the 2nd Battalion in Singapore and was captured with the Battalion in 1942, spending the rest of the war in Japanese prison camps. He became the Quartermaster of the 1st Battalion, and retired with the rank of major.

armed with *assegais* were no match for modern technology, skilfully handled by trained and reliable soldiers. Captured Zulus stated that they had been overwhelmed by the noise as much as the impact of the bullets and shrapnel that tore into them. It took less than half an hour before the Zulus lost heart and broke.

The wavering Zulus were struck by the 17th Lancers, who left the square to disperse and destroy the Zulus, who turned and fled, closely pursued by Lancers and mounted irregular units. The Zulu army no longer presented a credible threat, and although some small-scale actions continued for a few weeks, the war was effectively over. Ulundi fell to Chelmsford, who ordered the burning of the Royal *kraal*.

The Zulus lost over 1,500 men; the British, three officers and 79 men.

After his escape from Isandlwana, Essex's fellow officers had started to call him 'Lucky'. His luck continued when among the weapons surrendered by the Zulus was found in infantry sword, without its scabbard. The blade was inscribed '*Essex*'. It was Essex's sword, which he had left in his tent at the start of the Isandlwana battle.

Essex received the campaign medal for South Africa, with clasp '1879', and he was mentioned in official reports in the *London Gazette* for his work with the transport columns. Given the brevet rank of major, in January 1880 Essex boarded ship for Britain and some welcome leave.

ESSEX IN THE 1ST ANGLO-BOER WAR

Essex was to see South Africa again much sooner than he might have expected. This time he would face a foe expert in the use of firearms. Unrest with the Boers over the status of Transvaal had reached a point where armed insurrection seemed inevitable. The War Office sent out more troops to assist Major-General Pomeroy Colley, High Commissioner and General Officer Commanding South-East Africa. With all his South African experience, it was not surprising that Essex was selected to go.

On 9 December 1880 Essex boarded ship for South Africa. Before he arrived the Boers had opened fire on British troops at Potchefstroom, ending negotiations about the independence of the Transvaal. Transvaal was put under martial law, and Colley prepared to support the beleaguered garrisons in the Transvaal. The Boers, knowing that any attempt to relieve the garrisons must come through the pass at Laing's Nek, sent a force under Piet Joubert to seize the pass and fortify it. Laing's Nek and the approaches to it were dominated on both sides by high hills.

When Essex arrived in South Africa he joined Colley at Newcastle, on 2 January 1881. He was appointed Deputy Assistant Adjutant on Colley's Staff. Essex kept a journal in which he recorded the events of each day. His entry for 23 January describes Colley reviewing his troops:

His Excellency the Major-General reviewed the Natal Field Force this afternoon. The troops marched past and afterwards formed a square and were addressed by his Excellency. Orders were issued for the march of the Natal Field Force tomorrow.

Essex recorded the beginning of the advance:

The column marched at 5 am. The last wagon left camp at 7.30 am. About 3 miles from Camp Newcastle, a long and steep hill had to be climbed. On account of rain that had fallen during the week, the ground was soft, and this increased the difficulty. The wagons were taken up, one by one, by double 'spans' of oxen. About one half of the wagons had reached the top of the hill by 11 a.m. and were halted in order that the leading battalion might breakfast for 4 hours. It was not until 3.30 that the whole of the wagons had completed the ascent. A *laager* was formed about 5 miles from the late camp. This was completed by 5 pm.

Colley's Natal Field Force included a Naval Brigade that had rockets and two Gatling guns (these had been used to great effect against the Zulus at Ulundi two years before, but the Boers would never throw themselves against them as the Zulus had done).

The Natal Field Force crossed the Ingogo River and advanced to within five miles of Laing's Nek. A reconnaissance of the *nek* confirmed that it was held by the Boers. Colley camped at a farm just east of the road.

On Friday 28 January 1881 the troops rose at 3.30 a.m. to prepare for an attack on the Nek. The plan was to seize the hills on the east of the pass, from which the Boers on the hills west of the Nek could be neutralised, allowing passage through the Nek.

At 9.25 a.m. the artillery opened fire, and fifteen minutes later Colley sent the 58th Regiment to take Table Hill, which overlooked the pass. This would involve a long climb up the steep-sided hill against Boers in prepared positions. The column began to move forward, and Colley allowed his staff to go with it. As they were on horses the staff officers went to the front of the column. Colonel B.M. Deane, the senior officer present, led the 58th as they trudged up the increasingly steep hill.

At the top the Boers had dug a trench about 150 yards long with an earth parapet in front of it. They lined the parapet, while others were sited to fire into the flank of the 58th. The staff officers at the front of the men were an irresistibly inviting target for the Boers. Essex's helmet was sent spinning from his head, and his horse was hit, crumpling forward and throwing Essex over its head. Struggling to his feet, Essex expected to attract more fire but was not hit. The Brigade Major, Major Poole and Lieutenant Henry Dolphin lay dead, victims of the accurate Boer fire.

The 58th got within forty yards of the Boer positions but could go no further; within half an hour it was running out of ammunition. Essex, the senior officer present, realised that the situation was hopeless, especially as reinforcements were strengthening the Boer position. The 58th, by contrast, was losing men. There was no option but to withdraw, and at 11a.m. Essex ordered the bugler to sound the retreat. The withdrawal began on the right of the line, covered by two companies on the left which had borne the brunt of the engagement. Essex moved across to two companies of the 60th Rifles as the 58th withdrew. He moved these companies to the shelter of a ledge and from there directed their covering fire against the Boers until it was their turn to withdraw.

Essex was the only survivor out of the five staff officers who had set off so happily that morning. Once again his luck had seen him through a situation where so many had died.

Colley's despatch to the Secretary of State for War described the battle and included recommendations for men who had distinguished themselves. The *London Gazette* published details:

> Major Essex, who was with Colonel Deane in the attack on the hill, where his horse was killed under him, and distinguished himself by his courage and coolness, remained to the last, directing the companies that covered the retirement of the 58th regiment.

Essex was involved again on 8 February at the Ingogo River where Colley and his staff narrowly avoided being captured. Essex remained close to Colley throughout, carrying out his orders. After their withdrawal during the night, the only staff officers who remained alive were Essex and Colley's aide-de-camp (ADC). Essex, already known as 'Lucky' Essex was now being referred to as 'Bullet-Proof' and 'Indestructible'. He spent the day keeping close to Colley as they moved about the defensive position encouraging the men; and once again emerged unscathed. Colley reported that:

> Major Essex, Column Staff officer and Lieutenant B. Hamilton, 15th Regiment, my aide-de-camp, rendered me active and valuable assistance throughout the day.

H. Rider Haggard, the famous author, considered that Essex's exploits required more of an explanation than Colley had actually described:

> Of his staff officers, Major Essex now alone survived, his usual good fortune having carried him safe through the battle of Ingogo. What makes his repeated escapes more remarkable is that he was generally to be found in the heaviest firing.

While peace talks were being held, Essex was seconded to the 92nd. [12] Soon after his arrival a vacancy occurred for the rank of major. As a brevet major, Essex was senior to all the other captains in the regiment, and he was promoted to full major on 24 August 1881.[13] The 92nd spent a further year in South Africa before returning to Britain. Essex spent that time happily on regimental duties with the 2nd Battalion of his new regiment.[14] In April 1882 the 92nd sailed for Britain, where it eventually ended up in Edinburgh. It had been overseas for fourteen years.

Essex was appointed as instructor at the Royal Military College, Sandhurst, where his extensive experience must have been of great benefit to the gentlemen cadets. In February 1885 he was informed that he was to be posted to the 1st Battalion, The Gordon Highlanders when it returned to Malta from Egypt. The *Times* of 19 August reported:

> The troopship *Tamar* 4,650 tons and 2,500-horse power, embarked at Chatham on the 18 August 1885 officers and men for Alexandria. The *Tamar* will embark at Portland tomorrow. Major Essex 1st Battalion Gordon Highlanders, Lieutenant W. Booth and Lieutenant C.D. Winter, 1st Battalion Hampshire Regiment, and 141 non-commissioned officers and privates of the lst Battalion Dorset Regiment for Malta.

Essex oversaw the boarding of the troops on the single funnelled *Tamar*, which had carried him with the 75th to South Africa in 1871. He commanded the draft and saw their safe delivery in Malta.

In Malta Essex rejoined the regiment he had left as the 75th, in its new guise as the 1st Battalion, The Gordon Highlanders. It was totally different from the regiment he had known, but not unfamiliar, after his time with the 2nd Battalion. In May 1886, while still serving with the 1st Battalion, Essex was promoted to Lieutenant-Colonel, and informed that he would in due course assumed command of the 2nd Battalion, which was now based in Guernsey. He moved to the 2nd Battalion in 1887 as second-in-command until the Commanding Officer, Lieutenant-Colonel J.C. Hay retired in June.[15]

---

12 The 92nd was to be merged with the 75th on 30 June 1881 to form The Gordon Highlanders, so it was logical that Essex of the 75th should be seconded to the 92nd.

13 The vacancy was occasioned by the wounding at Majuba (and subsequent long convalescence) of Maj J.C. Hay. (See Volume IX, Chapter 17 for details of Majuba) There is no doubt that Essex deserved his substantive majority, but it must have raised eyebrows in the 2nd Battalion that he, an officer of the 1st Battalion seconded from the staff, was promoted into a 2nd Battalion vacancy.

14 Essex's Commanding Officer at this time was Lt-Col G.S. White, V.C.

15 Lt-Col J.C. Hay. The *Peeblesshire Advertiser* of 18th June, 1887, says: 'Seldom has a more picturesque and touching scene been witnessed than when Col. Hay took leave at Guernsey of the 2nd Battalion Gordon Highlanders (the old 92nd). Col. Hay is the oldest soldier in his Regiment, has served with it for thirty-two years in peace and war; been wounded in its ranks and has been its Commanding Officer. When the day came for severing the tie between the Colonel and those under him they determined to see him off with such an expression of love and respect as those who were present were not likely to forget. The Officers carried him shoulder-high to the gate of the Fort, where

Within two months of taking command Essex took the 2nd Battalion to Ireland, embarking on HMS *Assistance* for Belfast. The tour in Ireland was uneventful, and Essex saw out his tenure as commanding officer, leaving behind a happy, well-trained and efficient battalion.

Essex decided that, after commanding a battalion of The Gordon Highlanders, he would leave the Army, and after twenty-four years' service, on 1 July 1891, he sadly relinquished command of his battalion.

Edward 'Lucky' Essex, survivor of Isandlwana, Laing's Nek and Ingogo, lived until 1939, when he died in Bournemouth, aged 91. He had maintained his links with The Gordon Highlanders, being a faithful subscriber to the *Tiger and Sphinx*, to which he contributed on occasion. With him died an unexpected link between an epic battle in British history and The Gordon Highlanders.

Edward Essex

a carriage was awaiting; but the N.C.O.s and men would have no horses, and dragged it all the way to the pier, with twelve pipers to clear the way. At the pier officers, men, women and children all pressed for the last shake of the Colonel's hand. Then, the band playing, officers and men joining hands, '*Should auld acquaintance be forgot*' was sung and many a strong hand dashed away evidence of a tender heart, as the ship steamed slowly away amidst the cheers of Highlanders and islanders.' (*T&S, July 1925*.)

CHAPTER 19

A GORDON IN ABYSSINIA

IN 1940 Italy controlled Abyssinia, which it had conquered in 1936, as well as its 19th century conquests of Eritrea and Italian Somaliland. In August 1940 the Duke of Aosta invaded British Somaliland, whose long borders with Abyssinia and Italian Somaliland made defence impracticable. British forces evacuated to Aden. Italian East Africa bordered both British-held Kenya and Sudan, which was jointly controlled by Britain and Egypt; it also threatened the Suez Canal.

In January 1941, British forces launched a counter-offensive, moving into Eritrea from Sudan, attacking Italian Somaliland from the south and moving into Abyssinia. A British force, Gideon Force, commanded by Lieutenant-Colonel Orde Wingate, entered Abyssinia from Sudan, tying down substantial Italian forces and capturing strong points.

The Gordon Highlanders were not in the Abyssinian campaign, but one Gordon Highlander played a significant role. Major Hugh Boustead spent nearly ten years in Sudan, and had commanded the Sudan Camel Corps. He resigned from the army in 1935, when he was a company commander in the 1st Battalion, Gordon Highlanders in Edinburgh, to become a District Commissioner in Sudan. When war was declared he was recalled to the colours in the rank of Lieutenant-Colonel, tasked with raising a battalion of Sudanese troops for the campaign to drive the Italians from Abyssinia and East Africa. The extracts covering the Abyssinian campaign are from Boustead's autobiography *The Wind of Morning*.

In June 1940 Boustead was in Egypt where he attended some training exercises in the desert:

> After ten days of this Sir Arthur Smith sent for me and said, 'I would like you to meet General Wavell.' I was taken into the C. in C.'s room, where Wavell was sitting at his desk, his craggy face quite unreadable. He was about to speak to me when the telephone rang, and he picked up the receiver. He listened impassively, and in silence, and then put it back quietly. Turning to Smith, he said, 'That is to say that the Italians have come in'; he appeared unmoved at the news which committed his forces to action on two fronts against vastly superior numbers. Then he carried on with his interview with me. He asked me a number of questions about the Sudan, and went on, 'I understand that Platt[1] wants you to raise and

1   Commander of the Sudan Defence Force.

261

command the Frontier Battalion to cross the Abyssinian border. Have you met Sandford who is going into Egypt with a mission to raise the patriots?' I replied that I had had two or three talks with him in the past week. 'Well, Boustead, you'd better get on a flying-boat tomorrow morning and go down and raise your Frontier Battalion. Good luck to you. We shall hear more of you later.'

Raising the Frontier Battalion 'was no problem—young men of fine physique clamoured for enlistment in the new Patrol Companies'. Training presented problems—for example, the Nuba Company, with 270 six-foot jet-black hill men from the Nuba Mountains, had to be taught Arabic before working alongside the other companies. The companies were scattered over Sudan: the Eastern on the Abyssinian border, the Western a thousand miles away in Darfur, the others in Kordofan and the Blue Nile Province:

> To supervise and coordinate their training meant immense journeys followed by long hot days in the sun, on foot or horseback, watching the troops and setting and demonstrating exercises to the officers. The Sudanese officers were irregulars, like the men; the British were either regulars, or seconded from the Political Service, or planters from the Gezira Cotton Company. The Kaid[2] had picked them all personally—as he told me, 'I have chosen your officers for their toughness, adaptability and leadership.'

In late 1940 the situation in North Africa and the Middle East was ominous. In the Western Desert Wavell faced an enormous Italian army; Syria and Iraq were danger spots. In August the Italians had overrun the defences of British Somaliland, and their next target was Sudan. They had occupied the border towns of Kassala and Gallabat, and the way seemed open to Khartoum and the Nile, or up the Red Sea coast to Port Sudan.

Operating in the Abyssinian mountains would mean limited supplies, brought in on animal transport, and no reinforcements. Boustead trained his men to meet the enemy at close quarters while avoiding casualties and to control ammunition expenditure by strict fire discipline. He developed bold leaders, who could use ground, fire and movement and fire discipline. There would be a great deal of patrolling and the men were taught to operate, completely self-contained, in small groups.

On paper the Italians had overwhelming superiority, with nearly 300,000 men with tanks, aircraft and artillery against 7,500 men in Sudan and 10,000 in Kenya. Well supplied with ammunition and petrol, everything should have led them to strike across the 1,200 miles of frontier into Sudan, defended by three British battalions and 4,500 men of the Sudan Defence Force. The

---

2   Gen Platt.

Italians' biggest problem was in the 'occupied territory' of Abyssinia, with disaffected and bitterly resentful inhabitants. Some 14,000 Italian and Eritrean troops were tied down where Boustead would operate, in forts from which they emerged to sweep linking roads.

British strategy was simple: to invade Eritrea and bring to battle and destroy the main Italian armies; simultaneously to invade Italian Somaliland and Southern Abyssinia from Kenya; and to deny the enemy any reinforcements from his central position by raising and arming patriot forces to harass and destroy his garrisons in Abyssinia. The first task was accomplished by the 4th and 5th Indian Divisions after bitter fighting, and the second by General Cunningham's force of South African and East and West African troops. Part of the overall plan involved a small force, of brigade size, entering Abyssinia from the west to tie up Italian troops in the Gojjam area, bounded by Lake Tana in the north and the Abbai River (Blue Nile) in the east and south. This force was to be commanded by Lieutenant-Colonel Orde Wingate,[3] staff officer to General Platt. The backbone of this fighting force was Boustead's Frontier Battalion.

With his trained Battalion concentrated under his command, Boustead's main problem was transport for the march into Abyssinia. His route lay across a wasteland of stony ridges covered with thick waterless scrub, impassable to motor transport. The way led steadily upwards to the great Abyssinian Escarpment, 4,000–5,000-feet high and fully 2,000 feet above the hot wilderness below. They had to rely on camels to carry supplies, and weapons and ammunition for local patriots. Eventually 18,000 camels were used. Boustead found men for the camel transport in old friends of his Camel Corps days, who had served before mechanisation. They flocked to join him, and their long service in the Camel Corps bore fruit in the campaign.

The Frontier Battalion began its move into Abyssinia in November 1940 It was established on the Escarpment by January 1941 and prepared to meet Emperor Haile Selassie as he returned to Abyssinia. Wingate wanted to prepare a landing ground for the Emperor's return by air, but:

> the innocuous looking plain of white grass, which some staff officer had reported as eminently suitable for a landing ground, was in fact a huge bamboo forest with deep ravines beneath the canopy of leaves. The proposed [alternative] northern route for the Emperor in his lorry and my

---

3   Maj (later Lt-Col) Orde Wingate, 'staff officer to the Kaid', later became famous as the leader of the Chindits in Burma. Boustead found Wingate's strategic concept for the operations in Abyssinia arresting and brilliant, but his tactics impractical. Boustead relates 'Our relationship during the coming campaign was rendered more difficult by his acute lack of experience in dealing with anything but small bodies of men to whom he could give personal commands. This led to his interfering in the chain of command, which I would not stand for, and over which we had various violent altercations, since my own position in command of my battalion would have been insupportable if I had accepted his attitude.'

company and its camels led across a tangle of ridges and escarpments running north-west from Belaya.

Boustead flew to Khartoum to dissuade Wingate from the folly of his plan and urged him to follow the track that Acland's men (Acland commanded one of Boustead's companies) had cut. Boustead differed fundamentally with Wingate over the route chosen for the Emperor and the camel convoys, and he told him so. They argued for several hours:

> A further point of contention was the landing ground at Belaya, which Wingate said in an airy way could be constructed easily and quickly on the north-east of the mountain. I told him frankly that if this was his view, he was signally ignorant of mountain topography.

Wingate refused to alter his proposal for the Emperor's entry to Abyssinia:

> and only his own arrival at Belaya in late January on a jaded horse, without the Emperor, finally convinced him of the folly of his northern route which more than doubled the mortality of the camel convoys.

In February Boustead met up with Haile Selassie and the Ethiopian Battalion, which had lost most of its camels on its arduous journey. The campaign plan was revised, thanks to intelligence from Boustead's patrols. The main Italian force in the south, some 20,000 men in the forts of Burye, Dembecha and Debra Marcos would be attacked and isolated. This would pin down forces which might otherwise be used for the defence of Eritrea.

Boustead sent companies to different areas where they could operate against individual Italian garrisons. He enlisted local partisans (patriots), although rivalry of feudal chieftains meant constant mistrust among them. Although their military effectiveness was limited, and they did not make best use of the scarce British weapons with which they had been equipped, they still played an important part. Their existence prevented the enemy from carrying out reconnaissance patrols, and reinforced the Italians' siege mentality, keeping large forces immobile in the various garrisons:

> Gideon Force, as we were called, was to move first on to the fort of Matakal, some six miles east of Burye. Wingate's object was to stand astride the Italian lines of communication between Burye and Debra Marcos, and to harass the subsidiary forts. His strategy, and the psychological concept of this move, was typically imaginative; and it was decisive in its effect on the mind of the Italian commander.

Gideon Force achieved its aim of spreading concern and apprehension among the enemy, but Boustead had grave reservations about Wingate's cavalier deployment of his forces and flouting of basic military principles:

Wingate's concentration of his force achieved its purpose of alarming the enemy with exaggerated reports of its size: but to keep it concentrated ran counter to all he wanted to accomplish. We were a guerrilla army whose set policy was to rely on movement, on night operations carried out by small, mobile parties. Only in this way could we maintain the air concealment which would protect the force and ensure that its real size was not assessed by the enemy. On this policy security and surprise depended. Surprise was our offensive weapon.

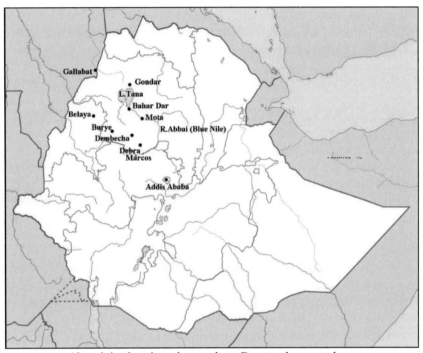

Abyssinia showing places where Boustead operated

But in the event Gideon Force moved down the Burye road with the Ethiopian Battalion leading, for political reasons, with no estimate of how far this four-mile camel column could march before daylight, with no plan for a day camp, no reconnaissance for cover from the air, or defence on the ground, over open downland where no cover was available. Moving as a military force, suffering all the risks of the most unwieldy form of mass transport imaginable, we outraged every military principle. Chance led our going; chance found our night camp; chance covered our day move, and some tolerant Deity protected us. In retrospect those days and nights remain the nightmare that they were at the time. They wore down men and animals at the beginning of a campaign characterised by its ardours and endurances. They aroused in me a fury at the military incompetence which would expose men to wanton and useless fatigue which would hinder not help operations.[4]

I rode with Wingate for a reconnaissance of the Burye forts. Viewed from a hilltop, the circle of low hills on which the forts sat presented a formidable appearance. Wire defences could be seen around the lower forts, a circle of low stone walls set in grassy mounds marked the crest of the positions. They were each manned by a battalion.

Wingate wanted to attack that night, but Boustead argued against this. Their forces were concentrated, vulnerable to bombers, and within easy striking range of enemy forts. If they lost their transport their fighting role would be fatally weakened. He argued that they were 'breaking every principle upon which we agreed for the conduct of the campaign'. Wingate finally heeded Boustead, and detailed the Ethiopian Battalion to harass communications between Burye and Debra Marcos. Boustead's Frontier Battalion would move by night to a point south of Matakal. The camel transport would stay at a safe distance, while the two companies, with mule and horse transport, would have a mobile striking role.

Boustead warned Wingate, who had ridden ahead with a Frontier Battalion platoon to reconnoitre, that the Sudanese soldiers, eager for battle, would inevitably become prematurely involved in broad daylight if he sent them on an independent reconnaissance of enemy positions. Later that day heavy firing was heard from the south. Boustead feared that his platoon with Wingate was in contact with the Italians, and this was confirmed when he found that, despite all his warnings, it had been sent on a reconnaissance and had come under fire from the Burye fortifications. Boustead felt that this 'precipitate and rash act' could have involved the destruction or capture of all of the camel transport. The daylight move was against their agreed principles and the decision of the previous evening.

Boustead went on foot to determine the situation. He found Wingate 'in realisation of the implications of his action, agitated and apprehensive'. Desultory firing was coming from the eastern forts, but the main risk was the sudden appearance of a motorised column from the Burye Garrison, three miles away up the metalled road on which the camel column had been drawn in broad daylight. Wingate was highly critical of the slow progress of the column, but Boustead retorted that Wingate had pointlessly precipitated a daylight action which could jeopardise the whole campaign.

Wingate headed east with the camel column; an anti-tank section leading to prevent an ambush on the main road. Boustead sent one of his companies

---

4   Wingate, characteristically, blamed everyone but himself. One officer on the force strung out about the countryside commented, 'Wingate was in a great temper. He cursed Boustead. He cursed Boyle. He openly said he was sick of the [Ethiopian Battalion].'

on a feint attack on the eastern fort to distract the enemy. The move was covered by mortars, whose fire brought down a heavy response. Every machine-gun and mortar in the fort opened fire and the wood where Boustead's mortars were concealed was a mass of flying twigs and branches as bullets whined and ricocheted through the trees. The attacking company worked forward in long grass, waiting for night. There was no question of close action in broad daylight, and once night fell their task of covering the withdrawal of the camel column would be accomplished. Before this happened, however, a force of enemy cavalry charged the company. The company commander and a Sudanese sergeant, firing Bren guns from the hip, drove off the horsemen, only twenty yards from their front and flank. The enemy left both men and horses dead and wounded.

Boustead's diversion had clearly disturbed the Italian commander, and Boustead felt that the threat of a night attack would add to his anxiety. He detailed one of his company commanders, with one platoon, to keep the Italians awake and on their toes throughout the night by desultory bursts of Bren and rifle fire, from positions widely dispersed along their fronts, and then to withdraw his men before daylight. The diversions were a great success. As Boustead linked up with Wingate and moved east, they could hear the roar of the guns in the Burye fort and see flares lighting the sky. The Italians fired off hundreds of thousands of rounds at the pin-prick probes, but the platoon mounting the diversion suffered no single casualty.

This was the pattern for the rest of the campaign. Boustead ensured that Italian forts and positions were harassed with mortar fire, which often set fire to buildings. The Italians' efforts to put out the fires offered irresistible targets to the Vickers guns of the attackers, which inflicted heavy casualties, and there were many desertions as a direct result.

When the Italians evacuated Burye to withdraw to Debra Marcos, a hundred miles to the east, Boustead agreed with Wingate that the Frontier Battalion should take up position overlooking Mankousa, leaving Wingate with three of Boustead's platoons on Mankousa Church Hill to observe. Wingate agreed to withdraw and rejoin the main body as soon as the move of the Burye garrison to Mankousa was confirmed. Boustead emphasised that his platoons should not be tied down in a fight, but should rejoin him as soon as the Italian withdrawal was confirmed. There was no question of fighting in daylight. Boustead moved after dark. An hour after daylight, as Wingate had not appeared and all seemed quiet, he moved the force towards Mankousa, keeping it concealed whilst taking up position to observe Mankousa. The road from Burye was 'black with enemy troops, in all some 10,000, preceded by four light armoured cars'. The Italian withdrawal was in full swing. As they watched, a large detachment broke away from the main body and surged up the hill to Mankousa Fort:

Mortar shells were falling thick and fast on Church Hill, which I sincerely hoped and prayed had been evacuated by Wingate and my platoons. Presently the relieving detachment was joined by the garrison and together they closed up on the main body.

After some time Wingate appeared looking particularly scruffy and rather shaken, having been caught by the mortar fire on Church Hill. I was angry that the platoons with him should have been uselessly exposed in this way and said so.[5] Wingate [went back] to Burye to tie up the administrative arrangements.

Moving at speed after the enemy, we caught up with them at three o'clock making camp on a hillside where they were proposing to spend the night. I turned the force off into a wood some thousand yards from the enemy and waited for dusk. That night [we] spent a rewarding evening shooting up enemy groups around their camp fires, beautifully silhouetted in the flames. Pandemonium broke out, and their firing in response was incessant. At about 4 a.m. I decided to put the force in a position round their rear from which we could harass them with fire as they moved out of the camp. The subsequent three hours spent shooting up their daylight move were exciting in the extreme. We broke into two parties, Peter Acland and myself moving well beyond their position to where we could get some really good shooting on to their lorries as they drove down the main road. Bill Harris moved in close to the exit of the night camp and after a very successful shoot was nearly taken by the cavalry. He had to run for it with his troops. Peter Acland and I were outflanked by a party of tough Eritreans and they nearly caught us.

When the Italian column eventually got away they left casualties strewn along the road. At 10 o'clock Johnson arrived from Mankousa with his company, and we continued the pursuit, leaving Bill Harris and his company, who had had a very tough night, to rest and follow us. He joined me about nightfall and I repeated the operations of the previous evening with Johnson's company, shooting up the enemy all night.

Boustead and his Frontier Battalion pressed on towards Dembecha. They were marching uphill through forests when they came over a rise to be greeted by a sudden burst of firing. They had come up to Dembecha Fort, and the enemy was holding a ridge in front of the fort in force. They spent two nights probing for a position from which to harass and attack Dembecha Fort,

---

5 There were frequent clashes between Boustead and Wingate. Although they were of equal rank, Wingate was in command of Gideon Force. While Boustead used every suitable opportunity to harass the enemy, he would not engage them when they had overwhelming superiority in numbers, as he had no means of replacing soldiers killed in action. On this occasion Wingate 'flew into a rage at Boustead, accusing him of cowardice' for not engaging the Italians, an accusation that was as unjust as it was unjustified.

but 'the enemy saved us the trouble by abandoning it and continuing their withdrawal to Debra Marcos. We came up with them on 13th March, and encamped in a wooded area while we reconnoitred':

Wingate and I had another disagreement: I told him I wanted to operate from the high ground to the north, and not from the low bush country south of the road, where the troops would be plagued with flies, and where we would get no observation by day for our operations by night. He disagreed: but when we rode forward to a copse on a high hill, with a fine view of Debra Marcos itself and the Gulit positions, the issued settled itself. We might well have been in the Perthshire Highlands, with moorland grassy slopes running down to a wooded river, and with the Chokey Mountains behind us to the North.

Active patrolling produced information about the enemy positions. The Italians did not sit behind their defences passively, and counter-attacked vigorously. With the intelligence gathered Boustead planned a series of attacks which would end in the fall of Debra Marcos on 3 April 1941, nearly a fortnight later. The attacks were launched on enemy positions night after night; each from a different point and on a different fort, made with bomb and bayonet—and mortars when practicable. Boustead's men withdrew before daylight to rest, only to attack another fort the next night:

Each night attack was preceded by an afternoon reconnaissance which I made with the officers and senior N.C.O.s of the company. We would move out at 3 p.m. and go under cover to a position from which we could survey the glacis of the fort which was the object of the night's attack. There I would point out the targets. We rode down with horse holders to hold the horses well out of sight. Then I sent back to bring up the force to where they spent the early part of the night. They were fed before they left and came on foot quietly; no fires allowed.

Each night attack was launched between midnight and 3 a.m. I would remain at a vantage point with Very pistols and give the signal for withdrawal. In the meantime I would wait with a small escort suffering gruelling anxiety as to what was happening. The Sudanese troops were instructed to attack and then when firing was opened to lie down and move on again as firing stopped. This required discipline and courage; it was so easy once lying down to remain like that. The orders were to assault the trenches up to the point of bayonet and bomb and then to withdraw. It was essential that the withdrawal should be carried out and the forces well clear before daylight, when they could be caught by machine-guns or ridden down on the open hillsides by cavalry.

Nearly all these forts were equipped with long sweeping glacis in front of them. Lying in position I would see and hear the firing going on, a tremendous crackle which would last perhaps ten minutes, and I wondered how these chaps could live on the open slopes. But it was all high, being fired at night without sights, and then the Sudanese soldiers would move forward until the next burst opened. Later there would come a crash of the bombs and one or two shots from the trenches.

These incessant night attacks cost us some casualties, though very few in comparison with what daylight assaults would have involved.

Rumours came that the Italians would abandon Gulit, fall back on Debra Marcos and withdraw down to the Abbai River. Patrols were still met by heavy machine-gun fire from Debra Marcos, though one of the outlying forts was abandoned. Night attacks kept pressure on the Italians:

I was camped out on a high down, overlooking Debra Marcos, and it was with enormous satisfaction that I saw on the morning of 3rd April the Ethiopian flag flying from the Citadel. It was reported that Ras Hailu had taken over from the Italians (hence the flag) but that he intended to resist to the last with several thousand Colonial troops. I dictated a letter telling him to hand over the town and surrender. [He] sent a vague answer. I sent another letter telling him peremptorily that he must surrender or air and land action would be taken against him. At the same time I put in patrols to occupy the Abima Fort and moved forward to the Citadel with a few men. Ras Hailu met me at the gates, dressed in the uniform of an Italian General with three or four rows of ribbons. [He] finally agreed [to surrender] and said he would move out the same evening, and handed over the keys of the Citadel.

I had only three platoons with which to ensure the surrender, whereas Ras Hailu had some several thousand Colonial troops. Looting started that night and I woke next morning to peer out of the window of the Citadel when shots were fired. I saw our guards shooting looters from the walls; three looters had fallen by the side of the hospital while walking away with blankets and the soldiers who picked them out from the Citadel walls were looking very pleased with themselves. The remainder fled and we suffered very little further trouble.

I received splendid news from Henry Johnson whom I had sent some days earlier with three platoons of No 1 Company and a mortar section to intercept enemy withdrawing from Debra Marcos to the Abbai River crossing. With the skill that he showed throughout the campaign he had successfully ambushed twenty-eight enemy lorries escorted by two armoured cars on the road fifteen miles east of Debra Marcos. The surprise was complete and only three lorries escaped.

On 6th April the Emperor arrived, accompanied by Chapman Andrews, from the Foreign Office, and Wingate. I had the troops on parade, the Ethiopian Battalion on one side and the Frontier Battalion on the other. After hoisting the Ethiopian flag the Emperor made a speech congratulating the assembled troops.

The fighting was not over. The withdrawing Italians managed to cross the Abbai after bribing a local chieftain who had been tasked to block their route. The company Boustead had sent waded across the Abbai, carrying kit and guns on their heads, as the river was too deep for loaded animals.

Having seen Johnson safely across the Abbai, Boustead returned to Debra Marcos and the following day went to visit Jarvis and No 3 Company, which was still pinning down Torelli's force at Bahar Dar. It took a week, over very rough country, for Boustead to reach Jarvis:

> I found Brown short of mortar ammunition which we ordered up with all speed. I said, 'It is essential to get Torelli out and to operate on him as we have been doing at Debra Marcos every night, and attack with bombs, rifle and bayonet.' Jarvis was delighted, and got going at once. A fortnight later after eleven night attacks during which some six Italian officers and 268 other ranks were killed and wounded, including Torelli himself, the enemy force was evacuated by dhow to Gondar.

When Boustead got back to Debra Marcos after setting Jarvis off on his task, he received an emergency operation order from Wingate instructing the Frontier Battalion to move with all speed to Mota Fort carrying the minimum weight. Boustead set off on 18 April with two platoons of No 1 Company, and with the main column following:

> The road led over the Chaigul Pass, a 14,000-foot pass through the Chokey Mountains. As we went up the cold became intense and the men from the Sudan plains suffered mountain sickness. A high wind rose, followed by snow which then worked up into a blizzard. The men only had one blanket for covering and we spent a miserable night below the pass shivering with cold and suffering from mountain sickness.

The soldiers recovered quickly after they had crossed the pass and come down to a lower altitude into the sun. The camel transport was brought over the same route with few casualties—a remarkable feat for animals brought up in the Sudan plains.

Everyone was ready to attack Mota Fort when Boustead received a signal from Wingate informing him that Nos. 2 and 4 Companies would be withdrawn forthwith, leaving only two platoons of No. 1 Company and the mortar platoon for operations.

When the depleted force reached Mota Fort it was found to be a strong position, and the commander refused to surrender when summoned. Boustead records what happened next:

I did not fancy a night attack with bomb and bayonet: instead, our platoon kept up harassing fire all night while the mortars were dug in. Next day the mortars kept up a steady fire, despite enemy counterfire, and after most buildings had been set ablaze, the Italians had had enough and surrendered. All the Eritrean troops in the garrison and their N.C.O.s agreed to enlist in the Emperor's army, and the Italians, nineteen officers and W.O.s, marched back with us to captivity.

On 21st May the Italians asked for terms of surrender. In the intervening period Johnson, with a small force of Sudanese, had pressed the enemy in wet and in fine weather, in daytime and at night, though he and his men were short of rations, in torn clothing and with worn-out sandals. Italian demoralisation was complete when Thesiger[6] moved by forced marches to attack from the north at Debra Sina.

On 23rd May Johnson, with twenty-five men covered by three Bren guns, began to disarm the enemy. The white nationals in the Carabinieri were allowed to keep their arms as honours of war and for self-protection. The total bag was 1,100 whites, 7,000 Colonial troops, 200 native women and one white woman. And it rained all day. For Johnson's force the campaign was over.

The capture of Mota Fort on 24 April 1941 was Boustead's last Ethiopian operation. In April the Eritrean campaign ended on the capture of Massawa on the Red Sea, and in May official resistance in Ethiopia ended with the Duke of Aosta's capitulation. Gideon Force's mission had been successful. It had tied down fifty-six Italian battalions, leaving only the equivalent of seventy-one battalions to face the main British force of five divisions fighting in Eritrea and south-east Abyssinia. Eritrea fell early in April 1941, and on 6 April Addis Ababa fell to General Cunningham. Wingate had tied down superior Italian forces, engaging them when advantageously possible, and sapping their will to continue through incessant pin-prick attacks. The tactical genius and driving force behind these operations and their successful execution was Hugh Boustead.

Emperor Haile Selassie recognised Boustead's contribution to his restitution on his throne and bestowed the Abyssinian Order of St George on him for his conduct of the campaign. In January 1942 Boustead was awarded the D.S.O. for the operations leading up to the capture of Debra Marcos. It was a remarkable achievement for a Gordon Highlander called back to the colours out of retirement.[7]

---

6 Wilfred Thesiger, grandson of Frederick Thesiger, Lord Chelmsford, British commander during the Zulu War of 1879, who lost 1,400 troops at Isandlwana.

7 For details of the life and career of Hugh Boustead see Chapter 38.

CHAPTER 20

GORDON HIGHLANDERS IN VIETNAM

THE Vietnam War ran from 1960 to 1975. What started as an attempt by Communist North Vietnam to destabilise South Vietnam, and ultimately to assimilate it into a one-nation Communist State, rapidly escalated into a full-scale war between Russian-backed North Vietnam and (dubiously) democratic South Vietnam, aided by the Free World Military Assistance Force (FWMAF), made up of South East Asia Treaty Organisation (SEATO) members the United States, Australia, New Zealand, South Korea, Thailand and the Philippines. The United Kingdom, an original signatory of SEATO, declined to send forces to aid South Vietnam, a protocol member of SEATO. Some in Britain felt that this political decision not to honour its obligations, pragmatic though it might have been, brought great dishonour upon the country—and upon its Armed Forces. Many British soldiers, having completed their engagement or resigned from the British Army, made their way to Vietnam, most of them having joined the Australian Army. Among them were two Gordon Highlanders.

Private Nigel Burnett, son of Gordon Highlander Colonel K.M. Burnett, O.B.E., served in Vietnam with the 7th Battalion, The Royal Australian Regiment, during its second tour in Vietnam, 1970–71. As a rifleman in a platoon he took part in many operations (each lasting from three to six weeks) in the jungle.

Captain Derek Napier resigned from the British Army in 1968, leaving the 1st Battalion in Minden, where he had been Intelligence Officer. He enlisted in the Australian Army and was posted to the 7th Battalion, the Royal Australian Regiment (7 RAR), joining it in Sydney in June 1968. In 1969 he was posted from 7 RAR to 5 RAR in Vietnam, to replace an officer wounded in action. He joined A Company as its second-in-command, and flew in by helicopter to join it in the jungle. The 5th Battalion was battle-hardened. Shortly before Captain Napier joined his company, 5 RAR had fought a decisive battle to clear the village of Binh Ba (close to the Australian Task Force Headquarters) that had been occupied by regular soldiers of the North Vietnamese Army. Supported by armoured personnel carriers (APCs), D Company, 5 RAR, fought through the village, inflicting devastating casualties on the enemy, who, withdrawing with their wounded, left 93 dead behind.

Captain Napier took part in all of A Company's operations from August 1969 to February 1970, when 5 RAR was relieved by his original battalion,

7 RAR. Like most operations in the jungle, much of the time was spent moving slowly and carefully through thick undergrowth, searching for signs of the enemy, and lying in ambush on tracks where the enemy could be expected. Contacts, when they happened, were short and intense, and Captain Napier was particularly lucky on one occasion when, after lying in ambush for some days, fruitlessly up to that point, the order was given to move out. Situated at the rear of the ambush position, Captain Napier stood up and prepared to pick up his heavy pack. Unseen by him, a party of Viet Cong was approaching, only some ten to fifteen metres away. Fortunately for Captain Napier, the Company Medical Orderly, a former SAS soldier, spotted the enemy and with a quick aimed shot killed the first one, at which the others turned and fled.

Captain Napier had another lucky escape when travelling on top of an APC. As they moved through a rubber plantation the APC plunged through some loose barbed wire, left over from a former defensive position, when Captain Napier noticed an anti-personnel mine tangled in the barbed wire. As the APC progressed, the wire, tangled in its tracks, was drawn along the top of the track. As the mine grew closer, Captain Napier tried to alert the APC commander, but the engine noise made communication impossible, and, inevitably, the mine went off. There was a considerable explosion that damaged the tracks of the APC. Had Captain Napier not been leaning inboard towards the commander, he would have taken much of the blast that went upwards from the track.

When 7 RAR relieved 5 RAR in February 1970, Captain Napier returned to 7 RAR and remained in Vietnam for another year. After a spell as a Liaison Officer with the American 199 Light Infantry Brigade in Long Kanh province, he returned to 7 RAR as a company second-in-command and stand-in company commander. He also did a spell as Liaison Officer with the Vietnamese Regional and Local Forces.

Living in a South Vietnamese village was a fascinating experience. As part of a small team of three Australians and five Americans in a wired-in compound defended by South Vietnamese Local Forces (locally recruited volunteers) Captain Napier worked with the South Vietnamese military commander of the area and the American military adviser to ensure that Australian operations were coordinated with South Vietnamese operations so that there could be no possibility of a clash between Australians and South Vietnamese forces. This was not always easy, as the South Vietnamese local forces, really little more than a not very professional 'Home Guard', usually agreed to all proposals, then went and did their own thing.

On one occasion, to foster good relations and better understanding between Australians, Americans and Vietnamese, the village chief and the senior South Vietnamese military commander (who was the District Chief) invited Captain Napier and his American counterpart to a banquet in the village chief's home. Entering the small house, they found their Vietnamese hosts, some other South Vietnamese officers and an interpreter. Sitting cross-legged on the floor in a corner was a very old Vietnamese peasant, head down and seemingly asleep. On a low table was spread out an array of local delicacies—fish, duck, vegetables, pastries and, on a large platter in the centre of the table, a vast pile of rice and sultanas.

The District Chief offered everyone drinks. In a former French colony, it was not surprising that the drink offered was a very fine cognac. In the Far East cognac was always drunk with ice, and the glasses passed round already had ice in them. Captain Napier knew that the ice factory at the edge of the village drew its water from a stream which ran through the padi fields surrounding the village, fields that were well trampled by both buffaloes and the peasants who worked them. He took pains to ensure that the cognac was poured into his glass until it reached the rim, not so much in an attempt to get as much cognac as possible but as a medical necessity, in the hope that the alcohol would kill off the bugs and bacteria that inhabited the ice!

After a halting conversation conducted in broken English through a Vietnamese interpreter, or in schoolboy French (French was still widely spoken throughout Vietnam) the District Chief invited Captain Napier to make the first inroads into the feast, starting with the rice and sultanas, but first he clapped his hands loudly and called out a command in Vietnamese. At this the old peasant in the corner raised his head, picked up a palm leaf sitting beside him, and started to wave it over the table. At the first pass, all the sultanas on the rice rose up in a cloud and buzzed around the room. Faced with a pile of rice on which hundreds of flies had been gorging themselves, Captain Napier stoically delved deep into the centre of the rice pile in the hope of finding some rice that the flies had not sampled!

When he was a Liaison Officer Captain Napier had yet another narrow escape. He was driving his stripped-down unarmoured Land Rover through the coastal village of Long Phuoc Hai, intending to check the road—little more than a dirt and sand track—that led from the village to the shore line. Coming behind him were three APCs from 7 RAR. As he came to another road that led out of the village he saw a police checkpoint on it and decided to speak to the police manning it. He pulled off the road and drove towards the checkpoint, and the APCs behind him continued on the road. He was just pulling up at the checkpoint when a large explosion occurred, and he saw that the first APC had been blown onto its side. He moved to the incident immediately and found that the APC had driven over a large mine, planted probably the night before, in the loose sand that formed the road. A large hole had been blown through the armoured underside of the APC. There had been four Diggers (the common name for Australian soldiers) in the vehicle: the driver, the commander and two soldiers sitting on top. The driver was lying, half out of his hatch, with a hole in his chest through which air bubbled through the blood as he breathed. He had been thrown against one of the steering tillers, which had penetrated his chest. The vehicle commander was lying outside the vehicle, his leg shattered when it hit the edge of the hatch as he was thrown out. One of the Diggers who had been on top was picking himself up, some twenty yards away, where he had been thrown by the force of the explosion, unharmed but very shaken. The other Digger lay beside the APC, apparently untouched, until it was seen that one side of his head had been cleanly sliced off by a piece of shrapnel. If Captain Napier had not turned off to visit the police checkpoint his Land Rover would have been the first vehicle down the road, and there would have been very little of it left. It was a narrow escape for him, though a tragedy for the soldiers in the APC.

The damaged APC is recovered after hitting a mine near Long Phuoc Hai

Captain Napier served with 7 RAR for the whole of its second tour in South Vietnam, from February 1970 to February 1971, making his tour with both 5 RAR and 7 RAR a long twenty-one months. He then spent a year as an instructor at the Jungle Training Centre at Canungra, in Queensland, before returning to Britain in 1972 and rejoining The Gordon Highlanders.

276

SECTION 9

THE LIGHTER SIDE

ONE of the most endearing characteristics of the British soldier is his sense of humour. Even in the most desperate of situations he will see the funny side of something. Sometimes it can appear macabre, but it keeps people going when times are tough. During the Falklands campaign in 1982 a soldier in the Parachute Regiment stood on a mine and suffered serious injury. 'I've lost my leg,' he cried. 'No you 'aven't, mate,' came the reply 'it's over 'ere!'

Although a sense of humour was universal throughout the Army, it had its regional variations. Within Scotland it varied greatly, from the rapid-fire patter of the Glaswegian to the slower home-spun humour of the Doric north-east.

CHAPTER 21

Sense of Humour

THE Gordons' sense of humour was obvious from the very earliest days. They could laugh at everyday situations, at hard work and exhausting campaigning, at triumph and adversity, and above all, at themselves. Sometimes their sense of humour was all that kept them going and was the 'last round in their pouch'.

Drilling the MacDonalds

Sergeants can be the bane of a soldier's life. Making fun of soldiers (usually without malice) was a normal part of the sergeant's make up:

> While the Highlanders were being marshalled to arms for the defence of our common country, companies might be seen here and there at drill. English then was not so common as it is now in the Highlands, and the Gaelic instructions in the use of arms have formed the theme of many a ludicrous story. Here is 'calling the roll'.

> The company consisted largely of MacDonalds, and there was some difficulty in distinguishing different men from each other. They were known by certain cognomens. No doubt this recorded version is exaggerated; but it is not improbable:

> Sergeant (bawling at the top of his voice):

> > 'Donald MacDonald *mor* (big)?'
> > (No answer, the man being absent.)
> > 'I see you're there so you're right not to speak to nobody in the ranks.'
> > 'Donald MacDonald *ruadh* (red)?'
> > 'Here!'
> > 'Aye, you're always here when nobody wants you!'
> > 'Donald MacDonald *fada* (tall)?'
> > (No answer.)
> > 'Oh, decent modest lad, you're always here, though like a good sodger, as you are, you seldom say nothing about it.'
> > 'Donald MacDonald *cluasan mor* (big ears)?'
> > (No answer.)
> > 'I hear you, but you might speak a little louder for all that!'
> > 'Donald MacDonald *ordag* (thumb)?'
> > 'Here!'

'If you're here this morning it's no' likely you'll be here tomorrow morning. I'll shust mark you down absent; so let that stand for that.'

'Donald MacDonald *casan mora* (big feet)?'

'Here!'

'Oh, *Tamorst*! You said that yesterday; but wha saw't you? You're always here if we take your own word for it.'

'Donald MacDonald *odhar* (yellow)?'

'Here!' (in a loud voice).

'If you was not known for a big liar, I would believe you; but you've a bad habit, my lad, of always crying "Here!" whether you're here or no, and till you give up your bad habit I'll shust mark you down absent for your impudence. It's all for your own good, so you need not cast down your brows, but shust be thankful that I don't stop your loaf too, and then you wad maybe have to thank your own souple tongue for a sair back and a toom belly.'

'Attention, noo, lads, and let every man turn his eyes to his Sergeant.'

T&S, December 1934.

Gordon Highlanders would converse on equal terms with men of every rank and distinction. The following took place in 1814, in France:

While the Gordons were marching at ease one day, the left hand man of the rear section, Jock Webster, hearing the sound of a horse's hoof on the turf, looked over his shoulder, 'an' wha but Wellington ridin' cannily by.' Jock brought his firelock smartly to the shoulder, calling out, 'Hoo far will ye tak' us, my Lord?' 'How far do you want to go, my lad?' 'To Paris, by God!' and Wellington rode on laughing.

The Life of a Regiment, Volume I, pp 329–30.

The Gordon Highlander, while solicitous about wounded comrades, would happily joke with them about their wounds and seemingly mock them. One way of coping with death and horrific wounds, and to minimise their initial impact was to make light of them. John Downie, wounded at Waterloo, recalled such an occasion:

When he was making his way to the rear, they came on a man McIntosh, who was one of the Duchess of Gordon's recruits; he was sitting on a dead horse, and, pointing to his leg shattered by a cannonball, said, in Gaelic, 'What can I make of that?' 'Mind, lad, ye got a kiss from the Duchess o' Gordon for that,' was the rather unfeeling reply.

The Life of a Regiment, Volume I, p 397.

The Gordon Highlander could joke when dealing with the enemy:

> In Spain spare ammunition was being stolen. One night, Peter Stewart
> on sentry, saw a calf kept getting near to the ammunition carts. It had
> rather odd action, and Peter challenged, when the creature answered with
> a prolonged 'Bo,' which had something of the human voice about it. He
> fired; it fell; 'Bo noo, ye beggar,' said Peter, and a Spaniard in a calf's
> head and hide was his bag.

The Life of a Regiment, Volume I, p 397.

Before the arrival of the railway, tourists in the Highlands were not
numerous. Laughing at the unsophisticated way of life of the locals was an
unfortunate attribute of some of them:

> I remember another of these veterans in Inverness; no man was better
> known in the Highland capital than the *Saighdear dhu* (black soldier). A
> keen sportsman, he followed his favourite pastime without much regard
> to legal rights. He varied his occupations by occasionally helping drovers
> with their cattle. One day while thus employed he was overtaken on the
> Fort Augustus road by some English men, who, with an assumption of
> superiority too common among a certain class of British tourist, began to
> chaff and interrogate the simple native they took him for. In reply to their
> questions he told them the cattle were going to Falkirk Tryst. 'What will
> they be worth there?' 'They'll no' do badly if they bring ten pund a head.'
> 'Only ten pounds! That's nothing to English prices. If you take them to
> London, my good fellow, you'll get twenty!' 'If you'll tak' Loch Ness to
> Hell,' retorted Donald, 'you'll get a shilling the glass for the watter!'

The Life of a Regiment, Volume II, p 3.

This tale is reminiscent of the party of tourists who, while admiring the
Highland scenery, asked an old Highlander what the views were like from
the top of a nearby mountain. 'Oh, ye can see a fair way fae up there,' said
the old man, 'outside the Highlands themsel'.' One tourist, thinking to make
fun of the old man, asked, 'How far can you see? As far as London?' The old
man looked at him, and replied, 'Och aye, on a clear nicht ye can see the
Moon.'

The pride of a young officer, resplendent in his uniform, was punctured
by an Irish down-and-out:

> A young officer found himself the centre of a little crowd, and thinking
> that in full Highland dress he was worthy of their admiration, he paused
> to gratify it, when an old fellow approached him, hat in hand, and with
> pleading accent said, 'Av ye please, sor—I'm a poor man—would your

honour, sor, give me' (the officer's hand sought his sporran) 'your breeches, sor, *when ye've done wid them*!'

The Life of a Regiment, Volume II, p 81.

Being in the public eye means that the slightest slip in behaviour is evident to all and the subject of amused comment. The following incident took place in Edinburgh in 1855:

> An incident which occurred to the writer shows how different were the ideas of society as to after-dinner conviviality to those of the present day. He dined at the Royal Company of Archers Hall as the guest of a gentleman well known for his legal acumen and his literary talent. The dinner hour was about six, and on leaving in the light of a summer evening no cab was at hand. The host was not very steady on his legs, and had to take the arm of his guest, who was conspicuous in gold epaulettes and dirk. Many and various were the remarks of the passers-by such as, 'Eh, losh keep's a', woman, here's the Shirra' fou—wi' a sodger!' On which that official, striking an attitude, exclaimed, 'Is it not hard that the Sheriff of Edinburgh is the only man in the city that can't get drunk with impunity!'

The Life of a Regiment, Volume II, pp 83–4.

Cricket has bemused many. A game that can take up to five days to complete, in which, to untutored eyes, nothing appears to happen for long periods, leaves many bewildered. To its adherents it is a sublime game of tactics and strategy. To Gordon Highlanders of 1861, however, it was a source of sheer frustration!

> Cricket, which was beginning to make its way in Scotland, as golf was becoming popular in England, was played by the officers, and they gave some bats, balls, and stumps to the men, by whom, however, the game was at first rather imperfectly understood. Two soldiers were seen practising, and the bowler managed to hit the wicket more than once. At last the batsmen shook his fist at him, saying, 'I'll tell ye what it is, Sandy—an ye ca' doon thae sticks again after me juist pittin' them up, I'll bash yer heid for ye.'

The Life of a Regiment, Volume II, p 71.

In the 18th century tea was the preserve of the rich and not the drink of the common man. By the second half of the 19th century it was more readily available and popular with all classes. Not everyone saw it as a welcome addition to the soldier's diet, and the suggestion that it should replace whisky was not universally shared:

Since the Crimean War several changes had taken place in the life and habits of the Regiment. Tea, when introduced in Scotland, was denounced by the Lord President of the Court of Session as an abominable drug, and drinking it a pernicious custom likely to destroy the nerve of the people; they also feared, if allowed to take the place of ale, it would prove injurious to agriculture by destroying the market for barley. Notwithstanding these prognostications, 'the new China drink' became popular among all classes, and bread and tea now replaced more nutritious meal and milk on the men's breakfast-table. Excess in strong drink, which had become comparatively rare among the gentry, was also less common in the ranks. The dram, formerly offered at breakfast in the houses of Highland gentlemen, was still the fashion among older farmers, but the old soldier no longer considered his 'morning' as the best refreshment after parade. Some, indeed, were abstainers, but the opinion of the majority was expressed by one to whom an advocate of total abstinence was expatiating on the delights of the tea-table and the pity of spoiling good water by mixing it with whisky. The soldier, wishing to be polite, agreed, saying, 'no doubt good water is a good thing, and too much whisky—'specially bad whisky—is not a good thing; but for my part I never saw a very cheerful party around a pump!'

The Life of a Regiment, Volume II, pp 75–6.

Life in 19th century India did not help ladies to grow old gracefully. The climate, disease, and above all the hot sun, gradually turned young newly married beauties into more severe versions of their former selves. By the time they were wives of senior officers, they were imposing, but had left beauty behind!

At Jullundur they were visited by Shere Ali Khan, Amir of Afghanistan, on his way to meet the Viceroy. He saw the regiment reviewed, and forty men fired 200 rounds volley firing, with only seven misses. The Amir, in the butts, was astonished, and spoke to the men, saying, 'Very good, brave boys, very good; well done.' It is said that when the officials went out to meet the Amir on his arrival, they were accompanied by the senior ladies of the station; on which His Highness remarked, 'I see your custom is the same as ours at Kabul, where on such occasions we leave our young beauties at home.'

The Life of a Regiment, Volume II, p 91.

Reform of Army punishment was generally seen to be an improvement in the soldier's conditions of service, but not all reforms were welcomed by the more law-abiding soldiers:

The severe penalties in civil life had been much modified since the early years of the century, but it was only in the reign of George IV that Sir James McIntosh brought in a measure for abolishing the punishment of death in cases of stealing property to the value of five shillings. In the army corporal punishment had, in 1847, been reduced to a maximum of fifty lashes, confined to a few disgraceful offences, and was done away with in 1868, except on active service. It was abolished in 1881—a form of punishment no longer suited to the times, but not disapproved by old soldiers, for the offender's duty did not fall on his comrades as it did when he was imprisoned. When punished a man was not called in question for anything he chose to say. 'Odd, sir, ye micht hae peety on a puir drucken cratur like yersell!' was, on one occasion, the remark of a culprit to the senior officer on parade, who had the reputation of being a two-bottle man.

The Life of a Regiment, Volume II, p 91.

Renowned for their sense of humour, the Irish have also been the butt of others' humour. The following shows an incomplete understanding of the rationale for numbering regiments:

There was a story concerning an Irishman who joined the 75th. When asked why he had done so, the reply was that 'he had a brother in the 76th and wished to be near him.'

T&S, March 1937.

Soldiers will complain about anything. In this case from 1879 the soldier's complaint goes back to the day he joined the Army:

The camp was 8,000 feet above the sea, and the cold was intense. We remained there until 1st December, when we returned to Sherpur. The men, cold and weary, had arrived at that stage of fatigue when singing and joking had ceased, and as the Gordons broke the ice to cross the river, Major White overheard the soldier near him, 'My God, I wish I had the sergeant that 'listed me by the lug the noo!'

The Life of a Regiment, Volume II, p118.

Many amusing comments come in moments of extremis. The soldier in this 1880 incident escaped death by a matter of inches, but his response kept his comrades amused long afterwards:

The fighting was continuous, the troops being stopped by water-courses or walls, from which they fired. Private Chapman cautiously raised his head for a shot, when, to the astonishment of his comrades, 'the Loon,' as he was called, jumped up, dancing about like a madman, with smoke coming out from a hole in his helmet, crying, 'My heid's aff, chaps!' It appeared that he carried his pipe and lights in his helmet, and a bullet had ignited the matches and set his hair ablaze, he being more frightened than hurt by this close shave.

The Life of a Regiment, Volume II, p 151.

The same campaign produced the following incident:

Many incidents illustrated the nature of the fight, and on such a stage tragedy goes hand-in-hand with comedy. 'What are you doing there, McKenzie?' cried Sergeant-major Ross. 'Takin' a deid man oot o' the watter before he'll be drooned!' replied the Highlandman.

The Life of a Regiment, Volume II, pp 150–1.

Night marching could be mind-numbing and, when marching along a railway, monotonous in the extreme. But the Gordon Highlander could still come up with a sardonic comment:

After dark the monotonous tramp became very tiring and the stored heat of rails gave the thirst of a lifetime: it was one of the most exhausting efforts of the campaign. The regular distance-posts gave rise to argument about kilometres covered and to come. At last a lamentable voice was heard: 'Aw drat they killameeters, killameeters; can some ane no kill a *dhoby*[1] for a change!' which caught the fancy of the Indian veterans and lasted the battalion for a long time.

The Life of a Regiment, Volume III, p 244.

The resigned humour of the British soldier, weary and hungry after days trying to bring the enemy to battle, is illustrated in this comment by a Gordon Highlander during the Boer War:

The night was black, the track invisible, several deep streams had to be forded, and all were thoroughly exhausted when the bivouac, four miles short of Pilgrim's Rest, was reached about 2 a.m. The sentiments of all were perfectly expressed by one hero who, roused, as he supposed, about ten minutes after he had lain down, exclaimed: 'There's to be nae rest for this pilgrim, ony wy!'

The Life of a Regiment, Volume III, p 214.

Sometimes a joke can be too funny, leading the perpetrator into the hands of the Regimental Police—but if it is memorable enough, it is worth it! The

---

1   *Dhoby* or *dhob*i was a term brought back from India. It means washing or laundry, and the *dhobi wallah* was the man who did the washing. In this case the word *dhoby* is a contraction of *dhobi wallah*.

Gordons always had 'characters' who accepted regimental retribution as the price of a good laugh. Every generation could point to regimental characters who seemed to 'get away with it':

> Private 'Cock' Stewart was a smart, capable soldier in the 2nd Battalion in India, 1910. An inveterate practical joker, he often ended in the hands of the Regimental Police. A Boxing Tournament was held in Cawnpore in the gymnasium. As the Regimental Sergeant Major was about to announce the last fight, a man walked into the ring dressed in white shorts, as black all over as 'the proverbial ace of spades' and challenged all-comers for 500 rupees a side. Everybody was nonplussed. It was some time before it dawned that it was a joke, when the Provost-Sergeant hustled the challenger to the Guard Room.
>
> It seems that 'Cock' and some friends were confined to barracks, and after answering their names at 10 p.m. had returned to their barracks room, where 'Cock' made a wager that he would go to the boxing and appear as Jack Johnson (the famous Negro boxer). With numerous tins of blacking his friends had turned him into a fearsome portrait of Jack Johnson, when he went to the gymnasium to interrupt the tournament with his impromptu appearance. The Battalion cheered and applauded as he was marched away.

T&S, March 1932.

For many years the Gordons were known as the 'cheesy' Regiment, although few outside the Regiment knew how this came about. Other regiments soon picked up this epithet, and often used it to mock the Gordons. What they did not realise was that the original mockery was self-generated, and typified the innate ability of the Gordons to laugh at themselves. This account records the genesis of the epithet. The incident took place on the Somme in November 1916.

> Side by side leading up from the main ration dump at Albert ran a railway embankment and a concealed sunken road. On the top of the embankment, from which the rails had long since gone, was a track. One night the ration party of an English regiment was on this track with rations, including an enormous round of cheese, on a hand cart. The ration party of 7th Gordons was on the sunken road, abreast of the English group. The cheese fell off the English ration cart and rolled down the embankment, accompanied by yells and curses from the English ration party.
>
> What ensued was related by a Sergeant of the 6th Gordons who, with true Donside modesty, not wishing to take all the honour of winning the war, gives credit to the 7th for their 'glorious action'.

We didn't go in for flashy stunts,
We merely played our part.
But were as hard a lot to stop
As any that did start.
But oh the Seventh from Deeside
Earned fame o'er all the seas,
By their famous stand on the awful night
When they killed the charging cheese.

A noble band the rations bore
Up from the peaceful rear.
Alert each man to his duty grim
And strangers all to fear,
And little recked of the part they'd play,
Or how hard would go the fight,
When they alone would stem the foe
On that now historic night.

They marched along, a silent band
By the side of a lonely hill,
When sudden the evening's quiet was rent
By a sound both loud and shrill.
Each heart beat high in its manly breast
For each scarred warrior knew
That sound could mean but one only thing –
The *Bosche* had broken through!

Halted the band and the Quarty spoke:
'Ye lads whom I now command
Have a part to play, a noble part
For the sake of our Motherland'.
Then he turned his face to the charging foe
And he yelled o'er the evening air,
Like a clarion blast his voice pealed forth
'Halt! Halt! Halt who goes there?'

The foe rushed on while the Quarty grim
To his shoulder raised his gun.
He swore aloud that he alone
Must kill the leading Hun.
The rifle spoke, the bullet flew,
Its course was quickly sped,
And in half the time it takes to tell
The charging foe lay dead.

The ration party shouldered arms
And went to find their prey.
They wanted to share the foeman's goods,
For such is a Quarty's way.
But joy within their hearts was quelled
And curses rent the breeze
When Quarty found to his dire dismay
That he'd shot a bloody cheese.

Now this is a tale of long ago
Which is remembered still
By the sweats of Banff and Donside
Who the old Sixth ranks did fill.
And if e'er you want to start a row
And crave mercy from your knees,
Just say to a man from the stalwart Seventh
'Hey Jock! Fa shot the cheese?'

T&S, 1991.

The Army taught soldiers the subjects that enabled them to sit for the Army Certificate of Education, at levels III, II and I, thereby making them eligible for promotion. Extracts below from *The Tiger and Sphinx* show some interesting answers to classroom questions!

The solar system is a way of teaching singing.

A corps is a dead man; a corpse is a dead woman.

A myth is a female moth.

When you breathe you inspire; when you don't breathe you expire.

Examinations assessed progress of individuals, who produced unusual and often imaginative answers to questions on subjects that had been taught:

Fort George is ¾ belonging to the Gordons and the other ½ to the Seaforths. It was built in 1646 on sand in the Moray Firth, and it sinks four inches every year.

Fort George is a very cold place, there is the Murry Firth all round except at Ardersier where there is the *Star and Shaws*. It was built for Napoleon, but they sent him to St. Helena which was a better place.

The 92nd was rased [sic] by the forth Duck of Gordon ably assisted by the beautiful Dutch Jean.

T&S, January & May 1925; May 1932; June 1935.

This cartoon dwells on the gullibility of a recruit on sentry—and his clear appreciation of the relationship between his Sergeant Major and the Commanding Officer!

Recruit: 'Halt, mon! Dae ye no ken there's nae civilians allowed in here?'

Commanding Officer (*in plain clothes*): 'But, don't you know that I am the Commanding Officer?'

Recruit: 'Och, indeed! Weel ye had better get oot o' here, for the Sergint-Major has been roarin' on ye aal roond aboot the place.'

The following tales may well be apocryphal, but that they are based on real characters and incidents in The Gordon Highlanders is beyond doubt. They hark back to the time when young boys were enlisted into the army. The reference to Wee Sandy travelling down to Aldershot to join the Battalion could refer either to the tours of the 2nd Battalion at Bordon, 1925–28 and at Aldershot 1931–34 or to that of the 1st Battalion at Aldershot, 1938–39. The Bandmaster of the 1st Battalion, WO1 W. Williams was appointed in 1938 and continued until 1955, while the Bandmaster of the 2nd Battalion, WO1 A.H. McPherson, was in post from 1928 to 1934. The tales appeared in the *Tiger and Sphinx* in 1952, when Bandmaster Williams was still serving in the 1st Battalion, and it is most likely that it is he who narrated them, which would therefore date to the 1st Battalion's Aldershot tour in 1938–39:

It was a Wednesday afternoon, some years ago, when the Band Sergeant ushered into my office a wee, red-haired, freckle-faced nipper, dressed in short trousers and blue jersey.

'The new boy, Sir,' said Sergt. B Flat, pushing the lad towards my table, from behind which I merely had a view of tousled red hair and twinkling mischievous blue eyes set in a freckled, begrimed face.

'What's your name, laddie?' I asked.

'Gordon Hamish Allister McKay, Sorr,' came the reply in the broadest accent I have ever heard.

'Have they given you a number yet, Boy?'

'Ay. Sorr, but I canna mind it the noo.'

'Well, that's one of the first things you should remember. Where do you come from?'

'Foggieloan, Sorr.'

Appealingly, I turned to the Band Sergeant.

'That's a wee placie in Aiberdeenshire, Sorr. It's nae sae far fae where I come fae.'[1]

Being new to the Regiment and to Sergt. B Flat's strange tongue, I gathered that wee McKay would need my deepest concentration.

'You travelled all the way down on your own, McKay?' I asked.

'Aye, Sorr, and I walked aroon a great muckle station in London withoot getting lost, and fun ma' way tae anither een ca'd Waterloo ma'sel, and then I speered ma way tae Aldershot fae there, Sorr.'

Wildly I glanced at my band sergeant, who quickly realizing that 1 was once again suffering from Foggieloanitis' supplied a lucid interpretation.

---

1   'Foggieloan' is the name by which the village of Aberchirder is locally known. This has confused visitors to the area for many years. There is a stretch of moorland north of the village, which was named Foggieloan Moss from two Gaelic words *foidh* (peat moss) and *lòn* (meadow), so 'Foggieloan' means 'peaty or boggy meadow'.

'Well, you're a Gordon Highlander now, Lad. You are in the finest Regiment in the British Army, in fact in the whole world. You understand what that means, Boy?'

'Aye, Sorr. My father was in the Gordons, Sorr.'

'Good. What battalion did he serve with, do you know?'

Wee McKay scratched his tousled head for a second.

'I dinna ken onything aboot battalions, Sorr.', he said. 'I heard him speak aboot India, Palestine, Gibraltar, Singapore and Edinburgh. He was jist a Gordon Highlander, Sorr.'

'Out of the mouths of babes and sucklings,' I thought.

'Well, I'm sure you'll want to be as good a Gordon as your dad, so there are one or two things I want you to remember.'

I then proceeded to tell him how to behave as a good Gordon and noted that he was listening intelligently and absorbing the points I emphasized. Finally I said:

'The Band Sergeant will take you to the Boys' Room, where you will find about twenty youngsters about your own age, and later he will give you a clarinet which you will have to work hard to learn. Before you go, I want you to remember that if you get into any trouble at all, see Sergt. B Flat, and if he cannot help you, come straight to me, and if you think it is serious enough to see me straight away, don't hesitate to come. All right?'

'Yes, Sorr.'

'All right, Sergeant, take him away and get him settled in.'

'Very good, Sorr. C'mon, McKay.'

I saw nothing of McKay for about a week or so, but heard that the Gordon Hamish Allister had been shortened to 'Sandy' and that he had suffered the ordeals of inoculations and vaccinations, plus the initiation ceremony of being a member of the Boys' Room.

There being no stock uniform to fit him, he had flitted round the Battalion like a Peter Pan, doing his drills and schooling, etc., and had been found near the guard room at 2200 hours one evening complete with whitewash bucket and brush, looking for the Last Post. Some eight or nine days later I was spending a Thursday evening sitting in a cosy chair before my sitting room fire, when a timid knock came at the back door. My wife was at the Married Families' so, reluctantly, I put down my book and went to the door, where I saw standing on the doorstep, wet through to the skin, the diminutive form of Boy McKay, forlorn and dejected as a drowned kitten.

'Come in McKay. Warm yourself at the fire. I'll see if there's a cup of tea in the pot.'

291

'Thank you, Sorr,' said Wee Sandy, and stepping inside the kitchen, brought half the mud of Aldershot and a gallon of rain with him. Timidly he sat on the edge of my proffered chair, and I gave him a cup of luke-warm, more or less stewed tea.

'Well, lad, how're you liking it in the Regiment?' I asked.

'I'm liking it fine, Sorr,' piped up Wee Sandy.

'You've been playing football and hockey, I hear, and doing very well at school. That's the stuff, boy, keep it up.'

'The fitba' is a' richt. Sorr, but I canna get the hang o' that there hockey game. A' they funny rules hae fair got me scunnered, Sorr.'

I understood the gist of this bewildering speech, but was not acquainted with the 'scunnered' part of it. Nevertheless I felt that he was feeling more at ease and said:

'Now, lad, what brings you to see me in such weather?'

'Well, Sorr, ye ken the morning when I first joined the Regiment?'

'Yes, McKay. I remember well,' I replied.

'Ye telt me then that if iver I got intae ony trouble I wis tae come and see ye, Sorr.'

'That's quite right, boy, I hope it's nothing serious?'

'Michty me, it's serious a'right, Sorr,' replied the worried-looking Sandy.

'Jings,' I thought, picturing all that could happen to bring a wee lad out in such weather seeking my aid. Forcing a cheerful smile to my face, I said:

'O.K., McKay, out with it lad, and let's see if I can help you.'

'Well, Sorr, can ye lend me half-a-croon?'

T&S, August 1952.

Wee Sandy soon established himself in the Regiment. His impish grin and ready wit made him many friends, and even the Senior N.C.Os. had a word for him when they saw him off duty.

One Sunday morning the Orderly Sergeant of H.Q. Company sent for Sandy and, handing him a sealed envelope, said: 'Tak this tae the Orderly Sergeant of 'A' Company as quickly as you can.'

'O.K., Sergeant,' said Wee Sandy, and off he went as fast as his wee legs could carry him. After half an hour he found 'A' Company's Orderly Sergeant in the Sergeants Mess.

'Sergt. McSporran telt me tae gie ye this as quick as possible. Ah've been a' roon the place keekin for ye,' said Wee Sand.

Sergt. Cheyne opened the envelope and read the contents. 'This is no for me, McKay. It's for the Orderly Sergeant o' 'B' Company. Double awa' roon and find him.'

Sandy turned about smartly and doubled off on his search for Sergt. McFee, eventually tracking him down in one of the barrack rooms, three storeys high. Puffing and blowing at his exertions, he handed the envelope to Sergt. McFee. 'Here's an important note fae Sergt. McSporran o' HQ. Company, Sergeant' puffed out Wee Sandy.

'Thanks,' said Sergt. McFee, and after reading it turned to McKay. 'Ye've come tae the wrang place, McKay. This is no fae me ava'. It's fae the Orderly Corporal o' Don Company. Awa at the double and gie it him. Ye'll nae doot find him in the Cookhouse.'

'Oh jings, that's the ither side o' the barracks' thought Wee Sandy, and was out of the room like a shot. The rain was pelting down by the time he reached the Cookhouse.

'Is the Orderly Corporal o' Don Company here please?' asked the wee loon, as he stood outside the Cook Sergeant's office. A cook told Sandy that he had missed him by about two minutes. 'I think he's awa tae the M.T. sheds,' came a voice from inside the Cookhouse. Off Sandy doubled on his search, and managed to catch up with Cpl. Strachan just as he came out of the M.T. lines. 'Am I richt glad tae see ye, Corporal,' puffed Wee Sandy, and repeated his tale of 'Important message fae the Orderly Sergeant o' H.Q. Company.'

After a quick glance at the note, Cpl. Strachan turned to Sandy: 'Ah'm afraid this isna' for me, McKay. Ye'll hae tae find the Orderly Sergeant of 'C' Company. I think he's in the Sergeants Mess.'

'Oh fegs; Ah've been there already.' and off he doubled back to the Sergeants Mess.

Knocking at the door of the Mess for about five minutes without an answer, and knowing that this must be an important message, he timidly stepped inside. 'Fit the 'ell dae ye want, McKay?' came a roar from the Provost Sergeant, who was just about to sink a pint of McEwen's. 'Get outside and knock at the door and wait until you're answered.' Wee Sandy nearly jumped out of his skin and was outside the door standing in the rain for another five minutes. 'Jock' Tamson, one of the Mess waiters, came and asked him what he wanted.

'Will ye tell the Orderly Sergeant of 'C' Company that I hae an important message for him, please,' whispered Sandy.

Shutting the door in his face, Tamson went into the Holy of Holies and Wee Sandy kicked his heels in the rain for about another ten minutes, whilst Sergt. Milne finished a game of darts.

'Well, McKay, and fits this important message ye hae for me?' asked Sergt. Milne.

'Ah dinna ken, Sergeant.' whispered the frightened Sandy. 'But it must be verra important, as ah've been a' roon barracks wi' it, and ah'm fair drookit. Dinna tell me it's nae for ye. Ah've walked ma boots doon tae the uppers running roon wi' this message.'

'Oh aye, it's for me aricht, but ah'm afraid ye'll hae some mair walking tae dae. Awa' tae the H.Q. Company stores and give the message tae 'Busty' McKay, the storeman. He'll tell ye fit tae dae.'

'Thanks, Sergeant,' and once again Wee Sandy made his weary round of the barracks. Stepping into the Company stores he espied the genial 'Busty' sitting in the middle of a bunch of his cronies, playing a quiet game of solo.

'Sergt. Milne sent me roon wi' this and ye're tae tell me fit tae dae. Busty' croaked Sandy. Reading the note, Busty turned to his gang and roared with laughter. 'Ye're a richt Dunderheid, Sandy. Hoo lang hae ye been running roon wi this *important* message?' he spluttered out. 'Jings. I started just before the N.A.A.F.I. break, and if I hae any mair running tae dae, ah'll miss ma dinner,' answered the wee lad.

Handing him the note, now crumpled and bedraggled looking, Sandy read 'Send Wee Sandy from one place to the other with this note just to keep him out of mischief.'

'Well, ah'm jiggered', muttered Wee Sandy. 'Missed ma N.A.A.F.I. break, and ma breeks and sheen are wet through. Jings, ah never thocht it wis a leg pull.'

'Niver mind, Sandy, ye'll be able tae dae the same when ye're a sergeant', came Busty's laughing reply.

T&S, November 1952.

For many years after the end of the Second War there were tales of Japanese soldiers who held out in remote jungle areas and, from time to time, re-emerged to make a belated return to Japan. Gordon Highlanders who had endured years as captives of the Japanese were not surprised at the fanaticism that kept those forgotten sons of a vanished empire in the jungle. Their response after all those years was a gentle one:

A Japanese soldier emerges from the Malayan jungle many years after the Second World War. He is duly flown home to be reunited with his wife.

After an emotional reunion, with much ritual bowing, the husband asks his wife, 'Honourable wife, have you been faithful to me?' To which she replies 'Honourable husband, I have indeed been faithful to you'.

The husband continues, 'Honourable wife, I think you lie. I have heard you've been living with a Gordon Highlander from Inverurie'.

'Fa tellt ye that?' she demands.

T&S, 1992.

The sense of humour that ran like a thread through the Regiment, sometimes led Gordon Highlanders to parody routine events in the expectation (and hope!) that they could do so without being caught!

In each detachment life slipped into a simple routine where all too often just being seen was the justification for the task. The UN forces had developed a series of obligatory drills for detachments in a variety of scenarios. If a car with a UN flag passed, the sentry must salute; if a visitor came to the post he must be given a brief, parrot fashion. The Jocks, as ever, fell in with the procedures and carried them out smartly and conscientiously, but sometimes added their own variations. At one post, some distance from the main road, the sentry was silhouetted against the sky. The Jock on sentry would march out to his saluting position, turn his back to the road, and salute with his left hand, secure in the knowledge that the passing VIP would not be able to tell the difference against the bright background.

The Life of a Regiment, Volume VII, p 59.

Gordon Highlanders were always ready to mock their fellows, as this example from *Bydandy*, the light-hearted battalion newspaper, during the tour in Armagh in 1972 makes clear.

'Whaur's Dungannon, Wullie?'
'Dinna ken.'
'Whaur's Belfast, Wullie?'
'Dinna ken.'
'You're thick, you are. D'ye no ken whaur ony place in Ireland is?'
'Whaur's this Ireland? Is it ony wey near Torphins?'
'Ye're in Ireland, ye stupid lookin' goat.'
'Ach, Ah thocht this wis Armagh.'
'Armagh's a toon in Ireland, eejit!'
'Ah weel, ye live an' learn a' the time.'
'Wullie, whit's yer job in the Battalion?'
'Ah'm in the Intelligence Section!'

The Life of a Regiment, Volume VII, p 90.

Humour was not the preserve of the other ranks, and officers were quite prepared to poke fun in situations which had lost all perspective. This was particularly true in Ireland, where memories of grievances, real and perceived, were kept alive for years after they had occurred:

Major Nigel Oxley was involved in a heated discussion about British 'meddling' in Ireland with a group of Republican activists, who had launched into a lengthy tirade that covered the Easter Rising of 1916, the potato famine of the 1840s, the Plantation of Northern Ireland with Scots settlers, the Battle of the Boyne in 1690, the oppression of the Catholic population by Oliver Cromwell in the 1650s and the English assumption of Overlordship of Ireland through the machinations of an English Pope in 1155.

'But you Irish started it all!' stated Major Oxley, with a twinkle in his eye.

'How d'ye mean?' queried the puzzled Irishmen, disturbed that they stood accused.

'Well, it all started when you Irish came across and pillaged Scotland in the seventh and eighth centuries', stated Major Oxley.

'Ah now, ye're living a bit in the past Major, aren't ye?' was the Irish response!

The Life of a Regiment, Volume VII, p 113.

As had happened so many times before, in this 1974 incident in Singapore, one Gordon Highlander was the butt of another's joke:

> Private John 'Tanner' McSeveney[2] was a good, dependable side drummer in the Drums and Pipes, but his bugling left something to be desired. Despite tuition by the Drum Major, Staff Sergeant Brian Huntington, and regular practice, he found bugling one of the harder and less enjoyable parts of his job. It was not surprising, therefore, that he regarded his turn as Duty Drummer less than enthusiastically. The Duty Drummer had to sound all the routine bugle calls during the day and was heard by the whole Battalion.
>
> The day came when his worst nightmares were realised. It had started off reasonably well, and the early calls during the day had posed no problems. When it came time to blow the call for Commanding Officer's Orders, the RSM, WO1 Hutton, even gave him a bottle of juice to wet his lips before he marched out to sound the call, which turned out to be perfectly acceptable. Feeling more confident, he played the Half Hour Dress call for the guard and the Quarter Hour Dress. Then came the big one—Retreat. Taking post outside Battalion HQ (and beside the Military Band barrack block) he launched into the call. It was terrible. His mouth dried up, notes cracked and the call was a travesty.
>
> The Military Band, hanging over their balcony, convulsed with laughter at the attempt and McSeveney, in frustration and humiliation,

---

2 Pte McSeveney was a fine drummer, who later transferred to 4th Royal Tank Regiment as Drum-Major. He ended his service as a recruiter in Inverness, coincidentally working for Lt-Col Derek Napier, and was tragically killed in a road accident shortly before completing his Army service.

threw them a most unmilitary gesture with one hand as he saluted with the other.

'Stand still that man!' came a stentorian roar from Battalion HQ. To his horror, Private McSeveney saw the Battalion Second in Command, Major Graham, moustache bristling, emerge from his office. 'That was disgraceful, McSeveney. I don't ever want to hear bugling like that again. Now, play it again, properly.'

This time, under the watchful, glowering eye of Major Graham, McSeveney managed to get through the call with no major mishap. Falling out, he marched off the square dreading the inevitable interview with the Drum Major that would follow next morning.

Pouring out his woes to the Duty Piper, Corporal Alexander 'Cy' Cruickshank, Private McSeveney was really fed up. 'Never mind,' said Corporal Cruickshank, 'ye've only got twa calls tae go, First Post and Last Post. Ye'll manage them nae bother. Come on doon tae the NAAFI and we'll hae a game of snooker till it's time.'

Corporal Cruickshank's concept of a game of snooker included a steady supply of Tiger beer, which was not perhaps the best preparation for a nervous bugler who had already blotted his copybook that day. As the time approached for First Post Corporal Cruickshank said, 'Dinnae worry aboot First Post, save your lips for the big yin at ten o' clock. There's naebody aboot, so naebody'll ken you've missed yin oot.'

Thinking this very sound advice, young McSeveney had another game of snooker then made his way with Corporal Cruickshank to the Guardroom some ten minutes before Last Post was due to be sounded. 'Ah'm still no' happy aboot playing Last Post,' he confided to the piper, 'it's aye been difficult for me.'

'Dinnae worry aboot a thing', replied Corporal Cruickshank. 'Ah'll play it fur ye. Ah'm nae bad at bugling and Ah've done it fur drummers afore.'

'Thanks, Cy,' said the pathetically grateful McSeveney, 'that's great. Ah owe ye wan!'

When the Guard fell in under the watchful eye of the Duty Officer, WO2 Dave Green, Private McSeveney and Corporal Cruickshank fell in at the side, but contrived to ensure that they were in shadow so no-one could see as Corporal Cruickshank took up the bugle.

'Duty Drummer, Sound Off', called WO2 Green and Corporal Cruickshank began. To McSeveney's horror the sound was appalling, a succession of strangled, discordant notes that bore no relation to any tune ever written, and sounded more like a dying pig than a foray into music. Cruickshank, an inveterate prankster, had never played the bugle before in his life! After what seemed an eternity he handed the bugle back to the dumbfounded drummer, struck up his pipes and marched off, leaving McSeveney rooted to the spot and the Guard clinging on to each other as they laughed uncontrollably at the debacle. Even the Duty Officer could hardly repress a grin as he ordered the hapless McSeveney into the cells. As McSeveney remarked woefully when the cell door slammed on him, 'Never trust a piper, especially wan that says he can play the bugle!'

The Life of a Regiment, Volume VII, pp 146–7.

Food, in one guise or another, has always been a staple part of soldiers' discussion and when one Gordon Highlander attempted an unusual meal it attracted inevitable comment:

The Pipe Band became as adept at jungle warfare as the rifle platoons. Some even tried to live off the jungle itself. Private Jeff Harper[3] caught a snake and decided to make it into a stew. Remembering the survival lessons from the Jungle Warfare School, he skinned it, cleaned it and diced the meat before cooking it in his mess tin with some gravy and an onion. As his fellow bandsmen looked on, he spooned the first helpings into his mouth, smacking his lips and uttering expressions of enjoyment and appreciation. This lasted for only a minute or two, however, before his face turned a delicate shade of green and, choking back his culinary masterpiece (which threatened to make an unscheduled reappearance) he fled into the jungle, which reverberated with noises of regurgitation. On his return he found little sympathy from his friends. 'Ah telt ye tae hae the Irish Stew,' mocked Corporal 'Cy' Cruickshank, 'at least ye ken whaur it's been!'

The Life of a Regiment, Volume VII, pp 152-3.

Some soldiers rise to the occasion when a witty response is required. The following exchange took place on a Dargai Day parade at Nee Soon Barracks in Singapore in 1974:

It was a fine day, and the parade took place in front of hundreds of spectators. The Inspecting Officer was the Commander of 28 Infantry Brigade, Brigadier David Russell, who presented Long Service and Good Conduct Medals to the RQMS, WO2 Jim Melville, the TQMS, WO2 Jim Sharp, WO2 Ian Mitchell, Sergeant Gardner of the Army Catering Corps, and Lance Corporal Jimmy Bond. As Brigadier Russell pinned the medal on Lance Corporal Bond's chest, it fell on the ground and the clasp broke.

'Oh, I'm terribly sorry,' said Brigadier Russell, horrified that such a thing could happen.

---

3   Jeff Harper in due course became Drum-Major of the 1st Battalion.

'That's orl right, Sir,' replied Lance Corporal Bond, an irrepressible Kentishman who was one of the Battalion characters, 'it was broken service anyway!'

The Life of a Regiment, Volume VII, p 158.

The Gordon Highlanders' sense of humour was not confined to individuals, but could express itself on a wider scale with officers, warrant officers and soldiers playing their part. The following example is from 1977, during the Gordons' tour of Belfast:

On 1 April a worried subaltern, Lieutenant E D J Chalmers, came into Major Napier's office in Support Company to report that one of his Jocks, Private Semple, was absent.

Absence without leave was a serious offence in Northern Ireland, where the possibility that a missing soldier might have been abducted and murdered by the IRA could never be discounted. Colonel Graham had told the Battalion in no uncertain terms that he viewed absence seriously, and that offenders could expect little sympathy from him. By and large the Gordons took the message to heart, and there were very few instances of absence without leave throughout the tour. This made Private Semple's offence all the more heinous, and Major Napier's brows furrowed as he listened to the details.

Private John Semple was a cheerful, cocky little Glaswegian who frequently found himself in trouble through his inability to resist having the last word. His record sheet was full of minor misdemeanours and he was no stranger to the disciplinary process. If anyone were going to absent himself, Semple would be near the top of the list. Despite all this, he was a good operational soldier, with shrewd tactical awareness, aggressive determination and courage. He was a typical Glaswegian, and nothing could keep his spirits down for long. The most crushing dressing down would be followed by a grin and a humorous remark. Semple could be infuriating, but it was difficult to remain angry with him for long.

As Major Napier fumed he noticed the CSM, WO2 Bill Murdoch, gesturing to him behind Ewan Chalmers' back. Realising that all was not as it seemed, he dismissed the hapless platoon commander, reminding him that he was responsible for his soldiers and instructing him to report back whenever Semple turned up.

'Semple isn't absent.' said the Sergeant Major, 'He's hiding in his locker. It's an April Fool joke on Mr Chalmers.'

'Is it, now?' replied Major Napier, 'well two can play at that game! When Semple finally shows himself, throw him in close arrest, don't let him explain anything, and march him in to see me. Meanwhile, we'll let Mr Chalmers sweat on it for a while!'

He telephoned the Guard Room and spoke to the Provost Sergeant, Sergeant Ian Bruce, explaining the joke, and saying that, in due course, he would send Semple down under escort. Would he throw Semple into a cell and keep him for a short while until the joke was sprung on him? Sergeant Bruce, knowing Semple, thought it an excellent idea and agreed willingly.

Some twenty minutes later there was a commotion outside the Company Office and a white-faced Private Semple was marched in by Sergeant David Duncan, his platoon sergeant.

'So!' roared WO2 Murdoch, 'You've come back, you horrible little man! Right—in to the Company Commander now. Keep your mouth shut—you can do your explaining to the Major! Corporal Masson, fall in as escort. Semple, belt and bonnet off. Now fall in!'

Knocking on Major Napier's door, WO2 Murdoch popped his head inside. 'I've got Private Semple here, Sir.'

'Right, Sarn't Major, march him in.'

'Prisoner and escort, quick march, Le', Ri', Le', Ri',—Left Wheel—Right Wheel—Mark Time—prisoner and escort, Halt! Left Turn! Stand still, Semple, what are you swaying about for? Keep your mouth shut!'

The bewildered and distinctly unhappy Semple was marched in at the double and marked time in front of the desk, knees pumping up and down like pistons, until the Sergeant Major's command to halt. The seemingly irate major gave the trembling soldier a thunderous look, then launched into a tirade that grew to a crescendo, all the while thumping the desk with his fist and sending papers flying to the floor.

'I've had enough of you, Semple,' he shouted, 'you're nothing but trouble. I've given you the benefit of the doubt up to now, but this time you've gone too far.' By this time he was standing, and leaning forward over the desk, staring into the eyes of the unfortunate Semple, who, with injured innocence, tried to make a final attempt at explanation.

'But Sir, . . .' he began.

'Keep your mouth shut when the Major's talking to you, you miserable little man!' bellowed the Sergeant Major.

Semple lapsed into an unhappy silence and stood, miserably dejected, as the Company Commander went on. 'It's the Guard Room for you, laddie, and then up before the Commanding Officer—and I wouldn't like to be in your shoes when he sees you!' He picked up the telephone to warn the Guard Room that the joke was about to go into its next phase.

'For ony sake, dinnae send him doon here,' came the reply,—we've got a car bomb at the Main Gate!' On cue, the camp alarm siren went off.

With the climax of his practical joke ruined, and with buildings emptying of their occupants, Major Napier stood up and looked at Private

Semple. 'We've got to fall in for a roll call now, Semple, so we'll adjourn this little discussion for the time being, but before we go there's just one more thing I want to say to you—April Fool!'

Semple looked at his Company Commander for a full ten seconds before his face sagged and the realisation that he had been fooled dawned on him.

'Now, fall in with the platoon, Semple, and you'd better make your peace with Mr Chalmers—he thought you'd gone over the wire!'

The Life of a Regiment, Volume VII, pp 205–7.

The north-east soldier was the backbone of The Gordon Highlanders. Lance Corporal Andy Thomson's dry humour, calm approach and assessment of his passenger's mood were typical of those fine soldiers:

During one tug-of-war competition Lance Corporal Andy Thomson was chatting to a member of one of the RUC teams. 'What do you do?' asked the policeman.

'Oh, Ah'm the Commandin' Officer's driver.' came the reply in a slow, North-East drawl.

'My now, that's interestin'. What's he loike?'

'Weel, when he's in a guid mood, he's aye lauchin' an' smilin'; when he's in a bad mood Ah jist ignore the auld bugger!'

The Life of a Regiment, Volume VII, p 229.

The Duke of Rothesay (Prince of Wales), Colonel-in-Chief of The Gordon Highlanders, met Gordons of all ranks on many occasions. They found him easy to get on with, interested in them and their families and concerned about their welfare. They, in turn, treated him with respect, affection and an unaffectedness that must surely have pleased him. During the Royal Family's annual stay at Balmoral in 1980, the Gordons provided the Royal Guard. Part of the duties involved assisting with shoots as beaters, ghillies, ponymen and others:

Private Stanley Marr was a ghillie. He frequently accompanied the Duke of Rothesay on the hills, looking after his equipment and guns. At their first meeting the Duke asked 'What's your name?'

'Stan' came the answer.

'Is that your surname?' asked the Prince.

'Oh, sorry, Sir,' replied a flustered Marr, 'it's Private Marr, Sir.'

'And what do you want me to call you?' asked the Prince.

'Jist call me Stan' came the reply.

'Oh, all right Stan.'

301

The day came when Marr accompanied the Duke of Rothesay up on to the moors, jumping into the back of the Landrover that carried the party. On previous trips Private Marr had eyed the Prince's packed lunch, prepared by the cooks at Balmoral Castle, and had drooled over smoked salmon sandwiches, dressed pheasant with salad, game pie and other culinary delights. He was philosophical, however, and content with his own packed lunch—a standard Army 'haverbag' of cheese sandwich, hardboiled egg, apple and bag of crisps.

As the Landrover lurched over rutted tracks and bounced across the moor Private Marr cushioned himself on the rucksacks and jackets carried in the back. In the manner of soldiers everywhere he made the most of whatever was available to make himself as comfortable as possible. Arriving at the destination he jumped out, helped the Prince into his jacket, and got his equipment and guns ready.

After a good morning's shooting, the party returned to the Landrover for lunch. Unpacking his rucksack, the Prince opened his packed lunch to find a congealed object, squashed into one motley, flattened mass.

'Good Lord,' exclaimed the Prince, 'What on earth has happened to this?'

Stan Marr never turned a hair. 'Never mind, Sir,' he replied, holding out his brown paper bag, 'hae mine.'

The Life of a Regiment, Volume VII, pp 297–8.

The funniest comments are often ad-libbed, in response to events of the moment. Not everyone can rise to such an occasion, but the Gordons from the north-east produced more than their share of those who could. Colour Sergeant Mick Kelbie was one such, during an exercise in Germany in 1987:

The highlight of every exercise was the clearing of a farm during which the pig-sty was set alight. This was the only building that was allowed to be set on fire, and German units always made the most of the opportunity to inject realism into the exercise. During a visit to the Gordons' exercise the German Commandant, escorted by Colour Sergeant Kelbie, stopped to watch the assault on the farm. As he watched the assault go in, amid smoke and flames from the burning outhouse, he remarked to his escorts, 'When our troops carry out this assault we usually have a soldier in a flame-proof suit who runs out of the building, on fire!' At that very moment Corporal B F Wales came running out of the building, beating frantically at his combat suit, which was in flames. As he rolled in the dirt to smother the flames, Colour Sergeant Kelbie remarked dryly, 'Aye, we dae that tae, but we dinnae wear thae silly suits!'

The Life of a Regiment, Volume VII, p 229.

SENSE OF HUMOUR

For 200 years Gordon Highlanders laughed at misfortune, mischance, mistakes, deprivation and discomfort. They laughed at success and failure, victory and defeat, friends and rivals, and most of all at themselves. At times, particularly in captivity, which was sometimes brutal and cruel, but always hard to bear, it was hard to keep a sense of humour, but that sense of humour was never far beneath the surface, and sometimes it was all that was left to keep them going. But it never failed them.

SECTION 10

O WAD SOME POW'R THE GIFTIE GIE US
TO SEE OURSELS AS OTHERS SEE US

EVERY regiment worth its salt believes that it is special—and better than the others. This is understandable and excusable, when building up regimental pride and spirit is a major part of the regimental system. If a regiment is to justify its boast, however, it must demonstrate it, because it will not come about if based solely on chest-beating assertions such as:

> 'Here's tae us! Wha's like us?
> Damned few, an' they're a' deid!'

The best testimonials to a regiment's worth come, not from within its own ranks but from outsiders. Throughout its existence The Gordon Highlanders proved their worth time and time again, in war and peace. Recorded in the following section are what other people said of the Regiment. Rather than stick to a strict chronological list, I have grouped the comments as far as possible into similar categories.

CHAPTER 22

AS OTHERS SEE US

THE first recorded instance of empathy with the local community comes from Ireland in 1798, when the 92nd (still numbered 100th) was sent at short notice to counter the rebellion that broke out on 23 May. The rebellion was followed in August 1798 by French invasion to encourage further insurrection and rebellion.

The performance of some British troops—regular and militia—at times involved harsh treatment of the population, whom the soldiers saw as aiding and abetting the rebels and revolutionary France. This treatment, indiscriminate and usually unjustified, bred resentment and hostility among the Irish. That it was in response to similar bad conduct by rebels was lost on those who suffered. 'The dreadful cruelties of the rebels had given rise to reprisals on the part of the troops, and especially of the yeomanry of the country, and the peasantry were subjected to all the horrors of civil war. The exceptional conduct of The Gordon Highlanders at this time has been a matter of honest pride to the regiment ever since'. (*The Life of a Regiment*, Volume I, p 42):

> *R.O., August 19th.* 1798:—Lieut.-Colonel Erskine is extremely happy that the following letter from the Dean of Ferns to the Marquis of Huntly, expressive of the good conduct of the regiment during their stay at Gorey, should be inserted in the Regimental Orderly Book:—
>
> My Lord,—I have the honour of enclosing to you that part of the proceedings in the last Vestry held in Gorey wherein your Lordship and your regiment are mentioned. This mark of our respect and gratitude should have been sooner expressed and conveyed to you, had not our calamitous situation delayed the calling of a Vestry, which we conceived the most regular mode of expressing our sentiments collectively. It may be pleasing to your Lordship to hear that, in the attendance of my parish, I have heard all the poor loud in the praise of the honesty and humanity of the privates of your regiment. They not only did not rob them of the wretched pittance that was left by the rebels, but refused such trifling presents (of provisions, etc.) as were offered them, saying their King paid them nobly, and enabled them to supply every want at their own expense.
>
> I have the honour to be,
> With great respect,
> Your Lordship's obedient Servant,
> (Signed)   Peter Brown, Dean of Ferns

We, the loyal inhabitants of the parish and vicinity of Gorey, in Vestry assembled, beg leave thus publicly to acknowledge the goodness and humanity evinced by the Marquis of Huntly during his short stay amongst us. We are proud to add that during that short stay rapine ceased to be a system, and the confidence of the people in the honour of government began to revive. We should be wanting in gratitude if we omitted our testimony that the humanity of the colonel was emulated by the soldiers, and we request the 100th Regiment to accept our thanks for the moderation and honour which marked the conduct of every individual officer and private who composed it.

> (Signed) Peter Brown, Rector.
> J. Jerman, Churchwarden.

Further testimony to the high character of the Gordon Highlanders is given in the *History of the Rebellion*. After describing the devastation and plundering sustained by the inhabitants, without distinction of loyalist or 'croppy,' the author continues:—'On the arrival of the Marquis of Huntly, however, with his regiment of Scottish Highlanders, the scene was totally altered; its behaviour was such as, if it were universal among soldiers, would render a military government amiable. To the astonishment of the (until then miserably harassed) peasantry, not the smallest trifle would any of these Highlanders accept, without payment of at least the full value.'

The Life of a Regiment, Volume I, pp 42–3.

In June 1799 The Gordon Highlanders (now known as the 92nd, having been renumbered from 100th in 1798) was selected to take part in the expedition against the French in Holland. The following was published in Orders at Monkstown:

At a meeting of the inhabitants of Athlone and vicinity, on the 15th June 1799, Thomas Mitchell, Esq, in the chair, the following address to Lieut.-Colonel Erskine, commanding His Majesty's 92nd Regiment in this Garrison, was unanimously agreed to.

Sir,—We heard with concern that his Majesty's 92nd Regiment, which you have commanded in this garrison, has been ordered to march for the purpose of joining those troops intended for a foreign expedition, but however we may regret your departure, we are not surprised that a regiment so eminently conspicuous for its steadiness and discipline should be selected for an arduous enterprise. We have during your continuance amongst us experienced a polite attention from the officers of your regiment; and the uninterrupted peace and tranquillity which have prevailed in this town and neighbourhood evince the attention of the soldiers under your command.

Permit us, therefore, to return you our thanks, and to request that you will convey the same to the officers, n.c. officers, and soldiers of your regiment.

By order of the meeting,

(Signed) Thomas Mitchell.

Stationed in Ireland in 1830, the 92nd once again showed that discipline, appreciation for the needs of the community and fellow-feeling did not go unnoticed:

Maryborough, 7th June 1830.

Sir,

We, the undersigned, magistrates of Maryborough district, at Petty Sessions assembled, avail ourselves of this, the earliest opportunity of expressing our high approbation of the conduct of the Ninety-Second Highlanders, quartered in the town of Maryborough for the last twelve months. In justice to the excellent character of the men, we feel called upon to testify that not a single complaint was made by the inhabitants against any of them, and that their conduct was uniformly correct and exemplary.

The general zeal and intelligence of the officers, supported by the steadiness and discipline of the men, when co-operating with the civil power, particularly during the last winter (in suppressing outrages, which, unhappily, extended to our hitherto peaceable county), demand our cordial thanks; and we beg that you will be pleased to make known to the officers and men these our sentiments, and to assure them that their services will long be gratefully remembered by every respectable inhabitant of this town and vicinity.

We have, etc.   (Signed)   W. Perceval, J.P.

D. O'Donoughue, J.P.

Matt. Cassan, J.P.

The Life of a Regiment, Volume II, p 19.

That this behaviour was natural to the men of the 92nd, even when far from the eyes of their commanding officer, is shown by the following testimonial to the training, conduct and good sense of all concerned:

The Bench of Magistrates assembled at Petty Sessions in the Court House, Nenagh, November 1830—Lord Dunalley in the chair.

The undersigned magistrates have observed with great satisfaction the uniformly regular and soldier-like conduct of the detachment of His Majesty's 92nd Highland Regiment during the period they have been at Nenagh, under the command of Captain Bayly, a conduct which reflects great credit on the system, discipline, and interior economy established in that corps, and has merited not only the notice and approbation of the gentlemen of this part of the country, but also secured for the individuals of this detachment the admiration and cordial regard of all classes of the inhabitants of Nenagh, as strongly manifested on the departure of the troops for Dublin. The magistrates, feeling it to be their pleasing duty to mark their approbation of such good conduct, request their chairman may be pleased to communicate these their sentiments to Lieut.-Colonel MacDonald, commanding the 92nd Regiment.

The Life of a Regiment, Volume II, pp 20–1.

During the latter part of 1832 and into 1833, the 92nd was frequently employed in aid of the civil power, to keep the peace and enforce the collection of tithes; in these duties the conduct of the discipline of The Gordon Highlanders was constantly approved by their superiors. The Commander of the Forces, Lieutenant-General Sir John Byng, thanked them for 'the judicious dispositions made, for the excellent discipline and proper spirit' displayed, and expressed 'regret that the service on which they were employed should have been of so harassing a nature'. Major-General Sir Thomas Arbuthnot, commanding the district, reported:

It was most pleasing to him to find that the manner in which the regiment and its detachments are in the habit of comporting themselves towards the inhabitants of the country, and the very soldier-like manner in which they perform their duties has made them bodily and individually respected and looked up to by the magistrates and gentry residing in the vicinity of their quarters.

The Life of a Regiment, Volume II, p 24.

In July 1833 the 92nd was ordered for Gibraltar and the detachments were recalled. The six service and four depot companies were inspected by Sir Thomas Arbuthnot, who expressed his regret at losing from his command a regiment 'which had gained universal respect and esteem for the manner in which it had executed the numerous and trying duties which it had been called upon to perform'. Further testimonial was received:

Fermoy, 8th August 1833.
The under-mentioned magistrates and other principal inhabitants of the town and neighbourhood of Fermoy, having heard with sincere regret that the highly distinguished Regiment under your command has received orders to embark for foreign service, cannot permit them to depart without expressing the high sense they entertained of their uniform exemplary

conduct during the protracted period of their being quartered in this Garrison, which has been such as to create a very general feeling of admiration and detachment; and they Further beg you to accept this expression of their esteem for the Regiment, and their best wishes for its future welfare.

Signed by   The Earl of Ennismore,

Major-General H.G. Barry,

and many others.

To Lieut.-Colonel MacDonald
   92nd Highlanders.

In 1851 the 92nd was posted to Corfu from Ireland, when it received a testimonial addressed to 'Lieut-Colonel Atherley, the Officers, N.C. Officers and Men of the 92nd Highlanders':

We, the undersigned, cannot permit your departure from Kilkenny, where you have been quartered for twelve months, without testifying our sincere regret upon your removal, at the same time taking occasion to express how much that regret is enhanced, owing to the uniform urbanity of the officers and the steady and peaceable demeanour of the men, which has won upon the regard and gained the esteem of all.

Satisfied that such conduct as your regiment has pursued here will always uphold the honour of the British army and the credit of the Empire, we have only earnestly to hope that the 92nd Highlanders may be protected through all perils and dangers, safely to return home, so that you may again earn, amongst your brother civilians, the same respect and detachment which is now so deservedly borne away from all classes here.

Signed by   Michael Hyland, Mayor,

The Earl of Desart, and eighty of he

nobility and gentry of the

County and city of Kilkenny.

14th Feb. 1851

The Life of a Regiment, Volume II, p 51.

Appreciation of the 92nd was marked wherever they went. In 1861 they were stationed in the city of Perth:

On their return to Stirling in May 1861, the Provost and magistrates of the city of Perth addressed a letter to Captain Macbean,[1] commanding the depot 92nd Highlanders, in which they express 'our sense of the peculiarly excellent and orderly character of the soldiers belonging to that gallant regiment during the time they have been quartered here. The best

---

1   Later to command the Regiment; and later still to become Colonel of the Regiment.

evidence of this is to be found in the fact that the city authorities have not been troubled with a complaint against any one of them, which is more than can be said for the soldiers of any depot quartered in Perth for very many years'. They attribute the good understanding between the inhabitants and the soldiers to the high state of discipline of the latter, 'and tender our best thanks to yourself and the officers, n.c. officers, and privates under your command for so pleasing a state of matters'. The letter concludes by an expression of gratitude to Captain Macbean for his 'many acts of kindness in connection with public objects in this city, and for those deeds of philanthropy which so well mark the character of the Christian gentleman and the Christian soldier'; and with good wishes to all—'we feel assured these sentiments are shared by the entire community over which we preside, and who will part with the 92nd with much regret'.

William Imrie, Lord Provost.

The Life of a Regiment, Volume II, pp 84–5.

For their calm and compassionate work in civil communities dating back to Ireland in 1798, Gordon Highlanders won recognition in every station they occupied. This was no less true during the Boer War than it had been a century before:

[In 1902] Mrs. Van Niekirk, Krugersdorp, wife of the burgher, testifies to the 'kindly treatment of the Dutch women and children by the British troops.' She described how the town was held by troops, up to 10,000 at times, and of all sorts; how the women, at first afraid, soon discovered that they could go about freely. During six months that she was in Krugersdorp she never heard of a single instance where a woman was treated with the slightest disrespect; the bearing of officers and men was invariably deferential to women and kindly to children. 'Last July a detachment of Gordon Highlanders camped on the veldt for a week in front of my house, which stands almost alone on the outskirts of the town. My husband was away. The nearest camp fires were not a dozen yards from my gate; yet I never experienced the least annoyance, nor missed from my ground so much as a stick of firewood. I could multiply instances: if I had not seen, I could not have believed that a victorious army would behave with such humanity and consideration.'

The Life of a Regiment, Volume III, p 435.

The example quoted above was not a 'one-off', but a true reflection of the natural instincts of The Gordon Highlanders. It was repeated in different theatres in different wars, with the same lack of rancour and respect for non-combatant civilian populations of former enemies. The population of Germany, crushed and defeated in May 1945, could be forgiven for feeling fearful and apprehensive in anticipation of their treatment at the hands of the occupying forces—British, American, French and Russian. As they had shown over the years, however, it was not in the nature of Gordon Highlanders to be vindictive or vengeful towards defenceless civilians. The following is a striking testament to their innate moderation, courtesy and even-handedness:

> May I, as a German, say a word of praise about the kindness of Scottish soldiers.
>
> During the summer of 1945, when Germany was at the mercy of soldiers from many countries of Europe and U.S.A., I came into contact with the Gordon Highlanders.
>
> They showed a kindness of heart not hitherto experienced, and they will not be forgotten in the North-West of Germany. As soldiers, they are magnificent.
>
> Their attitude towards a defeated enemy—at a time when it was easy to sneer at us—will remain unforgotten. Scotland may be proud of her soldiers.
>
> Paul E. Orth

Daily Record, November 1957.

German civilians looked upon Scotsmen from a stereotypical viewpoint; and were ready to make fun of their perceived tightness with money. The realisation that this stereotype might not be true dawned when The Gordon Highlanders were posted to Celle. The following appeared in the *Hannoversche Presse* in August 1958:[2]

The Scots are not like that at all

Their thriftiness is known all over the world. Philipp does not want to publish any new Scotch jokes, but he is of the opinion that there might be some connection between the debate concerning the Budget of the British Forces in Germany and the transfer of 500 Scotsmen to Celle. By their thriftiness the Scots will manage to make good the deficit.

They started right away at the day of their arrival. Originally it was planned that the 500 Scots were to get out at the main station and march through the town. Philipp on hearing this was sceptical. Considering the

---

2   On their arrival in Celle in 1958 the Gordons took the unusual (in those days) step of inviting local German civilians and dignitaries to a cocktail party in the Officers Mess. Easy and relaxed, the Gordons quickly put their guests at ease and formed friendships and contacts that were developed to mutual benefit over the next three years. When they left Celle in 1961 the people of Celle showed how much they appreciated the Gordons when they presented an engraved silver cigarette box to the Regiment, an unusual gesture at that time. It was a very real testament to the good relations and sense of fellowship enjoyed by the citizens of Celle and The Gordon Highlanders. Only one year later another Scottish regiment, after a brawl in Minden, became infamously known by the Germans as the 'Poison Dwarfs'.

present high costs of shoe repairs, the Scots would think this over. And there you see, the business-like thinking Commander had an idea. He made the soldiers travel on to the station Celle-Vorstadt and then get out. Almost 2 km of wear and tear of shoes were saved. Multiplied by 500 the result of two pairs of new soles. This is a pure deed of thriftiness.

Much admired were the nice skirts which belong to every Scotsman just as sleeve protectors belong to every official of the finance authorities. Seeing the soldiers' kilts for the first time little Thomas asked 'Uncle Philipp, why do the soldiers wear skirts?' Philipp thought this over for a while and since he could not think of anything he replied: 'Naturally for economical reasons. You see it is like this. If one wears trousers they have to be ironed. One needs an iron, and to be able to use it, electricity. Since the Scots do not wear trousers they do not need an iron and do not use any electricity. With the prices for electricity of today this again means real thriftiness.' That was clear to Thomas. Out of sympathy he asked for a Scots kilt for his next birthday.

First contacts with the new troops have shown that the Scots are very economical but by no means mean. Philipp went to have a glass of beer with Otto in the evening. There were some Scots at the next table and four more arrived soon afterwards. Otto whispered, 'That will be a big order, one bottle of lemonade and four glasses, all of it to be paid by the Corporal.' That is what you think—four whole glasses of beer were taken to the table by the waiter. 'You better get a pound of Pfennigs from the Bank in order to be able to hand out the right change,' Otto said grinning. The waiter just smiled, in a way only waiters can smile:—'The Scots are not like that at all, they give more tips than some of those who go round telling Scotch jokes.'

Otto remained very silent for the rest of the evening. When we paid our bill, he gave a 20 Pfennig tip for the first time in his life. Who after all would like to be known as being more Scotch than the Scots!

T&S, December 1958.

For a public duties battalion in Edinburgh, ceremonial guards were an integral part of the programme. To The Gordon Highlanders such duties, interspersed with the myriad tasks heaped upon the Battalion by Headquarter Scotland, came as second nature. Rehearsals for parades, their immaculate turn out and their obvious regimental pride enabled them to carry out such tasks in public with ease:

On 24 May [1966], the Battalion were represented by the Guard of Honour for the opening of the General Assembly. The Guard was under the command of Major Gordon-Steward and was inspected by the Lord

High Commissioner, Lord Birsay, who later commented most favourably in a letter to the Commanding Officer:

'The Guard of Honour at St Giles on the first morning paraded with a very high standard of efficiency. The House Guard was at all times extremely smart and turned out beautifully to salute on my leaving and returning to the Palace (of Holyrood House). Your Military Band was quite excellent and on many occasions our guests said how much they had enjoyed the pieces played. We also greatly enjoyed the Pipes and Drums each morning at the Changing of the Guard and were most indebted to four of your Pipers who turned out at short notice to play at the first banquet when the Edinburgh Police Pipe Band were held up abroad.'

The Life of a Regiment, Volume VII, pp 141–2.

There were times when criticism was levelled at The Gordon Highlanders. If the criticism was justified the Regiment accepted it and worked hard to put right any faults or deficiencies. Sometimes the criticism was unjustified, and the Regiment felt it was unfair. The only thing to do was demonstrate by performance the character and high standards that were the hallmark of the Regiment:

In May 1978 the 1st Battalion moved from Northern Ireland to Chester, where it came under command of Headquarters North-West District in Preston. The initial reception from some of the staff at the Headquarters seemed less than cordial, and highly critical of the Battalion. When the Commanding Officer questioned this reception, he found that the Headquarters had received some outstanding Special Investigation Branch (SIB) enquiries and Courts-Martial. The Headquarters did not take into account that the SIB enquiries related to contact reports which the police in Northern Ireland had not had time to follow to a conclusion, and that the Courts-Martial included a case of desertion from several years earlier, whose subject had just returned to the fold, and that the others were an accumulation of comparatively minor offences which had had too low a priority in the busy atmosphere of Northern Ireland for the legal authorities to follow them through. Justified complaints by the Battalion, supported by their Colonel-in-Chief, The Duke of Rothesay, about the injustice of charging poorly paid soldiers, accommodated up to 30 miles from Chester, for the transport costs of bringing them to and from the barracks, did not endear the Battalion to the Staff at Headquarters. It did not take long, however, for the Gordons to demonstrate their efficiency, effectiveness and discipline, and from then on it gained excellent reports for its work in the District, the GOC, Major-General Peter Sibbald recording:

I was impressed with the spirit, courtesy and general attitude of all ranks. I doubt I have ever seen a battalion run better. The relationship established with Chester and the local Press is quite first class and I congratulate all concerned. 1 Gordons is a battalion which is always a pleasure to visit. The hallmarks are enthusiasm, cheerfulness and courtesy. All ranks are well motivated, cheerful and have a practical 'get on with the job' attitude.

The Life of a Regiment, Volume VII, p 271.

The Gordon Highlanders prided themselves on being hospitable and friendly. This applied, not only within a Services environment, but to local communities wherever the Regiment was based. In 1984 the Gordons were once again in Germany, based at Deilinghofen near Hemer:

Wherever the Gordons went during Exercise 'Spearpoint' they won the confidence of the local German communities and enjoyed lavish hospitality. As far as 'A' Company was concerned one village showed its hospitality to such an extent that the CQMS reported that no army rations were consumed for a whole day! For local communities, which experienced great disruption and not a little damage during large exercises, to show such friendliness to an exercising unit spoke volumes for the innate courtesy and consideration shown by the Jocks in all their dealings with the host population.

The Life of a Regiment, Volume VII, p 348.

ACTIVE SERVICE

One of the most outstanding commendations of The Gordon Highlanders came from Winston Churchill, whose description of their performance at Doornkop in 1900 reinforced the Victorian view of The Gordon Highlanders as being something special:

The honours equally with the cost of the victory, making every allowance for skilful direction and bold leading, belong to the 1st Battalion Gordon Highlanders more than to all the other troops put together. The rocks against which they marched proved to be the very heart of the enemy's position. The grass in front of them was burnt and burning, and against this dark background the khaki figures showed distinctly. The Boers held their heaviest fire until the attack was within 800 yards, and then the ominous rattle of concentrated rifle fire burst forth. The advance neither checked nor quickened. With remorseless stride, undisturbed by peril or enthusiasm, the Gordon Highlanders swept steadily onwards, changed direction half left to avoid an enfilade fire, changed again to effect a lodgement on the end of the ridge most suitable to attack and at last rose up together to charge. The Boers shrank from the contact. Discharging their magazines furiously and firing their guns twice at point-blank range, they fled in confusion.'

There is no doubt that they are the finest regiment in the world. Their unfaltering advance, their machine-like change of direction, their final charge with the bayonet, constitute their latest feat of arms the equal of Dargai or Elandslaagte.

The Life of a Regiment, Volume III, pp 179–80.

Operations in the field during the Boer War were hard on men, weapons and equipment. Soldiers might look ragged, scruffy and dirty compared with those in barracks, but as long as they kept their weapons clean and functioning, and followed battle procedure, they were operationally effective. A captain rejoining the 1st Battalion from other work wrote home that his men were:

admirable veterans, a nomad crowd one moment, a disciplined corps the next; smart under arms, rifles beautifully cared for, duties properly performed. But on the march nomads, efficient, quick, quiet, a chaos of complete order; no orders given because everything so perfectly understood; no attention paid to certain details because everything so perfect without. As efficient in things warlike as man could wish: as ragged a crew as only a soldier who has seen service can conceive. No new coats, spats, or shoes since October, so coats are torn, stained, weather-beaten: slept in, rained on, muddied, washed; bleached, patched, pieced. Faces darkened to a rich brick from which fair moustaches standout white, necks swathed in comforters or handkerchiefs; buttons gone, replaced anyhow; at night you see balaclava caps, daytimes all sorts of headdresses replace helmets lost or shot through—Tam o' Shanters, bushranger felts of sorts. Kilts faded to drab, with frayed, torn, patched, stained aprons, many missing or half away; boots and shoes of any sort, many very far through indeed.

The Life of a Regiment, Volume III, pp 221–2.

The First World War was an ordeal for every battalion that fought in it. Gordon Highlander battalions did well, and though they suffered heavy losses at times the survivors rebuilt the battalions and maintained the standards set by their predecessors. Their efforts were not always recognised, but some commendations do stand out:

Brigadier-General F.J. Heyworth remarked that he found it hard to pick individual battalions for praise, but that he desired 'to notice the gallant conduct of the 6th (Territorial) Battalion the Gordon Highlanders' at

Neuve Chapelle. Joining a seasoned brigade, it had shown itself fully
qualified to keep up the standard; the 20th Brigade was proud to have the
battalion in its ranks.

The Life of a Regiment, Volume IV, p 41.

The Gordons wore the kilt throughout the First World War. There is no
doubt that it preyed on the minds of the Germans:

> The kilt was often condemned, perhaps justly, as unsuitable for trench
> warfare, but it had its moral value. The prisoners—253 taken by the
> brigade—declared with fervour that they wished to give themselves up to
> 'the English' of the 17th Division and by no means to kilted men.

The Life of a Regiment, Volume IV, p 72.

Gordon Highlander battalions, both Regular and Territorial, distinguished
themselves during the First World War, so much so that when 6th Gordons
was sent from 20th Brigade in 1916, the brigade commander made an
impassioned plea to retain it:

> Since the arrival of the specially selected Territorial units, a number of
> brigades had consisted of five or even six battalions. They were now all
> to revert to the standard pattern. The 6th Gordon Highlanders was the
> battalion which had to go and was selected for a spell on the lines of
> communication. Brig.-General Deverell made a strong plea for its
> retention. 'The battalion is a fine one in every respect', he wrote. 'It has
> proved its worth in active operations, in the trenches, in billets and on the
> march. I can always be certain that any duty demanded will be carried out
> in the most thorough manner. The offensive spirit is high in the battalion.
> The dash and spirit of this battalion is accentuated by its close connection
> in this brigade with the 2nd Battalion.

The Life of a Regiment, Volume IV, p 73.

Two Gordon battalions, the 1st and 5th/7th, fought at Alamein and in the
pursuit of the retreating Afrika Corps in 1942:

> On 14th November Major-General Wimberley, commanding the
> Highland Division, paid a graceful tribute to the Gordons. Writing to their
> Colonel-in-Chief he informed His Royal Highness that the two battalions
> of his Highland regiments serving in the Division had 'fought in the best
> traditions of their great past'. He continued: 'Actually as I write a well
> turned out Gordon Highlander guard in the kilt, with a piper playing *The
> Cock of the North*, has mounted outside my caravan.'
> Untried in battle before they attacked at El Alamein, the Highland
> Division were now war-hardened and desert-hardened. Of the two

battalions of Gordon Highlanders their Brigadier (Brigadier D.A.H. Graham) wrote to the Colonel of the Regiment: 'All your lads are in excellent heart and ready to take on anything that may be before them. They are a grand lot.'

The Life of a Regiment, Volume V, pp 145, 155.

The 2nd Battalion was recognised in Normandy in July 1944:

The divisional commander, Major-General G.H.A. MacMillan[3] added his word of pride in what his troops had achieved, and writing to the Colonel of the Regiment on 5th July the commanding officer said:

'The Battalion is out of the line and having a well-earned rest. Our first introduction to battle has been a very hard test: we had a week of hell from the multiple mortars. The one thing we can say is the Battalion did all they were told to do . . . the Jocks behaved in their usual grand way.'

The Life of a Regiment, Volume V, p 271.

INSPECTION REPORTS

Praise from a commander is always welcome, but never more so than when that commander has no hesitation in criticising regiments that do not live up to the expected standard:

On the 17th April [1805] the Battalion was inspected. Field officers and staff in white breeches and boots, the other officers in Highland dress; and Major-General Hope, in Orders of the 18th, expressed the highest approbation of the 'complete and efficient appearance of the 92nd Regiment yesterday, as well as the precision with which the Battalion moved,' and he 'requests Lieut-Colonel Napier to express to the officers and men his sense of the diligence they have bestowed on the several field duties, and of the proficiency to which they have attained.'

This was the more satisfactory, as General Hope is by no means so complimentary in his Order to a regiment he had inspected the previous day.

The Life of a Regiment, Volume I, p 117.

After distinguishing itself in the Napoleonic Wars the 92nd showed that it could maintain its standards in peacetime. The following comments are gratifying, if somewhat ironic, considering that the 92nd was about to embark

---

3   Gen MacMillan's son commanded 1st Gordons, 1971–73, and left the Army as Lt-Gen Sir John MacMillan.

on a disastrous posting in the West Indies, where yellow fever carried off more soldiers than it had lost in the wars:

> In October [1817], Major-General Burnet complimented them on their appearance, drill, precision of firing, etc., and particularly remarks 'the well-regulated system of interior economy which prevails in the corps,' and that the detachments he visited were in the best order.
>
> On the 28th April 1818 they were inspected by Major-General Sir Sydney Beckwith, who issued a very complimentary order, mentioning their 'soldier-like and respectable appearance,' and that he was equally gratified with that of the detachments, 'but no less was to be looked for from a Regiment who have always preserved their regular military habits under the most trying circumstances.'

The Life of a Regiment, Volume II, p 2.

Serving in India, in 1859 the 92nd won respect for consistency and professionalism:

> At Jhansi the regiment was inspected, and afterwards H.R.H. the Commander-in-Chief remarked on the 'excellent and most satisfactory report of Brigadier-General Sir Robert Napier upon this distinguished corps, which deserves great praise.'
>
> Sir Robert afterwards endorsed his opinion of the regiment by placing his two sons (the late Lord Napier of Magdala and his brother), when appointed to the Indian army, with the 92nd as a good school of duty.
>
> Lord Clyde also reported, after inspecting the regiment in December 1859, that 'their state of the highest order, after the recent continuous and arduous duties, reflects great credit on every rank of the corps.'

The Life of a Regiment, Volume II, p 70.

On arriving at a new station a regiment might expect its annual inspection reports to improve year by year as it gained experience and honed its training to the expectations of its brigade and higher commanders. It was almost unheard of to achieve the desired results at the first attempt! The 2nd Battalion did just that:

> In August [1905] the remarks of the Lieut.-General on his Inspections were received. He found the barracks in perfect order, the sanitation as good as possible—'showing the great care exercised in this splendid corps. This no doubt accounts for the absence of serious sickness at a time when other British troops in Peshawar are suffering a good deal.' He found that musketry left little to be desired and that the battalion was highly efficient in the science. Cynics will agree that it is natural for the

last report at any station to be very flattering, but for the first to be so eulogistic seems almost unnatural!

The Life of a Regiment, Volume III, pp 369–70.

A year later, the 2nd Battalion showed that the high standards it had set had been maintained:

> [In 1906] the yearly 'Confidential Reports' were received, and not an adverse word was to be found in them: 'A well-trained battalion in grand physical condition. Fit for service in every respect. I have seen it subjected to very severe marching tests and it has always commanded my admiration.' 'It would be hard to find a better turned-out regiment or one better disciplined.' 'The most marked characteristic of this splendid Regiment is its *esprit de corps*.'

The Life of a Regiment, Volume III, pp 371–2.

For their tour in the British Army of the Rhine (1967–71) the Gordons were equipped with the FV 432 armoured personnel carrier, and quickly became adept at working with tanks, artillery and engineers in the highly specialised mechanised role:

> The Gordons received an excellent report in 1970 from the Fitness For Role Inspection. In it Brigadier Creasey wrote:

> > 'Whatever I have seen done by The Gordon Highlanders during the past year has been done well, done properly, done in a professional manner and done cheerfully. I consider them to be the most experienced and probably the best mechanised Battalion in the British Army of the Rhine.

> > In Minden the Battalion has established excellent relations with the local German population. This has been due to the good behaviour and good discipline of the soldiers, and the excellent work of the Military Band.

> > I set the battalion the task of mounting and carrying out a ceremonial parade. As I would have expected this parade was excellent. The turnout and bearing of the individual soldier was immaculate. Every soldier I spoke to answered up well and cheerfully, and it was obvious that all concerned had a great pride in their Battalion and the results achieved.

> > Throughout the year the Battalion has taken part in every aspect of sporting life with determination and vigour; the highlight of 1970 being the success of the lightweight tug-of-war team in the Army finals. I am satisfied that all ranks are tough and fit as befits an infantry battalion.

From my inspection and from the ancillary inspection reports it is clear that a high standard of administration is being maintained.

My inspection day was most successful, and I was delighted with everything I saw and heard. The results reflected the high standard shown throughout the year.

I congratulate the Commanding Officer and all ranks on a highly successful year and inspection day. I rate the Battalion as fully fit for war.'

The Life of a Regiment, Volume VII, pp 35–6.

The standards that The Gordon Highlanders set themselves were high. These were apparent to all who saw them at work in daily routines and on operations, but documented acknowledgement was usually found only in annual inspection reports. The 1978 report, when the Gordons were on an eighteen-month tour in Belfast, was in no doubt about their effectiveness:

February saw the Annual Administrative Inspection where the Battalion's administration was scrutinised by teams from 39 Infantry Brigade and the Battalion was inspected by the Brigade Commander. The administrative organisation was found to be sound, providing the excellent support that had kept the rifle companies so well maintained.

Bearing in mind the high rate of deployments of companies and the heavy and constant usage of equipment [the serviceability] figures were quite outstanding. They reflected great credit on the TQM, Captain Strachan, the MTO, Captain Hutton, and all the technicians, storemen and drivers who had maintained the equipments throughout the year. The Inspection Report stated that the Battalion had achieved:

. . . 'the highest standards of operational and administrative efficiency and maintained them over a year of intense pressure. In the process morale has been sustained at a high level, and skilled leadership at all levels has ensured a close knit, happy and thoroughly professional unit devoting its efforts wholeheartedly to suppressing terrorism in Belfast. The Regiment can be proud of its achievements.'

The Commander Land Forces (CLF), Major-General R B Trant, added:

'I am very well aware of all the pressures which have fallen on 1st Battalion The Gordon Highlanders this past 12 months, and indeed throughout their whole tour in Northern Ireland.

I fully endorse this excellent report by the Commander 39 Infantry Brigade. The Battalion is well led, totally effective operationally, soundly administered with high morale.'

The Life of a Regiment, Volume VII, pp 241–2.

Non-operational soldiering in Chester provided challenges much different from those on active service in Northern Ireland, but the Gordons took them in their stride and impressed observers with their effectiveness, professionalism and regimental spirit:

Training for Northern Ireland started in March and ran side by side with preparation for the 'Annual Report on a Unit' inspection. This was conducted on 27 March [1979] by the GOC North-West District, Major-General P F A Sibbald, O.B.E.

. . . the Battalion was addressed by the General, who was well pleased with what he had seen during the day, and congratulated all present for an excellent parade. He also remarked on the enthusiasm, keenness and cheerfulness displayed by the Battalion throughout the time it had been in Chester. He was aware of the high regard in which the Gordons were held throughout North-West District. The report indicated that the Battalion was sound and had maintained standards in all areas. Among the General's comments in the Report were:

'I was impressed with the spirit, courtesy and general attitude of all ranks during the inspection and on other occasions. I liked what I saw on the day of the ARU although objectives were necessarily limited. The prime characteristics, noted by all inspecting officers, were enthusiasm, fitness and keenness.

The document inspections were very good indeed and I congratulate those responsible for the standard of production of the ARU file. The Orderly Room is clearly in good order.'

On public relations, General Sibbald was particularly complimentary:

'I doubt I have ever seen a battalion run better. The relationship established with Chester and the local Press is quite first class and I congratulate all concerned.'

General Sibbald went on to say:

'The Parade mounted for the ARU was long, complex and done in adverse conditions. The standard of both turnout and drill was excellent and bodes well for the visit to Scotland in June. I congratulate those who have worked up to this parade and the steadiness and bearing of soldiers on parade.

1 Gordons is a battalion which is always a pleasure to visit. The hallmarks are enthusiasm, cheerfulness and courtesy. All ranks are well motivated, cheerful and have a practical "get on with the job" attitude. I see the battalion going from strength to strength.'

The Life of a Regiment, Volume VII, pp 270–1.

In 1982 the 1st Battalion was at Kirknewton, west of Edinburgh. A severe winter, with long periods of sub-zero temperatures, had frozen all the radiators in the accommodation huts after the boiler broke down. Pipes had burst and all huts were flooded. The Battalion was dispersed to different diverse locations while the camp was repaired. It did not return to Kirknewton until March 1982, a month before the annual inspection!

On April 20 the GOC, Lieutenant-General Sir David Young, carried out the annual inspection. Some of the younger officers found out the hard way that looking busy is an important part of a subaltern's day. While watching 'A' Company carrying out Grade 1 training, the Chief of Staff, Colonel R T Gurdon, noticed the Platoon Commanders, Lieutenant Simon Blake and Second-Lieutenant Charles Everett, watching their soldiers going through their Weapon Training Test. Colonel Gurdon promptly told them to go and be tested as well! Nothing daunted, they threw themselves into the Test and passed with flying colours, Second-Lieutenant Everett even gaining a Distinction.

General Young examined all facets of the Battalion's activities, and was clearly pleased, particularly with the way in which every officer, NCO and Jock to whom he spoke responded with confidence and pride in his Regiment. His concluding remarks in the report were:

The Battalion can be justly proud of a year of fine achievements, and I have no hesitation in reporting them completely fit for role.

The Life of a Regiment, Volume VII, pp 320–1.

COMMENTS FROM OTHER MILITARY SOURCES

In 1799 the 92nd was in the British force assembling for the expedition against Holland, which was held by the French. No less an outsider than Major-General John Moore commented approvingly on the 92nd:

[The 92nd] embarked at Cove of Cork, landed at Dover on July 30th, and encamped at Barham Downs, where the troops for Holland were assembling under Lieut.-General Sir Ralph Abercromby. The regiment was in the 4th Brigade, consisting of the 2nd Battalion 1st Royals, and the 25th, 49th, 79th, and 92nd Regiments, under Major-General Moore. In describing the composition of the Army and of his own Brigade, General Moore, in his diary, says:—'The Guards are certainly a fine body of men. The regiments of the line are in general but poor, and few of them are formed or disciplined. The 92nd (Highlanders) are an exception—they are excellent.'

The Life of a Regiment, Volume I, p 52.

It is a matter of great regimental pride that the 75th, which in 1843 had no connection whatsoever with the 92nd Gordon Highlanders, distinguished itself in South Africa during the third Kaffir War and throughout its twelve-year tour in that country:

The 75th was clearly held in high esteem:

> Frontier Orders, Grahamstown, *13th May* 1843.—The Colonel Commanding on the frontier cannot part with a corps that has been so distinguished for a long and valuable service in this Colony without requesting Major Hall, the officers, n.c. Officers and soldiers of that excellent regiment to accept his acknowledgements for conduct which is as honourable to the corps as it has been of advantage to the Colony.
>
> General Orders, Headquarters, Cape Town, *6th July* 1843.—His Excellency the Commander-in-Chief cannot allow the 75th Regiment to leave his command without expressing to Major Hall, the officers, n.c. officers and soldiers of that corps his highest approbation of the good conduct and good services rendered by the regiment during the long period of duty in this Colony.

The Life of a Regiment, Volume II, p 211.

Posted once again to Ireland in 1866, the 92nd left behind a high reputation and much appreciation:

> March 1st, 1866.—The regiment embarked at Portsmouth on H.M. troopship *Simoom* for service in Ireland, and landed at Kingston on the 5th. They proceeded by rail to the Curragh, but after three days returned to Royal Barracks, Dublin, where the Greys were also quartered. On the regiment's departure from Aldershot, Major-General Lord Henry Percy, V.C., reported, 'that during the time the 92nd have been in the brigade under my command, I can report most favourably of them; they are well drilled, their conduct sober, orderly, and soldier-like, discipline good, and all that one can desire in a well regulated corps.'
>
> General the Hon. J. Yorke Scarlett, commanding the division, reported, for the information of H.R.H. the Commander-in-Chief, to the same effect, adding—'They left camp without an absentee or a drunken man, and were placed in the train within seven minutes from the regiment entering the station.'

The Life of a Regiment, Volume II, pp 87–8.

Lieutenant-Colonel C. Greenhill Gardyne, author of the first two volumes of *The Life of a Regiment*, heard the following tribute to The Gordon Highlanders in Afghanistan in 1879:

In the summer of 1880 I was at a party in London where the ladies were making much of a wounded Lancers officer, and begging him to relate his warlike experiences. With military modesty he avoided speaking of his personal achievements, but I heard him describe in graphic language the conduct of the Gordon Highlanders, which he had witnessed—'as if one was looking from the stage of the theatre at the gallery. That was the grandest performance I ever saw.' I mentioned that I had once been in the 92nd, when he remarked, 'It is a most extraordinary regiment. They are always ready for work—they always turn out as neat as new pins—their discipline is strict, while the good feeling between officers and men is remarkable.' He was Captain Scott Chisholme, who remained in the saddle and brought his regiment (the 9th) out of action though severely wounded in the charge at Siah Sang on this occasion. He was killed commanding the Imperial Light Horse at Elandslaagte, 1899.

The Life of a Regiment, Volume II, p 128.

To be singled out by a Commander-in-Chief, a regiment must have distinguished itself consistently by its high standards, training, discipline and, most of all, by its dash and daring when in contact with the enemy:

In a letter to Lieut-Colonel Parker, General Roberts[4] said, 'You must be proud of commanding such a Regiment, which I am sure it is second to none, and which I sincerely hope I may have with me if ever I am fortunate enough to hold another command on active service'; and when made a GCB he, like Sir John Moore, chose a Gordon Highlander as a supporter for his coat of arms, the other being a soldier of the 5th Gurkhas.

The Life of a Regiment, Volume II, pp 157.

Commendations by officers in fellow regiments show an appreciation for consistently high standards:

A testimony to the character of the battalion was in a memo dated July 17th, 1899, by Captain (now Major-General) Cookson, late Bengal Cavalry, who was in charge of the Jeypur Imperial Service Transport during the Tirah Campaign. He says that the Gordon Highlanders were remarkable for their readiness to help under all circumstances, that he never asked an n.c.o. or private of that regiment to lend a hand with fallen kits, etc., without a cheerful answer and ready help. He was not with their brigade, but they never asked if the baggage belonged to their own battalion or to others. 'It's not the baggage of my regiment' or 'my

---

4   Later Field Marshal Lord Roberts of Kandahar, V.C., K.G., K.P., O.M., G.C.B., G.C.S.I., G.C.I.E., V.D.

company' was an answer he never got from any of the Gordons, and he remarked their extraordinary *esprit de corps* and good discipline.

When staying in 1912 with Sir Pertab Singh,[5] Maharajah Regent of the Jodhpore State in Rajputana, the latter, on hearing that Major [A.D. Greenhill] Gardyne belonged to the Gordon Highlanders, kept repeating 'Very fine regiment, very grand regiment, I saw it often in Tirah, very fine the regiment, all Sahibs'; and related the following incident:—'During an action in Tirah, Sir William Lockhart, on whose staff I was serving, went to observe from the signalling post of the Gordon Highlanders, but as the hostile fire became severe we made Sir William move; but I stayed and talked to the men and offered them cigarettes. One man reached out to take a cigarette when a bullet struck his hand aside; he smiled, stretched out the other hand with a cigarette, lit it, and then looked at his wound. A very cool man, a very good man, quite like Rajput.'

The Life of a Regiment, Volume II, pp 305–7.

Going from operations in the field to mounting a ceremonial guard was not easy. Leaving behind a relaxed approach to many regimental duties and routines, and adjusting to a formal, disciplined and prescribed routine, brought with it psychological change from a situation where at any moment a soldier could find himself engaged with the enemy to one where there was no immediate threat to life. A good soldier would make that transition, but only with discipline and professionalism:

On 10th September [1901] one hundred picked men under Captain Macneal relieved a Cameron Highlander detachment as Headquarter Guard to the Commander-in-Chief. 'I was ordered to supply 12 men of 5ft. 9in.; my dozen averaged 5ft. 9¼ in., the tallest being 6ft. 2in.'

'When we lined up facing the Camerons we formed a dreadful contrast to them. They were magnificently turned out while we hadn't seen a button-brass or a tin of polish for two years. A fortnight later new kilts and jackets, new bandoliers, new shoe-brushes, brass-brushes, button-brasses, blanco. The turn-out became the smartest and cleanest I have ever seen, we even polished the iron toe and heel-caps of our shoes! We were very proud of being K's Guard,[6] though we didn't see much of him, but we thought him a great man. I never heard either Bobs or him adversely criticised.'

---

5   Sir Pertab Singh was an outstanding figure in India for half a century, and the best example of the ancient and splendid Rajput chivalry. He fought for the Empire in Tirah, in China, and in France and Palestine in the Great War, and his feats in sport and horsemanship have not been surpassed by any Briton. His description 'quite like Rajput' was the highest praise he could give.

6   Kitchener of Khartoum.

On relief of the guard, the Military Secretary wrote to the Colonel: 'The company has been a great comfort in every way, and the Chief is very sorry to lose it. In their duty, general behaviour, and bearing, all ranks have left nothing to be desired.'

The Life of a Regiment, Volume III, p 334.

Every Gordon Highlander had a particular role. Specialist training enabled Gordons to provide the administrative and logistical backup that supported the infantry soldiers at the front. Among these were the signallers,[7] who were highly trained:

On 18th May [1902] General Spens expressed in a most eulogistic letter to the Commanding Officer, his thanks for the services of Gordon signallers whom he had had with him for long. 'What we should have done without them I don't know; they were experts; their work frequently necessitated them being exposed to great danger, but they never faltered. Their record was beaten by none and they were invariably praised by every Staff officer who employed them. Sergt. Austin was in charge.'

The Life of a Regiment, Volume III, p 336.

When the 2nd Battalion left India in 1912 it was sent on its way with affection and praise:

Sir James Willcocks said good-bye to the Gordons; he told the men that he had served with the regiment before the colonel joined, and before most of them were born. 'You were a grand regiment then and I believe you are as good today.' His eloquent words ended with a God-speed— 'and God help the enemy that stands in front of you!'
. . . from the commanding officer of the Dogras.
'It is a great pleasure in the Indian Army to be alongside a British regiment which one can always hold up as a pattern to one's men. I am sorry to say this is not always the case. But I can honestly affirm that since they came here there has never been a single occasion on which we have not been able to say, 'Copy the Gordons.'

The Life of a Regiment, Volume III, p 406.

In 1920 the 1st Gordons, under the command of Lieutenant-Colonel C.J. Simpson, who had been wounded at Mons and was taken prisoner subsequently, joined the Army of the Black Sea and served in Turkey until November 1921:

---

7   Before wireless communication, signalling in the field was carried out using semaphore, the signaller holding a flag on a short staff in each hand. In order that the flags might be seen at a distance, the signaller often had to stand in a prominent position, exposed to the enemy.

On 20th November the 1st Gordons embarked for Malta. [Commander-in-Chief] Sir Charles Harington came on board to say farewell. In a letter to the commanding officer he wrote:

> I hope you will accept for yourself and convey to all ranks my grateful thanks for all you have done to uphold the honour of the British Army in Constantinople. I have watched with great pleasure the standard of your Battalion rising daily towards your well-known pre-War level. That level can only be reached by real hard work on the part of the officers, W.O.'s and N.C.O.'s and by the loyal support of the men which you enjoy. I congratulate you on your achievement and on the many trophies which you have won in this command.

The Life of a Regiment, Volume V, p 8.

The 1st Battalion won praise eight years later from the retiring Commander-in-Chief, India, Field Marshal Sir William Birdwood, who had seen the Gordons during their tour, and who appreciated his farewell from the Regiment after his final inspection:

November 26th, 1930.

My Dear Bell,

> On leaving Delhi, I send you a line to tell you how very glad I am to have been able to see something of your Regiment—the gallant old 75th—during my last few days service in India. I thought it was extraordinarily kind of you turning the Regiment out as you did to line the road, when I left you after my last inspection; while I can assure you that I very much appreciated seeing the really fine Guard of Honour which you did me the honour of providing on my departure.
>
> I need not tell you again how fully I hope that all possible good fortune and happiness may be before you and all ranks during your time in the Khyber, and for many years hence.
>
> Yours sincerely,
(Sgd.) W. R. Birdwood.

T&S, January 1931.

Appreciation of the work of the Gordons in Belfast in 1976–8 sometimes came from a lower level, that had seen them at first hand on a daily basis:

Support Company worked closely with 45 Commando and its supporting Gunner Battery, 79 (Kirkee) Commando Light Battery, whose commander wrote to Major Napier:

> 'Just a note to thank you and your Jocks for your help over the last four months. It has been a real pleasure having your platoons under command, and we all have a lasting impression of a first rate company,

whose standards of professionalism and enthusiasm have been an example to all of us. I hope you lot don't join the Scottish Army!'

The Life of a Regiment, Volume VII, p 229.

The Gordons found themselves once more in Northern Ireland in 1979 on an eventful four-month tour that saw them successfully policing Armagh and the towns in the county. Their performance on that tour emulated that of the highly praised 1976–8 tour:

Before the Battalion departed, the Commanding Officer received a message from the CLF, Major-General J M Glover:

'I write to thank you and congratulate you on all that the Battalion achieved during these last four hard months. The Battalion has done splendidly in the face of many frustrations. Whenever I visited I was hugely impressed with the robust cheerfulness and professionalism of your Jocks. They are wonderful soldiers. You can look back on your tour in North Armagh with real satisfaction.'

The Life of a Regiment, Volume VII, p 287.

When, in 1980, a party of Gordons led by Lieutenant D.N.F. Stewart visited the 48th Highlanders of Canada—the Gordons' affiliated Canadian regiment—the trip proved to be a great success:

The Jocks enjoyed the visit immensely. They got on well with their hosts and appreciated the hospitality lavished on them. They, in turn, made a favourable impression on the Canadians. In a letter to Brigadier MacMillan, the Honorary Colonel of the 48th Highlanders, Colonel Frank McEachern, wrote:

'As Honorary Colonel of the 48th Highlanders of Canada, I had the very great pleasure of meeting the contingent of Gordon Highlanders sent over to Canada a couple of weeks ago. May I say how greatly impressed I was not only by their bearing and deportment, but also by how very articulate and knowledgeable they were in conversation.

As Senior Aide-de-Camp to the Lieutenant Governor of Ontario, I was also present at a reception given by the Lieutenant Governor for these young men and those present, including Her Honour, were most impressed by them.

I do hope this will be a first step towards a closer contact between the two Regiments. We of the 48th Highlanders are always conscious and proud of our affiliation with the Gordons and this visit strengthened that tie. Personally, having worn the Gordon Tartan as a cadet at St Andrew's College, it gave me a very great thrill to see the kilt again.'

The Life of a Regiment, Volume VII, pp 288–9.

In 1989 the Gordons provided the Castle Guard for Edinburgh Castle during the Edinburgh Military Tattoo. The Guard upheld all the best traditions of The Gordon Highlanders:

The work on the Castle Guard and on the Tattoo had not gone unnoticed, and there were many tributes to the Gordons' bearing and cheerfulness, and the high standards that they had maintained. The Chief of Staff at Army HQ Scotland wrote:

'I would like to put on record how impressed we were by the NCOs and soldiers who composed the Guard over this period. At all times they were efficient, diligent, smart and very quick to react to any turnout. Their whole demeanour was a credit to their parent unit.'

Lieutenant-Colonel (Retired) L P G Dow, O.B.E., the Tattoo Producer and last Commanding Officer of The Cameronians, wrote to Colonel Price, saying:

'I really have been most impressed. I would happily put the clock back 42 years and start life again in your Battalion.'

The Life of a Regiment, Volume VII, p 428.

In 1990 the 1st Battalion made another tour in Belfast that saw the soldiers patrolling the streets and winning the respect, grudging or otherwise, of the population. Once again the Gordons met the high standards that their predecessors had set:

Text of a letter from Commander Land Forces:

'I wish to thank all ranks for their splendid efforts over the past five months in West Belfast. The Gordons adopted a thoroughly professional and tenacious approach which has been a significant contribution to PIRA's recent lack of success in the Belfast area.

'Your Battalion Headquarters was well organised from the start, and maximum advantage was always gained from the information available. I was particularly pleased with the excellent relations fostered with the RUC and other agencies as I know the complications that can arise in this area.

'Not only was the Battalion noted for its operational abilities, but also for its excellent administration. The Echelon support was first class throughout and you can take credit for a number of important improvements to the welfare infrastructure and the overall state of maintenance. These improvements will certainly be of benefit to future battalions.

'The Battalion had a most successful tour and maintained just the right attitude throughout. The Gordon Highlanders have a thoroughly well deserved reputation for excellence and I was very pleased to have had the Battalion in Province during my tenure as Commander Land Forces. Please pass on my thanks and congratulations to all ranks, including your reinforcements, for a job thoroughly well done.'

The following is the text of a signal from General Officer Commanding Northern Ireland to the Commanding Officer:

'CLF joins me in sending you our sincere thanks for the excellent work you and your Battalion have done throughout a difficult but most successful tour. You have made a very positive contribution to the campaign over the past five months and all ranks deserve much credit for the diligent and professional manner in which they carried out their duties. Please convey our gratitude to them all. We wish you a pleasant leave and a safe return to Inverness.'

The Life of a Regiment, Volume VII, pp 469–70.

In 1994 the 1st Battalion, The Gordon Highlanders, returned from Berlin to Edinburgh for the unwelcome amalgamation with The Queen's Own Highlanders that would bring to an end 207 years of glorious history. Right to the end they maintained the high standards that had so dignified their predecessors for two centuries:

On 8 March there was a farewell Retreat by the Drums and Pipes and Regimental Band, followed by a Cocktail Party. The Brigade Commander, Brigadier Bromhead,[8] wrote to Colonel Chant-Sempill. His remarks summed up his regard for the Gordons:

'I write to thank you for two outstanding events in Berlin.

The Charlottenburg Parade and march past were exceptional performances. It is difficult to put into words the impact that has on Berlin and our image in this city—but you did The Gordon Highlanders and our army proud that day. The Beating of Retreat last evening was also absolutely top quality.

Thank you, the Battalion, The Drums and Pipes and Band. You have been wonderful ambassadors not only for The Gordon

---

8 Brig David Bromhead was the great-great-nephew of Lt Gonville Bromhead, who won the Victoria Cross at Rorke's Drift in 1879.

Highlanders but, of course, for the Army, Scotland and the United Kingdom as well.

I am grateful—thank you.'

In a letter to the Colonel-in-Chief, The Duke of Rothesay, Brigadier Bromhead had this to say about The Gordon Highlanders:

'They are an outstanding Battalion, tough, fit and disciplined. Their time in Berlin has been an unqualified success. I know all amalgamations are tough, but their impending disappearance is particularly sad. They are an exceptional Regiment.'

The Life of a Regiment, Volume VII, pp 532–3, 534.

POSTSCRIPT

Just before publication of this volume, the following article appeared in the Aberdeen *Evening Express*. It is a touching reminder of how The Gordon Highlanders could fight with courage, determination and fortitude against a dogged and ferocious enemy, yet show compassion, kindness and humane behaviour towards that same enemy when he could no longer fight on:

A German war veteran who was shot by the Gordon Highlanders – and then had his life saved by them – has received a 90th birthday gift from the North-east museum dedicated to the regiment.

Karl Hunold was an 18-year-old paratrooper in the German 6th Parachute Battalion when he was badly wounded by soldiers of the 5/7th Battalion, The Gordon Highlanders on March 31 1945. His battalion was defending the town of Rees in northern Germany when they were crossing the road and were hit by machine gun fire. Karl was the only survivor.[9]

Karl was bleeding in a ditch when the commander of a Gordon's scout car saw him and shouted: "Friend, five minutes, doctor." Bleeding heavily from a lower leg wound, a field ambulance crew applied first aid before taking Karl to a field hospital for further treatment that saved his life. Surgeons managed to save his leg.

Eight weeks later Karl was still in the hospital when another British soldier appeared in his ward, asking for the 'one from Wuppertal' – Karl's home town. Communicating through gestures the soldier told Karl he was going to Wuppertal and would deliver a letter to his parents, who knew he was missing. Karl never learned the names or found a way to show his gratitude to the men who saved his life.

---

9   The town of Rees fell to the Gordon Highlanders and Black Watch on 25 March. 1st Gordons fought through the town. 5th/7th Gordons, having crossed the Rhine east of Rees, attacked the German defences on the east side of Rees.

But his stepson, Roland Goerz, a Lieutenant Colonel in the German Army, discovered the men were Gordon Highlanders. He contacted the Gordon Highlanders Museum asking if they could send a 90th birthday greeting. The Museum obliged.

Colonel Charlie Sloan, chairman of the Museum, said: 'The Museum decided to send a greeting and a present of a quaich so he could toast the regiment. Karl still holds the men who saved his life in his memory and he speaks of them in the highest regard. We were quite uplifted by this story. This is the first time we are aware of ever receiving a request for this sort of thing.'

Col Sloan said the Museum would be sharing Karl's story with visitors. He said: 'One of the Museum's volunteers, Jim Glennie, 90, was wounded while serving with the Gordon Highlanders in 1944 and he was treated by the medical service of the German Army. We think it is going to be quite nice to tell the story from the other side. It makes you realise that there is humanity in the heart of darkness.'

Karl, when he toasted the regiment with single malt Scotch whisky, also took the time to remember soldiers of all sides who were not lucky enough to survive the war and reach a ripe old age. Karl, who received the Iron Cross for bravery, was shot twice before March 31, 1945. He turned 90 on August 3.

Lt Col Goerz said: 'The handover of the birthday card and the gift had exactly the effect me and my wife intended. The birthday card and, much more, the quaich touched him deeply and for a moment Karl was back on that very day in the area of Rees. It was hard for him to express his emotions and to find words. Karl never expected to receive birthday congratulations by the unit of those men, not to speak of a gift. The Gordon Highlanders provided a great and very hard to describe joy, enabling him to close this open chapter in the story of his life and memories.'

Lt Col Goerz said Karl feels 'extraordinarily honoured' that his experiences of that day will find a place in the Museum. He added: 'It makes him very proud and very happy to express his gratitude in this way to all those who, by their humanity and display of comradeship among soldiers across enemy lines, enabled him to celebrate his 90th birthday. Karl was also deeply touched when he learned there was a man in Scotland, who shared the same fate. We also took time to remember all soldiers of both sides, who were not lucky like Karl or the guide of Gordon Highlanders Museum, to survive the war and reach an old age.'

Aberdeen *Evening Express*.

SECTION 11

SPECIAL FORCES

BRITAIN'S special forces units have their genesis early in the Second World War after the evacuation of the British Expeditionary Force (BEF) from Dunkirk. With the British Army unable to confront the German army anywhere in Europe, the only way to hit back was by using small, specially trained groups in hit-and-run raids designed to inflict damage, raise morale at home and, more importantly, to tie down German forces by forcing them to defend all their positions and equipment, especially on the long coast line. Many such units were proposed; and some were formed. Prominent amongst them were the Commandos, the Parachute Regiment and the Special Air Service (SAS). Other branches of Special Forces included the Special Operations Executive (SOE).

The Gordon Highlanders were involved in special forces from the very beginning.

CHAPTER 23

GORDON HIGHLANDERS IN SPECIAL FORCES

WINSTON Churchill specified the need for new units that, when Britain was unable to mount major offensive actions, would attack the enemy, inflict damage on him and not allow him to relax his guard on any point of the long defensive line that he was forced to man:

> The completely defensive habit of mind, which has ruined the French, must not be allowed to ruin all our initiative. It is of the highest consequence to keep the largest numbers of German forces all along the coasts of the countries that have been conquered, and we should immediately set to work to organise raiding forces on these coasts where the populations are friendly. Such forces might be composed by self-contained, thoroughly equipped units of say one thousand up to not less than ten thousand when combined.

> Enterprises must be prepared with specially trained troops of the hunter class, who can develop a reign of terror first of all on the "butcher and bolt" policy. I look to the Chiefs of Staff to propose me measures for a vigorous, enterprising and ceaseless offensive against the whole German occupied coastline.

The Second World War, Volume II, pp 214, 217.

Shortly after Dunkirk, volunteers for these special force units were called for, and men who longed to take on the Germans rather than wait in Britain while the country built up its armed forces responded in large numbers. Many Gordon Highlanders volunteered and from the earliest actions some of them were present. The Gordon Highlanders, as a regiment, were ordinary men who did extraordinary things. The Gordon Highlanders who volunteered for the special forces were extraordinary men in extraordinary units. Over one hundred Gordons (including men from their affiliated Regiment, the London Scottish) volunteered for special forces and forty-four of them were killed in action. All did their duty to the best of their ability, and did it well. Among them were some whose service was above and beyond the call of duty.

11 COMMANDO

The first special forces units raised were the Commandos. Eleven units, each called a 'Commando', were raised in different parts of Britain in July 1940. Two of these Commandos, 9 and 11, were raised from Scottish Command and Scottish units. In those earliest days Gordon Highlander (including London Scottish) volunteers appear to have been sent to 11 (Scottish) Commando, which very quickly was brought up to strength. The new unit soon got down to the task of training for role.

Chosen to lead the 11th (Scottish) Commando was Lieutenant-Colonel Richard Pedder of the Highland Light Infantry (HLI), a no-nonsense officer with a mind of his own who knew exactly what he wanted. Volunteers for 'special service of an undefined hazardous nature' were requested throughout Scottish Command. From those who applied, he ruthlessly culled officers and men he thought unsuitable.

Although not the first to be raised, 11 (Scottish) Commando was the first to reach operational strength. Colonel Pedder set up his headquarters in the Douglas Hotel in Galashiels, where he selected his officers and interviewed the men, who came from all over Scotland. Some were regular soldiers, others were conscripts fresh from basic training. Those selected were put through their paces with a month-long training period. Anyone found lacking was returned to unit (RTU). It was the only punishment necessary.

Piper James Lawson of The Gordon Highlanders joined the Commando from the Gordons' depot in Aberdeen. After arriving in Lamlash on Arran he recalled:

> 'I was standing at the window of the digs and was watching a troop marching along the road. They turned down the old pier, blowing up their Mae Wests, then jumped off the end of the pier and swam ashore. I was convinced I was in a madhouse.'

Piper Lawson (photo) later composed the first two parts of the tune *The 11th (Scottish) Commando March*. Until that time *Scotland the Brave* had been the regimental march and this new march was written to be played before *Scotland the Brave* to give the Commando its own identity.

Morale was high: the 11th (Scottish) Commando adopted the glengarry as headdress with a distinctive black hackle supported by the badge of the man's home regiment. Eventually, and despite some Army Council opposition, a green beret became standard for all Commandos. However, 11 (Scottish) Commando retained their glengarries until disbandment.

After some false starts, when operations were called off, often at the last minute, 11 (Scottish) Commando found itself in its first major action against the Vichy French in Syria.

THE BATTLE OF THE LITANI RIVER

In April 1941 Germany was fomenting insurrection in Iraq. The Vichy Government allowed Syrian airfields to be used by German planes in transit to the combat zone. There was a real possibility of a German takeover in Syria. To counter this threat, the Allies decided to advance into Syria, led by the 7th Australian Division, with two Indian Brigades, two brigades of British cavalry and the Free French Brigade in support. Against them were 53,000 French and colonial troops, well equipped with artillery, tanks and armoured cars.

The Vichy French had a strong defensive position on the Litani River where the vital Quâsmiyeh bridge was known to be mined. It fell to 11 (Scottish) Commando to land north and south of the Litani River and capture the bridge to facilitate the progress of the Australian 21st Infantry Brigade, which was leading the advance.

The Commando attack was frustrated when they arrived at the mouth of the Litani River, in brilliant moonlight, as there was a heavy swell running which made lowering and unhooking the landing craft very difficult. All elements of surprise had been lost.

The Vichy French retired to defensive points on the Litani River line and blew up the Quâsmiyeh bridge. The whole Commando force would now be landed north of the Litani River. The main attack would seize the enemy defensive positions overlooking the Litani river from the rear. A smaller party would seize the Kafr Badda bridge to the north, which was still intact. They were to disrupt communications, prevent enemy reinforcement and resupply and reinforce the centre party.

Under cover of artillery the Australians would build a pontoon bridge. They would then cross the Litani with their light armour to advance through the Commando positions.

On 9 June 1941, the northern party (six officers and ninety-six men in three landing craft) reached the beaches with little opposition. They advanced across very flat, open country. The most northerly group was detailed to take the Kafr Badda bridge, which was well defended by the enemy, with four machine-gun posts flanking the bridge approaches and commanding the surrounding area. These were reinforced with armoured cars. An intense action followed.

One of this group was Gordon Highlander Lance Corporal (later Squadron Sergeant-Major) D.R. Tait, who won a Military Medal for his part in the Battle of the Litani River.[1] Two enemy armoured cars had claimed heavy casualties amongst the Commandos. Tait, armed with an anti-tank rifle, ran over open ground towards the enemy until forced to take cover in a

---

1   A year later he was to win a Bar to his Military Medal when with the SAS in North Africa.

shallow shellhole, where the enemy concentrated their fire on him. He scrambled out of the shellhole and in open ground, in full view of the enemy, took careful aim and opened fire. His first shot caused an armoured car to burst into flames, and as he swung the weapon round to fire on the second car, it turned and fled at high speed.

The Kafr Badda bridge was in the hands of the Commandos by 6 a.m. It had not been mined and was captured intact. The position was reinforced against counter-attack and a large number of prisoners was collected and placed in the hills to the east.

The expected counter-attack arrived around noon in the form of eight armoured cars. The Commandos held them at bay for four hours, when a further six armoured cars arrived from the east. Unable to hold the position against the armoured cars, the commandos split into two groups and withdrew in separate directions. One group followed the coast and eventually got trapped in a barbed wire entanglement surrounding enemy machine-gun positions. After taking several casualties they were forced to surrender. Lance Corporal Tait refused to surrender. He swam out to sea, along the coast and across the mouth of the Litani to safety.

The headquarters troop with Colonel Pedder had landed further south, where they crawled off the beach through a dry stream-bed and crossed the road without being detected. Disrupting communications as they went, they made for the barracks that was their target. They captured a number of prisoners but came under heavy machine-gun and mortar fire. They were pinned down until one of their sections put these weapons out of action. They reached a rise north-east of the barracks where they again came under heavy machine-gun fire and accurate sniping, which caused a number of casualties. Colonel Pedder ordered a withdrawal to try to contact the main force which should have been to the south. In returning to lower ground with better cover, Colonel Pedder was killed.

All officers in the headquarters party were either killed or seriously wounded and the R.S.M., Gordon Highlander Lewis Tevendale,[2] assumed command. He planned a withdrawal to the Litani River but realised that enemy activity would make this difficult. The remaining men positioned

---

2   WO1 Tevendale won the Distinguished Conduct Medal for this action and for subsequently escaping. He was commissioned and, after further service in the Middle East, transferred to Ceylon, where he trained troops in partisan tactics against a possible Japanese invasion. Capt Tevendale took part in the second Chindit expedition in 1944. He built a fort in the Burmese jungle and named it *Aberdeen*' Maj-Gen Orde Wingate flew in one day and asked Tevendale why he had named it so. Tevendale replied, 'Because your good lady comes from there, sir, and so do I.' Tevendale gained a formidable reputation in the Chindits. During one action, he held up an entire battalion of Japanese with his Sten gun, covering the withdrawal of two columns of which he was the Second in Command.

    In retirement he owned a pub, 'The Gordon Highlander', in Aberdeen. The inner glass door was engraved with the regimental crest. The door is now the inner front door of The Gordon Highlanders Museum. His son was a sergeant in the 1st Battalion in the 1960's and 1970's.

themselves above the main road to the barracks and consolidated their situation, waiting for an opportunity to withdraw and in the meantime, disrupting enemy communications. The battle raged all afternoon but eventually they were surrounded and captured.

AFTERMATH OF LITANI

Despite being outnumbered, and suffering incredible misfortune and difficulties, 11 (Scottish) Commando held the line long enough for the Australians to cross the river and continue their advance to Beirut. Their bravery was not without cost; of 406 men who landed 130 were killed or wounded in nearly twenty-nine hours of fighting, for which they only had ammunition and food to last eight. The death of their Commanding Officer, Lieutenant-Colonel Pedder, and so many others was a disaster from which 11 Commando never recovered. Of the twenty-two Gordon Highlanders who took part, five were killed.

The Litani River battle was among the hardest fought of the operation, and despite winning four Military Crosses, two Distinguished Conduct Medals, a Military Medal and two Mentions in Despatches for their courage and bravery at Litani River it was clear within days of the Commando returning to Cyprus that it would be disbanded, a fate that had already befallen both No. 7 and No. 8 Commando.

On 1 September 1941, 11 (Scottish) Commando was ordered to disband. The Commando was down to nine officers and 250 other ranks. Volunteers were called to remain with the Commandos, but only five officers and 110 other ranks decided to stay. Most of the others sought opportunities to fight the Axis forces in other organisations, particularly L Detachment, SAS, under David Stirling.

L DETACHMENT, SAS

The origins of the SAS (Special Air Service) lie in the unit formed in July 1941 by David Stirling and originally called L Detachment, Special Air Service Brigade: the 'L' designation and 'Air Service' name being a British disinformation campaign to deceive the Germans into thinking there was an airborne regiment with numerous units operating in the area. L Detachment was the forerunner of the SAS. A number of Gordon Highlanders volunteered for L Detachment and took part in Operation *Squatter*, its first, disastrous mission against Axis airfields at Gazala and Tmimi, when, parachuting in extremely high winds, the force was dispersed and unable to carry out its task. Sergeant Jock Cheyne[3] was in one flight, along with fellow Gordon

---

3   Cheyne distinguished himself at the Battle of the Litani River by taking command when his troop officer, Lt Bill Fraser, had been hit and concussed.

Highlander Sergeant Jeff Du Vivier.[4] Of the fifty-four men who set off that night, only twenty-one returned. Cheyne did not return. His comrades had to leave him at the drop zone, as he suffered a broken back in landing and could not be moved. He was never seen alive again. Cheyne's loss was deeply felt by David Stirling, with whom he had been great friends. Private Douglas Keith, a Gordon Highlander from Auchinblae, Kincardineshire, was also killed on Operation *Squatter*, one of L Detachment's thirty-three casualties.

The failure of Operation *Squatter* led Stirling to abandon plans for further parachute operations, but it did not deter the embryonic SAS from carrying out further operations against German airfields, using the Long Range Desert Group (LRDG) to transport them to drop-off points near the airfields. One such raid, against the airfield at Agedabia, was led by Gordon Highlander

Lieutenant Bill Fraser, (photo) whose five-man section included Gordon Highlanders Corporal Bob Tait (who had won the Military Medal at Litani), Sergeant Jeff Du Vivier (who was to win the Military Medal for this action) and Corporal Jack Byrne (who was to win the Distinguished Conduct Medal after escaping from a German prison camp and returning to Britain). On 20 December 1941, the section was dropped off north of Agedabia airfield. Tait led, navigating by compass under cover of darkness. They hid the following day and could see aircraft taking off and landing on the horizon. After last light on 21 December they moved out; Tait led the section, Fraser was second, with Byrne bringing up the rear. Byrne carried a Thompson sub-machine-gun, the others Smith & Wesson .45 revolvers. Just after midnight, they located aircraft near the airfield's perimeter fence: German Messerschmitt ME109Fs and Italian Fiat C42s. Aircrew slept underneath their aircraft. After carefully laying explosives, the section crept away. They had gone only a few hundred yards when a large explosion went off, followed by others. Enemy fire in response was all trained skywards in the belief that they were being subjected to an air raid. Fraser's section spotted an additional seven ME109s, which were also blown up, just before the base's ammunition dump erupted in a huge fireball. Byrne's account reads:

> Whilst Bill and I were running hard towards the fighters, I squeezed the time-pencils of two of the bombs and for good measure jerked the pull-switches; the bombs should now explode in fourteen seconds. It took only a moment to place a bomb on each plane—all ME 109Fs, apparently

---

4 Du Vivier was from the London Scottish, which at that time was part of The Gordon Highlanders.

brand new, each one having a canvas-type horse-blanket strapped around its fuselage.

Bill stood watch at the wingtip of each plane whilst I placed the bombs. Twice he held out a hand to take the tommy-gun from me but I pretended not to notice. When we got to the seventh fighter, I ran straight past it, putting the last bomb on the eighth whilst Bill remained standing by the seventh fighter, shouting his head off until I displayed an empty hand.

As we turned to run back to the others, the first four of the fighters went up in flames almost together, and within seconds all eight were burning fiercely, the planes being so close together that one well-placed bomb in the centre of the row would probably have destroyed the lot.

By the time they got back to the rendezvous with the LRDG, it was almost daylight. Fraser's section had destroyed 37 aircraft, and they got back to Jalo just in time for the advance Christmas party that Stirling had laid on for the whole detachment.

SAS

By September 1942 L Detachment had carried out a number of successful attacks on German airfields, destroying large numbers of enemy aircraft. The 1st SAS was created on 28 September, with Lieutenant Bill Fraser as second in command of A Squadron. Fraser commanded SAS forays into Tunisia in the final days of the Axis in North Africa.

In 1942 Lieutenant Bill Fraser was awarded the Military Cross. He went on to command No.1 Troop, Special Raiding Squadron (SRS) in Sicily and Italy during 1943, including at the battles of Bagnara and Termoli. He was wounded at Termoli when a German shell hit a truck carrying SRS troops into battle. Eighteen were killed: the worst loss of life the SAS had suffered up to that point.

Promoted to Captain/Temporary Major, Fraser commanded A Squadron, SAS Brigade, during the Normandy campaign. By this point, he was one of the most experienced operators in the SAS, known for wearing his Gordon kilt to impress the locals! Du Vivier and Tait continued to serve under him during this period.

Operation *Houndsworth*, run by Fraser, aimed to impede German troop movements, disrupt their communications, particularly the railway line between Paris and Lyon, and prevent them from reinforcing their offensive against the Normandy bridgehead. Their main base was in a forest clearing in the Morvan: a region of rolling wooded hills in the middle of Burgundy. The operation had been in place since D-Day and in the first three weeks, the SAS, in collaboration with the local French Maquis, had cut the railway no fewer than twenty-two times. Jeeps were airdropped in at the beginning of July 1944 and in subsequent operations were used in raids to cut the railway line (in which six trains and fifty wagons were wrecked), to attack synthetic petrol plants and ambush enemy columns.

By early September these operations against strategic targets had made a large area uninhabitable to the enemy. The Germans sent an infantry battalion and an armoured car to flush the squadron from the forest; but the armoured car proved no match for a hidden six-pounder and the infantry soon lost heart.

Gordon Highlander Sergeant Cornelius McGinn won a Military Medal for leading two wounded men to safety after their jeep bumped into a German convoy near Lucy-sur-Yonne in early July 1944 and a close-quarter shoot-out ensued.

Fraser saw *Houndsworth* as a significant military success, although it led to harsh German reprisals against the local population.

In March 1945 Bill Fraser and A Squadron crossed the River Rhine at Wesel. Within forty-eight hours they ran into a party of Canadian Paras pinned down by an enemy Spandau machine-gun that turned its attention to Fraser, hitting his jeep—the lead vehicle. A bullet smashed into his hand, causing the jeep to somersault out of control. Luckily, Fraser emerged alive and was evacuated to a field hospital.

He was awarded a Bar to his Military Cross—and a Croix-de-Guerre.

SERGEANT JACK BYRNE RETURNS TO THE FRAY

Captured in North Africa in March 1942, Sergeant Jack Byrne was a reluctant prisoner; after a number of attempts he succeeded in returning to Britain via Sweden in August 1943.[5]

After six months of recuperation Byrne was sent to Achnacarry for Commando training. Months of arduous work followed until he was posted to 6 Commando, part of the 1st Special Service Brigade, in the rank of Lance Sergeant.

In May 1944, Byrne went into a sealed camp on the south coast of England in preparation for D-Day. On 6 June 1944, 6 Commando landed on Sword Beach, to infiltrate through enemy positions and link up with the 6th Airborne Division. After heavy hand-to-hand fighting, Byrne and his fellow Commandos achieved their objectives and captured significant numbers of prisoners, many of them Russians. Stiff fighting continued until Byrne was wounded in the knee. He went into action again at Maasbracht in Holland, crossing the Rhine in March 1945 and, after ferocious close-quarter fighting, at the capture of Wesel. On 4 April 1945, 6 Commando fought its way across the Dortmund-Ems canal and into Osnabruck, before capturing Leese on 8 April and, in their last action, capturing the vital bridge over the Elbe-Trave Canal on 29 April.

---

5   See Volume IX, Chapter 13.

After the War Byrne was demobilised. He joined the Kenya Police, serving with them until 1948, when he rejoined 1st Battalion, The Gordon Highlanders. He went with the Gordons on their tour of Malaya, before volunteering for the Malaya Police. In 1953, Byrne's career as a Police Lieutenant was brought to a violent and painful end by a terrorist who fired his heavy-calibre revolver straight into his stomach at point-blank range. Unbelievably, Byrne (photo, when serving in Malaya Police) survived and the terrorist was apprehended.

The *Tiger and Sphinx* commented:

> 6 Platoon's ten-day patrol, when Sergt. Byrne, DCM, beat his Platoon Commander, Lieut. Carmichael,[6] to the draw and got his bandit.
>
> Sergt. Byrne is due to leave us shortly to join the Malayan Police as a police Lieutenant, and we shall sadly miss his dry humour and his grumble at not being able to get out more often to hunt down bandits.

STUART CHANT ON THE ST NAZAIRE RAID

Lieutenant-Colonel Stuart Chant-Sempill, O.B.E., M.C., was a proud Gordon Highlander,[7] although, ironically, he never served in any Gordon battalion. Known before his marriage as Stuart Chant, he joined the Artists Rifles (now 21 SAS) as a private soldier in 1936 and was commissioned into the Royal Army Service Corps in October 1939. He served in France and Belgium with the British Expeditionary Force until evacuated from Dunkirk in May 1940. He volunteered for special service and joined 5 Commando, where he met two Gordon Highlanders, Keith Bell and Max Norman,[8] who introduced him to the Regiment. He rebadged as a Gordon in 1941:

> In 1942 Chant (photo below) was attached to No 2 Commando in preparation for one of the most secret and dangerous missions of the War—the raid on St Nazaire, at that time the largest dry dock in the world, and the only dock on the eastern Atlantic seaboard big enough to service Germany's capital ships. The dock also provided pens for nine U-boats with five more in the course of construction. The aim of the raid was to

---

6 Lt Jimmy Carmichael was mentioned in despatches for gallantry on this tour.

7 Chant's son, Lt-Col Hon I.D.W. Chant-Sempill, was the last Commanding Officer of the 1st Battalion before the amalgamation with The Queen's Own Highlanders in 1994.

8 Lt-Col A.M.B. Norman and 2Lt K. Bell.

destroy the dock facilities so that the German Navy would be unable effectively to continue the Battle of the Atlantic.

The plan was to drive a converted American destroyer, HMS *Campbeltown*, into the port's main lock having sliced through antisubmarine nets and other obstacles. Accompanying torpedo boats were to make for the submarine pens while the commandos on *Campbeltown* landed and attacked dock facilities

On 26/27 March 1942, Chant was in charge of a demolition team assigned to destroy the main pumping house, and embarked on the *Campbeltown*. As the destroyer approached the dry dock at 20 knots under intense enemy fire, some sailors and commandos on deck were killed and others wounded, including Chant, who was hit by shrapnel. Once *Campbeltown* had rammed the gates Chant and his team ran over the decks, now sloping at 20 degrees, clambered over the debris and dropped 18ft on to the quayside, each man carrying his 60lbs rucksack of demolition equipment. They raced to the main pump house, blew open the huge steel doors, descended into the cavernous pump house, laid their charges with a 90-second fuse and fled. Outside, they paused for breath and then moved on—just before the explosion hurled huge blocks of concrete where they had been standing.

On reaching the rendezvous with the other demolition teams they found that the boats to evacuate them had been destroyed by intense German fire. The Commandos, many wounded, decided to link up with the Resistance and escape to Spain. As they withdrew into the town Chant was shot in the knee, immobilised, and taken prisoner shortly afterwards.

The Germans assumed the raid was only a partial success, having killed 169 British and wounded and captured 200. They reoccupied the area in strength and because of many delayed charges causing later explosions shot many of their own workmen having mistaken them for British soldiers. *Campbeltown* was also packed with five tons of ammonal, fused to explode a short time later and four hundred Germans were killed when she blew up as they gathered round to assess the damage caused by the ramming.

The British raid on St Nazaire was recognised by the award of five Victoria Crosses, the highest number for any single action in the Second World War. Stuart Chant was awarded the Military Cross.

Stuart Chant (in helmet) captured after being shot in knee

Chant was moved to a hospital in Rennes, where a French surgeon removed the bullet from his knee without anaesthetic. He was moved to Spangenberg Castle (Oflag IX AH) where he met up with officers from the 51st Highland Division who had been captured at St Valery. He was moved to Rotenburg am Kulda (Oflag IX AZ) from where he attempted two escapes. First he hid in a truckload of potato peelings, but was detected by a guard dog and surrendered for fear of being bayoneted where he lay. On the second occasion he was one of 60 British prisoners who built a tunnel 20ft below the camp and 75 yards in length. Their getaway had to be postponed to await a moonless night and during that time they were betrayed by an informer.

Chant was repatriated as a *grand blessé* (an exchange scheme for wounded prisoners). He was the first officer to return to Britain after the St Nazaire raid, which until then had been given little publicity. German propaganda had described the raid as a failure. To counter this, Chant was one of a small group of officers sent by the War Office to America to lecture US audiences about their experiences.

T&S, 1991.

SPECIAL OPERATIONS EXECUTIVE

Geoffrey Hallowes

Born in 1918, Geoffrey MacLeod Hallowes was educated in Switzerland and at Cambridge but left in 1939 before taking his degree. He took the train to Aberdeen and joined The Gordon Highlanders. Commissioned and posted to the 2nd Battalion in Singapore, he took part in the Gordons' action against the Japanese in Johore and in Singapore.

That Hallowes managed to escape from Singapore was fortuitous, as officers and men were forbidden to leave their positions. When the island surrendered on 15 February 1942, he was one of four officers sent in pairs to carry the ceasefire order to garrisons in the islands of Balang Mati and Pulau Brani. They were told that, after delivering the order, they could stay with the troops and surrender or try to escape. Hallowes and Major Nick Nicholson of the Royal Engineers found a 14-foot dinghy with two paddles, in which they crossed to the islands, located the British units and passed on the order. Rather than wait to be taken prisoner they set off in their dinghy, but after losing a paddle when it broke, eventually landed on an island south of Singapore. Here they found four stranded British soldiers who had fled Singapore but had lost their boat when it sank. These men had two oars and pooling their resources, the party, now numbering six, set off again. Japanese planes circled the area and they feared that they would be attacked, but the planes left them alone and they made their way to another island where they bought coconuts and fruit. On the third night a storm arose and they were swept onto a reef but managed to pull off and make the shore. There they found one of Ivan Lyon's food supply dumps. On the following day disaster struck when their boat sank, but they got ashore safely. They negotiated with a Chinese junk to take them to Sumatra and arrived there a week after escaping from Singapore. Meeting up with other British refugees they got into a truck that struggled through the jungle, and arrived at Padang on 28 February 1942. A British destroyer which had been in the Battle of the Java Sea called in to refuel and they were taken aboard. They reached Colombo on 5 March 1942.

Reaching Bombay, Hallowes was employed as a staff captain on administrative duties. He escaped this by volunteering for the Special Operations Executive (SOE) and attending the special forces training school at Haifa. He joined the Yugoslav section of SOE's Force 133, based in Cairo, but, being a fluent French-speaker, was posted to Peterborough, where the 'Jedburgh' SOE teams were training. Each team comprised one British or American officer, a French officer and a radio operator. Ninety-four teams were parachuted into France in the days and weeks after D-Day to co-ordinate sabotage by the French Resistance.

Hallowes's team, codenamed 'Jeremy', comprised himself, Lieutenant Henri-Charles Giese and their radio operator, Sergeant Roger Leney. Fifteen such teams were sent by sea to Algiers and flown from there to southern France. Team 'Jeremy' was dropped on the night of 24 August 1944. It was met on the dropping zone by the remarkable Virginia Hall, nicknamed *La dame qui boite* (the limping lady).

Hall, an American citizen, had lost the lower part of her left leg in a shooting accident. She had entered Vichy France by boat in 1941 and established the SOE network in the Haute-Loire. Leaving Leney with her to establish a radio link with London, Hallowes and Giese set out for Le Puy, the local headquarters of the Gaullist *Forces Françaises de l'Intérieur* (F.F.I.). He called for an arms drop for this group, estimated to be some 1,500-strong. But when the drop took place there were weapons for only 100 men, giving Hallowes some difficulties with distribution.

With the F.F.I. concentrating on liberating towns and villages already vacated by the Germans, Hallowes turned his attention to delaying the escape across the Rhône of German units trying to head eastwards for home. To achieve this, he persuaded the Haute-Loire F.F.I. commander to move those of his men who were armed, by this time the majority, north to Vichy.

On return to Britain in late September 1944, Hallowes was sent to join SOE's Special Planning Unit 22, examining the feasibility of infiltrating German-speaking Poles and selected former German prisoners-of-war into German-held territory and Germany itself. He was responsible for the German ex-prisoners part of the operation, working from liberated Brussels and later from Hamburg.

Some useful work was achieved in the form of short-range intelligence gathering on behalf of the British 21st Army Group as it advanced into Germany in early 1945 and, later, investigating the activities of the Soviet Army in occupied Germany. Hallowes was awarded the Croix de Guerre for his services in France in 1944 and was mentioned in despatches on his return from Germany in 1945.

Hallowes later married the Anglo-French Resistance heroine, Odette Sansom, GC, MBE, who had served and fought gallantly in Occupied France, had been captured, tortured by the Gestapo and imprisoned in Ravensbruck.

Ivan Lyon

Ivan Lyon was serving in the 2nd Battalion, Gordon Highlanders in Singapore in the early years of the Second War. In 1942, before the Fall of Singapore, he was attached to the Special Operations Executive(SOE) and served with the SOE until his death in 1944. He was tasked with setting up escape routes through Sumatra, which he did successfully. He avoided capture and reached Australia, where he found that his wife and infant son had been captured when the Japanese intercepted a boat carrying refugees from Singapore. They were taken to Japan, where they spent the war as civilian internees, and survived to return to Britain after the war. Lyon, meantime, threw himself into the fight against the Japanese. Details of his remarkable exploits are found in Chapter 40 of this Volume, and in Volume IX, Chapter 14.

SECTION 12

THE VICTORIA CROSS

GORDON Highlanders were awarded nineteen Victoria Crosses, one of the highest totals of any infantry regiment (excluding those merged in the mass reorganisations carried out from the 1950s onwards). These awards dated from the Crimean War through to the Second World War.

The Gordon Highlander V.C.s are listed in this section. Citations are given and where possible, further details about the recipient and the actions that led to the award. The V.C.s are given in chronological order of award.

CHAPTER 24

CRIMEA AND INDIAN MUTINY

T HE 92nd (Gordon Highlanders) produced one of the earliest winners of the Victoria Cross. The new medal for gallantry was awarded to Private Thomas Beach of the 55th Regiment, one of more than 300 N.C.O.s and men of the 92nd who volunteered to serve in regiments in Crimea.

London Gazette 24th February, 1857

Private Thomas Beach

Thomas Beach, Private, 55th Regiment. For conspicuous gallantry at the Battle of Inkerman, 5th November, 1854, when on piquet, in attacking several Russians who were plundering Lieut.-Colonel Carpenter, 41st Regiment, who was lying wounded on the ground. He killed two of the Russians, and protected Lieut.-Colonel Carpenter until the arrival of some men of the 41st Regiment.

After the Crimean War Thomas Beach, (photo) like so many Gordon Highlanders who had volunteered to serve in other regiments in the war, returned to the 92nd. He was invested with his Victoria Cross by Lieutenant-General Sir James. Fergusson, GOC Gibraltar in July 1857.

A Forfarshire man, Beach left the army in 1863 and returned to Dundee, where, like so many ex-soldiers before and since, he found difficulty in adjusting to civilian life. When he died, aged only 40, it was from severe alcoholism,[1] and he was buried in an unmarked grave in Dundee's Eastern Necropolis. There he lay, unrecognised and unremarked, until 2003, when an inscribed bench commemorating him and his bravery was dedicated by Royal British Legion Scotland, which launched a fundraising campaign to erect a permanent memorial.

---

1 It was not until the late twentieth century that the stresses facing soldiers returning to civilian life after having experienced the horrors of war were recognised as 'Post Traumatic Stress Disorder' (PTSD). Whereas today soldiers suffering from PTSD receive counselling and treatment, in earlier days their only recourse was to alcohol.

To The Gordon Highlanders' great regret Beach's Victoria Cross was purchased by the Maharaja of Patiala in the 1920s and is one of five V.C.s in the Sheesh Mahal Collection in Patiala, Punjab, India.

London Gazette, 11th November, 1862

Colour-Sergeant Cornelius Coghlan

Cornelius Coghlan, Sergeant, 75th Regiment. Dates of Acts of Bravery: 8th June, 1857; 18th July, 1857. For gallantly venturing, under heavy fire, with three others, into a serai occupied by the enemy in great numbers, and removing Private Corbett, 75th Regiment, who lay severely wounded. Also for cheering and encouraging a party which hesitated to charge down a lane in Subjee Mundee, at Delhi, lined on each side with huts, and raked by a cross fire; then entering with the said party into an enclosure filled with the enemy, and destroying every man. For having, also, on the same occasion, returning under a cross fire to collect dhoolies and carry off the wounded; a service which was successfully performed, and for which this man received great praise from the officers of his regiment.

Cornelius Coghlan (photo) was born in Eyrecourt, Galway in June 1828. He joined the 75th (Stirlingshire) Regiment,[2] and served for 21 years. For his actions in the Mutiny, 1857–8, he received the Victoria Cross and Indian Mutiny Medal with clasps 'Delhi' and 'Relief of Lucknow'.

The first date on his citation was 8 June 1857 for Badli-ki-Serai. The second was 18 June 1857, for Subjee Mundee.[3] In September 1857, at Delhi, when his officers were killed, he encouraged his men by word and example to return to the attack. This resulted in victory and the Kabul Gate was stormed and taken. This was so noteworthy that a memorial tablet and

---

2   Coghlan was probably enlisted when the 75th was stationed in Ireland in 1846–49, within a year or so of Pte Patrick Green.

3   The same action in which Richard Wadeson won his V.C. The 75th therefore won two V.C.s on that day.

monument were erected over the gate. Included in the inscription was the name of Colour Sergeant Cornelius Coghlan. He was wounded in the knee during the capture of Delhi. Queen Victoria wrote a personal letter to him complimenting him on his bravery and lamenting that she could not personally present him with his V.C. He was invested with his Victoria Cross by Major-General Sir William Hutchinson at Devonport on 31 January 1863.

Coghlan served thirteen years in India as Private, Colour-Sergeant and Sergeant-Major. He served for 21 years as Sergeant-Major in the 3rd Connaught Rangers permanent staff. He died on 14 February 1915.

London Gazette, 24th December, 1858

Lieutenant Richard Wadeson

Richard Wadeson, Lieutenant, 75th Regiment. Date of Act of Bravery: 18th July, 1857. For conspicuous bravery at Delhi on the 18th July, 1857, when the regiment was engaged in the Subjee Mundee, in having saved the life of Private Michael Farrell, when attacked by a sowar[4] of the enemy's cavalry, and killed the sowar. Also on the same day for rescuing Private John Barry, of the same regiment, when wounded and helpless, he was attacked by a cavalry sowar, whom Lieutenant Wadeson killed.

Richard Wadeson (photo) was born in Lancaster in 1826. He enlisted in the 75th in 1848, and was obviously a very capable soldier, because, by the time of the Indian Mutiny in 1857 he had become the 75th's sergeant-major. His conduct at the Battle of Badli-ki-Serai on 8 June 1857 led him to be promoted to Ensign. On 18 June Captain Brookes, with 200 men of the 75th, attacked the enemy-held village of Subjee Mundee and dislodged a strong force of cavalry and infantry after some fierce hand-to-hand fighting, in which Lieutenant Crozier and three men were killed, sixteen wounded and one was missing. For his part in the fighting Ensign Wadeson was awarded the Victoria Cross.

---

4   Sowar – Indian cavalryman.

At the storming and capture of Delhi in September 1857, Wadeson again played a full part and was severely wounded.

It is to the credit of the sense of honour and value of merit shown by the officers of the 75th that when Wadeson was senior lieutenant, several officers junior to him had applied to purchase their companies, and would have been promoted above him, as he could not afford to purchase. This they refused to do and, on the next vacancy, he was promoted captain.

Wadeson rose through the ranks steadily; lieutenant in September 1857, captain in 1864, major in 1872, lieutenant-colonel in 1875 and colonel in 1880. He commanded the 75th from 1875 to 1880. As colonel on half-pay he was appointed Major and Lieutenant-Governor of the Royal Hospital, Chelsea in 1881. He died in 1885.

A brass memorial was placed in the Royal Hospital, Chelsea that reads:

To the memory of Colonel Richard Wadeson, V.C., Major and Lieutenant Governor of this Hospital from 1881 to 1885. Previously for 35 years in Her Majesty's 75th (Stirlingshire) Regiment (now the First Battalion of the Gordon Highlanders), passing through all ranks to the command of the regiment. Died in the Hospital, 24th January, 1885, aged 58 years. This tablet is erected by the Board of Commissioners of the Hospital on behalf of the In-pensioners, as a record of their affection and respect.

London Gazette, 26th October, 1858

Private Patrick Green

Patrick Green, Private, 75th Regiment. Date of Act of Bravery: 11th September, 1857. For the act of bravery recorded in a General Order issued by the Commander-in-Chief in India, of which the following is a copy: 'General Order. Headquarters, Allahabad, 28th July, 1858. The Commander-in-Chief in India is pleased to approve that the undermentioned soldier is presented in the name of Her Most Gracious Majesty, with the medal of the Victoria Cross, for Valour and daring in the field, viz., Private Patrick Green, Her Majesty's 75th Foot, for having, on 11th September, 1857, when the piquet at Koodsia Baugh, at Delhi, was hotly pressed by a large body of the enemy, successfully rescued a comrade who had fallen wounded as a skirmisher.

(signed) C. Campbell, General, Commander-in-Chief, East Indies.

Little is known about Patrick Green, who was born in Ballinasloe, County Galway, in 1824. The 75th was stationed in Ireland from 1845 to 1849, at which stage Green would be in his early twenties and ripe for enlistment. The 75th depot company, with its recruiting parties, was in Ireland along with the regiment, and indeed remained there after the 75th left for India.[5] Green (photo) was clearly a resourceful, brave and accomplished soldier, and he reached the rank of Colour-Sergeant. He died in 1889, aged 65.

5   *The Life of a Regiment*, Volume II states that 'During these two years [1845–6] a large number of Headquarter recruits had been enlisted' and 'At Dublin, in 1848, the establishment was augmented to 1,000 rank and file, and recruits were rapidly obtained.'

CHAPTER 25

NORTH-WEST FRONTIER

London Gazette, 3rd June, 1881

Major George Stuart White

George Stuart White, Major, 92nd Regiment (Gordon Highlanders). Date of Act of Bravery: 6th October, 1879. For conspicuous bravery during the engagement at Charasia on the 6th October, 1879, when, finding that artillery and rifle fire failed to dislodge the enemy from a fortified hill which it was necessary to capture, Major White led an attack on it in person. Advancing with two companies of his regiment, and climbing from one steep ledge to another, he came upon a body of the enemy strongly posted and outnumbering his force by about eight to one. His men being much exhausted and immediate action being necessary, Major White took a rifle and, going on by himself, shot the leader of the enemy. This act so intimidated the rest that they fled round the side of the hill and the position was won. Again on the 1st September, 1880, at the Battle of Kandahar, Major White, in leading the final charge under heavy fire from the enemy, who held a strong position supported by two guns, rode straight up to within a few yards of them, and seeing the guns, dashed forward and secured one of them, immediately after which the enemy retired.

George White (photo) was born in Portstewart, County Down, in 1835. Commissioned in the 27th Foot (Inniskilling Fusiliers) in 1853, he served in the Indian Mutiny. He transferred to the 92nd in 1872. By 1879 he was second-in-command. He was awarded the Victoria Cross for two separate actions, eleven months apart. This makes him one of the first double V.C. winners, (a distinction he shares with Cornelius Coghlan, whose V.C. was for two separate actions at Badli-ki-Serai and Delhi), and he would have been awarded a Bar to his V.C. had that system been in place in 1879. More detailed accounts of the actions that led to his V.C. are below:

Charasia, October 6, 1879

Skirting the East of Charasia, White found the enemy taking cover among the trees, and holding the hills to the right and left of the gorge. His three guns were soon in action, and, with skirmishers thrown out among the gardens and trees, drove the enemy to the shelter of sangars they had built. Our artillery made beautiful practice, one shell dismounting an Afghan gun and killing two horses near it, while others dispersed the enemy and prepared the way for the infantry attack. This was led by Major White, who, at the head of only fifty Highlanders charged the first hill, on which several hundred Afghans were strongly posted, outnumbering his force by about eight to one. It was perilous, and looked, perhaps, impossible; but that word is not recognised in the Gordons' vocabulary. The Highlanders went up in skirmishing order, climbing from rocky terrace to rocky terrace under a severe fire of musketry, and the enemy waited in the protection of his sangars,[1] as if to receive them at the point of the bayonet; but when they were within six yards the Afghans turned and fled, and were shot in the back as they made for the next hill. The success of this bold attack was mainly due to White's personal gallantry, of which the following is an instance. Not caring to expose his men, who were rather blown, in a particularly steep bit of ground which was enfiladed by a few Afghans securely placed in the rear of some rocks, he took a rifle from one of the soldiers and 'stalked' the enemy, followed by his leading files. Cautiously climbing, he reached the rocks forming a natural sangar behind which they were concealed, and as he showed himself they jumped up and ran, doubtless in the belief that he was the leader of many. 'Look out, sir,' cried a soldier behind White as the Afghan officer stayed to fire; but he missed his aim, and as he turned the Major shot him through the back, and some of the 92nd took his sword and gave it to the leader. This hill was named 'White's Hill' in the memory of his daring.

The guns were now able to advance nearer the pass, and the Major having given his men breathing time, and being reinforced by 100 men under Major Hay[2] and Captain D.F. Gordon, he again went forward and captured the other hills in gallant style. It was at this juncture that White was enabled to send on two companies of the Gordons, under Captain Oxley, by whose timely aid the determined foe were at length driven from this point of vantage also. The troops followed up their success and advanced at the double, while our guns shelled the shaken masses. The

1   Sangar - a temporary fortified position with a breastwork originally constructed of stones.
2   Maj J.C. Hay, who commanded the 92nd companies at Majuba, and who went on to command the 2nd Battalion, The Gordon Highlanders (1885–87). See also footnote 14 to Chapter 18.

Afghan right and centre gave way completely, and by 3.45 we were in possession of the whole ridge. The first objective having been thus gained, the troops, pivoting on their right, brought round their left, and advanced against the now exposed flanks of the enemy's left wing; at the same time White advanced from his position in front of the gorge, and a little after 4 p.m. had gained possession of the pass and twelve Afghan guns. Completely outflanked and enfiladed, the left wing of the enemy made but little resistance, but abandoning the height had retired across the river, pursued by the small body of cavalry attached to White's force, and by a party of the 92nd under Major Hay.

The Life of a Regiment, Volume II, pp 108–9.

On 1September 1880, eleven months after Charasia, Roberts's army lay outside Kandahar where it faced the Afghan army, which was in position along a range of hills from the Baba Wali Kotal on its left to Pir Paimal Hill and village on its right:

Baba Wali Kotal, 1st September 1880

At the other side of the Baba Wali Kotal the Afghans made another determined stand. Ghazis in large numbers flocked from the rear to an entrenched position on the plain; the enemy's guns on the Baba Wali were brought to bear on our men, who were also exposed to the fire of artillery from their front. The advanced companies of the 92nd, led by Major White, were lying under fire behind a line of willows, having a small bank and in some parts a ditch, which, however, gave little protection. White, who was on horseback, could see the muzzles of the guns right in front of him in a natural position of great strength; he could see the enemy were in solid columns a good distance behind their artillery, and he felt that if these masses had time to deploy, and lined the watercourse and bank where their two guns were in position, they could not have been defeated by a frontal attack without great loss and delay. Now was the time to take it by storm. He rode along the line, a conspicuous mark to the enemy, saying, 'Now, men, we've got to chalk a "Ninety-two" on these guns!' The signal was given, and they advanced with a rush in extended order over the level but fire-swept intervening space, supported by a portion of the 2nd Gurkhas and 23rd Pioneers, and covered by the fire of the screw-gun battery. Once they halted and laid down for a minute to take breath, then the Major called for 'Just one more charge to finish the business,' when, with a yell rather than a cheer, they up and at it, the pipers swelling the sound as their comrades raced for the guns. Many fell, but the gallant Major seemed to bear a charmed life as he rode on in front, put his horse at the ditch, and with difficulty scrambled up the opposite bank as his men

360

jumped into the water. An Afghan, who fired at him as he did so, was killed with others where they stood; but their gunners left the guns, and Bandsman Gray sat waving his helmet on one, while a Gurkha, who had joined White's men in the charge, put his cap on the muzzle of the other, and catching the Major's stirrup, said to him in Hindustani, 'Write down my name, Sahib, for the Order of Merit,' which he afterwards got.

The Life of a Regiment, Volume II, pp 152–3.

George White commanded the 2nd Battalion, The Gordon Highlanders (1881–5); was Commander-in-Chief in India (1893–8); and commanded at Ladysmith throughout the siege (1899–1900). He was Governor General of Gibraltar (1904–8) and Governor of the Royal Hospital, Chelsea. He died in 1912, having achieved the rank of Field Marshal.

London Gazette, 18th October, 1881

Lieutenant William Henry Dick-Cunyngham

William Henry Dick-Cunyngham, Captain, The Gordon Highlanders. Date of Act of Bravery; 13th December, 1879. For conspicuous gallantry and bravery displayed by him on the 13th December, 1879, at the attack on the Sherpur Pass, in Afghanistan, in having exposed himself to the full fire of the enemy, and by his example and encouragement rallied the men who, having been beaten back, were at the moment wavering at the top of the hill.

Dick-Cunyngham was a 28 year-old lieutenant in the 92nd Gordon Highlanders during the Second Anglo-Afghan War. He was promoted to captain after the action that won him the V.C., which is covered in *The Life of a Regiment*:

Lieutenants Grant and Dick-Cunyngham, with their men, were in rear of Forbes' section, below the rocks held by the enemy, whose numbers were rapidly increasing, but they were separated from Major White and the rest of his command by a spur of the hill, Lieutenant E.C. Bethune's company being on the left; on getting close to these rocks they found themselves enfiladed from another sangar on their left by a heavy fire in addition to that from their front. With the naked eye those below could see the Afghans crowding upon them in the bravest manner; a bullet at fifteen or twenty yards struck the metal top of Grant's sporran with such force that it knocked him over, apparently killed (though he was soon able to pick up the rifle of a wounded man and returned the compliment). Two of the three officers were down, the breathless men were falling under the furious fire; there was naturally a momentary hesitation, but it was only for a moment, for Dick-Cunyngham rushed forward, waving his sword, and called out, 'Don't retire, come on, lads, follow me!' With a wild shout on they went and rushed the sangar, jumping into it, Cunyngham first. Some of the Ghazis fought desperately, but their red standard went down, its defenders shot or bayoneted, and the rest were driven over the further side of the hill.

The Life of a Regiment, Volume II, pp.124–5.

William Henry Dick-Cunyngham, (illustration, as Lieutenant-Colonel) of Prestonfield, near Edinburgh, joined the 92nd in 1872 in the rank of 'sub-

lieutenant,' and served in the Afghan war of 1879–80. He served in the Boer War of 1881 but was not at Majuba. One of the most truly beloved officers who ever belonged to the Regiment, the following eulogy gives the universal feeling of those who knew him: 'The *beau idéal* of a Highland officer, there was not a man or woman who had a bad word to say about him. His heart was as true as steel, his manner courtesy itself. In kilt and bonnet, with a moustache so light that it seemed almost white against the bronze of his face, with a mountaineer's figure and swing, he caught every eye.' (*The Life of a Regiment*, Volume II, pp 58, 60.)

Dick-Cunyngham commanded the 2nd Battalion in India and South Africa. He was killed by a stray Boer bullet at Ladysmith in January 1900.

London Gazette, 20th May, 1898.

Piper George Findlater

George Findlater, Piper, The Gordon Highlanders. Date of Act of Bravery: 20th October, 1897. During the attack on the Dargai Heights on the 20th October, 1897, Piper Findlater, after being shot through both feet, and unable to stand, sat up, under heavy fire, playing the regimental march to encourage the charge of the Gordon Highlanders.

George Frederick Findlater (photo) was born at Turriff, Aberdeenshire, where his father had a croft and a meal mill, and a family of six sons and five daughters. In 1888 George enlisted in the 2nd Battalion, The Gordon Highlanders when, seeing little adventure in farm work, he took the Queen's shilling in Aberdeen.

The 16-year-old was big for his age and did his basic training in Castlehill Barracks. He joined the 2nd Battalion in Ireland where he studied music at the Curragh Camp with the intention of becoming a regimental piper. After service in Ceylon, Piper Findlater was posted to the 1st Battalion in India and he took part in his first action at the Malakand Pass where a tribesman's bullet clipped off the heel of his boot.

The Gordons won world renown at the battle of Dargai, and Findlater was one of many singled out for special attention. The following account of the battle shows why:

> On reaching the edge of the open ground, the Highlanders took cover while the mountain guns bombarded the well-defended summit for three minutes. Lieutenant-Colonel Mathias addressed the Highlanders, 'The General says the hill must be taken. The Gordons will take it!'. The bugle sounded *Advance*, the pipers began to play, the officers unsheathed their broadswords and their Colonel, with his second-in-command, Major Macbean, on his right and Lieutenant Gordon on his left, led the attack. The Highlanders, bayonets fixed, advanced into the hail of bullets. Major Macbean fell wounded through the thigh and, dragging himself to the shelter of a rock, encouraged the battalion. As he raised his water bottle to his lips he found that it was empty due to a bullet which had pierced it and was still rattling about inside. Lieutenant Lamont was killed in the first rush and Lieutenant Dingwall fell, wounded in four places. Many men were hit three or four times by bullets which passed through pouches, clothing and tunics. Piper Lance Corporal Milne was shot through the

lung[3] and Piper Findlater was hit in the left ankle. A second bullet hit his chanter while a third went through his right foot. Findlater was one of five Gordon pipers at Dargai. The pipe-major [Brown] was unable to continue after being hit in the chest. Findlater claimed that he did not hear the order to play *Cock o' the North*, which is a march. He chose to play a strathspey, *The Haughs of Cromdale*, which he thought more suitable. He felt sick with pain after he was shot but played on, while a murderous hail of bullets poured from the rifles of the Afridis entrenched on the heights. His action encouraged the men facing the riflemen on the Heights, and spurred them on to achieve what the onlookers and trapped infantry had come to think impossible.

Findlater was feted when the Gordons returned home.:

> Findlater was brought back to Britain to recover from his wounds at the Royal Victoria Hospital at Netley, Southampton. On Saturday, 14th May, 1898 Queen Victoria travelled from Windsor to present Private Findlater with his Victoria Cross.
>
> The Queen, seated in her bath-chair went into nearly every ward. When she reached Findlater she asked where he came from. 'Aberdeenshire' he replied. Sir John McNeill repeated the answer to the Queen, who remarked 'Oh! Another Aberdeenshire man.' In response to the Queen's enquiry as to whether or not he would have to give up soldiering, Piper Findlater replied quietly, 'Yes, your Majesty, I'm done for, and I'm very sorry that I'll not be able to serve longer with my regiment.'
>
> Piper Findlater sat beside Private Vickery, who was also being awarded the Victoria Cross. When Piper Findlater tried to stand for the presentation of the medal he was motioned by the Queen to remain seated. She said a few words to him and then, rising from her chair with the help of an Indian attendant, pinned the Victoria Cross on his chest,[4] commending him at the same time for his bravery.

www.craigcross.co.uk

Findlater retired from the army soon afterwards. He re-enlisted in the First World War and was appointed pipe major of the 9th Battalion, but due to ill health he had to retire in 1915. He spent the rest of his life as a farmer and died in 1947 aged 70.

---

3 LCpl Milne was awarded the Distinguished Conduct Medal.
4 Queen Victoria's visit to Netley Hospital on 14 May took place before the official announcement of Piper Findlater's Victoria Cross. The announcement did not appear in the *London Gazette* until 20 May. It was very unusual for the medals to be presented before the official announcement of the award.

London Gazette, 20th May, 1898

Private Edward Lawson

Edward Lawson, Private, The Gordon Highlanders. Date of Act of Bravery: 20th October, 1897. During the attack on the Dargai Heights on the 20th October, 1897, Private Lawson carried Lieut. K. Dingwall, The Gordon Highlanders (who was wounded and unable to move), out of a heavy fire, and subsequently returned and brought in Private McMillan being himself wounded in two places.

Newcastle-born Edward Lawson (photo) joined The Gordon Highlanders at the age of 17 (this would have been late 1890 or early 1891). He did his

initial training at Castlehill Barracks in Aberdeen and was then posted to the 2nd Battalion at the Curragh in Ireland. He was sent to the 1st Battalion in India in 1893.

When Lieutenant Dingwall fell wounded in the assault on the Heights of Dargai, Lawson ran to him and carried him to a place of safety. He turned back to continue the attack but was hit twice. He then found Private McMillan who was more severely wounded, and brought him to safety.

This was not his only act of bravery. On another occasion, after one of his comrades was hit by a bullet and fell into a dried up river bed, Lawson carried him safely to camp.

A fellow-Gordon said: 'Lawson was always a decent fellow but very rash and reckless: he would stick at nothing.' He served throughout the Boer War and was discharged from the Army in 1902 with a good conduct badge and a £10 V.C. pension. He went on to serve in the Reserve.

Edward Lawson died in 1955, aged 82, and was buried in Heaton Cemetery, Newcastle.

CHAPTER 26

BOER WAR

London Gazette, 6th July, 1900

Captain Ernest Beachcroft Beckwith Towse

Ernest Beachcroft Beckwith Towse, Captain, Gordon Highlanders. Date of Acts of Bravery: 11th December, 1899; 30th April, 1900. On the 11th December, 1899, at the action of Magersfontein, Captain Towse was brought to notice by his commanding officer for his gallantry and devotion in assisting the late Colonel Downman, when mortally wounded, in the retirement, and endeavouring when close up to the front of the firing line, to carry Colonel Downman on his back; but finding this not possible, Captain Towse supported him till joined by Colour-Sergeant Nelson and L/Cpl. Hodgson. On the 30th April, 1900, Captain Towse, with twelve men, took up a position on the top of Mount Thaba, far away from support. A force of about 150 Boers attempted to seize the same plateau, neither party appearing to see the other until they were but one hundred yards apart. Some of the Boers then got within forty yards of Captain Towse and his party and called on him to surrender. He at once caused his men to open fire, and remained firing himself until severely wounded (both eyes shattered), thus succeeding in driving off the Boers. The gallantry of this officer in vigorously attacking the enemy (for he not only fired, but charged forward) saved the situation; notwithstanding the numerical superiority of the Boers.

Born in 1864, Ernest Beachcroft Towse intended join the Royal Navy, but went into the Army instead, joining the 3rd Seaforth Highlanders in 1883. Two years later he was gazetted in the Wiltshire Regiment, transferring to The Gordon Highlanders the following year. He went with the Gordons to Egypt, Malta, Ceylon and India. He served in the Chitral Relief Force and was at the storming of the Malakand Pass, for which he received the India Medal with the Relief of Chitral clasp. In 1897 he was at Dargai. He received two further clasps to the India Medal.

Towse, who was a strikingly good-looking man ('the only soldier who could wear a monocle and not lose by it!'), had established a reputation not only for fearless leadership and great consideration for his men, but also for remarkable powers of endurance and determination. Once, when hunting elephant in the jungles of Ceylon, he trailed and made his kill, but he and his tracker became separated and he could not find his path back to camp. All that was edible was the proof of his kill—the elephant's tail—and on this raw and unappetising dish he subsisted for four days as he wandered in the jungle seeking and eventually finding his way to camp!

Like George White in Afghanistan, Beachcroft Towse (photo) was awarded the Victoria Cross for two separate actions, nearly five months apart. On 11 December 1899 at Magersfontein he displayed gallantry and devotion in assisting his mortally wounded Commanding Officer, Lieutenant-Colonel Downman.[1] He tried to carry him on his back whilst under fire but this proved impossible so he remained with Downman under very heavy fire. When the firing slackened, and assisted by two N.C.O.s, Towse carried his colonel to the nearest medical post, some 1,000 yards to the rear. Lieutenant-Colonel Downman died next day of his wounds. Towse was specially mentioned for his bravery in Lord Methuen's despatch on the battle.

On 30 April 1900, Major-General Ian Hamilton's troops met strong opposition from General de Wet's forces holding positions astride Hout Nek. Five miles south-west of the Nek was a large, plateau-like, 600-foot high hill known as Mount Thaba, which the Boers were not holding in any strength. Hamilton realised that with this hill in his possession, the Boer defences on Hout Nek would not only be overlooked, but outflanked. Major-General Smith-Dorrien's 19th Brigade was ordered to capture it. The Shropshire Light Infantry and Kitchener's Horse gained a foothold along the southern crest, but could make no further progress in the face of increasingly heavy enemy fire from the northern end of the hill, which the Boers were rapidly reinforcing. The Gordon Highlanders and two companies of Canadian Infantry were sent to reinforce the troops on the hill, but a concerted advance was out of the question and progress could only be made by small parties advancing independently, using cover from the bushes and rocks. A party of

---

1 To the Boers, Downman would have stood out as a senior officer. 'The Colonel was killed immediately. He would not wear a kilt, and stood up to wave the Battalion on with his stick.' Quote from *With the Gordon Highlanders to the Boer War & beyond*, by L. Gordon-Duff.

ten Highlanders and three Kitchener's Horse, led by Towse, was well ahead of the other groups. Clearly visible to Hamilton and Smith-Dorrien, they worked their way up a spur on the eastern side of the plateau, unaware of a larger enemy force who could also be seen climbing the same spur from the opposite side. To the anxious watchers below it was obvious that neither party knew of the presence of the other. Smith-Dorrien says:

> It was evident to us that they were unaware that working towards them was an overwhelming force of Boers, some 150 strong. This force we had seen for some time, and so unlike Boers and so like our own troops were their movements that they were within a few hundred yards of Towse's party before we realised that they were Boers. Then the 74th Field Battery and the R.H.A. guns poured shell into them at 3,400 yards. We saw the forces, only about 50 yards apart, suddenly discover each other, for both were approaching a crest-line from opposite sides. It looked as if our small party must be annihilated, when these few men of the Gordons rushed forward and poured in a terrible fire before which the Boers recoiled and fled. This gallant act saved us the hill. Had the Boers driven this small party back our task, difficult as it was, would have been more difficult. That scene is as clear to me today as when it happened twenty-four years ago. From where I stood in the plain with my Commander we could see the whole side of the hill, and I have often wondered why that small brave force rushed forward and not back, and why they weren't all killed. It was soon evident that they were very much alive, for they maintained their position while the enemy withdrew down the hill.

Memories of Forty-eight Years' Service, p 192.

The Life of a Regiment comments:

> The Boer counter-attack was composed of foreigners, adventurers who had served in their own national armies. It was commanded by Colonel Maximoff, a Russian, who called on Towse to surrender. Regimental versions credit Towse with the most forcible language of refusal; the War Diary states that his men fixed bayonets as they charged: seven of the little band, just half, were killed or wounded; Towse wounded Maximoff with a shot from his carbine, but was struck by a bullet which destroyed his sight. General Smith-Dorrien recommended him for the Victoria Cross, which he received.
>
> Smith-Dorrien wrote: 'I shall never forget the pathetic sight of the stricken Towse, shot through both eyes; certain he would never see again, not a thought for himself, but plenty for his men, hoping that he had done his duty, and with it all so cheerful and apparently happy. He spoke as

quietly and as lucidly as if he was in the best of health. He spoke most highly of the behaviour of Kitchener's Horse.'

The Life of a Regiment, Volume III, pp 159–60.

Beachcroft Towse's performance on Mount Thaba clearly impressed Smith-Dorrien, who, on receiving a letter from Towse thanking Smith-Dorrien for recommending him for the Victoria Cross, replied:

> You thank me for having recommended you for the V.C. which is very nice of you. But in doing it I merely did my duty, not a duty which amongst the sad thoughts of your blighted life gave me pleasure, that I could bring forward your name for that much deserved reward, feeling at the same time that by so doing I should be repaying to a very small extent the credit I, as your Brigadier, gained by your preventing with a handful of men against overwhelming odds, the Boers from establishing themselves on the summit of Thoba Mountain. Never have I watched anything so exciting, your tiny force working up one side and several lines of Boers moving to meet you up the other. Apparently neither side saw the other, but your force gained the highest point first and unflinchingly held your ground. We from below suddenly saw the Boers recoil and then retreat and although we did not actually see them off the Mountain for another 20 hours, they never made any further headway thanks entirely to the bravery and front shown by a very small party of the 1st Gordon Highlanders under you. Poor old chap. It's a sad subject that it should have ended the way it did but since you with your uncomplaining nature have made the best of things and are doing your best to enjoy your life, we your friends must try to think you are really happy.

[This is a fine example of the principle followed by good commanders that blame goes up the chain of command while credit goes down.]

> His soldiering days over, Towse did not allow blindness to daunt him. 'Blindness,' he said, 'can either master a man or a man can master blindness.' He taught himself a whole range of accomplishments and, having overcome his disability, he began the great work of his life— helping the blind.

> He joined the National Institute for the Blind in 1901 when the total income was £9,700; in 1944, when ill-health forced him to resign the chairmanship after twenty-three years, it was more than half a million.

> During the First World War, his wife, at his behest, wrote to King George V's Secretary and asked if Beachcroft-Towse could go to France to look after blinded soldiers. King George agreed, and he was appointed Staff Captain, without pay and allowances, at the Base. By making brief notes in Braille of the patient's wounds and the address of the next-of-kin,

he remembered each individual case and wrote to parents, wives or friends, telling them all about their men. He would work far into the night at his Braille typewriter and rarely snatched more than a few hours sleep. He was mentioned in Sir Douglas Haig's despatch in June 1916 for his devoted services and was awarded the 1914 Star, the War Medal and the Victory Medal.

In 1900 Queen Victoria presented his V.C. to him and made him Sergeant-at-Arms. King Edward VII reappointed him in 1902, and in 1903 he was admitted to the Honorary Corps of Gentlemen-at-Arms in which he served until 1939. He was on guard at the lying-in-state of Queen Victoria, King Edward VII, Queen Alexandra and King George V.

Beachcroft Towse was made a C.B.E. in 1920 and a K.C.V.O. in 1927, in which year he became a Knight of Grace of the Order of St. John of Jerusalem. He died in 1948 aged 84.

T&S, February 1949.

London Gazette, 20th July, 1900

Captain Matthew Fontaine Maury Meiklejohn

Matthew Fontaine Maury Meiklejohn, Capt., Gordon Highlanders. Date of Act of Bravery: 21 Oct. 1899. At the battle of Elandslaagte, on the 21st Oct. 1899, after the main Boer position had been captured, some of the men of the Gordon Highlanders, when about to advance, were exposed to a heavy cross-fire, and, having lost their leaders, commenced to waver. Seeing this, Captain Meiklejohn rushed to the front and called on the Gordons to follow him. By his conspicuous bravery and fearless example he rallied the men and led them against the enemy's position where he fell, desperately wounded in four places.

Matthew Meiklejohn, son of Professor Meiklejohn of St. Andrews University, was born on 27 November 1870, and educated at Fettes College, Edinburgh. He joined The Gordon Highlanders in India in June 1891, and four years later saw his first active service at the relief of Chitral. In 1897 Meiklejohn was slightly wounded when the Gordons took the heights of Dargai. He saw more fighting during the Tirah campaign for which received the India Medal with three clasps.

On the outbreak of the South African War the 2nd Gordons came with the Infantry Brigade sent from India, and Meiklejohn was with them as a Lieutenant. The 2nd Battalion was part of Sir George White's Natal Field Force that came under siege at Ladysmith, but before that they fought the battle of Elandslaagte on 21 October 1899. In this significant battle, which shook the Boers, driven from their positions by the unrelenting advance in the face of heavy fire, the Gordons suffered heavily casualties; their Commanding Officer, Dick-Cunyngham, was put out of action as were many other officers. Captain Meiklejohn, seeing that the men hesitated through loss of leadership, went forward and exhorted the Gordons to advance on the enemy. Whilst leading them in a very exposed position he was shot several times and badly wounded. In his *History of the South African and Transvaal War*, Louis Creswicke tells the story of Matthew Meiklejohn:

Among the heroes of Elandslaagte was Lieutenant Meiklejohn of the Gordon Highlanders. (photo) This young officer, one of the 'Dargai boys', helped the charge in an endeavour to embarrass the Boer flank. Supported by a party of Gordons, Meiklejohn waved his sword and cried out to his party hastily gathered around him. But the Boer ranks were alert, and poured in a deadly fire on the gallant band. Lieutenant Meiklejohn received three bullet wounds through his upper right arm, one through the right forearm, a finger blown away, a bullet through the left thigh, two bullets through the helmet, a snick in the neck, while his sword and scabbard were literally shot to pieces. He has lost his right arm but, happily, being left-handed it is hoped he may remain in the profession he is so well calculated to adorn.

Brought back into Ladysmith, which was shortly afterwards invested by the Boers, he shared the privations of a close and exhausting siege. Meiklejohn, now a captain, survived his wounds, but lost his right arm.

Despite the loss of his arm Meiklejohn remained in the Army and served on. In 1901 he was Garrison Adjutant at St. Helena, then returned to enter the Staff College. He served on the General Staff at Army Headquarters, and was promoted to major. Major Meiklejohn died on 4 July 1913, after an accident in Hyde Park when his horse bolted. Handicapped by having only one arm, Meiklejohn just managed to steer his horse into the rails bordering Rotten Row, opposite Knightsbridge Barracks, in order to avoid some children and their nurse, who probably would otherwise have been killed or seriously injured.

The mother of these children wrote to the *Times*:

As my nurse was the only eye-witness of the tragic accident which led to Major Meiklejohn's death, I think it right to acquaint the public with her story. She and my children were in Hyde Park on Saturday afternoon, 28 June. They had reached a spot opposite to Knightsbridge Barracks, and, as they were walking along the path, Major Meiklejohn, on his runaway horse, suddenly came upon them from between the trees. In order to avoid danger to the children, he turned his horse against the railings, which he must have known he could not clear. He thus gave his life for theirs, and added one more to the long roll of his brave and unselfish deeds.

T&S, February/March 1974.

In 1974 Major Gordon Harper, former Gordon Highlander who had emigrated to Australia, having read an account of Meiklejohn's death in the *Tiger and Sphinx*, wrote to the magazine to clarify the incident and add some further detail:

I was very much interested to read the item relating to the late Major Meiklejohn, V.C., with an account of his fatal accident in July 1913.

From the latter, however, it might be supposed that he was riding for pleasure. Probably few people are now alive who saw the whole picture. The following additional information, from one who was present may therefore be of interest.

I remember clearly the hot summer afternoon, with the chestnut trees in bloom in Hyde Park. Major Meiklejohn was on duty taking the annual inspection of the University of London contingent of the Officers Training Corps. A cadet lance-corporal at the time, I was in the front rank of my section and saw what happened. His horse was very restive, and when the band struck up it bolted. There was a large crowd of spectators which he succeeded in avoiding with considerable skill (he had only one arm) and deliberately turned his galloping steed to the rails, to his own grave hazard.

There was a thud. The parade was halted. Colonel Sir Wilmot P. Heringham, commanding the medical unit on parade, was called to the unconscious officer, and my immediate commander Captain A.E. Webb-Johnston (surgeon, Middlesex Hospital) was also summoned from his post. An ambulance was called, and Major Meiklejohn was conveyed to the hospital where he died from his injuries.

P.S. By ironic coincidence the tune playing for the March Past was *The Galloping Major*.

T&S, August/September 1974.

London Gazette, 20th July, 1900

Lieutenant William Robertson

William Robertson, Sergeant-Major (now Quartermaster and Honorary Lieutenant), The Gordon Highlanders. Date of Act of Bravery: 21st October, 1899. At the Battle of Elandslaagte, on the 21st October,1899, during the final advance on the enemy position, this Warrant Officer led each successive rush, exposing himself fearlessly to the enemy's artillery and rifle fire to encourage the men. After the main position had been captured, he led a small party to seize the Boer Camp. Though exposed to a deadly cross-fire from the enemy's rifles he gallantly held the position captured, and continued to encourage the men until he was wounded in two places.

William Robertson (photo) was born at Dumfries in 1865. He joined The

Gordon Highlanders in 1884 and served with the 2nd Battalion in India and South Africa. At Elandslaagte, as Regimental Sergeant-Major, he led his men in rush after rush. To encourage them he fearlessly exposed himself to a heavy bombardment of artillery and rifle fire. With the objective captured, Robertson gathered a small party, went on to seize the Boer camp and, despite being wounded twice, held it against desperate Boer efforts to retake it. This second act of courage was observed by General Ian Hamilton who wrote: 'No better V.C. was ever won than William Robertson's. There was no vainglory, but the danger was incurred in a cool and reasoned spirit for a military end of real importance.' Robertson, promoted to Lieutenant, received his decoration from the hands of Queen Victoria at Osborne.

In addition to the Victoria Cross he gained the Queen's Medal for South Africa with clasps for Elandslaagte, Ladysmith and Cape Colony. On his return home in 1900 he was given the freedom of Dumfries. When war broke out in 1914 Robertson rejoined, but as he was then nearly fifty years of age, active service at the front was denied him. He was employed as Recruiting Staff Officer at Edinburgh, promoted Lieutenant-Colonel, and finally retired as a full Colonel. He continued to an advanced age to do much voluntary work for disabled ex-Service men. He was chairman of Lady Haig's Poppy Factory in Edinburgh and vice-chairman and honorary treasurer of the British Legion in Scotland. Created an O.B.E. in 1917, he was promoted C.B.E. in 1946.

He had three sons and a daughter. His second son, Ian, was killed at Beaumont Hamel. William Robertson, V.C., died in 1949.

London Gazette, 10th August, 1900

Corporal John Frederick Mackay

John Frederick Mackay, Corporal, Gordon Highlanders. Date of Act of Bravery: 20th May, 1900. On the 20th May, 1900, during the action at Doornkop, near Johannesburg, Mackay repeatedly rushed forward, under a withering fire at short range, to attend to wounded comrades, dressing their wounds while he himself was without shelter, and in one instance carrying a wounded man from the open under heavy fire to the shelter of a boulder.

John Mackay (photo) was born in Edinburgh in 1873. On 20 May 1900, during the action on Crow's Nest Hill, Johannesburg, Corporal Mackay

repeatedly dashed forward under heavy rifle fire to attend to wounded comrades of the 1st Battalion Gordon Highlanders. He carried Private Forbes from heavy fire to the cover of a boulder, bound his wound, left him and aided another wounded man under heavy fire, his belt-plate being cut in two by a bullet.

Mackay's courage at Doornkop was not a solitary act of bravery. Less than two months later, on 11 July 1900, he carried out a similar act to that which won him the Victoria Cross at Doornkop. During the attempt to save the guns at Leehoehoek, Captain D.R. Younger was mortally hit by Boer rifle fire. Corporal Mackay, 'already "mentioned" twice for gallant deeds, saw from the right *kopje* Younger lying, dashed out, managed to hoist him on his back and carried him behind the left *kopje*; all this was under the concentrated fire of several hundred rifles at 800 yards.' *(The Life of a Regiment*, Volume III, p 220).

John Frederick Mackay served in the First World War and rose through the ranks to Lieutenant-Colonel, transferring to The King's Own Scottish

Borderers on receiving a commission. He also served in the Argyll and Sutherland Highlanders and in the Northern Nigeria Regiment. He died in Nice on 9 January 1930.[2]

London Gazette, 28th September, 1900

Captain William Eagleson Gordon

William Eagleson Gordon, Captain, Gordon Highlanders. Date of Act of Bravery: 11th July, 1900. On the 11th July, 1900, during the action near Leehoehoek, a party of men, accompanied by Captains Younger and Allan, having succeeded in dragging an artillery waggon when its horses were unable to do so by reason of the heavy and accurate fire of the enemy, Captain Gordon called for volunteers, and with the greatest coolness fastened the drag rope to the gun, and then beckoned to the men, who immediately doubled out to join him, in accordance with his previous instructions. While moving the gun Captain Younger and three men were hit. Seeing that further attempts would only result in further casualties, Captain Gordon ordered the remainder of the party under cover of the *kopje* again, and, having seen the wounded safely away, himself retired. Captain Gordon's conduct under a particularly heavy and most accurate fire at only 600 yards range was most admirable, and his manner of handling his men most masterly; his devotion on every occasion that this battalion has been under fire has been remarkable.

William Eagleson Gordon (photo below) was born on 4 May 1866, the son of a doctor, at Homehill, Bridge-of-Allan, Stirlingshire. On 6 June 1888 he joined the 1st Battalion, The Gordon Highlanders. He was with the Chitral Relief Force, taking part in the Malakand assault. Promoted to captain in June 1897 four months later he was in action at Dargai. He was adjutant from 1899 to 1903.

In the Boer War he was severely wounded at Magersfontein in 1899. On 11 July 1900, during the action near Leehoehoek, the General issued orders for withdrawal; the instruction reached Lieutenant-Colonel Macbean about 2.30 p.m. Close to Battalion Headquarters lay Turner, the artillery subaltern, with three wounds. On hearing the order, he burst out, 'Oh, you *can't* leave my guns'. Colonel Macbean assured him he might rest easy and called for volunteers to bring them under cover. Despite the rocky ground and the

---

2 During the Great War the military authorities searched for a 'wanted' man posing as an officer, wearing the Dargai, South African, Nigerian, Great War and Victoria Cross ribbons. Mackay was the only officer entitled to that remarkable row of medals. In London a member of the Army Provost Marshal's staff challenged him in a West End restaurant one evening, confident that he had caught the imposter. To his embarrassment he found he had caught 'the real thing'.

carcasses of the horses, the first effort under Captain D.R. Younger succeeded in running in a limber.

Captain Gordon went out, attached a drag-rope to a gun and beckoned to the waiting volunteers. Ten, with Captain Younger, rushed out and tailed on,  but the enemy were ready, their deadly fire swept the group and instantly men fell, among them Captain Younger mortally hit. Captain Allan joined the party, but it was plain that the effort was vain and Gordon ordered the men to take cover to avoid further casualties. He saw the wounded taken to a place of safety and then retired himself. He received the Victoria Cross from Lord Kitchener at Pretoria, on Peace Thanksgiving Day, June 1902.

Captain Gordon took part in actions in the Orange Free State and at Paardeberg in 1901 where he was slightly wounded. He was involved in many actions and mentioned in despatches three times. He was promoted to major in January 1907 and was a brevet colonel when appointed ADC to the King in October 1913.

In the First World War he was captured with the 1st Battalion but was released in 1916 as an exchange. From September 1917 to 1920 he commanded No. 1 (Midland) District, Scottish Command. He died in London on 10 March 1941.[3]

London Gazette, 8th August, 1902

Captain David Reginald Younger

David Reginald Younger, Captain, The Gordon Highlanders. Date of Act of Bravery: 11th July, 1900. This officer, during the action near Krugersdorf on 11th July, 1900, volunteered for and took out a party which dragged a Royal Artillery waggon under cover of a small *kopje*, though exposed to a very heavy and accurate fire at only 850 yards range. He also accompanied the second party of volunteers who went out to try and bring in one of the guns. During the afternoon he was mortally wounded, dying shortly afterwards. His cool and gallant conduct was the admiration of all who witnessed it, and, had Captain

---

3   W.E Gordon's son, 2Lt C.M.B. Gordon, joined The Gordon Highlanders in 1933, but was killed the same year in a car practising for races at Donnington Park.

Younger lived, the Field-Marshal Commanding-in-Chief in South Africa would have recommended him for the high award of the Victoria Cross at the same time as Captain W.E. Gordon, of the same regiment.

David Reginald Younger was born in 1871. He was educated at St Ninian's School, Moffat, and Malvern College. He joined the 1st Battalion, The Gordon Highlanders in 1893, was with the Chitral Relief Force and the Tirah Field Force, taking part in the assaults at the Malakand Pass and Dargai. He was with the Kimberley Relief Force, was at Magersfontein and was mentioned in despatches. He distinguished himself in the operations between 28 February and 13 March 1900.

On 11 July 1900 he was part of a group of brave men who attempted to save some artillery guns under heavy fire. He was the first to gather a party of men who managed to drag an artillery wagon under cover. Then Captain Gordon went out to save a gun and managed to fix a rope to it. He called for help and Captain Younger (photo) and others went out to try and drag it in but had to give up after Younger and three others were hit by Boer bullets. Captain Younger died later that day.

Younger clearly deserved the Victoria Cross, but he very nearly did not receive it. At that time the Victoria Cross was only awarded to living recipients. It was only after a number of Boer War incidents where British soldiers died after acts of courage worthy of great recognition that a new precedent was set whereby the Victoria Cross could be awarded posthumously. Younger's was one of the first posthumous V.C.s.[4] He was buried at Krugersdorp under a marble cross erected by his brother officers.

---

4   The Hon Frederick Roberts, son of Field Marshal Earl Roberts, was wounded at Colenso and died 24 hours later. His V.C. was 'gazetted' on 2 February, 1900 and he was given a posthumous medal. There was some anger that he had been treated as a special case, and the families of others just as worthy asked why their relatives could not be given a posthumous V.C. even though they had died many years earlier. In August 1902 Edward VII approved the award of six posthumous V.C.s (including Younger's) for acts of bravery in the Boer War. The families of men who had died in six similar cases between 1859 and 1897 campaigned for them to be awarded the V.C., and in 1907 the precedent was accepted. Crosses were 'gazetted' and delivered to the families of the men. The controversy surrounding Roberts's decoration meant the precedent for posthumous V.C. awards had been established, and in 1920 the rules were formally rewritten.

CHAPTER 27

1ST AND 2ND WORLD WARS

London Gazette, 18th February, 1915

Drummer William Kenny

William Kenny, No 6535, Drummer, 2nd Battalion, The Gordon Highlanders. Date of Act of Bravery: 23rd October, 1914. For conspicuous bravery on 23rd October, 1914, near Ypres, in rescuing wounded men on five occasions under very heavy fire in the most fearless manner, and for twice previously saving machine-guns by carrying them out of action. On numerous occasions Drummer Kenny conveyed urgent messages under very dangerous circumstances over fire-swept ground.

William Kenny (photo) was born in Malta in 1880. He enlisted in the 2nd

Battalion, The Gordon Highlanders. The Victoria Cross was awarded for numerous acts of bravery rather than one outstanding display of courage.

In addition to the Victoria Cross Kenny won: the Queen's South Africa medal with bars, King's South Africa medal with bars, 1914 Star with bar, British War medal, Allied Victory medal, Delhi Durbar medal and the Cross of St George (Russia). He was also mentioned in despatches. His Victoria Cross and medals are at The Gordon Highlanders Museum, Aberdeen.

William Kenny died in 1936 in London, aged 56. In 1999 The Gordon Highlanders London Association erected a new headstone at his grave in the Corps of Commissionaires plot at Brookwood Cemetery.

The following pen picture of Kenny was written by his friend Sergeant W.M. Allan. The 2nd Battalion was in Cairo when war broke out and did not land at Zeebrugge until 7 October 1914. In its ranks was Drummer William Kenny, the bass drummer in the Pipe Band (later Drum Major). Kenny, known to his friends as 'Paddy', was one of the 'characters' who appear in every good unit. It is easy to regard Victoria Cross holders as larger-than-life heroic figures, forgetting that most of them were ordinary men displaying extraordinary courage in difficult situations. They were soldiers who shared all the qualities and weaknesses that typified their comrades. Sergeant Allan's reminiscences give an affectionate portrait of a Gordon Highlander who, like all good soldiers in a close-knit team, made the best of the situation in which he found himself:

> As his Section Sergeant, it might not come amiss if I were to write a few reminiscences of the doings of this brave and gallant soldier during the early days of the war in 1914. 'Paddy,' as he was known to one and all, carried the bass drum in the Pipe Band in pre-war days.[1] On going overseas he was appointed as bugler and runner to the Company Commander of 'A' Company, Capt. J.L.G. Burnett, now Major-General Sir James Burnett, of Leys, and was attached to my Section. Being of a witty and humorous disposition, he naturally was the life of not only his Section but of the whole Platoon.

> On handing over the drums at Ostend,[2] Paddy retained the ticken bag[3] of the bass drum, also his drum belt, which, with haversack and water bottle, comprised his whole equipment. Paddy was a picture of a soldier, with his erect figure, ruddy complexion, big flowing moustache, and his keen, witty smile. I am sure he made the heart of many a Belgian maiden flutter. He always had plenty of admirers marching beside him at the head of the Platoon.

> During the retreat from Ghent to Ypres, and up to the 29th October, 1914, the ticken bag and Paddy's haversack were used as the section's larder. Many a nice plucked fowl, hare, or hunk of bacon found its way into that ticken bag to await the opportunity to 'drum-up.' We all had to take a turn of carrying the bag on the march, and it was often very bulky. In his haversack he carried pepper, salt, and always a few onions.

> On arrival at Ypres from Ghent, we occupied partly dug trenches beside the village of Zanvoordte. During the consolidation and wiring of the trenches we were much worried by enemy snipers, who took heavy toll. During this period Paddy was continually on the move, carrying messages to and from Headquarters, which was at a farmhouse behind the

---

1 Kenny carried the bass drum on the 400-mile march from Kolaghat to Dinapore in 1910 'In the narrow streets closely lined with people, the Bengali police officer riding ahead, the pipes playing, the six-foot drummer (Kenny) in his leopard-skin swinging his sticks and banging the big drum, the dense lines of white-clad natives began to sway and bend, salaaming, salaaming to the drum, to the mounted officer, to the whole column, but most of all to the big drum. Word went out that it was the regiment's God!'

2 The drums of the 2nd Battalion were discovered by the Germans when they occupied Ostend, and removed to Germany. They were finally returned to the 2nd Battalion in 1932. See Chapter 13.

3 The drums came complete with ticken covers. Ticken was a strong, closely woven linen or cotton fabric. It was usually twilled, and woven in stripes of different colours.

line. On the morning of the 21st October, a section of 'C' Company, in a scrap with some enemy cavalry who had occupied a farmhouse in front of their line, had a few men wounded. Cpl. 'Cockney' Robertson was mortally wounded. It was Paddy who carried 'Cockney' in, and helped to bring the other wounded men in.

On the traverse on the right of our fire-bay, Paddy used to throw his drum belt. One morning a sniper's bullet landed beside the belt. Every morning afterwards Paddy, when the bullet arrived, used to sing out to the sniper and signal a hit or a washout for a miss. On three occasions the sniper put a bullet through the belt. It was the glint of the sun on the brass hook on the belt that the sniper aimed at.

Early on the 23rd October our Platoon was withdrawn from the front line to a ditch a few hundred yards behind. The ticken bag came into action once more. Tim McBain and Paddy went along the ditch to a farmhouse and cooked a nice meal. We had just dispatched the meal, when a runner came along the ditch with orders for the Platoon to proceed to Headquarters. On arrival we found our Brigadier on a white horse ready to lead us into action.[4] We formed up and with Nos. 1 and 3 Platoons leading in open order we advanced up the ridge in the direction of a wood. There was quite a lot of shell fire during the advance, which caused a few casualties, but the worst part in the advance was the crossing of an open field to get to the wood, our objective being the trenches on the reverse side of the wood, which was held by 'D' Company and The Border Regiment.

No. 2 Platoon had orders not to follow the other Platoons over the open ground as the situation was now in hand. Paddy, who had returned to Headquarters with a message, was on his way back with a message to the Company Commander, and had to cross this open field. A German machine-gunner located low down in the valley had the range to a nicety. Although the situation was serious, we could not avoid laughing at Paddy, who, with bullets striking amongst his feet from the machine-gun, was jumping in the air like a bucking mule. Yet he had time to stop, turn towards the German and put his fingers to his nose, and then run for the shelter of the wood, with a spray of bullets following him. How he was not hit beats me.

On his return journey he saw wounded men from other Platoons. He treated the machine-gunner with contempt, and made journey after

---

4   Two points to note here. The Brigadier was on his horse on the battlefield, a familiar sight in the British Army from its earliest days, but one that would very soon become a thing of the past, and secondly, the Brigadier was about to lead his men into battle. British Generals in the First World War have attracted much adverse criticism, often misplaced and unjustified, but most displayed great courage, both physical and moral, and many of them died on the battlefield.

journey over the fire-swept field. On returning to the section he was shocked to find his pal, Tim McBain, badly wounded. Tim stopped a piece of shell about the stomach whilst lying next to me. Paddy would have no denial; he would fetch a stretcher, and he returned with two Scots Guards and a stretcher, making no attempt to take cover. He personally saw Tim to the dressing station, but he died next day. He showed great bravery when we carried tools up to 'D' Company after dark. We arrived during an enemy attack. Things did not look good.

On the 27th October the Division was withdrawn from the line. Our 'billets' were in a field. Just before dawn Paddy got a fire going. An empty biscuit tin was used to boil the tea, and Charlie Thornton got a dish from a dog's kennel, with the inscription, 'Drink, puppy, drink,' on it. This was used to fry bacon for fifteen men. Everything was going good, but the smell of bacon frying was too much for many hungry warriors, who were wondering where their breakfast was going to come from. Fred Stewart, our C.Q.M.S., came over to bluff Paddy, and says, 'Drummer Kenny, in the name of the King, I demand half of that bacon to feed men of the — Regiment who are attached to 'A' Company.' Paddy, without looking up, lifts up his clasp knife, and replies: 'In the name of J— C—, if you don't beat it I will * * * you!'

On the night of the 28th October we occupied trenches on the Menin road. In the early morning of the 29th we were called to Headquarters, on a sunken road. When the German attack began it appeared that the Grenadier Guards on our left were bearing the brunt. Our Company Officer came running to Headquarters and reported that owing to the German advance he had to make new dispositions. On being asked by the Commanding Officer if these men (meaning No. 2 Platoon and the Scouts, Signallers, etc.) would be useful, we were ordered to follow the Company Commander.

On arriving at the scene we found that the Grenadiers, supported by our 3 Platoon, were hard pressed to stop the Germans advancing through a wood. On the signal from Lieut. P. McKenzie to reinforce, we were soon in the thick of it. It was difficult to see what was doing owing to smoke from burning haystacks, which the wind was blowing in our direction, but it appeared that the attack was well supported. Mr. McKenzie, the only officer present, was trying his utmost to organize a counter-attack to drive the enemy from the wood. Suddenly the enemy came on again and took the wood. A machine-gun was left behind, with the belt still sticking in the feed-block. This was too much for Paddy so off he went into the wood and retrieved the gun before the Germans could take it, and brought it out of action.

It was about this time that Lieut. Brooke arrived, and a dangerous situation was saved, for we drove the enemy back and occupied the Grenadiers' trenches again. Lieut. Brooke[5] was killed just as we got into the trench.

W.M. Allan.

T&S, March 1936.

London Gazette, 18th February, 1915

Captain James Anson Otho Brooke

James Anson Otho Brooke, Lieutenant, Gordon Highlanders. Date of Act of Bravery: 29th October, 1914. For most conspicuous bravery and great ability near Gheluvelt, on the 29th October, in leading two attacks on the German trenches under heavy rifle and machine-gun fire, regaining a lost trench at a very critical moment. He was killed on that day. By his marked coolness and promptitude on this occasion, Lieut. Brooke prevented the enemy from breaking through our line at a time when a general counter-attack could not have been organized.

Otho Brooke (photo) was born in 1884, the son of Sir Harry Vasey Brooke, K.B.E. and Lady Patricia (*née* Moir-Byres) of Fairley, Countesswells, Aberdeenshire. He was an outstanding cadet at the Royal Military College, Sandhurst, winning the Sword of Honour[6] in 1905 before following in his father's footsteps and joining 2nd Battalion, The Gordon Highlanders.

At Fayet, while carrying a message from his colonel, Lieutenant Brooke noticed Germans breaking through part of the line. He gathered 100 men around him and led them in a charge against the advancing Germans, saving the situation and many British lives. He twice led attacks on the German trenches under heavy rifle and machine-gun fire and retook a trench that had been lost. After the action which gained

---

5   Lt James Otho Brooke also won the Victoria Cross during this action.
6   He carried this sword into battle in the action that won him the V.C. The sword is now in The Gordon Highlanders Museum. After the war Brooke's sister, Irene, married Lt (later Lt-Col) R.G. Lees, whose gallant and distinguished conduct while a prisoner-of-war of the Japanese was remembered with gratitude and affection by the men of the 2nd Battalion, and of other regiments who were captives along with him.

him the Victoria Cross, he went back to bring up support, and while doing so, was killed by a German sniper. His promotion to captain was notified posthumously.[7]

London Gazette, 6th September, 1917

Private George McIntosh

No. 265579, George McIntosh, Private, 1/6th Battalion, Gordon Highlanders. For most conspicuous bravery on 31st July 1917 when, during the consolidation of a position, his company came under machine-gun fire at close range. Private McIntosh immediately rushed forward under heavy fire, and reaching his emplacement, he threw a Mills grenade in to it, killing two of the enemy and wounding a third. Subsequently, entering the dug-out, he found two light machine-guns, which he carried back with him. His quick grasp of the situation and the utter fearlessness and rapidity with which he acted undoubtedly saved many of his comrades, and enabled the consolidation to proceed unhindered by machine-gun fire. Throughout the day the cheerfulness and courage of Private McIntosh was indomitable, and to his fine example in a great measure was due the success which attended his company.

George Imlach McIntosh (photo) was born in Buckie in 1897. In addition to his Victoria Cross he was twice mentioned in despatches in the First World War. He was presented with the Victoria Cross by King George V in Glasgow.

In the Second World War he enlisted in the Royal Air Force. He was a Flight Sergeant on an airfield in England when it was attacked by German bombers. McIntosh ran into some burning hangars and carried out injured airmen, saving their lives, until he collapsed from smoke inhalation. He accompanied crated aircraft to Russia on an Arctic convoy that was attacked by submarines and aircraft. He

---

7 Brooke's younger brother, Capt Henry Brian Brooke, joined the 2nd Battalion, Gordon Highlanders after Otho Brooke's death. At the Battle of Mametz, despite being wounded twice, he continued to lead his men. He suffered a third fatal wound and died on 24 July 1917.

displayed great leadership when the ship was hit and on fire. His efforts played a large part in saving the ship from the flames. He was once again mentioned in despatches. He ended the war as a Warrant Officer. Made a Freeman of Buckie in 1955, in 1960, as the only living Gordon Highlander V.C. (and the only Territorial Army Gordon Highlander to win the V.C. in the First War), he took the salute at a passing out parade of recruits at Gordon Barracks, Bridge of Don in Aberdeen.[8] He died in 1968 and was buried in Buckie.

London Gazette, 4th September, 1919

Lieutenant Allan Ebenezer Ker

Allan Ebenezer Ker, Lieutenant, 3rd Battalion, Gordon Highlander. For conspicuous bravery and devotion to duty. On the 21st March, 1918, near St Quentin, after a heavy bombardment, the enemy penetrated our line, and the flank of the 61st Division became exposed. Lieut. Ker, with one Vickers gun, succeeded in engaging the enemy's infantry, approaching under cover of dead ground, and held up the attack, inflicting many casualties. He then sent back word to his Battalion Headquarters that he had determined to stop with his Sergeant and several men who had been badly wounded, and fight until a counter-attack could be launched to relieve him. Just as ammunition failed his party was attacked from behind with bombs, machine-guns and the bayonet. Several bayonet attacks were delivered, but each time they were repulsed by Lieut. Ker and his companions with their revolvers, the Vickers gun having by this time been destroyed. The wounded were collected into a small shelter, and it was decided to defend them to the last and to hold the enemy as long as possible. In one of the many hand-to-hand encounters a German rifle and bayonet and a small supply of ammunition was secured, and subsequently used with good effect against the enemy. Although Lieut. Ker was very exhausted from want of food and gas poisoning, and from the supreme exertions he had made during ten hours of the most severe bombardment, fighting and attending to the wounded, he refused to surrender until all his ammunition was exhausted and his position was rushed by a large number of the enemy. His behaviour throughout the day was absolutely cool and fearless, and by his determination he was materially instrumental in engaging and holding up for three hours more than 500 of the enemy.

---

8   Lt-Gen Sir Peter Graham, as a subaltern, commanded the 'McIntosh, V.C.' Platoon at this parade.

Allan Ebenezer Ker (photo) was born in Edinburgh in 1883. Educated at Edinburgh Academy and the University of Edinburgh, he was commissioned into The Gordon Highlanders on 11 June 1915. In August 1916 he was attached to the Machine-gun Corps and went to France with the 61st Battalion. The action that won him the Victoria Cross took place on the first day of the German offensive, when under-strength British battalions were battered and overrun by Germans in overwhelming numbers. Ker's dogged defence held off the German attack in his area for most of that first day, inflicting heavy casualties on the attackers. By the end of the war, Ker had been promoted Captain in The Gordon Highlanders and retired shortly after. In the Second War he served as a major in the Chief of the Imperial General Staff's department. He died in London in 1958 aged 75.

London Gazette, 10 August 1944

Private George Allan Mitchell

In Italy on the night of 23rd and 24th January 1944, A Company of the London Scottish[9] was ordered to carry out a local attack to restore the situation on a portion of the main Damiano ridge. The Company attacked with two platoons forward and a composite platoon of London Scottish and Royal Berkshires in reserve. The Company Commander was wounded in the very early stages of the attack. The only other officer with the Company was wounded soon afterwards. A section of this Company was ordered by the Platoon Commander to carry out a right flanking movement against some enemy machine-guns which were holding up the advance. Almost as soon as he had issued the order, he was killed. There was no Platoon Sergeant. The section itself consisted of a Lance Corporal and three men, who were shortly joined by Private Mitchell, the 2-inch mortarmen from Platoon Headquarters and another private.

During the advance, the enemy opened heavy machine-gun fire at point blank range. Without hesitation, Private Mitchell dropped the 2-inch mortar which he was carrying, and seizing a rifle and bayonet, charged, alone, up the hill through intense spandau fire. He reached

---

9   The London Scottish was a part of The Gordon Highlanders.

the enemy machine-gun unscathed, jumped into the weapon pit, shot one and bayoneted the other member of the crew, thus silencing the gun. As a result, the advance of the platoon continued, but shortly afterwards the leading section was again held up by the fire of approximately two German sections who were strongly entrenched.

Private Mitchell, (photo) realising that prompt action was essential, rushed forward into the assault firing his rifle from his hip, completely oblivious of the bullets which were sweeping the area. The remainder of his section followed him and arrived in time to complete the capture of the position in which six Germans were killed and twelve made prisoner. As the section was reorganising, another enemy machine-gun opened up on it at close range. Once more Private Mitchell rushed forward alone and with his rifle and bayonet killed the crew.

The section now found itself immediately below the crest of the hill from which heavy small arms fire was being directed and grenades were being thrown. Private Mitchell's ammunition was exhausted, but in spite of this he called on the men for one further effort and again led the assault up the steep and rocky hillside. Dashing to the front, he was again the first man to reach the enemy position and was mainly instrumental in forcing the remainder of the enemy to surrender. A few minutes later, a German who had surrendered, picked up a rifle and shot Private Mitchell through the head.

Throughout this operation, carried out on a very dark night, up a steep hillside covered with rocks and scrub Private Mitchell displayed courage and devotion to duty of the very highest order. His complete disregard of the enemy fire, the fearless way in which he continually exposed himself, and his refusal to accept defeat, so inspired his comrades that together they succeeded in overcoming and defeating an enemy superior in numbers, and helped by all the advantages of the ground.

On 23 January 1944, the day after the Allied landings at Anzio, the British had to gain a firm foothold on the hills to the rear of the town and beachhead. Ordinary soldiers and very often junior officers thrown into a new area had no idea of the strategy of the operation and little comprehension of the tactics.

They knew simply that they had to attack a hill, a ridgeline, a bridge, building, village or wood. One soldier who, single-handed, achieved much but did not live to see the results was Private George Mitchell of The London Scottish. Mitchell's courage and determination can only be wondered at, but just as significant is how he assumed command of a leaderless platoon and, through his example, inspired it to achieve extraordinary results. To survive a maelstrom of German machine-guns, rifles and grenades only to be killed by the cowardly act of a German who had surrendered, was outrageous. The German was justifiably shot by one of Mitchell's comrades. George Mitchell is buried in the Commonwealth War Graves Commission Minturno War Cemetery overlooking the Garigliano River and Damiano Mountains, which he had done so much to capture.

CHAPTER 28

THE ONES THAT GOT AWAY

THE nineteen Victoria Crosses won by The Gordon Highlanders form a commendable and distinguished total. As in every regiment there were occasions when Gordon Highlanders carried out acts that were worthy of the Victoria Cross, but of which those in command were not aware. Some were recommended for the Victoria Cross but the Awards Committee did not feel that their actions were sufficiently unique or outstanding. Some Gordon Highlanders were recommended for the Victoria Cross but were not awarded the decoration for reasons that appear arbitrary and on occasions spurious.[1] Some performed heroic acts that were not witnessed by anyone who could have written a citation.

Too senior

Hugh Henry Rose (illustration), later Field Marshal Lord Strathnairn, was present at the Alma and Inkerman, and his bravery earned the admiration of the Russians themselves. He was recommended for the recently instituted Victoria Cross, but the proposal was turned down on the grounds that, being a Brigadier, he held too high a rank to be given the award.

---

1   After Dargai, in addition to the Victoria Crosses awarded to Piper Findlater and Pte Lawson, the Commanding Officer, Lt-Col Mathias, was recommended for the award. Sir William Lockhart's Despatch recorded '. . . the gallant conduct of Lieut.-Colonel Mathias, C.B., in leading his battalion to the assault of a most difficult position at a critical period of the fight when previous attempts had failed. . . . I recommend this officer for the Victoria Cross.' However, it having been decided by the War Office that neither general officers nor officers commanding battalions were eligible for the Victoria Cross, Colonel Mathias did not receive it.

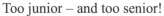

Too junior – and too senior!

Ian Hamilton was twice recommended for the Victoria Cross: first for Majuba, 1881—disallowed because he was too young, 'and would have plenty more chances'; then for Elandslaagte in 1899—disallowed because he was 'too senior—he was commanding a brigade'.

No-one witnessed it

Decorations awarded are well-deserved, but many instances of gallant conduct, which should have been rewarded with a decoration, go unnoticed. Soldiers accept this, but can be forgiven for feelings of regret and disappointment when bravery that they have witnessed is not appropriately recognised. A Royal Artillery officer wrote about an incident during the British advance north from the Somme in September 1918:

> On the road to Wassigny an incident worth noting was at a place where we passed below a railway. Evidently the Germans had been taken by surprise here, for a good few casualties were lying round about, both our own and the Germans. I have never heard a dead man cheered before, but this actually happened at this spot, for lying on a grassy part just off the road was a Gordon Highlander surrounded by five Germans. To look on those bodies and the position each was lying in, passers-by could not but imagine that the Gay Gordon had made great use of his bayonet but was caught by a sniper in the act of trying to account for a sixth German, for a bullet in the temple had ended his career. To see and pass a scene like this made the British patriotism rise, and we fellows of the RFA cheered a dead hero. An action fit for a V.C.

T&S, February/March 1971.

Second best?

There was a strict policy of 'rationing' awards, and brigades and divisions were given an allocation to be awarded as the commander decided. The recommendations inevitably outnumbered the allocation, and many highly deserving actions went unrewarded. Recommendations were often downgraded, with a lesser decoration being awarded in lieu. In this case, the Distinguished Conduct Medal, a prestigious decoration in its own right, was awarded instead of the Victoria Cross:

1944 – 5th/7th Gordons, V.C. recommendation

The Gordons pressed forward and were soon across the river. In the houses on the further side, however, S.S. troops offered a determined resistance and progress was slow. It was here that Private Redican proved his worth. His platoon were in an awkward position and at a critical moment he opened covering fire with his Bren gun, keeping it in action after being wounded in both legs. He was recommended for the Victoria Cross and eventually received the Distinguished Conduct Medal.

The Life of a Regiment, Volume V, p 289.

Private Redican's citation, approved by General Montgomery, enlarges on the account in *The Life of a Regiment*. Giving further proof of a resourceful, determined and extremely courageous young man, it reads:

In Lisieux on 22 Aug 44, 'C' Coy, 5/7th Bn. The Gordon Highlanders were holding the line of a street. They were ordered to send forward a patrol to the line of the railway which was held by enemy S.S. troops. When the patrol had reached the objective, the enemy opened up at point-blank range with spandaus and with grenades under intense fire half the patrol managed to reach a ruin. The enemy fire then increased in violence and movement towards the objective seemed quite impossible.

At this stage, Pte. Redican, entirely on his own initiative, seized a Bren gun and leapt into the open under a hail of enemy fire. Standing up completely exposed to the enemy he started firing at them from the hip, burst for burst. Very shortly he was hit in both legs. He fell to the ground but again seizing his Bren, he reloaded and continued firing although seriously wounded and in great pain.

This great act of gallantry drew the attention of the enemy on him and him alone. Taking advantage of it, the remainder of the patrol moved to a flank and neutralised the enemy's fire. Pte. Redican's heroism and utter contempt for death could not have been surpassed and undoubtedly saved the lives of his comrades.

The one that got away

Major Ivan Lyon[2] (photo) was awarded the D.S.O. for Operation *Jaywick*,[3] which he commanded and led. Many thought that this should have

been the Victoria Cross, for which he was recommended by two separate influential people, John Curtin: Prime Minister of Australia; and Lord Selborne, Minister of Economic Warfare in the British Government and the head of the Special Operations Executive. Lord Selborne wrote to Ivan Lyon's father:

> 'I tried to get your son the V.C. Colonel Lyon richly deserved to have received [it] . . . he was absolutely fearless.'

The recommendations were turned down because the Awards Committee did not feel that the action was deserving of such an honour. The same committee had no hesitation in awarding two V.C.s to the crews of midget submarines which attacked and crippled the German pocket battleship *Tirpitz*, a comparable exploit, although one carried out with far more sophisticated and effective equipment than that used by Ivan Lyon's party. It is interesting to speculate on what would have happened to a recommendation supported by the Prime Minister of Great Britain, Winston Churchill, and a senior member of his cabinet; say Lord Beaverbrook. It is hard to imagine such a recommendation being turned down! Little wonder that The Gordon Highlanders regarded this Victoria Cross, denied to one of their greatest heroes, as 'the one that got away'.

---

2   Ivan Lyon was a distant relative of Lt A.P.F. Lyon, who was killed at Bertry in 1914.
3   The attack on Singapore Harbour in 1943 that sank seven ships with a total gross tonnage of over 30,000 tons, using limpet mines placed by raiders in canoes. See Chapter 40.

SECTION 13

THE BACKBONE OF THE REGIMENT

THE character and reputation of a regiment are formed by the warrant officers, non-commissioned officers and men. Officers can provide leadership, inspiration and example, but it is the acts of the men in the ranks that determine how a regiment will perform. The reputation for excellence that The Gordon Highlanders gained was due in large part to the manner in which its soldiers responded to their officers and fought with great courage on every battlefield. Magnanimous in victory, unbowed in defeat, caring and compassionate to non-combatants, they were worthy representatives of the Highlands and north-east of Scotland from whence they sprang. They were the real backbone of the Regiment.

CHAPTER 29

THE MAGNIFICENT MEN THAT YOU GET FROM SCOTLAND

THE men who fought in India and in the Napoleonic Wars were the sons and grandsons of men who had fought at Culloden. Highland traditions of courage, fellowship, courtesy to strangers and hospitality were second nature to them, and although courage was the quality most demanded of them in those years, the others were not forgotten.

Patriotic contribution of the 75th

The 75th in India, facing an enemy that could destroy an East India Company army that included British regiments, was concerned enough about events in Europe that its soldiers (and officers) made a remarkable gesture of support for the British government and their comrades in arms:

> To—Lieut. Alexr. McCall, adj 75th Reg. Bombay
>
> Sir,
> We the non Commd Officers & Privates of the 75th Rt (with deference to your opinion as to the propriety of it) request the favour of your presenting the enclosed to Col Hart.
> We beg leave to be Sir, with respect
> Your obidt humble servs
>
> (Signed on behalf of non Comd officers & Privates of the 75th Reg)
>
> June 24 1798   D. McIntosh, Sgt Major
>
> To—Col. Sir G. Naughton Bt
>
> Sir.
> We, the non Commd Officers & Privates of the 75th Regt, animated with a wish to certify our fidelity & attachment to our Sovereign & anxiously concerned for the security of that Govert by which we are not only supported but enjoy so many blessings, & considering ourselves at all times in defending it, but being from our situation removed from our Mother Country where, at this arduous crisis our Personal Service might be useful, with the most respectful deference to your opinion propose a months gratuity from each rank as a donation towards the support of the war in which we are engaged.
> We beg leave to be
> Your most obid humble sevts
>
> Bombay June 24 1798   Signed as above

The Officers of the 75th Regt, sensible of that spirit & loyalty which the non Comd officers & Privates have so well expressed in their letter to Col Hart, are happy to follow the example by subscribing for the same purpose a months pay.

For the Officers,

G. V. Hart Col., Comd 75 Reg.

Glimpses of the men who established the reputation of The Gordon Highlanders appear in the pages of *The Life of a Regiment*:

> Many feats of individual bravery were performed [at Aboukir Bay, 1801], and long remembered. It is still told in Lochaber how Donald Cameron, a man remarkable for his great strength, was attacked by a French dragoon, when Donald, carrying the Frenchman's blow, transfixed him with his bayonet, and lifting him from the saddle threw him over his shoulder among his comrades, crying, '*Sin agibh fhearaibh, spéic a dh'Abercromby!*' ('There, men, is a blow for Abercromby!'). Donald, when he left the Regiment, was often visited by the Duke of Gordon (who, as Marquis of Huntly, had been his colonel) when passing through his Lochaber estates, and would press on his old commander the best his cottage afforded, treating him with the respectful familiarity characteristic of the old-fashioned Highlander. Donald Mor Og[1] came of a fighting family. His father, Donald Mor Cameron, carried Lochiel's standard at Prestonpans. In crossing the moss then existing there, at the beginning of the action, the men got out of order, and Lochiel ordered them to halt and dress their ranks, when Donald Mor cried, '*An Diabhul "halt" na "dress" bhios an so an diugh; leigibh leisna daoine dol air an aghairt f'had s'tha iad blath!*' '*Gum beannachadh Dia thu,*' answered Lochiel, '*biodhmar a thathu agradh!*' 'The devil a "halt" or "dress" will there be today; let the men go on while their blood is up.' 'God bless you, let it be as you say,' and the clan rushed on to victory.

The Life of a Regiment, Volume I, p 83.

> Among the wounded [at Mandora] was McKinnon the bard. Sergeant MacLean, a friend and admirer of the poet, found him insensible, but seeing that he still breathed, had him conveyed on board ship, where he recovered and composed two poems, one describing the landing in Egypt, the other the battles of the 13th and 21st of March, which are still the admiration of the lovers of Gaelic poetry.
> Corporal Alexander McKinnon the bard was born in 1770 in Morar, and enlisted in the Gordon Highlanders in 1794. He was 5 feet 10 inches,

---

1 *Mor* is Gaelic for 'big' or 'large', while *Og* is Gaelic for 'young'. Thus 'Donald Mor Og' is literally 'Donald Big Young' or colloquially 'Big Donald the Younger'.

and a man of great strength, amiable disposition, and a very good Gaelic scholar. When he composed a song or poem he would repeat it to his comrades for their approval of his description of the incidents. His songs were sung by the Gordons in many a bivouac and barrack, and did much to keep up the traditions and *esprit de corps*. They are still repeated in the West Highlands.

The Life of a Regiment, Volume I, p 96.

The British musket of the Napoleonic Wars was the latest version of the 'Brown Bess' (used from 1720 until 1853, when a rifled percussion-cap musket was introduced). The Napoleonic Wars musket was introduced in 1797. A trained soldier could fire three shots a minute while less experienced troops averaged two. The effective range was 80–100 yards, but it was most effective under fifty yards when fired in volleys. It was not accurate, and it took an exceptional shot to hit a target over fifty yards. Private Norman Stewart was an exceptional shot, and a great character:

> Perhaps Private Norman Stewart summed up the performance of his comrades [at Egmont-op-Zee] as well as a more official dispatch, when he told an English enquirer, 'Ilka lad shot a shentleman to hersel.'

The Life of a Regiment, Volume I, p 60.

A pensioner of the 92nd used to tell of two men of such bad character that none of their comrades would speak to them, who deserted to the enemy. One of these men found himself in the front rank of a French battalion, within hail of the 92nd; the French, not trusting deserters, placed them in front, where, not daring to be taken, they were bound to fight. The regiment had lately been served out with hose tartan; the deserter, in bravado, stuck on his bayonet the piece of red and white cloth, and impudently waved it at his old corps. The colonel's attention being drawn to it, turning to the men he said—'Will some one send a pill with my compliments to cure that scoundrel's impertinence!' Norman Stewart and another crack shot knelt and fired, the 'pill' went home, and the deserter's flag was lowered for ever.

The Life of a Regiment, Volume I, p 248.

At the desperate defence of Alba de Tormes in 1812, Norman Stewart played his part with typical confidence and daring:

> While the 92nd were lining the wall, and exchanging shots with the French skirmishers, who were firing briskly, Private Norman Stewart, an extraordinarily good shot who was separated by some little way from his comrades, placed his bonnet on a stone to look as if it was still on his

head, which, however, he carried to a safe distance; and proceeded to fire at the enemy with his 'Brown Bess,' which he lovingly called his 'wife', and if a Frenchman advanced nearer than he liked, would say, '*Dia, mar dean thu* "halt" *gheibh thu pog o m'bhean*' ('By G—d, if you'll no' halt, you'll get a kiss o' my "wife" '). When the French retired Norman took up his bonnet, which was a hopeless wreck; he tried it on amidst the laughter of his comrades, which attracted the attention of Colonel Cameron, who scolded him for destroying his necessaries; but, hearing how it happened, gave him a kindly clap on the shoulder, saying in Gaelic that he would give him a new bonnet—'Aye, or two if you want them.'

The Life of a Regiment, Volume I, pp 255–6.

Norman Stewart's luck finally ran out during the fierce fight at the Pass of Maya in 1813, when The Gordon Highlanders won undying fame for their dogged stand against overwhelming odds:

Among the veterans who died at Maya was Private Norman Stewart, the best shot in the battalion, with which he had served in all its many fights. He was a favourite both with his officers and fellow soldiers, a great character, and, as one of his old comrades said, 'had not as much English as would put the pot on the fire.' When an officer complimented him on his soldier-like behaviour in his first engagement [at Egmont-op-Zee], implying, however, that he had hardly expected it, Norman replied, '*Cha'n 'eil fhios de'n claidheamh a bhios 's an truaill gus an tairnear e*' (It is not known what sword is in the scabbard till it is drawn). He did not like his first musket, because it kicked, and because it was a 'widow,' for its former owner had died; but when he got a new one he called it his 'wife,' and woe betide the French skirmisher who came within reach of her kiss!

The Life of a Regiment, Volume I, p 298.

Gordon Highlanders showed devotion to duty, and to their comrades, refusing to leave the battlefield when wounded. Many of those paid the ultimate price for their loyalty:

An order was issued early [on] the 30th [July 1813] for all men who could not keep up with their Battalion to be sent to the baggage. He selected three from his company; two went with apparent goodwill, but William Dougald respectfully told him he would rather die than leave his comrades. He had been hit three times by spent bullets on the 25th, and though not much minded at the time, the wounds had become so inflamed by subsequent exertion that on the 30th he could scarcely drag his right leg after him. 'I shall never forget the exertions he made to keep up with his companions, and the admirable manner in which he performed his duty in action till stretched a lifeless corpse on the heights of La Zarza.'

John Brookes, one of the two who quitted the company agreeable to order, had been struck by a musket ball on the 25th; it had been turned aside by his leather-stock, but his throat became so inflamed that by the 30th he could hardly speak. The brave fellow having obeyed orders with apparent alacrity, his officer was astonished, on going into action, to see him only a few paces in rear on his way to rejoin his company, but had no time to take notice of his disobedience at the moment; and Brookes conducted himself with his usual spirit and gallantry, till another bullet struck him on the same place and killed him on the spot. The third man, Hugh Johnstone, had rejoined the company along with Brookes, and soon after was very severely wounded. He was carried to the rear, but subsequent movements placed him in the enemy's hands, where he remained without medical aid till the French retreated next day, when his master sent a party to carry him to La Zarza. They attended to him, but he was exhausted from loss of blood, and expired in his comrades' arms, with a smile on his countenance. 'Such was the premature fate of as good a soldier and faithful servant as ever graced the ranks of the British army.'

The Life of a Regiment, Volume I, pp 304–5.

The British Government was never generous when it came to paying its soldiers. As a British regiment serving in India, the 75th was administered by the Honorable East India Company. It was unusual for soldiers to refuse extra pay, particularly after the unsuccessful siege of Bhurtpore in 1805, which had proved so costly to the 75th in men lost:

The zeal and cheerfulness which animated the Highlanders is shown by a regimental order issued by Major Archibald Campbell dated 'Camp before Bhurtpore, 13 February 1805':

R.O.—The Commanding Officer listened with much satisfaction to the very handsome declaration of the men of the 75th who declined receiving any payment for working in the trenches, but as that duty has been required of them oftener than he expected, and as the other European corps are in the habit of being paid for it, he has also directed that it should be drawn for the men of this regiment, whose willing and regular behaviour at all times entitles them to every indulgence, and is exceedingly creditable to themselves.

The Life of a Regiment, Volume II, p 202.

The men of the 92nd (and all the Highland regiments) did not fit the common perception of a 'brutal and licentious soldiery' wallowing in drinking, gambling and debauchery. While this view was jaundiced and exaggerated, it had some basis in fact. Highlanders, whose reasons for joining the Army—loyalty to clan, chieftain, local area and family—differed greatly from what brought other men into the Army, so often displayed a moderation and prudent consideration lacking in their military peers:

> The Highlanders did not forget the old folks at home. When there were neither savings banks nor postal orders it was not easy for a soldier to send money. According to Sergeant Robertson, most Gordon Highlanders belonged to the estates of their officers, and they seem to have entrusted to them, as their natural guardians and friends, the money they wished to send to their parents. In Captain Cameron's letters I find constant reference to this practice, mentioning the sums belonging to each man, with his name or the by-name by which he was distinguished at home from others of the same name—as '*Ewen dubh Tailear*,' '*Ewen dubh Coul*,' both men of the name of Ewen Cameron.

The Life of a Regiment, Volume I, p 79.

More than a century later the same characteristics could be found in men of The Gordon Highlanders serving in Ireland:

> The folk showed them the traditional Irish kindness and hospitality unless religion or politics stepped in. Indeed, the old kindly feeling towards the Scot, perhaps particularly to the Highlander, was often manifest during this tour of service. When leaving Cork an officer writes: 'Many of the people expressed their great regret at losing us, who had behaved so well during our three years' stay; "we are sorry to be losing such gentlemen."' Similar testimony from the post office just outside barracks: 'Bedad,' said the Postmaster, 'they are the best ever I see in Cork! I do more in the Savings Bank on one pay night than in six months with any other Regiment.'

The Life of a Regiment, Volume III, p 346.

That the men of the 92nd were Highlanders, aware of a history that was often portrayed as romantic but also tragic, is clear from their reaction on coming across links with a past that was still recent enough for them personally to know men who had taken part:

> On the 29th October [1815] the encampment on the banks of the Seine was broken up, and the regiment marched to St Germains, where they were billeted. Here they were able to visit the Palace in which they were led to understand that Prince Charles Stuart had died. Lieutenant Innis [probably Lieutenant Hector Innes], in a letter to his mother, says: 'Many of our Highlanders were greatly affected on entering the chamber where

their Prince died.' But it was not, however, really 'Bonnie Prince Charlie' who died there, but his grandfather, James II (VII of Scotland). The incident, however, shows how fresh the memory of the '45 remained in the sentiment of many of the men, though they served King George III so loyally.

This sentiment was aptly expressed to George III, who, wishing to see one of those who had been out in the '45, a grim old McDonald from Knoydart, known as *Raonull Mor a' Chrolen*, was presented to His Majesty, who remarked that no doubt he regretted having taken part in the Rebellion. 'Sire,' promptly replied McDonald, 'I regret nothing of the kind'; but the King, who had been taken aback by this bold answer, was completely softened when the old man added, 'What I did for the Prince I would have done as heartily for your Majesty if you had been in the Prince's place.'

The Life of a Regiment, Volume I, p 388.

Promotion from the ranks was rare in the early days of the Regiment, but it was possible. Sergeant Graham, leading the Forlorn Hope at Seringapatam in 1799, having gained the top of the breach, fully expected to be rewarded with a commission, cried out 'Success to Ensign Graham' (the picture shows Graham, correctly dressed in the trousers that the 75th wore in India, but carrying the Union flag in its post-1803 form!) before falling dead, shot through the head. Sergeant Donald Ross, who plunged into the thick of the enemy on the ramparts and was wounded by eight sabre cuts, survived and was honoured with a commission. In the 19th century it was common for deserving senior N.C.O.s to be commissioned, to carry out  administrative duties as Quartermaster, but sometimes particularly able and deserving N.C.O.s acted as rifle company officers, leading soldiers[2]:

---

2   CSgt Hector MacDonald, after a particularly gallant action in Afghanistan in 1879, was reputedly offered either a Victoria Cross or a commission. He chose the commission, served as a company officer in the 92nd and went on to achieve the rank of Maj-Gen.

On the 14th November [1841], Sergeant-major Donald MacQueen was promoted Ensign in the 92nd. He became quartermaster, and finally retired on full pay with the rank of captain. He became tacksman of Blinkbonnie, on the Brodie estate, where 'the captain' was much respected, and often called upon to settle differences among neighbours. I spent a day with him there, and he told me that he had been herd on that very farm before he enlisted; he had also been 'look-out' for smugglers in the hills, before illicit distillation was put down; as soon as he was eighteen he walked off and enlisted with the nearest party of the 92nd. His account of his promotion was characteristic. One day Colonel MacDonald had been giving them the rough edge of his tongue at drill, and was afterwards standing with the adjutant in the square when Sergeant-major MacQueen passed. The colonel called him. 'I dare say,' he said, 'you think I was rather hard on you today, sergeant-major? There are some men that are not worth damning, but I'll make something of *you* yet!' When some time after, the colonel went to the Horse Guards and asked that one of three death vacancies should be given to a sergeant, he was told that they were already promised to others. He expostulated roundly, saying that those who had borne the rough should have a share of the smooth, and that if he could not reward deserving n.c. officers he would resign his command; it ended in the sergeant-major being gazetted senior of the three.

The Life of a Regiment, Volume II, pp 33–5.

The men of the 92nd in Afghanistan in 1879 were well-trained, experienced and proud Gordon Highlanders. The system allowed men who re-engaged at the end of their service to be drafted into other regiments. The men of the 92nd were not prepared to be arbitrarily sent away from their comrades and the regiment they loved:

On 14th February 1881, on being presented with the Freedom of the City of London and a sword of honour by the Corporation, Sir Frederick Roberts emphasised the advantage of having seasoned troops, and instanced the 92nd, whose sergeants averaged fifteen, corporals eleven, and privates nine years' service. He mentioned that between the first and second phases of the Afghan War some 150 men of the Regiment, whose period of service had expired, expressed readiness to re-engage on the express condition that they were not to be transferred to another regiment, according to the 'Brigade' system. The authorities allowed a special relaxation of the rule, with the result that these men, 'when every tried soldier was worth his weight in gold,' remained in the service.

The Life of a Regiment, Volume II, p 157.

James Ross (photo), whose letter describing the march to Kabul in 1879 appears in Volume IX, Chapter 15, typifies all that was best in the Gordon Highlander. He served a full career in the 92nd before retiring back to Scotland, where he forged a successful second career. He appears in a photograph titled 'Sergeants of the 92nd Gordon Highlanders, Afghanistan, 1879' (*The Life of a Regiment*, Volume II, facing p 110) where he is shown as 'Sergeant-Major James Ross'. He was, in fact the most senior non-commissioned rank in the battalion.[3] We know more about him from a letter sent by his granddaughter to Regimental Headquarters. He was clearly a considerate, humane man who made a mark in his post-regimental life as Governor of a Reform School in Aberdeenshire:

8th June, 1979

My Dear Captain Lumsden,

I never knew my grandparents—my grandfather died in 1901 when my father was 16, and my grandmother in 1916, but I heard many tales of him. He was quite a character: strict but fair and I think had a 'soft centre'. He waxes quite poetic when he talks of the Delhi Princess Lala-Rook— and he seems to have had a sense of humour. After he retired he was Principal of a Reform School in Aberdeenshire where his ideas on how to deal with delinquent boys were years ahead of his contemporaries. He disapproved of flogging but it being the law had to superintend its administration, but he stood by the boy and talked to him gently while the punishment was meted out: one famous 'bad boy' was sent to this Establishment having set alight the training ship he had been sent to for correction (I cannot remember the name of the ship but it used to lie off Tayport).[4] Under my grandfather's guidance he reformed enough for my grandfather to persuade the CO of the time that he should join the

---

3   A non-commissioned rank of Sergeant Major, indicated by four chevrons surmounted by a crown, had existed from the early 19th century. Infantry battalions had one Sergeant Major until just before World War 1 when the introduction of the Company Sergeant Major led to the rank of 'Sergeant Major' becoming 'Regimental Sergeant Major'.

4   The ship referred to was HMS *Mars*. The author's great-grandfather served on *Mars* as a Petty Officer after he left the Royal Navy.

Regiment, where he conducted himself well! Some years after my grandfather's death he called on my grandmother in Dyce in full 'Regimentals' to pay his respects and stood in front of my grandfather's photograph with tears streaming down his face, saying 'If it hadna been for the Captain I'd have spent my life in gaol'.

My grandfather disagreed with the policies of the Aberdeenshire Civic worthies, and he resigned. As he left, the boys lined the drive and their pipe band led him off the premises!

I recall meeting one splendid old officer—a General Robertson I believe—who served with him. I was with my father watching the victory parade in 1945 from the steps of the Royal Scottish Academy in Princes Street in Edinburgh when my father introduced me to this old gentleman in a wheel-chair. He did not need to be reminded who my father was although it must have been years since they'd met—as my father was so very like his father. The general asked him what his boy (my brother) was doing and on being told that he was serving in the 8th Gurkhas was most disapproving that he had not gone into the Gordons, and when my father said that he didn't have private means, General Robertson said 'Nonsense! We didn't all have private means you know!'[5] My father retired abashed!

I hope you enjoy reading what it was like to be a soldier in the second half of the nineteenth century. I am sending his pay-book too for you to look at. Take great care of these 'treasures'

Yours sincerely,

Patricia Robinson (nee Ross)

James Ross was promoted Quartermaster, 2nd Battalion, Gordon Highlanders in 1882.

T&S, Autumn 1979.

Scottish soldiers in the 20th century were universally known as 'Jocks'. This was not always so for Highland soldiers:

Although the number of Highlanders in the 92nd was certainly as great as in any Regiment, there is indirect evidence of the preponderance of Lowlanders, in the essentially lowland sobriquet 'Jock' (a word entirely unknown among the Gaelic people) in place of 'Donald' or 'Her nainsel,' the familiar appellations of Highland soldiers.

The Life of a Regiment, Volume II, p 181.

---

5   Lt-Col William Robertson, V.C., who died in 1949. After winning the V.C. at Elandslaagte in 1899 as Sgt-Maj, he was commissioned and rose to Lt-Col—without private means.

Gordon Highlanders had a 'good conceit o' themselves', and did not take kindly to suggestions that they might avoid the enemy, as the following exchange between a Gordon and a General illustrates:

On the 13th the General [Smith-Dorrien] paid a visit to the cheery wounded in hospital: among others to Private Doherty, reservist. 'Splendid fellow, has distinguished himself in every action', says Captain Allan. To Smith-Dorrien's encomiums on the conduct of the troops, Doherty shook a doubtful head: 'Aye, we may hae dune weel eneuch, but I dinna haud wi' yon rinnin' awa'.' 'Running away?' exclaimed the startled General, 'we didn't run away, we *retired* by order of the C-in-C!' 'Aye, sir, *you'll* maybe call it *retirin'* but *I* ca' it *rinnin' awa'*!'[6]

The Life of a Regiment, Volume III, pp 222.

Gordon Highlanders have always shown themselves ready to take advantage of any situation, particularly when food and personal comfort are involved. In the Boer War they were only too ready to grasp any opportunity that presented itself, as this example from the 2nd Battalion demonstrates:

Late in the evening they bivouacked close to Amersfoort, a poor village of fifty houses. The wagons did not arrive; the men had but a cardigan to reinforce their thin jacket; the night was bitterly cold and though fatigue parties brought up wood from the town, few got sleep.

The night is very clearly stamped on the memory of the 2nd Battalion veterans. Wherever two or three such are gathered there will be told the tale of how Corporal Angus bagged the General's blankets! To men of all corps, huddled round the poor fires or tramping up and down in vain effort to keep warm; hungry—for no supplies arrived till noon next day—the dark village proved an irresistible attraction. One might find a bush or a wall to keep off the icy wind, or even a stable with a sack or two—and why wouldn't one get a lie-down if one could? Corporal Angus was ambitious. He reconnoitred a fine house with lights and a stair on one side but with a dark window or two the other; he found an empty room with bed and bedding: he nipped off with all the blankets, curled himself up somewhere and slept serenely. The rest is legend.

Any General whose blankets thus vanished would be annoyed; the higher the General, the greater, I suppose, should be his wrath. Legend says that at first this wrath was beyond adjectives but that an interval

---

6   Doherty won the D.C.M. at Leehoehoek, where he carried a wounded gunner officer to safety, helped two others, and took part in the attempt to bring in the guns. He joined the Gordons in 1883, was with the 1st Battalion on the 1884 Nile Expedition and was discharged in 1891. He volunteered for South Africa in 1899. Discharged in 1906, he rejoined the Gordons in 1914. He was discharged as too old for service abroad, but went to sea as a deckhand on a minesweeper. He died in 1930.

elapsing before his camp commandant could point the finger of accusation at a particular corps, the General merely shook his big fist at the corps and did not try to smite the individual.

The Life of a Regiment, Volume III, p 198.

Gaelic has always been a source of confusion to those not familiar with it. From the belief that the Gaelic-speaking Highlanders were Irish to the assumption that they came from even further afield, the English in particular found it aurally confusing and somewhat 'foreign':

> Just at the end of the Aldershot tour the 2nd Division was mobilised to war strength, reservists were called up, large drafts furnished by the Militia battalions, horses brought in from every- or any-where. In the 1st battalion a very large proportion of the militiamen were West Coast Highlanders who spoke Gaelic among themselves; one evening a Staff Officer was visiting the bivouac and, hearing the men talking an apparently foreign-language, said to an officer: 'Who are these foreigners?' To which the officer replied: 'His Majesty's subjects from the West Highlands and Hebrides.'

The Life of a Regiment, Volume III, p 352.

If the men were the backbone of the Regiment, the non-commissioned officers and warrant officers were the cord that gave strength to the backbone, animated it and guided it. The following incident illustrating how a sergeant took the initiative and held the line took place during the Battle of the Somme:

> On the right the 12th Highland Light Infantry suffered very heavily while forming up, and failed in its assault. Two platoons of the 9th Gordons [Pioneer] were to dig two communication trenches begun by the explosion of a line of pipes or tubes. The right platoon was commanded by Sergeant G. Henderson, 'admirably commanded', as the report afterwards put it. Almost immediately after the waves of the assault had gone by men began to come back. Sergeant Henderson strongly suspected that the so-called Switch Line in front had not been taken. He therefore kept his men as far as possible under cover but gradually deepened the new trench. When it had reached a point within thirty yards of the German front line a machine-gun opened fire straight in front. This confirmed his view that the assault had not got in, so he prolonged the trench no further. To have finished it properly he would have had to get men extended on the surface. He did not do this, but deepened the trench to five feet in case it should be wanted later. Then he took his platoon to the empty British trench, manned the parapet, stopped all stragglers who came through, and

made them do likewise. He remained until 6 a.m. when a relieving battalion appeared.

This is a small incident, which does not find a mention in the history of the 15th Division, but seems worthy of description in that of the Gordon Highlanders. It shows how, where circumstances so often seem to control men rather than men circumstances, a sergeant who used his head could save lives while carrying out his orders to the extent that they remained practical. Sergeant Henderson was awarded the Military Medal and at a later date an Italian decoration.

The Life of a Regiment, Volume IV, pp 95–6.

National stereotypes were not affected by the carnage of the Great War, as this extract from the *London Evening News* shows!

I saw him on March 2nd, 1916, when we regained 'The Bluff', after attacks and counter-attacks which had been going on since February 14th. He was a Gordon Highlander making his way from the newly won position to the dressing station.

His left arm was badly hurt, a tourniquet consisting of one of his puttees had been applied, and with his right hand he was supporting the injured member. A clay pipe was in his mouth and a broad smile wreathed his face.

Jerry was showing his resentment at losing the 'rubber' by shelling the reserve line pretty heavily, and so Jock paused for a moment at my gun position which, dug well into the canal bank, offered a little shelter.

I asked him to stay until the stretcher-bearers came along. He replied: 'No, thank-ye, but I'll tak' a licht for my pipe. I've been out since Mons and been hit three times, but this is the first time I've had a Blighty, and I'm waiting for no d— stretcher-bearers.'

I remarked: 'Well, you have got a Blighty one this time, Jock.'

'Ay, mon,' Jock said, 'I'll lose my arm, but I come from Aiberdeen, and I'll do fine at the Kirk. They like one-armed men for takin' the collection.'

I gave Jock a light for his pipe and he went on his way.

T&S, January 1932.

Morale is often kept high, not necessarily through positive action by commanders, but by the refusal of private soldiers to let circumstances or their environment get them down:

A story told in the diary of the 6th Gordons may not be an example of the brightest type of humour, but it stands for a fortitude which staggers the mind. Marching back in the dark, and needless to say in rain, one man fell into a shell-hole full of water. 'He immediately commenced to quack like a duck, and the remainder of the platoon, following his example, quacked their way contentedly back to camp.'

The Life of a Regiment, Volume IV, pp 157–8.

This little tale, which shows the Gordon Highlander's ability to rise above appalling conditions with a ready quip, brings to mind the response of the platoon commanded by Lieutenant Clive Lyon in Borneo in 1965. After undergoing extensive and arduous jungle training before its first operational tour, the platoon was returning to camp led by the dignified, upright figure of their moustached platoon commander, who strode on, steadfastly ignoring his soldiers as they sang out the words of a popular song of the day,

'In the jungle, the mighty jungle, the lion sleeps tonight!'

Many Gordon Highlanders suffered wounds, both physical and mental, in the First World War. After the war most got on with their lives, in the Regiment or as civilians, but for some the effects of the war lasted for many years. Some had fought through the Boer War as well as the First War. The following is from the pensions column of the *Edinburgh Evening News*:

T.P. served in the Gordon Highlanders during the South African War, and was severely wounded. He was discharged pensioned, and re-joined during the late war. On his discharge he complained on numerous occasions of pains in his head, and on claiming to have his pre-war pension assessed on the same grounds as men disabled during the late war, he was informed that probably his stomach was out of order, which accounted for the head trouble. Up to the middle of last month, the pains became so severe that the man went and got examined at the Edinburgh Royal Infirmary, where he was X rayed. He was afterwards operated on, and a portion of a bullet was removed from the back of his head, where it had remained for 29 years.

T&S, September 1929.

Even after leaving the Army and settling into civilian life, Gordon Highlanders recalled to the colours brought with them the experience and camaraderie of years of service, as recalled by Major R.A.N. Ogilvie:

The following morning I was sent by rail to the Regimental Depot at Bridge of Don with a party of 30 N.C.O.s and young soldiers for the training cadre, with one sergeant to assist me in bringing back a draft of Reservists for the Battalion. We arrived at Aberdeen Station some 24 hours later—at 11.15 on the morning of Sunday, 3rd September [1939]. The first news to greet us was that we had declared war on Germany 15 minutes earlier. We marched the three miles to Gordon Barracks through deserted streets—Sunday morning in Aberdeen!

The Depot was a seething mass of men! Every square yard of the Parade Ground was packed—men awaiting kit, men with kit—the Depot was a beehive of activity, and coping well. The call-up was designed to bring reservists to the Colours in batches, so that they could be documented, medically inspected, kitted-out, and drafted in a simple operation. The Gordons' reservists had not waited for their call-up papers. They had all just reported in when they heard mobilisation announced on the wireless, determined to be back in the Regiment as quickly as possible! The sight was heart warming and very encouraging.

I took over the draft for the Battalion that afternoon—199 noisy, happy, exuberant reservists, impatient to be on their way! Behind the Depot pipers we marched to Aberdeen Station, pavements crowded all the way, the column 'cheered to the echo'! With myself at the head and my sergeant at the tail, I felt as if I owned the lot—I had only been commissioned for two months!

I got to know these reservists well, and my platoon was made up mostly of reservists. They were marvellous soldiers, as totally loyal and keen as any platoon commander could wish for, with an element, once trained to new ways and weapons, of excellent, steady N.C.O.s and men, true Gordons to the last drop of their north-east blood and Buchan tongue! They spent their evenings and spare time dismantling and reassembling newfangled Bren guns, competing one with another on the time taken.

From them I learned a new language—Scottish Urdu! They had, almost to a man, seen service in India on the North West Frontier. Breakfast started it—with *burgoo*, *char* and *chapattis*; dirty clothes went to the *dhobi-walla*; they talked of Landikotal, Rawalpindi and the Khyber! They were the salt of the earth.

T&S, 1990.

Gordon Highlanders found it easy to get on with locals. They did not abuse them, exploit them or patronise them, and they formed a particular rapport with children. The following example took place in 1943:

In Castiglione the 5th/7th were particularly comfortable, with running water and electric light at their disposal and a cinema to enjoy. Italian soldiery, some in civilian clothes, continued to come in, all of them war weary. The needs of the inhabitants were soon relieved by an official food distribution; meanwhile, the Jocks had been only too willing to sacrifice half their rations so that the children should not go hungry.

The Life of a Regiment, Volume V, p 216.

Peace-time soldiering in Germany after the Second World War gave little opportunity for Gordon Highlanders to display the courage of their war-time predecessors, but when the occasion arose, that courage was readily apparent:

The Commander-in-Chief, British Army of the Rhine, issued the following commendation for bravery for Lance Corporal David Allen:

During Exercise *Lorelei*, on 19 May, 1969, a farm in the village of Luerdissen was used as the location of a petrol replenishment point.

It was to this farm that Lance Corporal Allen drove his empty 600-gallon petrol tanker, accompanied in convoy by two other petrol tankers, one of which was partly full, and two empty petrol Stalwarts.

At the farm they were to meet and refuel their tankers from a 5,000-gallon petrol tanker. On arrival, this tanker was not there, so the five tankers parked alongside the barn and trees which enclosed the farm yard, which measured approximately 35 yards by 20 yards. Lance Corporal Allen parked his tanker near to an empty one, and the one that was partly full. The farmhouse was some 15 yards from his tanker.

After they had been in the farm yard for about 45 minutes, the RCT 5,000-gallon tanker full of civgas arrived to replenish the five tankers. It parked alongside the trees, opposite and about 25 yards from Allen's vehicle. An empty Stalwart then drew alongside it to take on fuel.

Lance Corporal Allen prepared his vehicle to transfer fuel from the large tanker. As is normal in turning the valve controls to take on fuel, a small spillage of about three pints of petrol escaped onto the ground. Suddenly the fire alarm was raised, and Lance Corporal Allen saw that this petrol spillage had been ignited. He immediately tackled the fire on his own but was unable to put the fire out. The flames spread rapidly to the valve controls at the rear of his vehicle and to the rear tyres.

Realising the danger of an explosion in his own tanker, which in turn might ignite the partly full tanker alongside or cause a further explosion in the empty tanker also near his vehicle, and the danger to the 5,000-gallon tanker then re-fuelling the Stalwart about 25 yards away, without hesitation he drove his flaming vehicle away from the fire and other tankers for some 70 yards into an orchard where he was stopped by a fence. With extinguishers brought to him by the other drivers he then managed to put out the fire in his own vehicle.

Lance Corporal Allen's disregard for his own safety from the start of the fire until it was brought under control and his presence of mind in driving the tanker away, avoided a serious explosion or series of explosions which would have caused untold damage to the farm, its occupants, the other seven soldiers in the area, and the other tankers.

The Life of a Regiment, Volume VI, pp 157–8.

The threat of death, in numerous unpleasant forms, was ever-present in Northern Ireland. On many occasions the person directly faced with the threat, and who had to deal with it, was a private soldier. On his training, calmness, presence of mind and readiness to act rested whether anyone would suffer or not:

Private J L Watson was on duty at the Main Gate, checking vehicles into the barracks. A green Ford Escort drew up on the other side of the dual carriageway, waiting for a break in the traffic before crossing over and entering the Main Gate. It was waved into the search bay while Watson went to check the driver's credentials.

The driver, a workman in the barracks, seemed uneasy and, contrary to normal procedure, wanted to collect his pass without having his car searched. Watson refused to allow this and instructed the driver to open the bonnet of the car. As Watson was searching the engine compartment the man grew agitated and asked to speak to him. There he told the sentry that a bomb had been placed in the boot of his car and that his family was being held hostage by armed terrorists. They had threatened to shoot his wife and children if he did not take his car to Palace Barracks and park it next to the Officers Mess.

Shouting out a bomb warning to the gate sentry, Watson ordered the man to get back into the car and to drive it out of the barracks. The man, patently terrified, steadfastly refused to do so. Here was a major dilemma. The driver appeared to be an innocent civilian, forced to carry a bomb by the threat of force against his family, and refusing to drive his car with its bomb out of the barracks. How could Watson make him do so against his will? On the other hand, if the car were not moved it would cause major damage to buildings, including nearby married quarters, and might kill and injure many people.

By this time the Guard Commander had alerted the Security Platoon and sounded the general alarm. He sent some members of the Guard out on to the road to halt the traffic, until the Security Platoon deployed out of the side gates on to the main road.

Watson resolved his dilemma very quickly. Faced with an apparent impasse he drew his pistol, cocked it and pointed it at the driver, saying, 'The IRA won't hurt your family—you've done your bit. But I'll bloody well shoot you if you don't get in that car and drive it across the road!' The driver looked at the pistol, black and menacing in the unwavering hand that pointed it at his head, then looked into the cold, implacable eyes that stared unblinkingly at him and came to his own decision. With a stifled sob he jumped back into the car, started the engine and reversed gingerly out of the gates.

To ensure that he carried out the instructions, Watson, aware that the bomb could explode at any moment, escorted the driver across the road towards waste ground on the far side of the dual carriageway. Once across the carriageway he tried to open a gate to the waste ground so that the car could be driven further away from the barracks and quarters area. The gate was padlocked, so Watson calmly ordered the driver out of the car and led him back across the road to the shelter of the barracks.

Inside the barracks everyone in the immediate area was evacuated and moved to a safer area, except for the sentries protecting the Main Gate from behind a blast shelter. The Operations Officer called for an ATO team and a team was on its way. It was too late, however, because some seven minutes after the car was driven on to the waste ground the bomb exploded (photo). Apart from a few shattered windows there was no damage inside the barracks and no-one was hurt. The driver was questioned by the RUC and then returned to his family.

The IRA had failed to cause death and destruction among the Gordons thanks to the alertness, courage and presence of mind of Private James Watson,[7] whose cool action had saved lives and prevented extensive damage to property. It was a vindication of the training and preparation that the Battalion had undergone before arriving in Belfast, and which it had maintained since.

Aftermath – the wrecked car after the bomb went off

---

7   Pte Watson was mentioned in despatches for this action.

Soldiers are used to discomfort, but it is how they bear it and react to it that defines how effective they really are:

> Colonel Graham visited his soldiers on the ground nearly every day throughout the tour. One Saturday afternoon, in the Falls Road, he noticed a young soldier, recently joined from the Training Depot. It was wet and miserable, with rain coming down in a steady downpour, and the young Jock was completely soaked. Going up to him, Colonel Graham chatted to him, and was soon satisfied that the new arrival was fully conversant with his duties and understood the hazards of operating in the Lower Falls. As he went to leave he remarked to the young Jock that he was sorry to see him so wet, and hoped he would get a chance to dry out. Without turning a hair the Jock replied in a broad Aberdeenshire accent, 'Ah weel, Sir, the rain only gaes skin deep', and went back to his task, as steady as a rock.

The Life of a Regiment, Volume VII, p 240.

The Gordon Highlanders understood soldiering. They knew that, on operations, their security rested on every man being alert at all times. No amount of training or experience would protect them if they let their attention wander, or their guard slip. In Belfast, in 1978:

> A sobering demonstration that the Gordons' standards had not slipped came when a patrol of 'B' Company was patrolling in the Cliftonville area. As they went down a road they covered, almost by second nature, a house that looked straight down the street. The Jocks ran in pairs to their next position, one man covering the windows of the house with his raised rifle. It was clear to any watcher that the house would come under immediate fire from the Gordons if anyone fired from it. That was standard procedure for all Gordon patrols.
>
> A few minutes later a patrol from the City Centre unit came down the same street. To the gunmen who had held their fire when the Gordons passed this appeared an easier target. They did not anticipate an immediate response against their position, and opened fire with an M60 machine-gun. A Gunner died in a hail of bullets. It was later confirmed that the gunmen had waited patiently for an easy target. Without doubt the professionalism and aggressive patrolling of the Gordons had persuaded them not to fire at them, and had saved a life.

The Life of a Regiment, Volume VII, p 246.

The public face of The Gordon Highlanders was never more apparent than when on public duties, providing the guard at Edinburgh Castle. They stood, smart and erect, while tourists of every nationality had their photographs taken beside them, and answered questions, many naive and silly, with grace and good humour:

> Despite the chilly weather there was no shortage of visitors to the Castle, and the Jocks on sentry found themselves the centre of attraction. When asked by a member of the French Rugby team why he had to stand in front of a sentry box all day, Private George Murdoch replied without hesitation, 'In case someone steals it!' Private Murdie, when asked by an American tourist the meaning of the motto above the portcullis on the Main Gate of the Castle—'*Nemo Me Impune Lacessit*'—replied with a straight face, 'Keep this passageway clear.'

The Life of a Regiment, Volume VII, p 290.

Professionally, the Gordon Highlander soldier showed himself as good as, if not better, than most. He revelled in new challenges and rose to the occasion, whatever was demanded of him. In Germany, faced with developing a new, airmobile role, he was in his element:

> Throughout the four year trial the Jock remained the bedrock of the Battalion. Airmobile operations gave free rein to his imagination, ingenuity and initiative. Though he might appear at first sight slow of speech and thought compared to some of his more street-wise contemporaries, the North-East Jock had a tenacity and ruggedness which made him peculiarly fitted for independent operations in small groups. Training ensured that he got the basics right, and impartial observers often remarked how well he performed in this field. He was encouraged to think about his craft, that of the infantryman, and one of the most revealing comments about this period was that the Jocks were so well trained that the Battalion was made up of 'thinking companies'. The Jocks anticipated what was required of them without being told. Common sense was the order of the day, and the Jocks could be relied upon to select the correct positions when moving into defence so that the platoon commander, on coming round to site the platoon trenches, usually found that the Jocks had unconsciously adopted the very positions that he would have selected. Camouflaging of defensive positions, routine in defence, first aid to battle casualties, ammunition conservation during fire fights and replenishment afterwards, the use of grenades and the fixing of bayonets at the right moment, were all carried out as if by second nature. Former platoon commanders, with memories of how they had to harry NCOs and soldiers to get these points right, will appreciate how much simpler life would be in such a 'thinking company'.

The Life of a Regiment, Volume VII, pp 388–9.

When duty was over the Gordon Highlander was as keen as any to get back to barracks and go out on the town. His eagerness caused some concern to Her Majesty The Queen:

> The ponymen had their chance to come to grips with their ponies. Training had not been possible as the Head Ponyman, David Muir, had been on holiday. It was not long before Gordon Highlanders could be seen trotting and cantering on the slopes of Lochnagar and around Loch Muick.
>
> There was no let up in the pace, and the ponymen worked hard bringing the shot stags off the hills.
>
> The pony section worked six days a week from dawn to dusk, with Sundays as a rest day. The section was split into teams of three, a walking ghillie and two ponymen. There was a tackman who polished and cleaned saddles and equipment, and a larder-man who quickly had to assimilate the skills of butchery and worked full time in the game larder.
>
> The ponymen worked hard, and looked forward to the few hours off that they could manage in the evening after the ponies had been groomed, fed and watered. On one occasion a Jock, kept late on the hillside and anxious to get back as quickly as possible, sprinted down the hill road with his pony, holding the bridle close by its head. The Queen remarked in concern to David Muir that she hoped the pony would not be worn out by being made to run so far. Her concern brought a dry retort from the Head Ponyman, 'The day one o' these ponies cannae outrun a Gordon Highlander'll be a sad day indeed!'

The Life of a Regiment, Volume VII, p 430.

It was always gratifying when people outside the Regiment acknowledged the calibre of the Gordon Highlander soldier. The following is an extract from a letter from WO1 P. Hanlon, A & SH, Regimental Sergeant Major of Army Headquarters Scotland:

> May I take this opportunity to thank you for the high standards shown by your Jocks whilst on duty at Craigiehall. The job is obviously tedious, but alas necessary, and the attitude of the Jocks is exactly what I would expect knowing the fine reputation of The Gordon Highlanders.
>
> The CSMs have been very helpful in a very difficult job. Please pass on my thanks to all for a job well done.

The Life of a Regiment, Volume VII, pp 475–6.

For more than two centuries the Gordon Highlander, from private soldier to regimental sergeant major, had carried out his duties, in peace and in war, conscientiously, reliably and effectively, without fuss and with humour. He faced drawbacks and successes, defeat and victory, impressive achievement and cruel imprisonment with the same steadiness and reliability. Without him there could have been no Regiment, and it is to him that the credit for The Gordon Highlanders' unrivalled reputation belongs. The Regiment could take great pride in truly having had, from the very beginning, such a strong and dependable backbone.

SECTION 14

REMARKABLE PEOPLE

BOTH the 75th and the 92nd, and from 1881 The Gordon Highlanders, produced many remarkable people. Every generation could point to men of great courage, of character, of achievement or just plain eccentricity. It would be impossible to describe them all, and this section comprises an arbitrary selection of some of them. Many readers will disagree with the selection, and will point out people who, they believe, should have been included. They are not wrong, and many Gordon Highlanders who deserve recognition in this section are not shown in it. But nobody could deny that those in this selection were indeed quite remarkable. I have written, in this section, of remarkable 'people' and not 'men' or even 'Gordon Highlanders', because the first person described is a woman, a remarkable woman, who is close to the heart of every Gordon Highlander.

CHAPTER 30

JANE MAXWELL, DUCHESS OF GORDON

JANE Maxwell, Duchess of Gordon (known to Gordon Highlanders as Duchess Jean), was a significant figure in the raising of The Gordon Highlanders. She was a complex character, devoted to the advancement of her children, and prominent in society and political circles in Edinburgh and London. Her act in traversing the Gordon estates, dressed in uniform, encouraging young men to enlist in the new regiment is the stuff of legend, but it did happen. If the 4th Duke may be called the Father of the Regiment for his financial support, his engaging wife is its Mother and, as such, is far better known than the Duke. It was she who encouraged recruits to flock to its banner, and this romantic episode makes her not only the earliest character in the history of The Gordon Highlanders, but also one of the most colourful:

Lady Jane Maxwell was the fourth child of Sir William Maxwell [of Monreith] and Magdalene Blair of Blair. Born in 1749 in Hyndford's Close, Edinburgh, where her mother had a second-floor flat, she was a boisterous girl; on occasions, with her sister Betty, riding down the High Street on the back of pigs turned loose from a neighbouring wynd. In 1767 she married Alexander, fourth Duke of Gordon, to whom she bore two sons and five daughters. She was a beauty,[1] with ready business sense, quick wit and a good nature, but 'singular coarseness of speech' (she knew the everyday speech of her fellow countrymen, and was quite prepared to use it, especially in 'polite company').

An intelligent and beautiful young woman[2], she fell in love with an army officer called Fraser (a relative of Lord Lovat) when she was sixteen but later learned that he had died in America. At seventeen she married Alexander, Duke of Gordon. While on their honeymoon, Jane received a letter from Fraser, who was alive, asking her to marry him. This, allied to the Duke's womanising, contributed to a less than happy marriage.

Jane, Duchess of Gordon with her son George, Marquis of Huntly

---

1   She had a nasty accident as a 14-year-old when playing in the High Street. She somehow got a finger of her right hand jammed in the wheel of a cart which moved away and tore her finger off. There is at Monreith House a letter written, left handed, by her after the accident explaining how it happened. Whenever possible she wore gloves in which a wooden finger replaced the one missing. One of these wooden fingers is still at Monreith House. In later life she used to explain the loss of the finger by saying it was a coaching accident.

2   At sixteen she was so strikingly beautiful that a song was written about her, *Bonnie Jennie of Monreith, the Flower of Galloway.*

She gave birth to her first son at the same time as her husband's mistress, Jane Christie, gave birth to a son. Both boys were called George, 'My George and the Duke's George' according to Lady Jane. She secured three dukes, a marquess and a baronet as husbands for her daughters. (So proud was she of this that she insisted on having it engraved on her tombstone.)

She helped to raise two regiments of Fencibles, single companies for the Fraser Highlanders and the Black Watch, and most significantly of all, the Gordon Highlanders. Doubt has sometimes been cast on whether she actually did offer a kiss to new recruits, as there is little contemporary corroborative written evidence to support this, but there was clearly an oral tradition, and it is in keeping with the character and temperament of one who as a girl rode down the Edinburgh High Street on the back of a pig! Whatever the truth, the Gordon Highlanders believed it, and treasured it as an endearing reminder of the remarkable woman who played such a prominent part in their genesis.[3]

Jane Maxwell is a prominent figure in eighteenth century social history. Her personal magnetism was in tune with the temperament of the stage. No sooner did she appear in any circle of society than she dominated it. Horace Walpole once called her 'The Empress of Fashion'. She held court in London and Edinburgh, where everybody who was anybody flocked to her salons. In London, her parties had a distinctive Scottish flavour, and she wore tartan while it was banned.[4]

Her personality was the subject of adverse criticism as it raised many jealousies, but she had some highly respected supporters. Robert **Burns** listed her as one of his 'avowed Patronesses'. She, in turn, admired Burns, and invited him to several of her drawing-room parties. On one occasion she told Sir Walter Scott that Burns was the only man whose conversation carried her off her feet. After some unpleasant and derogatory stories were spread about her, in April 1789 Burns wrote an angry letter to the *Gazetteer,* which had copied a sneering stanza, allegedly by Burns, from *The Star*. To the Editor of *The Star*, he wrote:

Mr Printer,

I was much surprised on being told that some silly verses on the Duchess of Gordon, which had appeared in a Paper of yours, were said

---

3   See the comment to a wounded Gordon recruited by the Duchess, in Chapter 21.
4   The Highland regiments had been exempted from the ban on Highland dress, but in London there was a horror of tartan and all things Highland. Jane, inspired by her son George, Marquis of Huntly, who had raised an independent company for The Black Watch, ordered silk tartan and determined to change the outlook of the capital. In no time, tartan became the height of fashion. This was an act that would have seen her fellow Scots in the Highlands charged with treason, and one that shows the supreme self-confidence of this remarkable woman.

to be my composition. As I am not a Reader of any London Newspaper, I have not yet been able to procure a sight of that paper. I know no more of the matter than what a friend could recollect; but this I know, I am not the author of the verses in question. My friend told me that the Printer himself expressed a doubt whether the poem was mine: I thank you, Sir, for that doubt. A Conductor of another London paper was not so candid when he inserted a disrespectful stanza on the same highly respectable personage, which he, with unqualified assurance, asserted to be mine; though in fact, I never composed a line on the Duchess of Gordon in my life. I have such a sense of what I personally owe to her Grace's benevolent patronage, and such a respect for her exalted character, that I have never yet dared to mention her name in any composition of mine, from a despair of doing justice to my own feelings.

I have been recollecting over the sins and trespasses of myself and my forefathers, to see if I can guess why I am visited and punished with this vile calamity, to be, at one time, falsely accused of the two most damning crimes, of which, as a man and as a poet, I could have been guilty—INGRATITUDE and STUPIDITY.

I beg of you, Sir, that in your very first paper, you will do justice to my injured character with respect to those verses, falsely said to be mine; and please mention farther that in the *Gazeteer and New Daily Advertiser*, of March 28, another forgery was committed on me, in publishing a disrespectful stanza on the Duchess of Gordon. I have written to the Conductor of that Paper, remonstrating on the injury he has done me; but lest from some motive or other, he should decline giving me that redress I crave, if you will undeceive the Public, by letting them know through the channel of your universally known paper, that I am guiltless of either the one or the other miserable pieces of rhyme, you will much oblige,

Sir, Your very humble servant . . .

The Gordons' marriage was unhappy. The Duke kept his mistress, Jane Christie, at Gordon Castle while he built a house for his wife at Kinrara,[5] on the River Spey, which became the smartest place to stay for anyone heading out of London for the summer. The marriage ended in 1805 but

---

5   Built around 1800, Kinrara is a handsome two-storeyed mansion that was extended around 1814 and again in 1839. The Duchess lived at Kinrara from July to November, spending the remaining months of the year in London. She laid out the picturesque landscape around the house and is buried half a mile to the southwest, the spot marked by her memorial. Kinrara passed to the Duke of Richmond and Gordon (for whom the earldom of Kinrara became a subsidiary title) after the death of the 5th (and last) Duke of Gordon. In the twentieth century Kinrara was let to the Earl of Zetland. It was sold to Lord Bilsland in 1929 and further altered in 1939.

the Duke did not pay Jane all the money to which she was legally entitled, and she was reduced to living in hotels. On her death in 1812 she was buried at Kinrara at her own request.

Am baile (Comhairle na Gàidhealtachd).

Kinrara

It has been suggested that, faced with the Duke's continued liaison with his mistress, Jane Christie, the Duchess of Gordon took up with Fraser, her former fiancé, whom she had believed killed in America but who had survived. It was rumoured that at least one of her daughters was the product of this liaison, and that when she was arranging her marriage with a peer of the realm, her response to the concerns of the father of the prospective husband about a reputed strain of insanity in the line of the Duke of Gordon was 'Don't worry about that, my Lord. I can assure you there is not a drop of Gordon blood in her!'

Sealed with a Kiss

Doubt has long been cast on whether or not Jane, Duchess of Gordon, actually kissed any potential recruit in her efforts to raise the Regiment. There appear to be no contemporary written accounts, but there are later accounts by people who were aware of the story at the time, the most telling being the comment to one of the soldiers recruited by the Duchess, after he had been wounded, to remember 'that he got a kiss from the Duchess o' Gordon for

423

that'. The following account includes a second-hand confirmation of the kiss story from the son of a man who was present when the Duchess was recruiting in Huntly and who claimed to have seen the kiss episode. What is even more interesting in this account is the suggestion that the Duchess was motivated to raise the Regiment as a bet with the Prince of Wales! There is no other evidence that this was indeed the case, but it would not have been out of character for Jane Maxwell! As to the date when this was written in the *Bath Herald* we can only conjecture, but if the writer's father turned down a £40 bounty from the Duchess he must have been of age to join the army in 1794. It is a reasonable assumption that the writer must have been born in the last decade of the 18th or the first decade of the 19th century, and his writing for the *Bath Herald* on such a subject is unlikely to have taken place before the 1820s at the earliest—and could have been any time in the succeeding forty years:[6]

> From a fragmentary MS, history of the Gordon family, which the late Provost Black[7] prepared for a new edition of Lachlan Shaw's *Moray*, I learn that Mr William Alexander wrote an article in the *Bath Herald* containing what is to me a new story about the raising of the Gordon Highlanders. It is stated that Jane Maxwell 'made a large bet with the Prince of Wales that she would raise a whole regiment of Highlanders in four months if he would appoint her son, the Marquis of Huntly, its colonel.' She did so, and 'gained her bet, which was said to have been sufficient to repay the expense of forming the regiment.' Mr Alexander was under no delusion about the recruits being got for nothing. He does not jettison the kiss story, but supplements it with the part played by money bounties. He says:

>> It is quite a true story that the Duchess recruited in person on horseback at markets on the Gordon estates, wearing a regimental jacket and bonnet, and offering for recruits the irresistible bounty of a kiss and a guinea. The writer was told by his father that he and his brothers were at a market in Huntly when the Duchess was there enlisting men for her son's regiment. As the time was drawing near when she had engaged to complete the enrolment, she was giving large bounties to recruits. She offered the writer's two uncles £40 each to enlist, which they declined. The same day the following well known

---

6 First published in 1792, the *Bath Herald* amalgamated with the *Bath Register and Western Advertiser* in 1793 under the title *Bath Herald and Register*. The name *Register* was dropped in 1800, and it was known as the *Bath Herald* until 1862 when it amalgamated with the *Bath Ex*press, becoming the *Bath Express and County Herald*. The article must therefore have appeared prior to 1862.

7 The 3rd Edition of Lachlan Shaw's *History of the Province of Moray* was published in 1882. The Provost Black referred to is presumably James Black, Provost of Elgin, who could have provided material for the 1882 edition.

event occurred. The Duchess offered £40 bounty to a handsome young man to enlist. He declined the £40, but said 'If your grace will allow me to kiss you, I will enlist without any other bounty,' thus offering £40 for a kiss of the beautiful Duchess. 'Come along, my lad,' answered the Duchess, and, throwing her arms round his neck, kissed him in the presence of hundreds of people.

J.M. Bulloch.

Aberdeen Journal, April 1910.

Jane Maxwell, Duchess of Gordon, helps to raise The Gordon Highlanders

Jane Maxwell's recruiting flag when raising the 2nd Battalion in 1803

Reverse of Jane Maxwell's recruiting flag

The Duchess of Gordon's Bonnet

Among many prized exhibits in The Gordon Highlanders Museum, one, of which all Gordon Highlanders are proud, is the original bonnet that Jane Maxwell, Duchess of Gordon, wore when she traversed the Gordon estates to recruit men for The Gordon Highlanders. Few regiments had so romantic a beginning, and an artefact that was at the very heart of that beginning is precious indeed. The article below explains how the bonnet finally came into the possession of the Regiment:

How many Gordon Highlanders stop to think how fortunate the Regiment is in possessing an origin so personal and picturesque as theirs? In many regiments we know practically nothing of how they were raised beyond the bald fact that they came into being to meet some national emergency. We know neither how nor where they were raised: they 'belong' nowhere, as Americans say. On the other hand, The Gordons very distinctly 'belong', for they are 'thirled' to the region where they were raised in 1794 by the 4th Duke of Gordon, aided by his dashing wife, Jane Maxwell, while their elder son became the first Colonel of the Regiment.

Tradition has it that Jane Maxwell, the flamboyant consort of the 4th Duke, went recruiting for the Gordons to the feein' markets, mounted on a white horse and wearing a special bonnet, and that she kissed the recruits who responded to her salute and the guinea she is said to have held between her teeth. It is difficult to prove this story, which was not told at the time, but cropped up later. Curiously enough, the kiss story, when attributed to her daughter, Lady Madeline Sinclair, when recruiting for the Caithness Fencibles at the same period, was repudiated by her husband, Sir Robert Sinclair, as a libel on the lady, concocted by rival recruiters. But every wise student knows how unwise it is to jettison tradition out of hand, for, as a rule, it will be found that if not true to the letter it is true in the spirit. What is absolutely true is the traditional statement that the Duchess did wear a special kind of bonnet, and that her world-famous headgear is now at Gordon Barracks, encased in a glass case.

You can understand that it is anything but easy to 'redd' up such a story, which goes back to 1794. But it is less easy to understand that it is very difficult to get an accurate account of how the Regiment came to get possession of this bonnet, which should be its mascot, a hundred years later, for it was in 1895 that the bonnet was acquired.

Nobody knows who made the bonnet, but it is clear that, after wearing it, the Duchess retained it in her own possession. It came into the possession of her son, the 5th Duke, who was the first Colonel of the Gordons. From the Duke, who died in 1836, it passed to his Duchess, the highly religious Elizabeth Brodie, who was as different from her dashing mother-in-law as chalk is to cheese. The Gordon estates fell to the Duke's sister, the Duchess of Richmond, and his widow betook herself to Huntly Lodge, taking the bonnet with her. When she died there in January, 1864, the bonnet was left to her housekeeper, who left it to a kinsman, Adam Hutton, a shepherd, who was one of her Grace's oldest servants. After Hutton's death it came into the possession of his eldest son, Thomas Hutton, who was born at Oxman, Roxburgh, in 1830, and, with a brother, is said to have been carried north with a younger brother in a creel swung on a mule's back. Thomas was a shepherd, and died at Bogincloch, Rhynie, in 1886. The bonnet then passed to his widow, Christina Maclachland, a native of Inveravon, who moved to Howtown near the village of Rhynie. In her home the bonnet was nearly destroyed. One of Mr. Hutton's grand-children, Mr. James Mackie, tells me that as a child he used to play with the bonnet in his grandmother's house. But, worse than that, Mr. Mackie remembers his own mother on one occasion making a patch quilt, and in her search for nice material pouncing on the bonnet. 'She was just putting scissors into it,' he says, 'when grandmother caught her, and she sure got a scolding for dare thinking of cutting up Lady (sic) Gordon's bonnet.' That is the first part of the pedigree of the bonnet.

The second chapter was supplied by Mr. Mackie, and it concerns John Innes (1851–1914), a guard on the Great North of Scotland Railway. He was the son of a crofter at Glenbarry, Banffshire, his mother being a sister of Mrs. Thomas Hutton. After learning the trade of a shoemaker, he joined the railway service as a porter at Waterloo Station, and subsequently served at Fraserburgh, Elgin, and again in Aberdeen, retiring in 1912.

One day, says Mr. Mackie, 'there rolled into Aberdeen two military men,' but he does not think they were Gordons. They had gone to the Criterion bar in Guild Street, and were 'more or less disputing' the story of the bonnet. I believe the year was 1894, and as that was the centenary of the Gordons, one can easily understand how the discussion about the bonnet arose. John Innes, who knew all about it, got into conversation with them, and convinced them that the bonnet was actually in existence. The information must have been of great interest to the manager of the bar, Sergt.-Major E.O.W. Hart, who had been a sergeant-major in The Gordon Highlanders, and subsequently instructor to the Volunteers.

The third chapter in the story concerns a visit to the Criterion by Capt. Henry Percy Uniacke (1862–1915),[1] who, on 5th May, 1914, wrote a short account of the incident. 'About 1895,' he said, 'there was a public-house in Aberdeen near the railway station which was much patronized by the men of the Depot, and where some got drunk. I thought the best thing would be to see the proprietor and ask him to put a stop to our fellows drinking too much. I had a satisfactory interview, and at the end he told me that he knew where the Duchess's bonnet was. After writing to New South Wales and Canada, the owner agreed to sell the bonnet. Capt. F. McConnell expressed a desire to present the bonnet to the 2nd Battalion, and it was bought accordingly.'

The link connecting the owner with it is supplied by Mr. Mackie, who says: 'In a short time (after the visit of Innes to the bar) my grandmother received a letter from military headquarters [Castlehill Barracks] regarding the bonnet, and if she had such a thing. My old grandmother, a real old-timer of the real Scottish type—I think I see her face yet—was so very proud of this letter and request. The bonnet was brought out, brushed and dolled up, parcelled and mailed without delay. It was the Duchess's bonnet; 'glad to let you have it.' I don't believe she ever entertained one thought of commercializing on the thing. In course of time she received £10 from headquarters, for which she was well pleased.' The regimental property inventory contains a Statement, signed by Thomas Hutton's widow, witnessed by her nephew, John Innes, and also by E.O.W. Hart, and counter-signed by P.M. Turnbull, J.P., 24th July, 1895, bearing on the history of the bonnet up to the time the widow got it, and ending with the words 'I now hand it to Sergt-Major Hart for presentation.'

I have told the pedigree of the Duchess' bonnet in detail as an example of the difficulty of getting down to what Mr. Cowper Powys called 'the bodkin of reality.' What will concern the Gordons much more is the fact that the bonnet is now safe and sound in the possession of the Regiment, which it helped to raise a hundred and forty-three years ago.

John Malcolm Bulloch

T&S, December 1937.

---

1 Lt-Col H.P. Uniacke took the 2nd Battalion to France in 1914. He was wounded at the first Battle of Ypres in 1914 and killed at Neuve Chapelle in March 1915.

The spirit of Jane Maxwell

There is a long tradition in Highland folk tales of the supernatural, ghosts and spirits, and the overlapping of reality and the other world. There are recorded instances of Gordon Highlanders who foresaw their own death, and others where some other sign was given of death and disaster. The following article appeared in the *Sunday Times* of 4 October 1936:

Sir,

My letter published on 9th August about regimental mourning for Sir John Moore has evoked so many interesting contributions that I am in hope some of your readers may be able to throw light on this story of a regimental wraith, communicated to me by a well-informed native of the back-o'-beyond Aberdeenshire district of the Cabrach.

Jane Maxwell, Duchess of Gordon, who is said to have helped to raise The Gordon Highlanders by giving a guinea and a kiss to the recruits, was buried at Kinrara, a lovely spot in the Inverness-shire parish of Alvie, where she spent the last sad years of her lively life. When the estate was sold a few years ago by the Duke of Richmond and Gordon, who bears the title of Earl of Kinrara, dating from 1876, the land containing the Duchess' grave was bought by the officers of The Gordon Highlanders.

My Cabrach correspondent tells me that an apparition appears at the Duchess' grave 'before dire disaster overtakes The Gordon Highlanders. It was seen before Magersfontein, and several times before and since, taking the form of a weeping lady with long fair hair.'

Is there any corroboration of this story, and have any other regiments a similar kind of wraith?

Bydand, Bloomsbury.

T&S, December 1936.

Memorial Ceremony on Speyside

The following article appeared in *The Tiger and Sphinx* in 1957. It covers an interesting ceremony at the grave of Jane Maxwell, Duchess of Gordon when her monument was refurbished. The grave and monument are still maintained by the trustees of The Gordon Highlanders Regimental Fund, and can be accessed with the permission of the occupier of Kinrara, currently Major Robin McLaren:

On 16th September [1957] at a simple, impressive ceremony at Kinrara, the memory of the wife of the Regiment's founder was honoured when a new granite plaque was unveiled to replace the original weather-beaten marble one.

The Monument and Grave stand in a fenced-off plot of ground, belonging to the Regiment, and it was here that Lord Bilsland, who owns the estate, spoke of Jane, Duchess of Gordon, as the force and focus of life around Badenoch for many years. She devoted her great energies and time to the welfare and happiness of the people she loved.

When she died in London on April 11th, 1812, she was, in accordance with her wishes, laid to rest in her favourite spot overlooking the bend of the Spey at Kinrara. She herself had composed the inscription, which she asked her husband to put on the monument.

The Colonel of the Regiment [Colonel W.J. Graham] thanked Lord Bilsland for his hospitality in entertaining the company and paid special tribute to his great generosity which, he said, had made it possible to renew the plaque.

Colonel Graham said that much had happened to the Regiment since 1794; we had had our triumphs and disappointments, our joys and our sorrows, but he was certain that the Duchess, her husband and their son could be proud of the Gordon Highlanders and of the part they had played in the formative years of the Regiment.

After the unveiling, Colonel Graham laid a wreath on the grave; of evergreens, tied with Gordon tartan ribbon, it had on it a plain crested card, 'From the Gordon Highlanders.' *Lochaber No More* was then played by Piper W. Cruickshank.

Among those present were Helen, Duchess of Northumberland (a direct descendant of Jane, Duchess of Gordon), Major-General E.C. Colville, Brigadier the Earl of Caithness, Colonel A. Milne and representatives from the Depot, 4th/7th Battalion, 5th/6th Battalion and The Gordon Highlanders War Memorial.

The following article appeared in *The Times* of October 4th, 1957:—

As I walked towards Kinrara along the banks of the Spey, among golden bracken and swiftly fading heather, I wondered what compulsion was urging me on so strange a pilgrimage—to attend the restoration of a tomb of a long-dead Duchess with whom I had no ties of kin or clan. But then this Duchess, Jane, Duchess of Gordon, was no ordinary woman; witty, brilliant and beautiful, in life she was a great personality, and after death something of a legend, so it seemed fitting to join with the Gordon Highlanders to pay tribute to her memory, and to read once again the inscription on her monument, now renewed after the weathering of 145 winters.

In May, 1812, the Duchess Jane was laid to rest in this small plantation beside the Spey—a spot chosen by herself because she loved it so well, within the grounds of her estate at Kinrara. Eighteen years previously had occurred the event with which her name has become forever associated—the raising of the Gordon Highlanders.

In the early summer of 1794 recruiting was going extremely ill for the Duke of Gordon's new regiment, of which his heir, Lord Huntly, was promised the command. Indeed, had it not been for the prompt action of the Duchess the regiment might never have got up to strength at all. Donning a regimental jacket and plaid of Huntly tartan and a specially designed feather bonnet (9in. high, made of blue silk velvet with red, white, and green dice at the border) she mounted a white horse, and rode to all the country fairs held in the wide expanse of the Gordon lands.

Between her lips she held a golden guinea, so that, in taking it, each man might be rewarded by her kiss! The result justified the means: on June 24, 1794, the regiment was embodied, 750 strong, under the name Gordon Highlanders.

The Duchess had tremendous fascination and charm. She was also a very clever woman and an astute politician. It is an irony of fate that posterity should remember her for only the one romantic episode of raising the Gordon Highlanders. She was the friend of William Pitt and, as a political hostess, as important to the Tories as the Duchess of Devonshire to the Whigs. Her considerable political acumen and tact can be estimated by the fact that, almost alone in Court circles, she succeeded in remaining on friendly terms with both King George III and his son, the Prince of Wales![2]

In this respect Sir Walter Scott has stolen some of the fame due to the Duchess, for Sir Walter was not the first to interest the Prince Regent in things Scottish. In London the Duchess of Gordon's love of dancing was well known; at her balls she had introduced Scottish dances, and it was she who taught the young prince, in his twenties, to dance, with great proficiency, the Highland reels.

[Her] last public act was to attend the Regency Fête given by the Prince Regent on June 19th, 1811. Still very beautiful, she wore 'a magnificent dress,' embroidered in white and silver, and held a reception of her own at the Pulteney Hotel before she left for Carlton House. Six months later she was stricken with mortal illness, and died in London on April 11, 1812, at the age of 63.

In accordance with her wish her body was brought to Kinrara for burial. The cortege took 23 days on the road, the hearse drawn all the way by six jet-black Belgian horses, and 'the most gratifying marks of

---

2   King George III adored her, and she supported the King, so she was allowed to promote her Scottish heritage more than others would have dared. She gave a ball at which she and the Duchess of York dressed in tartan when it was officially banned, and she arranged for the King to inspect troops dressed in tartan in Hyde Park. She arranged a truce between the King and his eldest son, the Prince Regent, who had run up enormous debts. She arranged for his debts to be met, and this enabled the construction of the Royal Pavilion at Brighton to be continued.

civility were shown to the attendants in all places through which they passed.' At Dalwhinnie, the southern limit of Gordon territory, the funeral party was met by Lord Huntly and a body of Gordon clansmen who followed the bier to Kinrara, and there 'encircled the ground in silence' as the funeral took place.

Duchess of Gordon's Memorial at Kinrara

Today it seemed possible to see them standing there again, as in the stillness of the valley the notes of the piper's lament rose to the hills. So it had been in 1812, so now, when on the simple grave a wreath was placed, bound with Gordon tartan. But today behind the grave stood the stone obelisk erected by the Duke of Gordon.

A Union flag covered the restoration, and when the flag fell away at the touch of Colonel Graham, Colonel of the Gordon Highlanders, the new plaque (gifted by Lord Bilsland, the present owner of Kinrara) was revealed. Instead of the old, worn, marble-cut words the inscription now stands out boldly in fine lead letters set in a one-ton block of granite, and, as on the original, it gives—at the request of the Duchess—the names not only of herself and her sons, but of all her five daughters and their husbands—four of whom were Peers—and their children.

So much for worldly glory, but the eye of the beholder travels down from the plaque and the obelisk to the grass-covered grave below, and the mind remembers those words of the Duchess, written in sorrow and in anger eight years before her death: 'I am Duchess of Gordon, and I have done as much credit to the name as any Duke ever did.' That is the epitaph by which she should be remembered.

A fascinating woman, may she rest in peace in the silence of Speyside.

T&S, November 1957.

CHAPTER 31

SOME EARLY COMMANDING OFFICERS

THE men who commanded The Gordon Highlanders were generally accomplished soldiers who led from the front, cared deeply about their men, and put their welfare and well-being as one of their first priorities. Of the many who had the honour to command the Regiment, a few from the early years are illustrated below. Inclusion in this selection does not imply that those omitted were less deserving or less distinguished, only that in such a small selection many will inevitably be left out.

ERSKINE OF CARDROSS

A number of commanding officers of The Gordon Highlanders (both the 75th and the 92nd) died leading their troops. The first to die in action was Lieutenant-Colonel Charles Erskine of Cardross[1] at Alexandria in 1801. Charles Erskine, who joined the 100th Regiment when it was raised in 1794,

---

1   The title comes from Cardross, Port of Menteith, and not from Cardross on the River Clyde. Charles Erskine, a grandson of the Earl of Kincardine, was descended from the Earls of Buchan.

had served in the 25th, 16th and 77th regiments in the war against Tipu Sultan in India and against the French in Martinique. He was the senior major in the new regiment, and took charge when the commanding officer was not present. He cared about his soldiers, whose welfare and well-being were as important to him as training and professionalism. In 1795, while exercising command in the absence of the Marquis of Huntly, Erskine displayed his enlightened approach to discipline, which was that:

> the discipline of the 100th Regiment should be carried on as pleasantly as possible during the short time he is to have the honour of commanding it, and he begs to assure them that nothing in his power shall be wanting that can contribute to their comfort and happiness. He takes the same opportunity of informing the n.c. officers and soldiers that he will be happy to show them every indulgence consistent with propriety.'

The Life of a Regiment, Volume I, p 30.

In May 1796 the Marquis of Huntly became Colonel of the Regiment, and Erskine, promoted to lieutenant-colonel, took command of the 100th. On returning from leave in 1797 he regretted that his first orders should be for courts-martial for 'rioting in the streets and unsoldierlike conduct'. Erskine's regret was genuine, and, while he had no compunction in punishing wrongdoers, he much preferred achieving discipline through encouragement and example. He would consider a soldier's general conduct and would remit corporal punishment whenever possible:

> A soldier of the 28th is sentenced to 1,000 lashes for desertion. These brutal punishments in the army were only a reflection of those in civil life, at a time when men were hung [sic] for stealing sheep, and when an unfortunate debtor was confined in a crowded and loathsome jail till his debt was paid, which often meant till his life's end. Colonel Erskine and his officers seem to have had a great aversion to corporal punishment, and though the law obliged regimental courts-martial to order it, the culprit's captain often begged him off, and the commanding officer would appear to have been glad of a good reason for remitting that part of the sentence.

> *R.O., May 1797.*—Lieut-Colonel Erskine has always pleasure in attending the request of officers in favour of any man of general good character who may be unfortunately confined under sentence of court-martial, but begs they will not apply in favour of one whose crime is such as makes it incompatible with his duty as commanding officer to forgive. He has told the regiment a thousand times, and he once more repeats it, that he will forgive no man whatever who is guilty of being drunk on guard, sleeping on his post, of being abusive to n.c. officers, or of stealing.

R.O., August 26th.—At the regimental court-martial held this day, was tried Alex. Kenedy of the Light Company for refusing to go sentry when ordered by the corporal, for which he was ordered to receive 300 lashes. On account of his character, the commanding officer pardons him on this occasion; but he desires the regiment to remember that nothing but Kenedy's remarkable good character would induce him to forgive his disobedience of orders, which no plea whatever can justify, and any soldier who receives an order that may be improper, will always get redress by complaining through the regular channel.

The Life of a Regiment, Volume I, pp 35–6.

Erskine did not like inflicting corporal punishment on his men. At Athlone several soldiers were sentenced to flogging by regimental court-martial, but because of 'the strong application of his captain,' or 'on account of many recommendations in his favour,' the corporal punishment was more often than not remitted. At the same time Erskine urged officers not to request leniency for men who were guilty of a serious breach of military discipline. One of his reasons for not flogging a man seems rather original:

R.O., May 19th, 1799.—Corporal Buchanan of the Light Company is reduced by court-martial for allowing sentries to relieve each other. For particular reasons which appeared, the court did not sentence him to corporal punishment, which the commission of such an unmilitary crime would certainly have merited. The lieut.-colonel is sorry that the corporal, of whom he entertained so good an opinion, should have so far forgot himself, and hopes it will be a warning to him in future. At the same court-martial was tried Donald McKinnon, for allowing himself to be relieved without the corporal, and he was sentenced to one hundred lashes. The punishment awarded is so trifling for an offence attended with so bad consequences, that the commanding officer remits it entirely.

The Life of a Regiment, Volume I, p 47.

Erskine's concern for the well-being of his men, regret when they went astray and readiness to rehabilitate men who showed that they had reformed is consistently shown:

August 30th, 1797.—Lieut.-Colonel Erskine hopes that the melancholy accident that happened last night to Robert Chisholm of Captain Gore's company, and the consequences that are likely to follow to William Henderson, who was the cause of his death, will prevent soldiers of the regiment making free use of their hands; for even if Henderson should escape with his life, for which he must be tried, it must be dreadful for any honest man that, by unjustifiable violence, he has been the cause of another man's death.

December 16th.—That any man who may unfortunately have got into a scrape, or who has merited to be returned as a bad character, may have an opportunity of recovering himself, Lieut.-Colonel Erskine will call for a return on the 4th June next, when he and every officer will be glad to hear of any reformation, and every man will be returned as a good character who has behaved well in the intermediate period.

The Life of a Regiment, Volume I, p 37.

Even when not in action and suffering losses to the enemy, regiments found their numbers reduced by a steady attrition through disease and illness, and through the discharge of time-expired men. These losses were made up by drafts of new recruits and by trained men volunteering from Fencible regiments. Erskine went to great lengths to ensure that these men were made to feel at home in the Regiment and were properly equipped and trained. In 1798 sixty-four men from the Perthshire Fencibles, which had been disbanded, volunteered for the 92nd (the 100th having been renumbered earlier that year):

R.O., January 14th, 1799.—Lieut.-Colonel Erskine particularly desires that officers and n.c. officers will pay the greatest attention to pointing out to those men of the Perthshire Fencibles who have just joined the duties required of them, and that, until such time as they are perfectly acquainted with their characters, they will treat them with that kindness and lenity which every recruit not acquainted with the system of the regiment is entitled to. They are all to receive enough plaid tartan for a kilt, and of hose tartan for two pairs of hose. They are not to be charged with the kilt and hose served out to them.

The Life of a Regiment, Volume I, p 46.

Soldiers had stoppages put on their pay for many things, such as cleaning equipment, replacement of worn-out uniform or damages. Erskine tried to keep stoppages to a minimum:

R.O., March 7th, 1799.—Lieut.-Colonel Erskine is extremely sorry that the charges to be made against the men on the 24th inst. shall be so heavy, but as he knows every good soldier prides himself on the neatness of his head-dress, and particularly every Highlander on the smartness of his bonnet, he is confident they would wish that their money should be disposed in that way, rather than in many others, in which neither their own pride nor the credit of the regiment is concerned. He is the more convinced of this from the expense of the bonnets not being nearly so great as in any other Highland regiment that he has heard of, which will show that he has attended as much as possible to their cheapness.

The Life of a Regiment, Volume I, pp 48–9.

In 1799 the 92nd took part in the expedition to Holland. The Marquis of Huntly rejoined his regiment, taking command in the field, but left effective command to Erskine. In Regimental Orders he, 'desires that all reports may be made to Lieut.-Colonel Erskine, as if he had the whole command of the regiment. The lieut.-colonel will fill up all vacancies of non-commissioned officers, and in every respect consider himself as commanding, except with respect to signing returns, which must be done by Lord Huntly himself.'

During the campaign, which was the first serious active service that the 92nd saw, the Regiment acquitted itself with distinction, earning its first battle honour, 'Egmont-op-Zee'. The Marquis of Huntly was wounded; and full command again devolved upon Erskine. So well did Erskine perform in this capacity that he was, for a time, given command of the Brigade.

In 1800 the 92nd sailed to Minorca, where Sir Ralph Abercromby's army for Egypt was assembling. Here they found the 42nd Royal Highlanders 'who received them with hospitality characteristic of the Scot abroad. Wine flowed, the quaint streets of Mahon re-echoed Highland toast and song, and many a Highland head ached next morning!' Erskine's approach to discipline is shown by his response to his men's Highland festivities:

> *R.O., August 8th.*—The lieut.-colonel will not take any particular notice of the irregularities which happened last night, on account of the men meeting so many of their friends, but he expects not to have anything more happening of the same nature.

The Life of a Regiment, Volume I, p 78.

The 92nd landed at Aboukir Bay in 1801. A few weeks before they reached Egypt, Erskine took sent a letter to his sister in Scotland on a ship returning to Britain. It was the last letter he was ever to write.

Envelopes were not used in the early 19th century. The pages of the letter were folded to make a narrow package and sealed with wax. The address was written on the outside of the package, along with any instructions or last-minute additions. This letter from Erskine is headed by the address details and forwarding instructions written by Erskine. The comment shown in square brackets was clearly added later. Erskine's sister's name, which begins with the letter 'M', is indecipherable on the original.[2] The Lord referred to is the nobleman after whom the Elgin Marbles were named:

---

2   Erskine had five brothers and six sisters: Janet, Matilda, Ann, Marion, Rachel Euphemia and Christian. Only one brother, David, the third son, survived. The eldest, John, died in India, Charles

11th Jany 1801

Miss M— Erskine
Cardross, Stirling, N.B.[3]

Send some of your letters as usual, and enclose one, now and then, to Lord Elgin at Constantinople

[The last letter received from him—he died of his wounds the 25th of March 1801]

On Bd the Stately in Marmorice Bay
Coast of Coramania. 11th Jany 1801

My Dear M—

I was made extremely happy by the receipt of your letter of the 18th Novr which came to hand a few days ago I was much envied for receiving it, as few of so late a date from Scotland, have arrived. I dined in company with Sir Ralph Abercromby the day I got it and I was happy that you mentioned his family being well, as he did not receive any letters at all by that conveyance. I wrote to my Father on the 1st Jany and enclosed it to Lord Elgin to forward it overland. In that letter, I mentioned the little likelyhood there was of sending any letters by sea, it being generally understood that no ships were to be sent home from this part of the world, untill near the period when we should be ready to proceed to Egypt. But Lord Keith, who, the world says, is sometimes capricious, has changed his mind, and now proposes sending one off immediately, and as I lose no opportunity of writing, I sit down to write a few lines to you. The letter which you say Annie wrote to me about a fortnight before your's, I have not yet received, nor many others which I find have been written. They will all make their appearance in a lump, some months hence perhaps.

We are now enjoying one of the finest Climates I have ever been in. It is winter with us, as with you, with this difference, that it is as hot here at present, as it is in Scotland in the month of July, with the mornings and evenings so cool, as to make a fire very comfortable. A good many of the sick of Different Regts, men of the 92nd amongst the rest, were landed, and encamped, and the mildness of the climate, I am happy to say, has recover'd them wonderfully. But the Climate is almost all we can boast of, for there is nothing to be got, but wood & water, except a few

---

in Egypt, James, a lieutenant in the Navy, died in the explosion that destroyed HMS *Queen Charlotte* in 1800 and William, the youngest, died when a major in the army. The opening of the letter to 'My Dear M—' suggests that it was addressed to Marion, as Matilda was married and presumably lived away from Cardross.

3   The initials N.B. stand for North Britain, the patronising and not very complimentary way in which Scotland was referred to at the time, when the term 'England' was generally used to denote both England itself and the whole of the United Kingdom.

miserably lean cattle, which are scarcely worth the killing—and now and then a few fowls. You may therefore believe, that we are anxious, for many reasons, to take our departure, and to finish the work on which we are going, as soon as possible. The sooner we go, my Dear M— the sooner we shall return, and I am in great hopes, that I shall be able to pass the latter end of this year with my friends in Scotland.

I was glad to hear of William's having accepted Genl Myers' offer, as he is certainly much better with him than with such a Regt as the 16th as long as it continues doing nothing. I feel very much obliged to the Myers' for their kindness to Wm. The General's son is upon this Expedition. He's a fine lad, and I regret, from being constantly on Board Ship, that it is not in my power to shew him any attention.

You say that you were all alarmed about the reports of the Plague having got into the Army, and of our Storms at Sea. You must pay no attention to the foolish Newspaper Reports. If you do, you must be constantly uneasy as so many goodnatured people, who disapprove of this expedition, would rather spread bad, than good news, respecting it. I am not Politician enough to know what effect a Rupture with Russia is likely to have on our operations in the Mediterranean. I hope that nothing will occur to put a stop to the Egyptian Expedition, as it would be a great disappointment not acting in that Country, after having heard so much about it.

I have never seen Lt. Henry of the 27th Regt, but knowing that he was in that Corps, and that he was son to John Henry, I made enquiry about him, and was glad to hear a very favourable report from the Comg Officer of his Regt. The 27th was left at Malta, being so much reduced by sickness as to be unable to proceed on the Expedition. The Abercromby's, The Hope's, The Ramsay's &c. are all in good health. Major Ramsay has been complaining often, but is now well.

It is supposed that we shall leave this so as to arrive on the Coast of Egypt by the end of this month or beginning of next.

God bless you all.

And believe me my dear M—

Ys most Affectionately

Chas Erskine

I rejoice to hear that my Father and Mother continue so well. Offer my condolence to John Sands for his recent loss.

Gordon Highlanders Museum.

The army landed at Aboukir Bay on 8 March 1801, in the face of determined French resistance, and the 92nd, 'did considerable execution, and pursued the enemy for some distance'. Five days later the 92nd, with some

350 rank and file, faced the French at Mandora. In a hard-fought and bloody battle, tin which the 90th[4] and 92nd bore the brunt, the French were defeated:

> Sergeant D. Nicol in his *Journal* says that at one time at Mandora the 92nd was in danger of being surrounded. Ammunition for the two guns failed and the guns were sent to the rear. Five companies were in line, the others being extended to the left among bushes towards the lake. The Colonel ordered the men not to fire till they could see their enemy's feet as they advanced from a hollow in front. When the order to fire was given, 'like magic it dispelled the gloom from our countenances. Every man did his duty manfully. We encouraged each other, firing, and at the same time praying, for soldiers do pray, and that fervently, on such occasions.'

The Life of a Regiment, Volume I, p 87.

The cost was high. The 92nd had eleven officers, eight sergeants and 119 rank and file killed and wounded: among them was Erskine of Cardross:

> struck by a grape-shot that mangled his thigh. At first hopes were entertained of his recovery, but he sank after the amputation of the limb and died in a few days. He had asked his brother officers to let him carry to the grave a gold locket which he wore round his neck, containing a lock of his sister's hair and of the lady to whom he was engaged.
>
> In 1894 a soldier of the garrison of Alexandria, while employed on some excavations in the sand, found the skeleton of a man, having only one leg and with a gold locket on the neck. He wrote mentioning the circumstance to the *Times* newspaper, and Colonel Erskine's story being well known both to his regiment and his family, there was no doubt the remains were his. They were re-interred in consecrated ground at Alexandria, and a suitable monument to his memory erected at the mutual cost of the officers of the Gordon Highlanders and Mr Erskine of Cardross, the locket being kept by the latter as an heirloom.[5]
>
> 'In him the Service lost one of its best officers,' wrote an officer of his regiment, and there can be no doubt that his thorough knowledge of his profession, his high sense of duty, the impartiality with which he carried on discipline, combined with his kindness and attention to the welfare of his men, had the best effect on the character of the regiment, with which he had served since it was raised.
>
> On the death of Erskine, the command devolved upon Major Napier.

The Life of a Regiment, Volume I, p 90.

---

4   Perthshire Volunteers, later 2nd Battalion, Cameronians.
5   The last letter ever written by Sir Ralph Abercromby to a private individual was to Lt-Col Erskine's father, James Erskine of Cardross, telling him of his son's wound.

Memorial to Erskine of Cardross at Alexandria

So died Lieutenant-Colonel Charles Erskine of Cardross, a commanding officer who, through his understanding of his men, concern for their well-being, compassion and humanity, and courageous leadership helped to establish the high standards of discipline, professionalism and fighting qualities that were to distinguish The Gordon Highlanders throughout their history.

HON JAMES MAITLAND

The first commanding officer of the 75th Highland Regiment to be killed in action was Lieutenant-Colonel James Maitland (illustration), who assumed command in 1804. James Maitland was the fourth son of Colonel Richard Maitland, who in turn was the third son of Charles Maitland, 6th Earl of Lauderdale. Richard Maitland fought at Quebec in 1759.

James Maitland led the 75th in Lord Lake's campaign against Holkar. The 75th was in the unsuccessful siege of Bhurtpore,[6] and Maitland commanded the main attack on 9 January 1805. Despite courageous and determined assaults, the attacking force could not secure the fiercely defended breach, and 'the gallant Maitland' fell at the head of his troops:

> Some men got into the ditch, but the water was breast high, and notwithstanding the inflexible ardour and repeated efforts of the gallant Maitland, who fell near the summit of the breach, the greater part of the troops, exposed to an incessant enfilade fire of grape could not face the deep water; and those that did so were powerless to storm the walls. Lieut. Col. Maitland being killed, officers and men falling fast, and there being no hope of crossing the ditch, the column fell back.

75th Regiment Record Book.

---

6   For details of the Siege of Bhurtpore see Volume IX, Chapter 3.

James Maitland died without issue, but his father's brother, Captain Hon. Frederick Lewis Maitland of Rankeillour, was the ancestor of Maitlands who served in The Gordon Highlanders throughout the years, including those of the Makgill-Crichton-Maitland and Maitland-Makgill-Crichton branches of the family. [7]

ALEXANDER NAPIER OF BLACKSTONE

The 92nd lost another commanding officer, in 1809. Like Erskine of Cardross, Alexander Napier of Blackstone was one of the original officers in 1794. He had been a Lieutenant in the 7th Fusiliers and was the senior captain in the new regiment.

Blackstone lies to the west of Paisley, but there is no trace now of the original house. In its day the spelling varied, sometimes being shown as 'Blackstoun,' and sometimes as 'Blackston'. The account below shows how the town of Paisley and the house of Blackstone, both staunchly loyalist, suffered at the hands of Charles Edward Stuart's Jacobite army in December 1745 as it retreated back to Scotland after reaching Derby. The interesting part of the account is the mention of Alexander Napier of Blackstone, presumably the father or grandfather of the Alexander Napier of the 92nd:

---

7   Two Maitlands, Captain S.C. Maitland, killed in South Africa in 1900, and his brother, Lt-Col C.A.S. Maitland of Dundrennan, were from a different family.

The douce burghers of Paisley began to panic when they heard that the wild Highland army of Bonnie Prince Charlie was about to march into the town. The panic was real, since the town was a loyal supporter of the Hanoverian government.

On Saturday, 28th December, 1745, Paisley folks heard that Prince Charles was in Glasgow, only seven miles away. There, he levied clothing from its citizens for his ragged regiment of wild, hungry, Highland soldiers, and they feared he would soon be in Paisley.

Local farmers, fearing their cattle would be slaughtered by the hungry, Highland army, drove their herds to the hills around Lochwinoch. On the following Sunday, between 150 and 200 of the rebel army marched through Paisley on their way to a raid on nearby Blackston House. One of their officers first left a letter at Bailie Fulton's House in Causeyside.

As well as demanding that meat and drink be sent to Blackston House to feed the Highland raiding party, the letter commanded that two of Paisley's senior bailies, Kyle and Park, attend a meeting in Glasgow.

The deputation duly arrived on Monday in Glasgow. They were told that a fine of £1,000 had been imposed on Paisley. If not paid, the town would be looted and pillaged. This had already happened to the nearby mansion of Blackston, the home of distinguished soldier, Alexander Napier, a Hanoverian officer who had succeeded in harassing the rebel army. Old scores were settled at Blackston.

paisley.org.uk

When Erskine of Cardross was promoted to Lieutenant-Colonel and given command of the Regiment, Napier was promoted to major, and took command when Erskine was on leave.

In August 1796, when a secret expedition was planned against a target in the Isle of Elba, Napier, in temporary command of the Regiment, made a plea 'in consequence of the unanimous wish of the officers and men,' for the 100th to be included in the attacking force:

Major Napier requested the Commander-in-Chief to permit the whole regiment to take part in this service, to which he received the following reply:—'The Commander-in-Chief is sensible of the zeal and laudable motives which have induced the officers and men of the 100th Regiment to offer their services on the present occasion, and he desires Major Napier to express his best thanks to them, as well as his assurance that he will be ready at all times to testify his satisfaction at their general good conduct and appearance, although circumstances will not, at this time, allow him to avail himself of their services to the extent they offer them.'

The Life of a Regiment, Volume I, pp 31–2.

Like Erskine, Napier had the well-being of his men, and the encouragement of their good behaviour at heart, and he looked for ways to reward good conduct:

R.O., Gibraltar, May 26th, 1797.—Major Napier, wishing to establish in the regiment a badge of honour for those men who have never been found guilty by a court-martial of any crime or irregularity since the Regiment was embodied, requests officers commanding companies will send in a list to his quarters of such as come under that description.

Napier fought with the 92nd in the Helder campaign where they won their first battle honour; 'Egmont-op-Zee'. He went with them to Egypt, where he took command after Erskine was killed at Mandora. He commanded the 92nd, by that stage mustering little more than 150 effective men, at the battle of Alexandria, where, for the first time in the Napoleonic wars, a British army faced a French army and defeated it.

Napier was confirmed in command of the 92nd when the Marquis of Huntly's recommendation was endorsed by the Duke of York:

R.O., September 16th.—The Marquis of Huntly has requested Lieut.-Colonel Napier to inform the regiment that he was much pleased with the accounts he had of their conduct, and that no person could be more gratified by the credit the 92nd acquired in Egypt than himself. His Lordship has also enclosed a letter from the Duke of York to be put in Regimental Orders.

Horse Guards, *30th May 1801.*

My Lord,—I have to acknowledge the receipt of your Lordship's letter of the 24th inst., and I need not assure you how sincerely I unite with you in regretting the loss of so deserving an officer as Lieut.-Colonel Erskine of the 92nd Regiment. I have ever entertained too high a sense of the gallant services of that Corps not to have recommended on this occasion that the step should go in the regiment, of which His Majesty has been pleased to approve.

I am, My Lord,
Yours,
Frederick,
Commander-in-Chief

Accordingly, Major Napier was promoted to lieutenant-colonel and Captain John Cameron to major. Napier was to command the 92nd for the next eight years.[8]

---

8   The men of the 92nd presented Napier with a fine sword. It was lost after he was killed, but it turned up, in auction, in the late twentieth century. It was purchased with funds provided by former Gordon

Napier shared Erskine's concern for the well-being of his men, and his approach to discipline, which was fair and reasonable, and not harsh. There was a system to redress wrongs, and Napier approved of this, although he insisted that redress should be sought through the proper channels. In doing so he brought home to the men of the Regiment that his strictures applied to his officers just as much as to them!

> *R.O., July 10th.*—Complaints having been made in an irregular manner by Captain Watt's company, Lieut.-Colonel Napier admonishes the men, 'who know perfectly the proper mode to be adopted when they feel themselves to be aggrieved. It appearing, however, that some negligence has taken place on the part of Captain Watt, Lieut.-Colonel Napier has reprimanded him in presence of the field-officers and captains of the Battalion.'

The Life of a Regiment, Volume I, p 118.

During the campaign in Denmark in 1807 Napier showed his courage, quick thinking and ability to seize an opportunity:

> One day about this time, as our Colonel was taking a ride to see what was going on, he fell in with 40 waggons carrying ammunition, under the charge of a small party of Danes; and, upon telling them that there was a great army close at hand coming up, he captured the whole, and brought them prisoners to the regiment.

Sergeant Robertson's Journal.

The presence of wives and families on campaign was common at this time, and they fell under the command of the commanding officer for discipline. Napier maintained a strict discipline, but as always, showed consideration where warranted:

> The Danes and Scots had many tastes in common, especially the love of liquor and music. There was a good deal of drunkenness, which Colonel Napier attributes to the practice of the women bringing brandy and wine from Roskeld, 'and Mrs Semple of the 1st Company having been found in the act, her provisions are to be stopped'; and in the case of another, whose conduct had been still worse, 'it was the intention of Lieut.-Colonel Napier that she should be drummed through the quarters of the regiment, but out of respect to the character of her husband, the lieut.-colonel will be satisfied with her disappearance for ever—and he gives her forty-eight hours to do so.'

Highlander Arnold Henderson and the National Museum of Scotland. It is now on display in the National War Museum in Edinburgh Castle.

The Grenadiers seem to have given the commanding officer nearly as much trouble as the ladies. The parish clergyman's ducks having been found in their cantonments, the corporal and twelve men, in whose apartment the ducks were discovered, have to furnish a guard and prevent any Grenadier passing out till the culprit who stole the poultry has given up. And the officers of the company are not to leave their cantonments.

The Life of a Regiment, Volume I, pp 133–4.

Napier led the 92nd in Sir John Moore's army that landed in Portugal in August 1808, and then advanced into Spain. When Madrid fell in December and Moore's army was in danger of being cut off, the 92nd was in the army that undertook the retreat to Corunna. The retreat was conducted successfully, but the army suffered severely and losses were heavy. The 92nd under Napier could take some comfort from the fact that its losses, although heavy, were lower than any other unit apart from the 1st Guards. When Moore's army stood and defeated the French at Corunna it did so while sustaining heavy losses in its command structure. General Sir John Moore was killed; Major-General Sir David Baird, who commanded the division in which the 92nd served, was seriously wounded—losing an arm; but, for the 92nd, the greatest loss was of its Commanding Officer, Lieutenant-Colonel Alexander Napier of Blackstone:[9]

We now heard, for the first time, that Sir J. Moore was no more, and that Sir David Baird was severely wounded. But what added most to our grief, was the death of Colonel Napier of the 92d, whom every man in the regiment adored, and to whom he was more like an affectionate father than a commanding officer.

Sergeant Robertson's Journal.

JOHN CAMERON OF FASSIEFERN

John Cameron of Fassiefern was from a similar mould to Erskine and Napier. He lived for his regiment and his men, although he was a strict (but fair) disciplinarian. Like his predecessors he stands out as an inspiring and charismatic leader.

John Cameron (illustration below), eldest son of Ewen Cameron of Fassiefern, was born in 1771 at Inverscadale. He had two elder sisters, one married to McDonald of Glencoe and the other to McNeill of Barra, and one younger sister, married to Macpherson of Cluny. He had two younger brothers. As a child Cameron was nursed by the wife of one of his father's tenants, whose son, Ewen McMillan, his foster brother, followed him

---

9   For an account of the retreat and Napier's death see Volume IX, Chapter 6.

faithfully through the wars, and was with him when he fell at Quatre Bras. He was educated at the Grammar School of Fort William, and by a private tutor, and he went on to the University of King's College, Aberdeen.[10] Unless otherwise attributed, all quotes in this chapter are from the *Memoir of Colonel John Cameron of Fassiefern.*

After a short time apprenticed to a lawyer in Edinburgh, in 1793 he persuaded his father to purchase him a commission in the 26th Regiment (Cameronians), but instead of the 26th, he entered as Lieutenant in an independent Highland company which was afterwards incorporated into the 93rd Regiment. In 1794 the Marquis of Huntly called on Fassiefern and offered his son John a captain's commission in the regiment that he was raising—The Gordon Highlanders. Fassiefern declined the offer on the grounds that he could not raise the number of men to entitle his son to such a rank, whereupon Huntly offered the rank without any stipulation or condition, saying he would be glad to have John Cameron a captain in his regiment although he brought not a single recruit.

---

10 The Marquis of Huntly, who was born in 1770, was a good friend of John Cameron and actively sought his services when the Regiment was raised in 1794. It is possible that this friendship started during Cameron's time at university in Aberdeen.

Touched and inspired by such generosity, Fassiefern approached his Chief, Lochiel, and his son-in-law, McNeill of Barra. With their aid the full complement was quickly gathered, and Cameron joined the Regiment with a hundred good men. When the Regiment mustered at Aberdeen the Lochaber men showed the influence of the clan feeling under which they had consented to go to war. When it was proposed to draft them into separate divisions of grenadiers and light troops, they declared that they would neither be separated from each other, nor serve under any captain except Cameron. It required all Cameron's persuasion to get them to submit to the rules of the service, but, promising that he would always watch over their interests in whatever division they were ranked, he prevailed on them to submit. None of them ever had cause to reproach him with forgetting his pledge.[11]

Cameron went to Gibraltar with The Gordon Highlanders. While there a dispute arose between him and a fellow officer, Lieutenant (afterwards Sir John) Maclean, that led to a duel. Fortunately, each escaped without serious injury, and this was the only instance in which Cameron had a hostile encounter with a brother officer.

Cameron had a sense of honour, common in Highland society, and this was displayed at the desperate defence of Alba de Tormes in 1812. Before one of the French attacks, a French officer of high rank approached so close to the position of the 92nd that several muskets were levelled at him. Cameron, disdaining to take such an advantage, promptly forbade the firing of a shot. 'It was Soult who was thus saved; and strange, indeed, are the "chances of war". The dreadful carnage of the 92nd at Maya, the loss of thousands of brave men through the bloodstained passes of the Pyrenees, might have been saved had not Cameron, at this moment, stayed the deadly weapons of his soldiers.'[12]

Wounded on more than one occasion, Cameron never flinched from placing himself at the forefront of battle to share the perils that faced his men. His letters to his father, Ewen Cameron, catalogue the wounds he received. In 1799 he wrote of the wound he received at Egmont-op-Zee:

> Late in the evening I received a slight wound in the knee; you may easily suppose it is a slight one, when I remained an hour with the Regiment, charged once with them after I got it, and did not leave till they forced me to the doctor. The clutching the doctor had at me to get out the

---

11 These men joined the army solely from attachment to, and confidence in their leader, and a clan spirit that in the course of less than fifty years produced more than 70,000 soldiers. During that time the prejudice against *enlisting* was stronger in the Highlands than anywhere else, for there was then a deep dislike, or even hatred of the 'red army' of the King's troops, who were still associated with all the sad and savage scenes that followed Culloden. Only the influence of respected leaders in the paternalistic clan system could have led so many Highlanders into the ranks of the army.

12 *The Life of a Regiment*, Volume I, p 255.

ball was infinitely worse than the wound itself and disabled me so much that I was obliged to be moved back to the cantonments.[13]

At Arroyo del Molinos in 1811, Cameron observed a lieutenant, who had assumed command of a company when its captain was wounded, making a false movement in deployment. Cameron, 'as was his custom when displeased, struck his left breast with his right hand in which he grasped his sword. The order had barely left his lips when a French bullet struck him on the right hand, shattered his middle finger, passed through the hilt of his sword.'[14]

Writing to his father of the battle of the Pass of Maya, Cameron again made light of a wound, although Sergeant Robertson recorded that he was 'severely wounded':

> I had the left elbow cleared of coat & shirt but only grazed near the bone, my right arm wounded but by no means severely my worst wound was a ball through the Right Thigh luckily it passed right through & did not touch a bone or artery. I am doing remarkably well though I have been travelling every day since to get some quiet place but hope to join the Regt. soon again.

Ewen McMillan, his foster brother, who fortunately escaped unhurt, had led him from the battle and guided him to some shelter where his wounds were dressed. At the Nive in 1813 he again downplayed a wound in a letter to his father:

> I have escaped for once with a slight scratch or two not worth mentioning.

The wounds he received in action are testimony to Cameron's courage and leadership. A further illustration of these qualities is given by the number of times his horse was shot from under him. Sergeant Robertson, writing of the battle of the Pass of Maya, comments:

> During the action the men were calling out to the Colonel [Cameron] what he thought of his cattle now; and when his horse was killed and himself severely wounded he was told that it was nothing but a touch of the oxen's horns.

Cameron, having been shot in three places himself, wrote to his father:

> My poor horse was also shot in three places, right through the shoulder through both hips & out at the off one & through the leg. But after all he carried his saddle 3 miles, I was hurt to lose the poor brute, as he almost

---

13 He seems to have made light of this wound purposely, as he was laid up a long time by it.
14 *The Life of a Regiment*, Volume I, p 225.

seemed to enjoy the fight & was as steady as a rock untill he got the wound through the shoulder, when I was obliged to dismount.

At the Nive in December 1813 he wrote to his father:

But I shall be ruined by horse flesh. The horse Cambell sent to me was killed under me. This is the third horse I have lost in this country I have lost more than a hundred pounds Sterling more than they will allow me. . . . my horse which had been wounded before was shot through the heart & fell dead, with me under him, our people were then retiring a little, & I should have been left there, as with every exertion I could not get from under him, had not my Orderly Corporal [Ewen McMillan] observed my situation & run & drawn me out, while in the act the French were so close that one of them took him by the neck one of our fellows shot the scoundrell dead & the Corporal even took the saddle with him.

Cameron was firm with his men and demanded the highest standards from them. He was a strict disciplinarian, but was always fair. That he cared deeply about his men, not only those he had brought to the regiment with him, but all Gordon Highlanders, no matter their origin, was clear. Writing to his father after the landings at Helder in 1799 his distress at losses due to an accident with a boat is evident:

One very melancholy circumstance took place as we landed in this country. A boat, carrying part of Captain Gore's company of ours, overset, by which means 1 sergeant and 14 privates of ours, a midshipman and 7 seamen were drowned. I am extremely sorry to say two of the men were Barra men, Donald McKinnon and Alexander McLeod—poor fellows, their fate was really hard.

Writing of a battle before the advance to Egmont op Zee Cameron comments on the 92nd's losses:

Only one man killed, and Captain Ramsay and six or seven men wounded. The man killed was, poor fellow, a Uist man of my company. I also had a man wounded, a Skye man.

Describing the losses at Egmont-op-Zee he said:

You will see by the papers the loss we have sustained; it is painful and horrible to me to think of it. There is, I hope in God, not much fear for the wounded officers and men, as any of them that were severely wounded died from the coldness of the night in the field. Of the poor lads that left the country with me, as far as I can yet learn, there is killed—Alexander McPhee and Angus McPhee, and Duncan Rankin; wounded—Sergeant McKinnon, Corporals Duncan and Richard Evans. Lieutenant D.

MacDonald,[15] Duncan's[16] friend, is amongst the worst wounded of the officers that have survived. He has got two thrusts of a bayonet through his breast. Of my company I do not exactly know the loss, but when I left the field I could find but five or six of them that were not either killed or wounded . . . Ewan Cameron, Glensuilach, being pretty severely wounded, though now doing well. His brother Allan, Glencoe's old servant, died of his wounds the day after the action; little Dougald Cameron, from Dochanassie, fought like a lion that day; though wounded in three different places, one being through and through his body, he refused to quit the field till the action was over.

During the retreat from Burgos in November 1812, the British army suffered from cold, wet conditions and shortage of food, and discipline in some regiments suffered. Not so in the 92nd, which maintained its structure and discipline despite the arduous conditions. Cameron lamented the sufferings of his men. In a letter to General Hope he stated:

From 27th October to 20th November, we were exposed to greater hardships than I thought the human frame could bear. Mine, I know, was very near yielding to it. In most inclement weather, with the canopy of heaven for our covering, wet, cold, and hungry, we were generally marching day and night, especially during the 16th, 17th, and 18th. Fifteen poor fellows of the 92d fell down, and were lost. My heart bled for them.

In 1813 writing to his father from the heights near Bayonne, Cameron lamented the loss of one of his officers.

Let Major Charles MacPherson of the barracks department in Edenr (a great Friend of Duncan's) know that his Nephew Lieut. Duncan MacPherson (whom I had put in charge of a Company a few days before) has falen nobly, cheering his Company to the charge, waving his bonnet in one hand, & his sword in the other. We had just rattled a French corps of Grenadiers down a hight by bayonet in great style when I halted the 92nd to draw breath, when Duncan came to tell me That the French in force had far outflanked our right, Lieut. Mitchell at the same time, telling me, they had far outflanked our left I had scarcely time to say 'Then Gentlemen we must charge them again' when in attempting it, both fell, & Two finer fellows never served their King & Country. Mitchell being also a young man of very superior accomplishments his brother was at the same time wounded but did not quit the Field during the day he is also a

---

15 Lt Donald MacDonald of Dalchosnie, who recovered from his wounds and commanded the 92nd at Waterloo.
16 Cameron's younger brother, Duncan.

Lieut. in the Regt. . . . . I had almost forgot to mention to you that poor Stronachreggan's son fell fighting most nobly nearby at the same time with Mitchell & MacPherson. None of our country lads were lost, indeed there are now scarcely any to lose.

At the fording of the River Nive in 1813.

> Cameron's favourite piper was hit by a ball, and fell down by his side. He at once stopped to render assistance, and, on finding that his assistance was of no avail, he exclaimed, in the saddest tone, that the loss of twenty of the regiment would not be so severely felt by him as that of this one man!

Cameron did not live to see the final defeat of the French at Waterloo, but he led the 92nd in their determined and glorious action at Quatre Bras; the opening act of the Battle of Waterloo. In both actions, Quatre Bras on 16 June 1815 and Waterloo on the 18th, The Gordon Highlanders added to the reputation they had built through the twenty-one years of their existence, and established themselves as one of the outstanding regiments in Wellington's army. They lived up to the highest expectations that Cameron of Fassiefern (and the Marquis of Huntly, Erskine of Cardross and Napier of Blackstone before him) had of them; his influence felt in his presence and in his memory. When the call to arms came in 1815 Cameron left his aged father to join the 92nd at Cork, and at the beginning of June had reached Brussels, where eight battalions were placed under his command. These he brought to such a high operational standard and public presence as to call forth unqualified admiration at the reviews which took place. On 15 June he attended the celebrated ball given by the Duchess of Richmond (a sister of the Marquis of Huntly). Late in the evening he was requested by the Duke of Wellington to march with all speed on Quatre Bras, and was directed to withdraw privately from the ballroom:

> By 2 p.m. he was in front of the enemy . . . With fearful odds against them, labouring under many sore and heavy disadvantages, they again and again repelled the French, led on by the fiery Ney. It was, however, at a terrible sacrifice that the British repulsed the French on that day. The noble 92d was dreadfully thinned; many gallant officers, and about 300 privates, were struck down. But the loss which the survivors, which the army generally, as well as [Wellington] himself, regretted most deeply, was that of their Colonel, who here 'closed his life of fame by a death of glory.' . . . The regiment lined a ditch in front of the Namur road. The Duke of Wellington happened to be stationed among them. Colonel Cameron, seeing the French advance, asked permission to charge them. The Duke replied, 'Have patience, and you will have plenty of work by

and by.' . . . At length, as [the French] began to push on to the Charleroi road, the Duke exclaimed, 'Now, Cameron, is your time—take care of that road.'

He instantly gave the spur to his horse; the regiment cleared the ditch at a bound, charged, and rapidly drove back the French; but while doing so, their leader was mortally wounded. A shot fired from the upper story of the farm-house passed through his body. His men raised a wild shout, rushed madly on the fated house, and inflicted dread vengeance on its doomed occupants.

Ewen McMillan speedily gave such aid as he could. Carrying him, with the aid of another private, beyond reach of the firing, he procured a cart, whereon he laid him, carefully and tenderly propping his head on a breast than which none was more faithful. The life-blood, however, was ebbing fast, and on reaching the village of Waterloo, McMillan carried Fassiefern into a deserted house by the roadside, and stretched him on the floor. He anxiously enquired how the day had gone, and how his beloved Highlanders had acquitted themselves. Hearing that they had been victorious, he said, 'I die happy, and I trust my dear country will believe that I have served her faithfully.' His dying words were in Gaelic, 'that mountain tongue, the first which he had heard in youth.'

Memoir of Colonel John Cameron of Fassiefern.

There was one putative slur on Cameron's memory and on The Gordon Highlanders. Many years later rumours surfaced that the wound Cameron suffered at Quatre Bras, from which he died later that day, was inflicted by one of his own men. In *Records of Argyll, 1885* (seventy years after the event) Lord Archibald Campbell wrote:

> There is a story current at Dunstaffnage, which used to be told by an old pensioner who lived on the estate and belonged to the district, that Colonel Cameron of Fassifern, of the 92nd, who was shot at Quatre Bras, was shot by one of his own men who was a bad character, and whom he had had flogged a few days before.

Greenhill Gardyne, in Volume I of *The Life of a Regiment*, alludes to the story and comments: 'whereas, though the captain of a ship could, in former days, order a man to be flogged, no officer, of whatever rank, had such power in the army. The colonel could order a soldier, for certain crimes, to be tried by Court-martial; and the Court, if the prisoner was found guilty, could condemn him to corporal punishment according to the law as it then existed, but the colonel could not.' The sole source of this allegation comes from 'an old pensioner who lived on the estate and belonged to the district'. There is no indication as to who this pensioner was, or indeed if he had served in the

92nd. If the story was wrong in respect to Cameron's power to order a flogging, what credence should be given to the rest? Cameron was known to be strict, but fair, respected and admired by his officers and men. There is no contemporary evidence from anyone who was actually there that he was shot by one of his own men. Had it happened, the men around the perpetrator must have seen it, and it is inconceivable that men who trusted and respected their commanding officer would have stood by and done nothing, yet there is no account of any disturbance in the ranks or protest that would have been noted by their N.C.O.s and officers. Sergeant Robertson, who was quite prepared to record the shortcomings as well as the strengths of The Gordon Highlanders, had criticised Cameron earlier in his *Journal*. In the days after Waterloo, he would have heard the battle tales, rumours and scandals discussed by the survivors, but he makes no mention whatsoever of Cameron being shot by one of his own. Nor do the two officers, Lieutenants Hope and Hobbs, who kept diaries, or Captain Winchester, who later recorded his account of Quatre Bras and Waterloo (each of whom would undoubtedly have been aware of any talk of such an event) make any reference whatsoever to it in their diaries, letters and accounts of the battle. Much of the fire against the 92nd was coming from the upper storey of a farmhouse, and Sergeant Robertson states: 'The lieutenant-colonel at this time was coming up as fast as he could ride, having been shot through the groin.' Captain Winchester confirms this incident: 'Here Colonel Cameron received his mortal wound on which he lost the power of managing his horse; the animal turned round and galloped with all his speed along the road until he reached Quatre Bras, where Colonel Cameron's groom was standing, with his led horse. The horse then suddenly stopping pitched the Colonel over his head on the road.' To be shot through the groin while astride a horse, the shot must have come from above. A shot that caused a groin wound fired by a man close by on the ground would almost certainly have hit the horse also and would probably have passed through Cameron's thigh. There is no record of Cameron's horse being wounded, or any reference to a wounded leg. Logically, therefore, the burden of evidence suggests that the shot was fired from above. This, allied to the absence of any mention of such a significant act by those who were present can only lead to the reasonable presumption that there is no truth in the allegation.

In Colonel Cameron the Gordon Highlanders lost an officer who had served with them in every campaign except Corunna; he had commanded a battalion since 1806, and had led them 'always to honour and almost always to victory.' His influence had a lasting effect on the character of the regiment. A strict disciplinarian, he understood that prompt obedience could be enforced without worrying officers or men, and that discipline and drill made his soldiers cool and hardy in times of danger and difficulty. He was respected by his officers, to whom his manner was rather reserved and distant. He did not shirk responsibility, and 'never allowed the rights or comforts of his men to be disregarded or lost sight of by any one; they considered him their best and never-failing friend, and reposed the most implicit and unbounded confidence in him as a commander'. The effects of his fiery nature were never more severely felt than by the officers of the commissariat if his men suffered from any neglect at the hands of that department. His officers and men had nothing to fear if they did their duty.

A most respectable old soldier, John Downie, used to speak of him as being much liked by the good men, 'though he made us do our duty'; 'a splendid soldier'; 'his only fault, his reckless bravery'. The late Sir Duncan Cameron having heard it stated that his brother sometimes carried discipline to excess sent for two Ballachulish men who had served in the 92nd. The first was a cunning calculating customer, whose desire was to please by speaking smooth things, and he made out the colonel's character to be so perfectly angelic that Sir Duncan, seeing through him, ordered him off without even showing him the hospitality for which his house was famous. The other was a manly old soldier, who spoke as he thought and felt. Sir Duncan questioned him, '*Dé nis an scorsa duine a bha 'nam bhrathair?*' '*Innsidh mise dhuibh a Shir Donnachdh; se Duine gasda, foghainteach, àilidh, a bha 'n Colonel Ian, fhad 'sa bha gnothaichean a dol gu math, ach 'se fior dheamhan a bh'ann 'nuair a rachadh camadh na corraige air aimreidh.*' ('Now, what sort of a man was my brother?' 'I will tell you, Sir Duncan. Colonel John was a fine, brave, splendid man when duty was well done [business went well], but the very devil when anything went wrong [*lit.* when the bending of the finger].') Sir Duncan asked no more questions. '*Ni sin an gnothach*' ('That is enough'), and dismissed him to his dinner in the hall with a £1 note in his pocket. In short, Colonel Cameron may be described as one who used his authority 'for the punishment of evil-doers, and the praise of them that do well'.

He was a born leader of men, besides being a true Highland gentleman, devoted to the music and poetry of his country.

The Duke of Wellington thus expressed himself in his dispatch to the Secretary of State, transmitting the list of killed and wounded at Quatre Bras and Waterloo:

> Your Lordship will see in the enclosed lists the names of some most valuable officers lost to His Majesty's service. Among them I cannot avoid to mention Colonel Cameron, of the Ninety-second, and Colonel Sir Henry Ellis, of the Twenty-third Regiments, to whose conduct I have frequently drawn your Lordship's attention, and who at last fell

distinguishing themselves at the head of the brave troops which they commanded.

Notwithstanding the glory of the occasion, it is impossible not to lament such men, both on account of the public and as friends.

The Life of a Regiment, Volume I, pp 358–60.

Monument to John Cameron of Fassiefern at Kilmallie

CHAPTER 32

MARQUIS OF HUNTLY, FIFTH AND LAST DUKE OF GORDON

A S eldest son of the 4th Duke of Gordon, George Gordon was Marquis of Huntly. A soldier from his earliest days, he served with the 3rd Guards (Scots Guards), 1st Royals (Royal Scots), 35th (Royal Sussex), 42nd Royal Highlanders (Black Watch) and of course The Gordon Highlanders. He led the Gordons in their first major action, where he was wounded. (He carried the musket ball in his back for seven years, until it was removed by surgery.) He was a genial man, easy to get on with and well regarded by all, from courtier to crofter. At home in social and Court circles, he was also a man of the people. He understood Highlanders, speaking Gaelic fluently and sharing their sense of humour! He became Duke of Gordon in 1827 and was highly regarded in the Gordon lands. When he died in 1836 his funeral ceremonies were major occasions in London and in Scotland:

> George, fifth and last Duke of Gordon, eighth Marquess of Huntly, and thirteenth Earl of Huntly died in London on 28th May, 1836. When he died his dukedom became extinct, though his marquisate passed to the fifth Earl of Aboyne, while his estates, worth £30,000 a year, passed to his sister, the Duchess of Richmond, who gave the famous Waterloo Ball in 1815. But if he had no children of his own, he has had thousands of them as members of the Gordon Highlanders, raised by father and mother, of whom he was the first Colonel.

The Duke, born at Edinburgh on 2nd February, 1770, was a soldier all his life. He could hardly have been otherwise, for he was born into a world that was absorbed in the problem of raising men to fight France. He was commissioned as Ensign in the 35th Foot in 1790, and later that year got a Letter of Service to raise an independent company for the Black Watch. He was given command of the company in the Black Watch in 1791. In 1792 he was Captain Lieutenant in 3rd Foot Guards (now Scots Guards). In 1794 he was appointed Lieutenant-Colonel in the 100th (afterwards 92nd Gordon Highlanders) of which he became Colonel in 1796. He was promoted to Major-General in 1801, to Lieutenant-General in 1808 to General in 1819. He became Governor of Edinburgh Castle in 1827, and was also Colonel of the Scots Fusilier Guards (now Scots Guards), the Royal Scots and the Black Watch.

John Malcolm Bulloch

T&S, June 1936.

An old wound

While commanding the 92nd at Egmont-op-Zee in 1799 Huntly was wounded by a musket ball and was taken from the field of battle. The wound troubled him for some years:

The Marquess saw much of Aberdeen in 1803–06, when on the North British Staff. His Helder wound gave him trouble, seven years after he received it. In Aberdeen on 8th April, 1806, he got an attack of fever, with severe pain, 'in that part of his back where suspicion lay that an extraneous body was lodged. This hourly increased, and a fluctuating tumor made its appearance. On pressure, a hard substance was felt, which pointed out the necessity of its removal. On Friday the 10th a simple incision was made into the tumor, and along with three ounces of purulent matter, a piece of leaden bullet was discharged, ragged in its surface, pointed at one end, about the size of a small raisin flattened. His Lordship bore the operation with his well known fortitude 'and (said the *Aberdeen Journal*) it must be very pleasing to all ranks of people to know that this noble, gallant officer, who has so long suffered violent attacks of pain, from having bled in his country's cause, has now every prospect of a complete recovery; but with a heart still ardent to expose himself again to danger, when his services are required. Let Britain have confidence, when she has such sons.' In a few days his doctor assured him that he could take his 'accustomed exercises' on horseback. He was popular with the garrison in the town, which at that time was not the Depot of the Gordons.

T&S, June 1936.

GEORGE GORDON, MARQUIS OF HUNTLY

An accomplished mimic

George Gordon always felt at home on his Highland estates, where he mixed freely with his tenants, speaking with them on friendly and equal terms. He spoke Gaelic, English and the Doric of the north-east, and was fluent and comfortable in each. He had a remarkable ability to disguise himself, in dress, posture and speech, so well that even close acquaintances could be fooled:

George, fifth Duke of Gordon, as Marquis of Huntly was the first Colonel of the Gordon Highlanders. Although long separated from the regiment officially, the connection was continued by many friendly ties, and it is not out of place, in the history of a Highland regiment, to notice the death of one whose position was so exceptional in the Highlands, particularly in the districts from which that regiment was principally recruited; and where he is still remembered for his generous sympathy with the peasantry, and his friendly personal intercourse with all classes. He was in the habit of giving one of his agents a sum to be distributed in alms to the poor of the neighbourhood, but hearing that the money was not so applied, he one day appeared in beggar's rags at his almoner's door, and, with the trembling voice of age, solicited alms. A servant told him to be gone—'No beggars allowed here!' In the well-feigned accent of the country he was pleading his necessity, when the master appeared and sternly ordered him to be gone, or he would set the dog at him! When in the next annual accounts the usual charge for 'incidental charities' appeared, the Marquis drew his pen through it, and reminded his agent with a severe rebuke of his conduct to the beggar.

One of a party, when his power of counterfeiting character was the topic of conversation, bet that he could not be deceived. The wager was accepted, and in a few days a sturdy gaberlunzie, in rags, doffed his bonnet to the gentleman, whom he met in his avenue. After answering a few questions in the dialect of the district, he was sent to the Hall, where he was served with an ample meal. On quitting the house he took care to cross the Laird's path and make his bow.

'Well, old boy, how did you fare in the hall?'

'Vara middlin',' replied the beggar; 'naething but cauld beef, soor bread, and stale ale!'

Enraged at this impudence, the Laird called some of his men and threatened to have him punished, when, like the 'Gudeman of Ballengeich,' Huntly

Let a' his duddies fa'
And stood the brawest gentleman that was amang them a'.

461

The men of Lochaber were not, in the early nineteenth century, the quiet, railway-riding, up-to-date people of today. Rent days, shinty matches, weddings, fairs, and funerals were all festive occasions where liquor flowed, and quarrels were settled by a fight. The Rev. D. MacColl, was factor on the Gordon estates there, but in his absence the Duke sent a gentleman from his lowland property to collect the rents, telling him to be sure to have an ox killed and a cask of whisky broached to regale the tenants. The agent gave the entertainment *first*, with the result that Highland blood was up; he fled in terror, and returned empty. His Grace, who understood his Highland tenantry, laughed and said, 'Never mind, I'll go with you next time,' which he did. The rents were willingly paid, *after* which another ox and cask of whisky were provided, and all went home happy and cheering their popular landlord.

He was a keen deer-stalker. Those who visited for that sport have described life at Glenfeshie—box-beds, two in a room, the fare the produce of hill and stream, dinner announced by the *piobreachd*; in the evening, music from the ladies, reels to the violin. The Duke and his Highland friends wore Highland dress on the hill and in the evening. Every guest was expected to sport at the least a vest of Gordon tartan.

After 1815 the best farms on the Gordon estates in Badenoch and Lochaber were occupied by retired officers, among them Colonel Mitchell and others of the 92nd. These were constant guests at Kinrara and Glenfeshie, and at Gordon Castle. Nor were the rank-and-file forgotten. Sgt MacKinnon, a Banavie man, who left a leg in Spain, was postmaster at Kingussie, a situation obtained for him by the Duke, and his daughter, named Johanna Cameron, after 'Fassiefern,' still (1900) occupies the house built for him, and relates how His Grace danced at the house-warming. To this day sons of old 92nd soldiers occupy their fathers' holdings on what were the Gordon estates;[1] for the Duke's vast lands in Badenoch and Lochaber, with the exception of Kinrara, were sold. It is not surprising to find that on his farewell visit to Badenoch a scene of the wildest enthusiasm took place, or that for years after his death 'the memory of the fifth and last Duke of Gordon' was drunk in solemn silence at public dinners. The other estates went to his nephew, the Duke of Richmond. The Dukedom of Gordon became extinct.[2] The title 'Marquis of Huntly' went to the Earls of Aboyne.

The Life of a Regiment, Volume II, pp 27–9.

---

1   Thirty years after the war some £2,000 was paid to pensioners at Kingussie on a single day. Many of these men had vests made of their regimental red jackets, on which they wore their medals on these occasions.

2   The Duke of Richmond was created Duke of Gordon in 1876.

George Gordon, 5th Duke of Gordon

Service to Scotch whisky

George Gordon, Marquis of Huntly, has a special place in the history of Scotch whisky. Deeply troubled by the whisky smuggling and related lawlessness of his Highland compatriots, Huntly thought that the Government could curtail the lawlessness by making it profitable to produce whisky legally, and so proposed this in the House of Lords. The Excise Act of 1823 was passed, legalizing the distillation of whisky in return for a license fee of £10 and a set payment per gallon of proof spirit. Smuggling died out almost completely over the next ten years. A great many of the present-day distilleries stand on sites used by illicit distillers who went legitimate. The Excise Act of 1823 thus laid the foundations for the Scotch whisky industry.

THE LIFE OF A REGIMENT

Funeral of Fifth Duke of Gordon

The military aspect of his career was emphasized at his funeral in London, which was on a very lavish scale, almost as a State occasion. As the Gordon Highlanders were in Malta, they took no part in it.

The Duke's body was removed from his London home in Belgrave Square to Greenwich on 3rd June, with 'imposing ceremony, one of the most grand and imposing spectacles ever witnessed in this country.' (*The Times*)

The procession moved through crowded streets to Greenwich, where the coffin was lowered on to the Royal Barge and rowed out by blue-jackets—Nelson's old boatswain at the helm—to the Government steamer *Firebrand* in midstream. The Scots Guards band followed in a barge, playing the *Dead March* in *'Saul'* while the regiment as a whole was drawn up on the platform facing the Thames.

The *Firebrand* sailed north, passing Aberdeen on Sunday, 5th June, and landed at Speymouth on Monday, 6th June. The coffin was taken to Gordon Castle, to lie in state till Thursday, 9th June, when it was taken to Elgin, where the Gordons had been buried for generations, and deposited in the vault where his ancestors lay.

The austerely beautiful granite statue of the Duke in the Castlegate, erected in 1844,[3] made the features of the Duke familiar to all Aberdonians. Its inscription reads:

George,
Fifth and Last
Duke of Gordon,
Born 1770
Died 1836
First Colonel of
92nd Gordon Highlanders.

His father and mother raised the Gordons, he was their first Colonel, and he did his soldiering in the field with them. He was immortalized as regards his experience in 1799, when the Gordons gained their first battle honour 'Egmont-op-Zee', by Mrs. Grant of Laggan's[4] song, *'Oh, where, tell me where, has your Highland laddie gone?'*

John Malcolm Bulloch

T&S, June 1936.

---

3   The large statue was the first to be sculpted from a single piece of granite. It now stands in Golden Square, Aberdeen. Its previous site at the Castlegate is now occupied by the Gordon Highlanders statue, erected in 2011.
4   Mrs Anne Grant, Scottish poet and author.

CHAPTER 33

SERGEANT DAVID ROBERTSON

O NE of the most interesting accounts of The Gordon Highlanders in the years 1800 to 1815 is *Sergeant Robertson's Journal*, in which Sergeant David Robertson relates his experiences in the actions in which the Regiment was engaged. His *Journal* is an invaluable source of information about the Napoleonic Wars, seen from the ranks as opposed to the different viewpoint given in the memoirs of officers who took part. Mr A.J. Henderson, a former officer of The Gordon Highlanders, compiled these biographical details:

Robertson, son of Alexander and Christian Robertson was born in Dunkeld, Perthshire, in about 1777. After service in the Atholl Company of Volunteers and the Caithness Highlanders, he volunteered into the 92nd (Highland) Regiment of Foot, being attested at Cork on 7th of July 1800, and he remained with it for the rest of his military career.

On 12th December 1800 he joined the 92nd in Malta and went with it to Egypt. On return to Britain he was promoted Corporal on 7th December 1803. He was promoted Sergeant on 17th October 1807 while on the expedition to Denmark. He went to the Iberian Peninsula in 1808 and took part in the retreat to, and battle of, Corunna in 1808/9. On the Regiment's return to Britain he accompanied it on the expedition to Walcheren in 1809, and after that, returned with the 92nd to the Peninsula in 1810.

In the Peninsula he was present at the Battles of Fuentes d'Onor (1811), Arroyo del Molinos (1811), Almaraz (1812), Defence of Alba de Tormes (1812), the Pass of Maya (1813), Vittoria (1813), the Pyrenees (1813), Nivelle (1813), Nive (1813), Orthes (1814) and Toulouse (1814).

On 25th September 1813, Robertson was appointed Colour Sergeant, a rank which he held until 12th May 1815 when, for reasons unknown, he reverted to the rank of Sergeant.

On Napoleon's abdication in 1814, the 92nd returned to Britain and was stationed in Ireland, until April 1815, when it went to join Wellington's Army in Flanders.

On the night of the 15th June it was rushed to the village of Quatre Bras to try to stem the surprise attack of the French under Marshal Ney. Robertson was wounded, but returned to duty as soon as he was able.

> In this attempt I received a wound in the head, while in the act of cheering the men forward. I was very sick for a short time, and was sent to the rear under the care of the surgeon, where I got my wound

dressed, and remained till morning; and when I awoke I found I was able to join the regiment again. On account of this wound I was reported dead, and my old companions were rather surprised at my return.

Sergeant Robertson's Journal.

The following extract is from the Preface to the Second Edition of *Sergeant Robertson's Journal*, by Mr A.J. Henderson:

Of Robertson as a person we know little, as unlike diarists he leads straight into the narrative of the story of his military life and gives us no initial clue to his origins and upbringing. However, a document at the Public Record Office at Kew shows that when he was admitted to a pension of 1s 10d on his discharge on 22nd June, 1818, he was 41 years of age, 5ft 9ins tall, had fair hair and complexion, grey eyes and was a shoemaker by trade. This document also shows him as having enlisted in the Caithness Highlanders on 5th April, 1795, and as having transferred to the 92nd Foot on 7th July, 1800.

Col. C. Greenhill Gardyne in his history of the 92nd, *The Life of a Regiment*, gives Robertson's Christian name as Duncan, but the above document, as well as both the muster and medal rolls at the PRO, shows that it was in fact David, and as some other writers have taken their cue from Gardyne and also referred to him as Duncan, it is nice to have this opportunity to set the record straight.

Robertson had the good fortune to serve in the Army during one of the most epoch making periods in our history, and under three of our greatest Generals in the campaigns in which their reputations were made, namely Abercromby, Moore and Wellington. Many veterans of these wars have left memoirs of their experiences, but for the most part they were Officers, whose views of life naturally were rather different to those of the men they commanded. Robertson, however, belongs to that smaller group of writers who came from amongst those who form the vast bulk of an army, the rank and file. As he states in his preface, Robertson kept his *Journal* throughout his service and eventually published it in his own natural words, unedited by anyone with literary pretensions. We are therefore lucky enough to have views which are clearly his own and from which we are able to learn the opinions of the Generals themselves, and these are not always flattering! In the same way Robertson, although proud of the Regiment in which he served, is not averse to criticising it. This is the work of an honest, hardworking soldier who committed his thoughts to paper exactly as they occurred.

Sergeant Robertson's Journal, Preface to the Second Edition.

Survivor of Waterloo

After Quatre Bras on 16 June 1815, during which its Commanding Officer, Colonel John Cameron of Fassiefern, had been mortally wounded, the 92nd marched to Wellington's chosen position near Mont St. Jean. On 18 June the Regiment played a gallant part in the Battle of Waterloo. At one point in the battle, due to the loss of officers killed or wounded, Robertson was in command of two companies, a heavy responsibility for a sergeant, but one that he shouldered willingly and carried out effectively.

Robertson was one of the depleted band of Gordon Highlanders who marched to Paris after Waterloo, after which they returned to Britain:

> We remained in Paris till November, when we were shipped for England, and shortly after our arrival, were ordered for Scotland. On the road we were treated with great kindness, and entertained with hospitality in almost every place on the way, until we came to Edinburgh, from whence we marched to Ireland. I remained with my regiment here till 1818, when, owing to a disappointment in my promotion, and the increase of my family, I applied for my discharge, which, after some delay, was at last granted. Having got a pension for my services sufficient to support me, I finally wended my way to the place of my nativity, where I live in peace, far removed from those scenes of bloodshed and misery which it has been my lot to witness, and which I have thus attempted to describe.

Sergeant Robertson's Journal.

Robertson may have been justified in his disappointment at lack of promotion, for he had been a sergeant since 1807, had carried out all the duties demanded of him and more, and had commanded companies in battle. He felt that preference was given to men from the parts of the country from which their officers came, and he may well have been right. There are numerous examples, quoted as good man-management, of officers taking a particular interest in the men who had joined with them from their own areas, but this inevitably meant that men of ability from other parts of the country on occasions missed out on advancement:

> This 'disappointment' may actually have saved Robertson's life, as the following year, 1819, the 92nd was posted to the West Indies where it was decimated by disease, and many veterans of Egypt, Denmark, the Peninsula and Waterloo perished.

> In 1809 he married Margaret Crerar, and by her had eight children. Robertson did not live to receive a Military General Service Medal as he died in 1846, just prior to its issue, to those still living, in 1847.

A.J. Henderson.

Sergeant Robertson's Journal is a valuable account of the wars in Egypt, the Peninsula, France and Waterloo, and an absorbing insight into the life of the ordinary soldier during those wars. That the *Journal* was published at all is fortuitous, as the original draft, which Robertson entrusted to a friend for comment, was lost, and was only found by chance many years afterwards:

On his return to the place of his nativity, in 1818, a number of friends expressed a desire that he should publish a work so fraught with interest to them, and to the country in general. After repeated solicitations, he so far complied with their request as to commence to get it ready for publication. Not being satisfied, however, with the state in which it was, he gave it into the hands of a literary friend that he might give it that polish which he was desirous it should have, before it went forth to the public. But, as the grim monarch will raise his messenger as readily on the downy-bed as on the bloody battle-field, before the work of revisal had been commenced, the friend into whose hands the MS. had been committed was suddenly cut off; and in turning over his effects, the Author's labours had happened to be mislaid, and were considered as lost. After a lapse of twenty years, however, they were accidentally discovered, and safely returned in the same state in which they had at first been left by the Author.

Sergeant Robertson's Journal; Preface to the First Edition.

CHAPTER 34

THE MACDONALDS OF DALCHOSNIE

THE Gordon Highlanders had many examples of members of the same family serving in the Regiment. Sons succeeded fathers and grandfathers, nephews followed uncles, and brothers served alongside brothers. When the 92nd was raised Lieutenant George Gordon (natural son of the 4th Duke of Gordon) was the younger half-brother of the first Commanding Officer, George, Marquis of Huntly. It was 1798, however, before the first member of a remarkable family joined the 92nd. The MacDonalds of Dalchosnie played a major part in the military history of Scotland. No fewer than nine of them served in The Gordon Highlanders, but they had been making their mark for more than a century before the 92nd was raised. They gave military service over many generations, fighting for James VII, the Old and Young Pretenders and in the British Army.

The MacDonalds were staunch supporters of the Stewart line and fought in all the actions in Scotland for the Stewart cause. Allan MacDonald (First of Dalchosnie) (1)[1] fought under Viscount Dundee at Killiecrankie in 1689. His sons John (1) and Donald (1) served in the Atholl Regiment in support of the Old Pretender in 1715; Donald being executed at Preston. John's second son, Alan (2) was also out in 1715 and died in prison in Manchester. Two more of John's sons, Alexander (1) and John (2), were out with the Young Pretender in 1745 and both were killed at Culloden in 1746. Alexander had two sons, Alan (3) and John (3), both of whom were out with the Prince in 1745. Alan died of wounds and John MacDonald was the only male member of the family who came through the '45 alive. John had three sons and a daughter, Alexander (2), William (1), Donald (2) and Julia. Alexander (2) had five sons of whom three—John (4), Alexander (3) and James—served in the 92nd. Donald (2) commanded the 92nd at Waterloo and had two sons, William (2) and Alan (4), who served in the 92nd. Julia married Captain Alexander MacDonald of Moy and their son Ranald also served in the 92nd. Of Alexander's (2) sons, John (4) went on to command the 92nd and ended his career as a General; Alexander (3) died of wounds at the Pass of Maya in 1813; and James saw service in the Peninsula. General Sir John MacDonald (4) had four sons, of whom two, Alistair MacIan (who as General, commanded the forces in Scotland) and John Alan, both served in the 92nd.

---

1 As the same Christian names appear from generation to generation I have marked the names in Arabic numerals in chronological order.

Donald MacDonald

Donald MacDonald (2), the youngest son of John MacDonald (3), the survivor of the '45, was gazetted to the 92nd in 1798. He was a good officer who understood his men. John Cattanach of Badenoch, 'spoke much of his captain, MacDonald (Dalchosnie); he and many other officers constantly spoke Gaelic to them, and would give news from home to those from their own districts'. Donald MacDonald suffered his share of wounds while fighting for The Gordon Highlanders. At Egmont-op-Zee in 1799 he took part in the furious hand-to-hand conflict with the French that lasted three-and-a-half hours. *The Life of a Regiment* states: 'It may be observed that this is one of the few instances on record of crossing bayonets by large bodies. Even the supernumerary rank of the 92nd on this occasion was bayoneted.' MacDonald, who fought with great bravery, received bayonet wounds in the breast while defending himself against the united attacks of three French soldiers.[2] At Arroyo del Molinos in 1811 he was seriously wounded. Cameron of Fassiefern, commanding the Regiment, wrote: 'poor Captain Donald MacDonald is most dangerously wounded, having his left leg broke, and wounded under the right knee'. Amputation was proposed as the only means of saving his life, but he produced a brace of pistols and threatened to blow out the brains of the first surgeon who attempted to amputate his legs! The surgeon took the hint, and saved the legs. When Cameron was killed at Quatre Bras and Lieutenant-Colonel Mitchell, who succeeded him, wounded, Donald MacDonald took command. Although wounded at Quatre Bras, he led the 92nd throughout the day at Waterloo and was at their head when they broke the French column, 3,000 strong, that threatened to pierce the British line. He remained in command for the remainder of the campaign, leading the 92nd to Paris and, when it returned to Britain, on its triumphant march through Edinburgh to the Castle. Having handed command back to Lieutenant-Colonel Mitchell when the latter returned, recovered from his wounds, Lieutenant-Colonel MacDonald retired on half-pay in 1818; fortuitously before the 92nd embarked on its disastrous tour in the West Indies, where it lost more men to yellow fever than it had in the Napoleonic Wars. Lieutenant-Colonel Donald MacDonald, C.B. died in 1829 'of the effects of his wounds after years of suffering'. Of him the *Edinburgh Morning Advertiser* of June 1829 reported: 'The deceased was a complete soldier. Few officers have seen more service or had their bodies so severely shattered by their country's enemies. His deeds will live long in the remembrance of his relatives and old companions in arms. May every

---

2 Cameron of Fassiefern, in a letter to his father, describes this wounding: 'Lieutenant D. MacDonald, Duncan's friend, is amongst the worst wounded of the officers that have survived. He has got two thrusts of a bayonet through his breast.'

Highland warrior bear in recollection the heroic exploits of their intrepid countryman, and like him when duty calls them to the mortal combat, tread in the paths of honour and of duty.'

JOHN MACDONALD

Donald MacDonald's nephew, Alexander (3), was a Lieutenant in the 92nd when he died of wounds received at the desperate battle at the Pass of Maya in 1813. Had Alexander lived he would have witnessed at La Zarza, only five days later, a remarkable display of courage and daring by his elder brother, John (4), who would one day command the 92nd:

> When the 92nd retired from the ridge, a Portuguese battalion was ordered to cover the retreat, but their conduct proved an exception to the generally conspicuous gallantry of their countrymen. In the valley, between the ridge and the rocks to which the 92nd retired, were some houses which should have been held by the Portuguese, but of which they allowed the French to get possession, taking the shortest road to safety. Enraged to see this post lost by the bad behaviour of his men, their colonel rode up to the standard-bearer, snatched the flag from his hands, and galloped to within 100 yards of the houses, where he remained for a considerable time with shot flying about his ears, while he waved the colour round his head to induce his men to follow. The gallant young colonel (he was only captain in the British army) was a Highlander, he had both an uncle and a brother in the 92nd, and it was with the greatest difficulty their officers could prevent the Highlanders from breaking away to render their countryman the aid which his Portuguese refused; but the orders were peremptory, and soon they had the pleasure of congratulating the young commander on his hairbreadth escapes from the danger in which his gallantry had placed him, for his cloak and clothes were pierced in several places by musket balls. He was John MacDonald of Dalchosnie, and he many years afterwards commanded the Gordon Highlanders.

The Life of a Regiment, Volume I, p 305.

John MacDonald (4) joined the 88th Regiment in 1803. He was with them in the expedition to Buenos Ayres in 1804, and was twice wounded at the storming of Monte Video. From 1808 to 1814 he served in the Peninsula, Pyrenees and South of France; first as Captain in the 88th and afterwards as Lieutenant-Colonel of the IVth Portuguese Regiment. He was at Busaco with the 88th, and took part in the retreat to Lisbon and in the defence of Torres Vedras. He commanded his Portuguese regiment at the relief of Badajoz, and took part in the battles of Albuhera and Vittoria. In the Battle of the Pyrenees in July 1813, he was severely wounded. On recovering from his wounds he took command of his regiment and took the fortified Rock of Arolla, after desperate fighting. In recognition of his services he was permitted to wear on his crest a flag with the word 'Arolla' inscribed on it. In the assault he was again severely wounded. In April 1814 he took part in the Battle of Toulouse. In 1817, on account of ill-health, he retired with the rank of Lieutenant-Colonel on half-pay, but he was again placed on full pay in 1819 in the 91st Regiment, of which he became Lieutenant-Colonel in 1824. In 1828 he was appointed to command the 92nd Regiment, which was in a poor state after a debilitating and disease-ridden tour in the West Indies under commanding officers who were not of the regiment. MacDonald, himself a Gaelic-speaking Highlander with an innate understanding of Highland soldiers, very quickly brought the 92nd back to its accustomed standard. While commanding the 92nd he fought one of the last duels to take place in the Army.[3] Like all good commanding officers, MacDonald was firm, insisting on discipline and professionalism, but fair. He looked for merit where it was to be found and rewarded it accordingly.

When John MacDonald handed over command of the 92nd in 1846 he had been in command for some eighteen years. While this had denied promotion to some senior Gordon Highlanders, it had been of lasting benefit to the 92n: 'His system of interior economy was acknowledged by the men to have made service in the regiment most comfortable, for though he insisted on a smart and soldier-like appearance, he studied to prevent any unnecessary expense to the soldier. Of a kind and generous though fiery nature, he was not a man to be trifled with, and could be severe on either officer or soldier where severity was required; but like the old Highland chiefs, he would never allow one of his people to be wronged.'[4] He was highly regarded throughout the Army, not least by the Duke of Wellington. Greenhill Gardyne says: 'Feared by the bad men, he was liked by the good, and I never heard one who had served under him speak of Colonel MacDonald without respect.'

Once, coming out of church in Glasgow, some of the men put on their bonnets before leaving the building. MacDonald rebuked them: 'Have ye no respect to the House of God and be damned to ye?' On another occasion he had pitched into the officers very severely on parade, and their silence at lunch was the measure of their resentment, which the colonel observing, said, 'Gentlemen, I thought that ye knew by this time that the old man's bark is worse than his bite,' and all went well again.

MacDonald commanded the 92nd in Ireland, Gibraltar, Malta, West Indies, Scotland and took them back to Ireland, where he was promoted Major-General in 1846. In 1848 he was appointed Commander of the Forces and Lieutenant-Governor of Jamaica, but on the breaking out of rebellion in Ireland he was selected by the Duke of Wellington to take command of the

---

3   An account of this duel is in Chapter 11.
4   *T&S*, Volume II, p 46.

force sent to suppress the disturbance. He remained in Ireland, with his headquarters at Kilkenny, until 1854. While preserving a high state of discipline, General MacDonald was exceedingly popular with the Irish population. Major-General MacDonald was promoted to Lieutenant-General in 1854, appointed Colonel of the 92nd in 1855, made K.C.B. in 1856 and promoted to General in 1862. He died in 1866.[5]

John MacDonald had two brothers who also served in the 92nd: Alexander (3) and Captain James. Lieutenant Alexander MacDonald served with the 92nd in the Peninsula and the Pyrenees, and died of wounds received at the Pass of Maya in 1813. He was the original of 'Alistair MacDonald' in Grant's *Romance of War*. Captain James MacDonald served in the Peninsula and died unmarried in 1840.

Sir John had four sons, of whom Alastair MacIan (afterwards General) and John Alan (afterwards Captain) served with the 92nd. His other sons were Charles, who served as a captain with the 93rd Highlanders at Alma, Balaclava and Lucknow, and was killed in the attack on the Begum's Palace in India in 1858; and Donald (3), who served as a captain with the 79th in the Crimea till the fall of Sebastopol, in the second siege and storming of Lucknow, and in many other engagements of the Mutiny.

ALASTAIR MACIAN MACDONALD

John MacDonald's eldest son, Alastair MacIan MacDonald, joined the 92nd as Ensign in 1846 and became Lieutenant in the following year. He served as aide-de-camp to his father, from 1848 till 1854. He was appointed aide-de-camp to Sir John Pennefather in 1854 and served with him in Crimea, being present at the Battles of Alma, Inkerman and Sebastopol. He was twice wounded. He was aide-de-camp to the Duke of Cambridge. Promoted Major-General in 1877, in 1881 he was Commander of the Forces in Scotland. He retired in the rank of General:

Alistair MacDonald retired to Dunalastair, at the head of Loch Rannoch, where he conceived the idea of having a steam yacht to run a public service up and down the loch as well as for his own private use. The boat, the *Gitana*, was built in sections at Rutherglen and assembled at Loch Rannoch. She was an iron hulled craft 90ft long and weighing some 54 tons, equipped with a 25 hp steam engine and licensed to carry 360 passengers. She was launched in June 1881 in front of a large and exuberant crowd, but though there was great enthusiasm from the people of Rannoch there was stony hostility from the local landowners, who

---

5   This famous old Highland Warrior died in his native land, and the old colours of his regiment hung for some years over his tomb in the Episcopal Church at Kinloch Rannoch. It is much to be regretted that no portrait of him suitable for reproduction appears to exist. *The Life of a Regiment*, Volume II, p 88

would not allow the General to build a pier at the west end of the loch and neither was he offered safe anchorage at the east end. So the idea of running a public service was abandoned and the *Gitana* was used merely in a private capacity for the General and his friends. The boat was moored for the winter near Kinloch Rannoch, exposed to the elements. In December 1881 a large storm caused the *Gitana* to drag her anchor and she was washed up on the shingle at the head of the loch. She was refloated with some difficulty. When the next great storm came on January 5th 1882, the new mooring remained firm but the severity of the storm smashed some of her elaborately etched saloon windows. The waters poured in and the *Gitana* slowly sank from sight to the muddy waters below. There she remained, about 100 ft from the surface for the next ninety-six years.

In 1972 divers discovered the boat in an upright position, and in an excellent state of preservation. In 1978 the *Gitana* was raised, repaired and refitted. The boat was moored in the same exposed part of the loch as when first launched, and in December 1983 heavy gales caused her to drag her moorings and she was battered to pieces against the shore.

From the *Perthshire Diary*.

General Alistair MacDonald died unmarried in 1910. In the surviving branch of the MacDonalds of Dalchosnie, the descendants of Lieutenant-Colonel Donald MacDonald, there were no surviving sons to carry on the name and the 114-year tradition of illustrious service in the 92nd.

Gitana on Loch Rannoch

CHAPTER 35

Two Gordon Field-Marshals

Field-Marshal Hugh Henry Rose, Lord Strathnairn

A MONG the officers who have held the appointment of Colonel of The Gordon Highlanders, there have been two who reached the highest rank in the British Army.

Hugh Henry Rose, Lord Strathnairn, was born in 1801 in Berlin, where his father, Sir George Henry Rose, was in the diplomatic service. He came of a distinguished family, the Roses of Kilravock in Nairnshire.

After service with the 19th Foot, Major Rose joined the 92nd in 1829 and over the next ten years served with the Regiment in Ireland, Gibraltar and Malta. In Ireland, he quelled a serious riot at Cullan, Tipperary. In Malta, where cholera killed a number of the troops, Rose, with the Regimental surgeon, Dr. Paterson, was indefatigable in caring for the stricken. Writing to Lieutenant-Colonel MacDonald, on leave in Scotland, Rose mentions by name several men, a woman and a child who had died of cholera, and that 'no expense has been spared in attending to their wants. The men are in capital spirits, and it is a pleasure to see the way they attend to one another.' In this outbreak one sergeant, six privates, three women and a child died.

In 1840 he was sent on a military and diplomatic mission to Syria, where he spent eight years. On one occasion he was twice wounded in an engagement with Egyptian cavalry; on another, during an outbreak of religious persecution, he showed great courage in evacuating a party of

Christians from a monastery on Mount Labaron and personally escorting them through hostile country to Beirut.

When war with Russia broke out Rose went to Crimea as Queen's commissioner to the headquarters of the French forces. He was again wounded. He was present at the Battles of the Alma and Inkerman, and his bravery earned the admiration of the Russians themselves. He was recommended for the Victoria Cross, which had recently been instituted, but the proposal was turned down on the grounds that, being a brigadier, he held too high a rank to be given the award!

After the Crimean War, Rose, who had been knighted for his services, went to India, where he won fame commanding the Central India Field Force during the Mutiny. In April 1858, with 1,500 men, of whom 500 were Europeans, he defeated an army of 20,000 under the redoubtable Tantia Topi, and a few days later captured the strong fortress of Jansi. He had fewer than 400 men killed and wounded, whereas the rebels lost 5,000 in killed alone. Early in May, Rose attacked Koonch, which he took after a battle fought in a temperature of 110 degrees in the shade. Later that month, with an army weakened by sickness due to great heat and hard marching, he captured Kalpi from an enemy force ten times the size of his. In June he crowned his achievements by a series of victories culminating in the capture of Gwalior. The resistance of the rebels in Central India collapsed, and the brilliant and exhausting campaign came to an end.

In 1860 Rose became Commander-in-Chief in India in succession to Colin Campbell, Lord Clyde, and from 1865 to 1870 he was Commander-in-Chief in Ireland. He was raised to the peerage in 1866 as Baron Strathnairn of Strathnairn and Jansi, and in the same year accepted the colonelcy of the 92nd; an appointment which he relinquished three years later on being made Colonel of the Royal Horse Guards. In 1877, in recognition of his long and distinguished service, he was promoted Field-Marshal.

Field Marshal Hugh Henry Rose, G.C.S.I., K.C.B., Lord Strathnairn, died in 1885. Unmarried, his title became extinct. An equestrian statue cast from guns captured by the Central India Field Forces in 1858 was set up to his memory in London, but in 1933, after the reconstruction of Knightsbridge Underground Station, it was moved to store. Sir Osbert Sitwell, referring to the statue, wrote: 'The only thing that most Londoners know about this forgotten general is that a bird sometimes nests in his plumes!' Yet Lord Strathnairn was one of the most successful military leaders of his time: brave, resourceful, able, and conscientious, and his name deserves to be remembered with pride.

TWO FIELD-MARSHALS

Field-Marshal Sir George Stuart White

The second Gordon Highlander Field-Marshal was Sir George Stuart White (born 1835), an Irishman from County Antrim, who joined the 92nd after serving in the Indian Mutiny with the 27th (Inniskilling Fusiliers):

After twenty-six years in the Army, as a Major, he achieved distinction in the Afghan War of 1879. During Sir Frederick Roberts' advance from Charasia to Kabul the British force was threatened by a strong body of Afghans, advantageously posted on the heights above a gorge. White led a party of Gordon Highlanders in a daring attack against the numerically superior enemy, and succeeded in clearing the hills and securing the pass. For his conspicuous gallantry on this occasion and in a later action at Babi Wali Kotal, near Kandahar, when he led the Gordons in capturing enemy guns by a charge across open ground swept by enemy fire, he was awarded the Victoria Cross. Thereafter his rise was rapid. Having commanded the 2nd Battalion, Gordon Highlanders 1881 to 1885, he enhanced his reputation in the Burmese War of 1886, on the North-West Frontier, and in Baluchistan. For his services he was knighted. Appointed Commander-in-Chief in India in 1893, he was responsible for the conduct of the Chitral and Tirah Expeditions of 1895 and 1897.

On the outbreak of the South African War in 1899 White, aged 64, was sent to prevent the invasion of Natal. The strength and skill of the enemy was not realized, and the task proved impossible; but White, by his resolve to hold Ladysmith, kept a considerable body of Boers engaged in siege. It is for his defence of the beleaguered city that his name is now chiefly remembered. The odds against him were great and the situation desperate. At one point General Buller, discouraged by the ill-success of the war, suggested it would be wise for the city to capitulate, but White to his lasting credit, replied, 'The loss of 10,000 men would be a heavy blow to England; we must not think of it.' All the efforts of the investing army to dislodge him failed, and on 28th February, 1900, the city was relieved. The defence of Ladysmith ranks as one of the heroic episodes of British history, and White, like Baden-Powell, who had successfully held out at Mafeking, was enthusiastically acclaimed at home. His health, unfortunately, had been impaired by the rigours of the siege.

After the War, White was Governor of Gibraltar, and in 1903 became a Field-Marshal. Two years later he received the Order of Merit. On his return to England in 1908, he was appointed Governor of Chelsea Hospital, where he died in 1912, aged 76.

A battalion of the Gordon Highlanders,[1] whose Colonel he had been for fifteen years, took part in his funeral procession through London, and the officers and warrant officers of the Regiment were ordered to wear mourning for a month. He was buried in his native Antrim, and is commemorated by an equestrian statue in Portland Place, London.

T&S, February 1954.

White had a fund of regimental anecdotes, of which the following is an example. Talking of some of the old characters he had known in the Regiment, he told of one of the old incorrigibles with scores of 'drunks' against him, such as no longer exist in the sober army of to-day. One day he came across this man as a prisoner awaiting disposal at the Orderly Room and said, 'Hallo, what's brought you here again?' 'Jist twa o' the polis, sir.' 'Um! drunk again I suppose?' 'Yes, sir,' shaking his head sorrowfully, 'baith o' them.'

Another story is recorded by Colonel C. Greenhill Gardyne, who stayed with White when he was Governor of Gibraltar. Kaiser Wilhelm II had visited Gibraltar; and when driving with White, having asked permission to smoke, he turned to the latter's ADC to ask for a light, which the aide could not supply: on which the Kaiser turned to his host:— 'How is it that a British Staff Officer cannot produce a match?' to which White replied, 'Because, sir, the British Staff is matchless.'

The Life of a Regiment, Volume II, p 315.

---

1   This would be the 1st Battalion, stationed in Colchester at that time.

CHAPTER 36

IAN HAMILTON

I AN Standish Monteith Hamilton is one of the most remarkable Gordon Highlanders. In a military career which saw active service in every corner of the Empire, in some of the most memorable actions in India, South Africa and during the First World War, he met with success and defeat in battle, achievement and failure in command. He was an unfailing friend of the soldier, whose welfare and well-being were uppermost in his mind. The end of his active military career was associated with failure at Gallipoli, a failure that had more to do with political decisions, poor intelligence and lack of resources than the lack of command ability attributed to Hamilton by those who chose not to share the blame. His greatest achievement was the establishment of the British Legion, which arose out of his recommendations in a report published in 1919 but not actioned by the Government until Field Marshal Lord Haig was tasked to implement it. To Haig and Hamilton belong the credit for forming the Royal British Legion, but to Hamilton belongs the credit for its genesis.

Pedigree

Ian Hamilton was born in Corfu on 16th January 1853, the son of Captain Christian Monteith Hamilton,[1] commanding the Grenadier

---

1   Capt C.M. Hamilton commanded the 92nd from 1865 to 1869.

Company of the 92nd Gordon Highlanders. His mother was Maria Corinna Vereker, daughter of the 3rd Viscount Gort. He was a cousin of Lord Gort, V.C.,[2] the 6th Viscount Gort. By birth he was a mixture of Highland Scot and West Irish—a Celt on both sides. The family was a branch of the Scottish Hamiltons of Westport, and Sir Ian was conscious of the advantages of being born and bred a Scot. His mother died when her second son, Vereker, was born and the children were brought up by grandparents at Hafton House, Dunoon, and in Glasgow.

Joins 92nd

Aged 14, Hamilton entered Wellington College, then in its early years. From Wellington he went to Sandhurst, and in 1872 was gazetted to the Suffolk Regiment. The next year he transferred to his father's regiment, the 92nd Gordon Highlanders, and for sixty-six years served the Regiment in one capacity or another, until he relinquished the appointment of Colonel of the Regiment in 1939. To his dying day he followed the fortunes of the Gordon Highlanders with the keenest interest.

Beginning with the Afghan War of 1878–80, he saw active service in every campaign in which the Empire was involved throughout his career, with the exception of Tibet. He was at Charasiah, and the occupation of Kabul. An early exploit brought him to the notice of Lord Roberts. With fellow subaltern, Lieutenant St John W. Forbes,[3] he made his way into a signalling post that had been rushed by the Afghans. The two subalterns recovered the arms and equipment, and held the post until relief arrived. They then organized a pursuit and killed the leader of the Afghan raiders.

In 1881, the 92nd Gordon Highlanders were on their way to Britain from India, but as a result of a telegram Hamilton sent to Sir Evelyn Wood, advertising a 'splendid battalion eager service much nearer Natal than England,' Hamilton and three companies of Gordon Highlanders found themselves in the disastrous battle of Majuba[4] instead of disembarking at Southampton.

In 1884 Hamilton was with the 1st Battalion on the Nile Expedition and was present at the Battle of Kirbekan. He was promoted brevet major. In 1886–7 he was on the Burmese Expedition and was promoted lieutenant-colonel. In 1895, whilst on the staff of Sir George White, himself a Gordon Highlander, he took part in the Chitral Relief campaign and came once more into close contact with the 1st Battalion.

---

2   He was a first cousin of Standish William Prendergast Vereker, killed at Isandlwana, whose father, the 3rd Viscount Gort, was Hamilton's uncle. He was a first cousin, once removed, of George Standish Gage Craufurd, another distinguished Gordon Highlander.

3   Forbes was to be killed shortly after, gallantly charging a group of Afghans on the heights above Kabul. See Volume IX, Chapter 15.

4   See Hamilton's account of the battle in Volume IX, Chapter 17.

Reaches rank of General

In 1897 renewed trouble on the North-West Frontier of India resulted in British forces being assembled at Nowshera and Peshawar, and one under Sir Bindon Blood was dispatched towards the Malakand Pass, the other being sent from Jamrud for use against the Afridis in Tirah. Hamilton (illustration) was given a brigade, but an accident prevented him from taking part. Later, however, he commanded a brigade which included the 1st Battalion, until the cessation of hostilities in 1898. He distinguished himself, showing great personal bravery, at Elandslaagte and Wagon Point during the Boer War.

From 1904 to 1905, Hamilton was the military attaché of the British Indian Army serving with the Japanese army in Manchuria during the Russo-Japanese War.

Perhaps his greatest service, to the Indian and British Armies, was in rewriting musketry regulations, with emphasis on speed and precision. So well were the lessons learned that at Mons, in 1914, the Germans thought British soldiers were all armed with machine-guns. By 1914 Hamilton had reached the rank of General.

Gallipoli

In March 1915 Kitchener appointed Hamilton to command the Allied Mediterranean Expeditionary Force to gain control of the Dardanelles straits and capture Constantinople. He was 62 and had been in charge of land defences in England. Whilst a senior and respected officer, more experienced than most, he was considered too unconventional, too intellectual and too friendly with politicians to be given a command on the western front. He left London at thirty-six hours' notice to take up his command, with no opportunity to take part in planning the campaign. Poor intelligence reports grossly underestimated the strength and willingness to fight of the defending forces. It was conceived that a force of 70,000 would be adequate to overpower the defenders quickly.

Hamilton (photo below) had to organise armed landings. He had no specialised landing craft, the disparate troops he had been given had no training and supplies had been packed in ways which made them difficult to access for landings. Hamilton believed that the navy would make further attacks during the landings. The navy, anticipating losses and rejecting the idea that loss of ships was tactically acceptable, declined to mount another attack. The Turks had been allowed two months to prepare ground defences and they used the time effectively.

Although the campaign ended in withdrawal, it nearly succeeded. The

Turks stated that on two occasions their Government withdrew to Asia in the belief that the British would be in Constantinople within days. On Gallipoli the flower of the Turkish Army was destroyed, leaving only less-experienced troops to bar the way in Palestine.

On his return Hamilton was offered the post of Commander-in-Chief, Ireland, where the political situation was tense. This he declined, saying: 'I refuse to be made a scapegoat twice.' He was offered the Northern Command of England, but declined, 'to give a younger man a chance.'

He remained on the Active List as Colonel of the Gordon Highlanders—in those days a life appointment. Born in the Regiment, he had hoped to die 'wearing the tartan with the yellow stripe'; but, aware that Major-General Sir James Burnett of Leys, Bt., would soon be 65, the new retiring age, Hamilton resigned in 1939 and recommended Sir James in his stead. He regularly visited the Service and Territorial battalions of the Gordons, flying in two-seater machines of Scottish flying clubs.

Twice denied V.C.

Ian Hamilton had a reputation for courage, gallantry and initiative, qualities which, with his gaiety, quiet dignity in adversity and his far-sightedness, won the admiration of those who knew him and the envy—and sometimes malice—of those who did not. He was mentioned in despatches ten times, and awarded the D.S.O., C.B., K.C.B., G.C.B. and G.C.M.G. He was twice recommended for the Victoria Cross: for Majuba in 1881—disallowed because he was 'too young, and would have plenty more chances'; and Elandslaagte in 1899—disallowed because he was 'too senior—commanding a brigade.'

British Legion

In 1918 a conference of all three Services, with Hamilton as chairman, was convened 'to report upon questions affecting the interests of those who have served and are serving' in the Forces. The report made recommendations to unite ex-Servicemen (and women) who were forming separate groups, each with a political bias. At least half of the members were to be of rank below commissioned officer—a revolutionary suggestion in those days.

The report forwarded to the Government was pigeon-holed till, rivalries between ex-Service associations becoming bitter, the Government implemented Hamilton's report and recalled Lord Haig from a holiday in South Africa to rally ex-Service men and women into one non-political body. Thus were born the British Legion and the British Legion, Scotland. The latter was, in fact, the elder.

Thenceforward Hamilton devoted himself to his old comrades-in-arms. He visited branches, attended functions, and meetings whenever questions of principle were involved: he was indefatigable and never spared himself to help the ex-Service cause in any way he could.

He became President of the British Legion, Scotland, in succession to Lord Jellicoe, an honour he greatly valued and retained to the day of his death. At the last annual conference he attended, in 1947, he was presented with the Freedom of Inverness. Immediately after these ceremonies he attended the Provost's luncheon, listened to the story of his personal encounter with the Loch Ness monster, drank a (large) dram with the Pipe-Major and another with the Bandmaster—all accomplished in a single day by motoring 300-odd miles to and from Blair Drummond—this in his 95th year.

Writer and orator

Sir Ian Hamilton was a man of great literary ability and a gifted writer. His irrepressive gaiety and, charm won the affection and admiration of people in all walks of life. He was a brilliant public speaker, a shrewd and kindly psychologist with a keen sense of humour and a sympathetic understanding of the trials and tribulations of the rank and file. To ex-Servicemen he was more than a hero.

General Sir Ian Hamilton died in London on Sunday, 12th October, 1947, aged 94.

At the unveiling of his memorial in St Paul's Cathedral in 1957, Sir Winston Churchill recalled that he first met Hamilton sixty years before when they were both returning from India. The general's career, he said, had stretched across some of the greatest days of the Empire—from the Afghan War of 1878, through South Africa, the Nile, Burma, the frontier wars of India in the 1890s, to, above all, the Boer War.

'He has described some of those days himself,' said Churchill, 'in the most lively and readable though characteristically modest words. From them, however, and from the memory of those who knew him, emerges the picture of a brilliant and chivalrous man who reached the highest positions in the Army and came to command one of the great endeavours of the First World War.

'Sir Ian Hamilton served his country well, and it is most fitting that he should be honoured here in St. Paul's Cathedral among the illustrious men whose deeds have lighted the pages of our history with their records of courage and patriotism.'

Ian Hamilton was well described by a friend who had long known him as 'the most personally courageous man I have ever seen in action and in the ordinary soldier's life an officer of singular charm and courtesy.'

T&S, 1948, February 1953, May 1954, March 1958.

CHAPTER 37

STANDISH CRAUFURD

G EORGE Standish Gage Craufurd was born in 1872, the eldest son of Sir Charles Craufurd, 4th Baronet of Kilbirnie, and the Hon Isolda Caroline Vereker, eldest daughter of the 4th Viscount Gort.[1] Like Ian Hamilton, he was educated at Wellington College and the Royal Military College, Sandhurst.

Craufurd would have been aware of the military career of his cousin, Ian Hamilton, in the 92nd Gordon Highlanders. The amalgamation of the 92nd with the 75th (Stirlingshire) Regiment in 1881 brought a further link with the Regiment through his great-uncle Robert Craufurd, who, as senior captain, commanded the 75th Highland Regiment in its early days in India, and, as General Robert Craufurd, commanded the Light Division during the Peninsular War until killed at the Siege of Ciudad Rodrigo. It is more likely, however, that it was Standish Craufurd's connection with Ian Hamilton that made him join The Gordon Highlanders, into which he was commissioned in

---

1   Isolda Caroline's aunt, Maria Corinna Vereker, was Ian Hamilton's mother. Hamilton, was therefore Craufurd's first cousin once removed. Maria's brother John became the 5th Viscount Gort, father of Field Marshal Lord Gort, V.C., the 6th Viscount, who was Craufurd's first cousin.

1892. As a lieutenant in the 1st Battalion he took part in a number of actions on the North-West Frontier, including the Gordons' world-famous action at Dargai, where he was wounded.

Boer War

In 1899 the 1st Battalion went to South Africa, where, Craufurd, commanded 'A' Company at Magersfontein, Paardeberg, Poplar Grove,

Driefontein, Houtnek, Vet and Zand Rivers, Doornkop,[2] Belfast and Lydenburg. From March 1901 to July 1902 he commanded the Gordon Highlander company in the 6th Mounted Infantry, and then the 6th Mounted Infantry itself.

In May 1901 a Mounted Infantry force, 300 strong commanded by Major Sladen, which included Craufurd's Gordon Highlander company, captured 45 Boers, 120 wagons and a number of Boer women. Having sent a party to report the success to Lieutenant-Colonel De Lisle, commanding the Mounted Infantry, Major Sladen was expecting De Lisle's main force to join up with him.

Captured

Shortly before noon, just when De Lisle might be expected, large bodies of horse were observed to the west; they came on on two sides in regular formation and were thought to be Bethune's troops.[3] Sladen sent out Captain Craufurd and Lieut. White[4] to inform and direct them.

As Craufurd approached on foot he suddenly found himself within twenty yards of a line of Boer scouts lying on the grass; escape was impossible and he threw his bandolier high in the air in surrender; his action was seen and the alarm given at the laager. On the other flank White

---

2   See Craufurd's account of Doornkop in Volume IX, Chapter 17.
3   Lt-Col E.C. Bethune, late of the 92nd Gordon Highlanders.
4   Lt John White, son of Gen (later Field-Marshal) Sir George White.

was similarly taken, was stripped of his boots and clothes and told to clear off; he did so, away from the scene of the fierce action which now began.

The Life of a Regiment, Volume III, pp 298–9.

After his capture Craufurd went through the horrifying experience of being sentenced to death, but circumstance and Boer reluctance to shoot him enabled him to escape with his life:

> Taken to De Wet and De la Rey and questioned, he answered in the Taal (Cape Dutch, which he had learned well), and the Dutch nurse whom he had suppressed in the morning accused him first of having violated the Red Cross and then of being a renegade Cape Dutchman! His answers were defiant, the Boer leaders appear to have lost their tempers, and he was told off to be shot out of hand, when, as he was being led away, the women of the laager who had been silent witnesses of the cross-examination, suddenly made a rush and surrounded him, declaring that he had done his best for them in the morning, they didn't believe a word of it and he should only be shot over their bodies. De la Rey handed him over to two guards for further enquiry: when the final relief began he made a bolt and escaped the bullets fired at close range by men who, he believes, preferred to miss!

The Life of a Regiment, Volume III, pp 298–300, 332.

Craufurd took part in the mounted infantry operations in Cape Colony, Orange River Colony and Transvaal. For his service in South Africa he was awarded the D.S.O.

He attended the 1903–04 course at the Staff College, Camberley, qualified by special selection on a Commander-in-Chief's nomination for service in the field. In 1905 he was appointed ADC to his cousin, Lieutenant-General Sir Ian Hamilton. From 1905 to 1908 he was a staff officer with the West African Frontier Force and took part in operations in southern Nigeria. For this work he received a letter of appreciation from the Secretary of State for the Colonies. After West Africa he returned to the 2nd Battalion, The Gordon Highlanders in India, where he served from 1908 to 1910, and took part in the 400-mile march that the Battalion made as a political gesture during a time of civil unrest.

Service with Royal Navy

Craufurd was employed (1910–3) as an intelligence officer at Jask, the naval base that controlled access to the Persian Gulf through the Strait of Hormuz. He was engaged in co-ordination and liaison between the Royal Navy and the Army of India, in patrols and operations in the Gulf and on the mainland to intercept gun-runners supplying Baluchi and Afghan traders with

European arms and ammunition, smuggled from Muscat for the Pathan tribes on the North-West Frontier. The force was also tasked to protect the Indo-European telegraph lines and stations. Craufurd took part in operations at sea and on land. For these services he was appointed a Commander of the Indian Empire (C.I.E.) and awarded the Naval General Service Medal. (This medal was awarded to only four Army officers, but it took a lengthy correspondence between Navy and Army before Craufurd's medal was awarded.)

On completing this tour Craufurd returned to the 2nd Battalion, The Gordon Highlanders, then stationed in Cairo. Returning to Britain on leave, Craufurd and Major A.D. Greenhill Gardyne, travelling through Syria, were shown Hittite antiquities by an archaeologist named T.E. Lawrence, who had already made a local name for himself for influence with Arabs and Kurds.

First World War

Craufurd went to France with the 2nd Battalion as second-in-command. He took part in the first battle at Gheluvelt, where he led the Brigade counter attack, and, having taken command of the Battalion after Lieutenant-Colonel Uniacke was wounded, led it at the battle at Zwartelan Woods, where he was wounded. His letter to his mother was dictated by him that same night:[5]

1st November 1914

My Regiment has had a pretty bad time and is much reduced. I think it kept the enemy back all right. Personally after taking command yesterday I was hit by shrapnel this morning in the arm. The wound is in no way serious. Could you write to Lady Saltoun expressing sorrow at Simon Fraser's death and admiring Willie Fraser's pluck.[6] Write to Towse[7] to tell him the Regiment has done splendidly but not many of us left '*pro tem*'.

Love to all.

I am writing for Major Craufurd as he is hit in the forearm.

MW Blackburne, Chaplain 8th Bde.

Major Craufurd is in no danger, the wound is nothing and will heal rapidly.

---

5   Craufurd papers, The Gordon Highlanders Museum (GHPB 2369).

6   Simon Fraser was a younger brother of Capt Alexander Fraser, Master of Saltoun (captured with the 1st Battalion in August 1914); he was killed at Gheluvelt with the 2nd Battalion. Another brother, William Fraser, also served in 2nd Gordons. He went on to command 6th Gordons in 1917 and ended the war commanding the 1st Battalion. He achieved the rank of brigadier and commanded 24 Guards Brigade in Norway, 1940. He was wounded in both wars, was awarded the M.C. and D.S.O. in the First World War and mentioned in despatches in the Second.

7   Capt E. Beachcroft Towse, who was blinded while winning the V.C. in 1900 and who worked tirelessly on behalf of wounded, and particularly blinded, soldiers. See Chapter 26.

After convalescence in Britain he returned to 2nd Gordons in time to take part in the Battle of Neuve Chapelle and the attack on Aubers Ridge, where he was once again wounded, this time severely. Back in Britain, he described the wound to his mother:[8]

21st March 1915

I will now explain my wound. I have had two arteries severed, one a main one. I was fortunately bandaged by our doctor at once, but even so bled to exhaustion on the battlefield and on arrival home had to be operated on as soon as possible to unite the arteries and save my arm being amputated at the socket. It is now a week since the operation and the tube and stitches are out today.

I may possibly be able to go for a drive on Wednesday or Thursday. I am gaining strength every day. Though far more serious than my last wound it is far less painful. This is, I believe, the best War Hospital for Officers in London.

I am rapidly improving—no longer feel exhausted at seeing people or writing letters.

Not easy to write against one's knees in bed!

The Somme

On recovering from his wounds Craufurd commanded 1st Gordons from November 1915 to November 1916, when the Battalion took part in the recapture of The Bluff in February 1916, the actions in the Battle of the Somme around Delville Wood in July, Guillemont in August 1916 (in each of which Craufurd was wounded)[9] and the Ancre in November 1916. As an experienced regimental officer Craufurd took particular care over the welfare of his men. The following letter to his mother shows the lengths to which he went to obtain comforts for his men:

8 January 1916

Both Alister Gordon and I talked over the provision of comforts for the men and decided that the time had now come to organise it properly with an old officer at the head. The work of the ladies of the Regiment last winter filled a much needed gap, but the war is of so uncertain duration we felt it time to place things on a less amateur basis. Mrs Baird asked if you would work for this Battalion or if she should continue, but

---

8   Craufurd papers, The Gordon Highlanders Museum (GHPB 2369).
9   'At some point he was shot at, and his life was saved because the bullet hit and lodged in the large flat flashlight torch which was in a pocket of his coat. I still have the torch, with the bullet embedded in it.' From correspondence with *Sir Robert Craufurd*. (Sir Robert Craufurd generously donated the torch, and other Standish Craufurd artefacts to The Gordon Highlanders Museum.)

I wrote to her, and Alister to Mrs Uniacke saying we had asked Captain Brooke of Fairley[10] to organise things for both Battalions, though we are asking the aid of ladies in the Regiment in the collection of comforts for him to forward. Where not otherwise stated by the donor the two Regular Battalions pool our comforts as we have pooled our funds.

At the same time it is my province as Commanding Officer to beg for my Battalion! From Annbank[11] I beg for a gift of sago—about £1 worth would do the Battalion for one day.

We have condensed milk, and a little pudding is a great change for the mess in Billet. We are having your curry in stew for dinners today.

Craufurd commanded 1st Gordons throughout the Battle of the Somme although they did not take part on the opening day, 1 July 1916. While Craufurd wrote regularly to his mother and father, he kept his letters to inconsequential matters and family matters, and did not divulge much about military affairs or the desperate fighting in which he and his men were involved. The letter written on 16 July 1916 bears this out. The 'minor part' that his Battalion played is brought into perspective by Corporal Robertson, Craufurd's runner, who was close to him throughout the action, and whose diary entry for 14 July follows Craufurd's letter:

16th July 1916

We have been taking so far a minor part in the second phase of the offensive, which is moving gradually forward. I have seen our other Battalion again in action, the third time in our history we have been working practically side-by-side. The weather is fine but very cold for July.

Though the gunfire is incessant it is hard to believe that a battle which may well turn out one of the turning points in world history is being fought. All over the battlefield are German dugouts which make comfortable temporary Headquarters.

PS. Could you please send me a box of soup squares, they would be much appreciated.

From Corporal Robertson's diary for 14 July:

3.0 a.m. The second phase of the B.P. has commenced. Attack on 40 mile front. Germans are 1,000 yards from here. What a terrific bombardment. Never saw anything like this before. The German lines are a mass of flame. Germans sending up red, blue, green and yellow flares. The uproar is awful—guns wheel to wheel about 200 yards behind us.

---

10 Father of Capt James Anson Otho Brooke, V.C.
11 The family home in the small village of Annbank in Ayrshire.

They are firing directly over our heads. Hundreds of guns. The bigger ones ditto only further behind. Several of our boys bleeding at nose and ears with concussion. No reply from other side. Thank the Lord—they are biding their time or retiring. Another move. 4.0 a.m. Dark yet. We shift nearer, 300 yards behind the barrage and lie down. Don't feel too happy as there are always some of our shells falling short, and that gets us. Our attacking line are 100 yards ahead. 4.20 a.m. Signs of dawn. Our barrage lifts and drops 300 yards further on. Our boys charge. We lie still. Two H.E. burst short, two of our boys killed, one wounded on my left. 6.0 a.m. Things a bit quieter. All our planes up seeing what's what. Decipher one Morsing, attack successful especially by French on our right. Good. That will save us, perhaps. Orders to 'dig in', we will get it later on. 7.0 a.m. Prisoners coming in carrying their own wounded. They say it is 'Hell'. Some look as if they have been right in it. It's awful. You haven't a sporting chance in this war. 9.0 a.m. We shift on again to where the Germans were at 4.0 a.m. this morning. What a mess (Edge of Bazentin Wood). Not many dead. They must have hooked it—wise men. No fire from enemy so far—he must be shifting his guns back. 10.0 a.m.—More drum fire from the French 75s on our right. No peace for Jerry. About 12 shells land in amongst us. Nearly got a nose cap all to myself—heard it singing, then the dull thump as it banged into the earth. Evidence of the retirement—dismantled guns—limber wagons—shells and food. Collar some German sausage. Very tasty. Cram pockets as no sign of our side feeding us. Things quiet—odd shell up to 4 p.m. Saw our cavalry going into action. Fine sight. They have waited 17 months for this. Indians look fine. Later—a lot of them got caught in barbed wire—rotten for horses. Our objective is Longueval. A shell skiffed by while writing this—burst 40 yards off. One officer and one man wounded. 6 p.m. Just had a dozen H.E. over. One killed—ten wounded.

The letters below cover Craufurd's last action in command of 1st Gordons. Although wounded on several occasions, he had survived eleven major attacks when so many of his contemporaries had not:[12]

12 November 1916

I am going into my twelfth big action in this war with the Regiment tonight. If anything happens remember no other of our old Regulars can say the same. I am told it is almost certainly the last time I command the Battalion in action as its Colonel.

Meanwhile memory suddenly harps back to my first big attack as Colonel when we passed through Poperinghe in the snow to attack

---

12 Craufurd papers, The Gordon Highlanders Museum (GHPB 2369).

through the moonlight onto the Bluff, while many an unknown khaki figure wished us good luck, for all knew the meaning of the march.

19 November 1916

We went into action a week ago and stayed in the trenches for another five days. This was a bit of a strain. Now we are in reserve and hope to get out of the line for a month's rest in a week or ten days time. Our attack failed owing to mud and mist but our casualties are not really heavy under the circumstances.

In places the mud was knee deep and in one or two shell holes even thigh deep and once the attack was broken up the mist hindered rather than helped. Weather has been very cold and today we had snow. Today, however, is milder.

I suppose we shall wait for a settled spell of frost before we attack again. It is the battered condition of the ground from shelling which makes the mud so bad. It has all been tossed and torn for weeks past and the ground has no solidity. The artillery now on both sides has died down—everyone glad of a respite I expect—ourselves included.

Commands brigades

From November 1916 until March 1917, Craufurd promoted to the temporary rank of Brigadier-General, commanded 3 Infantry Brigade. From September 1917 until March 1919, he commanded 18 Infantry Brigade throughout the German offensive of March 1918 and the British counter-offensive that broke the German Army and led to the Armistice that ended the war. He fought 18 Brigade at Cambrai and Premy Ridge[13] and was wounded at St Quentin. Despite the wound he continued to command his brigade. During the first day of the German Offensive he led 18 Brigade in a stubborn defensive action that inflicted heavy casualties on the attacking Germans, but at the cost of crippling casualties. This earned great praise from Army Commander General Byng.[14] In a letter written on the third day of the offensive, Craufurd implies that his brigade lost more than ninety percent of its strength in opposing the German attack:[15]

---

13 One of the other brigades in 6 Division, 71 Infantry Brigade, was commanded by Brig-Gen P.W. Brown, D.S.O., a fellow Gordon Highlander and father of Col D.H.W. Brown, who commanded the 1st Battalion from 1969 to 1971.

14 'I cannot allow the 6th Division to leave the Third Army without expressing my appreciation of their splendid conduct during the first stages of the great battle now in progress. By their devotion and courage they have broken up overwhelming attacks and prevented the enemy gaining his object, namely a decisive victory.' *Byng.*

15 Craufurd papers, The Gordon Highlanders Museum (GHPB 2369).

March 23rd [1918] Night

So far all right. We were still in the line & took the full brunt of the offensive. Brigade reduced to the size of a weak battalion,[16] did magnificently.

We have been taken out last night but still in the battle area and within long-range of the guns and liable to be called into the fight any moment.

I really think the stand of the brigade in our sector [on the] first day had a great influence on our part of the field. The battle, as we always knew, has been very severe—probably one of the biggest battles ever fought. Otherwise as an opening phase, enemy's barrage came down quite suddenly at 5 a.m.

Craufurd commanded 18 Brigade until the Armistice and as part of the British Army of Occupation in Germany until 1919. He was invested as a Companion, Order of St. Michael and St. George (C.M.G.) in 1916 'For services rendered in connection with Military in the Field'. In 1919 he was invested as a Companion, Order of the Bath (C.B.) 'For valuable services rendered in connection with operations in France and Flanders'. He was appointed ADC to King George V and Brevet Colonel 'For distinguished service in connection with military operations in France and Flanders', and mentioned in despatches four times.

Craufurd's post-war service saw him in the rank of Brigadier-General commanding Brigades in Scotland and India. He retired as an Honorary Brigadier-General in 1928 and was appointed Deputy Lord Lieutenant and Justice of the Peace for Ayrshire. In 1939 he succeeded to the title of 5th Baronet Craufurd of Kilbirnie, Ayrshire.

Craufurd served once again in uniform during the Second World War as Commanding Officer of the Ayrshire Home Guard from 1940 to 1942 (when he reached the age of 70).

Brigadier-General George Standish Gage Craufurd, Bart, C.B., C.M.G., C.I.E., D.S.O., ADC, a remarkable man who deserves a place in the pantheon of Gordon Highlander heroes, died on 6 January 1957. When he was buried, the piper at his funeral was the son of Piper George Findlater, V.C., the Dargai hero who, like Craufurd, was wounded at that battle.

---

16 Of the three battalions in the brigade only 8 officers and 110 men remained out of a total of some 1,800.

CHAPTER 38

HUGH BOUSTEAD

H UGH Boustead was remarkable in many ways. In an action-packed life he spent fourteen years in The Gordon Highlanders. Although relatively few of these were spent with either of the Battalions, he felt himself so much a Gordon Highlander that in 1978, aged 83, he marched with fellow Gordon Highlanders, serving and retired, at the farewell parade for the Colonel of the Regiment, Lieutenant-General Sir George Gordon-Lennox. In the First World War he fought in the Royal Navy and in the trenches of the Western Front. He fought for the White Russians against the Bolshevik Red Army in 1919, and led a battalion of Sudanese soldiers against the Italians in Abyssinia during the Second War. He commanded a company in the Sudan Camel Corps between the Wars and later commanded the Camel Corps. He was a colonial administrator in Sudan and adviser to Arab rulers in the Arabian Gulf. He was an Army boxing champion, an Olympic athlete and a member of the 1933 British Everest Expedition. An accomplished author, his autobiography, *The Wind of Morning*, is a modest and inspiring account of his experiences. The extracts quoted below are all from *The Wind of Morning*.

Born in 1895 in Ceylon, the son of a tea planter, Hugh Boustead was educated at Cheam School, the Royal Naval College, Osborne,[1] and the

---

1   Throughout his life Boustead came across people who achieved fame and renown in many spheres. At Osborne he slept next to another cadet, George Archer-Shee, who was the real-life model for the eponymous victim of Terence Rattigan's play, *The Winslow Boy*.

Britannia Royal Naval College at Dartmouth[2] before joining the cruiser HMS *Hyacinth,* the Flagship of the Cape Station in South Africa as a Midshipman (photo).

In 1914, soon after war was declared, *Hyacinth* was sent across the Atlantic to intercept the German squadron that had inflicted a heavy defeat on the Royal Navy at Coronel, but the Navy brought the Germans to action at the Falklands and destroyed them before *Hyacinth* arrived. Thereafter, she patrolled the east coast of Africa in search of the German cruiser *Konigsberg*, which was attacking British shipping. On 14 April 1915 the cargo ship *Rubens*, disguised as the Danish steamer *Kronberg,* approached Manza Bay, ten miles north of Tanga in German East Africa. Intelligence reports indicated that a cargo ship carrying timber and flying a Scandinavian flag would be at a given position at a given time. Under the timber were arms and ammunition for German troops in German East Africa; *Hyacinth* was to intercept and capture this ship. What followed was an episode that the Royal Navy would prefer to forget.

Hyacinth (photo) plotted her course and arrived at an interception point just before the appointed time; the horizons were clear, and there was no sign of another vessel. The Navigator checked his position and discovered that he had made an error, placing *Hyacinth* 25 sea-miles south of where she should be. A signal from naval intelligence advised that the *Rubens* would enter Manza Bay the following morning. After steaming north *Hyacinth* spotted the *Rubens* next morning and engaged her with 6-inch guns. The *Rubens'* crew abandoned ship and rowed ashore. *Hyacinth's*

gunners blasted *Rubens* for over an hour and sent a boarding party to seize the hulk, but the party returned, having been machine-gunned by German Askaris (African soldiers) on the beach. The party reported that boarding was impossible because of a fierce fire raging on deck, and that the ship was

2   While at Dartmouth Boustead's teacher of English and History was George Mallory, who, along with his climbing partner Andrew Irvine, was to die attempting to reach the summit of Everest in 1924.

sinking. Satisfied that the mission had been accomplished, *Hyacinth* departed for Zanzibar and declared victory, but the Germans had deceived the Royal Navy. They had scuttled *Rubens* in shallow water and started a deck fire using petrol. Although part of it was under water, the cargo was intact and was later recovered by the Germans.

Boustead was on *Hyacinth* in the naval force that bombarded and sank *Konigsberg*, which had taken refuge in the Rufiji River. This was the extent

of Boustead's naval active service, and after a succession of boring routine patrols, and wanting to play a more active role in the war that was raging in Europe, he secured a change of employment by the unusual (and frowned-upon) step of deserting from the Royal Navy and enlisting in the South African Scottish regiment (photo), with which he went to France in 1916. Survival in the trenches owed much to luck. Boustead's first brush with death came during the Battle of the Somme in 1916:

> The trench offered little shelter. The balloons continued to watch us and presently a salvo of 5.9 inch shells pitched over us, quickly followed by a short bracket. I thought, 'The next one will be ours.' And it was. Although a shell pitched in the middle of the section, the three of us in the centre escaped any hurt other than a tremendous shock and blast which blew the equipment off our shoulders, our steel hats away, and poured tear gas in great clouds all over the trench. Coughing and spitting and weeping, and blinded by tear gas, we could hear those of our comrades who were wounded moaning under the debris. Six of the section, three on either side of us, were utterly destroyed, torn to pieces, and six more were wounded.'

It was only a matter of time before Boustead was wounded, and the Fates seemed determined that he should suffer:

> When night fell I moved into one of our trenches on the edge of Delville Wood when suddenly a heavy shrapnel barrage opened on the trench. It was a deep trench with safe dug-outs on the sides where I had hoped to get some sleep after a meal. The last thing I remember was a tremendous bang on the head. I was woken in the early morning by a South African Scottish sergeant standing on me. He was an enormous man called Maclean, of about fifteen stone, and this brought me to. My head

was throbbing and my hair was covered in blood from a cut in my skull. My steel helmet was caved in on top, evidently by shrapnel. Maclean picked me up and I had the head treated at the dressing station. After some aspirin I was O.K.

I rejoined my platoon back beyond the orchard trench again, only to come out that evening for a rest in the Longueval Road, lying in holes cut in the bank and hoping for the best. The shelling was almost incessant, but the snipers had done the main work and the toll of death among the South African Brigade was very heavy. On the morning of the 18th there was a sudden alarm and dropping with sleep we fell in on the road after daylight, with orders to go back to the orchard and the woods. A barrage came down at that moment and of the thirty men left of the original two hundred and fifty in my company, four were wounded. I was blown across the road, and went back to the Bernafay dressing station with a hole through my kilt and thigh. At the dressing station I asked to go back to the line since the wound was a light one, but the doctors said the wound was poisoned and this meant Etaples at least and possibly England.

My main relief at being hit was the chance to sleep. For five days and nights we had hardly slept at all and at times I was conscious of a longing to get hit anywhere to be able to sleep. It was late July and within a week I found myself back in the London General Hospital with hundreds of others wounded in the Somme streaming in daily.

The South African Scottish played a gallant part in the fighting at Delville Wood in the Battle of the Somme, but lost ninety percent of its original number killed or wounded in four days of bitter fighting. Boustead returned to France as a Second-Lieutenant in charge of the South African Scottish sniper and intelligence sections. On the eve of the Battle of Arras in 1917 he was tasked with laying out tapes in no man's land to mark the start point from which the leading companies would advance at Zero Hour:

As soon as dusk fell I was out with the snipers with the tape and by about ten o'clock we had the line laid. Then I had to get the two companies into their positions, followed by a re-check right down the line before reporting to the Colonel.

On reaching the left-hand post I began to question them in a whisper asking if all was well. There was no reply, though they were all lying exactly as I had left them. I shook one or two and thought they were all heavily asleep. I found the Section Commander and shook him but no answer. It was very dark apart from the flares. I thought this was strange and began to examine the corporal with a small torch. He was quite dead from a shrapnel shell which had burst straight over the shell-hole they were occupying. His whole section had been killed by the same burst and were lying as I had left them.

Boustead, in charge of the snipers, was never far from the action during the protracted battle. Once again chance intervened:

> I led my snipers out behind the leading company, who had deployed and were moving in extended order across an open plain with rifles at the port. We moved out in file, taking advantage of a low wall and the last of the houses for cover.
>
> I felt a bang on the outside of my left thigh as if it had been hit by a log of wood. I fell into a shell hole full of icy water and snow. Alongside was a young medical student, Hugh Leith, one of the brightest of my snipers. As sniping officer, because of perpetual night patrols, I was not wearing the kilt, but breeches, and I could feel them filling with blood. On taking them down I saw blood spurting out of the main artery. Leith opened my field dressing and applied it as a tourniquet to the wound; had he not done so I would have died within minutes. We lay in the shell hole, shivering with cold, our feet in icy water, while eight-inch shells poured round us. I told my sergeant to take the snipers on, and lay watching in anguish while the German machine-guns from the chemical works kept up a heavy fire which cut the advance company down like swathes of corn under a sickle.
>
> All the stretcher bearers had been killed and the only wounded who could get back were those who could walk. I got hold of a stout South African from the Cape Regiment who had been hit in the arm and could support me with his other arm. We moved back to a place called the Candle Factory, some mile or so down the Scarpe River which was the nearest dressing station. It took us about an hour and a half. The doctor looked at my wound and asked me how I got back to the dressing station. When I told him I had walked he would not believe it.

Boustead was evacuated to England where surgeons saved his leg. He was awarded the Military Cross, which was presented by King George V.

On returning to duty Boustead was sent to the Indian Army in Mesopotamia, but, as hostilities there had effectively ceased, he pressed to be returned to the South African Scottish on the Western Front and rejoined them in September 1918 until end of the war in November 1918.

After the war Boustead volunteered to fight with the White Russian Army against the Bolshevik Red Army. He was as an instructor with the infantry, and he trained the Cossacks of the Don Plastun Brigade in the Lewis gun. Although officially a non-combatant, Boustead accompanied the brigade on campaign and took part in several actions. His Lewis gunners proved decisive when faced with Red Army cavalry:

I was riding with the left-hand company, who were marching through breast-high grass. We were some eight hundred yards from the wood when the scouts came running back. Before [we] had time to deploy, three squadrons of Red cavalry burst from the forest, with sabres already drawn, and it looked as though we were trapped.

It was a bad moment, but Sergeant Sultricov, an intelligent Roumanian Lewis gunner, saved the situation. Rushing his two gun teams to the left of the column, which had had no time to extend, he fired the guns from the men's shoulders, one man supporting each gun on his shoulder. Owing to the high grass, this was the only effective way of working the Lewis gun.

This was the first cavalry charge I had seen, and it was the first action for most of these young Plastunis. It looked at one moment as if nothing could stop the dense mass of horsemen, and their determined rush with flashing sabres and cheering shouts was enough to cause an intense state of 'wind up', even amongst old soldiers. The line of cavalry looked as if they were almost on top of us. But the effect of the Lewis gun fire was devastating. Sabres flew, and horses reared and fell on their riders; through a cloud of dust the screaming of the horses and the shouts of their riders were loud in our ears.

The enemy melted under the fire at this range. As those in the rear turned and fled, they were followed by bursts from the other two machine-guns that had by now opened up.

The Plastunis could hardly believe their eyes. Hardly a man had fired a shot from his rifle. It was all over in two minutes, and each man could thank Sergeant Sultricov for his life. The confidence this action inspired in the Lewis guns was most fortunate. One stoppage at so short range would have been fatal, but as they were Sultricov's guns, the stoppage did not occur.

Ordered to retire to avoid being encircled by Red cavalry, Boustead sought opportunities for his Lewis gunners:

As the retirement was completed, I went to the top of a haystack with Colonel Efanov, where we could see for miles. We watched the enemy's scouts, also on haystacks, with their horses hidden behind, firing on our scouts as they advanced.

We sent for a Lewis gun, and kept up a heavy fire on them. We could see them jumping from the top of the haystack into the saddle, and galloping away when the fire became too hot.

With the White forces in retreat, there was plenty of work for the Lewis gunners. Boustead took command of one of the companies after all Russian officers had been killed or wounded:

I went forward with the right hand company. As we crossed the ridge, a hail of fire swept over our heads; like all partially trained troops, the Red infantry was firing too high. But the shrapnel barrage was effective, and as we advanced and closed the range, the enemy rifle and automatic fire was too intense to go forward. All three company officers were hit, two being killed outright. Then I saw a cloud of dust moving to our right flank—three enemy squadrons making the first outflanking move. The two Lewis guns were having stoppages because the gunners were excited and hurried, and the position looked bad

Highton came forward to me over the ridge, and I was able to send him off with a message to Colonel Efanov that the company had to retreat or be surrounded. I gave the order myself, since there was no Russian officer left; miraculously the stoppages cleared and our gunners opened up a devastating fire on the cavalry, who had been confidently advancing in close formation.

We managed to get back across the ridge, to see a long line of enemy infantry advancing towards us from Kardail. They drove us from the front, halting to fire as they came, while the cavalry, on both flanks now, herded us like sheepdogs.

We made a halt at a line of haystacks. From their tops we had a fine field of fire covering the retreat of the left flank. I got some guns into action, cursing in my few words of Russian the gun teams who had left their magazines where they had used them instead of bringing them in to be re-filled. Vasili spotted an ammunition cart slipping away and galloped after them with my revolver, to drive them back to the line.

This stand inflicted a vital check on the enemy advance.

General Holman, commanding the British Military Mission received letters from the Commander of the Don Plastun Brigade and from the Divisional Commander, saying that at Kardail the day had been saved by the action of the right flank and by the success of the Lewis guns.[3] General Holman recommended Boustead for a second Military Cross.

In addition to the British Military Cross, Boustead was awarded the very rare order of St. Vladimir with Bow and Cross Swords by the Russians, the equivalent of the D.S.O. His gallantry during the First World War and when serving with the White Russians led to the King pardoning his earlier desertion from the Royal Navy.

On return from Russia Boustead applied to remain in the Army, and studied Russian at Oxford. He describes this period:

---

3   Other sources reported that Boustead was not only present during the battles fought by the Plastun Brigade, but that he actively took part in the fighting; on one occasion engaging enemy cavalry with a Lewis gun fired from the saddle of his horse.

I decided to stay in the army, and I was recommended for a regular commission. This would take some time, and in the meantime, as Captain in the South African Scottish, I was at a loose end. My old friend Hugh Seymour had been at Oxford before the war, and was going up again to complete his degree. He persuaded me to see the Provost of Worcester, his College. My interview went off alright, although I had been brought up in anything but an academic atmosphere, and it seemed curious to meet an elderly gentleman with no contacts whatsoever with the world I knew. I had to sit an exam, and then was accepted. I decided to read Russian, since my colloquial knowledge had been good enough to take me all around the Don.

Boustead was a natural sportsman, and would try his hand at any sport. He excelled at boxing, and entered:

the Army Championships at Aldershot, where I won the Lightweight after knocking my opponent through the ropes. While sitting in the dressing-room getting my breath back, the Director of Physical Training asked me where I was going. He said I was remarkably fit, and that I ought to put my name down for the Modern Pentathlon trials at Aldershot in June. I had never heard of this, but he explained that it consisted of riding, running, shooting, fencing and swimming, and that the Olympic Games in Antwerp was the objective. I was full of enthusiasm.

The Inspector of Physical Training in the Army (Boustead's 'Director of Physical Training') was Colonel Ronald Campbell, C.B.E., D.S.O., a Gordon Highlander and a former boxing champion. Campbell encouraged Boustead to enter for the Modern Pentathlon trials (Boustead passed easily and was later made Captain of the British Olympic Pentathlon team for the 1920 Olympics) and also put his name forward to The Gordon Highlanders. Boustead consequently joined the Regiment. His sporting prowess flourished in the Gordons and he became a physical training instructor. He trained and led the Regimental boxing team, and had personal success in boxing championships.

In the Gordons Boustead served in the 1st Battalion under two commanding officers: Lieutenant-Colonel C. Ogston, who had also served in Russia with the British Military Mission, and Lieutenant-Colonel H. Pelham Burn, described by Boustead as:

an outstanding C.O. in every way. He had an overpowering and commanding personality, a very practical approach to any problem and was the finest trainer of officers and men that I have come across. I have never ceased to be grateful for what I learnt from him of the art of training troops. When I came to command a company of the Camel Corps in the

Sudan, and later the Camel Corps itself, I remained very grateful to Pelham Burn for opening the door to one of the most fascinating aspects of Army life, the capacity to train troops skilfully and realistically for war.

After serving in Turkey and Malta with the 1st Battalion, Boustead was nominated by Colonel Campbell for a post at Sandhurst in charge of physical training.[4] He was considered for the British pentathlon team for the 1924 Olympics, but Fate intervened. In a motorcycle accident he broke his left arm, and by the time he had recovered the Olympics were over and the posting to Sandhurst had fallen through.

Although he enjoyed serving with the Gordons, the disappointment of losing the job at Sandhurst that he would have relished led to his becoming restless and tired of the rigours of a regimented lifestyle. This prompted him to accept a posting in 1924 to the Sudan Camel Corps.

Boustead spent the next ten years in Sudan, initially as a company commander in the Camel Corps and latterly as Commander of the Camel Corps. He spent much time in remote areas of Sudan and learned the language and customs of the people. He grew to love the country and the people and did much beyond his military duties to enhance the life of the local population. He gained the respect of the people, of the civil administration and of the military authorities, and came to be regarded as an extremely valuable asset in the running of the vast territory.

One of the benefits of serving in Sudan was that British officers got three months leave each year.[5] Boustead used his leaves to travel and indulge in various sports and activities, including sailing, trekking and mountain climbing. His climbing experience led to him being invited to join the British team in the 1933 attempt on Everest.

In 1934 Boustead's time in Sudan came to an end. Amid great scenes of affection and appreciation the local chiefs and their people took leave of him, while those at the head of the civil administration paid him fulsome compliments and noted his suitability for employment.

After ten years in which he had enjoyed much freedom of action, Boustead found regimental duty in a garrison city a poor substitute:

> When my leave was up, I returned to my regiment, the Gordon Highlanders, in Edinburgh. One miserable, cold grey day in February 1935, I was commanding a company of seventy men on guard duty in Edinburgh Castle, and thinking back to sunlit days on the steppes of

---

4   The officer he was to take over from at Sandhurst was fellow Gordon Highlander Capt C.M. Usher, Scottish international rugby player, international fencer and aggressive boxer. Usher was another man who led a varied and interesting career that saw him participate in significant and crucial wartime events. See Chapter 39.
5   In 1931 he returned to Britain on leave, and met up with old Gordon Highlander friends at the annual Regimental Dinner in London.

Kordofan, with a whole country to secure and some 1,200 under command. Out of the blue came a telegram. It read:

> 'For Major Boustead, Gordon Highlanders, from Civil Secretary, Sudan Government. I am authorised to offer you an appointment in the Sudan Political Service, the rank of District Commissioner, and the appointment of Resident of Zalingei Emirate in Darfur, provided that you will resign from the Army.'

It seemed that all my hopes had materialised and I sat down and wrote a reply saying, 'Have resigned and gratefully accept the appointment you offer.' Then I went into see the Colonel.[6] He looked at these two telegrams and laughed and said, 'We realise you were sold to the Sudan, and did not think we would be able to hold you.'

For the next five years Boustead guided the development of a vast area, encouraging, demonstrating and persuading the local chiefs and their tribesmen to improve education, agriculture, care of livestock, husbanding and improving water supplies, and the exercise of fair and impartial justice. He never tried to impose systems or methods, but always endeavoured to work towards getting the people to accept them and adopt them under their own volition. He lived a simple life, and when visiting communities, observed their customs and habits, eating what they ate, and treating them with respect. He also had an eye to the future government and administration of the district by the inhabitants:

> During this period John Owen and I worked together intensively training the chiefs' sons when they were on leave from school. We dressed them simply in white damur (local cotton) *gibba* and shorts, with a green turban as a distinguishing mark for a chief's son. They were nicknamed either Green Hats or the *Abu arbain* (Fathers of Forty), because they received forty piastres, about eight shillings, a month. When I went on trek, they sat on top of the lorry; and at each chief's centre they had to prune the forest trees around the area in the early morning and check over all the books of schools, courts and health centres. They poured tea for the elders and their fathers, and attended all conferences. On the return journey from tour they were dropped off the lorry to find their own way home on foot, forty or fifty miles across country, within a time limit. There would be bets on the way home as to who would be dropped off, and every time the lorry stopped I would see Ahmed or Ibrahim or Yussef nudging each other with a laugh to indicate it was the other's turn. This somewhat Spartan training paid a hundred-fold; in later years many of these lads

---

6   Lt-Col J.M. Hamilton.

became a driving force in the development of the district. I looked on this training as vital for the future; the reward came after the war when, after a further final period of training with me, they were fit to join their fathers as administrative executives to their regions.

When war came in 1939 Boustead, an experienced soldier, was recalled to the colours. He raised, trained and commanded a battalion of Sudanese troops, the Frontier Battalion, which he led into Abyssinia as part of Wingate's Gideon Force. In Abyssinia he conducted extensive operations against the Italians in the campaign that led to the Italian defeat and surrender. For his leadership, skill and operational effectiveness during the campaign he was awarded the Abyssinian Order of St George by Emperor Haile Selassie, and in January 1942 was awarded the D.S.O. by His Majesty King George VI.[7]

Boustead saw the war out on security duties in Eritrea, commanding the Border Force, which grew to a brigade group, with a regular camel company and a mounted infantry company in addition to three battalions of the Sudan Defence Force (including his old Frontier Battalion). In July 1945 he returned to his old district at Zalingei. His arrival back in the district was memorable:

> I was met by a crowd of Fur chiefs and their followers. Whenever in the past I had left Zalingei on leave, and again on my return, a band of horsemen would escort me to and from a certain wadi, about four hours' ride away. On this occasion it was a special welcome, and we rode along with singing and cheering and volleys of shots, the chiefs curvetting their horses. '*Chefalhal, Inshallah Kheir, Murhabha, El Hamdalillah*' (How are you? Pray God you are well, Welcome, Praise be to God). It was indeed a homecoming: all week the welcome and the feasting continued.

Boustead soon picked up the reins again, and worked hard and persistently on improving the lot of the people:

> As soon as I had time to get the courts straight I turned my whole attention to the Green Hats—the chiefs' sons whose education I had started ten years ago, and who were now young men ready to be trained to hold their fathers' areas. I found this stimulating. They were a most promising lot of young lads, keen to learn and to help. With them I was able during the succeeding five years to set up sub-grade schools, to increase the dispensaries and improve village hygiene throughout the whole district, and to improve the road system.

Visitors to Boustead's bungalow could be startled by his habit of frequently blowing a whistle when he needed a servant to bring him a glass

---

7   An account of this campaign is in Chapter 19.

of water, but he explained in his charming way that this was the only practical signal to draw attention. He worked tirelessly for his people, despite a debilitating attack of cerebral malaria which led to a stay in hospital (some hundreds of miles away) and a further month to recover his strength.

In March 1949, Boustead's time in Sudan came to an end. He was then invited to accept the position of Resident Adviser in the East Aden Protectorate (an area loosely called the Hadhramaut). When the time came to leave Sudan the people showed their appreciation and respect with a memorable farewell:

> It was with great reluctance when the time came that I rode out for the last time on the road to Fasher with the one hundred and fifty chiefs and followers who had come to greet me on my return after the war. They rode out with me much further than the normal point, and our goodbyes and good wishes were fervent.

The Hadhramaut takes its name from the great Wadi Hadhramaut in the interior, an enormous watercourse which only flows after the occasional rains, but is adequately watered by wells. Boustead found his task different from that in Zalingei:

> I found the position of Resident Adviser a very delicate one, in comparison with the role of District Commissioner in the Sudan. There the D.C. was the executive, and his effectiveness could be measured by the results which he, and only he, could achieve in his district. The Adviser and his staff are there to advise the Executive and not to usurp its authority. This may mean slow progress when new ideas and approaches have to be put across tactfully to provincial governors and heads of departments, but it means that when new developments are finally underway, they are not 'gimmicks' enforced by an outsider, but flow naturally from the local administration.

Over nine years in the Hadhramaut Boustead encouraged the local administration to introduce improvements in the life of the people. When he arrived the area was recovering from a famine that resulted from crop failure. It was decided to rebuild dams and drop-weirs in the Hadhramaut Valley in order to maintain the water level:

> At the same time I was advised that an irrigation scheme for small pumps should be put into operation with all speed to make the whole Wadi self-supporting in its principal staple crop, wheat. At the same time the date palms in the valley would benefit enormously by increased water. The next four years of my stewardship were devoted to this task as one of the priorities of the many and urgent calls for the country . . . Day and night I and my Political Officer were up and down the Wadi in the burning

summer of 1950, watching the progress of those projects, directing and encouraging. I used to travel from village to village, collecting all the population of the surrounding district, and address them in the late afternoon when their day's work was done. Gradually they became more responsive, and as we learnt more ourselves and the pump owners thus became better at overcoming their difficulties, results began to show. From that year on, the pumps increased in the Wadi by a hundred to a hundred and thirty engines a year, and there were nearly 1,200 when I left nine years later. The danger of famine had completely passed and the pump owners were actually exporting wheat to the West Aden Protectorate, a thing never known in the history of the Hadhramaut. Reflecting on these matters, I was enormously struck at the people's willingness to accept advice in a way which I have never found in the Gulf States of Arabia.

As Resident Adviser Boustead inevitably got involved in the politics of the Protectorate and with the potential use of force when the occasion demanded, such as in October 1950:

I had reached the capital of the Wadi Duan and was lodged in the village of Masna. I was sleeping in the Naib's house, about a third of the way up the 1,500 foot cliff which formed the wall of the Wadi. About one o'clock in the morning I heard banging on the door. [It was] an officer of the Hadhramaut Bedouin Legion carrying a letter marked urgent in red in Arabic on the envelope. He said, 'I have come from Sultan Awad, and there is great disturbance in Mukalla.' I deciphered the letter by lantern light; written in Arabic, in Awad's own hand, it began, 'The matter is very serious. You must please come at once to Mukalla. There is opposition to Sheikh Qadal's appointment as State Secretary and there is a meeting of four thousand people in front of my house this afternoon at four o'clock. If you do not come there may be bloodshed. The situation is very dangerous and I am preparing the troops.' Kennedy, who knew Mukalla, had left on a mission, and the young officer who was in the town had only just arrived. Sultan Awad's house was in the Residency grounds. I thought that perhaps it would be better to let the matter settle itself. Then I thought, 'The youngster will not know what to do. He may well think that he must help Awad and call out the army; so I must go down and deal with this personally.'

The Naib was awake and was giving coffee to the officer. I told my Sergeant to get the kit together and the Naib to get porters. We left his house and scrambled down to the wadi bed, then had a stiff climb by lantern light up the other side of the Wadi Duan. It was four o'clock in the morning, and a full moon was in the sky. My Ford V8 tourer was waiting at the top of the cliff with the lorry. We set out at once on the 150-mile drive to Mukalla across the rolling rocky steppe land of the *jol*. We drove over the 7,000-foot range that separates the plateau from Mukalla without stopping, reaching the town at 9 a.m. I was greeted by my young officer who said, 'I've been anxiously waiting for you. I've got the army to stand by.' I had done a good deal of thinking during the drive and was determined that there must be no crisis which could lead to any sort of disturbances during the Sultan's absence, particularly not in the Residency courtyard. Should that happen, the Crown Prince would undoubtedly throw the blame onto the Resident, and probably the Residency would be burned down as happened in Cyprus. So I told this young lad not to worry but to tell the army to stand down since I would not use it at any cost. I said, 'I will see Sheikh Seif at ten o'clock so please arrange to bring him along and be present yourself.'

Boustead, using charm, diplomacy and logic, outmanoeuvred those wishing to foment unrest, and a peaceful acceptance of law and order was obtained. He was under no illusion as to where the tension had originated:

I have no doubt that Sheikh Seif's intention was to precipitate a riot in which the Resident would be involved. He was undoubtedly deeply disappointed at my refusal to acknowledge that there was any crisis which required immediate settlement.

Even in the Hadhramaut Boustead came across unusual, often well-known figures, although on occasion he was unaware of their background and celebrity:

I was just about clear, when I looked up to see an anxious-looking chap in white shorts and white shirt, carrying a BOAC handbag. I asked, 'Can I help?' And he said, 'I am Hammond Innes and I sent you a wire asking you if I could visit you.' I replied, 'I'm very sorry, nothing has come here and I am just about to leave in the car waiting below to attend a major tribal gathering in the mountains of Duan. But first do tell me what you do.' He looked somewhat surprised and said, 'I write.' I then asked him whether he would like to accompany me on trek if he had the time. He jumped eagerly at this and I got my servants busy producing some warm clothes and a camp bed and bedding whilst I introduced him to the Ministers.

The interest of the journey was increased by Hammond Innes' lively and fascinating company. It was a cold, starlit night with no dew and before going off to sleep I asked him what sort of sales he had for his books. He replied, 'About fourteen million readers in America alone.' . . . At one o'clock I woke and was surprised to see Hammond Innes writing at what was evidently a diary. He was still writing at two. In the morning I asked him if he always put down the day's happenings and what would come of it eventually. He said, 'Yes, I invariably do, enough to convey an absolute picture of what I saw, if necessary five years later. For it may be as long as that before I'm able to turn to that particular scene and transform it into a story.' The subsequent days spent with him are vividly described in a chapter of *A Harvest of Journeys* which was not published until six or seven years later.

Without being patronising, Boustead took a great interest in the people, and would go to great lengths to help them:

Sultan Hussein bin Ali was a small man, quiet and reserved, with agreeable manners. His brothers were not distinguished, but his cousin Abdullah was a lively and promising lad of eighteen. His burning wish, encouraged by the Sultan, was to become a doctor: at this time all doctors in the Protectorate were Indians apart from the Health Adviser, who was British. So we sent him to England to learn English as a first step, and when I went on leave I visited him in Norwich. He asked whether I knew the cathedral. When I said no, he said eagerly, 'I must show it to you before lunch, it is too remarkable,' and so I had the great pleasure of being shown round one of the masterpieces of our Christian heritage by a charming and intelligent young Moslem.

I went back to London determined to get him into a university, and was subsequently able to introduce him to Alan Lennox-Boyd,[8] who was enormously impressed by him. He helped him with introductions to relations in Dublin, where he took a good degree. After a period as a house surgeon in England, Abdulla returned to the Kathiri State, where ever since he has been Medical Officer to his people.

Originally appointed in 1949 on a two-year contract as Resident Adviser, Boustead's contract was renewed several times, but after nine years he felt that it was time for a change, and that a change would be good for the Protectorate. In 1958 Britain advised the Sultan of Oman to set up a Development Department, and Boustead was asked to take on the job of Development Secretary. Once again he had to take leave of people with whom he had developed close working relations and deep friendships:

It was with a rather sad heart that I spent my final three months touring in the Duan and Hadhramaut Valleys and along the coast. Wherever I went there were huge farewell parties and dinners where a hundred or more people would assemble over goat meat and rice, or over exquisitely

---

8   Lennox-Boyd was Colonial Secretary in the British Government.

cooked Hadhrami meals in the Wadi, which the Sultans and the Seiyids knew so well how to serve with all the tastes of Java and the Indies in the food.

In Mukalla the forces were all present for a final parade, with most of the townspeople watching. After the state band had played 'The Queen', I was presented by the Sultan with a superb sword inlaid in gold. Then on to the Kathiri State, where there was another presentation in front of the army and police with crowds and bands. It was extremely exacting, at the same time very warming, to leave such friends behind.

In my farewell speech to the people at Mukalla, I said:

> 'I thank you all for the friendliness, kindness, courtesy and patience you have shown me and my officers over these years and I wish you all and your States the peace, progress and prosperity that you deserve. I am sure that, if and when oil is found, your Rulers will use its wealth with the wisdom and interest that you have shown in running your Governments. It has been my privilege to serve you through the happiest years of my life. I leave with thankfulness for having had these years, but with the inevitable distress at leaving such friends.
>
> 'There is one end, our works live after us and by their fruits we should be judged in days to come. If we have worked well and faithfully, then it is well.'

Boustead spent three years as Development Secretary in Muscat and Oman. Muscat was in a deplorable condition, due to local unrest against the Sultan's rule. There were no medical services. A British diplomat who accompanied Boustead on a tour of Muscat told the Sultan that, in twenty years' experience in the Middle East, he had never seen a people so poverty-stricken or debilitated with diseases capable of treatment and cure. This led to the building of some twenty health centres and dispensaries throughout the Sultanate.

Rebel bands shot up convoys and planted mines which caused many casualties. Boustead's first priority was to get a road built into the Shargia, the wild south-eastern province of Oman. The road was built, despite corrupt officials who charged exorbitant rates for the workmen they provided and then charged the workmen two-thirds of their wages. Work was threatened by rebels who planted mines.

Nothing could be achieved without the approval of the Sultan. Boustead was disturbed to find that letters asking for early decisions had not even been opened, so he resorted to an old ruse, 'and thereafter wrote to tell him I was proposing to do so-and-so, and would go ahead unless I heard to the contrary within the next ten days'. He proposed a programme to build primary schools in each Province HQ to instruct the sons of the leading Sheiks and Province Governors, who would play an active part in the Administration:

> The Sultan would have none of this. He said to me cynically one day, 'That is why you lost India, because you educated the people.'

Boustead achieved much in Muscat and Oman, but felt that he had been prevented from doing everything he hoped to achieve by official indifference and lack of enthusiasm. He wrote:

> There was an enormous lot to do in Muscat to complete the programme. I spent the whole of the burning summer of 1961 touring in the field, completing health centres and dispensaries, building roads and spreading the agricultural and pump gospel through the interior. Physically it was probably the most trying experience I had in the Middle East. The heat in the interior was intense. Lying in a tent, I found most trying of all the burning dry winds which seemed to sear right through one, and left me with a perpetual thirst and skin desiccated by the heat.
>
> Muscat was insufferably hot and I realised the full force of a Persian saying that 'the sinner who goes to Muscat has a foretaste of what is coming to him in the after world'. When October came round I had completed three years and I left for a month's leave in Kenya before taking up the post in Abu Dhabi.[9] I was not sorry to say goodbye to Muscat and Oman.

The morning before paying his first ceremonial call on Sheikh Shakhbut, the Ruler of Abu Dhabi, Boustead received a letter from Edward Heath,[10] the Foreign Secretary's representative in the House of Commons:

> Since I had a chance of seeing something of your devoted work in the Sultanate last winter, I have been all the better able to appreciate how much you have done in getting the whole development programme under way in the face of great difficulties. I should like you to know how much we appreciate your work in the Sultanate and I take your success there to be earnest of great things in your next uphill job.

Sheikh Shakhbut greeted Boustead warmly, having been told officially that Boustead was 'an officer of considerable seniority and experience', and that he and his Agency would be entirely independent, not subordinate to Dubai as had previously been the case. Sheikh Shakhbut was flattered and extremely pleased at this recognition of his rising influence and position in the Gulf.

---

9 Boustead had been offered the post of Political Agent at Abu Dhabi, which was blossoming into a rapidly developing oil state.

10 Later to become Prime Minister of the United Kingdom.

As in Eastern Aden, Boustead set about achieving improvements in the infrastructure and welfare of the people through persuasion and encouragement, rather than assumption of direct responsibility; always endeavouring to enable progress to be made through the efforts of the Sheikh's administration. One of his first achievements was the building of a pipeline to bring water from the interior.

Persuading Sheikh Shakhbut to fund development projects was a problem. The elderly Sheikh had spent his life living frugally. Years of poverty and an inborn reverence for money made him unwilling to finance long-term projects. A major project to develop a port fell through when the Sheikh was politically outmanoeuvred in a dispute with Qatar over ownership of an island. The Sheikh, in a rage over losing possession of the island, delayed all development plans. Boustead pointed out that the loss of the island was largely the Sheikh's own fault, through his lack of interest and failure to prepare the sound legal case that would have proved his ownership.

Boustead established good working relations with the Sheikh's brother, Zaid[11] (subsequently Ruler of Abu Dhabi), who was the Ruler of Buraimi, the finest agricultural area in Abu Dhabi. Zaid was popular and enlightened, adored by his people. He had a kind word for everybody and was generous with his money. Boustead was struck by all that had been done in his hometown and in the Buraimi area for the people. Zaid was a charismatic leader who understood politics and would work with and learn from the British.

Boustead's friendship with Sheikh Zaid developed, and he spent many days with him, hawking on the dunes during the bustard season. He was not averse to joining in the sports enjoyed by Zaid's people:

> Hawking, riding and camping with Zaid formed the most pleasant interludes during my years in Abu Dhabi. After hawking all morning and a delicious lunch of bustard baked in sand, the afternoons would be spent with his followers in foot races, wrestling and competing in the long jump. There was an amusing incident when a very tough young tribal retainer came up to me and asked me whether I knew how to wrestle. I was sitting on the sand at the time and the others looked at me to see my response. I jumped up quickly and before Mohammed bin Amri had time to think I had thrown him on his back with a cross buttock and fell sharply on top of him. All the followers were vastly amused and pulled his leg for being thrown by the Political Agent.

Boustead appreciated that Zaid had the intellect, education and ability to be a successful and forward-thinking Ruler. The hawking expeditions

---

11   Otherwise known as Sheikh Zayed bin Sultan Al Nahyan.

allowed them to spend many evenings around the fire in the lonely desert, drinking coffee and discussing development in both infrastructure and welfare that new and growing oil revenues provided for Abu Dhabi. Boustead's logical and reasoned arguments did much to convince Zaid that the future of a progressive and moderate Abu Dhabi would depend upon his guidance and direction. These discussions would bear fruit in a few years.

Zaid was loyal to his brother, Shakhbut, but aware of his shortcomings. Shakhbut was considerate and courteous, but at heart a tribal Bedouin, aware of his impoverished early days. Although oil revenues were increasing, he was reluctant to spend on development or the well-being of the people. He was persuaded to put the money into banks that had been set up in the country. He invited Boustead to look under his bed and tell the world that he had not got the money stashed away there. 'They will believe you,' he said, 'if you tell the reporters.' Boustead replied that while he had every confidence that the money was deposited in the bank, Shakhbut 'must not ask the manager to show it to you every day!'

It was clear in political circles that if Abu Dhabi were to progress, Shakhbut would have to go, and be replaced by Sheikh Zaid. After much discussion and encouragement, Boustead persuaded Zaid that what he saw as an act of disloyalty to his brother would actually be for the benefit of his country. Zaid, reluctantly, agreed to the coup. Lieutenant-General Sir John MacMillan, who was Brigade Major at the time, recalls unlocking the safe in his office and giving his commander his sealed orders, 'and the Scouts[12] were called in and briefed for the coup the following day. That night Zaid got cold feet, and it was called off. He had sworn to his mother that he would never do anything to harm his brother, and felt he couldn't go through with it.' This loyalty and family feeling was typical of Zaid, to whom honour and integrity were the mainstays of his character. Boustead, whose tour of duty in the Gulf was coming to an end, did not reproach his friend, but offered him the friendship and counsel that he had always enjoyed, rebuilding Zaid's confidence and self-belief. Boustead's faith in Zaid was unshaken and would bear fruit before long. (Photo below—Boustead inspects Trucial Oman Scouts.)

Within a year the coup took place, without bloodshed, and the development could at last begin. Abu Dhabi became a model of enlightened, prudent use of its resources under a humane, moderate and tolerant Ruler. This was a significant event that affected the development of the United Arab Emirates and their relationship with the Western world in general and the United Kingdom in particular. The smooth transition of power, the political outlook of Abu Dhabi and the benign and popular influence of Sheikh Zaid

---

12 Trucial Oman Scouts.

over four decades owed much to Hugh Boustead's presence, persuasive powers and empathy with the indigenous peoples.[13]

In July 1965, aged 70, Boustead retired, after twenty-five years in Sudan and sixteen in Arabia. He was knighted in the New Year's Honours List.[14] He had no home in Britain, and only a small pension. The offer of a temporary job as an adviser in Sudan led to his touring Europe and North Africa before going on to Sudan. He was entranced by Morocco and decided to retire there, so he bought a house with splendid views of the Riff ranges. An invitation from the Emperor of Ethiopia to be his guest at the twenty-fifth anniversary of the liberation from the Italians took him to Addis Ababa, where he met many friends from the Abyssinian campaign. When the time came to say goodbye, Emperor Haile Selassie gave each of his guests who had served him in the Gojjam campaign a silver cigarette case emblazoned with the Imperial Arms in gold.

Boustead heard from Sheikh Zaid, his good friend, now Ruler of Abu Dhabi. Zaid invited him to spend the winter with him and Boustead gladly agreed to join him in January 1968 when the work in Sudan would be finished. In Sudan he met many friends:

> Passing through Kas village, I called in on the *shartai*'s Court, which was in session. The open Court House which Beaton and I had designed in 1936 was still in use; the young *shartai*, who had been one of my 'Green Hats' and had now succeeded his father, was trying a case, sitting with his back to me. As soon as I stepped out of the Land Rover, the accused, witnesses, the Court Elders and peons came rushing out without a word to the President and started to hug me in the usual Sudani fashion when greeting an old friend. Basi Deldum, the young *shartai*, turned

---

13 Zaid ruled Abu Dhabi until his death in 2004. President of the United Arab Emirates (UAE) and a moderate but visionary leader of his desert people. Zaid was the principal architect of the federation of seven emirates formed when Britain withdrew from the Persian Gulf in 1971. It became the longest and most successful example of regional integration in modern Arab history. Zaid's foresight ensured that the UAE's citizens went from poverty to riches in less than a generation, without losing their cultural or religious heritage. The freedom of worship offered to Christians, and allowances made for expatriates to follow Western ways, helped fuel development. Pious and disciplinarian, Sheikh Zaid never forgot his desert origins, his Islamic faith or his youthful passion for traditional sports and conservation.

14 After Boustead died British MP Richard Luce, son of Sir William Luce, the Political Resident in the Persian Gulf who authorised the coup that brought Zaid to power, claimed that no one had a greater impact in cementing relations between the British and the Arabs than Boustead.

round in bewilderment at the sudden disappearance of the entire courtroom, and then followed them. It was some time before we could re-assemble the Court, when I suggested that I should sit and have tea with them. The incident was a fitting climax to a heart-warming visit.

After a happy visit to Abu Dhabi, where he was given a warm welcome by Sheikh Zaid, Boustead returned to Tangier where he started to write his memoirs. This task was interrupted by an invitation from Sheikh Zaid to go back to Abu Dhabi and take charge of his stud of ninety or so mares, foals and stallions. Boustead was more than happy to accept this invitation.

In 1978 Colonel Sir Hugh Boustead, K.B.E., C.M.G., D.S.O., M.C. accepted an invitation to return to his old Regiment, The Gordon Highlanders, in Chester. Along with a host of Gordons young and old, marched past the Colonel of the Regiment, Lieutenant-General Sir George Gordon-Lennox. Boustead was accommodated in the Officers Mess. After the parade he was one of the distinguished guests at a formal dinner in Chester Town Hall. He met old friends and made new ones among the serving officers, few of whom were aware of what an extraordinary man they had in their midst. The author was one of those, and he remembers Boustead as a quiet, unassuming, charming and courteous man.

In a remarkable life, Hugh Boustead was moulded by the situations in which he found himself. It is best to leave the final words to him:

> To those of us who fought in the First World War as we were stepping into life at eighteen or nineteen, the experience was indelible. The war stands like a great peak on the horizon of one's life; the lengthening perspective of the years never seems to have taken one much further from it. To be still alive at the end of it was almost unbelievable, and the fact of survival gave me an even greater zest for life. I have never ceased to be thankful for the gift of life, and in turn life has been good to me.
>
> I learned, too, the worth of comradeship in shared danger, and the resources of the human spirit. That spirit can be the same, I found, in Cossack or Sherpa, in Sudanese farmer or Ethiopian patriot, in Arabian *seiyid* or Bedouin nomad. Honour, courage, unselfishness and a good heart stamp the true man whatever his land or race. These are not just military qualities, though no good soldier lacks them. I found them just as frequently in ordinary life when fortune led me from soldiering to administration.
>
> There can be few deeper satisfactions than to have played a part in helping a country or a people forward—to a life of peace, under an honest government with justice administered under the rule of law, with education for the young, with medical care for the sick. We can never accomplish all that we hope to do, but to have left something better than

we found it is our due return for the gift of life. As I said to the people of Mukalla when I bade them farewell, 'There is one end, our works live after us and by their fruits we should be judged in days to come. If we have worked well and faithfully, then it is well.'

On 14 April 1980, eleven days before reaching the age of 85, Hugh Boustead died. Frustrated naval officer, gallant infantry soldier, dashing mounted soldier, guerrilla fighter, Olympic sportsman, Everest mountaineer, distinguished colonial administrator and political adviser, and accomplished author, he had lived life to the full and packed enough experience in his long life to satisfy half-a-dozen ordinary men.

CHAPTER 39

CHARLES USHER

CHARLES Usher (known more commonly in The Gordon Highlanders as 'Dougie' Usher) was a member of the eponymous Scottish brewing and whisky distilling family. Educated at Merchiston Castle School in Edinburgh, he excelled at sport and showed an aptitude for languages. From Merchiston he went to Sandhurst and was commissioned into The Gordon Highlanders, joining the 1st Battalion in 1911.

When war broke out on 4 August 1914, Usher, a platoon commander in the 1st Battalion, went to France with the BEF. He took part in the Battalion's stand at Mons and in the subsequent retreat of the BEF, cut disastrously short when most of the 1st Battalion, along with detachments from other units, was left behind when the order to continue the retreat failed to reach them and they were overrun by the advancing German Army. Usher was wounded in the head shortly before the Battalion was captured.

Usher spent the rest of the war in German prison camps and in internment in Holland in 1918. While in prison camp he organised physical fitness programmes that kept prisoners active and fit, helped to write and produce an illustrated magazine (copies of which were laboriously handwritten and

516

drawn), practised and developed his piping[1] and Highland dancing skills, and even helped to build a (very short) nine-hole golf course inside the barbed wire of the prison camp! He made a number of attempts to escape, but each one was frustrated. While in prison camp he wrote letters to his mother that contained coded intelligence on German troop movements and German morale that his mother passed on to the War Office. During his internment in Holland he organised physical fitness training and events. After the war he was made an Officer of the British Empire (O.B.E.) for his work with his fellow prisoners.

After the First World War Usher returned to The Gordon Highlanders and served in both the 1st and 2nd Battalions as a company commander, officer in command of the Regimental Depot, second-in-command of the 2nd Battalion and ultimately as Commanding Officer of the 1st Battalion.

Usher commanded the 1st Battalion from 1938 to 1940. He took the Battalion to France with the BEF, but handed over command to his successor before the start of the German *blitzkrieg*. Promoted to Colonel, he was appointed Area Commandant St Malo; one of the Channel ports chosen for the reception of munitions. This posting was short-lived, however, and on 1 April 1940 Usher returned east to command a sub-area of the Lines of Communication. His task was to keep the troops at GHQ and in the three Corps of the BEF supplied with men and material; and to handle personnel going the other way—sick, wounded or due leave.

Usher quickly got to grips with the disparate and wide-spread collection of men and material. An efficient system was quickly introduced, ensuring that equipment, supplies and men got to their destination, whether forward to their units or returning for replacement, repair or leave. As with everything he did, Usher set up and maintained an effective system. He was everywhere: ensuring that officers in charge of the various activities understood their duties and responsibilities—and were working efficiently. He also met the soldiers carrying out these tasks, encouraged them and made sure they were kept up-to-date with the situation at the Front. He got by on a few hours' sleep every night, and had boundless energy.

The German *blitzkrieg* was a complete success, and the BEF found itself pushed back to Dunkirk, where it got itself into some semblance of order and was evacuated from the beaches over a nine-day period from 26 May to 4 June 1940. Dunkirk, however, was not a panic-stricken flight of a defeated army scrambling to get away from the pursuing Germans. Although bloodied and disorganised, the BEF was still a disciplined force, and it kept the Germans away from Dunkirk while the evacuation proceeded. This was achieved by forces, some of them ad hoc and hurriedly assembled, that held

---

1   Usher was an excellent piper who had been tutored by Pipe Maj G.S. McLennan (who, in 1929, shortly before he died, composed one of his very last tunes in honour of Usher).

and guarded the approaches to Dunkirk that the Germans would have to use. One of these forces, Usherforce, was commanded by Colonel Dougie Usher (in the local rank of Brigadier), and its task was to hold and block the road to Dunkirk from the south. This road ran through the ancient fortified town of Bergues (map), and Usher made this the critical centre of his defensive line.

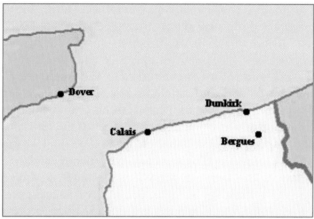

The land around the town was easily flooded, low-lying and criss-crossed with ditches. It was impassable by tanks or guns except on conspicuous built-up roads, with ditches either side, which well-sited guns could make unusable. Usherforce consisted of one under-strength infantry battalion (6th Green Howards), one Royal Artillery Regiment and two Royal Artillery Batteries and a number of disparate non-combatant units. Opposing him were the *Liebstandarte* Division[2] and the *Gross Deutschland* Regiment.[3] A steady stream of British Army troops, in various degrees of order, made its way through Bergues on its way to Dunkirk. Usher took arms and ammunition that he needed from some of these troops, and also persuaded some of them to remain with him and fight, allowing him to release non-combatant and support troops back to Dunkirk. For five days Usher held Bergues against everything that the Germans could throw against him; infantry, armour and air. When, on 30 May he was ordered to hand over to the French and withdraw all his troops to Dunkirk, he did this without significant loss. He remained in the heavily shelled area at Dunkirk, helping to organise the beaches until all the men under his command were clear. Only then did Usher and Private Carle, his driver/batman, finally leave the beach and try to find a ship. Carle was a non-swimmer, so, with full packs on their backs, Usher took Carle on his back and swam with him to seven boats—two of which were bombed when they were on board—before finding one to get them home, where they landed on 1 June.

---

2   The 1st SS Panzer Division.
3   Four battalions of motorised infantry.

Having safely arrived back in Britain, Usher was awarded the D.S.O., but, despite the expectations of all who had served under him, he was not offered a higher command. Instead, he was told that his services were no longer required. He was given a commission in the newly formed Home Guard and made responsible for all of Scotland north of the Great Glen.

In 1944 Usher's facility for foreign languages, particularly French, allied to his considerable charm and diplomatic skills, led to his being reinstated as a Colonel in the Regular Army and trained as a Civil Affairs Officer, ready to take on the task of re-establishing local government and public services in France after the planned invasion. The original plan had been for Usher to move directly to the city of Caen and start work there, but the timetable fell badly behind as the Germans put up strong resistance and held Caen, which was an important centre of communications. Two extremely heavy air raids on Caen, one on D-Day and one on 9 July, devastated the city, reducing some quarters to nothing more than heaps of rubble. The Germans still held it, however, and remained entrenched in the southern half of the city when Usher and his team arrived. While heavy fighting continued in Caen, Usher set up a civil administration of loyal French officials and used military resources to get water and electricity supplies re-established. Thanks to Usher's organising ability, tact and diplomacy, charm and persuasion and steely determination, the daily life of a French city that had been brought to its knees by over a month of bombing, bombardment and fierce fighting was brought back into being and the rebirth of a thriving community assured.

Usher's work in re-establishing civil government and local services in Caen was repeated in 1945, when he took his team into the German city of Minden while fighting was still going on. From April 1945 to June 1946 he was the effective military ruler of the large region around Minden (photo). Finding non-Nazi Germans, he built up local government teams that worked under his direction re-establishing democratic systems of local and regional government that started the long process of rebuilding the economy of a defeated nation. Usher was spectacularly successful, gaining the respect, admiration and co-operation of a cowed and defeated people.

Usher returned to post-war Britain in 1947 where, as he had reached the age of fifty-five, he was discharged from the Army. He found gainful employment when he was appointed Director of Physical Education at the University of Edinburgh, taking over in that post from another former Gordon Highlander, Colonel R.B. Campbell. During his time at Edinburgh University Usher continued the good work started by his predecessor and developed it further. He encouraged students to take part in physical activity, organising easily accessible and achievable programmes in the gymnasium that allowed students to join in and drop out according to their own timetables. He encouraged and developed University sport, both team and individual activities, and the University thrived on it.

In 1959, when he was 68, the University Senate reluctantly concluded that he would have to retire. When they came to the gymnasium to inform him of their decision, he received the news balancing on his head, with arms outstretched, on the high beam!

Usher was a natural sportsman, excelling at many different sports, outstanding in some. While still at school he was approached by the Scottish Rugby Union to play for the Scottish team, but wise counsel persuaded him to wait. He was selected for the Scottish rugby team in 1912 (after he had introduced the game to The Gordon Highlanders) and was also given a trial for the Scottish hockey team. As hockey and rugby internationals were played on the same day, Usher had to choose one or the other, and he chose rugby (although he was to play hockey for The Gordon Highlanders for many years). He was capped at rugby for Scotland and played for the national team up until the start of the First World War. Following his return to duty in 1919, he resumed his rugby career when he played for the Mother Country (the forerunner of the British Lions) against New Zealand in the Inter-services and Dominion Tournament. He played for Scotland again, and captained the national side on a number of occasions, gaining sixteen caps in the rugby career that had been interrupted by the War. How many caps he would have won had the War not intervened is a matter of conjecture. He was a skilled, aggressive boxer, and he trained The Gordon Highlanders' boxing team. One of his boxers, Private Jack Garland, was the bantamweight Army Champion, 1927 and 1928, Imperial Services Boxing Association Champion, 1927 and 1928, Amateur Boxing Association Champion, 1928, and represented Great Britain at the 1928 Olympic Games.

Usher's sporting pedigree was acknowledged when he was appointed team manager of the Scottish team in the 1950 British Empire Games and the 1954 British Empire and Commonwealth Games. In 1950, as Scotland could not afford to send a fencer, Usher, who had fenced for Scotland in the 1920s, stood in and represented his country in the individual *épée*. He scored three wins and three defeats for fifth place in the elimination pools, fighting for the first time with an electric *épée*.

Colonel Charles 'Dougie' Usher never lost his affection for The Gordon Highlanders. He attended and helped to organise the annual Officers Dinners that were held in Edinburgh, usually at the North British Hotel. On one occasion there was confusion over the number of officers attending. The formally dressed Head Waiter was adamant that the extra numbers could not be squeezed into the dining room, and it looked like disappointed subalterns would have to leave and find somewhere else to dine. Usher took the Head Waiter aside and, with a fatherly arm around his shoulders, chatted softly and amicably to him. In no time at all the Head Waiter had been charmed into opening a nearby room, fitting it out with a properly set dining table, and sitting the delighted young officers in a room of their own where they could enjoy themselves away from the eyes of the 'old and bold'. They came through to the main dining room for the speeches and were vociferous in their praise of the old soldier who had given them such a splendid evening. It was another example of the charm, diplomacy and powers of persuasion of a remarkable man.

Charles Usher died in 1981. In adversity and triumph he had maintained the high standards that he had set himself from the beginning. He had served his country, his fellow men and above all his beloved Gordon Highlanders, faithfully, loyally and with total commitment. He was, indeed, an inspiration to all who knew him and those who came after.

CHAPTER 40

IVAN LYON

IVAN Lyon, son of Brigadier-General Francis Lyon, RA,[1] was a distant relative of Lieutenant Alexander Lyon,[2] killed near Bertry in August 1914.[3] He was commissioned into The Gordon Highlanders in August 1935, and went with the 2nd Battalion to Singapore in 1937. In 1941 Captain Ivan Lyon was attached to the Intelligence Corps, and worked in the Special Operations Executive (SOE). Before Singapore fell in 1942 he helped to set up an escape route to Padang on the west coast of Sumatra. The route went by sea from Singapore to the Indragiri River on the east coast of Sumatra and up river to Ringat. From there, using tortuous road and rail routes, it crossed the central mountain range and on to Padang. His pastime of ocean sailing in the boat he shared with his good friend, fellow Gordon Highlander Captain Francis Moir-Byres, had taught him about local tides and currents. He remained in the area for some considerable time after Singapore fell, assisting stragglers who had got off the island, and he helped many Allied soldiers to escape.

On one occasion he was bringing a launch alongside the jetty at Ringat when he misjudged his approach and bumped into a fishing boat. This

---

1   Brig-Gen Francis Lyon, C.B., C.M.G., C.V.O., D.S.O., Croix de Guerre was ADC to General Sir George White during the siege of Ladysmith in 1899–1900, and a good friend of Gen Sir Ian Hamilton, who had been a brigade commander during the siege.
2   Both could trace their ancestry back to David Lyon of Cossins, who died at Flodden in 1513.
3   Volume IX, Chapter 20.

unleashed a tirade of colourful Australian abuse from a civilian, Bill Reynolds, on board the fishing boat. After suitable apologies Lyon was soon sharing a beer with the Australian, who became a great friend and collaborator in planning the raid that would make Lyon famous. The fishing boat was the Krait, the craft on which his legendary fame would be based. His activities in organising the escape route and assisting escapers led to the award of MBE for this work. He left Padang for Ceylon in a native *proa* and was employed on the staff in India. His wife and baby son Clive,[4] who had been evacuated to Australia in February 1942, sailed to join him in India, but their ship was intercepted by a German raider and they, along with the crew and other passengers, were handed over to the Japanese. They were taken to Japan where they spent the remainder of the war in a prison camp at Fukushima.[5]

From India Ivan Lyon made his way to Australia. Determined to take the fight to the Japanese, he did so in a most remarkable way, organising and leading Operation *Jaywick*, an attack in two-man canoes on Japanese shipping in Singapore harbour:

1943—Operation *Jaywick*

The great naval base at Singapore fell to the Japanese on 15th February, 1942, and under the name of Shonan, was brought into use for operations against Burma, India and Ceylon.

When Australia had recovered from these events, British and Australian brains decided that, while land operations in New Guinea were in progress, a raid would be made against shipping in Singapore harbour. An ex-Japanese craft, the *Kofuku Maru* renamed *Krait*, 70 feet long with a speed of 6½ knots, which had carried refugees from Sumatra to India was allotted to carry the limpeteers[6] as near as possible to the scene of operations.

The party was Major I. Lyon, The Gordon Highlanders; Lieutenant D.N. Davidson, R.N.V.R.; Lieutenant R. Page, A.I.F.; Ldg. Seaman K.P. Cain, R.A.N.; Ldg, Stoker P. McDowell, R.N.; Ldg. Telegraphist H. Young. R.A.N.; Corporal A.G. Morris, R.A.M.C.; Corporal A. Crilly, A.I.F.; A/B B.A.W. Falls, R.A.N.; A/B A.W. Jones, R.A.N.; A/B A.W. Huston, R.A.N.; A/B F.W. Marsh, R.A.N.; and A/B M. Berryman, R.A.N.[7] (photo below)

---

4   Clive Lyon was commissioned as a Gordon Highlander in 1964, and spent a year in the jungles of Borneo as a platoon commander, during Confrontation with Indonesia.

5   The site of the modern nuclear power station that was damaged in the tsunami of 2011.

6   The attack was to be carried out using limpet mines attached to the hulls of the Japanese ships by the raiders in canoes, hence the name 'limpeteers'.

7   A.I.F.; Australian Imperial Force; R.A.M.C.; Royal Army Medical Corps; R.A.N.; Royal Australian Navy; R.N.; Royal Navy; R.N.V.R.; Royal Naval Volunteer Reserve; A/B; Able-Bodied Seaman.

After commando training the party left Western Australia on 2nd September, 1943, in the *Krait* (photo), which carried rubber canoes, limpet mines, arms and rations. The ship headed north, passed through Lombok Strait, turned north-west through the Java Sea and took the party to within 21 miles of Singapore. The canoes had stores for a week and limpet mines. The crews set off for the island of Dongas, eight miles from

Singapore, that was to be the forward base. On September 22nd the three canoes, manned by Lyon and Huston, Davidson and Falls, and Page and Jones, arrived at Dongas, the crews exhausted by the long paddle. A rest day was spent examining the harbour for targets.

On the night of 26th September, the limpeteers paddled silently into Singapore harbour and stealthily approached their targets. At times they were swept along the wharves by the tide, but No. 1 canoe placed two limpets under the engine room and one on the tail shaft of the *Shinkoku Maru* a 10,000-ton tanker lying in the Examination Anchorage.

Canoe No. 2 twice crossed the boom into Keppel Harbour searching for suitable targets, ignoring two smaller ships. Three ships were selected, the *Hakusan Maru* 2,917 tons, the *Kisan Maru* 5,077 tons, and the *Taisyo Maru* 6,000 tons being mined.

Canoe No. 3 quietly moved about, examining ships and sentry posts, and placed limpets against the *Nasusan Maru* 4,399 tons alongside Bukum Wharf, *Yamagata Maru* 3,807 tons in Bukum Roads and a steamer in the Examination Anchorage.

By the next dawn the attackers were back at Palau Sambu Island. Seven distinct explosions were heard and soon intensive Japanese air and sea patrols were seen.

When darkness fell on 27th September the three canoes set off to rendezvous with the *Krait* at Pompong, 36 miles from Singapore. For a time, as no contact was made, the party feared that they had missed their mother ship, and discussed plans to proceed independently to Australia, some 2,000 miles away. The *Krait* (photo), however, discovered them

later, having missed them in the darkness. Course was set for Exmouth Gulf which they reached on the 19th of October. There had been no personnel lost.

The *Kisan Maru* and *Hakusan Maru* stayed at the bottom of Singapore Harbour, whilst the *Yamagata Maru*, *Taisyo Maru* and *Nasusan Maru* were later repaired and returned to service, the first named to be sunk on 16th April, 1944, and the latter on 24th June, 1944. The *Shinkoku Maru*, the 10,000-ton tanker, was repaired but was sunk by U.S. aircraft on 17th February, 1944.

All the limpeteers were either decorated[8] or mentioned in despatches, and one can imagine the strain that Lieutenant Carse and his crew of seven were under cruising the *Krait* in enemy waters for 10 days.

T&S, September 1960.

---

8   Ivan Lyon was recommended for the V.C., but awarded the D.S.O. for this operation.

In 1944 a second raid on Singapore harbour, Operation *Rimau*, was planned, again commanded and led by Ivan Lyon, now Lieutenant-Colonel. Reports for some time after the war suggested that it had been a complete failure, and that those not killed in action were later given a hero's death by the respectful Japanese. This account of Operation *Rimau*, by Lynette Ramsay-Silver, author of *The Heroes of Rimau*, casts doubts on earlier 'official' accounts of what actually happened. Constant through every account is the courage and dedication of the men who took part, but Ramsay-Silver sheds new light on how the men actually died. She relies for much of her chronological account on Cyril Wild's account *Expedition to Singkep*. Her analysis of Japanese and local accounts is where a new view of the story is found. Ivan Lyon is the only Gordon Highlander connection, but it is fitting that the story of those gallant British and Australian servicemen is clarified.

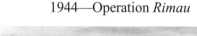

1944—Operation *Rimau*

On 11 September 1944 the British submarine *Porpoise* (photo) slipped quietly from Fremantle, bound for Indonesian waters. On board were 23 Australian and British members of Operation *Rimau*.[9] Their destination— Japanese held Singapore. Their mission—to penetrate the harbour in one-man submersible craft and blow up 60 enemy ships. The party was confident. The previous year six of them, including Commanding Officer, Lieutenant-Colonel Ivan Lyon, had carried out a similar raid—Operation *Jaywick*—which had damaged or sunk seven ships.

Nineteen days later, the submarine commander farewelled the raiders at Pedjantan Island, promising to return 38 days later. A handful of Chinese and Malays and the conquering Japanese were the only people ever to see the 23 again.

T&S, 1992.

---

9   *Rimau* is the Malay word for 'tiger', which was appropriate, as Ivan Lyon had a large tattoo of a tiger on his chest!

On 28th September the submarine stopped and seized a local junk, *Mustika*, and Lyon's men loaded their stores from it on to Merapas Island. After that the plan went badly wrong. On 10th October, hours before the raid, the junk was challenged by a local police patrol boat as they approached Singapore. One of the commandos opened fire, compromising the entire operation.

Lyon ordered the junk back to Merapas Island, where it and the raiding party's secret stores were destroyed, but he made one last-ditch effort to salvage the mission. In the early hours of 11th October Lyon and six men penetrated the Harbour and mined three ships. He then dispersed his men, but the pursuit this time was hot and furious.

The submarine was to pick them up from Merapas on 7th November, almost a month away. The raiding party passed through Pangil Island, but their presence was betrayed by a local man. On Soreh Island the Japanese caught up with them, and in a series of pitched gun battles, in which he killed more than 60 of the enemy, Lt-Col Ivan Lyon and Lt Bobby Ross were eventually killed by a hand grenade as they were trying to cover the escape of wounded members of their party.

www.worldnavalships.com

Lynette Ramsay-Silver's account continues:

Unlike Operation *Jaywick*, the story of Operation *Rimau* was destined to remain a mystery for almost 50 years. With little evidence available, it has long been accepted that the *Rimau* raid was an unmitigated disaster. According to the scant official post-war records, not only was the entire party lost but the raid was an abject failure. It was further stated that ten men who had been captured had talked too freely, giving information to the enemy. Although these ten had been executed, it was held that the Japanese had done so reluctantly and only after trying the accused before a legally constituted court which found them guilty of war crimes. The official reports stated that the beheadings had been carried out in a style befitting Samurai warriors. The fate of 11 of the party was unknown.

Although journalist Ronald McKie, when writing a fictionalised account of Operation *Jaywick* in 1960 made an attempt to uncover the truth about Operation *Rimau*, he was less than successful. Hampered by a lack of detail and access to official documentation, and led astray by self-seeking Japanese concerned in the affair, it would perhaps have been better if he had waited until further research had been carried out. With his unreferenced account simply reinforcing the many rumours that abounded, theory soon became fact.

Shrouded in mystery and distorted by hearsay, Operation *Rimau* would doubtless have remained a mishmash of fact and fiction had former

Commando Major Tom Hall been a less stubborn individual. Alerted by a chance remark in 1958, Hall (aged 24 at the time) determined to find out precisely what had happened on the mission and the ultimate fate of every one of the 23 men, two of whom were rumoured to have paddled from Singapore to Timor. His self-imposed search, arduous and frustrating, took him 31 years. In 1988 using his wealth of meticulously recorded documents, it was my privilege to begin to unravel the story which, two years later, would lead to the publication of *The Heroes of Rimau*.

Major Hall's evidence meant a rewrite of accepted history. To overturn such a well-entrenched story would not be easy. To research previously unknown history is hard enough—to re-write what many see as the gospel truth is extremely difficult.

Previous publication of certain 'facts' by unscrupulous individuals who had access to Hall's early, but incomplete research material, and who had breached his confidentiality, had not helped. Neither had a feature film, financed with Japanese money. Endorsed by a returned servicemen's organisation (which believed at face value that the plot was drawn entirely from documented evidence), the film was long on action but pitifully short on fact. In 1988, a brief Department of Defence publication on Operation *Rimau* had added to the confusion. Written from material deposited by a film company, it contained as fact the same fictitious film scenarios to which Major Hall, in his capacity as consultant, had objected violently, forcing the cancellation of the film.

It is unfortunate that, being in the public domain, such erroneous material resurfaced in a television mini-series. Included is the ludicrous assertion that Lyon—who knew his wife was in an internment camp in Japan—was obsessed with attacking Singapore because she was imprisoned there. Many were seduced into believing not only that activities depicted on the screen actually took place, but that the raid failed and the captured men were reluctantly executed in true Samurai style. Nothing could be further from the truth.

Major Hall's evidence reveals that a raid on enemy shipping took place on the morning of 11 October 1944; that it was born not from personal revenge but from a deep and patriotic love of God, King and Country; that almost all the information allegedly volunteered by the *Rimau* men was already known to the Japanese; that the men who were beheaded were put through a sham trial on trumped-up charges for no other reason than to save the collective Japanese face; that the execution, far from being a ceremonial occasion was carried out by lowly prison guards whose swordmanship left much to be desired; that almost all the party might have been saved had the pick-up team done its job properly and had the submarine commander carried out his orders; that the post-war investigation into the disappearance of the *Rimau* men and the fate of those beheaded was incompetent; and that the Australian Army, in seeking to distance itself from an operation deemed to be a failure, issued statements that reinforced the myth that those executed had committed war crimes. It also reveals, for the first time, the fate of every man attached to the party, including the pair who reached Timor—not by canoe but in a native sailing boat.

Collecting the evidence was difficult. Once a document was located its veracity was checked wherever possible with material from another source. In many instances, this cross-referencing ironed out longstanding ambiguities and amplified information which otherwise would have been too scant. This was especially useful in piecing together evidence such as that required to prove that the raid had indeed taken place. I cite this particular example in detail to indicate the lengths to which Major Hall went to ensure that his research was based on fact, and fact alone.

The initial information, that seven men including Lieutenant-Colonel Ivan Lyon had raided enemy shipping came from Japanese messages. These signals, now in Washington DC, had been secretly intercepted and decoded shortly after transmission, by Americans who had cracked the Japanese cypher. Major Hall realised that this information required verification to ensure that the *Jaywick* raid of 1943 (carried out by Major Lyon and five men) was not being confused with an attack carried out by Lieutenant-Colonel Lyon and six men in 1944. This was achieved by locating a war crimes interrogation report, part of a 1,500-page file into the investigations of two missing Australians, neither from Operation *Rimau*. During lengthy interrogations in 1947, forty-eight Japanese officers recounted to Allied investigators the details of people who had passed through their hands in Surabaya, Java, where two missing Australians were known to have vanished. One of the prisoners whom they recalled was *Rimau*'s Douglas Warne, who had been captured and taken to Surabaya. The Japanese were adamant that Warne had revealed that he was one of the raiders but had failed to reach his objective owing to the strong rip-tide.

Major Hall, although elated to discover that the raid had been carried out (and that, according to the Japanese, three ships had been sunk) felt that such a startling claim, flying in the face of accepted history, required supporting evidence which did not come from Japanese sources. In 1981 he travelled to Indonesia where he located eyewitnesses to the events of October 1944. The locals were happy to answer questions and revealed that, at dawn the morning after the *Rimau* team had been involved in a fight with Japanese collaborators (i.e. the morning of 11 October), they heard violent explosions off Samboe Island, about 16 kilometres from

Singapore. Hall then decided to have every wreck in Singapore Harbour and the Roads plotted on a huge naval chart. Once this had been done, he set about the tedious and lengthy task of eliminating each wreck from information supplied by Singapore, British and American authorities. When he had finished, there were three wrecks for which no one could account. They lay off Samboe Island, precisely where the local Indonesians said they would be.

The exhaustive cross-checking used for written evidence was also applied to that from Indonesian eyewitnesses. Tapes of all conversations were checked in Australia to ensure that the translations were correct. The information from one eyewitness was cross-checked against that given by another. Such was the total recall of these people that the most minute details were independently corroborated. When Major Hall complimented the Indonesians on their prodigious memories, they had stated simply 'It was important to remember. One day we knew that someone would come back to ask about the white men'.

It was on this trip that Hall discovered the remains of one of the missing *Rimau* men at Merapas Island—the submarine's rendezvous point. Hall managed to bring the skull back to Australia, where forensic analysts revealed that it belonged to one of two men—Sergeant Colin Cameron or Sub-Lieutenant Gregor Riggs.

Further detail was obtained from Hiroyuki Furuta, the Japanese interpreter during the *Rimau* men's interrogation and trial. In 1957 Furuta wrote an article for a Japanese magazine about the capture and trial of the men. This article was translated by the Foreign Office, which believed it to be an accurate account. Unfortunately, not only had Furuta written the account from memory 13 years after the event (he had destroyed his diary before the Allies arrived in Singapore). He had also been elastic with the truth—inventing names and dates, substituting the identity of one man for another, having the victims shot rather than beheaded, repeating hearsay when he had no direct knowledge and generally embroidering the facts to make the account palatable for Japanese consumption.

Rather shamefaced that statements in his article had been taken literally, he rewrote his original version. Aware that this new account still left much to be desired, he then amended the amended version. Not surprisingly, many (including Ronald McKie and the makers of the previously mentioned films) were misled by Furuta, particularly in regard to the beheadings. Although he had not witnessed the men's deaths, he wanted to believe that they had been accorded a ceremonial execution as his superiors had claimed and which an Allied investigating officer was hoodwinked into believing. The official testimonies of two Koreans at Outram Road Gaol where the 10 men were held, as well as a grisly exhumation report on the bodies, belie this outrageous claim. It became obvious, on examining Furuta's evidence, that his version of events required cross-checking, claim by claim.

Factual statements made to investigating officers by the Japanese could be misleading. The assertion that 'by coincidence all four parties met on Sole Island where they had a clash with the Japanese. During the engagement Lt Colonel Lyon and Lt Ross were killed' has led to some erroneous statements. The first is the assumption that 'all four parties' meant all the *Rimau* team split into four, when the Japanese actually meant the occupants of four folboats (three containing two men and one containing Douglas Warne). This is confirmed by other Japanese and Major Hall's eyewitnesses. The remainder of the party was safely back at Merapas and was not involved in the fighting. The second assumption is that an island named Sole existed. No one could find it in 1945. Nor in 1960 could Ronald McKie. He simply picked an island on a map, named it Sole Island and arranged the action to suit this fictitious location. The island where Lyon and Ross died was Soreh. The Allied translator, in making the usual allowances for Japanese pronunciation, adjusted it to Soleh, which was then transcribed as Sole. And Sole it has been ever since, despite the fact that no island by that name exists.

Anxious to see the islands for myself and to check the statements collected in 1981, I went with Major Hall to Indonesia in 1989. Never once did those interviewed in 1989 deviate from their previous stories. Indeed, even more details came to light. We found two new eyewitnesses and knew what areas of inquiry required amplification. With the interviews completed and accompanied by the Indonesians, we visited all the places where the *Rimau* men had been. Travelling by small native boat to reach the more inaccessible islands, we clambered through thick jungle to stand on the same place that Ivan Lyon and his men stood almost half a century before.

However, it was when we reached Merapas that we received our greatest shock. Eyewitness Achap was going carefully through his information when he suddenly pointed to a tree and announced, 'And that is where I buried the other one'. Some frantic questioning elicited the fact that by 'the other one' he meant the companion of the man whose skull Major Hall had taken home on the previous visit. Believing in 1981 that the Major had found what he was looking for—the remains of a fictitious uncle (Hall's cover story)—Achap had neglected to tell him that there had been a second man.

Through the interpreter we learned that the 'soldier' had literally run for his life, only to be trapped on the end of a small spur. Turning to face his pursuers, he had been shot three times in the chest. Pitched backwards, he had landed not far from where Achap, who had been taken along by the Japanese as a human shield, was standing.

Achap had time to carefully examine an engraved silver bracelet which the dead man was wearing. Apologising that as the writing was foreign to him he was able to remember only a couple of letters, Achap drew in Major Hall's notebook a symbol which we recognised as being that of the Royal Naval Volunteer Reserve, followed by G.....S. Achap could not possibly have known that one of the two men left on Merapas was Sub Lt Gregor Riggs of the R.N.V.R. Since Riggs was buried beneath the tree, we now knew that the skull recovered earlier belonged to Sergeant Colin Cameron.

Achap's revelation about Rigg's burial solved one last mystery. In October 1945 an Allied search party had found the grave, marked with a wooden post and an oriental inscription, which led them to believe the deceased was Japanese. Word about the grave had previously filtered through to Furuta, whose imagination had worked overtime. Altering the site to Soreh (photo) and the victims to Lyon and Ross, who still lay where they had fallen, he told Allied investigators that the pair had died in a blaze of glory (which was true) and that the Japanese had 'made very fine graves for them' (which was not).

Rimau men *were* marked by very fine graves—erected by the War Graves Commission. The bodies of the ten who were beheaded were recovered and reinterred in Singapore's Kranji War Cemetery, as were the skeletal remains of Lyon and Ross. Before long, two more fine graves will be erected in Kranji. As a result of Major Hall's dedicated research and the evidence cited in *The Heroes of Rimau* the War Graves Commission has already located the previously unidentified burial sites of Lieutenant-Commander Donald Davidson and Corporal A.G.P. Campbell, who died together on the tiny island of Tapai. We are most gratified to learn that their graves, along with the rest of their comrades, will be marked with headstones befitting *Heroes of Rimau*.

T&S, 1992.

Death of Ivan Lyon

The following account of the death of Ivan Lyon appears in several versions from different sources of varying reliability. As none of the party survived the war the account could only have come from Japanese after-action reports, interrogation of the survivor (Corporal Stewart) and accounts from local civilians. It has been established that civilian memories of the events were remarkably detailed, more than forty years later. What is not in doubt is that a determined resistance was put up, and that Ivan Lyon died in the fierce fighting. The account is in keeping with his character, his reputation and his actions since the Japanese invasion of Malaya.

Lyon died on the tiny island of Soreh on 16 October 1944, whilst fighting a rearguard action to cover the evacuation of two injured members of the *Rimau* party. Discovered by a Japanese landing crew, Lyon—together with Corporal Clair Stewart and Lieutenant Robert Ross, the injured Private Archie Campbell and Lieutenant-Commander Donald Davidson—engaged the Japanese in battle, killing and injuring seven. The remaining Japanese escaped. Knowing that they would come back in a matter of hours with reinforcements—and that there was no possibility of island-hopping to safety with two injured and exhausted comrades—Lyon made the decision to dose the injured Davidson and Campbell with morphine, and set them on their way towards the nearby island of Tapai, where other members of the Rimau party were known to be holed up.

Lyon set about creating rudimentary defences, taking into account the position of a Malay household. The danger of involving the occupants of the shack in the forthcoming battle led Lyon to switch position away from this location, a formidable task given that the tiny island had little significant cover, and was almost indefensible in daylight. Lyon and Ross climbed a large tree, having first equipped themselves with a good supply of ammunition and grenades. Corporal Stewart was positioned in a stone-lined ditch, about 30 metres to their left, together with a cache of grenades and ammunition for the silenced Stens that all three carried.

The Japanese returned two hours later, approximately 110 strong. For almost four hours the Japanese suffered heavy losses, unaware that their enemy was firing from high above them, as well as being caught repeatedly by the grenades thrown by the unseen Stewart. At midnight, Japanese soldiers finally caught sight of the tiny muzzle flashes from the silenced Stens. Grenades were thrown into the trees; Ross and Lyon fell from the branches, killed by grenade shrapnel. They had accounted for over sixty dead and wounded Japanese. Stewart remained undiscovered on the island, but was marooned as his folboat had been taken by the Japanese. He was eventually caught and taken to Singapore, where he was executed.

Headstone of Ivan Lyon at Kranji, Singapore

SECTION 15

TROOPSHIPS

THROUGHOUT the years The Gordon Highlanders and their constituent regiments, the 75th and 92nd, saw service in Europe, Africa, the Caribbean, the Middle East, India and the Far East. Until the 1960s they travelled to these parts by troopship or by Royal Navy warship. The names of some of these ships keep recurring, often over long periods. On occasions we have accounts of these journeys, some of which are recorded below. It is perhaps worth looking at some of the ships that carried the 75th, the 92nd and The Gordon Highlanders to their destinations, where The Gordon Highlanders saw many of their number pay the ultimate price for policing the Empire and keeping the peace.

CHAPTER 41

TROOPSHIPS

RAISED for service in India, the 75th was sent there in 1787, and would have travelled in hired transports. As the whole Regiment moved together a number of ships would have been used exclusively for this purpose. We have no record of these ships, but the *Memoirs of Sergeant Kenward*, who travelled out to India little more than a year after the 75th made the journey, gives some idea of such a voyage.

Drafts of reinforcements travelled in East Indiamen along with civilian passengers, as the following passage describes:

TROOPSHIP TO INDIA, 1789

110 Recruits embarked on the *Ponsborne* Indiaman in February 1789 among which was myself, and after a tedious passage of better than six months arrived at our destination, having in the course of the voyage only called at St. Iago, the Canary Islands for a trifling refit, for which we suffered in a Gale a few days before.

Here we remained about a fortnight and proceeded on our Voyage without any particular Occurrence until arrival off the Cape of Good Hope. It was there God awaited us in order to call such as lived in their sins to a sincere repentance and to convince us that the good success of a Voyage depends solely on Heaven. We were however happily delivered from our fears after about a Fort-night buffeting with furious winds and seas, without any material Injury by the calm and moderate weather which succeeded, and which accompanied us the remainder of the Voyage.

We buried (or rather cast overboard,) during the Passage only one soldier and a sailor, owing no doubt to the humane care and attention of the Captain of the ship whose name was Thomas. He was certainly a most excellent character, which was a great mercy to us, having no Officer on board to whom had it been necessary we might have appealed to check the Tyrany of a Vicious Commander.

Memoirs of Sergeant William Kenward.

Passage in an Indiaman was more tolerable than in the hired transports that took the 75th to India, such as that described below:

Kenward was right to be thankful for a relatively safe and uneventful voyage in a well-found East Indiaman, even though soldiers had to travel in the steerage, all other accommodation being reserved for paying civilian passengers. Conditions on troop transports were usually appalling, and to quote Fortescue,[1] 'In truth it is difficult in these days to realise the perils and discomforts patiently endured by officers and men in leaky transports, when frequently they could not sleep dry for weeks together. Not the least of the dangers was the drunkenness and incompetence of the masters and mates, which on at least one occasion compelled a captain of infantry to take command and navigate a ship from the West Indies to England.'

Memoirs of Sergeant William Kenward (Editor's comment).

The following description of a convoy carrying troops from India to Britain in 1806, the year before the 75th returned, gives a vivid account of the perils that faced ships in the face of nature at its most violent:

John Shipp, who was in the Indiaman *Lord Duncan*, described the storm as follows: 'We were overtaken by a terrific hurricane, which blew for two days without a pause. During the course of it the *Lady Castlereagh* seemed certain to be lost. She was about a quarter of a mile from us, and we watched her as she heeled over so violently that at one time we could see the whole of her keel. There was a shout of horror from all of us at the sight of it, and our Captain said she would never right herself. But the next wave brought her up, and though she rolled, and pitched, and laboured dreadfully she kept afloat. Some of her masts were carried away, but which I do not now recollect. She was the only vessel in the fleet to suffer much damage.'

Memoirs of Sergeant William Kenward (Editor's comment).

Kenward transferred from the 75th to the 76th in 1806 and returned to Britain with the 76th. The ships travelled in a convoy, which assembled at Ceylon, 'being the Rendezvous appointed for Homeward bound ships from China, Bengal, Bombay and Madras'. Kenward mentions men from regiments departing India being drafted into other regiments. In this instance, the drafted men had obviously elected to go to a regiment returning to Britain rather than go to Egypt with their own regiments:

I shall now take my leave of this quarter of India and proceed with my reader towards Bengal, having received orders for Embarkation and vessels being arrived to transport us we with raptures obeyed the order and in a few days found ourselves again in Bombay Harbour, where we remained about a fortnight, but did not disembark. Here Detachments of the 61st and 88th Regts (left behind their Corps on their proceeding to

---

1   Author of the thirteen-volume *History of the British Army*, published over the period 1899 to 1930.

Egypt) joined us, being turned over to the 76th Regiment as drafts. The whole occupying four ships. We had a very unpleasant passage from Bombay, and our vessel (the *Jane*) in particular was in great danger of being lost, being very ill mand with Country Sailors, who owing to the rough treatment received from their Officers seemed rather to prefer death to life.

In the Bay of Bengal the vessel was caught in a squall under full sail, which the sailors could or would not strike until the Ship was laying on her beam ends. The Chief Officer was himself an Excellent sailor but a cruel Tyrant, and happily the squall (as is common in those seas) was but for a short duration.

Memoirs of Sergeant William Kenward.

One of the interesting things about British Army troopships in the eighteenth and nineteenth centuries is the longevity of their service, some carrying veteran soldiers who had not been born when they were launched.

HMS *APOLLO*

Regimental records do not name the ships that took the 75th to India in 1787. Likewise, the ships that took the 92nd to Gibraltar, to Holland and to Egypt in the same era are not named.[2] The first named ship we have which transported the 92nd was HMS *Apollo* (illustration), a Royal Navy 38-gun frigate built in 1805. *Apollo* took part in a number of actions in the

---

2 We do, however, have a letter written to his sister by Lt-Col Charles Erskine of Cardross, on the way to Egypt in 1800, on board HMS *Stately*, a 64-gun ship of the line converted for use as a troopship in 1799.

Mediterranean from 1807 to 1814. In 1810 she, with HMS *Audacious* and HMS *Vestal*, took the 92nd to Portugal. In 1839 *Apollo* was converted to a troopship, and in 1851, 41 years after her first voyage with the 92nd, took the 92nd from Ireland to Corfu. She went on to take British troops to the Crimea!

HIRED MILITARY TROOPSHIP (HMT) *SIMOOM*

Her Majesty's Troopship *Simoom* (photo) was built on the Clyde in 1849. She was laid down as an iron frigate but completed as a troopship, and served in this capacity until 1887. She carried the 92nd from Portsmouth to Kingston, Ireland in 1866, and part of the 75th from Natal to Cape Town and on to England in 1875:

> The right half battalion under Captain Bevan headed by the Band of the 32nd Regt. marched out of King William's Town to sail for home from East London on the troopship *Simoom*. Sandy the Piper (91st Regt.) who was well known all over Kafirland and whose services were always welcomed at Scottish festivities, headed the 75th with his bagpipes, a silver-mounted set which in 1863 had been presented to him as a token of regard for his services rendered on the top of a triumphal arch in Smith Street when Prince Alfred visited King William's Town in 1860. Among the adults and small boys of Fort Beaufort and on the farms and at hotels opened by discharged highlanders, Sandy the Piper whose name was Maclean and was ever fond of a dram or more, was in a seventh heaven of bliss as he led the 75th on to the *Simoom* at East London. Maybe he shed a few tears because his fellow highlanders were leaving him behind in the valleys and mountains of a wild Kafirland.

T&S, March 1964.

HMT *HIMALAYA*

When built for the Pacific and Orient line in 1853, the *Himalaya* (photo) was the largest steamer in the world and the most elegant. She was chartered, and then bought by the Navy, as a troop transport. She took troops to Crimea, and gained the battle honours 'New Zealand 1863–66', and, with her sister ship, *Tamar*, 'Ashanti 1873–74'. She took the 92nd from Glasgow to Portsmouth in 1865, the 75th from Gibraltar to Hong Kong in 1868, part of the 75th from South Africa to Britain in 1875, and in 1888 the 35-year-old veteran took the 1st Battalion, The Gordon Highlanders from Malta to Ceylon. Converted to a coaling hulk in 1895, she was sunk in 1940 by the *Luftwaffe* in Portland Harbour.

Henry Pridmore joined the 75th in 1864. He spent seventeen years in the 75th and seven in the 1st Battalion, The Gordon Highlanders. In 1868 the 75th was sent to Hong Kong on board HMT *Himalaya*:

> Our next station was Hong Kong, and as the Suez Canal was not then open to troopships we made the voyage by going round the Cape of Good Hope. On October 7th, 1868, we set sail on H.M. Troopship *Himalaya*, and we had several halts on the way, Ascension, St. Helena, Cape Town and Simons Town being the main ones in Africa. We stayed about a week in Simons Town, taking on coal and provisions, and each company went ashore daily for exercise. Just after leaving the Cape we ran into a storm. I shall never forget that night; the ship tossed and rolled and all her sails were torn, but she stood the test and we continued our journey towards Singapore, where we were amused by the black boys diving for coins and always managing to bring them up. Our next stop was the Island of Manila. Why we stopped there I cannot say, but our officers went ashore and returned with some Spanish officers, who looked round the ship. It

was on December 21st that we landed at Hong Kong after having been on board ship for 76 days.

T&S, May 1933.

The following account by W.H. Patterson, former Regimental Sergeant Major, of the move of the 1st Battalion, The Gordon Highlanders from Malta to Ceylon in 1888 is interesting, not only for its description of the accommodation, feeding arrangements and routine aboard a troopship, but of the troopship itself, HMT *Himalaya*: the veteran ship that had carried the 75th to Hong Kong in 1868:

We were on voyage from Malta to Ceylon on the *Himalaya*. She was one of the old vessels in which Tommy did his ocean travelling when the powers-that-be decreed a change of station and a sea voyage for the good of his health, and to keep him from getting rusty.

On those old troopers the comfort and convenience of the soldier was the last thing considered. The accommodation was limited; the food was absolutely the limit. Troopships were manned and managed exclusively by the Royal Navy, who regarded us as quite decent fellows ashore, but a positive nuisance afloat.

If it was an unhappy experience for us men, 800 of us cramped up like herrings in a barrel with barely room to stand up on that portion of the deck allotted to us through the day, and slung up in hammocks at night on the close, stuffy troop-decks, what must it have been for the women and children, many of the latter infants?

No bread was issued, though it was possible to buy it from the ship's canteen occasionally. No fresh meat was available. The rations were salt junk and ship's biscuit. Dinner was the same every day—pea-soup—in which salt junk was boiled, to season the soup and soften the tough meat. That fare was a trial to the troops; it was starvation for women and children.

Little provision was made for the very young children, but the married people could buy condensed milk from the canteen at fancy prices; even so, this was poor sustenance for a youngster, and pea-soup and junk was hardly the sort of food for an infant to thrive on. The women were not long before they got thoroughly fed up.

The married families were accommodated on the main troop-deck; their sleeping quarters separated from the men's by a solid bulkhead, pierced by a door guarded night and day by a sentry. They took meals on the same mess-deck as the men, but at separate tables. The mess-tables and seats were slung up to the roof, except during the night, when they were let down on to the floor, and at meal times, when they were lowered to the normal table height. During the first week at sea there was no trouble. Men, women and children were too sea-sick to bother about food. Presently, however, the voyagers began to sit up and take notice and renew their interest in life; then the fun began.

The ship's Orderly Officer went his rounds at dinner as usual accompanied by an orderly corporal, and the time-honoured question 'Any complaints?' received the equally hoary old response, 'None sir,' as we knew it was hopeless to expect anything better however much we complained. The women, however, though they might have put up with it for themselves and said little, the fact that their babies were suffering made them furious. They decided to stir things up.

To that end a big upstanding Aberdonian lady was deputed to launch the attack. On the fateful day her husband, a lance-corporal, was ship's Orderly Corporal, and accompanied the Orderly Officer round the mess-decks. He led the way between the tables, rapped with his cane and shouted 'Orderly Officer! Tenshun!' The Orderly Officer, a newly-fledged subaltern who had only joined the battalion a few days before we embarked, was a trifle self-conscious and more than a little bashful on his first encounter with Mrs. Tommy Atkins. He had been bad with seasickness too, and was rather white about the gills. Approaching the women's tables, he inquired, 'Any complaints?' and was answered promptly by the married lady deputed to speak, 'Yes, sir!' Pointing with her finger to the tureen in which the salt junk lay in slabs, greasy and repulsive, she leaned over the table and continued, 'Fit dee 'ee think o' that muck, sir, as meat fur bairns an' weemen?'

The young officer was taken aback, though doubtless he had his own opinion as to what the answer should be. However, the lady gave him little chance of saying anything; she proceeded very volubly, in the broadest 'Aiberdeen,' to state her opinion, punctuated by applause from the female members of her audience. The officer, unable to get a word in, got flustered. The Orderly Corporal rushed to the rescue. An old soldier, he was horrified to see anyone addressing an officer except in the position of 'Attention.' It added to his amazed indignation that it was his own wife who was doing it. Stepping forward, in his sternest regimental tones he addressed his better-half, 'Silence, Mrs.—, stand to attention when you speak to an Officer!'

His wife turned and gave him a look, one of those that linger in the memory. She never said a word, but seizing a slab of junk from the tureen, slashed him across the face with the greasy mess and knocked him head over heels in the gangway.

The officer, thinking he was next, turned and bolted, leaving the corporal to the tender mercies of his infuriated better half. She continued the motion, and flogged him with her greasy weapon till he too managed to get to his feet and made his exit at his best pace. The troops by this time were up on the tables viewing the engagement, and many were helpless with laughing. All enjoyed the fun except the victim and the unfortunate Tommy who received the salt junk full in the face when Mrs.— flung it after her departing hubby.

Poor — had to appear before the Commanding Officer[3] to answer for his wife's lack of self-control, and got his porter stopped for a week. After our arrival at Colombo someone got hold of a copy of a book just published, *How to be Happy tho' Married*, and sent it to him. He must have enjoyed reading it.

The other incident might have developed into a tragedy but as everything ended happily, it caused no end of amusement.

The regulations prescribed that after embarkation every company had to be detailed for duty. Some were 'Guards,' others 'Watches' whose duty was to swab down decks, pull ropes, and assist generally, under the direction of naval petty officers, in running the ship. The company had to furnish men as 'Ash Party'. Their duty consisted of drawing up by a hand windlass buckets containing hot ashes from the stoke-hole and emptying them into the sea.

One of the chaps on this duty was noted in the Regiment for the size of his feet. Though not a big man physically, his boots were outsize, but as the size of his foot-wear undoubtedly saved his life, even a handicap like big feet had its compensations in his case.

One morning, in response to the raucous bellow of the boatswain's mate, 'Ash Party, Up ashes', he found himself at the windlass. His part was to seize the bucket as it emerged from the lift, and tilt the ashes down the chute into the sea. Half-dazed with sleep, he, in tilting the bucket, allowed it to slip too far over; it overbalanced and was on the way to join its contents in the Red Sea. He hung on like grim death, and being on the light side and unsteady on his feet on the rolling ship, he overbalanced and fell into the chute. The opening was not big, but the bucket got through, and his horrified chums had reason for thinking he was well on his way, but his boots saved him (the Ash Party were allowed to wear boots, alone out of all on board, to save their feet from getting burned by hot ashes.)

Somehow, his feet got wedged in and, clinging to the bucket, hung suspended, half-in and half-out of the opening looking down into the waves rushing past the ship's side. The other chaps seized him by the ankles and tried to pull him aboard, but he would not abandon the bucket, and only did so after being howled at by his rescuers.

---

3   Lt-Col J.E. Boyes.

After he was pulled to safety, one of the party said to him rather angrily, 'You ***, why the *** didn't you let go the *** bucket?'

Brave — excitedly replied, 'Aye, an' *** well have to pay for it, eh? D'ye tak' me for a *** fool? '

Right enough, he had to justify himself for 'Losing by neglect one of Her Majesty's ash buckets,' but in the circumstances he did not have its value passed through his accounts.

T&S, May 1925.

HMT *TAMAR*

Her Majesty's Troopship *Tamar* was launched in 1863, ten years after *Himalaya*, to which she bore a striking resemblance. She carried troops until 1897, and then served as a supply ship in Hong Kong until 1941. *Tamar* was dual-powered with masts and a steam engine, giving a speed of twelve knots. She carried the 75th from Hong Kong to Mauritius, and on to South Africa in 1871. In 1874 she was part of the Naval Brigade during the Ashanti War. In 1875 she took some of the 75th from Gibraltar to Britain after HMT *Himalaya* had broken down. She was at the bombardment of Alexandria in 1882, prior to the landing of the British force that included 1st Gordons. In 1885 she carried a draft for the 1st Battalion, under Major Edward Essex, from Portland to Malta. In 1897 *Tamar* became the Hong Kong receiving ship, until replaced by the shore station, which was named HMS *Tamar*.

During the battle for Hong Kong in 1941 *Tamar* was scuttled to deny her to the Japanese. As the ship's superstructure became airlocked, the ship refused to sink for some time, until the Royal Artillery administered the *coup de grâce*. One of her masts was erected in Stanley, Hong Kong.

SS *NUBIA*

The *Nubia* was built in Greenock in 1894 for the P&O line, from whom she was hired as a troop transport. During the Boer War she was used as a troop transport and as a hospital ship.

Herbert Styles, Company Sergeant Major in 2nd Gordons, writes of the move to India in 1898. Rations clearly had not improved in the ten years since the 1st Battalion's move to Ceylon!

> The 2nd Battalion, under Lieut-Col. Dick-Cunyngham, V.C., embarked at Southampton on the transport *Nubia* on 6th September, 1898. Here a disastrous incident happened to me. After being told off to our messes, we were ordered out of the kilt and into white jackets and trews, and to proceed to our respective upper decks. I had a small leather purse, containing a sovereign, a half-sovereign, and some small change in the fob pocket of my trews. Whilst leaning over the rails on the forecastle deck, my purse slipped out and, dropping, lodged on the anchor chains round the bows of the ship. I laid down on the deck and a couple of friends held me by the ankles and I reached down for the purse, but, to my horror, just as my hand was almost touching it, the purse slipped off and sank into the cruel waters of the harbour, and there was I, faced with a long voyage and no money. I was heart-broken; thirty shillings was thirty shillings. I have never used a purse since.

We steamed off and made for Cowes, where the Royal Yacht *Osborne* with H.R.H. the Prince of Wales (the late King Edward VII), Colonel-in-Chief of the Regiment on board, came alongside *Nubia* and ordered her to slow down, and both ships then steamed along together for several miles. His Royal Highness sent several messages to Lieut-Col. Dick-Cunyngham. The crew of the Royal Yacht cheered, which was answered by the troops on board the *Nubia*. His Royal Highness then sent a last message wishing the Battalion God-speed and a good voyage, and ordered the *Nubia* to proceed on her voyage.

We proceeded to Queenstown to pick up a draft of Northamptons. We had a rough passage in the Irish Sea. I am a good sailor, but it was the nearest I have been to being seasick. One chap was terribly sick, and exclaimed, 'would give my deferred pay for a square foot of dry land!' (deferred pay was 2d. a day deducted from pay, and returned to the soldier on termination of his engagement. It was a nice nest egg for civilian life— a system greatly appreciated in those days, I am sure).

The principal diet was salt junk, and it was wonderful, after everybody had thrown off the effects of the seasickness, how one could make a good meal of it, if not actually appreciating it. We arrived at Bombay on 30th September, 1898, with 19 officers, 455 other ranks.

T&S, December 1934.

SS *PALITANA, SIRSA, WARORA, CHESHIRE, SALAMIS* AND *ASSAYE*

Palitana, Sirsa and *Warora* took the 2nd Battalion from India to South Africa in 1899. *Palitana* (photo) was a Clyde-built passenger cargo vessel, launched on 21 January 1886. She was hired from the British India Steam Navigation Company. The 2,600 ton *Sirsa* was built on the Clyde in 1883 for the British India Steam Navigation Company.

In September 1899 the 2nd Battalion was warned for service in South Africa, and in the same month was loaded into three hired vessels, *Palitana*, *Sirsa* and *Warora*:

> The troops sailed at once; Headquarters and five companies on the *Palitana* of 2,900 tons, the remainder on the 3920 ton *Warora* (photo) and

> the 2610 ton *Sirsa*, and the three companies and 60 mules that crowded her had a rough start, sail hoisted to steady her, and only three out of twelve officers at the first 'dinner meal'. *Palitana*, 'rolled horribly even in calm weather.'

> On 5th October, off Madagascar, a passing vessel announced to the *Sirsa* the outbreak of war, received with cheers; but on the 9th, after two days' real gale, with seas breaking on board freely, she reached Durban to learn that the news was premature. The *Palitana* was ahead, but the swell was too heavy for any ship to cross the bar, and both vessels tossed giddily till afternoon. (Many a Briton and many a Boer knew that sickening scend and heave of the Durban swell during the next two years. Many ships remained outside the overcrowded harbour and discharged personnel into lighters; if it was rough, men were shot into a wicker cage, swung outboard by the derrick, and dumped into the swaying lighter. Boer prisoners who had never seen the sea thought their last hour was come when subjected to this ordeal.)

The Life of a Regiment, Volume III, pp 10–1.

While the 2nd Battalion sailed to Durban in the *Palitana*, *Warora* and *Sirsa*, the 1st Battalion embarked on the SS *Cheshire* from Liverpool. The *Cheshire* was built in 1891 and was eventually sold in 1911.

Quotes in the account of the voyage are from *The Tiger and Sphinx*, with further indented quotes from the diary of Lance Corporal E.G. Chissel:

> The great *Cheshire* was a very different vessel to the two little 'B.I. boats' that conveyed the sister battalion to Durban; the troops on board

numbered 1,300. Very rough weather was encountered for the first week but thereafter the voyage was uneventful.

SS *Cheshire*

Friday 10th November 1899 – I awoke about 4.00 am feeling cold after my first sleep at sea and got up when Reveille sounded. A goodly number were sick as the sea was rough during the night. We had breakfast and dinner as usual the tea being made from condensed water (freshwater on ships is made from condensing boiled seawater). We had the greatest trouble to keep standing as the sea is very rough and the waves lashing over the ship.

Saturday 11th November – Got up 7.00am, had a wash. We paraded at 10.00 am for Medical Inspection. I saw a lot of dolphins leaping out of the water while I was on deck. The sea got a bit calmer but still made the ship swing, the dishes as well which, by the way, were made of tin. Some chaps still very bad with sickness.

Life on a troopship has improved since 1899. Settling in is always hurry and flurry, telling off to mess-tables and sleeping quarters, the daily issue and return of hammocks, company parade decks, telling off to boats; learning ship's standing orders, and a score of details more. A big ship was easy to lose one's way in, though electric light has simplified night movement since the days of lanterns.

Captain and subalterns of the day had a fine round of duty: guard-mounting on a rolling ship was a trial; so was ship's inspection at 10 a.m. by the 'Old Man', who trailed behind him as many personages of soldier and sailor as any land general! The watches had to be duplicated by soldiers; the army officer of the watch reporting periodically to the bridge; he accompanied the First Officer's rounds, and in oil-lamp days bumped hammocks and tripped over sleepers in alleyways and dark mess-decks. But hot coffee warmed subalterns in the small hours. The ship's adjutant had a 'job of work'—provost staff and ship's police; the innumerable sentries, stores and magazines, forbidden entries; sentries were seasick, and fell asleep after being so; where more than one corps was aboard, each blamed the other for errors or inefficiencies.

Lance Corporal Chissel's description of other troop ships at sea give some idea of the mobilisation and despatch of troops to South Africa:

> Sunday 12th November – We passed in mid-ocean the SS *Colombia* with the 10th Hussars on board. They sailed on the 5th and we on the 9th, by dinner time they were so far astern that we could only see the masts. Weather beautiful and the sea delightful. We had a false alarm of fire at 10.00am. Concerts are being given each evening and everyone seems to be happy.
>
> Monday 13th November – Got paid with two half-sovereigns which we could not change. Band played on deck during the forenoon. In the afternoon the SS *Bavarian* with 1,300 troops on board (Connaught Rangers and Dublin Fusiliers) passed about 100 yards from us and we exchanged cheers, their band playing the *Soldiers of the Queen* and ours *I canna leave the auld folks noo* and the pipers played two tunes. The signallers were signalling for about an hour. *Retreat* sounded just after they had passed. They were for the Cape from Queenstown.
>
> Friday 17th November – A drink of cold water is impossible as the water in the tanks was almost boiling. We passed Cape Verde at 3.00pm and near it was a canoe with four blacks aboard who gave us a cheer. The band played on deck at night and we received permission to sleep on deck during the night.
>
> Monday 20th November – A new sport in which there was a King and Queen, a Doctor, a barber and a big bath of water. The King sent for the younger Officers. Captain Macnab was the first called and questioned as to his trespassing on the King's domains. After answering all questions the King handed him over to the Doctor who gave him a pill of raw 'dok' (Docusate Sodium – a laxative!) and handed him over to the barber who shaved him and knocked the chair from underneath, letting him fall into the bath of water. This was done to a few more, then a few of us upset the whole lot – King, Queen and all into the bath, they did not expect it. The sport was for passing the Equator as we could not do so on Sunday.

On crossing the line Father Neptune, with Barber (Pioneer Sergeant Livingstone) and a court composed of the biggest men in the battalion, came on board with all proper ceremony. But hefty as they were, they were pretty weary of chucking people into the big sail-bath by the time the ship's officers ended the show by shooting monarch and court into the bath while a hose was turned on to the spectators.

There were fire and boat stations to deal with, and the first time the urgent shout of 'Boy overboard!' rang along the decks, with whistles and alarm-bell, and one thousand men rushing all ways to stations: the ship altering course to double back, steam blowing off, shouts as the boat is lowered—and the anti-climax when the 'b-u-o-y' comes aboard again, with the skipper timing the operation.

And on a war-voyage instruction set in as soon as things were fixed: instruction of young officers, musketry practice at targets swung from a spar astern, or even at bottles; lectures; care of feet, sun-blisters, waste of water, attempts to break into store room, good sermon at church parade.

Gordons on board SS *Cheshire* – note slouch hats![4]

Monday 27th November – Our Section were put on 2nd Relief of Watch going on from 12.00pm until 4.00pm. Then we had Medical Inspection. The day was rather misty and the ship had to go half speed and keep on blowing her fog horn.

Tuesday 28th November – The mist cleared and the sea and weather was beautiful. We paraded with straps on and canteens in our hands to see that all was complete, then we had our rifles, kits, helmets, and all our baggage to get packed, ready for disembarkation. Heat so oppressive I had to sleep on deck tonight.

Wednesday 29th November – About 9.00am we sighted a lighthouse on our left and a shoal of whales. We passed the lighthouse and rounding a corner, we beheld Table Mountain.

---

4   Slouch hats were issued on the voyage but were seldom worn in South Africa.

At last Capetown approaches. The baggage is 'broken out', sea-kits and hammocks handed in, kitbags stacked ready. Finally, time for a landing; mess-decks, utensils, mess furniture beautifully cleaned and handed over; ship's damages ridiculously small, even with the loss of hammocks and blankets! Last civilities to captain and crew; mutual cheers—out files the eager regiment and begins a new chapter.

The Life of a Regiment, Volume III, pp 89–90.

Salamis (above) took the 1st Battalion from South Africa to Britain in 1902 after the Boer War. Aberdeen built, she was completed in 1899. In 1900 she transported the New South Wales Naval Brigade to Shanghai to join the International Brigade to relieve Peking in the Boxer Rebellion.

Greenock built *Assaye* (below) was used as a Boer War troop transport, and continued as a troopship until 1928, when she was scrapped. Like *Salamis*, she took troops to China during the Boxer Rebellion and during the Boer War took General Cronje to St Helena as a prisoner-of-war. In 1914 she transported the 2nd Battalion from Cairo to Southampton for service in France. In 1924 she took some of the 1st Battalion to India.

The 1st Battalion was in Constantinople from 1920 to 1921. There is no regimental record of the ships which took the Gordons there, although there is a comment on the voyage to Malta in 1921 before the Battalion was quickly returned to Constantinople on an emergency deployment:

The Gordons had a stormy passage in an unseaworthy vessel which was obliged to seek shelter at Mudros before completing the voyage.

The Life of a Regiment, Volume IV, p 8.

HMS *EAGLE*, HMT *MARGLEN*, *DORSETSHIRE* AND *SOMERSETSHIRE*

In 1924 the 1st Battalion was sent on emergency deployment from Malta to Egypt, carried on board the aircraft carrier HMS *Eagle* (above).

The Battalion moved from Egypt to India in 1925 on board HMT *Marglen* (below) and HMT *Assaye* (the same ship that had taken the 2nd Battalion from Egypt to England in 1914).

All the Regiment's sea voyages during the 1930s were carried out on two Troopships, HMT *Dorsetshire* and HMT *Somersetshire*.

Dorsetshire (above) was built in 1920 and converted to trooping in 1927. A sister ship to *Shropshire*, she could carry 1,400 troops. She operated throughout the Second World War and carried her last troops from Liverpool to Korea. She was scrapped in 1954.

HMT *Dorsetshire* took the 1st Battalion from Bombay to Haifa in 1934 and the 2nd Battalion from Gibraltar to Singapore in 1937.

Somersetshire (above) was built in 1927 and carried 1,300 troops. In the Second World War she was converted to a hospital ship and in 1941 joined her sister ship *Dorsetshire* in evacuating wounded from Tobruk. In April 1942, in the Mediterranean, she was struck by three German torpedoes but did not sink. The crew re-boarded her and reached Alexandria on one engine.

From 1944 to 1946 she operated as a hospital ship, finishing up in the Pacific. In 1953 she carried troops to East Africa. She was broken up in 1954.

Somersetshire took the 2nd Battalion from Southampton to Gibraltar in 1934 and the 1st Battalion from Haifa to Southampton in 1935. The 2nd Battalion, writing of the trip to Gibraltar, said:

> The weather when we left was called, and there had been gale warnings on the wireless. The sea, however, was exceptionally smooth throughout the trip, and the *Somersetshire* does not roll appreciably. This did not prevent a large number of the passengers from being seasick, unfortunately, and the troop decks the first day out were, to say the least, treacherous to walk on. Everyone recovered before the end of the trip, and we disembarked in lovely weather.

T&S, December 1934.

HMT *EMPIRE HALLADALE*

The *Empire Halladale* (below) was formerly known as the *Antonio Delfino*. She was built for the Hamburg South American Line and sailed on the Hamburg to River Plate route until 1932. She was captured in Copenhagen in May 1945 and used as a troopship until broken up in 1956. In 1951 she took The Gordon Highlanders to Malaya.

The following account of the move to Malaya on the *Empire Halladale* in 1951 shows that, although troopships had become slightly more up-to-date, they were still overcrowded, with little space for training or recreation. This cynical and slightly jaundiced account nevertheless bubbles with the humour with which the Gordons graced every situation:

Those old Gordon Highlanders, who sailed before, behind, beneath and probably not infrequently secured to the masts of converted clippers in the old 'trooping' days, would doubtless regard with scorn the luxuries of modern troopship travel.

Hammocks have been replaced by strips of canvas lashed to tubular steel frames in tiers of three and sets of six. On a troop deck of 170 men it is perfectly possible for three or more to move simultaneously. There are meals for which there are only three successive sittings. Canvas windsails for ventilation have been replaced by blowers which produce an unfailing supply of cold air as far as Gibraltar and hot from there eastwards.

Nor, in this all-out welfare effort, has entertainment been overlooked. A talking cinema, frequently audible, operates on the after deck. A game of 'Crown and Anchor' is operated with unobtrusive selflessness by several members of the crew, who signed on specially for the purpose. For those of the thirteen hundred aboard who care to use their imagination to the extent of envisaging nets and quoits, deck tennis can be played on the forward well deck.

The only flaw in this floating Eden is lack of deck space. Of this, however, we may be hypercritical. We are nevertheless, preoccupied with the problem of training ourselves and a large number of new arrivals for imminent indulgence in a type of warfare new to most.

It is only by the most abstruse mathematical calculations and long hours of unremitting toil, that the Senior Major has succeeded in producing a programme which fills every minute of the day and crevice of the vessel with frenzied activity.

Figures may be found in cross-legged rows perched on washplace hand-basins, listening, like Yogis in meditation, to a four-day recital of the dangers that await us. The enthusiast, who at P.T. leaps not wisely but too far, may involuntarily join a class on the wireless set 68T. Instructors entwined in ladders or draped from derricks, harangue glutinous masses of soldiery, wedged between winches, on tropical hygiene. Practising drummers busily beat the paint off an air-shaft head. Pipers perched on life rafts coax harsh wails from sun-dried bags. The Band and Ladies' Choir are practising in the 'Recreation Room' to the accompaniment of fusillades from farther aft as 'D' Company open fire on jettisoned jam tins.

'Hullo How Baker Zebra One Four, say again, dammit. Over,' issues in sepulchral tones from a ventilator, thus indicating the presence of the Officers R.T. Class under the isolation hospital. The Adjutant, Regimental Sergeant-Major, Orderly Room Sergeant and volunteer R.A.F. clerk, entombed five decks down in a drying room eight feet by eight, compete distractedly with the thrumming of the Sergeant-Tailor's sewing machine perilously balanced on a hatch outside.

'Hyperbole,' those acquainted with the word may say, lifting an incredulous eyebrow. Yet it is a daily attested fact that, on the day of arrival at our first port of call, two captains were discovered sorting the ship's mail in the only available space—the port side and only lavatory on 'B' deck—thus causing an insoluble traffic problem throughout the ship from 'C' deck down to the bilges.

T&S, May 1951.

HMT *OXFORDSHIRE*

Built in 1957 on the Clyde, the 20,586 ton *Oxfordshire* (below) was the last purpose-built British troopship. She was a troopship until 1962, after which all major troop movements were carried out by air. *Oxfordshire* was sold in 1964. *Oxfordshire* took The Gordon Highlanders on their final move by troopship, to Kenya in 1961.

One hundred and seventy-four years after their first move by troopship The Gordon Highlanders set out on their last. The journey to Kenya in 1961 was the final curtain in the Gordons' long association with ships that had carried them across the globe and back. Ironically, after all the discomforts, overcrowding and monotonous rations of previous journeys this last one gave the appearance of having solved most of the problems that had bedevilled British troops at sea! *The Tiger and Sphinx* describes the last voyage:

The journey to Kenya in *Oxfordshire* was significant, for it was the first time for years that the Battalion had travelled abroad with all its families and the last time the Battalion would embark on a troopship.

The recent committee on Ministry of Transport trooping costs was highly critical of the expenditure in maintaining the three remaining troopships and there appears little doubt that the next year or two will see a change over to air trooping.

It will be a sad day when the sea trooping era passes away, for the recuperative effect of a sea voyage is extremely valuable and provides a welcome amenity and attraction amongst the more humdrum routine of normal military life. It is thus an important recruiting factor and the pleasures of a sea cruise are not to be discarded lightly in favour of the pure economic advantages of space age air travel.

Oxfordshire herself was a paragon among troopships and the old soldiers in the Battalion could hardly believe their eyes when they saw this 20,000 ton floating hotel and compared it with the veteran '*Empire*' boats of only a few years ago.

Canteen messing with a varied and adequate menu, spacious troopdecks and ample deck space together with the most modern of fittings and amenities all went to make the voyage a pleasant experience for the Battalion, and considering the enormous number of families and children aboard (over 100 families and 200 children) the administration succeeded in coping with the many problems of health and welfare admirably.

The ship's company were extremely co-operative and the whole organisation of the Bibby line who were the owners of the ship was the epitome of courtesy and efficiency.

T&S, March 1962.

A further, personal, account by Lance Corporal Woolridge gives a Jock's view of the journey:

We caught our first glimpse of her as she lay alongside the quay, a modern yellow funnel surmounting a gleaming white superstructure; she looked clean and new, and if a trifle on the small side, that was only to be expected with the *Queen Mary* lying between her and our train. We assembled on the platform a few yards from the tall white sides of our home for the next 17 days. We were soon on board and settling in; if a little cramped, we were on board ship and would make the best of it. Off came boots, puttees and kilts, on went soft shoes and trousers, then up to catch our last glimpse of the UK, and to wave to those on the quayside. Shortly afterwards we cast off and steamed down the Solent, the music of our Military Band and a solitary piper becoming ever fainter in our ears.

The first evening was spent drawing bedding, being detailed for working parties, unpacking, and stowing away cases and kitbags. We became acquainted with messing arrangements and some, on their first acquaintance with the sea, came off second best. After supper we consoled ourselves that although Scotland was many miles away McEwan's ale could be bought for 10d.a bottle; with that and Andy Stewart's records we spent our first evening until time to turn in.

Drums and Pipes play 1st Battalion on board HMT *Oxfordshire*

The sea was never really calm but the weather became progressively warmer as we headed south. Soon sickness became a thing of the past and we settled down to the ship's routine of sleep, meals, cleaning ship, and becoming acquainted with our fellow travellers. Some were surprised at the amount of cleaning that had to be done each morning but soon learnt that cleanliness was of paramount importance and after a few days even the ship's officers could find no fault with our work. On the third day we reached Gibraltar and the decks became hives of activity as we got ready to go ashore, then up on deck to catch our first glimpse of the 'Rock.' The foam-whitened sea gave evidence to the strength of the wind, as when the ship turned broadside on to enter Algeciras Bay she developed a pronounced list to port. Shortly afterwards the Captain regretfully cancelled shore leave, and disappointedly we changed into our B.Ds.[5] and returned to the upper deck to watch, if not to sample. The weather was chilly and cloudy and with only a Shackleton doing approaches there was little to relieve the monotony. We were glad to get under way again, looking forward to Aden for shore leave.

---

5   Battle Dress, the standard working dress of those days.

The Mediterranean disappointed many; the sun did not shine, it was cold and B.D.s were the order of the day. Day succeeded day, and until we passed the Sicilian Narrows we were rarely out of sight of the North African coast. How many realised they were passing over one of the most relentlessly fought battlefields of the last war, the death bed of the *Eagle*, *Ark Royal* and Manchester; the scene of the bravery of the *Ohio*? Some remembered the final collapse and surrender of the German Army at Cape Bon, a forbidding promontory, girt with cliffs and rocky coastline. Malta GC was passed during the hours of darkness, Pantellaria, a former E-boat base, could just be seen against the sky and then there was nothing except passing ships until the coast of Egypt came into sight three days later. The weather became warmer and we looked forward to the day when we could exchange B.D. for the lighter K.D.[6] Deck sports began, deck hockey, basketball, shooting, and tug of war; the Signal Platoon practised morse and the Pipers played their pipes in whatever space they could find, usually in the troop decks.

Finally we anchored off the entrance to the Canal where we were delayed for a while, but eventually we entered Port Said to await our convoy. President Nasser was in the city and the harbour was brightly illuminated, three destroyers making a particularly brave show: 'for Christmas' said one of the policemen put on board after we had moored.

No sooner had we moored than bum-boats surrounded us, ready to bargain and exchange a thousand articles; trading was loudly carried out, mainly in broad Scots, with the salesmen and ourselves trying to outdo each other as we bargained and haggled over each purchase. Wallets, bags, soft toys and photograph albums were the most popular purchases, but one of the latter, on being dissected, does not bear description.

Early next morning we left Port Said but after breakfast the upper deck was crowded with sightseers wanting to see as much as possible of this great engineering feat. Shouts were exchanged with canal workers, the few women seen received many a loud whistle, and binoculars were passed around as the other ships in convoy and the surrounding landscape were scanned. The countryside varied from featureless desert to verdant areas around the lakes. The Canal itself appeared to be in good condition with maintenance going on all the time. Of much interest was the airfield at the end of the Bitter Lakes containing many Egyptian Air Force MIG aircraft. It must have provided the constant patrols we saw in Egyptian waters.

During the afternoon we lay at anchor in the Bitter Lakes to allow a north bound convoy to pass; it contained many tankers, as did our own,

---

6   Khaki Drill, a lightweight material used for uniforms in hot climates.

and a P. & O. liner on the Far East run homeward bound. As we passed Port Tewfik an onlooker on the bank bade us a Merry Christmas, we in return wished him 'A Good New Year' and so we left the Canal and began to prepare for Christmas.

Disappointed though some of us may have been to have to spend Christmas at sea praise must be given to the ship's company who did their best to give us a pleasant day. For the troops there was a special dinner served by the Officers and Senior N.C.O.s with a free beer and cigarette issue, and for the children there was a cinema show followed by a fancy dress parade, the Captain forsaking the bridge to act as Master of Ceremonies for the occasion. Father Christmas also visited the ship and with the aid of the ship's and our own officers distributed presents to each child on board.

As the days grew warmer sunbathing was the order of the day. We reached Aden on the 27th and everybody prepared to go ashore. This time we were not disappointed, and as soon as clearance had been given the tenders made their way to shore full of eager sightseers. For many this was their first visit to a free port and the cheapness of the articles which could be bought was the subject of conversation for days afterwards.

Shore leave finished and we cast off our moorings to head for the open sea, due south for Mombasa, in Kenya. The weather remained fine but there was a fair sea whipped up by what must have been a 30 knot wind. It came from astern however and the forward speed of the ship did much to cancel it out. These were days of warmth and hours given to sun worship. Flying fish and porpoises were seen and sharks eagerly looked for. A few days out of Aden news of the Kuwait scare reached the ship together with the news that H.M.S. *Centaur* had been despatched from Mombasa to Aden. We eagerly watched for the approaching warships but unfortunately we did not sight each other. During this passage the stabilizers must have been stopped as the ship developed quite a roll in a reasonably high sea, but this time there was no talk of sickness, the sea, rough or smooth, had been accepted and was not worth bothering about.

On 31st December, Hogmanay, we reached Mombasa. Only the War Office could have picked such a date, but we tried to make the best of it. We were given a special dinner and beer issue, our third since Redford, and the New Year was seen in on the foc'sle which had been equipped with four bars. Unfortunately, the 'proper spirit' was lacking but we did our best to celebrate the occasion as it should be celebrated.

We left the ship in detachments over four days, and our last glimpse of her came from the train. *Oxfordshire* lay, stern towards us, waiting to take another human cargo, this time to take them home. *Oxfordshire* gave us a good passage and did not take advantage of stomachs unused to the sea as she might have done. Her Captain and crew did their utmost for us, and to them all we express our thanks and good wishes for the future when, her service completed, she returns to civvy street.

T&S, March 1962.

The voyage to Kenya in 1961 was the last time The Gordon Highlanders as a regiment moved by sea. Thereafter all moves were by air, although the Battalion did find itself at sea again during the Borneo tour in 1965. They returned from their first operational tour, in Sabah to their training base at Kota Belud on HMS *Albion*, a Royal Navy aircraft carrier. The voyage around the north-east corner of Borneo was scheduled over three days and two nights, but increased tension between India and Pakistan led to *Albion* being sent to the Bay of Bengal. Once the Gordons had been helicoptered on board, the ship set off. The Captain and crew of *Albion*, with typical Royal Navy hospitality, had planned two nights of partying and celebration for the Gordons, who had spent the previous four months in the jungle, but condensed it all into a single night's celebration. It was a battalion of sore-headed Gordon Highlanders that paraded next morning on the flight deck to be flown by helicopter to Kota Belud as HMS *Albion* (below) steamed past at full speed, without stopping.

APPENDIX 1

LETTERS OF SERVICE

75TH HIGHLAND REGIMENT

War Office
12th October 1787

Sir,

I have the honor to acquaint you, The King has been pleased to order that a Regiment shall be forthwith raised under your Command, for His Majesty's Service abroad. The Regiment is to Consist of Eight Battalion Companies, one Company of Grenadiers, and one of Light Infantry, together with an additional Company which is to remain at Home For the purpose of Recruiting. The Eight Battalion Companies to consist each of One Captain, Two Lieutenants, One Ensign, Three Serjeants, Four Corporals, Two Drummers and Seventy one Private Men; The Grenadier Company of One Captain, Three Lieutenants, Three Serjeants, Four Corporals, Two Drummers, Two Fifers and Seventy one Private Men; The Light Infantry Company of One Captain, Three Lieutenants, Three Serjeants, Four Corporals, Two Drummers and Seventy one Private Men; The additional Company of One Captain, Two Lieuts, One Ensign, Eight Serjeants, Eight Corporals, Four Drummers and Thirty Private Men.

The Regiment is to be under your Command as Colonel, with a Company, and to have One Lieutenant-Colonel, and One Major, each having also a Company together with the Usual Staff Officers. The Pay of the Officers is to commence from the date of their Commissions, and the Non-commissioned Officers and Private Men from the Dates of their Respective Attestations.

No more than Three Guineas is to be given to each Recruit, on pain of his Majesty's highest displeasure.

It is to be clearly understood, that none of the Officers who shall obtain Commissions in your Regiment, are to expect Leave to dispose of their present Commissions.

In Case the Regiment should be reduced after it has once been established, the Officers will be entitled to half pay.

As this Regiment is to be raised with a particular view to Serve in the East Indies His Majesty has been pleased to Consent that a certain proportion Officers viz.

The Lieut Colonel
Four Captains of Companies
Eleven Lieutenants and
Four Ensigns

shall be taken from the Officers of the Army, paid by the East India Company, who will hereafter receive Commissions from His Majesty, of a Date Junior to those which shall be given on this occasion, in the Respective Ranks, to the Officers belonging to His Majesty's Forces.

Government will allow a Bounty of Three Guineas per Man for every Recruit approved, with the assistance of which Bounty the Officers now to be appointed by His Majesty (exclusive of the Field Officers and Staff) will be required to raise a Certain proportion of Men or forfeit all Claim to the promotions intended for them.

The Names of the Officers, and the Number of Men each is to raise, shall be communicated to you, with as little delay as possible; in the meantime I am to acquaint you, that His Majesty is pleased to leave to you, the recommendation of One Captain, Two Lieutenants, and Two Ensigns, upon consideration of their raising the proportion of Men, specified in the annexed paper, as also the Nomination of the Adjutant, Quarter Master and Chaplain, who are not expected to contribute to the Levy.

Whatever Recruits shall be raised by the Officers who find Men for their Commissions beyond the required Number, or shall be obtained by your arrangements, and by the endeavours of the Officers under your Command, in the Ordinary Course of Recruiting, may be charged with the Regulated allowance to the Recruiting Officer, of Five Guineas for each Man Approved.

I am to add that it being required, that the Regiment shall be actually raised, and approved after being reviewed by the 25th of December next, every exertion on your part, and on that of the Officers of your Regiment, will be necessary that His Majesty's expectations on this head may not be disappointed.

> I have the honour to be
> > Sir
> > Your most obedient humble servant
> > > (signed) George Yonge

Colonel Robt Abercromby

75th Regiment Record Book.

APPENDIX 1

100TH HIGHLAND REGIMENT

War Office
10th February, 1794

My Lord,

I am commanded to acquaint you that His Majesty approves of your Grace's offer of raising a Regiment of Foot to be completed within three months upon the following conditions:

The Corps to consist of one company of Grenadiers, one of Light Infantry, and eight Battalion Companies.

The Grenadier Company is to consist of one captain, three lieutenants, four sergeants, five corporals, two drummers, two fifers, and 95 privates.

The Light Infantry of one captain, three lieutenants, four sergeants, two drummers, and 95 privates.

And each Battalion Company of one captain, two lieutenants, one ensign, four sergeants, five corporals, two drummers, and 95 privates;

Together with the usual staff officers, and with a serjeant major, and quartermaster serjeant, exclusive of the serjeants above specified. The captain lieutenant is (as usual) included in the number of lieutenants above mentioned.

The corps is to have three field officers, each with a company; their respective ranks to be determined by the rank of the officer whom your Grace shall recommend for the command thereof. If the person so recommended for the command is not at present in the army, he will be allowed temporary rank during the continuance of the regiment on the establishment but will not be entitled to half pay on its reduction.

His Majesty leaves to your Grace the nomination of all the officers, being such as are well affected to his Majesty, and most likely by their interest and connections to assist in raising the corps without delay; who, if they meet with his Royal approbation, may be assured they shall have commissions as soon as the regiment is completed.

The officers, if taken from the half pay, are to serve in their present ranks; if full pay, with one step of promotion. The gentlemen named for ensigncies are not to be under sixteen years of age. The quartermaster is not to be proposed for any other commission.

In case the corps shall be reduced after it has been established, the officers will be entitled to half pay.

The pay of the officers is to commence from the dates of their commissions: and that of the non-commissioned officers and private men from the dates of their attestations.

Levy money will be allowed to Your Grace in aid of this levy at the rate of five guineas per man for 1064 men.

The recruits are to be engaged without limitation as to the period or place of their service.

None are to be enlisted under five feet four inches, nor under 18 years or above 35. Growing lads from 16 to 18, at five feet three inches will not be rejected.

The non-commissioned officers and privates are to be inspected by a general officer, who will reject all such as are unfit for service, or not enlisted in conformity with the terms of this Letter.

His Majesty consents that on a reduction the Regiment shall, if it be desired, be disbanded in that part of the country where it was raised.

In the execution of this service, I take leave to assure Your Grace of every assistance which my office can afford.

I have the honour to be,

Sir,

Your most obedient humble servant

(signed) George Yonge

His Grace, The Duke of Gordon

The Gordon Highlanders, Their Origin by J.M. Bulloch.

The officers appointed to the 100th already held commissions, and came from other regiments or from half pay. Their experience and ability would allow the new regiment to achieve high professional standards of training and operational effectiveness very quickly. Of the original officers of the 92nd, those we know had military experience are listed below.

Lieutenant-Colonel

George, Marquis of Huntly, served in the 42nd Royal Highlanders (Black Watch) and 3rd Guards (Scots Guards) in Flanders and at the siege of Valenciennes.

Majors

Charles Erskine of Cardross served in the 25th, 16th, and 77th Regiments in the war against Tipu Sultan in India, and against the French at Martinique.

Donald MacDonald of Boisdale served in the 76th Regiment (Macdonald's Highlanders).

Captains

Alexander Napier of Blackstone from lieutenant in the 7th Fusiliers.

John Cameron of Fassiefern was an ensign in the 26th Regiment and a lieutenant in Captain Campbell of Ardchattan's Independent Highland Company.

Hon. John Ramsay, son of the Earl of Dalhousie, from lieutenant in the 57th Regiment.

Andrew Paton from lieutenant in the 10th Regiment.

Simon MacDonald of Morar served in the American War in the 76th Regiment (Macdonald's Highlanders).

Captain-Lieutenant

John Gordon of Coynachie from the 81st Regiment.

Lieutenants

Peter Grant from a Fusilier Regiment.

Archibald MacDonell from the 79th Highlanders.

John MacLean of Dochgarroch promoted from the 1st Royals (Royal Scots).

Ewan MacPherson from the 78th Highlanders.

George Gordon (illegitimate son of 4th Duke of Gordon) from the 6th Dragoons.[1]

Adjutant

James Henderson, came from an Independent Company.

---

1   George Gordon, half-brother to George Gordon, Marquis of Huntly. These are the two referred to by Jane Maxwell, Duchess of Gordon, as 'My George and the Duke's George'.

APPENDIX 2

FIRST MUSTER ROLL OF THE GORDON HIGHLANDERS

W E know a lot about the composition of the 92nd when it was raised. Its Highland character is quite clear.

When the Regiment was finally embodied, on 24th June, 1794, it had 750 rank and file. But its first official muster roll, or 'Description Register,' contains 914 names, for it includes subsequent enlistments, and some of the first recruits may not have reached the rendezvous at Aberdeen. The first description register—which the Gordons are lucky in possessing, the great majority of other regiments having long since lost or destroyed theirs—proves the overwhelmingly Scots character of the Corps. This document, preserved in a huge folio volume at the Depot, contains eight valuable facts about every man, in turn his name, date of enlistment, age, height, colour of eyes and complexion, birthplace, trade, and the date when he died or left. Of the 914 so biographed, only sixty-three were non-Scots, fifty-one being Irish, and one, a musician, German. The greatest number, 240, came from Inverness-shire, where the Duke had huge estates, Aberdeen standing second with 124, and Banffshire third with 82. The rest were supplied by twenty-four Scots counties, two coming from Wigtown, while Orkney sent one. All the officers without exception were Scots.

As to occupation, farm servants, entered as 'labourers,' were first with 442. The next-largest supply came from 185 weavers; there were 42 tailors, 31 shoemakers, 17 blacksmiths, and 13 wrights; while 89 other trades were represented. Again, there were 361 different surnames on the roll, 247 of them being 'Macs' of various kinds, headed by the MacDonalds with 40, the MacPhersons coming second with 35, and the Camerons third with 34. Strangely enough, there were only 16 Gordons.

The height of the recruits is another very interesting fact, correcting the common fallacy that the men of the early Highland regiments were gigantic fellows who could swing claymores almost as big as cabers. As a matter of fact, the average height of the 914 men in the Gordons was only 5ft. 5½ in. and only six of them were six feet or over, two of these being weavers and one a shoemaker: that is to say, sedentary fellows, who went to legs like 'tattie shaws.' The tallest man was David Wood, a Morayshire 'labourer' from Dyke, who was 6ft. 4 in., and who died within a year of enlisting. The average age was 23, the youngest being a boy of nine, Robert Watt, from Banff. The oldest recruit, a Haddington man, was 47 when he enlisted, and he served till he was 52.

J.M. Bulloch

T&S, December 1935.

An abbreviated version of the 'Description Register' to which Bulloch refers is shown below. In the 'Career' column the abbreviation 'Dis.' Stands for 'Discharged'. Some variations in spelling will be seen. This is undoubtedly due to the entries in the recruiting registers made by different recruiting officers, which were then transcribed to the Description Register

Name	Attestation Date	Age	Height	Birthplace	Trade	Career
ABRAHAM, William	May 22	28	5ft 7½ in	Annan	Labourer	Dis. 24/2/1799
ADAM, David	April 1	35	5ft 8in	Stirling	Stocking maker	
ADAM, James	April 18	30	5ft 7in	Paisley	Weaver	Dis. 20/5/1800
ADAMS, George	May 6	33	5ft 9½ in	Kirkliston	Labourer	
AITCHISON, Robert	March 27	37	5ft 7in	Use (Ewes) Dumfries	Sadler	
AITKEN, John	May 21	27	5ft 5½ in	Kilbarchan	Weaver	
AITKEN, Robert	April 3	21	5ft 8½ in	Paisley	Weaver	
ALLERDICE, James	March 5	22	5ft 9¾ in	Gamrie	Labourer	Enlisted by Lord Huntly; dis. 24/2/1799
ALLERDICE, John	March 29	28	5ft 5in	Gartly	Weaver	Enlisted by Lord Huntly; to 2nd Batt. 25/11/1803
ALLERDICE, William	March 31	13	4ft 7in	Aberdeen	Weaver	Enlisted by Lord Huntly; to 2nd Batt. 25/11/1803
ALLAN, James	—	18	5ft 4½ in	—	—	To 2nd Batt. 25/11/1803
ALLEN, James	June 10	33	5ft 5in	Dunshach-lan, Meath	Merchant	Dis. 27/5/1802
ALLEN, Jonathan	April 27	18	5ft 2in	Huntly	Weaver	Enlisted by Lieut Davidson
ALLEN, William	June 3	19	5ft 8in	Falkirk	Carter	Dis. 24/2/1799
ALLISON, James	March 20	34	5ft 3¾ in	Glasgow	Labourer	Dis. 4/5/1802
ANDERSON, Alex.	March 7	29	5ft 4in	Aboyne	Wright	Dis. 4/5/1802
ANDERSON, George	March 12	34	5ft 8in	Turriff	Weaver	
ANDERSON, James	May 2	18	5ft 4in	Paisley	Weaver	Dis. 27/5/1802
ANDERSON, James	May 7	19	5ft 3½ in	Colston, Cromar	Weaver	Dead 4/1/1799
ANDERSON, John	May 27	32	5ft 10¾ in	Aghadowey Derry	Cotton spinner	Dis. 8/6/1796
ANDERSON, Wm.	April 1	18	5ft 7in	Larbert	Mason	
ANDERSON, Wm.	—	19	5ft 11in	—	—	To 2nd Bn 25/11/1803
ANGUS, James	May 20	19	5ft 8in	Mortly [Mortlach]	Labourer	Dead 27/12/1799

Name	Date	Age	Height	Place	Occupation	Notes
ANNAND, William	April 4	15	5ft 3in	Bechelvail [Belhelvie]	Weaver	Dis. 24/2/1799
ARDBUCKLE, John	April 1	34	5ft 11in	Cambuslang	Sawer	Dis. 10/6/1795
ATINBOROUGH, Wm.	Nov 1795	18	5ft 6½ in	Dunbanon [Dunbennan]	Nailer	
BAILLIE, Francis	May 10	34	5ft 4in	Dores	Weaver	Dis. 9/6/1797
BAIN, Alexander	April 12	18	5ft 5in	Wick	Spoonmaker	
BAIN, William	May 21	35	5ft 4½ in	Kippen Stirling	Weaver	
BALFOUR, James	May 25	25	5ft 9½ in	Calduff Donegal	Butcher	To 61st Regt 28/10/1794
BANKS, George	April 16	35	5ft 5in	Glasgow	Shoe-maker	Enlisted by Lord Huntly; dis. 30/6/1798
BANKS, John	Feb 25	18	5ft 3in	Edinburgh	Shoe-maker	Deserted 16/6/1799
BARCLAY, Alex.	April 5	24	5ft 8½in	Leith	Labourer	Enlisted by Ensign Fraser; dead 3/2/1809
BAXTER, James	April 14	20	5ft 7½ in	Bellie	Weaver	Dead 18/2/1795
BAXTER, John	March 12	17	5ft 3in	Bellie	Labourer	Discharged
BAXTER, William	March 20	29	5ft 5in	Duffus	Black-smith	To 2nd Batt. 25/11/1803
BAXTER, William	Feb 14 1798	17	5ft 6in	Bellie	—	Enlisted by Lord Huntly
BEATON, Daniel	May 3	16	5ft 3½ in	Portree	Weaver	Dead 12/4/1799
BEATON, Murdoch	Sep 15	35	5ft 5in	Portree	Weaver	Dis. 20/5/1800
BEATTIE, Alexander	March 9	16	5ft 3in	Aberdeen	Servant	
BEATTIE, John	May 3	16	5ft 4in	Disercreal, Tyrone	Weaver	
BEATTON, Murdoch	May 9	35	5ft 4in	Connan	Labourer	Enlisted by Lieut McPherson; dead 6/11/1794
BEIDIE, William	Feb 28	29	5ft 6½ in	Benholm	Weaver	Sergeant, 1813
BERRY, Joseph	April 11	34	5ft 7½ in	Christ-church,	Wool-comber	Dis. 30Jun 1798
BETHUNE, John	Feb 22	28	5ft 8in	Kilmonivaig	Labourer	
BIGGAM, James	May 16	18	5ft 5½ in	Cambleton, Argyll	Taylor	Died 25/2/1809
BIRNIE. William	April 21	19	5ft 11½ in	Old Deer	Blacksmith	
BISSET, Robert	May 29	16	5ft 1in	Alloa	Weaver	
BLACK, Alexander	May 16	26	5ft 5in	Falkirk	Weaver	
BLACK, William	Feb 21	23	6ft 0in	Kintore	Sawer	Dead 31/5/1795
BLACK, William	May 10	35	5ft 6½ in	Kilmallie-vick, Argyll	Labourer	Late 74th Regt., 2 months' svc.
BLAIKIE, John	Oct 26	40	5ft 8½ in	Kirnton, Midlothian	Taylor	Late 61st Regt., 11yrs 2 months
BLAIR, Thomas	April 3	16	5ft 7in	Gifford, Haddington	Baker	Enlisted by Ensign Fraser; dead 5/10/1799
BOOTH, William	May 6	17	5ft 3½ in	Dundonald	Labourer	
BOYD, Adam	April 12	22	5ft 5½ in	Kilmarnock	Bonnet maker	
BOYD, Hugh	May 6	26	5ft 5in	Kilmally	Labourer	Dead 18/9/1795
BOYD, James	April 18	16	5ft 2in	Falkirk	Weaver	
BOYLE, Hugh	May 9	23	5ft 4½ in	Broad Island Antrim	Labourer	Dis. 4/5/1802

BOWIE, John	March 25	29	5ft 9 in	Ratho,	Servant	Dead 25/3/1808
BREMNER, Alex.	April 25	14	5ft 4 in	Stirling	Nailsmith	Enlisted by Lord Huntly
BREMNER, George	March 4 1795	15	5ft 0in	Bellie	Labourer	Dis. 5/8/1798
BREMNER, John	June 14	23	5ft 7½ in	Rothes	Labourer	Dead 7/10/1799
BRIMNER, Andrew	March 23 1798	16	5ft 2in	Speymouth	Labourer	Enlisted by Lord Huntly
BRODIE, William	April 17 1798	16	5ft 3½ in	Banff	Labourer	Enlisted by Lord Huntly
BROOK, John	June 29	16	5ft 3in	Old Deer	Cutler	
BROOK, Richard	April 14	16	5ft 3½ in	Paisley	Weaver	Dis. 20/5/1800
BROOK, Robert	April 28	21	5ft 6½ in	Peterhead	Labourer	To 46th Regt. 2/11/1794
BROWN, Æneas	April 29	17	5ft 4in	Depadlin, Londonderry	Labourer	Deserted 14/12/1797
BROWN, Andrew	April 14	—	—	—	—	Enlisted by Maj McDonald; dis. 3/11/1794
BROWN, Dugald	April 21	19	5ft 8½ in	Whitburn, Linlithgow	Gardener	Dis. 10/6/1795
BROWN, James	May 14	16	5ft 2in	Cairney	Labourer	
BROWN, James	July 7	26	5ft 6in	Deskford	Labourer	
BROWN, John	April 4	30	5ft 7in	Paisley	Weaver	Died of wounds at Harwich BROWN,
Malcolm	June 16	25	5ft 8½ in	Comrie	Taylor	Dead 15/2/1798
BROWN, William	March 2	25	5ft 8in	Inveravon	Shoe-maker	Dis. 24/7/1799
BROWN, William	May 10	18	5ft 3in	Cairney	Labourer	West Fencibles; 5½ months' service; dis. 9/6/1797
BRUCE, James	March 19	32	5ft 6in	Dundee	Labourer	Dead 27/8/1799
BRUKMIRE, John	May 1	18	5ft 4in	Temple Patrick, Antrim	Weaver	Dis. 1/2/1808
BRYCE, Robert	April 17	21	5ft 8½ in	Kinross	Weaver	To 2nd Batt. 25/11/1803
BUCHAN, John	April 17	17	5ft 2½ in	Dyce	Weaver	Dis. 24/5/1807
BUCHAN, John	April 25	28	5ft 7in	Glasgow	Labourer	
BUCHANNAN, Norman	May 15	22	5ft 10½ in	Skye	Labourer	Died of wounds 3/2/1800
BUCHANNAN, Thos.	April 28	15	5ft 2½ in	Alloa	Weaver	
CAIRNS, James	May 11	18	5ft 6in	Paisley	Shoe-maker	Prize List 1813
CALDER, Andrew	April 30	38	5ft 10in	Foveran	Labourer	Enlisted by Capt A. Gordon dis. 23/6/1800
CALDER, Marquis	May 31	16	5ft 6in	Watton,	Weaver	
CALDER, William	June 4	21	5ft 4½ in	Dunnet	Labourer	Dead 18/9/1795
CAMERON, Alex.	April 8	18	5ft 4in	Kilmally	Labourer	Enlisted by Capt J. Cameron
CAMERON, Alex.	April 10	19	5ft 5in	Kilmally	Labourer	Dis. 27/5/1802
CAMERON, Alex.	April 11	18	5ft 4in	Kilmally	Labourer	To 2nd Batt. 25/3/1803
CAMERON, Alex.	April 27	24	5ft 6in	Ardnamur-chan	Labourer	Enlisted by Capt J. Cameron
CAMERON, Alex.	May 6	19	5ft 8½ in	Kilmally	Labourer	Dead 28/8/1795

571

CAMERON, Alex.	May 20	18	5ft 3in	Kilmanivaig	Labourer	
CAMERON, Allan	Sept 14	24	5ft 8in	Kilmally	Labourer	Dead 11/10/1799[1]
CAMERON, Angus	April 9	21	5ft 4½ in	Mushirlock, Inverness	Servant	Enlisted by Lord Huntly; dis. 24/2/1806
CAMERON, Donald	April 9	22	5ft 5in	Kilmally	Labourer	Enlisted by Capt J. Cameron; deserted 16/6 /1799
CAMERON, Charles	May 6	16	5ft 4in	Kilmally	Labourer	
CAMERON, Charles	June 9	16	5ft 4in	Kilmally	Labourer	Ensign 18/2/1799
						"A most distinguished officer, 3rd Regt, J. McDonald." Dis. 6/3/1799
CAMERON. Charles	June 10	16	5ft 4½ in	Kilmally	Labourer	Dis. 30/6/1798
CAMERON, Daniel	June 8	34	5ft 3½ in	Morvain, Argyll	Labourer	Dis. 10/6/1795
CAMERON, Donald	April 22	17	5ft 2in	Kilmanivaig	Labourer	Enlisted by Lord Huntly; to 9th R.V. Batt. 15/10/1806
CAMERON, Dougald	April 27	22	5ft 7in	Kilmally	Farmer	Enlisted by Capt J. Cameron, Ensign, E. Mid'sex Militia
CAMERON, Duncan	May 2	19	5ft 4in	Kilmally	Labourer	Dead 12/10/1799
CAMERON, Duncan	May 13	18	5ft 5in	Kilmally	Labourer	Dead 20/11/1796
CAMERON, Duncan	May 27	16	5ft 3in	Kilmanivaig	Labourer	
CAMERON, Ewan	April 8	17	5ft 4in	Kilmally	Labourer	Enlisted by Capt J. Cameron; dead 23/12/1809
CAMERON, Ewan	April 12	20	5ft 5in	Kilmally	Labourer	Enlisted by Capt J. Cameron
CAMERON, Ewan	May 1	28	5ft 5in	Kilmally	Taylor	Dis. 31/10/1800
CAMERON, Ewan	May 10	22	5ft 5½ in	Kilmally	Labourer	
CAMERON, Ewan	May 24	18	5ft 6in	Kilmally	Taylor	Dead 2/11/1799
CAMERON, Hugh	May 7	16	5ft 3½ in	Fortingall	Labourer	
CAMERON, John	Jan 22 1795	16	5ft 2½ in	Alloa	Weaver	Dead 20/9/1809
CAMERON, John	March 5	25	5ft 4in	Kilmally	Labourer	Dead 22/10/1794
CAMERON, John	March 8	14	5ft 2in	Kiltarlity	Labourer	
CAMERON, John	March 14	19	5ft 3in	St Cuthbert's Edinburgh	Book-binder	
CAMERON, John	April 9	19	5ft 5in	Kilmally	Labourer	
CAMERON, John	May 1	21	5ft 5in	Kilmally	Taylor	
CAMERON, John	May 20	20	5ft 10in	Kincardine, Inverness	Taylor	
CAMERON, John	June 2	18	5ft 5in	Kilmally	Labourer	
CAMERON, Robert	May 21	21	5ft 4 in	Falkirk	Black-smith	Enlisted by Lord Huntly
CAMERON, William	June 13	32	5ft 4½ in	Abernethy	Labourer	Dis. 30/6/1798

---

1   Those who died on or after 11 October 1799 were killed at Egmont-op-Zee, or died of wounds from the battle (for three or four months after).

Name	Date	Age	Height	Place	Occupation	Notes
CAMPBELL, Andrew	March 12	24	5ft 9in	Muthil, Perthshire	Labourer	Deserted 6/4/1799
CAMPBELL, Charles	April 1	19	5ft 4in	Reay	Labourer	
CAMPBELL, Donald	March 25	34	5ft 2½ in	Redcastle, Ross	Twist miller	Dis. 27/5/1802
CAMPBELL, Donald	April 26	18	5ft 7in	Barra	Labourer	Enlisted by Capt J. Cameron
CAMPBELL, Donald	June 6	20	5ft 6½ in	Halkirk	Labourer	2nd Battalion
CAMPBELL, Wm.	March 31	18	5ft 6½ in	Farr	Weaver	
CAMPBELL, Wm.	April 1	21	5ft 6½ in	Dowrass, Sutherland	Labourer	
CAMPBELL, Wm.	June 14	19	5ft 5in	Reay	Labourer	To Reay Fencibles 24/4/1799
CARD, Francis	Aug 1	35	5ft 7½ in	Flamborough, York	Labourer	Dead 10/9/1797
CATHERWOOD, Don.	June 7	15	5ft 3in	Lisson, Tyrone	Taylor	Dead 12/10/1799
CATTANACH, Alex.	May 22	23	5ft 9in	Kingussie	Labourer	
CATTANACH, Donald	March 11	16	5ft 3in	Kingussie	Labourer	Dead 4/10/1799
CATTANACH, John	April 15	16	5ft 4in	Kingussie	Labourer	Enlisted by Lieut McLean
CATTANACH, Malcolm	May 3	22	5ft 6in	Kingussie	Labourer	Dis. 27/5/1802
CHALMERS, Alex.	May 5	15	5ft 1½ in	Glasgow	Weaver	To 2nd Batt.
CHAPMAN, James	April 14	30	5ft 11in	Kilbarchan, Renfrew	Weaver	
CHERRY, James	May 6	22	5ft 6½ in	Glasgow	Hosier	Dead 25/1/1799
CHISHOLM, Roderick	April 14	25	5ft 3½ in	Kilmorach, Inverness	Carpenter	Enlisted by Lord Huntly; dead 12/10/1799
CHRISTIE, John	March 5	16	5ft 4in	Strichen	Wool comber	
CLARK, Alexander	May 22	18	5ft 8in	Kingussie	Taylor	Ensign 19/2/1799; dis. 6/3/1799
CLARK, James	April 14	15	5ft 1½ in	Cross, Inverness	Labourer	Enlisted by Lord Huntly; to 2nd Batt. 25/11/1803
CLARK, William	May 26	18	5ft 7½ in	Lochwinnoch, Renfrew	Weaver	
CLARKSON, William	April 8	35	5ft 7in	Ecclesmachan, Linlithgow	Turner	Enlisted by Ensign Fraser dis. 1/4/1804
CLAURON, Robert	May 1	47	5ft 4½ in	Haddington	Labourer	Dis. 24/2/1799
COCHRAN, Walter	March 25	23	5ft 9in	Aberdeen	Flesher	Dis. 4/5/1802
COCK, James	May 5	16	5ft 3in	Alloa	Slater	
COCK, Richard	March 31	15	5ft 3in	Edinburgh	Hairdresser	
CONELY, Patrick	May 24	20	5ft 4in	Castle Blen, Monaghan	Labourer	
COUPER, John	July 16 1795	20	5ft 7in	Tarland	Gardener	Dis. 27/5/1809
COUTS, John	March 31	17	5ft 3in	Aberdeen	Taylor	
COUVILE, John	June 6	22	5ft 7in	Lisson, Tyrone	Weaver	Deserted 16/6/1799
CRAIG, John	April 13	15	5ft 3½ in	Glasgow	Labourer	Dis. 30/6/1799
CRAIGAN, John	March 25	18	5ft 4in	Rhynie	Labourer	Enlisted by Capt J. Gordon; dead 19/1/1799

Name	Date	Age	Height	Place	Occupation	Notes
CRAIGAN, William	April 3	15	5ft 3in	Cairney	Labourer	
CRAWFORD, Hugh	April 14	16	5ft 3½ in	Stewarton, Ayr	Weaver	
CROSS, Alexander	April 12	16	5ft 4in	Eastwood, Lanark	Weaver	
CRUICKSHANK, John	March 21	23	5ft 4in	Dunbennan	Mason	Dead 30/9/1809
CRUICKSHANK, John	April 29	27	5ft 3in	Glass	Labourer	
CRUICKSHANK, Wm.	April 5	18	5ft 6½ in	Glass	Taylor	To 66th Regt. 13/3/1798
CUMMIN, George	Dec 2	30	5ft 10in	Kirkmichael	Labourer	Dis. 1/2/1799, to be ensign in N. Fencibles
CUMMIN, James	April 7	33	5ft 11½ in	Elgin	Wright	Dis. 27/5/1802
CUMMING, James	March 28	34	5ft 6½ in	Clack-mannan	Weaver	Dis. 27/5/1802
CUNNINGHAM, John	May 26	25	5ft 9in	Ardhallan, Argyll	Wright	
CUNNINGHAM, Alex.	March 25	26	5ft 7½ in	Alisonford, E. Lothian	Servant	Dis. 7/6/1802
CUNNINGHAM, Wm.	March 26	23	5ft 9½ in	St Cuthbert's Edinburgh	Blacksmith	
CURRAY, Donald	May 17	20	5ft 6in	North Uist	Labourer	
DALLAS, William	March 24	29	5ft 5in	Golspie	Gardener	
DARLIN, David	March 12	17	5ft 5in	Edinburgh	Slater	Dis. 25/11/1804
DAVIE, John	April 21	24	5ft 9½ in	Terynissel Aberdeen	Labourer	
DAVIDSON, John	April 12	15	5ft 2in	Kinel, Angus	Labourer	
DAVIDSON, Paul	May 22	35	5ft 8in	Kingussie	Labourer	Dead 15/2/1795
DAVIDSON, Robert	July 11	23	5ft 6½ in	Stabletown, Cumb'land	Labourer	Dis. 20/5/1800
DAVIDSON, William	April 15	35	5ft 5in	Kingussie	Labourer	Dis. 10/6/1795
DAWSON, Thomas	March 25	20	5ft 6½ in	Inverness	Taylor	
DEANS, Robert	May 10	34	5ft 7in	Knockando	Weaver	Dead 4/11/1794
DERRACH, John	May 5	20	5ft 10in	Lech, Tyrone	Labourer	Dead 27/8/1799
DEUTALSOP, William	May 7	35	5ft 6½ in	Londonderry	Weaver	Dis. 9/6/1797
DEWAR, Andrew	July 1	21	5ft 3½ in	Dunfermline	Weaver	Dead 6/2/1802
DEWAR, Duncan	May 2	35	5ft 7½ in	Dall, Perth	Gardener	To 37th Regt 16/3/1798
DEY, Alexander	May 3	16	5ft 8½ in	Forgie	Labourer	Dead 24/1/1809
DICKIE, William	April 22 1796	35	5ft 9in	East Calder	Labourer	Dis. 30/6/1798
DIGNAN, John	May 25	—	—	—	—	Dis. 6/10/1800
DOBBIE, Alexander	March 2	22	5ft 9½ in	Bellie	Labourer	Enlisted by Lord Huntly; dead 12/10/1799
DOCHARTY, Simon	March 2	26	5ft 7in	Coumber, Londonderry	Weaver	
DONALD, James	May 14	16	5ft 6in	Old Deer	Weaver	Dead 12/10/1799
DONALDSON, Robert	May 24	30	5ft 8¼ in	Eastwood, Renfrew	Weaver	Dis. 20/5/1800
DOUGLAS, John	May 15	20	5ft 10½in	Kilpatrick	Taylor	Dis. 24/2/1799
DOW, James	March 20	24	5ft 5in	Alloa	Labourer	
DOWARTY, Simon	June 14	24	5ft 9in	St Ninian's, Stirling	Merchant	
DOWIE, James	May 28	15	5ft 1in	Linlithgow	Labourer	Dead 10/9/1809

DOWLIN, William	April 24	12	4ft 9in	Falmouth, Essex [sic]	Labourer	Dis. 4/5/1802
DOWNIE, James	April 16	35	5ft 7½ in	Glasgow	Black-smith	Dis. 30/6/1798
DOWNS, John	May 13	22	5ft 5in	Antrim	Labourer	
DUFFES, John	May 12 1798	—	—	—	—	Enlisted by Lord Huntly
DUNBAR, Alex.	March 28	16	5ft 3in	Duffus	Labourer	
DUNCAN, Edward	May 10	23	5ft 8¼ in	Saline	Weaver	Dis. 27/5/1802
DUNCAN, George	—	—	—	—	—	Enlisted by Lord Huntly
DUNCAN, James	May 10	22	5ft 10½ in	Saline	Weaver	
DUNCAN, James	May 16	24	5ft 6in	Montrose	Chaise driver	Dis. 27/5/1802
DUNCAN, John	May 16	15	5ft 2½ in	Kincardine O'Neil	Padler	
DUNCAN, John	May 26	15	5ft 4in	Dollar	Weaver	Dead 12/10/1799
DUNLOP, William	May 11	35	5ft 9in	Northquarter Lanark	Weaver	Dis. 10/6/1795
DURWARD, John	Feb 26	34	5ft 6½ in	Garvock	Black-smith	Dis. 30/6/1798
EDMOND, Thomas	June 11	29	5ft 3¾ in	Balfron, Stirling	Smith	Dead 16/10/1799
EISDALE, Thomas	April 5	27	5ft 10½ in	Stevenston	Miner	Dis. 27/5/1802
ELLIS, Alexander	April 26	33	5ft 4¾ in	Fordyce	Plasterer	Dis. 27/5/1802
ELLIS, Alexander	June 29	28	5ft 2in	Gartly	Mason	Dead 14/10/1794
ELLIS, John	March 11	17	5ft 10in	Cairney	Weaver	Dis. 27/5/1802
EVANS, Richard	April 18	23	5ft 7in	Northkep, Flint	Butcher	Transferred 10/8/1810
EWING, John	April 20	18	5ft 7in	Glasgow	Weaver	
EWING, Peter	Aug 28 1796	17	5ft 4in	Clunie, Aberdeen	Labourer	
FARLOW, Walter	March 3	35	5ft 6in	Donegal	Weaver	Dis. 20/5/1800
FEE, Henry	June 10 1795	—	—	—	—	Late 128th Reg. dead 13/3/1801
FERGUS, James	June 7	35	5ft 4in	Glasgow	Weaver	Dis. 30/6/1798
FERGUSON, James	April 14 1795	20	5ft 10½ in	Ardersier	Weaver	
FERGUSON, James	June 10 1795	—	—	—	—	Late 128th Reg; desert 23/3/1799
FERGUSON, John	May 2	35	5ft 5in	Kilmarnook	Weaver	Dis. 10/6/1795
FERGUSON, John	May 27	27	5ft 5in	Alva	Labourer	Dis. 9/6/1797
FERGUSON, Malcolm	—	26	5ft 5½ in	North Uist	—	Dead 10/9/1799
FERGUSON, Patrick	May 10	30	5ft 5in	Armagh	Sawer	
FERGUSON, Peter	April 27	21	5ft 9in	Kilmally	Labourer	To Ensign, Renfrew Militia
FERGUSON, Robert	May 8	18	6ft 0in	Cumber-nauld	Weaver	Dis. 23/6/1800
FIMISTER, Alex.	May 25	25	5ft 3½ in	Alves	Labourer	Dis. 9/6/1797
FINDLAY, Alex	—	—	—	—	—	Dead
FINDLATER, Wm.	April 6	20	5ft 7½ in	Fyvie	Taylor	Dis. 27/5/1802
FLAMINGHAM, Nicolas	June 4	25	5ft 5in	Stewarton, Tyrone	Labourer	
FLEMING, James	April 14	17	5ft 5½ in	Dunipace	Labourer	
FLEMING, John	April 7	20	5ft 7in	Dunipace	Wright	Transferred 24/3/ 1804

575

FORBES, Alexander	March 9	33	5ft 6½ in	Chapel of Garioch	Taylor	
FORBES, Alexander	April 25	25	5ft 4in	Daviot	Labourer	Dead 28/8/1806
FORBES, Andrew	April 16	12	5ft 0in	Newmachar	Labourer	Argyll Militia 31/12/1809
FORBES, Hary	July 19	20	5ft 3in	Strathdon	Labourer	Dead 22/12/1795
FORBES, James	April 9	18	5ft 8in	Inveravon	Labourer	
FORBES, John	Sep 16	22	5ft 4in	Strathdon	Labourer	
FORBES, William	March 20	17	5ft 4in	Kilmorack	Hatter	Dead 23/8/1795
FORDICE, Alexander	May 15	16	5ft 3in	Drumblade	Labourer	Dead 15/10/1795
FOREMAN, Andrew	March 22	17	5ft 3½ in	Crimond	Labourer	Dis. 10/6/1795
FRASER, Angus	Feb 28	20	5ft 3in	Inverness	Labourer	
FRASER, Charles	June 7	16	5ft 3in	Ardersier	Servant	
FRASER, Donald	March 12	23	5ft 9in	Calder	Labourer	Enlisted by Lord Huntly; dead 12/10/1799
FRASER, James	Feb 21	34	5ft 5in	Fordyce	Wool-comber	Dis. 27/5/1802
FRASER, John	March 29	16	5ft 2in	Ardersier	Labourer	Dead 12/10/1799
FRASER, John	April 16	32	5ft 8in	Kiltarlity	Labourer	Dead 19/10/1794
FRASER, John	May 6	28	5ft 6in	Dunfermline	Excise Officer	Dis. 30/6/ 1798
FRASER, John	May 20	16	5ft 3in	Beaulie	Spinner	
FRASER, Peter	March 6	26	5ft 7in	Huntly	Labourer	Dis. 20/5/1800
FRASER, Thomas	Feb 28	34	5ft 6½ in	Kirkhill	Weaver	Dead 11/2/1799
FRASER, Thomas	April 16	15	5ft 3in	Inverness	Labourer	
FRASER, Thomas	May 1	15	5ft 2½ in	Portsmouth	Weaver	
FRASER, William	April 14	17	5ft 5½ in	Croy	Labourer	
FRASER, William	May 7	16	5ft 4½ in	Daviot	Labourer	
FRASER, William	Aug 21	26	5ft 4¾ in	Kirkhill, Inverness		Enlisted by Lord Huntly
FRENCH, John	May 24	28	5ft 6in	Crawford-john, Lanark	Wright	
FYFE, William	May 8	18	5ft 5½ in	Huntly	Labourer	
GALLOWAY, Alex.	April 18	36	5ft 9in	Stirling	Weaver	Dead 12/10/1799
GARDNER, James	May 10	14	5ft 2½ in	Denny	Labourer	
GARDNER, William	April 18	21	5ft 7½ in	Glasgow	Weaver	
GEDDES, James	April 19	19	5ft 6½ in	Rathven	Labourer	Dis. 31/10/1800
GEDDES, John	April 7	22	5ft 11½ in	Raffin, Banff	Glass-blower	Transferred 10/8/1810
GEMBLE, John	April 4	24	5ft 5¾ in	Kilmarnock	Shoemaker	
GEORGE, Robert	July 16	16	5ft 3in	Marnoch	Labourer	
GEORGE, William	June 24	25	5ft 2in	Tunay? Banff	Labourer	
GIBB, Joseph	March 18	16	5ft 3in	Huntly	Weaver	To 2nd Batt. 25/11/1803
GIBSON, William	June 5	25	5ft 5in	Stewarton, Tyrone	Carpenter	
GILCHRIST, John	June 12	26	5ft 6¾ in	Paisley	Shoe-maker	Dis. 3/11/1795
GILLES, Alexander	May 14	23	5ft 3in	Rothes	Taylor	Transferred 10/8/1810

GILLES, Donald	May 30	20	5ft 5in	Durinish,	Weaver	Dead 12/10/1799
GILLES, Douglas	Aug 26	35	5ft 5in	Ardnamur-chan	Labourer	Discharged
GILLES, Duncan	June 22	32	5ft 4in	Ardnamur-chan	Chapman	Dis. 8/6/1796
GILLES, Duncan	July 3	20	5ft 4in	Glenelg	Labourer	
GILLES, Ewan	July 3	20	5ft 7in	Glenelg	Labourer	
GILLES, Hugh	April 26	18	5ft 5¾ in	Barra	Labourer	
GILLES, John	March 31	17	5ft 4in	Erles, Inverness	Weaver	Transferred 24/6/1805
GILLESPIE, John	April 23	25	5ft 3in	Aberdeen	Wool-comber	
GILLESPIE, William	April 23	25	5ft 3in	Stranraer	Wright	Dis. 8/6/1796
GORDON, Alexander	Feb 17	17	5ft 6in	Cairney	Labourer	Dead 4/11/1799
GORDON, Alexander	March 16	21	5ft 8in	Inveravon	Labourer	To 2nd Batt. 25/11/ 1803
GORDON, Alexander	April 19	17	5ft 5in	Mortlach	Labourer	
GORDON, Alexander	June 18	30	5ft 6in	Inveravon	Labourer	Dead 19/12/1795
GORDON, Charles	Feb 17	20	5ft 5in	Glass	Labourer	Dis. 26/2/1800, having found a man in his place
GORDON, Donald	May 21	21	5ft 5in	Inch, Inverness	Labourer	Dis. 27/5/1802
GORDON, George	March 12	26	5ft 4in	Cabrach	Labourer	Dis. (date not known)
GORDON, John	March 2	18	5ft 6in	Glenbucket	Weaver	To 2nd Batt. 25/11/1803
GORDON, John	April 6	16	5ft 4in	Inveravon	Taylor	
GORDON, John	April 18	34	5ft 4½ in	Cabrach	Shoe-maker	Dis. 18/6/1795
GORDON, John	June 24	17	5ft 3in	Rayne	Book-binder	Dis. 27/5/1802
GORDON, Peter	June 2	21	5ft 7in	Inveravon	Black-smith	Dis. 1/8/1803
GORDON, Peter	June 14	26	5ft 7in	Kirkmichael	Labourer	
GORDON, William	March 20	20	5ft 5in	Urquhart, Ross	Taylor	Dead 12/10/1799
GORDON, William	March 28	22	5ft 6in	Inveravon	Labourer	Transferred 25/11/1803
GORDON, William	April 16	19	5ft 8in	Inverury	Labourer	To 2nd Batt. 20/11/1803
Goudie, John	April 7	34	5ft 6in	Paisley	Weaver	Enlisted by Ensign Fraser; dis. 27/5/1802
GOW, Alexander	April 17	18	5ft 4½ in	Gamrie	Labourer	Dead 12/10/1799
GRAHAM, James	March 7	16	5ft 3¼ in	Glasgow	Weaver	
GRAHAME, Murdoch	July 12	19	5ft 4in	Snisort	Labourer	
GRANT, David	July 5	24	5ft 4in	Tarbet,	Labourer	Dis. 10/6/1795
GRANT, James	March 15	35	5ft 3½ in	Mortlach	Wool-comber	Dis. 10/6/1795
GRANT, James	May 24	15	5ft 3in	Glenduff, co. Down	Labourer	
GRANT, John	March 19	20	5ft 3in	Kirkmichael	Weaver	Dead 12/10/1799
GRANT, John	May 29	19	5ft 6½ in	Ruthven	Labourer	Dis. 26/5/1800

Name	Date	Age	Height	Place	Occupation	Notes
GRANT, John	Oct 29	—	—	—	—	From South Fencibles 5 yrs', 61st Regt 11yrs' service; dead 12/10/1799
GRANT, John	Sep 4 1797	20	5ft 7in	Inveravon	Labourer	Dead 12/10/1799
GRANT, William	June 10	23	5ft 4in	Inveravon	Labourer	
GRAY, James	March 24	31	5ft 6in	Kilmodack, Perth	Weaver	
GREACH, David	April 18	16	5ft 4in	Auchendore	Weaver	Dis. 23/6/1800
GREENHORN, John	May 26	28	5ft 8in	Polmont Stirling	Collier	Deserted 9/7/1794
GRIEG, Andrew	March 18	17	5ft 4½ in	Bachern, Banff	Labourer	
GRIEG, Francis	April 22	23	5ft 7½ in	Peterhead	Woolcomber	Transferred 24/6/1805
GRIEG, James	March 20	16	5ft 3in	Dundurcas	Labourer	
GRIEG, Thomas	April 24	14	5ft 2in	Laswade	Papermaker	
GUNN, Adam	May 10	34	5ft 4in	Kildonan	Woolcomber	
GUNN, Alexander	May 10	24	5ft 2½ in	Halkirk	Weaver	Dis. 24/5/1800
GUNN, George	Oct 29	—	—	—	—	From N. Fencibles 5 yrs, 61st Regt 11yrs; dis. 27/5/1802
GUNN, John	May 26	32	5ft 5in	Kildonan	Labourer	Dis. 10/1/1795
GUNN, Peter	March 21	19	5ft 11½ in	Huntly	Weaver	
HADGIN, Thomas	April 23	34	5ft 5in	Lisburn, Antrim	Weaver	Dis. 27/11/1795
HALBERT, Robert	April 9	29	5ft 11½ in	Irvine	Weaver	Dis. 27/5/1807
HALL, William	May 30	16	5ft 3½ in	Rhynie	Coalier	
HAMILTON, John	May 24	16	5ft 3in	Linlithgow	Shoemaker	Dead 6/3/1799
HART, Edward	May 27	18	5ft 7in	Cumber, Londonderry	Carpenter	
HAY, George	April 18	24	5ft 8in	Inverpeiling, Banff	Labourer	Deserted 9/6/1794
HAY, James	April 16	17	5ft 3in	Glenbucket	Weaver	To 2nd Batt. 25/11/1803
HAY, James	May 6	35	5ft 6½ in	Calder, Lanark	Weaver	
HAY, William	May 15	28	5ft 10¼ in	Rhynie	Labourer	Enlisted by Lord Huntly; dead 19/2/1799
HEMDRY, John	April 9	19	5ft 10in	Alloa	Weaver	Dead 12/10/1799
HENDERSON, Angus	April 30	15	4ft 11in	Kilmally	Labourer	
HENDERSON, Robt.	March 1	16	5ft 2in	Huntly	Labourer	
HENDERSON, Robt,	May 10	19	5ft 8in	Dunblane	Weaver	Dis. 8/6/1796
HENDERSON, Thomas	March 25	35	5ft 6in	Perth	Weaver	Enlisted by Ensign Fraser; dis. 30/6/1798
HENDERSON, Thomas	March 29	35	5ft 5in	Halkirk	Taylor	To 2nd Batt. 25/11/1804
HENDERSON, Wm.	April 25	17	5ft 5in	Stirling	Weaver	
HENDERSON, Wm.	May 11	20	5ft 7in	Thurso	Labourer	Dis. Aug/1805
HERKLESS, David	April 17	32	5ft 2in	Musselburgh	Shoemaker	Enlisted by Maj McDonald

Name	Date	Age	Height	Place	Occupation	Notes
HODGERT, Alex.	March 29	16	5ft 4½ in	Cambleton, Argyll	Weaver	
HOGG, George	March 24	28	5ft 9in	Clack-mannan	Carpenter	
HOLLINGWORTH, Andrew	Nov 3	39	—	St Paul's, Dublin	Musician	Late 46th Regt, 26 yrs' service; dead 8/1/1796
HORN, James	April 3	20	5ft 7in	Gartly	Labourer	
HUNTER, John	April 2	21	5ft 9½ in	Stow	Labourer	
HUTCHISON, JOHN	April 13	28	5ft 11½ in	Banefield Dunfermline	Weaver	Dis. 30/6/1798
HUTCHISON, Thomas	May 6	17	5ft 3½ in	Edinburgh	Sailor	
INNES, Alexander	June 10	18	5ft 7½ in	Inveravon	Labourer	
INNES, John	March 11	20	5ft 9in	Inveravon	Labourer	
INNES, John	March 13	21	5ft 4½ in	Wick	Confectioner	
INNES, Robert	May 27	34	5ft 6in	Kirkmichael	Labourer	Dis. 20/5/1800
IRVINE, James	March 17	30	5ft 5in	Armagh	Weaver	Dis. 27/8/1802
IRVINE, Matthew	May 9	21	5ft 9in	Ulco, Antrim	Labourer	
JACK, Coats	May 15	16	5ft 3in	Glasgow	Weaver	
JACK, James	April 4	26	5ft 10in	Glasgow	Weaver	Enlisted by Ensign Fraser; deserted 9/7/1794
JAMIESON, George	April 12	—	—	—	—	Enlisted by Maj McDonald; dead 6/12/1796
JAMIESON, James	April 30	19	5ft 9in	Feteresso	Labourer	Dead 12/10/1799
JAMIESON, James	June 15	34	5ft 4in	Greenock	Sheriff Officer	Dis. 30/6/1798
JARDINE, Samuel	May 17	19	5ft 8¼ in	Answorth, Stafford	Copper-smith	Deserted 26/7/1796
JOSS, John	April 3	28	5ft 6in	King Edward	Farrier	
KELLY, Walter	April 1	35	5ft 6in	Almadock, Perth	Slater	Dead 24/12/1795
KENNEDY, Alex.	April l0	17	5ft 5½ in	Kilmallie	Labourer	Transferred 21/10/1809
KENNEDY, Alex.	April 18	19	5ft 3in	Kilmanivaig	Labourer	To 95th Regt. 25/12/1803
KENNEDY, Angus	April 19	35	5ft 5½ in	Maybeg, Inverness	Miln Driver	Dis. 24/2/1799
KENNEDY, Ewan	April 5	18	5ft 5in	Kilmallie	Labourer	Dis. 1/2/1808
KENNEDY, Ewan	May 6	16	5ft 4in	Kilmallie	Taylor	
KENNEDY, John	Feb 22	21	5ft 10½ in	Boleskine	Labourer	Enlisted by Lieut McPherson
KENNEDY, John	April 18	35	5ft 5in	Kingussie	Labourer	Dis. 10/6/1795
KENNEDY, Neil	April 22	29	5ft 7½ in	Kilmanivaig	Labourer	
KERR, James	Feb 18	15	5ft 1½ in	Daviot,	Labourer	Dead 17/2/1799
KING, Richard	April 22	24	5ft 5½ in	Prestonpans	Mason	
KINMOUTH, John	March 25	22	5ft 5½ in	Dunning	Weaver	Dead 23/9/1795
KINNAIRD, Wm.	—	—	—	—	—	Prisoner in Holland; struck off, 31/5/1800
KNOX, John	May 15	26	5ft 8½ in	Renfrew	Weaver	To 2nd Batt. 2/11/1803
LAING, Alexander	Feb 22	26	5ft 5½ in	Aberdeen	Hair-dresser	Dis. 24/5/1800

Name	Date	Age	Height	Place	Trade	Notes
LAMONT, John	May 2	21	5ft 3½ in	Knapdale,	Weaver	Dis. 4/5/1802
LAPSLEY, William	Feb 25	18	5ft 4in	Midlothian	Weaver	Dis. 12/12/1803
LATTIMORE, John	March 27	29	5ft 5in	Antrim	Weaver	Dis. 4/5/1802
LEDINGHAM, Geo.	April 29	19	5ft 5in	Insch	Labourer	Dead 24/8/1795
LEGG, James	April 28	17	5ft 6in	Fordyce	Labourer	Deserted 4/9/1794
LEITCH, Alexander	April 21	16	5ft 4½ in	Nairn	Labourer	
LEITH, Andrew	March 17	19	5ft 5½ in	Grange, Antrim	Weaver	
LESLIE, George	April 3	16	5ft 3in	Rothes	Labourer	Dead 1/1/1796
LESLIE, Robert	May 6	20	5ft 6½ in	Ellistown, Ross	Weaver	Deserted 9/7/1794
LESLIE, William	—	16	5ft 10½ in	Mortlach	Miller	Dead 8/10/1809
LIDDLE, John	April 5	34	5ft 4in	Lanark	Labourer	Dis. 27/5/1802
LOAN, William	May 16	28	5ft 5½ in	Drummore, co. Down	Blacksmith	Enlisted by Lieut Stewart
LOURIMORE, Hugh	May 27	23	5ft 9in	Stanyfair, Antrim	Weaver	Deserted 9/7/1794
LOURIMOR, Wm.	May I5	36	5ft 6in	Banff	Labourer	Dis. 30/6/1798
LOURIMORE, Wm.	June 21	16	5ft 3½ in	Forgie	Stocking maker	
LUMSDALE, John	—	28	5ft 7½ in	Baillie, Banff	Labourer	
LYON, James	May 14	16	5ft 5in	Dundurcas	Labourer	
LYON, Robert	April 10	21	5ft 7in	Kilbride, Lanark	Baker	Dis. 20/5/1800
McAllister, Alex.	March 9	34	5ft 6in	Johnston, Renfrew	Weaver	Dis. 1/4/1805
McARTHUR, Peter	March 27	27	5ft 10½ in	Calder	Labourer	Dead 16/4/1796
McARTY William	May 16	18	5ft 6in	Brigh, co. Down	Labourer	Dis.10/7/1797
McBAIN, Alexander	March 18	16	5ft 4in	Moy,	Labourer	Sergeant
McBAIN, Angus	May 9	40	5ft 7¾ in	Moy	Labourer	Dead 14/2/1806
McBEATH, George	March 1	35	5ft 6½ in	Lathron	Labourer	
McCALLUM, James	April 8	29	5ft 6½ in	Alloa	Skinner	Dead Aug/1802
McCARMET, Donald	May 26	18	5ft 6in	Kilmanivaig	Labourer	
McCORMICK, Gilbert	March 27	22	5ft 8in	Killihoman, Argyll	Slater	Deserted
McCORMICK, Neil	May 8	28	5ft 5in	South Uist	Labourer	
McDERMID, John	May 10	15	5ft 2½ in	Islay	Labourer	
McDONALD, Alex.	March 15	17	5ft 10in	Dores, Inverness	Labourer	To 2nd Batt. 25/11/1803
McDONALD, Alex.	March 18	22	5ft 6in	Alvie	Shoemaker	Dead 22/2/1809
McDONALD, Alex.	April 21	19	5ft 4½ in	Rothiemurchus	Labourer	Dis. 30/6/1799
McDONALD, Alex.	April 30	21	5ft 7in	Ardnamurchan	Cotton spinner	
McDONALD, Alex.	May 1	38	5ft 6in	Inverness	Labourer	Dis. 24/1/1803
McDONALD, Alex.	May 10	20	5ft 7in	North Uist	Labourer	Dis. 27/5/1802
McDONALD, Allen	March 10	35	5ft 7in	Tyrie, Argyll	Labourer	Dis. 20/5/1800
McDONALD, Andrew	May 14	35	5ft 6in	Larbert	Shoemaker	Deserted 9/7/1794
McDONALD, Angus	May 29	18	5ft 4in	Bolleskine	Labourer	Dead 12/10/1799
McDONALD, Angus	July 13	25	5ft 7in	Glenelg,	Labourer	Dead 5/3/1799
McDONALD, Angus	Aug 25	16	5ft 0in	Ardnamurchan	Taylor	Dis. 27/6/1802

Name	Date	Age	Height	Place	Occupation	Notes
MᶜDONALD, Colin	March 4	12	4ft 11in	Petty, Nairn	Taylor	Dead 19/10/1794
MᶜDONALD, Donald	Aug 25	35	5ft 8½ in	Ardnamur-chan	Labourer	Dis. 27/5/1802
MᶜDONALD, Donald	Oct 18	16	5ft 2in	Ardnamur-chan	Labourer	Dead 20/8/1797
MᶜDONALD, Donald	Dec 18	34	5ft 6in	Small Isles, Inverness	Labourer	Dis. 24/5/1800
MᶜDONALD, Donald	Feb 24 1795	15	5ft 0in	Ardnamur-chan	Labourer	Dead 15/5/1796
MᶜDONALD, Dougald	April 30	19	5ft 10in	Ardnamur-chan	Cotton spinner	Dis. 20/5/1800
MᶜDONALD, Duncan	March 16	12	4ft 8in	Aberdeen	Labourer	To 2nd Batt. 25/11/1803
MᶜDONALD, Duncan	April 23	16	5ft 2½ in	Croy	Labourer	
MᶜDONALD, Ewan	June 22	19	5ft 0in	Ardnamur-chan	Carpenter	
MᶜDONALD, Hugh	March 15	22	5ft 3in	Canongate, Midlothian	Hatmaker	
MᶜDONALD, Hugh	April 21	16	5ft 3½ in	Inverness	Labourer	
MᶜDONALD, James	May 8	16	5ft 4¾ in	Nairn	Labourer	To 2nd Batt. 25/11/1803
MᶜDONALD, John	March 15	30	5ft 5½ in	Lairg	Wool-comber	Dead 12/6/1796
MᶜDONALD, John	March 28	19	5ft 7in	Laggan,	Labourer	Dead 2/9/ 1809
MᶜDONALD, John	April 18	16	5ft 3½ in	Kilinan, Argyll	Shoemaker	
MᶜDONALD, John	May 30	16	5ft 4in	Forres	Thread manufacturer	
MᶜDONALD, John	Sep 22	21	5ft 9in	Strathdon	Wright	Deserted 19/7/1799
MᶜDONALD, John	Oct 18	20	5ft 6½ in	Ardnamur-chan	Weaver	
MᶜDONALD, John	Nov 19	18	5ft 1in	Ardnamur-chan	Labourer	
MᶜDONALD, Neil	March 12	19	5ft 4in	Barra	Labourer	Trans 10/8/1810
MᶜDONALD, Neil	March 28	22	5ft 3in	Culloden	Labourer	Dis. 20/5/1800
MᶜDONALD, Robert	March 16	19	5ft 7in	Laggan	Labourer	
MᶜDONALD, Ronald	May 5	28	5ft 6in	South Uist	Labourer	To Ensign
MᶜDONALD, Ronald	Aug 2	20	5ft 4in	Bracadel, Inverness	Labourer	Dis. 1805
MᶜDONALD, Ronald	Dec 29	17	5ft 5in	Ardnamur-chan	Labourer	Dead 12/10/1799
MᶜDONELL, Donell	Feb 21	18	5ft 4in	Abertarfe, Inverness	Labourer	Enlisted by Lieut MᶜPherson
MᶜDONELL, Ewan	March 12	23	5ft 6in	Kilmanivaig	Labourer	Dead 12/10/1799
MᶜDONELL, John	March 9	17	5ft 4in	Kilmanivaig	Labourer	
MᶜDONELL, John	June 2	16	5ft 3½ in	Kilmanivaig	Labourer	
MᶜDOUGALD, Dougald	April 25	—	—	—	—	Enlisted by Maj MᶜDonald; dis. 10/6/1795
MᶜEACHIN, Angus	July 14	32	5ft 2in	Strath, Inverness	Labourer	Dis. (date not known)
MᶜEACHIN, John	June 21	18	5ft 0in	Ardnamur-chan	Labourer	Dead 10/11/1799
MᶜEWAN, James	May 19	17	5ft 5½ in	Losse, Perth	Wright	

Name	Date	Age	Height	Place	Occupation	Notes
MᶜFARLANE, Andw.	May 30	19	5ft 8½ in	Gorbals	Coal Hewer	Dead 12/10/1799
MᶜFARLANE, John	April 8	16	5ft 4in	Glasgow	Labourer	Dis. 24/1/1796
MᶜFINDLAY, Wm.	May 10	34	5ft 9½ in	Kilpatrick, Dunbarton	Nailer	Deserted 9/7/1794
MᶜGARVIE, Mundy	May 3	35	5ft 5in	Argyll, Tyrone	Labourer	Dead 7/10/1794
MᶜGHEE, James	May 7	34	5ft 5in	Ballieston, Antrim	Weaver	
MᶜGIE, James	June 10 1795	16	5ft 4½ in	Glasgow	Labourer	To 2nd Batt. 25/11/1803
MᶜGIE, William	Aug 26	17	5ft 3in	Insch, Aberdeen	Labourer	To 2nd Batt. 25/11/1803
MᶜGILVRAY, Ben.	March 11	16	5ft 0in	Bolleskine	Taylor	
MᶜGILVRAY, Ewan	July 7	36	5ft 7in	Ardnamur-chan	Labourer	Dis. 8/6/1796
MᶜGILVRAY, John	Dec 10	18	5ft 10½ in	Ardnamur-chan	Labourer	Dis. 20/5/1800
MᶜGLASHAN, Arch.	March 16	33	5ft 8in	Ardnamur-chan	Labourer	Dead 1/11/1796
MᶜGOWAN, Alex.	May 5	17	5ft 6in	Bocharn, Banff	Taylor	
MᶜGRATH, Henry	May 20	25	5ft 7n	Achirn, co. Down	Labourer	Dis. 10/6/1795
MᶜGREGOR, Alex.	March 2	30	6ft 0in	Laggan	Soldier	Dis. 24/1/1803
MᶜGREGOR, Alex.	March 19	16	5ft 3in	Cromdale	Labourer	
MᶜGREGOR, Alex.	May 23	16	5ft 4in	Nairn	Labourer	
MᶜGREGOR, Alex.	May 31	26	5ft 8in	Laggan	Labourer	Dis. 24/5/1800
MᶜGREGOR, Charles	April 2	20	5ft 7in	Inveravon	Labourer	
MᶜGREGOR, John	May 7	29	5ft 6in	Paisley	Weaver	Enlisted by Capt Napier; dis. 31/10/1800
MᶜGREGOR, Wm.	March 10	35	5ft 4in	Cabrach	Taylor	Dead 30/8/1796
MᶜGREWAR, John	June 14	17	5ft 4in	Bolleskine	Labourer	Dead 30/10/1795
MᶜHARDY, Charles	Aug 31	17	5ft 2in	Strathdon	Weaver	
MᶜINNES, Andrew	July 14	16	5ft 3in	Ardnamur-chan	Labourer	Deserted 26/2/1799
MᶜINNES, Donald	Sep 28	15	5ft 2in	South Uist	Labourer	Dis. 10/7/1797
MᶜINNES, Ewan	March 12	35	5ft 6in	Kilmallie	Labourer	Dis. 30/6/1798
MᶜINNES, John	June 5	35	5ft 4½ in	Ardriamur-chan	Labourer	
MᶜINTOSH, Andrew	March 18	16	5ft 3in	Ardersier	Labourer	
MᶜINTOSH, Angus	May 17	30	5ft 10¾ in	Petty	Labourer	Sergeant
MᶜINTOSH, David	March 7	15	5ft 0in	Pitsligo	Labourer	
MᶜINTOSH, Gardner	March 29	25	5ft 9in	Newbattle,	Minder	
MᶜINTOSH, James	April 1	16	5ft 5in	Midmar	Labourer	To 46th Regt 2/11/1794
MᶜINTOSH, John	March 4	20	5ft 6in	Abertarfe, Inverness	Shoe-maker	Sergeant
MᶜINTOSH, John	April 24	16	5ft 2in	Canongate,	Labourer	Dis. 4/5/802
MᶜINTOSH, John	May 22	19	5ft 0in	Kingussie	Labourer	Dis. 30/6/1798
MᶜINTOSH, Kenneth	Nov 3	26	—	Durness,	Weaver	Late 46th Regt 9 years' service; dead 12/10/1799
MᶜINTOSH, Lachlan	May 30	22	5ft 7in	Laggan	Labourer	Dead 22/11/1795

Name	Date	Age	Height	Place	Occupation	Notes
McINTOSH, Lachlan	June 2	22	5ft 7in	Kingussie	Labourer	Dead 18/10/1800
McINTYRE, Alex.	March 21	37	5ft 5in	Ardentalen, Argyle	Labourer	Sergeant
McINTYRE, Alex.	May 23	18	5ft 8in	Kingussie	Weaver	To 9th R.V. Batt. 29/11/1805
McINTYRE, Donald	April 17	23	5ft 3in	South Uist	Labourer	Dead 18/10/1799
McINTYRE, Ewan	May 21	28	5ft 6in	South Uist	Labourer	Dis. 8/6/1796
McINTYRE, Gordon	March 6	13	4ft 7½ in	Edinburgh	Goldsmith	To 66th Regt. 10/6/1795
McINTYRE, James	May 22	35	5ft 7in	Kingussie	Labourer	
McINTYRE, William	March 11	15	5ft 2in	Nairn	Labourer	
McINVINE, Duncan	May 5	34	5ft 6in	Kilcalminel, Argyll	Labourer	
McKAY, Archibald	May 15	18	5ft 7½ in	Hughall, Antrim	Inkle weaver	
McKAY, Donald	March 16	18	5ft 6½ in	Bellie	Labourer	Dead 29/10/1794
McKAY, Donald	March 25	19	5ft 7in	St Nicolas, Aberdeen	Shoemaker	
McKAY, Donald	May 8	21	5ft 3m	Cromarty	Stocking maker	Dead 10/6/1799
McKAY, Findlay	May 15	21	5ft 4½ in	Fullerman, Ross	Weaver	Dead 19/1/1799
McKAY, Hugh	March 28	18	5ft 4½ in	Thurso	Weaver	Dis. 27/8/1802
McKAY, John	March 12	16	5ft 5in	Thurso	Staymaker	Dis. 29/8/1796
McKAY, John	April 25	15	5ft 2in	Durness	Weaver	Dead 3/12/1799
McKAY, John	May 28	15	5ft 2½ in	Kilearnan, Ross	Labourer	Dead 12/10/1799
McKAY, John	June 10 1795	12	4ft 11in	Reay	Labourer	To Reay Fencibles for another man, 24/4/1799.
McKAY, Robert	March 27	17	5ft 4½ in	Kintail,	Weaver	Dis. 24/5/1807
McKAY, Robert	June 4	23	5ft 6in	Inveravon	Labourer	
McKAY, Stephen	March 1	19	5ft 4in	Edinburgh	Founder	Dead 22/12/1795
McKAY, Thomas	March 12	—	—	—	—	Enlisted by Maj McDonald; dis. 30/6/1798
McKAY, William	April 2	15	5ft 2in	Sutherland	Weaver	Dead 4/3/1799
McKEACHIN, Dun.	March 11	17	5ft 4in	Kilmallie	Labourer	
McKEACHIN, Hugh	April 21	18	5ft 4in	Ardnamurchan	Labourer	Dis. 24/2/1799
McKEACHNIE, Alex.	May 12	16	5ft 4in	Glasgow	Weaver	
McKENZIE, Alex.	May 5	19	5ft 4in	Ferintosh,	Labourer	
McKENZIE, Alex.	May 9	18	5ft 3½ in	Birnie	Labourer	
McKENZIE, Donald	May 23	14	5ft 2in	Rosskeen	Labourer	Dis. 30/7/1803
McKENZIE, Duncan	March 19	27	5ft 9in	Kilmallie	Labourer	
McKENZIE, John	Feb 18	13	4ft 10½ in	Cromarty	Labourer	To 2nd Batt, 5/11/1803
McKENZIE, John	March 18	19	5ft 6in	Bolleskine,	Armourer	Sergeant
McKENZIE, John	March 28	34	5ft 4in	Mortlach	Gardener	Dis. 24/2/1799
McKENZIE, John	May 6	22	5ft 6in	Liberton, Edinburgh	Labourer	Transferred 10/8/1810
McKENZIE, John	May 23	18	5ft 6in	Inverness	Labourer	
McKENZIE, Keneth	May 3	17	5ft 7½ in	Duthil	Weaver	

Name	Date	Age	Height	Place	Trade	Notes
MᶜKENZIE, Murdoch	Aug 12	19	5ft 7½ in	Lochcarron,	Piper	
MᶜKENZIE, Wm.	March 12	16	5ft 3½ in	Annis, Ross	Labourer	Dis. 24/5/1807
MᶜKERIN, Archibald	March 10	28	5ft 6in	Knapdale	Weaver	
MACKIE, William	May 15	16	5ft 2in	Marnoch	Weaver	Died in Ireland
MᶜKILLICAN, Ben.	May 8	20	5ft 6in	Pettie	Weaver	Dead 25/9/1795
MᶜKILLICAN, John	April 8	15	5ft 1in	Croy	Labourer	Discharged
MᶜKILLOP, Hugh	May 17	35	5ft 5in	Kilmore,	Weaver	Dis. 9/6/1797
MᶜKILLIP, John	March 22	16	5ft 3in	Bolleskine,	Labourer	Dis. 3/11/1795
MᶜKILLOP, John	May 4	16	5ft 4in	Lorn, Argyll		Dis. 27/5/1802
MᶜKINLAY, Duncan	March 20	28	5ft 9in	Lochgoil, Argyll	Labourer	Enlisted by Ensign Fraser
MᶜKINNON, Alex.	Dec 18	24	5ft 7in	Glenelg	Labourer	Dis. 27/5/1802
MᶜKINNON, Donald	March 11	17	5ft 5in	Kilmallie	Labourer	Dis. 31/10/1800
MᶜKINNON, Donald	March 12	19	5ft 5in	Barra	Taylor	Transferred 10/8/1810
MᶜKINNON, Donald	April 20	18	5ft 6in	Kilfinchan, Argyll	Labourer	Dead 27/8/1799
MᶜKINNON, Donald	June 23	30	5ft 5in	Muck	Labourer	Dis. 27/5/1802
MᶜKINNON, Donald	Aug 12	28	5ft 8in	Sleat, Skye	Labourer	
MᶜKINNON, John	May 2	22	5ft 3½ in	Mull	Labourer	Dead 12/10/1799
MᶜKINNON, John	Aug 20	19	5ft 2in	Ardnamur-chan	Labourer	Dis. 24/5/1800
MᶜKORMICK, Pat.	May 18	22	5ft 5in	Glenevy, Antrim	Labourer	Dis. 30/6/1798
MᶜLACHLAN, Wm.	April 3	28	5ft 8in	Kilpatrick	Weaver	Dis. 31/10/1800
MᶜLAMONT, James	April 5	28	5ft 4in	Colmonel, Ayr	Weaver	Dis. 4/5/1802
MᶜLEAN, Alexander	March 12	17	5ft 8½ in	Barra	Fisher	Enlisted by Capt J. Cameron; dead 6/10/1796
MᶜLEAN, Alexander	May 15	19	5ft 8in	Inverness	Labourer	
MᶜLEAN, Alexander	May 16	35	5ft 6½ in	Islay	Labourer	
MᶜLEAN, Allen	June 18	37	5ft 9½ in	Mervin, Argyll	Labourer	Dead 6/2/1797
MᶜLEAN Donald	May 18	16	5ft 0½ in	North Uist	Labourer	Dis. 27/5/1802
MᶜLEAN, Donald	June 5	35	5ft 9in	Ardnamur-chan	Taylor	
MᶜLEAN, Duncan	April 4	25	5ft 9in	Kilmuir	Labourer	Dis. 27/5/1802
MᶜLEAN, Findlay	March 14	24	5ft 6½ in	Laggan,	Labourer	
MᶜLEAN, John	Feb 18	34	5ft 4in	Alvie	Labourer	
MᶜLEAN, John	Feb 18	18	5ft 5in	Inveravon	Labourer	Dis. 1/2/1808
MᶜLEAN, John	March 12	20	5ft 8in	Barra	Labourer	Dead 3/2/1799
MᶜLEAN, John	June 6	15	5ft 4in	Ardnamur-chan	Labourer	Dis. 27/5/1802
MᶜLEARON, Alex.	March 12	18	5ft 5½ in	Inverary	Mason	
MᶜLEARON, Arch.	March 28	19	5ft 4in	Edinburgh	Wright	
MᶜLEARON, John	May 31	16	5ft 1½ in	Kincardine	Shoemaker	
MᶜCLAY, Charles	March 14	16	5ft 4in	Girvan	Weaver	Enlisted by Ensign Fraser; dead 12/10/1799
MᶜLEALLON, Arch.	May 15	23	5ft 7in	Inverness	Labourer	
MᶜLELLAN, Donald	June 20	30	5ft 4in	South Uist	Labourer	Dis. 8/6/1796
MᶜLELLAN, Donald	Aug 26	34	5ft 0in	Glenelg	Labourer	Dead 7/1/1799
MᶜLELLAN, Hugh	April 5	22	5ft 7½ in	Terfergus, Argyll	Weaver	Dead 29/9/1795
MᶜLELLAN, John	May 6	33	5ft 6in	South Uist	Labourer	
MᶜLELLAN, John	May 29	15	5ft 2in	Contin	Labourer	

Name	Date	Age	Height	Place	Occupation	Notes
MᶜLELLAN, Patrick	June 17	22	5ft 7in	Glasgow	Shoemaker	
MᶜLEOD, Alexander	March 12	18	5ft 4in	Troternish	Labourer	Dead 27/8/1799
MᶜLEOD, Alexander	May 20	26	5ft 6½ in	South Uist	Labourer	Dead 14/1/1799
MᶜLEOD, Hugh	—	22	5ft 6in	Durness	Taylor	Exchanged to Reay Fencibles for another man, 24/4/1799
MᶜLEOD, John	June 3	18	5ft 6in	Kilmuir	Labourer	Dis. 20/5/1800
MᶜLEOD, John	July 21	30	5ft 7in	Portree	Labourer	Dis. 27/5/1802
MᶜLEOD, Neil	May 19	28	5ft 5in	Durinish	Labourer	Dead 27/8/1799
MᶜLIESH, Donell	May 25	25	5ft 4½ in	Antrim	Labourer	Dis. 30/6/1798
MᶜLUSKIE, William	May 9	25	5ft 4in	Errageturan, Tyrone	Labourer	
MᶜMASTER, Allen	April 30	17	5ft 4½ in	Kilmallie	Labourer	To 2nd Batt. 25/11/1803
MᶜMASTER, Arch.	Nov 22	20	5ft 3½ in	Ardnamurchan	Labourer	Dead 12/10/1799
MᶜMILLAN, Alex.	March 10	17	5ft 4in	Kilmallie	Labourer	
MᶜMILLAN, Dougald	June 7	16	5ft 3½ in	Kilmally	Labourer	Dis. 31/10/1800
MᶜMILLAN, Duncan	April 3	26	5ft 6in	Kilmally	Weaver	
MᶜMILLAN, Duncan	July 26	11	4ft 0in	—	Labourer	
MᶜMILLAN, Ewan	March 10	22	5ft 9in	Kilmally	Labourer	
MᶜMILLAN, Ewan	April 5	30	5ft 10in	Kilmallie	Labourer	
MᶜMILLAN, Ewan	May 8	20	5ft 4in	Kilmallie	Labourer	
MᶜMILLAN, John	March 9	21	5ft 9½ in	Kilmallie	Weaver	Dis. 1/2/1808
MᶜMILLAN, John	March 12	20	5ft 6½ in	Barra	Labourer	
MᶜMILLAN, John	April 21	21	5ft 7in	Kilmallie	Labourer	Enlisted by Capt J. Cameron
MᶜMILLAN, John	April 22	21	5ft 6in	Down, co. Down	Tobacco spinner	Lost left arm dis. 29/1/1800
MᶜMILLAN, Lachlan	June 9	23	5ft 5in	South Uist	Labourer	Dis. 6/9/1802
MᶜMILLAN, Neil	June 8	22	5ft 8½ in	Kilmally	Labourer	Dis. 24/1/1803
MᶜNAB, James	April 5	32	5ft 6in	Aberdour Fife	Weaver	Dis. 20/5/1800
MᶜNAIR, John	June 2	18	5ft 4½ in	Kilmanivaig	Labourer	Dis. 8/4/1804
MᶜNEAL, John	April 26	17	5ft 6½ in	Barra	Labourer	Dead 12/10/1799
MᶜNEIL, John	May 15	17	5ft 6½ in	Greenock	Shoemaker	To 9th R.Y. Batt.15/10/1806
MᶜNEIL, Rodrick	March 12	19	5ft 4½ in	Barra	Taylor	Dead 12/10/1799
MᶜNICHOL, Donald	April 22	36	5ft 8in	Port of Menteith	Blacksmith	Dis. 27/5/1802
MᶜNICHOL, John	March 11	—	—	—	—	Enlisted by Maj MᶜDonald; dis. 30/6/1798
MᶜPHEE, Alexander	April 26	22	5ft 6in	Kilmallie	Labourer	Dead 12/10/1799
MᶜPHEE, Angus	March 12	23	5ft 5in	Kilmally	Labourer	Dead 12/10/1799
MᶜPHEE, Duncan	May 6	35	5ft 5in	Kilmallie	Labourer	Dead 18/11/1794
MᶜPHEE, John	May 13	22	5ft 7in	Kilmallie	Labourer	
MᶜPHERSON, Alex.	Feb 24	35	5ft 8in	Ardnamachan	Labourer	Enlisted by Lieut MᶜPherson
MᶜPHERSON, Alex.	May 12	34	5ft 7½ in	Ardnamurchan	Labourer	Deserted 24/2/1799
MᶜPHERSON, Alex.	May 23	26	5ft 4in	Laggan	Taylor	Dis. 24/5/1800

Name	Date	Age	Height	Place	Occupation	Notes
M^cPHERSON, Allen	May 13	12	4ft 9in	Ardnamurchan	Labourer	
M^cPHERSON, Alex.	May 30	17	5ft 6in	Kingussie	Labourer	Dead 24/5/1801
M^cPHERSON, Andrew	May 31	19	5ft 4½ in	Laggan	Labourer	To 2nd Batt. 25/11/1803
M^cPHERSON, Angus	March 5	28	5ft 5in	Laggan,	Labourer	
M^cPHERSON, Donald	March 5	17	5ft 4in	Kingussie	Labourer	
M^cPHERSON, Donald	March 15	17	5ft 4in	Kingussie	Labourer	Dis. 31/12/1795; dead 11/10/1799
M^cPHERSON, Donald	May 21	20	5ft 10in	Laggan	Labourer	
M^cPHERSON, Donald	May 22	27	5ft 8½ in	Kingussie	Labourer	Dead 8/1/1799
M^cPHERSON, Donald	June 3	25	5ft 9½ in	Laggan	Labourer	Dis. 14/10/1798
M^cPHERSON, Duncan	March 11	20	5ft 6in	Laggan,	Barber	Dis. 12/8/1797
M^cPHERSON, Duncan	May 23	30	5ft 8in	Laggan	Labourer	Dead 17/11/1794
M^cPHERSON, Duncan	May 30	16	5ft 3in	Laggan	Labourer	
M^cPHERSON, Ewan	March 14	30	5ft 4½ in	Laggan,	Labourer	Dis. 27/5/1802
M^cPHERSON, Ewan	June 10	14	5ft 0in	Laggan	Labourer	
M^cPHERSON, Hugh	March 3	24	5ft 6in	Laggan	Clerk	
M^cPHERSON, James	March 24	17	5ft 4in	Laggan	Labourer	Sergeant
M^cPHERSON, James	May 20	21	5ft 11in	Laggan,	Labourer	Dead 20/1/1796
M^cPHERSON, John	March 16	30	5ft 6in	Kingussie	Labourer	Trans 10/8/1810
M^cPHERSON, John	May 22	19	5ft 10½ in	Laggan	Labourer	Ensign 20/2/1799; dis. 6/3/1799
M^cPHERSON, John	May 30	20	5ft 4in	Durinish	Labourer	Dead 24/10/1799
M^cPHERSON, John	Aug 15	26	5ft 4½ in	Laggan	Labourer	Dis. 24/2/1799
M^cPHERSON, Lachlan	March 2	23	5ft 8in	Laggan,	Labourer	Dis. 14/10/1798
M^cPHERSON, Lachlan	April 6 1795	35	5ft 5in	Croy	Butcher	Dis. 30/1/1798
M^cPHERSON, Lachlan	May 16	20	5ft 7in	Laggan,	Labourer	Dead 4/9/1809
M^cPHERSON, Malcolm	March 16	22	5ft 5in	Kingussie	Labourer	Dead 4/1/1796
M^cPHERSON, Malcolm	June 2	29	5ft 11in	South Uist	Labourer	
M^cPHERSON, Peter	May 23	22	5ft 5in	Laggan	Labourer	
M^cPHERSON, Robert	March 14	16	5ft 4in	Laggan,	Labourer	Dis. 24/2/1799
M^cPHERSON, Thomas	March 14	28	5ft 7½ in	Inch	Labourer	
M^cPHERSON, Thomas	May 30	19	5ft 6in	Inveravon	Labourer	To 2nd Batt. 25/11/1803
M^cPHERSON, Thomas	June 14	18	5ft 3in	Laggan	Labourer	
M^cPHERSON, Wm.	Feb 22	16	5ft 3in	Kingussie	Labourer	
M^cQUEEN, James	Nov 12	16	5ft 4in	St Nicholas, Aberdeen	Labourer	Dis. 30/6/1798
M^cQUEEN, Malcolm	July 4	16	5ft 3in	Kilmuir	Labourer	
M^cROBBIE, James	March 16	17	5ft 4in	Aberlour	Labourer	Dead 24/10/1797
M^cSWEEN, Sween	May 30	23	5ft 6½ in	Snizort	Labourer	Dis. 20/5/1800
M^cTAVISH, Angus	March 12	25	5ft 5in	Bolleskine	Labourer	
M^cVEY, John	May 12	19	5ft 7½ in	Ramshorn, Lanark	Weaver	Dis. 27/5/1802
MAIR, Alexander	May 3	35	5ft 6½ in	New Milns, Ayr	Blacksmith	Dis. 10/6/1795
MALLOCH, George	May 15	15	5ft 3in	Negurting, Perth	Dieper bleacher	Dead 23/12/1795
MALVEN, Charles	April 17	27	5ft 9½ in	Diple	Mason	Dead 7/3/1809
MANSON, Andrew	June 9	32	5ft 9in	Thurso	Labourer	Dis. 27/5/1802
MANSON, Donald	March 16	16	5ft 3½ in	Obreck, Caithness	Labourer	Dead 26/10/1794

MANSON, Donald	June 4	16	5ft 4in	Olrig, Caithness	Labourer	
MARRINER, James	April 23	19	5ft 4in	Kilmore, co. Down	Labourer	
MARRON, John	April 1	17	5ft 3½ in	Antrim	Labourer	
MARSHALL, William	April 18	35	5ft 3½ in	Mortlach	Wool-comber	Dis. 30/6/1798
MARTIN, James	Feb 24	34	5ft 7in	Kinethmont	Wool-comber	Sergeant Dis. 30/6/1798
MARTIN, James	March 16	14	6ft 0in	Huntly	Ropemaker	
MARTIN, John	June 29	16	6ft 3in	Inerat, Inverness	Labourer	Dead 6/10/1799
MARTIN, Murdoch	July 28	26	5ft 8½ in	Tromper, Inverness	Labourer	Dis. 20/5/1800
MARTIN, William	March 29	34	5ft 10in	Glasgow	Weaver	Late 26 Regt., 9 yrs 9 months; dis. 24/2/1799
MASON, John	Dec 29	34	5ft 8in	Federessie, Kincardine	Wool-comber	Dead 15/5/1796
MATHISON, Alex.	May 12	29	5ft 4½ in	Clyne	Labourer	Dead 30/4/1796
MATHISON, Donald	July 13	22	6ft 5½ in	Snisort,	Labourer	Dis. 31/10/1802
MATHIESON, John	March 8	21	5ft 3in	Inverness	Weaver	Dead 12/10/1799
MIDDLETON, Alex.	April 16	17	5ft 4in	St Nicholas, Aberdeen	Baker	
MILLER, John	April 4	35	5ft 10in	Glasgow	Weaver	
MILLER, John	April 28	16	5ft 9in	Monklan, Lanark	Weaver	Dead 1/4/1799
MILLER, William	April 15	17	5ft 4½ in	Dunnet	Taylor	Dead 12/10/1799
MILNE, James	April 16	17	5ft 6in	Edinburgh	Slater	
MILNE, James	April 21	17	5ft 2in	New Machar	Combmaker	
MILNE, Laughlan	May 16	22	5ft 7in	Banff	Gardener	
MILNS, Patrick	May 15	32	5ft 7in	Rhynie	Labourer	
MIRRLEES, George	March 29	33	5ft 3½ in	Westkirk, Edinburgh	Wright	Dis. 24/2/1799
MITCHELL, Alex,	May 12	15	5ft 2½ in	Glasgow	Hairdresser	
MITCHELL, James	April 12	35	5ft 5in	Kenneth-mont	Shoe-maker	Dis. 30/6/1798
MITCHELL, John	March 29	24	5ft 7in	Borowness, Linlithgow	Weaver	Sergeant, dead 10/11/1809
MITCHELL, William	March 23	30	5ft 3½ in	Glasgow	Weaver	Dis. 30/6/1798
MITCHELL, William	April 19	17	5ft 2in	St Nicholas, Aberdeen	Weaver	Dis. 12/10/1805
MOCHRIE, John	April 12	26	5ft 4½ in	Forfar, Banff [sic]	Weaver	Dis. 23/7/1794
MOIR, James	May 22	22	5ft 7in	Rhynie	Labourer	To 2nd Batt. 25/11/1803
MONK, Archibald	May 10	24	5ft 7in	South Uist	Labourer	
MONRO, Hector	May 15	16	5ft 2½ in	Alness	Labourer	Dis. 3/11/1800
MONRO, Hugh	April 3	28	5ft 4½ in	Kenneth-mont	Wool-comber	Dis. 4/5/1802
Monro, Lewis	March 12	19	5ft 6in	Inveravon	Weaver	Dis. 10/6/1795
MONRO, William	April 13	—	—	—	—	Enlisted by Maj McDonald; dis. 27/5/1802
MONRO, William	April 24	16	5ft 3in	Clatt	Labourer	

587

Name	Date	Age	Height	Place	Trade	Notes
MONTAGUE, Thomas	April 26	16	5ft 4in	Arrigel, co. Tyrone	Weaver	Dead 31/10/1795
MONTAGUE, Peter	May 1	19	5ft 10½ in	Bavaigh, Derry	Labourer	
MONTAGUE, Thomas	May 16	30	5ft 5in	Argyle, co. Tyrone	Weaver	Dis. 9/6/1797
MONTGOMERY, Edw'd	April 14	19	5ft 8in	Shankle, Armagh	Sawer	
MONTGOMERY, Murd.	July 12	25	5ft 0in	Portree	Labourer	
MONTIETH, Ebenezer	April 25	12	5ft 2in	Stirling	Labourer	Dead 12/10/1799
MONTIETH, William	April 25	16	5ft 3in	Stirling	Gardener	Dis. 25/6/1809
MOODY, William	May 24	35	5ft 8in	Kilwinning, Ayr	Weaver	
MORE, David	April 17	19	5ft 9½ in	Leith	Labourer	
MORGAN, James	May 5	33	5ft 6¾ in	Dunfermline	Taylor	Dis. 30/6/1798
MORGAN, James	June 6	25	5ft 8½ in	Lisson, Tyrone	Weaver	Dead 23/6/1810
MORRICE, Robert	May 1	29	5ft 8in	Rothsay	Labourer	Dis. 27/5/1802
MORRISON, Alex.	April 26	24	5ft 3in	Barra	Labourer	Dis. 8/6/1796
MORRISON, Andrew	May 6	17	5ft 3½ in	Comrie	Labourer	Dead 12/10/1799
MORRISON, George	Feb 28	28	5ft 7in	Turriff	Threadtwiner	
MORRISON, George	Sep 16	16	5ft 4in	Eddira-chilles Sutherland	Labourer	Dis. 24/4/1799; exchanged for another man to Reay Fencibles
MORRISON, John	April 1	22	5ft 10¾ in	Turriff	Thread twiner	
MORRISON, Rodrick	May 24	17	5ft 2½ in	Harris	Weaver	Dead 22/2/1809
MORTIMORE, Wm.	March 1	27	5ft 10¾ in	Belly, Banff	Cabinet-maker	
MORTON, John	May 10	20	5ft 7½ in	Tormenny, Derry	Labourer	Dis. 28/8/1795
MOUR, John	May 27	30	5ft 6in	Campsie	Gardener	To 61 Reg., 28/10/1797
MUNRO, Donald	Feb 28	—	—	—	—	Dis. 24/2/1799
MURCHIE, James	April 5	30	5ft 8½ in	Bochern, Banff	Labourer	To 5th RV. Batt. 24/5/1807
MURDOCH, Alex.	April 9	23	6ft 7½ in	Down, Perth	Weaver	
MURDOCH, James	April 1	25	5ft 8in	Ruthven	Labourer	
MURDOCH, Malcolm	June 8	38	5ft 4in	Kilmadock, Perth	Weaver	Dis. 30/6/1798
MURRAY, John	March 5	33	5ft 3in	Cairney	Weaver	
MURRAY, John	April 22	28	6ft 5½ in	Strichen	Weaver	Dis. 27/5/1802
MURRAY, John	June 8	16	5ft 4½ in	Glasgow	Potter	
MURRAY, William	March 2	20	5ft 3in	Fordyce	Weaver	
NESS, Robert	April 14	21	5ft 8in	Auchter-muchty	Weaver	Enlisted by Lord Huntly; dead 22/7/1795
NEWLANDS, James	April 12	25	5ft 8in	Aberlour	Labourer	Dead 27/8/1795
NICHOL, Daniel	April 11	30	5ft 7½ in	Lesmaingo, Lanark	Weaver	Enlisted by Maj McDonald
NICHOL, William	May 1	24	5ft 4in	Mortlach	Weaver	
NICOL, John	June 30	16	5ft 2in	Banff	Stocking Weaver	

Name	Date	Age	Height	Place	Occupation	Notes
NICOLS, Robert	June 10 1795	29	—	Gibraltar	—	Late 32nd Regt, 18 yrs, 1 mth; 61st Regt, 1 yr. 10 months.
NICOLSON, John	July 16	34	5ft 4in	Snisort	Labourer	Dis. 30/6/1798
NICOLSON, John	Aug 6	34	5ft 6in	Portree	Farmer	Dis. 30/6/1798
NORRICE, Robert	June 8	15	5ft 3½ in	Glasgow	Potter	Dis. 24/5/1807
PARK, Daniel	April 1	26	5ft 7in	Calder	Slater	
PARK, John	May 23	34	5ft 4¾ in	Glasgow	Nailer	
PARKER, William	May 28	23	5ft 8in	Kilbarchan, Renfrew	Shoe-maker	To 9th R.V. Batt. 24/2/1806
PATTERSON, Alex.	May 23	18	5ft 8½ in	Stirling	Nailmaker	
PATTERSON, Andrew	April 18	17	5ft 2½ in	Redcastle	Spoon-maker	Dead 28/2/1799
PATTERSON, George	May 27	25	5ft 10in	Stirling	Nailer	Dead 24/12/1795
PATTERSON, William	May 23	21	5ft 11in	Stirling	Black-smith	Dis. 20/5/1800
PAUL, Robert	May 1	34	5ft 4½ in	Glasgow	Rope-spinner	Dis. 30/6/1798
PETRIE, James	March 18	35	5ft 9½ in	Biggar	Nailer	Dis. 30/6/1798
PETRIE, John	May 5	32	5ft 7in	Manmuir, Forfar	Taylor	Enlisted by Ensign Fraser
PETTIGREW, John	March 2	17	5ft 4in	Airdrie	Weaver	
PHILP, Charles	May 29	16	5ft 5in	Kenneth-mont	Taylor	Dead 9/7/1794
PIRRIE, William	May 17	35	5ft 5in	Ruthven	Labourer	Dis. 24/2/1799
PORTER, Hugh	May 9	26	5ft 7in	Bellivoi, Ireland	Weaver	Dead 12/10/1799
POWRIE, Robert	April 15	16	5ft 2in	Alyth, Perth	Shoe-maker	
RHAEBURN, Thomas	April 19	34	5ft 7in	Boyndie	Cattle Dealer	Dis. 10/6/1795
RAINEY, John	March 1	29	5ft 4in	Old Deer	Wool-comber	Dis. 10/7/1797
RALPH, James	April 25	16	5ft 2½ in	Alves	Labourer	Deserted 28/8/1797
RALPH, William	May 8	34	5ft 4¼ in	Alves	Weaver	Dead 6/8/1794
RAMSAY, Samuel	June 20	17	5ft 3½ in	Spynie	Labourer	Dead 23/2/1807
RANKINE, Donald	April 10	21	5ft 4in	Kilmally	Weaver	Enlisted by Capt J. Cameron; dis. 24/5/1807
RANKINE, James	March 28	18	5ft 4in	Airdrie	Weaver	Enlisted by Ensign Fraser; dead 5/10/1799
RANKINE, James	April 28	25	5ft 5in	Glasgow	Stocking-weaver	Transferred. 10/8/1818
REID, Alexander	Feb 28	20	5ft 6in	Thurso	Labourer	Dis. 30/6/1798
REID, Lawrence	March 24	32	5ft 3½ in	Pennycook	Weaver	
REID, William	May 27	31	5ft 6in	Larbert	Coalier	Dis. 27/5/1802
RELIE, Edward	May 29	34	5ft 8in	Ralduff, Cavan	Labourer	
RENNIE, David	April 6	16	5ft 4¾ in	Newcastle	Labourer	
RENNIE, John	July 1	17	5ft 3½ in	Fintry	Shoemaker	
RENNIE, Theodor	June 11	19	5ft 7½ in	Dumbennan	Farmer	
RETTIE, Alexander	March 8	26	5ft 0in	New Deer	Butcher	Dis. 30/6/1798
REYNOLDS, John	May 15	26	5ft 9in	Cabrach	Labourer	Sergeant
RIACH, John	March 11	19	5ft 4½ in	Aberlour	Labourer	

Name	Date	Age	Height	Place	Occupation	Notes
RIACH, John	June 13	24	5ft 6½ in	Strathdon	Labourer	Dis. 4/5/1802
RIACH, William	June 6	17	5ft 4in	Kirkmichael	Labourer	Dead 14/10/1795
RITCHIE, Robert	March 18	18	5ft 7½ in	Duffus	Labourer	Dis. 8/6/1796
ROBB, Colin	May 19	35	5ft 6in	Loggie	Labourer	Dis. 27/5/1802
ROBERTSON, Arch.	March 4	19	5ft 5in	Edinburgh	Copperplate printer	
ROBERTSON, Donald	June 2	28	5ft 5in	Inch	Labourer	Dis. 1/2/1808
ROBERTSON, Finlay	April 17	29	5ft 6in	Tain	Labourer	Transferred 24/1/1808
ROBERTSON, James	May 20	35	5ft 6in	Neilston	Labourer	Dead 13/6/1797
ROBERTSON, George	March 29	19	5ft 7in	Kairn, Aberdeen	Labourer	Transferred 19/5/1810
ROBERTSON, James	April 3	16	5ft 2½ in	Stirling	Weaver	Dead 1/11/1799
ROBERTSON, John	March 5	18	5ft 7½ in	Newhills	Labourer	Dead 29/9/1795
ROBERTSON, John	March 19	36	5ft 5in	—	Weaver	Left in England
ROBERTSON, Patrick	March 28	30	5ft 4½ in	Haddington	Wright	Dis. 30/6/1798
ROBERTSON, Robert	April 4	33	5ft 7in	Paisley	Weaver	
ROBERTSON, Wm.	Feb 24	33	5ft 6¾ in	Old Machar	Wool-comber	Dis. 27/5/1802
ROBERTSON, Wm.	May 12	—	—	Aberdeen	Mason	Dead 18/11/1796
ROBERTSON, Wm.	June 29	35	5ft 9½ in	Rutherglen	Weaver	Dead 27/11/1795
ROBSON, William	March 8	35	5ft 6in	Skene	Woolcomber	
ROGERS, John	April 16	28	5ft 3½ in	South Leith	Cork cutter	Enlisted by Maj McDonald; dis. 9/6/1810
RONALDS, Alex.	March 29	22	5ft 5½ in	Falkirk	Taylor	Enlisted by Ensign Fraser; dead 9/10/1799
RONALDS, Thomas	April 19	24	5ft 4½ in	Rhynie	Shoe-maker	Dead 1/3/1809
RONEY, Donald	May 24	22	5ft 6½ in	Killan, co. Down	Labourer	Enlisted by Lieut Stewart
ROSESIDE, John	April 9	22	5ft 9½ in	Campbleton	Weaver	Dis. 24/5/1800
ROSS, Alexander	May 12	18	5ft 5½ in	Forres	Labourer	
ROSS, Andrew	May 22	17	5ft 4in	Laggan	Labourer	Dis. 27/5/1802
ROSS, David	Feb 19	12	4ft 10in	Inverness	Labourer	
ROSS, David	April 12	25	5ft 3in	Inverness	Weaver	Dead 10/8/1810
ROSS, David	May 12	19	5ft 2in	Dornoch	Weaver	Dead 30/6/1798
ROSS, David	June 2	20	5ft 3½ in	Laggan	Labourer	
ROSS, Hugh	March 26	12	5ft 0in	Reay	Labourer	
ROSS, James	April 8	20	5ft 8½ in	Rosemeven, Ross	Black-smith	To 61 Reg., 28/10/1794
ROSS, John	April 16	16	5ft 2in	Old Machar	Weaver	Dead 31/10/1795
ROSS, John	June 7	22	5ft 3in	Daviot	Weaver	Transferred. 10/8/1810
ROSS, John	June 5	19	5ft 8in	Olrig	Labourer	
ROSS, William	April 4	18	5ft 2½ in	Croy	Labourer	Dis. 4/5/1802
ROXBURGH, John	May 28	35	5ft 9½ in	Newton Stewart	Shoe-maker	Dead 20/10/1799
RUSSELL, John	April 8	23	5ft 8in	Monkland	Weaver	
SCOTT, George	Feb 17	24	5ft 6½ in	Gartly	Labourer	To 2nd Batt, 25/11/1803
SCOTT, Robert	March 19	39	5ft 7in	Derry	Miller	Dis. 30/6/1798
SEEBRIGHT, George	Oct 27	—	—	—	—	Dis. 10/6/1795
SHAND, Alexander	April 12	20	5ft 10½ in	Speymouth	Labourer	

Name	Date	Age	Height	Place	Occupation	Notes
SHAND, John	April 5	30	5ft 5in	Turriff	Shoemaker	
SHAND, Robert	May 12	28	5ft 9in	Rhynie	Labourer	
SHANKS, George	April 25	29	6ft 0in	Glasgow	Shoemaker	To 61 Reg., 28/10/1794
SHANKS, Hugh	May 14	21	5ft 6in	Kilbarchan	Weaver	Dis. 30/6/1798
SHARP, James	July 5	21	5ft 5in	Invertown, Banff	Labourer	
SHARP, John	March 29	25	5ft 5in	Drumelzier Peebles	Printer	Dis. 27/5/1802
SHAW, Alexander	March 11	21	5ft 8in	Kilmorich, Argyle	Labourer	Dead 3/1/1799
SHAW, Peter	June 25	21	5ft 4in	Inerat, Inverness	Labourer	
SHEDDAN, James	April 8	16	5ft 2in	St Cuthbert's Edinburgh	Labourer	To 2nd Batt. 25/11/1803; dead 22/9/1809
SHORT, Alexander	May 17	35	5ft 4½ in	Glasgow	Shoemaker	Dis. 10/6/1795
SHUAN, John	April 22	18	5ft 4½ in	Lonmay	Labourer	Transferred 10/8/1810
SIBBALD, Thomas	April 22	28	5ft 11in	Broughton, Tweeddale	Shoemaker	
SIME, Daniel	May 21	30	5ft 8in	Maybole	Labourer	
SIME, David	June 6	18	5ft 5in	Dundee	Labourer	
SIME, John	May 10	27	5ft 6in	Elgin	Labourer	Dead 26/9/1795
SIMPSON, James	May 18	17	5ft 8in	Bellie	Labourer	
SIMPSON, Peter	April 3	19	5ft 7in	Old Machar	Combmaker	Dead 12/10/1799
SIMPSON, Thomas	May 2	17	5ft 3in	Edinburgh	Hairdresser	Dead 24/8/1798
SINCLAIR, David	May 9	20	5ft 7½ in	Stronsay	Wheelwright	
SINCLAIR, George	June 12	20	5ft 9½ in	Bower, Caithness	Weaver	
SINCLAIR, John	March 24	20	5ft 8½ in	Blackford, Perth	Mason	Transferred. 24/3/1804
SINCLAIR, Peter	March 9	16	5ft 5in	Reay	Labourer	Dis. 27/5/1802
SINCLAIR, William	April 12	37	5ft 8in	Reay	Wine Cooper	Dead 27/8/1799
SKEEN, Joseph	March 15	29	5ft 4½ in	Tarland	Woolcomber	
SKEEN, William	May 10	32	5ft 5in	Inverkeithnie	Hairdresser	
SLIMMAN, Andrew	May 15	26	5ft 11in	Falkirk	Miner	Transferred 10/8/1810
SMELLIE, John	May 3	34	5ft 11½ in	Dalserf, Lanark	Weaver	Dis. 30/6/1798
SMITH, Alexander	March 7	21	5ft 7in	Turriff	Weaver	Dis. 30/6/1798
SMITH, Alexander	March 18	21	5ft 7in	Dunlichity, Inverness	Labourer	Sergeant, dead 25/11/1795
SMITH, Alexander	May 1	—	—	—	—	Enlisted by Maj McDonald; dead (date not known)
SMITH, Andrew	April 19	—	—	—	—	Enlisted by Maj McDonald; dis. 8/6/1796
SMITH, Findlay	April 25	20	5ft 4½ in	Daviot,	Taylor	
SMITH, George	March 2	35	5ft 6½ in	Coldstone, Aberdeen	Woolcomber	Dis. 30/6/1798

SMITH, George	April 4	27	6ft 2in	Kilmarnock	Weaver	Dis. 24/5/1800
SMITH, John	March 28	32	5ft 4½ in	Strachan	Taylor	Dis. 10/6/1795
SMITH, John	March 31	37	5ft 9in	St Philip's, Gloucester	Labourer	Enlisted by Ensign Fraser; dis. 3/11/1795
SMITH, John	April 19	19	5ft 3in	Maryculter	Smith	
SMITH, Robert	March 19	34	5ft 8in	Newmilns,	Weaver	Dis. 24/2/1799
SMITH, William	April 14	20	5ft 2in	St Ninian, Stirling	Nailsmith	Dead 31/5/1799
SMOUT, George	May 2	21	5ft 8½ in	Ellon	Labourer	
SNADDOn, John	May 12	32	5ft 6in	Shaws, Fife	Weaver	Enlisted by Lieut McLean; dis. 10/6/1795
SOCHLING, C. Augustus	Nov 3	27	—	Hess, Castle Reutlin Germany	Musician	Dis. 16/5/1798
STEWART, Alex.	Feb 25	24	5ft 11½ in	Kilmanivaig	Labourer	Sergeant
STEWART, Alex.	May 3	23	5ft 8½ in	Mortlach	Labourer	Dis. 1/4/1805
STEWART, Alex.	June 11	34	5ft 5in	Portree	Labourer	
STEWART, Archibald	April 15	34	5ft 3in	North Uist	Wool-comber	Dis. 8/6/1796
STEWART, Daniel	March 20	23	5ft 8in	Blair Athol	Waiter	Adjutant 29/5/1806
STEWART, Donald	April 3	21	5ft 8in	Kirkmichael	Labourer	Dead 17/9/1809
STEWART, James	March 11	19	5ft 8in	Greenock	Labourer	To 9th R.V. Batt. 27/5/1807
STEWART, James	July 8	19	5ft 6in	Mortlach	Labourer	Dead 12/10/1799
STEWART, James	Sep 27	23	5ft 6in	Sleat, Skye	Taylor	Dead 12/10/1799
STEWART, John	June 4	33	5ft 6in	Kirkmichael	Labourer	
STEWART, John	June 6	24	5ft 10in	Inveravon	Labourer	
STEWART, John	Aug 26	33	5ft 4in	Kilmore	Labourer	Dis. 30/6/1798
STEWART, Lewis	June 5	35	5ft 6in	Inveravon	Labourer	Dis. 10/6/1795
STEWART, Norman	July 10	17	5ft 3in	Inverness	Labourer	
STEWART, Robert	March 4	16	5ft 4in	Cairney	Labourer	
STEWART, Robert	March 2	16	5ft 2in	Kirk-michael	Labourer	Deserted 27/6/1794
STEWART, William	Feb 25	36	5ft 7in	Fortingall	Labourer	
STEWART, William	April 26	20	5ft 10in	Glenavy, Antrim	Apoth-ecary	Dis.10/6/1795
STILL, George	April 17	27	5ft 5½ in	Aberdeen	Wool-comber	Sergeant, dead 21/1/1796
STRONACH, Thomas	Feb 27	20	5ft 4in	Cairney	Labourer	
SUTHERLAND, Angus	May 1	13	4ft 10in	Saggie, Sutherland	Labourer	Dead 13/10/1799
SUTHERLAND, James	May 10	17	5ft 5in	Thurso	Weaver	Dead 12/10/1799
SUTHERLAND, Wm.	Oct 22	—	—	Ardersier	Labourer	Dis. 30/6/1798
SYMERS, Andrew	Feb 24	23	5ft 7in	Keig	Weaver	
SYMONS, Alexander	May 31	16	5ft 7in	Cairney	Labourer	
SYMOns, James	April 18	18	5ft 5½ in	Keith	Shoe-maker	Discharged
SWAN, William	April 2	34	5ft 8in	Liberton, Edinburgh	Sawer	
SWANSON, David	June 14	16	5ft 3½ in	Elach, Caithness	Labourer	To 9th R.V. Batt. 15/10/1806

Name	Date	Age	Height	Place	Occupation	Notes
TAIT, Andrew	May 3	35	5ft 5in	Hilsborrow co. Down	Weaver	Dis. 24/9/1799
TAYLOR, James	March 20	17	5ft 7½ in	Bellie	Labourer	Dis. 10/6/1799
TAYLOR, John	May 3	19	5ft 5in	Forres	Hosier	Dead 12/10/1799
TEISDALE, John	April 8	16	5ft 4in	Dalserf	Weaver	Dead 28/8/1795
THOBURN, George	April 16	22	5ft 6in	Traquair, Tweeddale	Weaver	
THOMSON, Alex.	April 5	21	5ft 5in	Oldmacher	Weaver	Dead 10/1/1796
THOMSON, Alex.	April 5	34	5ft 5½ in	Kintyre, Argyle	Shoe-maker	Dead 8/1/1796
THOMSON, Alex.	Ma y 15	18	5ft 4in	Glasgow	Weaver	
THOMSON, David	April 21	—	—	—	—	Enlisted by Maj McDonald; dead 12/10/1799
THOMSON, David	May 6	23	5ft 8in	Falkirk	Labourer	Dead 22/5/1795
THOMSON, George	Feb 24	33	5ft 4in	Forgue	Taylor	Dis. 30/1/1798
THOMSON, James	April 8	16	5ft 4in	Westquarter Lanark	Weaver	Enlisted by Ensign Fraser
THOMSON, James	April 9	35	5ft 7¾ in	Dalserf, Lanark	Cotton Spinner	Enlisted by Capt Fraser; dis. 20/5/1800
THOMSON, James	May 12	34	5ft 3½ in	Elgin	Taylor	Dis. 10/6/1795
THOMSON, Peter	May 5	37	5ft 5in	Falkirk	Labourer	Dis. 27/5/1802
THOMSON, Thomas	April 10	35	5ft 7½ in	Lanbaden, Cardigan	Pensioner	Dead 29/5/1795
THOMSON, Thomas	April 24	26	5ft 6½ in	Humbie	Labourer	Dis. 20/5/1800
THOMSON, Thomas	Nov 3	31	5ft l0½ in	Annan	Labourer	Enlisted by Lord Huntly: late 81st Regt., 5 years 5 mths; 61st Reg., 11 yrs. 5 mths.; dis. 9/11/1796
TOD, Andrew	Oct 21	25	5ft 9in	Leslie, Fife	Confect-ioner	Dis. 16/3/1798
TOD, James	March 28	26	5ft 9in	Ellon	Labourer	
TUGH, Matthew	March 15	21	5ft 4½ in	Aberdeen	Servant	
TURNBULL, George	April 22	47	5ft 11in	Dunbar	Labourer	Dead 21/2/1795
TURNER, Alexander	May 21	18	5ft 6in	Glasgow	Blacksmith	
Turner, Archibald	May 23	15	5ft 2in	Glasgow	Nailsmith	Deserted 16/12/1798
TURNER, James	May 18	35	5ft 6½ in	Greenock	Black-smith	Dead 28/7/1795
URQUHART, Alex.	May 21 1795	19	5ft 3½ in	Cromarty	Taylor	Dead 18/6/1796
URQUHART, Donald	May 13	20	5ft 6½ in	Cromarty	Labourer	
URQHART, George	April 15	18	5ft 4in	Cromarty	Labourer	Dead 15/9/1809
URQUHART, John	May 24	38	5ft 5in	Invery Inverness	Stocking-maker	Dis. 10/6/1795
VICKERMAN, Fred.	April 3	25	5ft 5½ in	Edinburgh	Labourer	Transferred l0/8/1810
WALKER, James	April 25	15	5ft 2½ in	Gartly	Weaver	
WALLACE, George	March 2	19	5ft 4in	Edinburgh	Woolcomber	
WALLACE, John	March 6	16	5ft 4in	Gorbals	Weaver	
WANDS, William	May 15	17	5ft 6in	Botrifney, Banff	Labourer	
WATSON, Adam	April 23	22	5ft 5½ in	Duffus	Servant	

WATSON, John	March 8	23	5ft 5in	Cromarty	Taylor	Dead 12/10/1799
WATSOn, Thomas	March 20	19	5ft 8in	Gorbals	Weaver	To 46th Regt. 2/11/1794
WATSON, Walter	April 11	14	5ft 1in	Glasgow	Weaver	
WATSON, William	March 12	30	5ft 8½	Clack-mannan	Labourer	Dis. 31/12/1799
WATSON, William	May 23	18	5ft 8in	Slamannan,	Labourer	Dead 22/12/795
WATT, Alexander	March 29	27	5ft 8in	Crieff	Mason	Dead 4/2/1799
WATT, Alexander	April 27	28	5ft 8½ in	Keith	Hatmaker	To 9th R.V. Batt. 29/3/1805
WATT, James	April 10	16	5ft 4in	Stirling	Labourer	
WATT, John	March 17	22	5ft 7½ in	Gartly	Mill-wright	Dead 13/11/1795
WATT, John	March 20	20	5ft 8in	Crieff	Mason	Dead 17/11/1794
WATT, John	July 8	17	5ft 6in	Deskford	Labourer	Dead 23/12/1795
WATT, Nathaniel	March 1	24	5ft 7in	Rothes	Mason	Dis. 1/6/1803
WATT, Robert	May 24	9	4ft 1in	Banff	Labourer	
WEBSTER, Cusine	May 19	19	5ft 5½ in	Dunfermline	Weaver	Dis. 27/3/1802
WEIR, James	May 14	16	5ft 4in	Kirkintilloch	Weaver	Dis. 24/5/1800
WHITE, William	Jan 9 1795	16	5ft 3½ in	Glasgow	Weaver	Dead 18/1/1796
WHITEFORD, David	May 19	17	5ft 5in	Beith	Weaver	
WHITEFORD, John	May 14	16	5ft 4in	Beith	Labourer	
WHYTE, James	April 3	30	5ft 4in	Glasgow	Weaver	Dead 18/11/1797
WHYTE, James	May 18	18	5ft 4½ in	Falkirk	Coalhewer	
WHYTE, William	May 12	20	5ft 5in	Falkirk	Labourer	Dis. 20/5/1800
WILLIAMSON, Mal.	April 29	35	5ft 4in	Glasgow	Weaver	Dis. 10/6/1795
WILLIE, Wilson	April 22	22	5ft 10½ in	Govan	Weaver	
WILSON, Ewan	May 8	25	5ft 6in	South Uist	Labourer	
WILSON, Hugh	May 20	28	5ft 5in	Paisley	Weaver	Dis. 1/4/1805
WILSON, James	March 5	32	5ft 8in	Glass	Flax-dresser	Dead 24/2/1799
WILSON, James	May 18	23	5ft 3in	Bellie	Black-smith	Sergeant, dead 2/4/1798
WILSON, John	March 6	19	5ft 8½ in	Gravesend, Kent	Labourer	Deserted 24/9/1794
WILSON, Montgomery	April 25	16	5ft 3½ in	Liberton	Labourer	
WILSON, Robert	March 12	18	5ft 3in	Fyvie	Weaver	Dead 6/9/1796
WILSON, Thomas	April 25	12	4ft 10in	Stirling	Labourer	Dis. 24/6/1797
WILSON, William	March 30	30	5ft 11in	Keith	Game-keeper	Dis. (date not known)
WILSON, William	May 8	34	5ft 5½ in	Glasgow	Maltster	Dis. 9/7/1802
WOOD, Alexander	April 11	28	5ft 6½ in	Aberdeen	Wright	Dead 12/10/1799
WOOD, David	April 9	28	6ft 4in	Dyke	Labourer	Dead 20/3/1795
WOOD, James	April 20	35	5ft 7in	Glasgow	Shoe-maker	Enlisted by Ensign Fraser; Dead 13/10/1799
WRIGHT, Archibald	May 11	21	5ft 6in	Drumgoole co. Down	Weaver	Dead 10/6/1809
WRIGHT, James	March 17	15	5ft 3½ in	Clack-mannan	Weaver	To 6th R V. Batt. 24/6/1805
WRIGHT, Peter	April 20	14	4ft 10in	Glasgow	Pipemaker	Dis. 24/6/1797

YOUNG, James	March 1	20	5ft 8½ in	Ordiquhill	Brazier	To 6th R.V. Batt. 24/5/1807
YOUNG, James	Aug 28	30	5ft 4in	Slains	China Mender	
YOUNG, John	March 1	25	5ft 6in	Ordiquhill	Brazier	
YOUNG, John	March 28	20	5ft 6in	Gorbals	Slater	
YOUNG, John	April 26	34	5ft 7½ in	Irvine	Hatter	Dis. 20/5/1800
YOUNG, William	April 3	30	5ft 8½ in	Fenwick	Weaver	
YOUNG, William	June 24	14	5ft 2½ in	Paisley	Shoemaker	
YOUNGER, William	Feb 20	20	5ft 8in	Clack-mannan	Wright	

APPENDIX 3

COLONELS AND COMMANDING OFFICERS

COLONEL OF THE REGIMENT

75TH

General Sir Robert Abercromby	1787–1827
Lieutenant-General J. Dunlop	1827–1832
Lieutenant-General Sir J. Fuller	1832–1841
General Sir W. Hutchinson	1841–1845
Major-General S.H. Berkeley	1845–1858
Major-General Sir J.A. Clerke	1858–1870
Major-General D. Russell	1870–1872
Lieutenant-General J.T. Hill	1872–1881

92ND

George, Marquis of Huntly	1796–1806
Lieutenant-General Sir John Hope[1]	1806–1820
Lieutenant-General John Hope	1820–1823
Lieutenant-General Alexander Duff	1823–1831
Lieutenant-General Sir J.H. Dalrymple	1831–1843
Lieutenant-General Sir William Macbean	1843–1855
Lieutenant-General Sir John MacDonald of Dalchosnie	1855–1866
Field Marshal Lord Strathnairn (Hugh Henry Rose)	1866–1869
Lieutenant-General J. Campbell	1869–1871
Lieutenant-General G. Staunton	1871–1880
General M. Kerr Atherley	1880–1881

THE GORDON HIGHLANDERS (75TH/92ND)

Lieutenant-General J.T. Hill & Generals M. Kerr Atherley & J.A. Ewart (1884)	1881–1895
Lieutenant-General C.E.P. Gordon	1895–1897
Field Marshal Sir George White	1897–1912
General Sir Charles Douglas	1912–1914
General Sir Ian Hamilton	1914–1939
Major-General Sir James Burnett of Leys	1939–1947
Colonel W.J. Graham	1947–1958

---

1 Sir John Hope became 4th Earl of Hopetoun in 1816. He should not be confused with the John Hope who succeeded him as Colonel of the 92nd in 1820.

APPENDIX 3

Brigadier J.R. Sinclair, Earl of Caithness	1958–1965
Lieutenant-General Sir George Gordon-Lennox	1968–1978
Lieutenant-General Sir John MacMillan	1978–1986
Lieutenant-General Sir Peter Graham	1986–1994

COMMANDING OFFICERS

75TH

Colonel Sir Robert Abercromby	1787–1788
Lieutenant-Colonel J. Hartley	1788–1795
Lieutenant-Colonel G.V. Hart	1795–1799
Lieutenant-Colonel A. Cumine	1799–1804
Lieutenant-Colonel Hon J. Maitland[2]	1804–1805
Lieutenant-Colonel S. Swinton	1805–1815
Lieutenant-Colonel Sir Patrick Ross	1815–1821
Lieutenant-Colonel Sir John Campbell	1821–1824
Lieutenant-Colonel Viscount Barnard	1824–1826
Lieutenant-Colonel R. England	1826–1837
Lieutenant-Colonel P. Grieve	1837–1843
Lieutenant-Colonel R.D. Hallifax	1843–1849
Lieutenant-Colonel A. Jardine	1849–1858
Lieutenant-Colonel W. Radcliff	1858–1864
Lieutenant-Colonel C.E.P. Gordon	1864–1868
Lieutenant-Colonel T. Milles	1868–1875
Lieutenant-Colonel R. Wadeson	1875–1880
Lieutenant-Colonel D. Hammill	1880–1881

92ND

Lieutenant-Colonel George Gordon, Marquis of Huntly	1794–1796
Lieutenant-Colonel C. Erskine of Cardross[3]	1796–1801
Lieutenant-Colonel A. Napier of Blackstone[4]	1801–1809
Lieutenant-Colonel J. Lamont of Lamont	1809
Lieutenant-Colonel J. Cameron of Fassiefern[5]	1809–1815
Lieutenant-Colonel J. Mitchell	1815–1819
Lieutenant-Colonel Sir F. Stovin	1819–1821
Lieutenant-Colonel D. Williamson	1821–1828
Lieutenant-Colonel J. MacDonald of Dalchosnie	1828–1846
Lieutenant-Colonel J.A. Forbes	1846–1849

2 Killed in action at Bhurtpore.
3 Killed in action at Mandora.
4 Killed in action at Corunna.
5 Killed in action at Quatre Bras.

Lieutenant-Colonel M.K. Atherley	1849–1857
Lieutenant-Colonel A.I. Lockhart	1857–1865
Lieutenant-Colonel C.M. Hamilton	1865–1869
Lieutenant-Colonel F. Macbean	1869–1873
Lieutenant-Colonel A.W. Cameron	1873–1876
Lieutenant-Colonel G.H. Parker	1876–1881

92ND – 2ND BATTALION

Lieutenant-Colonel J.W. Gordon	1804–1806
Lieutenant-Colonel J. Cameron of Fassiefern	1806–1809
Lieutenant-Colonel J. Lamont	1809–1814

THE GORDON HIGHLANDERS (75TH/92ND)

1ST BATTALION

Lieutenant-Colonel D. Hammill	1881–1885
Lieutenant-Colonel F.F. Daniell	1885–1887
Lieutenant-Colonel J.E. Boyes	1887–1891
Lieutenant-Colonel T.S. Gildea	1891–1895
Lieutenant-Colonel H.H. Mathias	1895–1898
Lieutenant-Colonel G.T.F. Downman[6]	1898–1899
Lieutenant-Colonel F. Macbean	1899–1903
Lieutenant-Colonel H.H. Burney	1903–1907
Lieutenant-Colonel Hon F. Gordon	1907–1911
Lieutenant-Colonel F.H. Neish[7]	1911–1914
Major A.D. Greenhill Gardyne	1914
Major A.W.F. Baird	1914–1915
Lieutenant-Colonel G.S.G. Craufurd	1915–1916
Lieutenant-Colonel J.L.G. Burnett of Leys	1916–1918
Lieutenant-Colonel R.A. Wolfe-Murray[8]	1918
Lieutenant-Colonel Hon W. Fraser	1918–1919
Lieutenant-Colonel C.J. Simpson	1919–1921
Lieutenant-Colonel C. Ogston	1921–1923
Lieutenant-Colonel H. Pelham Burn	1923–1926
Lieutenant-Colonel I. Picton–Warlow	1926–1930
Lieutenant-Colonel F. Bell	1930–1934
Lieutenant-Colonel J.M. Hamilton	1934–1938
Lieutenant-Colonel C.M. Usher	1938–1940

6 Killed in action at Magersfontein.
7 Prisoner-of-war, Bertry.
8 Wounded in action.

Lieutenant-Colonel H. Wright[9]		1940
Lieutenant-Colonel K.G. O'Morchoe		1940–1941
Lieutenant-Colonel G.E. Malcolm		1941–1942
Lieutenant-Colonel H. Murray		1942
Major	J.M. Hay	1942
Major	J.E.G. Hay	1942
Lieutenant-Colonel H.A.F. Fausset-Farquhar		1942–1943
Lieutenant-Colonel J.D.C. Anderson		1943–1944
Lieutenant-Colonel W.A. Stevenson		1944
Lieutenant-Colonel H.C. H.T. Cumming-Bruce		1944
Lieutenant-Colonel J.A. Grant-Peterkin		1944–1945
Lieutenant-Colonel B.J. Madden		1945–1946
Lieutenant-Colonel B.J. D. Gerrard		1946–1948
Lieutenant-Colonel V.D.G. Campbell		1948–1950
Lieutenant-Colonel W.D.H. Duke		1950–1953
Lieutenant-Colonel J.E.G. Hay		1953–1956
Lieutenant-Colonel P.W. Forbes		1956–1959
Lieutenant-Colonel G.R. Elsmie		1959–1961
Lieutenant-Colonel B.C.A. Napier		1961–1963
Lieutenant-Colonel R.W. Smith		1963–1965
Lieutenant-Colonel J. Neish		1965–1968
Lieutenant-Colonel D.H.W. Brown		1968–1971
Lieutenant-Colonel J.R.A. MacMillan		1971–1973
Lieutenant-Colonel D.G.B. Saunders		1973–1976
Lieutenant-Colonel P.W. Graham		1976–1978
Lieutenant-Colonel C.H. Van der Noot		1978–1981
Lieutenant-Colonel G.H. Peebles		1981–1983
Lieutenant-Colonel A.I.G. Kennedy		1983–1986
Lieutenant-Colonel J.M.W. Stenhouse		1986–1988
Lieutenant-Colonel C.E. Price		1988–1991
Lieutenant-Colonel A.J.M. Durcan		1991–1993
Lieutenant-Colonel I.D.W. Chant-Sempill		1993–1994

2ND BATTALION

Lieutenant-Colonel G.S. White	1881–1885
Lieutenant-Colonel J.C. Hay	1885–1887
Lieutenant-Colonel E. Essex	1887–1891
Lieutenant-Colonel R.H. Oxley	1891–1895
Lieutenant-Colonel Hon J.S. Napier	1895–1897
Lieutenant-Colonel W.H. Dick–Cunyngham[10]	1897–1900

9   Prisoner-of-war, St Valery.
10 Killed in action at Ladysmith.

Lieutenant-Colonel W.A. Scott		1900–1903
Lieutenant-Colonel H. Wright		1903–1907
Lieutenant-Colonel G. Staunton		1907–1911
Lieutenant-Colonel H.P. Uniacke[11]		1911–1915
Lieutenant-Colonel J.R.E. Stansfeld[12]		1915
Lieutenant-Colonel A.F. Gordon		1915
Lieutenant-Colonel B.G.R. Gordon		1915–1916
Lieutenant-Colonel H.A. Ross		1916
Major	R.D. Oxley[13]	1916
Major	R.A.N. Tytler	1916
Lieutenant-Colonel P.W. Brown		1916–1917
Lieutenant-Colonel F. Makgill-Crichton-Maitland		1917–1918
Major	W. Gordon	1918
Lieutenant-Colonel A.D. Greenhill Gardyne		1919–1920
Lieutenant-Colonel P.W. Brown		1920–1921
Lieutenant-Colonel J.L.G. Burnett of Leys		1921–1926
Lieutenant-Colonel J. Forbes-Robertson, V.C.		1926–1930
Lieutenant-Colonel S.R. McClintock		1930–1934
Lieutenant-Colonel G.T. Burney		1934–1938
Lieutenant-Colonel W.J. Graham[14]		1938–1941
Lieutenant-Colonel J.H. Stitt[15]		1941–1942
Lieutenant-Colonel H.I. Bradshaw		1942–1943
Lieutenant-Colonel E.C. Colville		1943–1944
Lieutenant-Colonel J.R. Sinclair		1944
Major	R. Henderson	1944
Lieutenant-Colonel R.W.M. de Winton		1944–1945
Lieutenant-Colonel R.M. Neilson		1945–1946
Lieutenant-Colonel R.G. Lees		1946–1948

3RD BATTALION

Lieutenant-Colonel T. Innes	1881–1883
Lieutenant-Colonel J Turner	1883–1886
Lieutenant-Colonel A.G. Keen	1886–1889
Lieutenant-Colonel J.A. Man	1889–1895
Lieutenant-Colonel A.H Keith-Falconer, Earl of Kintore	1895–1906
Lieutenant-Colonel A.L.H. Buchanan	1906–1910
Lieutenant-Colonel A.H. Leith, Lord Burgh	1910–1917

11 Killed in action at Neuve Chapelle.
12 Killed in action at Loos.
13 Killed in action at The Somme. Son of Colonel R.H. Oxley, who commanded 2nd Gordons, 1891–1895.
14 Prisoner-of-war, Malaya.
15 Prisoner-of-war, Singapore.

Lieutenant-Colonel J.O. Forbes	1917–1919
Lieutenant-Colonel J.L.G. Burnett of Leys	1919
Lieutenant-Colonel J.O. Forbes	1919–1923

{Re-formed 1961 after merger of 5th/6th and 4th/7th Battalions}

Lieutenant-Colonel J. Shankley	1961
Lieutenant-Colonel K.M. Burnett	1961–1964
Lieutenant-Colonel E.E. Toms	1964–1966
Lieutenant-Colonel R. Bannerman	1966–1969

4TH BATTALION

Lieutenant-Colonel D.B.D. Stewart	1908–1914
Lieutenant-Colonel T. Ogilvie	1914–1916
Lieutenant-Colonel S.R. McClintock	1916–1917
Lieutenant-Colonel J. Rowbotham	1917–1918
Lieutenant-Colonel D.F. Bickmore[16]	1918
Lieutenant-Colonel S. McDonald	1918–1919
Lieutenant-Colonel P.W. Brown	1919–1920
Lieutenant-Colonel L. McKinnon	1920–1923
Lieutenant-Colonel C.D. Peterkin	1923–1928
Lieutenant-Colonel J.H.M. Gordon	1928–1933
Lieutenant-Colonel R.L.J. Henderson	1933–1935
Lieutenant-Colonel W. Philip	1935–1940
Lieutenant-Colonel R.A.G. Taylor	1940
Lieutenant-Colonel A. Milne	1940–1941

{became 92nd (Gordon Highlanders) Anti-Tank Regiment, Royal Artillery in November 1941}

4TH/7TH BATTALION

Lieutenant-Colonel A. Milne	1948–1950
Lieutenant-Colonel A.M. Milne	1950–1954
Lieutenant-Colonel J. Harper	1954–1957
Lieutenant-Colonel J. Shankley	1957–1961

5TH BATTALION

Lieutenant-Colonel J.L. Reid	1908–1910
Lieutenant-Colonel W. McConnachie	1910–1912
Lieutenant-Colonel Sir Arthur Grant	1912–1915
Lieutenant-Colonel M.F. McTaggart[17]	1915–1918

---

16 Wounded and captured, July 1918.
17 Prisoner-of-war, Fresnoy-le-Petit, 1918.

Lieutenant-Colonel G.A. Smith[18]		1918
Lieutenant-Colonel Lord Dudley Gordon		1918–1919
Lieutenant-Colonel A.D. Greenhill Gardyne		1919
Lieutenant-Colonel R.R. Forbes		1919–1920
Lieutenant-Colonel R. Bruce		1920–1924

{Assimilated 7th Battalion 1920; became 5th/7th Battalion 1924; re-formed as 5th Battalion 1939}

Lieutenant-Colonel A.D. Buchanan-Smith		1939–1940
Major	R.N. Christie	1940
Lieutenant-Colonel J. Clark		1940

{Merged with 7th Battalion 1940}

5TH/7TH BATTALION

Lieutenant-Colonel J. Milne		1924–1928
Lieutenant-Colonel R. Adam		1928–1932
Lieutenant-Colonel G.P. Geddes		1932–1936
Lieutenant-Colonel A.D. Buchanan–Smith		1936–1939
Lieutenant-Colonel D.W. Hunter-Blair		1940–1941
Lieutenant-Colonel H.W.B. Saunders		1941–1942
Lieutenant-Colonel J. Sorel-Cameron		1942
Lieutenant-Colonel J.E.G. Hay		1942–1943
Major	B.C.A. Napier	1943
Major	R.W.M. de Winton	1943
Lieutenant-Colonel J.E.G. Hay		1943–1944
Major	M. Lindsay	1944
Lieutenant-Colonel H.H.C. Blair-Imrie		1944
Major	M.H.H. du Boulay	1944
Lieutenant-Colonel G.D. Renny		1944
Lieutenant-Colonel C.F. Irvine		1944–1945

5TH/6TH BATTALION

Lieutenant-Colonel T.R. Gordon Duff		1948–1951
Lieutenant-Colonel F.G.E. Walford		1951
Lieutenant-Colonel M.H.H. Du Boulay		1951–1954
Lieutenant-Colonel R.W. Petrie		1954–1956
Lieutenant-Colonel H.R.R. Attwool		1956–1958
Lieutenant-Colonel W.C. Dewar		1958–1960
Lieutenant-Colonel K.M. Burnett		1960–1961

---

18 Killed in action at Arras, 1918.

6TH BATTALION

Lieutenant-Colonel A.B. Whitton	1908–1910
Lieutenant-Colonel C. McLean	1910–1915
Lieutenant-Colonel J.E. McQueen[19]	1915
Lieutenant-Colonel J. Dawson	1915–1917
Lieutenant-Colonel Hon W. Fraser	1917–1918
Lieutenant-Colonel A.A. Duff	1918
Lieutenant-Colonel J.G. Thom	1918

{Merged with 7th Battalion 1918; reformed 1920}

Lieutenant-Colonel Sir G.W. Abercromby	1920–1927
Lieutenant-Colonel R. Steuart–Menzies	1927–1931
Lieutenant-Colonel A.S. Fortune	1931–1936
Lieutenant-Colonel J.L. Ledingham	1936–1940
Lieutenant-Colonel P.T. Pirie	1940–1941
Lieutenant-Colonel J. Peddie	1941–1944
Lieutenant-Colonel J.B. Clapham	1944–1945
Lieutenant-Colonel P.J. Johnstone	1945

6TH/7TH BATTALION

Lieutenant-Colonel J.G. Thom	1918
Lieutenant-Colonel C.J.E. Cranstoun	1918

7TH BATTALION

Lieutenant-Colonel A.H. Farquharson	1908–1911
Lieutenant-Colonel R.W. Walker	1911–1914
Lieutenant-Colonel G.H. Bower	1914–1916
Lieutenant-Colonel H.S. Turnbull	1916–1917
Lieutenant-Colonel A.de L. Long	1917–1918
Major W.H. Newson	1918
Lieutenant-Colonel J. Menzies	1918
Lieutenant-Colonel R. Bruce	1918

{Merged with 5th Battalion 1920; re-formed 1939}

Lieutenant-Colonel J.N. Reid	1939–1940
Lieutenant-Colonel D.W. Hunter-Blair	1940

{Merged with 5th Battalion 1940; merged with 4th Battalion 1948}

8TH BATTALION

Lieutenant-Colonel A.L.H. Buchanan	1914

---

19 Killed in action at Loos.

Lieutenant-Colonel G. Staunton		1914–1915
Colonel	H. Wright	1915
Lieutenant-Colonel A.D. Greenhill Gardyne		1915–1916
Lieutenant-Colonel C.W.E. Gordon		1916

{Merged with 10th Battalion, 1916–18}

Lieutenant-Colonel J.H.McI. Gordon	1939–1940
Lieutenant-Colonel R.W.F. Johnston	1940–1943
Lieutenant-Colonel D.B. Anderson	1943–1944
Lieutenant-Colonel J.A. Campbell	1944–1945
Lieutenant-Colonel R.A. Cumberlege	1945
Lieutenant-Colonel A.M. Milne	1945

8TH/10TH BATTALION

Lieutenant-Colonel H. Pelham Burn	1916
Lieutenant-Colonel D. MacLeod	1916–1918
Lieutenant-Colonel J.G. Thom	1917–1918
Lieutenant-Colonel Lord Dudley Gordon	1918

9TH BATTALION

Lieutenant-Colonel W.A. Scott	1914–1916
Lieutenant-Colonel E.H.H. Gordon	1916–1917
Lieutenant-Colonel T.G. Taylor	1917–1918
Lieutenant-Colonel R.A. Wolfe-Murray	1919
Lieutenant-Colonel W.M. Stewart	1920

{Re-formed 1939}

Lieutenant-Colonel W.T. Murray Bissett	1939–1940
Lieutenant-Colonel A.D. Buchanan-Smith	1940–1941
Lieutenant-Colonel G.H. Anderson	1941–1942
Lieutenant-Colonel J.N.F. Blackater	1942–1945

10TH BATTALION

Lieutenant-Colonel S. MacDougall[20] of Lunga	1914–1915
Lieutenant-Colonel H.R. Wallace	1915–1916
Lieutenant-Colonel W. MacGregor	1916

{Merged with 8th Battalion, 1916–18}

Lieutenant-Colonel J.H.McI. Gordon	1940–1942
Lieutenant-Colonel G.W.A. Alexander	1942–1943

20 Killed in action at La Bassée.

APPENDIX 3

Lieutenant-C　ENTRENCHING) BATTALION

Lieutenant-Ord   1915–1916

　　　regor   1916–1917

Lieutenant-Co　11TH BATTALION

Lieutenant-Colexander   1940–1941

Lieutenant-Codson   1941–1942

　　　haw   1942

　　{11th

　　　bered as 2nd Battalion, May 1942}

BIBLIOGRAPHY

6th Gordons 1935 – 1945, Major J.C. Williamson (Abe
    Journal, 1946).
75th Regiment Record Book.   7–
A Sussex Highlander: The Memoirs of Sergeant Willia
    1828, (2005, Whydown Books, Sedlescombe).   of Jane
Am baile (Comhairle na Gàidhealtachd), (extracts co
    Maxwell, Duchess of Gordon).   1896).
An Octogenarian Literary Life, J.R. O'Flanagan (Co 1924).
Annals of an Active Life, General Sir Nevil Macread
Charles 'Dougie' Usher, Kenneth Usher (Amazon
Diary of John Cunningham, 92nd Regiment. (Tiger
Diary of Lance-Corporal E.G. Chissel, Andre Chi undee,
Historical Diary of The Gordon Highlanders, Lt-(
    John Leng & Co., 1914).   ke
History of the South African and Transvaal War,
    (Edinburgh: T C & E C Jack, 1901).
Letter from Erskine of Cardross to his sister, (Gl *lu War*
Lucky Essex, Graham Alexander (*The Journal o*
    Historical Society; December 2003).
Manuscript Records of the 75th Regiment, (GH R. McIan
McIan's Costumes of the Clans of Scotland, R.
    (London, Ackerman & Co., 1845).   ibald Clerk
Memoir of Colonel John Cameron of Fassiefe
    (Thomas Murray & Son, Glasgow, 1858). *r and Herald*
Memorials of Sanquhar Churchyard, Tom W
    Press, Sanquhar, 1912).   ace Smith-Dorrien
Memories of Forty-Eight Years' Service, Ge
    (Dutton and company, 1925).   one Browne
Notes on the Dress of the 71st Regiment, A
    (Glasgow: John Horn Ltd. 1934).   *Scotland: With a*
Observations on the Present State of the H Emigration, Thomas
    View of the Causes and Probable Cons & Co. 1806).
    Douglas, Earl of Selkirk (Edinburgh, J of Blackstone)
paisley.org.uk, (covering the life of Alexa
Papers of G.S.G. Craufurd, (GH Museu d recollection of my
Recollections of William Hannah (from *dia and then Burma*, by
    Father's War, through England, the (
    William Hannah Jnr, 2003).
Scottish Notes & Queries, May 1930.

BIBLIOGRAPHY

Sketches of The Character, Manners, and Present State of the Highlanders of Scotland; with details of The Military Service of The Highland Regiments, Major-General David Stewart (extracts known as *Annals of the Highland Regiments*) (Edinburgh, A. Constable, 1822).

Territorial Soldiering in the North-East of Scotland during 1759–1814, John Malcolm Bulloch (Aberdeen University, 1914).

The General Danced at Dawn, George MacDonald Fraser (Barrie & Jenkins, London, 1970).

The Gordon Highlanders, The History of their Origin together with a Transcript of The First Official Muster, John Malcolm Bulloch (Banffshire Field Club, 1913).

The Heroes of Rimau, Lynette Ramsay-Silver, (Pen & Sword, 1991).

The Journal of Sergeant Robertson, late 92nd Foot: comprising the different campaigns between the years 1797 and 1815, (Perth, J. Fisher, 1842, 2nd edition edited by A.J. Henderson; Maggs, 1982).

The Life of a Regiment – official history of The Gordon Highlanders,.
   Vol. I, Lt-Col C. Greenhill Gardyne, (Medici Society, 1901).
   Vol. II, Lt-Col C. Greenhill Gardyne, (Medici Society, 1901).
   Vol. III, Lt-Col A.D. Greenhill Gardyne, (Leo Cooper, 1939).
   Vol. IV, Cyril Falls, (Aberdeen University Press, 1958).
   Vol. V, Wilfrid Miles, (Aberdeen University Press, 1961).
   Vol. VI, C. Sinclair-Stevenson, (Leo Cooper, 1974).
   Vol VII, Lt-Col D.M. Napier, (Mainstream Publishing, 2010).

The Military Memoirs of an Infantry Officer, Lieutenant James Hope (Edinburgh, Anderson & Bryce, 1838).

The Pipes of War, Sir Bruce Seton and Pipe-Maj. John Grant (Glasgow, Maclehose & Co. 1920).

The Reason Why, Cecil Woodham Smith (Constable, London, 1953).

The Romance of War, James Grant (London, Routledge, Warne & Routledge, 1869).

The Second World War, Winston S. Churchill (Cassell & Co., 1949).

The Tiger and Sphinx 1894–1994, Regimental magazine of The Gordon Highlanders.

The Wind of Morning, Colonel Sir Hugh Boustead (Chatto & Windus, 1971), by kind permission of Mrs A.L. West.

The Aberdeen Journal.

The Aberdeen Evening Express.

The Aldershot News.

The Bath Herald.

The Daily Record.

The Dublin Evening Mail.

The Edinburgh Evening News

The Edinburgh Magazine.
The Edinburgh Morning Advertiser.
The Hannoversche Presse.
The Kelso Mail.
The London Evening News
The London Gazette.
The Madras Courier.
The Natal Advertiser.
The Perthshire Diary
The Sunday Times.
The *Times.*
With the Gordon Highlanders to the Boer War & beyond, Lachlan Gordon-Duff (Spellmount, Staplehurst, 2000).
www.bydand.com, (extracts covering the life of Jane Maxwell, Duchess of Gordon).
www.craigcross.co.uk, (extracts covering the award of the Victoria Cross to Piper George Findlater).
www.paisley.org.uk, (extracts covering the history of Blackstone House).
www.worldnavalships.com, (extracts covering Ivan Lyon's final operation).
Zulu Rising, Ian Knight (Pan Books, 2011), by kind permission of Ian Knight.

INDEX

Abbreviations used are shown at the end of the Index

mascot, 190.
Masson, Cpl, 300.
Mathias, H.H., Lt-Col, 169, 363, 388, 598.
Maximoff, Col, 368.
Maxwell of Monreith, W., Sir, 419.
Maxwell, D., Lt, 14.
Maxwell, Jane:
see Gordon, Jane Maxwell.
Maxwell, W.G., Capt, 124, 125.
Maya:
see Peninsular War.
Meiklejohn, M.F.M., Capt, 370–2.
Mellay, G., Ppr, 178.
Melvill, T., Lt, 245.
Melville, J., WO2, 298.
memorials and monuments:
5th Duke of Gordon, 464.
51st Highland Division, 130.
Erskine of Cardross, 442.
George Stuart White, 478.
Hugh Henry Rose, 476.
Ian Hamilton, 483–4.
Jane, Duchess of Gordon, 429–33.
John Cameron of Fassifern, 458.
Kabul Gate, Delhi, 354–5.
Richard Wadeson, 356.
Walter Charteris, 239.
Mentioned in Despatches:
Napoleonic Wars, 457–8.
Boer Wars, 169, 258, 367, 374, 376, 377.
Northern Ireland, 412.
WWI, 370, 378, 383–4, 482, 493.
WWII, 341, 345, 349, 488, 525.
Menzies, S.A., Lt, 179–80.
Menzies, J., 59.
Messes, 72–4, 101, 125, 151, 153, 170, 195, 198–201, 209,.218, 222, 240, 243, 292, 411, 514,
Methuen, Lord, Lt-Gen, 367.
Meyrick, St.J., Lt, 83, 84.
Michie, C., Maj, 255.
Michie, J.G., Rev, 24.
Middleton, Ppr, 160.
military bands, 155, 177, 189–94.

Military Cross (MC):
WWI, 65, 181, 488, 498, 500.
WWII, 98, 137, 186–7, 341, 343–4, 345.
Military General Service Medal, 468.
Military Medal (MM):
WWI, 407.
WWII, 136, 137, 339, 341, 342, 344.
Militia, 15, 41, 42, 51, 57, 105, 107–8, 110–1, 124, 171–2, 235, 307, 406.
Miller, J., Rev, 82.
Milne, LCpl, 168–9, 363.
Milne, Sgt, 293–4.
Milne, A., Lt-Col, 430, 601.
Milne, S.M., 34.
Milne, W., Ppr, 178.
mine incidents, 126, 274, 275–6, 277, 509, 523–5.
Minorca, 29–30, 438.
Minto, 4th Earl of, 170.
Mitchell, G., Lt, 454.
Mitchell, G.A., Pte, 385–7.
Mitchell, I., WO2, 298.
Mitchell, J., Ens, 20, Lt, 48, Lt-Col, 462, 470, 597.
Mitchell, J., 25.
Mitchell, Sgt, 174.
Mitchell, T., Lt, 453–4.
Mitchell, T., 308–9.
Modern Pentathlon, 501–2.
Moir-Byres, F., Capt, 522.
Moir-Byres, P., Lady, 382.
Montgomery, B.L., Gen, 175, 390.
Monro, C.G., 2Lt, 83.
Moore, J., Sir, Maj-Gen, 10, 47, 324, 326, Lt-Gen, 429, 448, 466.
Morris, A.G., Cpl, 523.
Morrison, A., Ch Const, 69.
Morrison, G., Maj, 67.
Morrison, M., Lt, 127.
mosquitos, 207, 212–3.
Mostyn, Capt, 245.
Muir, D., 415.
Munro, H., Sir, Lt-Gen, 23.

Abbreviations used in Index:

2Lt	Second-Lieutenant
AB	Able-Bodied Seaman
Adm	Admiral
Bn	Battalion
Brig	Brigadier
Brig-Gen	Brigadier-General
Capt	Captain
Ch Const	Chief Constable
Col	Colonel
Conf.	Conference
Cpl	Corporal
CSgt	Colour-Sergeant
CSM	Company Sergeant Major
Dmr	Drummer
Drum-Maj	Drum-Major
Ens	Ensign
HMT	Her Majesty's Transport
LCpl	Lance-Corporal
Ldg	Leading
LSgt	Lance-Sergeant
Lt	Lieutenant
Lt-Cdr	Lieutenant-Commander
Lt-Col	Lieutenant-Colonel
M.	Monsieur
Mme.	Madame
Maj	Major
Pipe-Maj	Pipe Major
Ppr	Piper
Pte	Private
QM	Quartermaster
Regt	Regiment
RSM	Regimental Sergeant Major
Sgt	Sergeant
SMS	*Seiner Majestät Schiff* (His Majesty's Ship)
Soc.	Society
SS	Steam Ship
Surg	Surgeon
Tpr	Trooper
Visc	Viscount
WO1	Warrant Officer 1st Class
WO2	Warrant Officer 2nd Class
WWI	World War I
WWII	World War II